Balzac and His World

FELICIEN MARCEAU

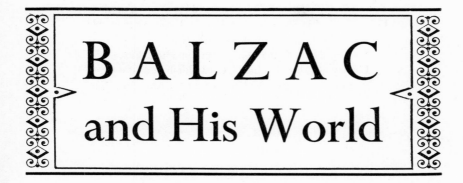

BALZAC
and His World

Translated from the French by DEREK COLTMAN

THE ORION PRESS · NEW YORK · 1966

CONTENTS

Contents

III
INDEX OF CHARACTERS IN
LA COMEDIE HUMAINE

PREFACE

THIS WORK is an essay. As things have turned out, that is exactly what it is: an attempt . . . That it is not a wholly successful one I would be the first to admit. In some places there are serious omissions, in others I have repeated myself. But I am of the opinion that if a thing is worth saying at all, then one should not be too particular about saying it twice. As for the omissions, I seriously doubt whether it is possible for any work on Balzac not to be guilty of them. There is something in Balzac that is not on an ordinary human scale: he is a whole world on his own. And everyone sees of the world only that which attracts, irritates or moves him: this one the woods, that one the old façades, another the may-bugs or the milkmaid's blue eyes. I once knew a Balzac enthusiast who swore by *Louis Lambert* and nothing else; whereas I have always found much more in *Illusions perdues*. I am well aware, for example, that Balzac has made forays into the realm of mysticism, and I have pointed this out. But I hope nothing more will be required of me than that. Mysticism bores me. Had I attempted to write about it in my turn, then without any doubt whatsoever this book would have included several pages of very dull writing. A scholar might well have written a more comprehensive account, but I am not a scholar. I am a novelist. There is one drawback with novelists: they are only able to write about things that interest them—deeply. And yet it is perhaps not a bad thing that it should be a novelist who, from time to time, writes about Balzac.

"It is important to have read Balzac, all Balzac," André Gide wrote in *Incidences*. "There have been writers who thought they could get away without doing so; afterwards, they have been hard put to see exactly what it was they were lacking; but their readers have seen it clearly enough." Just as Dostoievsky used to say: we all have our origins in *The Overcoat*, so three quarters of French novelists ought to say: we are all the sons of *Père Goriot*. What can we think of that Balzac has not already hit upon? Do you know where the first skis are to be found in French literature? In *Séraphita*.

I don't wish to start a literary squabble at this point about themes. Themes are public property. So that it is without even a hint of malice towards anyone in particular that I would like to suggest the idea of a

sort of genealogical table which would demonstrate that there is not
one theme, out of all the themes that have been used in French literature
for the past hundred years, that Balzac has not at least touched upon. His
les Paysans is already Zola's *la Terre*. His *les Employés* is the same book
as Courteline's *Messieurs les Ronds de Cuir*.* Balzac's Vautrin-Herrera
antedates Victor Hugo's Valjean-Madeleine, as well as Rocambole, as well
as Fantômas. *Le Lys dans la Vallée* is the same book as *la Porte Etroite*.
Une Ténébreuse Affaire, as has been pointed out a hundred times, is one
of the ancestors of the detective novel. But it is also the tragedy of a
conflict between two regimes, between two worlds, between Laurence de
Cinq-Cygne and Malin de Gondreville. Hardly anything need be changed
in order to make it into the tragedy depicted by Claudel in *l'Otage*, for
us to discern the figures of Sygne de Coûfontaine and the Baron Turelure,
the second of whom, like Malin, always floats back to the top under any
regime. Laurence de Cinq-Cygne and Sygne de Coûfontaine—it is never
a simple coincidence when words happen to resemble one another.† Proust
too has recognized all he owed to Balzac in the frequent references made
to him throughout his work. Vautrin and Rubempré already foreshadow
Charlus and Morel. The imprisonment of *la Fille aux Yeux d'Or* already
suggests the imprisonment of Albertine. In *Illusions Perdues*, in *Un Début
dans la Vie*, we are already introduced, long before Vallès, to the bachelor
and all his miseries. In *Splendeurs et Misères des Courtisanes*, the misfortunes of Lydie Peyrade, who is shut away against her will in a brothel, are
already material for a *roman noir*. Victurnien d'Esgrignon in the *Cabinet
des Antiques* and Savinien de Portenduère in *Ursule Mirouët* both suffer
from the same disease as Barrès' *Déracinés:* a bad upbringing aggravated
by transplantation. A young girl writes to a writer: it is the starting point
of Montherlant's *Jeunes Filles*, but it is also that of *Modeste Mignon*. And
I scarcely need mention the first page of Montherlant's *Célibataires*—a
perfect example of Balzacian exposition. *Les Petits Bourgeois*, the dinners
at the Pension Vauquer, Mme. Cibot's harangues, they all read like Henri
Monnier. Even, on occasion, like Raymond Queneau. The Marquis d'Es-

---

* "Clerks with balding foreheads, feeling the cold, cased in flannel, perched upon fifth-
storeys growing their flowers" (*Employés*, 953). Wouldn't you swear that was by
Courteline?
† I thought at first that I was the first to point out this parallel. Another illusion. During one of the broadcast conversations he had with Jean Amrouche, Paul Claudel himself said: "Balzac has had an influence, however unconscious it may have been, on
some of my plays. On *L'Otage*, for example . . . Toussaint Turelure is a Balzacian
character, and the whole Coûfontaine drama is undoubtedly impregnated with a decidedly Balzacian atmosphere." (*Mémoires Improvisés*, p. 308)

grignon is already the same character as Paul Bourget's *Emigré*. And there is also an interesting comparison to be drawn between Barbey d'Aurevilly's *Vieille Maîtresse* and the giant of Ville-d'Avray's *Béatrix*.

All this in a general sense of course, in the widest possible sense. I do not in the slightest wish to insinuate that if it had not been for Balzac Gide would not have written *la Porte Etroite*, or Montherlant *les Jeunes Filles*. By citing writers as different from one another as Claudel and Courteline, as Proust and Ponson du Terrail, by pointing out that Balzac has left his mark on all of them alike, I simply wish to give some idea of the scope of his world, to show how far and how wide he cast his shadow, and, at the same time, to offer some excuse for the omissions that will be found in this work.

And I should also like, simply, to make one last admission: in order to achieve anything like perfection in this essay I ought to have devoted my whole life to it. But I should still like to write one or two more novels.

Rather than attempt another biography of Balzac, or another historical account of his work, tasks that have already been performed both often and well, I have approached the *Comédie humaine* as a finished, a completed monument, in the same way as one approaches Notre-Dame or the temple at Angkor. I took up my stand right in the middle of it, and I looked around me. In this way I perceived the characters, then the society they formed, and finally, circulating through the characters and giving them life, certain themes. Hence the two main sections of this work. I thought at first that I need only treat of the themes themselves, but as I went along I realized that the result would hardly be intelligible if it were not preceded by a tour of the characters themselves, by some sort of reconnoitering of the society in which they lived.

As for the characters, there may be some astonishment occasioned by the fact that I have devoted a whole section, for example, to Mme. d'Espard or Claude Vignon while contenting myself with only a few references to, say, Sylvain Pons or César Birotteau, when both of these latter have whole novels named after them. This is, of course, partly due to my own enthusiasms, but above all it is because it seemed to me that the interest of both Sylvain Pons and César Birotteau had already been exhausted by Balzac himself, precisely because of the great importance he himself ascribed to them. Having said everything about them, and in both cases within the limits of a single novel, Balzac leaves the commentator almost nothing to add. Generally speaking, however, the same cannot be said of those characters who recur from work to work, whose personalities therefore develop and become gradually rounded out from novel to novel, whose lives include blanks that provide opportunities for conjecture, and whose traits, because they are so widely scattered throughout the whole, may profitably be collected and examined with greater attention. There are other characters discussed here that exemplify particular aspects of Balzac's technique, or his obsessions, or his vision of the world. Lastly, there are those that owe their inclusion in this inventory to the fact that a hundred years of being read and an occasional strangeness that has crept into some of the author's language in those years seem to me to have obscured their true nature. Balzac's tone, as we all know, is extremely reserved. Quite often it is almost as though he had intended his books to be read, as it were, on two levels. A boy of fourteen might well read *Une Passion dans le Désert* or *le Père Goriot* without seeing anything more in them than an exotic adventure and an unpleasant example of filial ingratitude. But when he reads them again ten years later he will realize with amazement that Rastignac is a gigolo, that Vautrin's speeches have strange undertones, and that the nature of the relations between the panther and the soldier are such as nature herself could not approve. These are only three rather obvious examples. There are many others. Balzac, who is generally thought of as the most unstinting of writers, is perhaps, on the contrary, the most reticent of all, and the one who leaves most for his readers to guess at.

Here and there, in the case of particular characters, I have also made occasional attempts to indicate where, as they say, "he got it all from." I have not done this simply for the pleasure of discovering a few "keys" that are not only without interest but were also discovered by others long before me, but in an attempt to shed some degree of light, feeble though it may be, on that mysterious operation, that strange translation that can make a novel from an anecdote and transform a mortal creature into an immortal creation.

Balzac no doubt had his reasons for including in his *Comédie humaine* several stories that take place in fairly distant times. These particular stories, which are not in any case among his most interesting, were useless for a work such as this, since my aim, one that has been shared by others, is to clarify the structure of the Balzacian world, a world that is essentially that of the first half of the nineteenth century. I have therefore limited myself to those works whose action does not precede the French Revolution—though including *Sarrasine*, which begins in 1758 but does not end until 1830, and allowing myself several incursions into the fascinating preface to *Sur Catherine de Médicis*. For the same reasons I have ignored *Séraphita*, which takes place in a far-off and somewhat cloudy Norway. It also happens to be a book that bored me stiff, though I apologize for not using a more seemly expression.

Even pruned to this extent, the *Comédie humaine* still covers a chronological period of sixty years, and the fact is by no means without importance. From *Illusions perdues* to *Cousin Pons* a great many things have changed, social customs have evolved, some characters have disappeared or grown old. In this respect I think it would be as well if I advise the reader to refer back occasionally to the following list of the various stories that make up the *Comédie humaine*, arranged, not according to their date of publication or the date when they were written, but according to the chronology of their plots.

PRE-HISTORY

Action		*Date of Composition*
1308	Les Proscrits	1831
After 1426	Jésus-Christ en Flandre	1831
1479	Maître Cornelius	1831
16th century	L'Elixir de longue vie	1830
1560	Le Martyr Calviniste, first part of "Sur Catherine de Médicis"	1841
1573	Le Secret des Ruggieri, second part of "Sur Catherine de Médicis"	1836
1591-1617	L'Enfant Maudit	1831-1836
1612	Le Chef-d'Oeuvre inconnu	1832
1758	Sarrasine (Ends in 1830)	1830
1786	Les Deux Rêves, third part of "Sur Catherine de Médicis"	1828

FIRST BALZACIAN GENERATION
(*Revolution—Empire—Restoration*)

Action		Date of Composition
After 1789	Les Marana	1832
1792	*Beginning of* La Rabouilleuse, (*main action of which between 1815 and 1839*)	1842
1793	Un Episode sous la Terreur	1831
1793	Le Réquisitionnaire	1831
1799	L'Auberge Rouge (*ends in 1819*)	1831
1799	Les Chouans	1827
1799	Une Passion dans le désert	1832
1799	Séraphita	1833-1835
1800	*Beginning of* La Vendetta	1830
Empire	La Maison du Chat-qui-pelote	1829
1803-1806	Une Ténébreuse Affaire (*ends in 1833*)	1841
1806-1833	Une Double Famille	1830-1842
1808	El Verdugo	1829
1809	La Paix du ménage	1829
1809-1823	Le Lys dans la Vallée	1835
1809	*Passages from* L'Envers de l'Histoire Contemporaine	1840-1848
1812	Adieu (*ends in 1819*)	1830
1812-1824	Louis Lambert	1832
1812-1824	La Recherche de l'Absolu	1834
1813-1824	La Femme de Trente Ans	1828-1844
Before 1815	*Various stories from* Autre Etude de Femme	1839-1842
Restoration	Gobseck (*ends in 1830*)	1830
1815	La Fille aux yeux d'or	1834
1815-1819	*End of* La Vendetta	1830
1816	La Vieille Fille	1836
1818	La Duchesse de Langeais	1834
1818	Le Colonel Chabert (*ends in 1840*)	1832
1819 approx.	La Bourse	1832
1819	Le Message	1832
1819	Ferragus	1833
1819-1820	Le Père Goriot	1833
1819-1823	Les Illusions perdues	1835-1843

Action		Date of Composition
1819-1823	César Birotteau	1837
1819	Eugénie Grandet	1833
1819	Le Bal de Sceaux	1829
1820	La Grenadière	1832
1820	Massimila Doni	1839
1821-1827	Le Contrat de Mariage	1835
1821-1831	La Messe de l'Athée	1836
Before 1822	Melmoth réconcilié	1835
1822	Facino Cane	1836
1822-1824	Le Cabinet des Antiques	1837
1822	La Femme abandonnée	1832
1822	Un Début dans la Vie (*ends in 1838*)	1842
1823	Les Paysans	1845
1823	Etude de Femme	1830
1823	Un Drame au bord de la mer	1834
1824-1830	Les Splendeurs et Misères des Courtisanes	1838-1847
1824-1830	Les Employés	1836
1824	Honorine (*ends in 1836*)	1843
1823-1835	Mémoires de deux Jeunes Mariées	1841
1825	Madame Firmiani	1831
1825	Le Curé de Tours	1832
1826	La Maison Nucingen	1837
1827	Pierrette	1839
1828	L'Interdiction	1836
1829	Le Médecin de Campagne	1832
1829	Modeste Mignon	1844
1829-1837	Ursule Mirouët	1841
1829-1843	Le Curé de Village	1837-1845

SECOND BALZACIAN GENERATION
(*Reign of Louis-Philippe*)

1830	L'Illustre Gaudissart	1832
1830	La Peau de Chagrin	1830
After 1830	Les Secrets de la Princesse de Cadignan	1839
1830-1837	Un Prince de la Bohème	1839-1845
1830-1840	Les Petits Bourgeois	—

| | | *Date of* |
Action		*Composition*
1831-1837	Gambara	1837
1832	Pierre Grassou	1839
1833	Une Fille d'Eve	1833
1833	Un Homme d'affaires	1845
1834	Albert Savarus	1842
1835	La Fausse Maîtresse	1842
1836	Z. Marcas	1840
1836-1839	Béatrix	1838-1844
1836	L'Envers de l'Histoire contemporaine	1840-1848
1836-1843	La Muse du Département	1843
1838-1844	La Cousine Bette	1846
1839	Le Député d'Arcis	1847
1844 approx.	Gaudissart II	1844
1844	Le Cousin Pons	1846
1846	Les Comédiens sans le savoir	1845

These dates are, of course, in some cases only approximate. For the dates of composition I have followed those given by Balzac himself at the end of each work. For the dates of the plots I have made extensive use of the table in Ethel Preston's book *Recherches sur la technique de Balzac*.

A collation of these two chronologies, the imaginary one and the real one, that of the plots and that of their dates of composition, gives rise to some curious observations. I have provided a note on this matter on page 233.

All the quotations, page numbers, etc. in this book refer to the ten-volume edition of the *Comédie humaine* published by the Bibliothèque de la Pléiade.

I

THE CHARACTERS

CHAPTER 1

The Recurrence of Characters

As is well known, Balzac's characters circulate from one novel to another. Some of them reappear in this way in up to ten or twenty different stories, the record in this field being held by Henri de Marsay and Horace Bianchon who, unless I am mistaken, are mentioned in twenty-five and twenty-four different works respectively.

Why did Balzac go about things in this way? one might ask. However, I myself am rather more inclined to wonder how he could have avoided doing so. From the moment when a novelist decides that he is no longer satisfied with the delineation of individual lives, that he wants to depict a society as well, then he must sooner or later be faced with that elementary social phenomenon of which any woman who moves at all in society expresses her awareness daily in the words: "Heavens, what a small world it is! You know, Paris is just a village!" So that, in principle, the recurrence of characters is no more than a transposition, in fiction, of the everyday social cross-reference. "You see the man dancing with Susie? Well that's Yvonne's ex-son-in-law. His wife is remarried to a dentist now." So that though there are grounds for astonishment at the effects that Balzac was able to draw from this technique, still the technique itself doesn't seem to me to merit much exclaiming over. I am quite ready to believe that if Balzac hadn't hit upon it, then some other novelist after him would soon have repaired the oversight.

What seems to me much more interesting is the way in which Balzac actually used the idea. To begin with, there can be no question whatever that he consciously intended this recurrence of characters to lend to the *Comédie humaine* a feeling of unity. But was he trying to go even further than that? Was he attempting to make his work as a whole into one single novel, a "serial" in which each individual work was a chapter? The answer is that he surely did not. If we take up any volume of the *Thibault* series, or of *A la Recherche du Temps perdu*, without having read the preceding vol-

[3]

umes, although we may still derive a certain pleasure from reading it, that pleasure is bound to be incomplete because there will be a great many things in the isolated volume that must of necessity remain obscure and unintelligible to us. And the reason for this is precisely the fact that *les Thibault* is all one novel. If, on the other hand, we take up *le Contrat de Mariage*, one of the books in which the record-breaking Henri de Marsay appears, our pleasure will still be complete even if we haven't read a single one of the other works in which that interesting young man appears. And the same is true of *le Père Goriot*. The novel is self-explanatory. Our edification is complete, even if we haven't already read *Gobseck*, in which Balzac gives a detailed account of the agonies through which Goriot's daughter is living at the same time. And this remains true even though those agonies are alluded to in *le Père Goriot*.

In this respect my opinion is wholly at variance with that of Claude Mauriac, who writes in his essay on Balzac, "*Aimer Balzac*": "How can we truly appreciate that admirable scene in *les Illusions perdues* in which Baron Sixte du Chatelet and Général de Montriveau meet at the Opéra . . . if we have not already read, and if we do not read again afterwards, *la Duchesse de Langeais*, in which all the reasons for Armand de Montriveau's great prestige are made clear? For his prestige is such that it is shared to some extent even by his companions, and in this case gives the otherwise rather colorless personality of the Baron du Chatelet a significance that *les Illusions perdues* alone cannot at all adequately convey, even though that significance is indispensable to an exact understanding of the book." I don't believe a word of it. One only needs to read through the scene to see that it tells us quite enough about Chatelet to understand all that is happening, even if we haven't read *la Duchesse de Langeais*. The same can be said of the moment in *le Père Goriot* when Mme le Beauséant asks the aforesaid Duchesse if she has heard any news of Montriveau. "To anyone not familiar with Balzac's world, these are just so many empty words," Claude Mauriac writes. Again he is in error. It is true that when he wrote the words in question Balzac was thinking of an episode that he had narrated in another novel, but it cannot be said that he insisted on his readers knowing that other novel, since he immediately takes the trouble to explain: "The Duchesse, who was generally thought to have been abandoned by M. de Montriveau . . ." (*le Père Goriot*, p.907). You will never find a phrase like that in *les Thibault*. And it would be out of place if you did, since the author of *les Thibault* has the right to assume that you have read all the preceding volumes. Balzac, on the other hand, by taking care to slip in this piece of information makes it clear that all we need to know in order to understand this particular scene is that Mme de Langeais has been abandoned by a lover. As for knowing why and how, that is something else, another novel altogether—and one that will, in its turn, be sufficient unto itself. In *Béatrix*, we are shown the workings of a little plot that has been hatched to throw Mme de Rochefide into the arms of La Palférine. To entice the prey, Balzac writes, Nathan "sang the praises of that personable and impertinent young man so well . . . that Béatrix, her appetite whetted by the poet's account, expressed the desire to . . ." etc. (*Béatrix*, p. 606). Whereupon the story of the novel continues. But the poet's eulogy of La Palférine does in fact exist, and Balzac published it. But he published it separately and under the title of *Un Prince de la Bohème*. "One of the most celebrated authors of the day was sitting . . . next to an extremely illustrious marquise . . ." There is no doubt that the two episodes are identical, and the two works are definitely linked; yet Balzac published them separately. We may certainly suppose that he would never have done such a thing if he had thought that the details given in the one were indispensable to our understanding of the other. Especially since both stories were written at more or less the same time. But it is extremely probable that Balzac himself sensed the danger threatening him, the danger of sacrificing the internal unity of each work to the unity of the *Comédie humaine* as a whole. And to him, saving the internal unity of the individual novels came first. In *Béatrix*, that unity would have been broken if he had inserted *Un Prince de la Bohème* as a long digression; in *le Père Goriot* it would have been broken if he had inserted the whole of *Gobseck* at some point. As it is, one can read *Gobseck* either before or after *Goriot*, *Un Prince de la Bohème* either before or after *Béatrix*, and it makes no difference whatever. The furthest one can go in this respect, in agreeing with Claude Mauriac, is to make an exception of *le Député d'Arcis*, of which the plot is curiously controlled by that of *Une Ténébreuse Affaire*, and of the long Vautrin epic that comprises *Goriot*, *les Illusions perdues* and *Splendeurs et Misères des Courtisanes*.

Furthermore, though we are today free to read the *Comédie humaine* in any order that pleases us, still it is permissible to suppose that Balzac, at the time of writing, did sometimes think of the readers of his own day, those readers who were going to read what he had written as soon as he had written it. In *la Femme abandonnée*, he shows us Mme de Beauséant finding consolation in a new love after being deserted by Ajuda. If we are to be logical about this matter, then the reader ought first to be acquainted with the details of that desertion, which are given to us in full in *Goriot*. The trouble is, however, that *le Père Goriot* didn't appear until two years after *la Femme abandonnée*. It seems unnecessary to add that Balzac could hardly have been expecting his readers to wait for the second of these two works before reading the first.

It will doubtless be answered that at that time Balzac still hadn't conceived the general plan of his whole work. But he had certainly done so by 1845, for it was in that year that he drew up a list of all his novels with a view to a complete edition. Now in number seventeen on this list (*Une Fille d'Eve*) Félix de Vandenesse is already a married man, while his childhood and first love (in *le Lys dans la Vallée*) do not occur until number thirty-three. Ernest de la Brière's marriage (in *Modeste Mignon*) takes place in number eight, while his forbears (in *les Employés*) do not appear until much later on—number fifty-three, in fact. So that it will be seen that Balzac himself set no store whatever by chronological order.

Let us also observe that such a chronological order would prove impossible to maintain. Take *la Rabouilleuse*. During the course of this novel, Joseph Bridau has to take a journey. The account of the journey exists, but once again it is given to us in another story—*Un Début dans la Vie*. This second story neither antedates nor postdates the other: it takes place at the same time. But suppose we put down *la Rabouilleuse* when we reached page 1043 in order to read *Un Début dans la Vie*. In the second story we immediately come up against Canalis. Should we now put down *Un Début* and go looking through *Modeste Mignon* for Canalis' previous adventures, and then put down *Modeste Mignon* in its turn because we have met with La Brière and go hunting through *les Employés* to find out about the forbears and early life of yet another new character? And should we not go on with page 1043 of *la Rabouilleuse* until we have finally finished with all these wanderings? If such were the case, then the *Comédie humaine* would necessarily appear to us as the most disorganized work of fiction ever produced on this earth, and one with the extraordinary drawback that we should be obliged to read it in its entirety before being able—and then only as we read it again—to comprehend its meaning and its development. And what would become of the unity and the enchantment we expect of a novel in such a work? No, it is obvious that, to Balzac, each one of his novels had its own separate meaning and internal unity. In each one of them, we are always provided with all the indispensable data necessary to understand it. *La Cousine Bette* is not a fragment, it is not a volume from some larger novel as *Albertine disparue* is, or as *la Mort du Père* and *Vorge contre Quinette* are. It is a novel.

However, it is a novel with windows onto a larger world—a novel with avenues, prospects, paths continually leading out of it if we choose to take them. We have made a beautiful journey, and now we are being shown all those things that the exigencies of time, of our guide, of the plot, prevented us from seeing at the time. In *le Père Goriot*, we made the aquaintance of Rastignac. Now we meet him again in *les Illusions perdues*. He is only a secondary figure in the second book, but a secondary figure we already know, one who opens a familiar prospect for us into the distance. As I have already pointed out, the recurrence of characters is simply a transposition into fictional form of ordinary gossip. But what is gossip, after all, but a window being opened, a sudden unexpected vista, the irruption into a closed drawing room of something happening elsewhere, of another environment, of a fragment of the sordid or riotous past? Not that these previous incidents are ever indispensable, but thanks to our knowledge of them a sudden ray of light will strike one of the characters, surround him with an unexpected aura, gild him, provide him with a shadow, throw him into relief and lend him a denser feeling of reality.

Here then we already have one of the results of this technique. Balzac has at his disposal a whole world of secondary characters, but secondary characters who also hold the rank of primary characters, who make their entrances not as blanks to be made something of but already charged with memories. It is a little like those farewell performances in which even the smallest roles are played by celebrated stars, or like the characters in *Parade* for whom Picasso designed costumes representing the cities from which they came. And it is this effect that enables Balzac to stage-manage what Mrs. Ethel Preston so aptly terms his *reviews**, those large assemblies of characters, those crowds that in the work of any other novelist would either remain entirely lifeless or else necessitate pages of introduction: his review of the Princesse de Cadignan's lovers (*Secrets de la Princesse de Cadignan*); the reviews of the various courtesans in *Un Début*, in *les Illusions perdues*, in *les Comédiens sans le savoir;* the review of the Nucingens' guests in *les Splendeurs* (p.718) or of the Grandlieus' in the same work (p.730). "Often the pretty Baronne de Macumer (née Chaulieu), the Duchesse de Maufrigneuse, Mme d'Espard, Mme de Camps, Mlle des Touches . . . were all to be found visiting there, on their way to a ball or on their way back from the Opéra. The Vicomte de Grandlieu, the Duc de Rhétoré, the Marquis de Chaulieu . . . , his wife, Madeleine de Mortsauf . . . , the Marquis d'Ajuda-Pinto, Prince de Blamont-

* Ethel Preston: *Recherches sur la technique de Balzac. Le retour des personnages.*

Chauvry, the Marquis de Beauséant, the Vidame de Pamiers, the Vandenesse brothers . . ." For the reader who has never read any other work by Balzac than *les Splendeurs* itself, this enumeration is already sufficient to evoke the image of a brilliant assembly. Those who know their author better are dazzled. In a few lines we have had set before us, not merely fifteen people whom we recognize, fifteen people with separate lives of their own, we have also had fifteen windows opened for us, fifteen sudden prospects of fifteen individual destinies. It is at such times that Balzac reaps the fruits of what he has sown. And he offers us a whole sheaf of memories: the love of Louise de Chaulieu, the passing fancies of Mme de Maufrigneuse, Mme d'Espard's intrigues, Mme Firmiani's charming marriage, Ajuda's cowardly desertion, the tragedy of *le Lys dans la Vallèe*, the genius of Félicité des Touches.

And at the same time, thanks to this simple enumeration of names, another and a very important character takes the stage: society itself. In this case, Society, that exalted world of the Faubourg Saint-Germain for which Rubempré was to go even as far as suicide. And the same can be said for the review of the dukes, in *le Cabinet des Antiques* (p.377), on the occasion of Victurnien d'Esgrignon's arrival in Paris: "the Dukes de Verneuil, d'Hérouville, de Lenoncourt, de Chaulieu, de Navarreins, de Grandlieu, de Maufrigneuse, the Princes de Cadignan and de Blamont-Chauvry all joined in the pleasant task of presenting to the king this charming remnant of so ancient a family." And observe that for the matter in hand one duke would have amply sufficed—indeed, it is a little difficult to envisage how all nine of them managed to take part in so simple a presentation. But the fact is, that this is what is so important in this particular book: the vision of society as a teeming, swarming entity. It pullulates on every side. Victurnien is not alone. He is part of an environment, one to which he is indissolubly attached by a thousand links and nine dukes. To his status as an individual there is added his secondary status as a member of society. There are certain of Balzac's characters, in fact, to whom he has contrived to give a certain reality by means of this secondary form of status alone. There is, for example, the Marquis de Ronquerolles. His role is minimal, and we possess only a bare minimum of details about him. But simply by the fact of his continual reappearance (Ronquerolles must be mentioned at least eighteen times), he achieves a kind of weight, he exists. Exactly like those people who end up by carving out a niche for themselves in society simply by dint of being seen everywhere all the time.

This secondary form of status does not only reinforce the primary existence of the characters, however; it also forces us to believe in their reality. And this is another effect that Balzac achieves with this technique: the recurrence of his characters becomes a form of proof. When a character we already know from an earlier novel reappears in a second one by the side of a new character, then the character we already know and believe in becomes in some way a proof of the reality of the new arrival. Or, at least, it activates that suspension of disbelief that is essential in reading a novel. Why should we refuse to believe in Victurnien when he arrives on the scene in the tow of the Duc de Grandlieu, whom we already know from a previous novel, and whom we therefore already believe in? It is like the sort of argument that goes: You believe in God, don't you? Good. Then why should you not believe in miracles? In *le Cabinet des Antiques*, Grandlieu is no more than a supporting character. But where the ordinary novelist would be obliged to devote ten lines or so to introducing him and making us accept him, Balzac (a) presents us with a character we already know, one whose mere name is sufficient to establish his existence, and (b) uses this previously established character as a guarantee for the reality of Victurnien, whom we have never met before. One stone, two birds.

There is a curious example of this use of the recurrence of characters as evidence in a passage from *la Vieille Fille* (p.303). In order to make us accept a certain episode in the plot of this novel, Balzac needs to convince us that little causes can frequently produce great effects. The idea itself having been expressed, it is then backed up by a series of examples by way of proof: "And look what happens then. The Duchesse de Langeais becomes a nun for want of the patience to wait a mere ten minutes, the judge Popinot waits until the next day before going to question the Marquis d'Espard, Charles Grandet comes back by way of Bordeaux instead of disembarking at Nantes." And in the same way, in *le Colonel Chabert* (p.1147), Derville quotes the example of Old Goriot when he wants to emphasize the cruelty of the world: "I once saw a father dying in a loft, without a penny to his name or a stitch of clothing, completely deserted by two daughters to whom he had made over incomes of forty thousand francs a year." The mechanism is quite obvious. Where we would say: impatience is always punished—look at Napoleon; Balzac says: look at the Duchesse de Langeais. The whole thing is simply a very clever piece of sleight of hand. For after all, what witness, what guarantee have we for this Duc de Grandlieu, for this Langeais story, this Grandet story, this Goriot story? No one but Balzac—the same Balzac who then has the gall to present them to us as proofs. Imagine a defendant saying to a magistrate: "But Your Honor, the proof that I was at home on the day of the crime is that I told you so yesterday." Is that a proof? Obviously not, though there is just one difference. Balzac hasn't merely told us about the Langeais case, or about the Goriot case: his talents as a novelist are such that he has made us believe in them. He has made us into his witnesses, as it were. So that these two examples have ceased to be mere literary allusions: they have become part of our own personal experience, part of our personal memories. For us, as for Balzac, the Duchesse of Langeais and Old Goriot have become as real as Napoleon, and as worthy of being cited as proofs. And Balzac, on his deathbed, summoned to his aid, not the real Dupuytren, but the imaginary Bianchon.

The most interesting thing of all to me, however, is that this technique, far from encumbering or hindering him in any way, has endowed Balzac with an extraordinary liberty of movement. He refuses to be held down by anything; he simply writes about any episode that suits him and ignores those that bore him. The story is never finished, but at the same time the author is never a prisoner of the "sequel." At the end of *Goriot*, Rastignac's interest as a character is far from being exhausted. We still don't know what will become of him, whether he is going to make his fortune, or how, or whether or not he is destined to grow tired of his liaison with Delphine. Yet all this is perhaps not worth a second novel. Instead, Balzac gives us all this information in various fragments. Rastignac's further career we are given in a series of allusions. His financial successes are swiftly narrated in *la Maison Nucingen*. His sexual temptations are made the subject of a short novella (*Etude de Femme*) and a short digression in *l'Interdiction*. His biography is completed, but almost imperceptibly. Time is there all right, but instead of expressing it in long chapters or in interminable tea-time chatter such as we find in English novels, Balzac tucks it away, this passing of time, this duration, in the "blanks" that separate each character's successive reappearances. When Balzac tells us, in *la Cousine Bette* (p.439), that Mme Hulot is busy about some charity presided over by Mmes Popinot, de Rastignac and d'Espard, the sentence at first glance looks insignificant enough. As far as the plot of *la Cousine Bette* is concerned, it is superfluous for us to know who these three women are. But if we have read the novels in which they appear, then here, in one brief phrase, is the completion of three separate biographies. What? Mme Popinot, a shop-keeper's daughter, the equal of the haughty Mme d'Espard? And Mme de Rastignac, has she no suspicion that this same Mme d'Espard once almost snatched her husband from under her nose? And Mme d'Espard! Presiding over a charity? Who would have believed it? And yet it is true that there was a time, in her younger days, when she occasionally assumed an air of piety. So time is always there. And this is his work. In that one line we have the equivalent of the chapter in which Proust shows us all his characters in old age.

At the same time, nothing is ever really over. Who is to say that Mme Popinot or Mme d'Espard have made their last appearance in that sentence? Perhaps they still have other words to say. Perhaps we shall see them in the next novel. Except for those who die (and who nevertheless sometimes still survive in memory or in the influence they have had on others), Balzac's characters never come to an end. Nathan's biography is not complete. Nor is Vautrin's. They move off into a zone of darkness. But how are we to know that they will not re-emerge? They have done so more than once before. Here, I think, we are touching upon one of the reasons, though only one among so many, why la Comédie humaine is of all works of prose fiction the one that undoubtedly approaches most nearly to real life. Only very rarely can we follow the lives of the people we know day by day. They reappear in our lives only at intervals. What have they been doing in the meantime? Darkness. Mystery. It is the same with Balzac's "blanks." They are not really blank, they too are filled with darkness: they constitute and render for us that ineradicable zone of mystery that always remains in every life and in every being. In life, too, nothing is ever finished off. By means of a technique that is, after all, simple enough in principle, Balzac has managed to break and dispense with an old convention, the convention that insists on a novel beginning at one fixed point and ending at another. Life never begins and never finishes. It is not a slice. There is always something before and something afterwards. Even birth and death are not really limits. I know that a great many novels do not really end on their last page, that their last sentences often leave the future an open question. In Balzac's works, this extension into the future exists even more strongly. Because we know that the characters may always return in another book, the author is in a way promising us the future and forcing us to think about it. This is another of the miracles in this writer's work: it leaves something for the reader to do himself. It stirs up his own powers of imagination, of deduction, of comparison, of astonishment. Sainte-Beuve (*Causeries du lundi*, November 15, 1834) has this to say about the recurrence of characters: "Nothing is more damaging to the curiosity that is produced by novelty, or to the charm exerted over a reader by the unexpected. At every turning in the road we find ourselves confronted with the same old faces." This, it seems to me, is a misapprehension. If I get into a train and find myself confronted with a childhood friend, surely my surprise will be greater than if I am confronted with a total stranger.

CHAPTER 2

A Brief Geography
of Balzac's World

FOLLOWING UP an idea first expressed by Balzac himself as early as 1839, two diligent writers named Anatole Cerfber and Jules Christophe had published by Calmann-Lévy in 1887 a *Répertoire de la Comédie humaine* that is, as it were, a Larousse of all Balzac's characters. It is an excellent piece of work, and the only exception that can be taken to it is that the authors have mistakenly included all the characters from certain uncanonical completions of novels that Balzac himself never finished. *Le Comte de Sallenauve, les Parvenus, la Famille Beauvisage*, a large part of *les Petits Bourgeois* and of *le Député d'Arcis*, all these are merely so many apocrypha, almost always amusingly and skillfully written, but nevertheless not by Balzac. And now, more recently, in 1952, Fernand Lotte has composed a very interesting *Dictionnaire biographique des personnages fictifs de la Comédie humaine*, published by Corti.

These two catalogues indicate that the *Comédie Humaine* includes more than two thousand characters—two thousand four hundred and seventy-two to be precise, says Marcel Bouteron. That is a great deal. It is an enormous number when you think that Balzac created them all alone. And yet it is also a very small number when you think that with the manpower of one decimated regiment he set out to depict the whole of society, town and country, Court and commerce, the world of high finance and the world of the press, of the law courts, of the moneylenders, of the drapers and of the tarts. In fact, thickly populated though it may seem, Balzac's world is a small one. Though, mark you, the world itself is a small one, as we know. Paris is indeed a village, and one where we are continually running up against the same people over and over again. But most of us only frequent two or three very distinct and quite small groups. Balzac, on the other hand, takes us with him into the most diverse environments, into the homes of people whose lives are entirely cut off from one another. Yet there are a great many links between them all the same. They have the same doctor, for example, the same notary, the same solicitor. Look at Desplein. He is a doctor with a very considerable practice, but we may all the same be permitted a little surprise at finding him at the bedsides of so many very different patients. He attends Chardon, who is poor, and Mme Desmarets, who is rich; Pierrette, who lives in Provins, Mme Mignon, who lives at le Havre, and Mme de Sérizy in Paris. He also attends Flamet de la Billardière, Mme Philippe Bridau, Nucingen, Mme de Bauvan, and Vanda de Mergi. Grindot is a good architect. At least one hopes he is, for he has a finger in every pie. He remodels Birotteau's house for him, he decorates the du Guénics', he advises Mme Schontz, he builds a house for Matifat, he is in charge of Florine's new establishment, and I don't know what else besides. So that despite the vast number of his characters we see that Balzac uses them all with the utmost economy, and his France sometimes reminds one of the Republic of San Marino. It is a country where everyone knows the others, where everyone is more or less related or linked in some way to everyone else, where everyone's life is somewhere or other dovetailed into the lives of all those around them. The first tenet of the Balzacian dogma is this: "In Paris, as in any country town, everyone knows everything." No one, for example, is unaware that Cardot gives Florentine five hundred francs a month, or that Camusot allows Coralie two thousand for the same period (*Illusions perdues*, pp. 726 and 724). Lucien de Rubempré goes to see the moneylender Samanon. They have never seen each other before. "You live with Coralie," Samanon tells him, "and your effects have been seized" (*id.* p.839). How does he know? Fraisier is merely an obscure neighborhood solicitor. Yet he knows all about the misfortunes that have befallen President Camusot's wife, as well as exactly who her family are and the role she played in the d'Espard affair (*Cousin Pons*, p.677). Mme Cibot is only a concierge, but she too knows what is going on: "Grandville? The one who used to live on the Vieille-Rue du Temple?" she asks (*id.* p.677). Nucingen falls in love with Esther: all Paris is immediately talking about it (*Splendeurs*, p.720). Rastignac starts paying court to Mme de Nucingen, and there is immediately not one tenant in the pension Vauquer who isn't aware of it.

These are all the results of the smallness of Balzac's world, but they are also the result of his heroes' remarkable indiscretion and extraordinary frankness. Henri de Marsay was once Mme de Maufrigneuse's lover. But is that any reason to tell his friends that she lives at a rate of two hundred thousand *livres* a year and that she owes "thirty thousand francs to Victorine and eighteen thousand francs at Houbigant's" (*Cabinet des Antiques*, pp. 391 and 392)? It is even difficult to decide which is the more astonish-

ing, that he should know these things, or that he should be telling them.
The frankness of most of the other characters is equally disconcerting.
You are penniless, Crevel tells the Baronne Hulot. Your husband took
Josépha away from me and I have sworn to avenge myself by taking you
in my turn. "Yes, you will be mine when the time comes . . . (I have)
caroused too often with your husband and a pair of lady-friends not to
have heard from his own rascally lips what you are worth . . . It is time
you learned, good and worthy woman as you are, that husbands, once
they are drunk, tell a great many things about their wives when they are
with their mistresses, things that make the mistresses laugh until you'd
think they were going to burst." (*Cousine Bette*, pp. 144 to 149) I know of
course that Crevel is a cad of the worst sort, but this kind of frankness and
indiscretion, though in differing degrees, is found everywhere in Balzac's
work. Mme Topinard once dispensed her favors to a theater manager who
later disappeared from the scene. "I was able to pay my respects, through
her, to my unfortunate predecessor," the new manager says. And he is
speaking to the husband! (*Cousin Pons*, p.781.) Before getting married,
Sylvie Rogron consults a doctor. The subject is evidently a very delicate
one. Yet she does not hesitate to talk about it to Vinet, even though she
has known him a rather short time. And she takes him into her confidence
with so little ceremony that Vinet is still able to catch up with two people
in the street who left the house before the conversation started (*Pierrette*,
p.723). Everyone discloses his or her schemes, ambitions and financial resources. There are only a very few sly fly-by-nights who refuse to reveal
to the first person they meet what the exact figure of their yearly income
is.

For Balzac the world began in 1815. "Since he was born in 1799," Sainte-
Beuve writes, "he was fifteen when the Empire finally fell. Thus we find
that he knew and experienced the Napoleonic era with all the clearsightedness and penetrating insight so peculiar to childhood" (*Causeries du
lundi*, September 2, 1850). This doesn't seem to me to be quite true. Balzac did make some incursions into the Napoleonic era, but he never described it. One has only to compare, for example, the ball given by Malin
de Gondreville in *la Paix du Ménage* and the Grandlieus' salon in *Splendeurs*. On the one hand we find an assembly of men and women, on the
other we are confronted with a homogeneous and completely organized
society. For Balzac, I repeat, the world as a socially organized entity did
not come into existence until 1815.
    At the top, at the very top, the keystone of this whole society, is the

king. Louis XVIII appears frequently. Charles X is mentioned. Then there is the Petit-Château, the world of the Royalists, the Ultras who have returned to Paris from exile, either abroad or on their country properties, the world of the dukes, "the Lenoncourts, the Navarreins, the Grandlieus" (*Illusions Perdues*, p.884), "the Chaulieus, the Navarreins, the Lenoncourts" (*Splendeurs*, p.729), not to mention those two oracles of snobbery, those two high-priestesses of bon ton, the Princesse de Blamont-Chauvry and the Duchesse d'Uxelles, and with them all their various relations, the Marquise d'Espard, who is a Blamont, the Duchesse de Langeais, née Navarreins, the Vandenesses, the Duchesse de Maufrigneuse, née Uxelles, Ajuda, who marries a Grandlieu, the Baronne de Macumer, who is a Chaulieu, Mlle des Touches, a cousin of the Grandlieus, Mme Firmiani, related to the Cadignans, Mortsauf, the husband of a Lenoncourt. These names constitute the most closed world it is possible to imagine, one to which neither money nor high office can assure lesser beings of entrée. Of all these families the Grandlieus alone have come to terms with the Empire. But the Grandlieus have five daughters to find husbands for. Who will cast the first stone!

Below this citadel, in imperceptibly widening circles, we find other milieux that are less strict, the drawing rooms of women whose berth is irreproachable but who are younger and less discriminating in their choice of acquaintances. Mme Firmiani receives Mme Rabourdin, Mme de Montcornet receives Nathan. Mme de Beauséant agrees to receive the Baronne de Nucingen. Without her husband, it is true. On the other hand, Nucingen is tactful enough to leave his wife at home when he goes to visit Mme d'Espard. For Mme d'Espard's is a political salon: to be admitted to it is a mark of financial or political power but by no means a social triumph. Mlle des Touches' literary salon enjoys the same privileges. The Duchesse de Maufrigneuse is able to meet Nathan and Vignon there, but it goes without saying that these two gentlemen will never set foot in her own house. It is by working up through salons of this sort that men like Marsay, Rastignac or Blondet insinuate themselves into Society. Only Rubempré, however, was ever to rise so high as to be received by the Grandlieus, an experiment in tolerance that turned out, in this case, to be less than encouraging, since Rubempré was to end up killing himself in prison. "You see what comes of receiving people of whom one is not completely certain," Grandlieu comments (*Splendeurs*, p.1097).

When we cross the thresholds of people like Mme de Sérizy we are crossing one of the invisible lines of longitude drawn by the pundits of snobbery. We are now in the world of the Grandvilles, the Bauvans, the

Soulanges—the hard-working section of the nobility, holders of high office in the state. The tone here is less legitimist. We meet many people who have accepted appointments or promotions from Napoleon. And some of the titles here were created by the Emperor himself.

Below, the bankers. You move a great deal in Society, Mlle de Grand-lieu says to Rubempré. "In Society?" he replies. "No, I've merely been dining out all week with a lot of bankers. Today with Nucingen, yester-day with du Tillet, the day before with the Kellers" (*Splendeurs*, p.735). These three names constitute the kernel of Balzac's financial world.

These hierarchies may well produce smiles. In practice, however, they are no more strictly adhered to in Balzac's works than they are a hundred years later in Proust's. Moreover, this elasticity was to increase even fur-ther after 1830. Under Louis-Philippe, the ruling class loses its concentra-tion. There is no longer an élite, instead there are several: the legitimist nobility, now a little less haughty, a little further from the corridors of power, the Orleanist nobility, and above all the bourgeoisie. Under the Restoration, this bourgeoisie was still an entity with very vague bounda-ries. Let us look in on a reception given by the Birotteaus in 1819, one for which the invitations were sent out after a great deal of reflection that had nothing to do with social prejudice or snobbery and everything to do with friendship and gratitude. Rubbing shoulders, we shall see a peer of France, an Emilie de Fontaine, a traveling salesman and a pharmacist. A visit to the Camusots, on the other hand, after 1830, enables us to sense that we are in the center of a new caste, a newly formed milieu that is based, not on birth any longer, but on money, on personal honesty and on family ties. A man like Popinot, who in 1820 was nailing up packing-cases, has now become one of the kings of this new élite, a group that includes the Camusots, the Cardots, the Crevels and the Hulots.

To one side, escaping all such classifications, there is the world of pleas-ure, which in the *Comédie humaine* more or less coincides with the world of art and letters. Here, we find actresses, courtesans and literary people all taking great pleasure in one another's company.

Except for this Bohemian world, the same social structure is prevalent in the provinces too. Worthy nobles like the d'Esgrignons in Alençon, the du Guénics in Guérande, the Listomères in Tours, the Bargetons in An-goulême. Then the bourgeoisie: Mlle Cormon in Alençon, the La Bau-drayes in Sancerre, the lotto games of the Grandets in Saumur, the par-venus in Soulanges, the middle class of Arcis.

CHAPTER 3

The Lions

Characteristics of the species.—Lucien de Rubempré (Coralie and Esther)—Eugène de Rastignac—Raphaël de Valentin—Henri de Marsay—Le Marquis de Ronquerolles—Armand de Montriveau—Maxime de Trailles—La Palférine—Franchessini—Charles and Félix de Vandenesse—Octave de Camps—Victurnien d'Esgrignon, Savinien de Portenduère, Paul de Mannerville, Godefroid de Beaudenord, Auguste de Maulincour, or the defeated lions—Varieties of the species—Exotic lions: Ajuda-Pinto and Henri Montès—Lions in the antechamber: Clément Chardin des Lupeaulx, Sixte du Chatelet and Martial de la Roche-Hugon—The bourgeois lion: Charles Grandet—The provincial lion: Amédée de Soulas. The dukes.

AT THE HEART of the *Comédie humaine*, cutting diagonally across plots and social barriers alike, we find the lion: The dandy, the masher, the elegant young man with his yellow gloves. He is a character with a long history in France. "The lion was once called a *raffiné*, a *muguet*, or *homme à bonnes fortunes;* later on, *muscadin, incroyable, merveilleux;* finally, *dandy* and *fashionable*," Frédéric Soulié writes. Balzac himself tells us: "After the *incroyable*, the *élégant* and the *merveilleux*, those three successors of the *petits maîtres*, there came the *dandy*, then the *lion*" (*Albert Savarus*, p.755).

But we must be careful: there are overtones of silliness, of affectation, of frivolity in these terms by which we might easily find ourselves misled. Balzac's lion is not just a fop. He is also a lion in the original meaning of the word: a carnivorous and predatory beast to be feared even in repose, for there is no moment when it is not seeking fresh prey to devour. Brummel and the Chevalier d'Orsay were dandies; dandies and nothing else.

[17]

Their waistcoats, their cravats and their affectation constituted a goal, an end in themselves. They sought for nothing beyond these things. And the same is true of the Chevalier de Beauvoisis presented to us by Stendhal in *le Rouge et le Noir*. He is a fop, and nothing more than a fop. The hungry animal in *le Rouge et le Noir*, the character with ambition is not the Chevalier, it is the little Julien Sorel, a young man who would never give two seconds' thought to his waistcoats if left to himself. On the one hand, the dandy; on the other, the social climber. In Balzac's works it is different: the two are combined. Henri de Marsay is a fop but he is also—and before everything else—a social climber; his foppery is nothing but a means by which the social climber hopes to gain his ends. In *le Cabinet des Antiques*, Marsay and Rastignac initiate the young Victurnien d'Esgrignon into the society of the lions. In *le Contrat de Marriage*, the same Marsay gives Manerville a dressing-down. At first sight these two scenes recall the episodes in *le Rouge et le Noir* in which Julien Sorel is given advice by the young Russian princes. But between Stendhal's version and Balzac's the tone has completely changed. In the one it is a question of love, of vanity; in the other it is a question of money, of power, of success. What should I do in order to make women love me? What should I do in order to merit my own self-esteem? What will people think of me? Those are the questions Julien Sorel asks himself. But Balzac's lions are incapable of such innocence. They don't give a damn about self-esteem, or indeed about anyone else's. Nor are they particularly concerned about love in general. As for obtaining mastery over themselves, the idea would not even occur to them. It is mastery over others they want. Women? Yes, they want to be successful with women, but only so that the women they have succeeded with can help them to conquer society, to achieve power, to become rich. Balzac's lions are the younger brothers of all those thirty-year-old colonels who followed Napoleon through Europe and helped him topple its social structures. Napoleon had vanished from the scene, but he had left a great, ruthless dream behind him. He had taught youth that the world owed it a debt, that everything was possible. But now that Napoleon was no longer there, the new young generation was emerging into a world where it was being continually hectored, a world ruled by old men, by a bunch of old dukes back from their exile abroad, by the old foxes who had known how to survive, by aging courtiers seasoned by their misfortunes. Balzac insists several times upon "the bondage to which the Restoration, so cluttered with eligible old men and aging courtiers, had condemned the young generation" (*Cabinet des Antiques*, p.377), "the gerontocracy under which everything in France is withering away"

(*Prince de la Bohème*, p.823), "the inertia and apathy to which they are being condemned by a lot of overweening old men" (*id.* p.831).

Since there is no longer any room for military ambitions, since the Pont d'Arcole is finished as a source of glory, these avid young men must find another way to their goal. What way is there left not closed to them by their aged competitors? Women. What is the best way of succeeding with women? Foppery. The Marsays and the Rastignacs therefore start looking to their waistcoats and cravats. But we must not be deceived by the means; the goal they are aiming at is still the same one towards which the Murats and the Lasalles were once able to charge on horseback. Fops, yes, but wearing their foppery as young men in other times might wear a pistol or their reputation for a right upper-cut. Those waistcoats are weapons. Or tools, as Rastignac puts it. "The tools with which we till our vineyards in these parts" (*Père Goriot*, p.917). There he is "in his trusty Milanese armor," Blondet says, as he catches sight of Rubempré dressed to kill (*Splendeurs*, p.662). "Armed with that beauty which is the body's intelligence, armed with that intelligence which is the grace of the soul," Balzac writes in *la Fille aux Yeux d'Or* (p.284). Weapons, the word recurs again and again. Dangerous weapons that kill those who get in the way, that wound heiresses to the heart, that sometimes even wound those who wield them if they are not dexterous enough; Manerville and Beaudenord for instance. It is easy to laugh at Rubempré's anguish when he arrives in Paris and discovers that his jacket is ridiculous and his nankeen trousers out of fashion; but his bitterness is the same as that of the young soldier who is champing at the bit because he has no regiment to lead to the conquest of Saragossa. "What woman could ever have guessed at the true shape of his handsome feet inside the villainous boots he had brought with him from Angoulême?" (*Illusions perdues*, p.607) Yes, we may laugh. But why? Do we laugh at the young writer who cries; "Ah! what publisher?" Or at the young Bonaparte when he cries: "Ah! what general?" "The fop is a colonel in the army of Love," Henri de Marsay says (*la Fille aux yeux d'Or*, p.287). Had he been born twenty years earlier, that fop would have become a marshal of France. Is it his fault if the age he lives in has offered him nothing but a battalion of women to maneuver with? "The regiment of women at his command" (*id.* p.287). Is it his fault if it offers him no other stepping stones to fame but swooning bodies? A regiment! the lion of 1800 cries. A rich woman! exclaims the lion of 1815. "We have progressed from the Deed to the Idea," Rastignac says (*Cabinet des Antiques*, p.381). Translation: we have progressed from the battles of Jena and Austerlitz to the battles in boudoirs, to the battles in the wings.

Nothing left but intrigue? Then long live intrigue! General Montcornet exacted tribute from Pomerania, Maxime de Trailles exacts tribute from Mme de Restaud.

These young men have many of the characteristics of soldiers: reckless-ness, comradeship, impatience for pleasure, contempt for danger, shame-lessness and indifference for their victims. Recklessness: they are all up to their eyes in debt and don't give a damn. "We have nothing to lose but the fortunes we are hunting," Blondet says (*Illusions perdues*, p.823). "At that time, there flourished a group of young men, some rich, some poor, all idle, called the *viveurs*, and they did in fact live with the most incred-ible recklessness . . . all eating up money as fast as they could lay hands on it, spicing this furious, though not foolish existence with the crudest of jests, there was no impossibility from which they would recoil, no mis-deed they would not consider an addition to their glory" (*id*. p.820). Comradeship: an honest officer like Montriveau finds it quite natural to help Marsay in his enterprises. Are they not all, after all, linked together by the freemasonry of the Thirteen? Their clamorous appetites: "To suc-ceed! To succeed whatever the cost . . . We are as ravenous as wolves" (*Père Goriot*, pp. 934 and 935). Contempt for danger: they fight duels, and they go to meet their opponents as though they were merely going for a walk. "A band of insolent upstarts," Raphaël de Valentin says, "who walked about with their noses in the air, talking empty nonsense, sitting down without a tremor beside any woman with an imposing air and bab-bling a lot of impertinences to her" (*Peau de Chagrin*, p.82). Shameless-ness: they have affairs with women and tell about them everywhere, shout them on the rooftops: "In Bohemia, secrecy is rarely observed in the mat-ter of passing love affairs" (*Prince de la Bohème*, p.833). Victurnien d'Esgrignon keeps all his friends up to date with the progress he is making with Mme de Maufrigneuse, and no one can fail to be aware of Savinien de Portenduère's liaison with Mme de Sérizy. "You know my obliga-tions," Rastignac says to Valentin, "and are therefore aware how much I would lose by changing the object of my love" (*Peau de Chagrin*, p.101). And in the *Député d'Arcis* (p.731), Maxime de Trailles says in so many words to this same Rastignac: You have ended up by marrying your mis-tress's daughter, and you certainly earned her. Lastly, their indifference: if a lion disappears from the ranks, next day he is already forgotten. Again, this is a military characteristic. Victurnien d'Esgrignon collapses, Savinien de Portuendère is thrown into jail, Beaudenord cannot stand the pace, Rubempré hangs himself: their friends merely joke about these events. Mme de Langeais dies. Oh, come on, Ronquerolles says to her lover, "let's throw her into the sea and forget about her" (*Duchesse de Langeais*, p.254). They are all bachelors, needless to say. Marriage is always the death of a lion. Either he marries badly, like Beaudenord, and this ball and chain around his ankle keeps him out of the running; or he marries well and retires from the arena to digest his prey in comfort. From then on his teeth are drawn. As with Rastignac.

Under the July monarchy the lions gradually disappear. There are still a few bohemians, like La Palférine, but between the bohemian and the lion there lies a gulf. La Palférine lives in a garret. Maxime de Trailles, even when his affairs were at their worst, was never without his manservant and his cabriolet. Ambitious young men under Louis-Philippe choose other weapons. They become lawyers, like young Hulot or Théodose de la Peyrade, or magistrates in the Courts of Appeal. The day of elegance is over: a simple black suit creates a better effect. No more impertinence of manner either: it is the hearts of the electorate these new young men are out to win. And no more amorous intrigues: hypocrisy and a serious demeanor pay higher dividends.

Lucien de Rubempré (Coralie-Esther)

Of all these young men it is Lucien de Rubempré who makes, or almost makes, the most astonishing career for himself. He fails, I admit, but he fails on the eve of marriage to a Grandlieu, and on the verge of appointment to the post of French Ambassador in Germany. Henri de Marsay was to become Premier and Rastignac a member of the cabinet, considerable achievements by any standard; but Marsay has an influential father and an income of a hundred thousand *livres* a year to start with, while Rastignac is related to Mme de Beauséant. Lucien, on the other hand, starts from nothing. He isn't even a genuine Rubempré, because Rubempré was in fact his mother's name. (There was also an Alberthe de Rubempré with whom Stendhal was once in love—which almost makes him a relative of Balzac, as it were.) Lucien's real name is Chardon, a common or garden name if ever there was one. He is the son of a pharmacist in Angoulême who dies without a penny. Mme Chardon exercises the modest profession of midwife, so she isn't of much help either. Lucien is therefore alone. He is good-looking and he writes verses: not a hand one would bid very high on! But Lucien uses those two trumps well: his poems procure him entrée into one of the more literary Angoulême drawing rooms, and his appearance enables him to seduce Mme de Bargeton. Though perhaps seduce is rather too strong a term. The lady talks to him about poetry and

Lucien answers her in the same vein. But when he returns home he hears his father's successor calling to him. "Hallo there, youngster," he hears. "And how's our health today then, lad? I've just been conducting an experiment with some molasses." (*Illusions perdues*, p.518) Lucien is irked by such remarks. He, after all, is a young man who takes himself seriously. He has been spoiled by too much admiration: from his mother, from his sister, from his friend David Séchard. Now he is being spoiled by Mme de Bargeton, who, without knowing it, is corrupting him. She first makes him give up a profession that is, in her eyes, unworthy of one beloved by the muses; then she comes between him and his family. Since she finds the idea of loving a midwife's son too much to bear, she gets rid of the midwife. "Dear child, lovers need no other family but themselves" (*id.* p.569). In the end, she kidnaps him. In 1821 they leave together for Paris. Lucien is something like twenty years old, the lady thirty-six.

Fatal journey: Paris and its marvels were to act upon them both like some corrosive chemical. The young poet's prestige begins to crumble, and that of the queen of Angoulême to flake. Beneath the great chandelier of the Opéra, confronted with lions like Marsay and the Vandenesses, Lucien is suddenly nothing but a "boy out on a spree in his Sunday clothes" (*id.* p.619). When compared with Mme d'Espard, Louise de Bargeton is nothing but a woman with "dry, blotchy skin . . . sandy haired, and worse . . . provincial in her speech, and above all badly dressed!" (*id.* p.611) Mutual disappointment. Mutual revelation. "And the eyes of both of them were opened, and they saw that they were naked." One senses clearly that it only needs one of them to cling to the other for the break not to take place. But it is only real lovers who cling. Or those who are really ambitious. Louise is not really in love: she is far more concerned with her vanity than with her heart. And Lucien's ambition turns out to be made of the worst possible stuff—indecisive, lacking in perseverance and unwilling to accept logical consequences. He has scarcely set eyes upon Mme d'Espard than he becomes inflamed with "an intellectual ardor" for her (*id.* p.620), one in which desire plays no part whatever. It goes without saying that Mme d'Espard hasn't so much as glanced at him; but his glances have wounded Mme de Bargeton cruelly and she deserts him. Deprived of both ladies, Lucien throws himself into his work with the same "intellectual ardor." "I shall live on sixty francs a month," he writes to his sister (*id.* p.630). He has, as a matter of fact, just spent two thousand francs on clothes, but people who are indecisive are usually also of short memory. He spends his days in the Bibliothèque Saint Geneviève, writes a novel and produces a few sonnets in which there is

some mention of Jesus shaking his wings. He also walks around Paris looking at the women there, "his heart heavy with its burden of blood" (*id.*
p.636). Perhaps, after walking a great deal, he also allowed himself to be
inveigled occasionally by one of the ladies sauntering in search of money,
but not too much of it, under those same arches in the Palais-Royal where
another ambitious young man had wandered thirty years before, a young
stranger like himself, not from Angoulême but from Ajaccio. "Her face
was pale and her limbs were shivering with the cold. But one has to live,
she told him. Neither you nor I know the name of the young girl that
Bonaparte took back with him one November night to his room in the
Hotel de Cherbourg" (Marcel Schwob, *Le Livre de Monelle*).

But will Lucien show more perseverance in his work than in his liaison
with Louise de Bargeton? Possibly, if he is given encouragement. In any
case, he finds himself torn between two friends, one good and one bad,
one honest and one a charlatan, a guardian angel and a demon. Daniel
d'Arthez and Etienne Lousteau. The first is a writer, the second a journalist, a fact that according to Balzac's personal cosmogony points up the
difference between them still further. D'Arthez proves the more influential of the pair at first. He introduces Lucien into his own group, where
the young man is received politely but without illusions. "There is a diabolical principle somewhere in you," Michel Chrestien tells him, "that will
enable you to justify in your own eyes all the things that are most contrary to our principles" (*id.* p.661). Lucien believes himself to be a writer,
but he does not have the perseverance, the pertinacity that characterizes
genuine evocations, that characterized that of Balzac himself. He grows
tired of literature. He drifts away from d'Arthez and falls back upon
Lousteau. He hurls himself upon the idea of journalism in exactly the same
way as he has already hurled himself successively upon Mme de Bargeton,
Mme d'Espard and then upon literature. It is his fourth new undertaking
in a matter of weeks.

Now, to Balzac, journalism is pure prostitution. Whenever he introduces us to a journalist there is generally a tart not far away. And indeed,
no sooner has Lucien set foot in a newspaper office than the rest of him is
lolling in bed with Coralie. Coralie, an actress at the Panorama Dramatique, is Camusot's kept woman—the corruption is beginning. Lucien lets
himself be drawn into this world. Is it his own money or Camusot's he is
spending when he buys himself those pretty shirts and those diamond
studs? He doesn't even think about it. It is left to Coralie to give him a
lesson in probity by sending Camusot back to his bales and his yardstick.
She then invites Lucien to live with her and sets about destroying him

completely. Firstly by the "collusion of interests" from which he benefits, secondly by her irremediable vulgarity. She's a good-hearted thing, Coralie, but she's a tart. After she's said about something that it's "good form" she has nothing left to say. Lucien sometimes regrets not seeing his writer friends any more. "Oh them," she says, "they look to me like nothing but a lot of suckers!" (*id.* p.785) Lucien becomes a journalist, writing without conviction, willing to express any opinion for money, using everything, his pen, his right of entry into theaters, for mercenary ends. The Royalists make overtures to him. What are you doing among all those liberals? Mme d'Espard asks him. Come over to us, we'll get you a court order making it legal for you to call yourself de Rubempré. "Lucien was won over in a moment" (*id.* p.796). He is still ambitious, but he is still indecisive, inconstant, thoughtless as well, too quickly swayed, too ready to relinquish the bird in hand for vague promises. "Dear Lucien, so ambitious and so unsuccessful," Esther is to write to him later (*Splendeurs*, p.977).

He is "a child chasing after pleasures and vain delights . . . ," Balzac tells us, "without any fixed plan, a slave to circumstances" (*Illusions Perdues*, p.867). He was given an opportunity with Mme de Bargeton: he allowed her to leave him. Another opportunity with his writing: he gave it up. Another opportunity with the liberals: he betrays them. "Be an ultra. After all, it's so much better form," Coralie exclaims (*id.* p.817). He yields, thereby earning himself the hatred of his former friends and the contempt of his new ones. It is not enough to turn one's coat, one must also do it for a good reason. Once he has compromised himself in this way, the royalists shrug off the promises they made to him with a laugh; the liberal critics get up a campaign against Coralie; the pair's creditors emerge into the open and start baying at their heels. It is the black period that all those with ambition eventually have to live through. All that is necessary is to lie low until the storm has passed. But Lucien is as deficient in patience as he is in perseverance. He signs some forged letters of credit. Coralie dies, while Lucien sits at her bedside writing bawdy songs to pay for her funeral.* Once again, Lucien is alone. He has no one left but Coralie's chambermaid, who is soon out on the sidewalk earning him twenty

---

* Balzac seems to have found this idea a very striking one. "Are you being forced to compose cheap songs to pay for your mistress's funeral cortege?" the antique dealer asks Raphaël de Valentin in *la Peau de Chagrin* (p.35). "Have I ever told you the story about the man who wrote drinking-songs so that he would have the money to bury his beloved mistress?" (Balzac: *Lettres à l'Etrangère*) If we are to believe what Werdet tells us in his *Souvenirs de la vie littéraire*, the thing did actually happen to Maurice Alhoy, one of the founders of the *Figaro*.

francs so that he can retreat to the safety of Angoulême. His downfall is complete. The erstwhile fancy-man is on the way to becoming a ponce.

Back in Angoulême, the forged letters of credit have brought about the ruin of David Séchard, by then Lucien's brother-in-law. Lucien repents of what he has done. But, as d'Arthez says: "I look upon periodic repentence as a great hypocrisy" (*id*. p.859). In reality, Lucien cannot tolerate not being admired any more. His presumption of his own worth is still sufficient to attract further malicious gossip and painful snubs, even in Angoulême, and he decides eventually to commit suicide. He is saved in the nick of time by the Abbé Herrera, who evidently has some sort of designs upon him. But what designs? It is a subject we shall return to when dealing with Vautrin, for the Abbé Herrera is none other, as we all know, than the ex-convict Vautrin. Desire for possession? A passion for exercising vicarious power through an intermediary? Homosexuality? A little of all three no doubt. Let us not forget for one thing that Lucien is a man-woman. "This man who is half a woman," Balzac says (*Splendeurs*, p.727). And it seems unlikely that he means only in character. Besides, what a handsome figure he must have cut when Vautrin caught sight of him on that road, elegant, melancholy, a great yellow flower dangling from one hand (*Illusions perdues*, p.1014). Vautrin sets him up in a fresh establishment, and the process of corruption continues. After having been kept by a woman, we now see Lucien being kept by a man.

Vautrin, of course, knows the times he is living in. He soon puts Lucien in the way of finding a rich mistress. No messing about, no trifling, a duchess! Lucien becomes the lover of Mme de Maufrigneuse, who, after a while, yields him up to Mme de Sérizy. There is no love involved in all this. Mme de Sérizy is easily fifteen years older than Lucien, and she is well known for bestowing her favors only on the commonest of men (*Duchesse de Langeais*, p.223). Can this mean that Lucien is common? I rather think it does. The Mesdames de Maufrigneuse and de Sérizy have already almost ceased to display any restraint in their behavior; yet the little propriety they do still have is nevertheless sufficient to irk Lucien. The deepest urges of his being require that his mistress be a whore. He misses Coralie. But he finds a replacement for her: Esther Gobseck, known as la Torpille, the great-niece of the moneylender. Esther is the daughter of a prostitute who died, as Blondet puts it, on the field of dishonor (*Splendeurs*, p.666), a prostitute herself in every sense of the word, now living in a high-class brothel after having been kept successively by old des Lupeaulx, d'Estourny, a Stavisky of that era, and several other willing dandies. Another Coralie did I say? Oh no, much worse. At least

Coralie had her profession to provide her with an alibi. Esther is simply a prostitute and nothing else. A few years earlier, Giroudeau had introduced her to someone as follows: "She has a voice that will extract a thousand-franc note from the very flintiest of hearts . . . After having gulped down the fortunes of two Englishmen, a Russian and a Roman Prince, Mademoiselle Esther is at present in the most appalling financial straits. All you have to do is give her ten thousand francs and she will be delighted" (*Rabouilleuse*, p.1093). "There isn't a woman in the whole of Paris," Lousteau tells us, "who can match her when it comes to saying 'Get out!' to some creature she's tired of" (*Splendeurs*, p.666). One day, talking about a watch that doesn't go, given to her by a customer in payment for favors received, she says: "It's pinchbeck—like what he got from me" (*Illusions perdues*, p.991). That's the kind of person Esther is. Someone is going to tell me that she is transformed, transfigured by her love for Lucien; but I don't believe it for a moment. It's true that Esther has a certain stature that Coralie always lacked, but she always remains a prostitute all the same. Doesn't Balzac himself tell us elsewhere that she still longs for the dark gutters she crawled out of (*Splendeurs*, p.692)? And after several years of Lucien doesn't she slip back rather too quickly into her old professional vocabulary? "My pretty little elephant," we find her saying to Nucingen (*id*. p.905). And then, in her admirable letter to Lucien: "Nini dear, I don't want you to start tearing your hair out and all that when you find out I'm dead" (*id*. p.978). No, we must just face up to the fact that there exists between Lucien and his tarts a bond that is never broken. After all, is he not something of a prostitute himself? Vautrin saw that right away, and despite his principles, despite his hatred for useless women, he allows Lucien this caprice. He treats him like a child, like a baby that must be kept amused. However, Vautrin takes certain precautions all the same: Esther has to be kept quiet, almost under lock and key. She only goes out at night, and scarcely has any life at all except during the few hours that Lucien comes to spend with her, between two social engagements, dressed in his red trousers and his turban (*Splendeurs*, p.707).

With Vautrin to guide him, Esther to assuage his desires and Mme de Sérizy to introduce him everywhere, Lucien becomes a force to reckon with. He has broken with his former bohemian friends, it is rumored that he is under the protection of the Grande Aumônerie and his books are successful. And yet, like some incredible precursor of Rimbaud, he doesn't care at all. The success is posthumous, he tells someone who congratulates him on it (*id*. p.711). And it's true. Lucien is now a man living on after his own death. Normally, he would have committed suicide. It is thanks to Vautrin alone that he is still alive, and Vautrin is keeping him going now by main force.

For all this success, however, the moment comes when there is not enough money. It is now 1829, and this is the crux of Lucien's career: he has just asked for the hand of Clotilde de Grandlieu, a young woman already past her prime, flat-chested, but a member of one of France's most powerful families. The father is reluctant. Let Lucien buy back the Rubempré lands and then we'll see, is his attitude. Then we must buy them back! Vautrin says. It will cost a million, but Vautrin intends to raise the sum by throwing Esther into the arms of Nucingen-the-rich-banker. And note that Lucien has no objections to the scheme whatever. In fact, he takes advantage of this unexpected vacation in order to be unfaithful to Esther with an English whore who happens to be handy. The only one to suffer is Esther. The years spent locked away in a brothel have damaged her understanding less than they have Lucien's flabby ambitions. She gives herself to Nucingen but kills herself immediately afterwards. Nucingen kicks up a great fuss, the police are called in and Lucien and Vautrin are arrested.

Are they finished? Not yet—an aunt of Vautrin's rushes to visit Mme de Maufrigneuse and Mme de Sérizy: save Lucien or your letters will be made public. For they had written him letters, poor ladies. "And what letters! . . . Street-walkers, when they write, express their beautiful sentiments with a certain amount of style, but great ladies, alas! who talk and behave with style and nobility all day long, write rather the way street-walkers behave" (*id*. p.1115). They both rush to the prison. Too late. Lucien is a weakling, one of those people who are destroyed by solitude. And besides, as I have already said, his vital spark is no longer in his own breast but in the hands of the hardy Vautrin. Separated from the strength that keeps him alive, Lucien crumbles, confesses everything that is required of him and hangs himself. Wretched creature! A little patience and he would have emerged a conqueror.

In that curious, spiteful and interesting book of anonymous memoirs—written in fact by a magistrate named Lambinet—published under the title of *Balzac mis à nu*, the author tells the story of a certain Duranton, the son of a wine merchant who had insinuated his way into various Parisian drawing rooms and succeeded in becoming the lover of Mme de Girardin. One day, finding himself very short of money, this Duranton asked his mistress to get him appointed to some post or other. The lady was at first annoyed by the request. Later she changed her mind, but too late. A letter was brought to her. She opened it, "gave a terrible cry, rushed out of her house without stopping to cover her head, ran along the public sidewalk, hailed a passing cab and eventually arrived at Duranton's lodgings. She called, knocked, had the door broken down, hurled herself into the room and fell senseless upon the floor. Duranton was hanging dead from the ceiling of his bedroom . . . M. de Girardin . . . managed to behave perfectly towards his wife. He took her home without any fuss . . . and lavished the most affectionate attention upon her." *

It is impossible while reading this story not to think of the episode in *Splendeurs et Misères* which describes Mme de Sérizy discovering Lucien hanging in his cell. Balzac, a great friend of the Girardins, must surely have been familiar with this incident in their lives, and he certainly remembered it. But he also drew his inspiration for the events in Lucien's life from another news term, one to which he alludes in *les Marana* (p.834). This story involved a certain Coralie Kaersmackers who was murdered in her bedroom by her lover, a captain in the army who, later on, also killed himself in his prison cell. This is an occasion where we are able to glimpse something of the actual process by which a novelist transmutes the details provided for him by real life. The Kaersmackers woman, if we are to go by her name, must have been either Belgian or Dutch. Like Esther. But her first name was to serve for one of Lucien's other mistresses. As for the captain, his suicide in the prison cell was to give rise to that of Lucien, while the crime he committed was to be used in the case of Esther's mother, the beautiful Dutchwoman who is murdered by a captain in her bedroom in the Palais-Royal (*César Birotteau*, p.411 and *Splendeurs*, p.676).

However, the essence of Lucien—and this is why I have given up so much space to him—is drawn above all from Balzac himself. It would be hard to imagine the sturdy Honoré as Vautrin's minion, it is true; but Lucien writing his novel in his wretched hotel room is nevertheless Balzac in his attic room on the Rue Lesdiguières where the rent was five francs a month. And the letters Lucien writes to his sister are also sometimes very like those that Balzac wrote to Laure de Surville. Balzac too tried his hand at journalism at one time. Like Lucien, he sometimes found himself tearing to pieces in one newspaper a work that he had lauded to the skies the day before in the columns of another. Like Lucien, he progressed from a sort of liberalism, though a very vague sort, to the most uncompromising

---

* *Balzac mis à nu ou les dessous de la société romantique,* taken from the memoirs of a contemporary, published by Charles Léger, Paris, 1928, pp. 117 to 126.

royalism. Indeed, the conversation that Lucien has with Mme d'Espard and the Duc de Rhétoré must, I imagine, owe something to the conferences that took place among Balzac, Mme de Castries and the Duc de Fitz-James "who put him in touch with Laurentin, the editor of a new royalist weekly." * In 1824, commissioned by someone or other, Balzac published a pamphlet on the laws of primogeniture that he signed with the initial D. This incident recurs in *Illusions perdues* (p.808): "Which of you would like to write a pamphlet demanding a revival of the laws of primogeniture? . . ." Finot asks. "How much are they paying?" Vernou inquires. "Six hundred francs. You can sign it: Count C." We should immediately add, however, that in Balzac's case the matter was on a somewhat higher plane. And this kind of transposition is rather rare. Generally speaking, the novelist puffs up, exaggerates his misfortunes when he fictionalizes them, whereas here the contrary is the case. But the resemblance between the character and his creator exists. Those sonnets, for instance, that Balzac attributes to Lucien in *Illusions perdues*, Balzac himself had already had published under his own name in *les Annales romantiques pour 1827-1828*, and Sainte-Beuve found them "harmonious and rhythmically pleasing." As for the novel that Rubempré publishes, it cannot fail to call to mind the three stories that Balzac grouped together under the title *Sur Catherine de Médicis*. "Have the courage to recreate for us the great and magnificent figure of Catherine," d'Arthez says. (*Illusions perdues*, p.650.) Doubtless an echo of the advice that Balzac himself received from his friend Jean Thomassy, who "urged him to give up writing those bad novels of his . . . and to devote himself to literary productions more elevated in their inspiration." † Unless it is perhaps an echo of the conversations that took place between Balzac and Alfred de Vigny at the time when Vigny was occupied with a new edition of *Cinq-Mars*. Lucien is Balzac. But a Balzac one stage lower than Balzac in real life, a Balzac without a genuine vocation, the Balzac of 1825, a Balzac, in short, without a *Comédie humaine*. And what is there left of Balzac today—except the *Comédie humaine?*

Eugène de Rastignac

A kept man, a forger, a dabbler in high-class pimping whose everyday companions are an ex-prostitute and an ex-convict, Rubempré is obviously not a particularly savory character. It's true that his marriage might have

---

* André Billy: *Vie de Balzac* (I, 141).
† J.-L. Arrigon: *Les débuts littéraires de Honoré de Balzac*, p. 150.

saved him from all this. But what if the marriage had not come off anyway? And even if it had, how far would the sinister Vautrin's influence still have been in evidence? Suicide or not, the fact that Lucien dies in prison is in no way astonishing. His whole life led towards that moment.

And yet: I don't know whether or not this is true of other readers, but I never find Rubempré either hateful or antipathetic. The main sentiment he inspires is one of pity. Because he is a victim, a child, bewildered, thoughtless, vulnerable, lost in a world that is too big for him. Even in his corruption he still retains a naïve and touching kind of enthusiasm. Rastignac is never touching, or at least only very rarely. He never descends as low as Lucien, we never see him in a magistrate's court; but there is a feeling that what keeps him out of it is more a fear of the police than any innate quality of honesty. Weak though he may be, Lucien is a nonconformist. Rastignac is a conformist, excessively so. He is always willing to come to terms right away. I don't know whether he pursued his law studies all that far, but certainly far enough to have retained a clear distinction in his mind between crimes, which are always dangerous, and the sort of dirty tricks that are petty enough to exclude any legal risk. It's true that he comes out with a challenging exclamation or two—such as the famous: "It's between the two of us now!" And that is indeed a handsomely expressed sentiment. As long as we go on and read the next two lines: "And as a first step in the contest to which he had challenged Society, Rastignac went to dinner at Mme de Nucingen's." Such is the extent of his famous challenge. Such are the man's limits.

We meet Rastignac for the first time in 1819, when he is a lodger in the Vauquer pension on the Rue Neuve-Sainte-Geneviève, the present Rue Tournefort. He is twenty-one and a law student at the Sorbonne. He is poor but determined: when he goes to a ball he works the whole of the rest of the night in order to make up for lost time (*Père Goriot*, p.873). His parents belong to the lesser provincial nobility, and we glimpse them occasionally in the drawing rooms of Angoulême (*Illusions perdues*, p.535). They have an income of three thousand francs a year and five children, which means that poor Eugène never has enough money even to take a cab. Why a cab, you may ask. Do students go to lectures in cabs? No, but Eugène is ambitious and wants to make his way into Society. Since he is Mme de Beauséant's cousin he is in a position to be received almost everywhere, but how can he walk into drawing rooms with muddy boots? The footmen snicker at him behind his back. Or at least he imagines they do, for there is nothing quite so sensitive as an ambitious young man without money. In short, Rastignac is ripe for his encounter with the devil. And the devil, it goes without saying, doesn't take long to appear. Like Lucien, though several years beforehand, he meets Vautrin. And Vautrin conceives the same passion for Eugène that he does later for Lucien; only in this case it is slightly less violent. Eugène is less good-looking for one thing. Blue-eyed, white-skinned, short rather than tall. Dark-haired, whereas Lucien is blond. And the accent! Rastignac is from Angoulême. Still, he has ambition, and that is enough to excite the ex-convict's interest in itself.

Unlike Lucien, however, Rastignac resists the iron will he has encountered. Because he is inherently honest, or because he is cautious? A little of both probably, but more because he is cautious, I suspect. We must not forget that though both young men meet the same devil they do not both meet him in quite the same circumstances. When Rubempré first encounters Vautrin he has already experienced most of the disappointments and all the cold water in his face that Parisian life has to offer, whereas Rastignac's feet are still dry. "My youth is still as blue as a clear and cloudless sky," he says (*Père Goriot*, p.942). There is despair in Rubempré's acceptance, despair and apathy. The apathy of someone who has come very close to death. But Rastignac isn't in despair, and indeed has no reason to be so. For him, Vautrin has appeared too soon. He needs to have gone through a few more ordeals to be really ready for this meeting. And since he has not lived through those ordeals, Rastignac keeps his wits about him. "Life and I are like a couple who are still only engaged . . . Vautrin has shown me what happens after one has been married ten years" (*id.* p.943). Is that the cry of a revolted conscience? Or is it merely that of a man who accepts the idea of corruption but isn't going to risk anything until he knows exactly what's at stake? Of a fledgling teetering on the edge of the nest? Certainly Rastignac's upbringing was more favorable than Rubempré's, since he had the authority of a father to guide him, whereas Lucien only had a mother. At one point, (*Rabouilleuse*, p.848) Balzac indicates to us that this fact is not without its importance. Poor as they are, the Rastignacs nevertheless live in the class they were born to. The Chardon-Rubemprés, on the other hand, have fallen below their original station. This is the cause, in Rastignac, of those scruples that are more like fears, those attacks of timidity, touching enough if you like, but not a sign of the best character. Vautrin is well aware of this. "We still have a few little swaddling bands of virtue clinging to us," he remarks (*Père Goriot*, p.991). In everything Rastignac does there is something sly, something reticent and calculating. Generally speaking, Balzac's heroes only think out loud—or at least we only know what they are thinking from what they say. Rastignac, on the other hand, knows how to keep quiet. He listens to inner voices. In *Père Goriot*, he subjects himself to a veritable examination of conscience. And several years later, in *Splendeurs et Misères des Courtisanes* (p.670), when Rastignac meets Vautrin again at the Opéra, Balzac writes, rather curiously: "At three that morning, des Lupeaulx and Finot found the elegantly attired Rastignac still in the same place, still leaning against the column where the terrible mask had left him. Rastignac had been confessing himself: he himself had been priest as well as penitent, judge as well as defendant. He allowed them to take him off to breakfast, and then returned home, completely drunk but without having spoken a word." It is these unexpressed thoughts no doubt that give Rastignac his catlike demeanor. He senses that Vautrin is an outlaw and a rebel, that there is a latent danger in being connected with such a man, and he is extremely circumspect as a result. He refuses with horror the opportunity of marrying the little Taillefer girl, when she becomes rich after a murder contrived by the ingenious Vautrin, but at the same time he writes letters to his sisters extorting all their little savings from them. We have the whole of Rastignac there: a man who recoils from crime, but not from actions that are petty and rather despicable.

Nevertheless, despite the fact that he shies away at first, the barbs of temptation have taken hold. Rastignac does not follow Vautrin, but he has skimmed off the cream of his advice. Especially since the ex-convict has found an unexpected ally: "He told me bluntly what Mme de Beauséant conveyed to me in a rather more elegant way" (*Père Goriot*, p.942). Rastignac is neither as brilliant nor as quick-witted as Rubempré, but all the same, once he has been told things twice he can grasp them well enough. The next rich woman he meets he sets his sights on. It turns out to be Mme de Restaud. Since she is already well provided for in this respect, Rastignac, keeping to the same family, moves on to her sister, Delphine de Nucingen, the wife of the famous financier. This time he is successful, and Delphine is prepared to set him up in an apartment on the Rue d'Artois, next to Saint-Philippe-du-Roule. Rastignac accepts. To hell with the laws of the Medes and Persians! And Eugène becomes a gigolo. Though not, it must be admitted, without a certain amount of wavering. His finer feelings come to the surface by the bedside of the dying Goriot—but for the last time. Finally he stands in the cemetery of Père-Lachaise and gazes down on Paris. "It's between the two of us now!" Like Lucien at the Opéra, when he says to himself: "This is my kingdom" (*Illusions perdues*, p.622). Almost the words of Satan on the mountain. Once Goriot is under the ground Rastignac immediately betrays him by "going to dinner at

Mme de Nucingen's." What he just followed to the grave was not the body of an old pasta merchant but his own soul, his own honor, his own youth.

And so we see Rastignac enthroned in the Nucingen household and, in consequence, with enough pocket money at his disposal to take his place in the circle of dandies. Does he have any genuine friends, though? I doubt it. We rarely see him doing anyone a good turn, and from time to time we even catch him revealing rather petty jealousies. It is Rastignac who discloses the truth about Rubempré's lowly birth when the latter comes to Paris, and then the facts about his misdemeanors when he returns to Angoulême (*Illusions perdues*, pp. 619 and 904). Later on, he feigns for this same Rubempré the liveliest of friendships, but that no doubt is the result of threats on Vautrin's part. He is also one of the few people who takes part in Lucien's funeral procession. He is almost alone behind Goriot's coffin and almost alone behind Lucien's too. Obviously a young man with a great weakness for hugger-mugger burials.

Everyone in Paris, it goes without saying, is aware of his new circumstances. "What have you got against M. de Rastignac?" the Comte de Fontaine asks his daughter. "Mme de Nucingen has made a banker of him," she replies maliciously (*Bal de Sceaux*, p.90). And Blondet too: "Rastignac's fortune is simply Delphine de Nucingen" (*Maison Nucingen*, p.597). The husband is also in the know. "I neffer tolt you you foss riticuluss ven you pegan tooing much vorse for your little Muhssyuh te Rastignac," he says to his wife in his own private language (*Splendeurs*, p.774). But Nucingen is in fact delighted at being able to delegate the deadly pleasures of home life. Now it is Eugène who takes Delphine out to the Bois, who has to put up with her migraines, her whims and her bad tempers. Prudently, like the sensible young man he is, he sails along in the wake of little, blonde Delphine with her white eyelashes. Does he love her? Perhaps. But one can sense that he is also eaten up with desires for other women. He would very much like to have an affair with Mme de Listomère (see *Etude de Femme*), but he hasn't the courage to follow up his opportunity. What if Delphine were to find out! I can recall a brief flirtation with Mme de Maufrigneuse (*Secrets de la princesse de Cadignan*, p.14), but it was undoubtedly the Duchess herself who took the initiative there. He sometimes risks an appearance in the world of pleasure, at Esther's (*Splendeurs*, p.863), at Suzanne du Val Noble's (*Illusions perdues*, p.785), but even on those occasions he remains cautious, aloof and pompous. He is the kind of man who is always watching himself, who refuses to compromise himself, who represses himself. *Etude de Femme* is in fact an almost clinical study of repression: a man writing to a woman, then absent-mindedly writing another woman's name on the envelope. Later on still, during the same year as his marriage, we also encounter Rastignac at Josépha's (*Cousine Bette*, p.200).

After a few years however, Rastignac begins to feel itchy. He's been in one place rather a long time, and his reward is a long time in coming. He has a tilbury and quantities of very handsome handkerchiefs, but no capital. In *l'Interdiction* he complains of the fact to Bianchon. He begins to think of leaving Delphine for Mme d'Espard, the same Mme d'Espard who has already proved so tempting to Lucien. In *la Peau de Chagrin*, we shall see him showing an interest in a certain widow from Alsace, encountered no doubt at Nucingen's, since the banker is also from Alsace. She says *my anchel*, but she is said to have an income of fifty thousand *livres* a year, a fact that goes a long way towards excusing her accent. He gives up the idea, however, when he discovers that the fifty thousand are in fact only eighteen thousand, and that the missing thirty-two thousand are made up for by an extra toe on her left foot. "I can't live with a woman who has six toes! People would know, I should be a laughing-stock." (*Peau de Chagrin*, p.146) People would know! As I said, in Balzac there is nothing people don't know!

It will be observed that Rastignac never for an instant considers achieving his ambitions by any means other than women. Rubempré does at least make the effort to write a book, then some newspaper articles. Rastignac does nothing. He himself admits that he is "as lazy as a lobster" (*id.* p.98). And though he is certainly cunning, can he be called intelligent? "No one has ever accused him of thinking up a good deal," Couture says (*Maison Nucingen*, p.596). According to Bixiou, he is "a fellow who never says a thing worth saying," but one who has the art, when necessary, of concentrating all his powers onto any affair that comes up (*id.* p.597). What kind of affairs? In *la Peau de Chagrin* (p.98), Rastignac explains his system: making connections. "I move around a lot, I push myself forward." When he is taking Raphaël de Valentin to the Comtesse Foedora's, he comes out with an admirably expressive remark: "You'll be quite comfortable there" (*Peau de Chagrin*, p.103). The remark of a gigolo.

Nevertheless, there is something rather disconcerting about the Rastignac of *la Peau de Chagrin*. He has a cordiality of manner that nothing in his earlier behavior has led us to expect. And he's untidy too. "There were some old socks hanging over the back of a luxurious divan" (*id.* p.148). One senses that Delphine is as clean as a cat; would she have tolerated such things? And again, in *Etude de Femme*, Rastignac appears as "a young

man as modest as he is thoughtless, full of good qualities and letting nothing show but his faults; passionate, yet always making fun of the passions"
(*Etude de Femme*, p.1049). That doesn't sound much like the Rastignac
we know either. I am inclined to believe that the Rastignac in these two
works is not entirely Rastignac. He is a convenience rather than a
character, a figure who is used in the first case to dispense certain necessary advice, and in the second as a hook to hang the storyline onto. He
could be replaced in either story by any young Parisian man about town,
and Balzac does not seem to have bothered unduly about his character,
merely brushing in lightly a few characteristics of the type he represents.

What does seem certain, however, is that there comes a moment when
Rastignac's fidelity to Delphine goes through a crisis. Doubtless Nucingen
senses the danger. What if his wife should suddenly renew her conjugal
affections? He decides to give his substitute the reward he has earned by
permitting him to benefit from the business deal that is detailed to us in *la
Maison Nucingen*. Rastignac becomes rich. From then on, Marsay is quite
prepared to refer to him as a "strange fellow who is beginning to get
somewhere" (*Contrat de Marriage*, p.198). Rather a condescending remark
from a man we have been seeing everywhere with Rastignac for several
years, in the Bois, at social events, in restaurants (*Illusions perdues*, p.624;
Cabinet des Antiques, p.377; *Rabouilleuse*, p.1113; *Ursule Mirouët*,
p.356). Be that as it may, Marsay takes him in hand, and Rastignac becomes one of the clique that seizes power in 1830. Three years later, we
see him as under-secretary of State (Une *Ténébreuse Affaire*, p.629). And
he marries Delphine's daughter, the traditional reward of the faithful gigolo.
"You're all right, you're lucky!" Maxime de Trailles says to him. "You've
managed to end up marrying the sole heiress of the Nucingen millions,
and you certainly earned them . . . Twenty years of forced labor!"
(*Député d'Arcis*, p.731). And Rastignac accepts these remarks as compli-
ment, without flinching. His marriage completes his career. He becomes a
member of the cabinet, a count and a peer. His wife is accepted by the
Grandlieus, then by Mme d'Espard (*Béatrix*, p.590, and *Député d'Arcis*,
p.731). He has an income of three hundred thousand *livres* a year (*Comédiens sans le savoir*, p.57). He provides dowries for his sisters, and one of
them marries Martial de la Roche-Hugon. His brother becomes a bishop
(*Député d'Arcis*, p.725).

Rastignac, as has often been pointed out, bears a distinct resemblance in
many ways to Thiers. Like Rastignac, Thiers was from the South and
always retained a hint of garlic in his speech. He was born in 1797, arrived

in Paris in 1821 and became a member of the new cabinet in 1830, so that his career in this respect runs almost parallel to Rastignac's. His furnished room in the Passage Montesquieu must have been very like the one occupied by Rastignac in the Vauquer pension, and his friendship with Mignet was very similar to Rastignac's with Bianchon. He also married a Mlle Dosne, the daughter of Mme Dosne. Thiers was a dandy too, and the newspapers of the day made fun of "certain blue cravats that dissolved the whole of Tortoni's into helpless laughter." * There is quite enough there to provide the basis for a character in a novel. We should beware of trying to push the parallel any further, however. Thiers is a quite different man from Rastignac. Certainly drawing-room intrigues played a certain part in his success, but there was also his work as a historian, his labors as a journalist, his erudition, his intelligence, all things singularly lacking in Rastignac, who was an idler, "a Jack of all trades and master of none" (*Peau de Chagrin*, p.98). Thiers would still have been someone who mattered, even without Mme Dosne. Rastignac without Delphine would never have amounted to anything. He might have found another Delphine, I admit, but he is first and foremost a gigolo all the same. His dandyism is, in consequence, a professional duty. Thiers' dandyism was merely a detail.

Nevertheless, in both men we can discern the same profound character trait: absence of heart and aridity of feelings. Thiers' merit resided above all in his intelligence, in his ability to see reality clearly. But his courage was a strictly intellectual courage. In 1870, the certainty of being in the right gave him the strength to face down the tumult that broke out in the Chambre. But on December 2, when he was arrested, he crumpled. "He cried out that he didn't want to die, that he wasn't a criminal, that he had been party to no conspiracy, that from that moment on he would have nothing more to do with politics." † Thiers had no real generosity of spirit. He saved France, but he was perfectly willing to accept the massacre of the communards. "M. Thiers combines an instinct for higher things with a rather inferior way of behaving in practice," Chateaubriand said. "When still quite young, at an age when it is usual still to have beliefs of some kind, he had already reached the extreme of political perversity in one leap," Emile Ollivier adds. Remove the instinct for higher things and you are left with Rastignac. If you reduce the scale as well, that is; for Rastignac is only a quarter of Thiers' stature. Though this does not do away with the resemblance. Thiers and Rastignac are both realists, both

---

* Henri Malo: *Thiers* (p.101).
† Henri Malo: *Thiers* (p.421).

men who understand everything except the incomprehensible, except those forces, at once too generous and too undisciplined to come within their comprehension, that open a way to the hearts of a people. Thiers restored France's frontiers, but it was to Gambetta that the French raised the statues. Neither Thiers nor Rastignac had any beliefs, they were content merely to reflect on the world as it was. However, this lack of profound convictions did at least mean that they were both free from ideological rancor. Thiers had a passport issued to a communard who had managed to escape the firing-squad, and Rastignac authorizes d'Arthez to have Michel Chrestien decently buried after his death in a riot (*Secrets de la Princesse de Cadignan*, p.24). It goes without saying, of course, that Balzac, since he died in 1850, could not have known most of the incidents in Thiers' career that I have mentioned here. But he foresaw them, and we shall be meeting other examples of this gift of second sight that he possessed. I shall only mention one of them at this point: a letter to Mme Hanska in which he discusses M. Prudhomme, the character then very recently created by Monnier. Balzac claims that he could have got much more out of this particular type, and goes on to explain what he means. It is impossible to believe that Balzac was not thinking of Thiers when he wrote this letter, as Thibaudet says, in his *Histoire de la littérature française:* "Everything is there: the Anzin mines as well as the love affair with his mother-in-law. Yet in 1830 the young and brilliant minister, Talleyrand's pupil and favorite, had absolutely nothing about him, either physically or morally, of the Prudhomme figure, at once so petty and so great, that M. Thiers was to become for his critics after 1871. It is as though Balzac, with the aid of his seven league boots, has anticipated history by forty years."

Raphaël de Valentin

I mention Raphaël de Valentin at this point because he appears to be a prefiguration of both Lucien de Rubempré and Rastignac. And a symbolic prefiguration too. As is well known, *la Peau de Chagrin* is one of those works in which Balzac treats his subject realistically and fantastically at the same time. Valentin sells his soul, like Faust, but he also lives on the Rue de Varennes, just a stone's throw from where Marsay also lives. In his "real" aspect, Valentin has a great many things in common with Eugène and Lucien. Like them, he begins by shutting himself away in an attic and living on croissants and cups of milk. Like them, he falls in love with a countess and suffers all the usual agonies of the penniless young man who wants to cut a figure in Society. "Only a young man without a penny," he says, "can know how much falling in love can cost in the way of gloves, coats, shirts, etc." (*Peau de Chagrin*, p.106). This is already Rastignac's remark in *Père Goriot* (p.899): "It takes a whole lot of gigs and high-polished boots . . . of white kid gloves at six francs a pair." And lastly, like Lucien and Eugène again, Raphaël sells himself. But whereas Lucien sells himself to dishonest newspapers and then to Vautrin, whereas Eugène sells himself to Delphine, Raphaël sells himself to the Devil. Their careers run parallel, only in Valentin's case everything becomes symbolic. "Evil, which in its poetic aspect is termed the Devil" (*Splendeurs*, p.727). Here, we see everything in its poetic aspect, we are confronted with the very essence of things, not simply with an illustration of them. The Comtesse Foedora "is, if you like, Society" (*Peau de Chagrin*, p.249). Pauline is man's dreams, his capacity for love, his vocation, his better self. We shall find all these symbols again, later on, in *Père Goriot* and *Illusions perdues*, but in those works they appear only in their everyday guise. The Devil becomes Vautrin, or Lousteau, or Delphine.* Pauline is to Raphaël what his vocation as a writer is to Lucien, or his law studies to Rastignac: the honest and unsullied path of duty. The Roman orgy of *la Peau de Chagrin* becomes a supper with Coralie. Instead of the Comtesse Foedora, we find Society itself with its thousand faces, the Society that must be conquered and is so difficult to come to grips with. Society: the Beauséants' ball, Clotilde de Grandlieu, the footman who conveys to Lucien in *les Splendeurs* that he has been ostracized by those who matter, and whose stupid face at that moment is also the face of destiny itself.

Nowhere, however, do we ever meet Raphaël de Valentin again. By 1831 he is dead without issue, followed into oblivion by Pauline and the Comtesse Foedora, who vanish like symbols driven out by reality.

Henri de Marsay

Lucien de Rubempré has the weaknesses of a pretty woman, Eugène de Rastignac is hampered by the scruples of an accountant. Henri de Marsay, on the other hand, has neither weaknesses nor scruples. In him we see the lion in the full meaning of the word, and the scars he leaves upon his victims are scored with royal claws. A rogue, Taine says. If you like, yes. There is something of Vautrin in Marsay; but a Vautrin who has never

---

* "That devil," Balzac writes of Vautrin. "Just as Rastignac when tempted by that devil recoiled, so Lucien succumbed" (*Splendeurs*, p. 727). "Is he the Devil?" Esther asks (*id.* p.706).

had a ball and chain around his ankle. He is Vautrin and Rubempré at the same time: he holds all the trumps that they have and none of their disadvantages. He is handsome, young, rich, and a bastard—which gives him plenty of elbow room. The future belongs to the bastards, André Gide wrote. Especially to bastards like Marsay, for he is not only a bastard, he also has a private fortune, good connections and the support of his parents. In short, he has all the advantages of a family without any of the disadvantages.

Born in 1792 or thereabouts—for the exact date is never made quite clear—Marsay is the son of a famous English statesman, Lord Dudley, and a young girl who later, when she discovers she is pregnant, finds a M. de Marsay who is old enough and poor enough to be persuaded to marry her. (Later, she becomes a widow and remarries with the Marquis de Vordac.) Henri de Marsay is brought up by his official father's sister, an old maid, and by the Abbé de Maronis, a rather odd sort of clergyman who "nurtured him upon his own experience, dragged him extremely rarely into churches . . . took him backstage in theaters occasionally, and on visits to courtesans rather often" (*Fille aux yeux d'Or*, p.271). Lord Dudley has settled enough money on him to bring in a hundred thousand francs a year, and this, when the time comes, permits him to cut a brilliant figure in society. He lives on the Rue de l'Université and keeps fourteen horses; he is also good-looking "with the beauty of a young girl, a beauty in itself soft and effeminate, but redeemed by a calm steady gaze, by eyes as savage and unbending as those of a tiger" (*les Illusions perdues*, p.614). Later on, he is to say in all simplicity: "I was one of the handsomest young men in Paris" (*Autre Etude de Femme*, p.218).

It is not long, needless to say, before such a paragon finds a taker. At seventeen Marsay is already undergoing his initiation in the arms of a "childless widow" whom he identifies, very chivalrously, only by her first name, which is Charlotte. Alas, this Charlotte betrays him in order to marry a duke.

It is rare for a man's first love affair not to assume some particular importance for him, for it not to weigh fairly heavily in the balance that decides his fate or the formation of his character. That this is the case with Marsay he informs us himself, since his account of this liaison is only given in response to Blondet's question: "Was there any fact, or thought, or desire in your early life that told you what your vocation was?" (*Autre Etude de Femme*, p.211) Immediately after this betrayal, Marsay says, "I realized that I was meant to be a statesman" and "as far as love is concerned, I became as atheistical as a mathematician" (*id.* pp. 216 and

218). And perhaps it also explains his cruelty. Having been so badly treated by his first woman, he goes on to avenge himself on all his subsequent mistresses.

We first meet Marsay in his twenty-third year, at the moment when, with the help of a series of mysterious cabs, he is the lover of Paquita Valdès, a plump Spanish girl who speaks English. This Paquita leads the life of a virtual prisoner—a theme we have already encountered before with Esther—and dresses up her lover in womens' clothes, a fact that becomes more easily explicable when we discover that she is also the . . . is "mistress" the right term? . . . of Marsay's own half-sister, the Marquise de San-Réal, née Porraberil.

In his *Dictionnaire des Personnages*, Fernand Lotte recounts these two affairs in the reverse order, which means that Marsay's first mistress was Paquita. According to the dates given he is correct in this: the affair with Paquita takes place in 1815, whereas the one with Charlotte occurs well on into the Restoration period (in one outburst of affection the duchess-to-be mentions Louis XVIII's Charter to the nation). But according to the ages Balzac gives, I am correct. The texts make it quite clear that Marsay was only seventeen at the time of his liaison with Charlotte (*Autre Etude de Femme*, p.212), whereas at the time of the affair with Paquita he is twenty-two (*Fille aux yeux d'Or*, p.272). Besides, everything about the liaison with Paquita indicates a man who is by no means inexperienced in such matters. In short, we are faced here with one of Balzac's rare chronological errors. And as for the allusion in *Autre Etude de Femme* (p.222), suggesting that Delphine de Nucingen was Marsay's "second," that too is an oversight. Even if we look at things in the best possible light and suppose a long and improbable period of chastity on Marsay's part, Delphine could still only have been the third.

The matter is in any case of small importance. What is important to remember is that Marsay was Delphine's lover before Rastignac, Coralie's before Rubempré (*Splendeurs*, p.794) and Mme de Maufrigneuse's before Victurnien d'Esgrignon (*Cabinet des Antiques*, p.403). Obviously the man for initiations. And the curious thing is that not one of these women has remembered anything good about him. "We never love the men who set themselves up as our tutors," Mme de Maufrigneuse remarks on his account (*Secrets de la Princesse de Cadignan*, p.18). And Coralie can't even mention his name without a shudder. A bad sign this: no man merely interested in his own pleasure could have left such somber recollections in his wake. Marsay must be cruel, fundamentally cruel. He must make his women pay dearly for the humiliation he suffered at the hands of the

Duchess Charlotte, even if we do not take into account the streak of natural cruelty that probably exists in him. He basks "in evil the way Turkish women do in their baths" (*Cabinet des Antiques,* p.391). "A genuine monster" (*Père Goriot,* p.978).

Furthermore, no matter what people may say, and no matter how much nobility may sometimes appear in the actions of cruel people, no one is ever going to persuade me that it is possible to be cruel without also being mean-spirited. And despite his aura of prestige, Marsay does sometimes reveal a certain meanness of character. With women he is spiteful; with men he is envious. Envious? What has he to be envious of? you may ask. But only someone very innocent believes that envious people need a reason for their envy! Marsay is not content to shine: he wishes to shine alone. Even the most modest of stars nearby is sufficient to irk him. "Get rid of Lucien," des Lupeaulx says to Finot. "Rastignac and Marsay never want to hear his name again" (*Illusions perdues,* p.853). Not that Lucien has ever harmed them in any way, mark you. He has achieved a certain success, and that is quite enough to set them against him. And then there is Victurnien d'Esgrignon. "De Marsay," Balzac writes, "watched d'Esgrignon *sinking* with inexpressible delight. He took pleasure in leaning an arm on his shoulder, in purring to him like a friendly cat while pressing down on him with the weight of his body so as to make him disappear from view all the sooner." And again, why? Could Victurnien have done him any harm? I doubt it very much, but Marsay "was jealous of the very public way in which the Duchess (de Maufrigneuse) had insisted on being alone with d'Esgrignon" (*Cabinet des Antiques,* pp. 390-391). There is something very petty about such posthumous jealousy. Marsay also detests Vandenesse, and for reasons that are apparently no more admirable than in the case of d'Esgrignon. With Manerville, however, it is true that he reveals himself as a faithful friend and devoted companion. In *le Contrat de Mariage,* when Manerville is already a ruined man, Marsay still attempts to save him. He sends him money and offers to take him into a sort of partnership in his own political career. Why? Is it genuine friendship, or does he see Manerville as a yes-man who might be of use to him? Is Marsay one of those men who cannot do without a confidant, who must always try to prolong the rather brief pleasures of love and intrigue in conversation? There seems good reason for thinking so, when one considers the delight he seems to take in keeping Manerville up to date with his love affairs in *la Fille aux Yeux d'Or.* Perhaps he is like Peter Schlemil, who wasted away because he had no shadow.

Like many corrupt people, Marsay is also a corruptor. A deliberate and systematic one, what's more. He preaches evil and takes pleasure in seeing it spreading around him. In this respect he is a direct offspring of Satan. He makes one think of Don Juan, of Valmont in *les Liaisons Dangereuses*, of Gaudet d'Arras in *le Paysan perverti*, of Lord Henry Wotton in *The Picture of Dorian Gray*, of Ménalque in *Les Nourritures Terrestres*, or of the hero of that curious little work by Edmond Jaloux entitled *Protée*. Seen from a distance, he is merely a fop who spends two hours a day at his dressing table, a playboy, "the regent of ribaldry," as Louise de Chaulieu puts it (*Mémoires de deux Jeunes Mariées*, p.222). But beneath this mask of apparent frivolity, what scabrous and mysterious secrets lurk! As early as 1814 Marsay is already a member of the Thirteen, that secret society made up of thirteen men drawn together by a common taste for "Asiatic pleasures" with Ferragus, an ex-convict, at their head. What complicities in evil does that membership alone not suppose? Marsay is present when Ferragus poisons Maulincourt (*Ferragus*, p.55); present when Montriveau attempts to carry off the Duchesse de Langeais from her convent (*Duchesse de Langeais*, p.253); present again—indeed, the principal actor—when it comes to carrying off Paquita Valdès. Is there any deed from which he has ever shrunk? It seems unlikely. Like some perverted Hippolytus, he sleeps with Arabella Dudley, his father's wife, and no doubt gives her the two children that Lord Dudley is innocent enough to take for his own. In fact, this bastard has a very strong sense of family: it will be remembered that he also slept with Paquita, his half-sister's mistress.

Beginning in 1827, Marsay starts to raise his sights. First of all, he marries. The bride is a Miss Dinah Stevens, found for him by his mother. She is "a delightful English old maid, with two hundred and forty thousand *livres* a year . . . sole heiress of a gouty old codger . . . who, in the not very distant future, is due to leave her another fortune at least equal to the one she already possesses . . . A young lady of thirty-six, if you please . . . with a red nose and eyes like a dead goat's . . . A creature that eats, walks, drinks, is capable of having children, looking after them, bringing them up perfectly, and, in short, behaves so exactly like a woman in every way that you might even be cozened into thinking she is one" (*Contrat de Mariage*, pp. 201 and 202). Such is the fortunate lady upon whom his choice has fallen as she appears in the eyes of her timid suitor. After such a description, we can hardly be astonished at the fact that she never appears in the various drawing-rooms where her husband still continues to shine. It is also permissible to suppose that he is unfaithful to her, though I must admit that I can find no text that openly states as much. There is certainly a point at which someone says of a girl destined to a career of prostitution that she has been promised to Marsay (*Splendeurs*, p.880), but it is possible that this is merely a manner of speaking, a quip, a jest thrown out on the spur of the moment. He also visits Mme de Maufrigneuse again (*Une Ténébreuse Affaire*, p.638); but there is no way of being certain that this is not a matter of mere friendship. In *les Liaisons dangereuses*, the two corruptors fall out. Valmont and Mme de Merteil declare war on one another. But one can imagine them just as easily not falling out, continuing to see one another with pleasure, sitting together by the fireside and regaling one another with their latest depravities.

However, I myself am more inclined to believe that after 1827 women no longer counted with Marsay. "There comes an age," he wrote, "when the most beautiful mistress a man can serve is his country" (*Contrat de Mariage*, p.200). He plots, he schemes, he intrigues, he maneuvers; he collects together a group of men who, being bound together by self-interest, will always make it their first aim to push one another to the highest places in the state. Their political program consists simply of seizing power for themselves. The method they employ is close teamwork. And the moment when it pays off is the removal of Charles X in 1830. There is nothing idealistic in all this. Marsay's team marches behind the man of a dozen oaths, the old fox, Talleyrand. "I sail in the lee of a certain prince who limps only in body and whom I regard as a politician of genius" (*id.* p.200). And if we accept that Marsay's character is modeled in some ways on Morny's, then Talleyrand is in a sense his grandfather. Cunning in the same way as the famous statesman, Marsay is bound to succeed. And succeed he does. When we meet him again in 1830 he is already Premier. He is, Balzac tells us, "the only great statesman to emerge from the July Revolution" (*Député d'Arcis*, p.726). "An immensely gifted statesman," he adds elsewhere (*Fille d'Eve*, p.26). But in 1833, Marsay dies, eliminated by the only adversary he was ever unable to best: God.

Marsay, Morny: names, births, careers, all have a similar resemblance. Morny, as is well known, was the adulterine son of Queen Hortense and Charles, Comte de Flahaut, himself the adulterine son of Mme de Flahaut and Talleyrand. Like Marsay, Morny was a bastard who reaped nothing but advantages from his bastardy: money without restrictions, patronage without responsibilities. Balzac had met him at Mme Gay's, and also at the house of the Countess O'Donnell, whose doors were always open to "that crowd of dangerous, unscrupulous men, almost outlaws, but witty, charming, only too clever at evading responsibilities, and including, among others, Cabarrus, Lamothe, who was to become Emile de Girardin, Morny, the two du Bourg brothers . . ." * These du Bourg brothers were two illegitimate sons later adopted by an old and ruined aristocrat who married their mother. This detail was to be used later in the creation of Marsay. Morny's father, Charles de Flahaut, had been forced to seek refuge in England, and during his stay there had married the daughter of Lord Keith. It is interesting here to observe the association of ideas—probably unconscious—by which the anglicized Flahaut is transformed into the English Lord Dudley, who is then endowed with some measure of the prestige attaching to the station of Queen Hortense by making him not just an ordinary lord but also a renowned and powerful statesman. We also find Dudley being obliged to escape from England for somewhat nefarious motives. This detail, which serves no particular purpose in the *Comédie humaine*, is probably nothing more than a reminiscence of Flahaut's exile in England, though in his case it was a perfectly honorable one.

I have already quoted one description of Marsay: "The beauty of a young girl, a beauty in itself soft and effeminate, but redeemed by a calm and steady gaze, by eyes as savage and unbending as those of a tiger." Here is another: "Possessed of great beauty, but a kind of beauty whose effeminate charm was lent austerity and strength by something soldierlike in his supple carriage and in his manly expression . . . From time to time a brief flame would flash from those two eyes that were normally as cold as steel." These are indisputably descriptions of the same man, yet the second is in fact a portrait of Morny, one handed down to us by Corentin Guyho in his book *l'Empire inédit*. Marsay has a taste for "Asiatic pleasures." Morny, if we are to believe this same historian, "believed in nothing, desired nothing apart from pleasure," he demanded "of life all the happiness that it is capable of bestowing while refusing to bow himself, in exchange for his pleasures, to the yoke of any moral duty whatever." Marsay accompanies Montriveau on his travels in the East. Morny took part in the Algerian campaign. Marsay adores any sort of plot or intrigue. While Louis-Philippe was still on the throne, Morny had already delivered a speech in defence of secret diplomacy. Marsay becomes Premier. Morny was to be a member of the cabinet and Speaker of the House. Besides, we have only to compare Marsay to Daudet's Mora (in *le Nabab*) and Zola's Marsy (in *Son Excellence Eugène Rougon*). Despite the differ-

---

* *Balzac mis à nu*, p.85.

ence in temperament among the three novelists, the resemblance nevertheless exists. These three characters were obviously all taken from the same
model.

Except that *le Nabab* and *Son Excellence Eugène Rougon* were both
written after the Duc de Morny's death, whereas Marsay occurs in the
Comédie humaine as early as *le Bal de Sceaux*, a work written in 1829.
And in *le Contrat de Mariage*, written in 1835, Balzac is already alluding
to his political career; yet Morny in 1835 was only twenty-four, a young
man no different from a thousand others. He had still not done anything
of note, and it seems unlikely that even he himself knew what path his
future was to take. His political career didn't begin until seven years later,
and it was a very modest début even then. Morny's real opportunity, his
real political career, did not become finally apparent until the rise to
power of his half-brother, Napoleon III. And Balzac was dead by then, so
that we do not even have to admit the supposition that he might have
retouched the texts. Here again—and the example is even more striking
than that of Thiers-Rastignac—we have a genuine case of second sight.
Marsay is Morny's horoscope. And if we re-read the famous letter in *Contrat de Mariage* in which Marsay explains the methods by which he intends to seize power we shall see that the technique he outlines is not that
of revolution but of the *coup d'état*. He is concerned, not with creating
civil disorders, but with infiltrating the Civil Service. And this technique
was in fact to be used not, as Balzac has it, in 1830, when there were street
riots and popular demonstrations, but on December 2, 1851, when the
Prince-President and his acolytes limited themselves to a mere modifica-
tion in the form of a power that, in fact, they already possessed. If Marsay
had lived, it would be easy to envisage him emerging from the Opéra on
the evening of that December 1, like Morny, in his evening clothes, not
even removing his gloves in order to sign the decree that would make him,
next morning, either a political outlaw or a conqueror. The novelist's gift
is often no more than an extra-lucid capacity for observation.

The Marquis de Ronquerolles

At first glance, Ronquerolles seems the most innocuous of men. A noble
of the second rank with an estate that brings in a fair income (*Paysans*,
p.14), his family connections are impeccable: one sister married to the
Comte de Sérizy, another who is the Marquise du Rouvre. He is also elegant as to his person, for his name is often bracketed with those of all the
most noted dandies of the day. On the surface, however, he seems to be a

more serious person than these companions. He is a deputy in parliament, and slightly left of center in his politics. He does not speak often, but when he does he speaks well. He is well received in society: we see him at Mme de Beauséant's (*Père Goriot*), at Mme d'Espard's (*Interdiction*), at Mlle des Touches' (*Autre Etude de Femme*). Special peculiarities: none, since we can hardly call having been the lover of Mme de Maufrigneuse a special peculiarity. There has been one great adventure in his life: he has been on a journey to the East with Marsay and Montriveau (*Contrat de Mariage*, p. 194). Though we must be careful not to confuse this journey with the expedition to Egypt and through "the unexplored regions of Africa" that is mentioned in *les Illusions perdues* (p.501) and in *la Duchesse de Langeais* (p.161). The trip to Egypt included only Montriveau and Chatelet, and it took place somewhere between 1815 and 1818, whereas the journey to the East occurred in about 1827. And it seems likely that it was undertaken only as a subterfuge, a front to give some element of likelihood to the expedition that was being planned as a means of removing Mme de Langeais from her convent. The most important thing to remember about it is the proof it gives us that Marsay and Ronquerolles were intimately acquainted. Why the devil then, when they meet in public, do they pretend not to know one another? (*Fille aux yeux d'Or*, pp. 273-274.) Is there some mystery there? There is indeed. To our stupefaction, we are suddenly informed one day that this Ronquerolles we had thought such a sedate fellow is a member of the Thirteen. Nor is he by any means a sleeping partner. On the contrary, he is unflagging in his personal exertions and devotion to the cause. It is he, for example, who takes upon himself the task of killing young Maulincour in a duel (*Ferragus*, p.51). And I am also fairly certain that it is he who takes care of Ferragus when the ex-convict is laid up in the wretched little room where he has taken refuge (*id.* p.96). Lastly, it is in his sister's house that the kidnapping of the Duchesse de Langeais is planned to take place. All this is food for thought indeed. What services must the other members have rendered him, how vulnerable must he be to blackmail if he is thus willing to further the nefarious schemes of an escaped galley slave, if he never for an instant hesitates to compromise in such affairs a career that must in fact be very dear to his heart?

I scarcely need to add that Ronquerolles is also a member of the clique that rises so swiftly to power after 1830. He is "one of the new dynasty's most able diplomats" (*Fausse Maîtresse*, p.11). He also appears later on in the role of a kind uncle providing an income for his niece, Mme du Rouvre's daughter. I don't know who it was he married, but his own two children both died, alas, of cholera. We also know that the lion in him sometimes made a reappearance, and that this sedate gentleman allowed himself at least one visit to the celebrated Malaga (*id*. p.48).

Armand de Montriveau

Montriveau, Balzac tells us, is "as simple as a child" (*Père Goriot*, p.875). He has the gravity, the seriousness, the logic of a child. He takes nothing lightly and thinks everything through to its conclusion. Life appears to him in the guise of a theorem, and what is more he is a colonel in the artillery—a very serious-minded lot, according to Balzac. Like Ronque-rolles, Montriveau is a liberal. He has served under Napoleon, though without much enthusiasm. He lives on the Rue de Seine, the prettiest street in Paris, so Léautaud tells us. In 1815, having lost patience with the Bourbons because they won't recognize his rank, he travels to Egypt with Chatelet. Having been captured by the Arabs and kept a prisoner for two years, he returns even more thoughtful than before. Then he falls in love with Antoinette de Langeais, who is what we would call, if we were being polite, a flirt. She is perfectly prepared to let a man love her, but when it comes to paying him his reward she never has any change on her. (This account of her character is somewhat brief. Further details will be found in the section headed Antoinette de Langeais.) Now let me see, thinks the logical Montriveau—and he begins to expound his arguments. Major, mi-nor, conclusion. But Mme de Langeais proves strangely unaffected by this geometry. So Montriveau has her kidnapped. By whom? By the Thirteen. Yes, that is what is so unexpected in this business: this honest artillery officer belongs to the Thirteen. One simply doesn't know what to think. If Montriveau could deceive us so, whom can we ever trust again? And again we ask, why? Does he too have a taste for those Asiatic pleasures? Is he another of those quiet and reputable men of whom we suddenly learn one day that they have been murdered in some dark and squalid hotel? His biographer offers us no explanations. There is simply the one bald fact: when Montriveau decides to kidnap Mme de Langeais, the Thirteen are at his disposal. However, the kidnapping does not, in fact, accomplish very much. Once the Duchesse is in his power, Montriveau discovers that he no longer wants her, and sends her home. But the Duchesse refuses to accept this turn of events, and we find her offering herself to him in every para-graph. Then, when her blandishments have proved no more successful than those of Potiphar's wife, she leaves Paris and disappears. Montriveau's passion immediately flames up again. What a contrary pair they make!

And eventually he finds the Duchesse again in a convent in the Balearic islands. He charters a brig with the intention of carrying her off a second time; but once more the Duchesse evades him; this time by dying. Quite frankly, it seems to be pushing flirtatiousness a little far. "Ah well," says Ronquerolles, phlegmatic as ever, "let's tie a cannon ball to each of her feet, throw her into the sea, and think no more about her than if she were some book we read when we were children" (*Duchesse de Langeais*, p.254).

In 1842, Montriveau is a peer of France. He has also been promoted to the rank of general, and we find him paying court to a Mme Rogron, one of the social ornaments of Provins who is only waiting for her husband to die in order to remarry (*Pierrette*, p.781). From Mme de Langeais to Mme Rogron! It hardly seems worth having been a member of the Thirteen for that. Though it is true that Mme Rogron was born a Chargeboeuf.

Maxime de Trailles, Charles-Edouard de la Palférine, Franchessini

With Maxime de Trailles, La Palférine and Franchessini we have moved down a rung. No big incomes here, no state emoluments, no landed property, or indeed property of any sort. There is just a façade. They have pretty enough waistcoats, these young men, but there is nothing in the pockets. They talk loudly all right, but that's because they have no money to talk for them. Between Marsay and Maxime de Trailles there lies the gulf that separates the adventurous lion from the adventurer. De Trailles is ravenous for success. Marsay merely has appetites. It's not at all the same thing.

To begin with, where did he spring from, this Maxime de Trailles, this "Archduke of Bohemia" (*Béatrix*, p.589) who of all these young men is the one who has most resolutely flung all scruples onto the rubbish heap, this rake who is so renowned as such amongst a whole company of rakes that people say "a worse rake than Maxime de Trailles" (*Employés*, p.870) just as they might say "more Catholic than the Pope"; "the ablest, the cleverest, etc., of all those young pirates with their yellow gloves, their cabriolets and their beautiful manners" (*Un Homme d'affaires*, p.806).

We have been nobles since François I, he says in *Béatrix* (p.590) and Counts since Catherine de Médicis. He himself was born in 1792 and has been a page to the Emperor (*Député d'Arcis*, p.726). All of which may be true. I say "maybe" because I find it odd that with all that family history he apparently possesses not a single uncle, not a single aunt, not a single cousin. Admittedly none of our other lions, with the exception of Ronquerolles, have any family either; but at least Balzac has taken the trouble to explain why. Marsay is a bastard. Lucien de Rubempré's and Eugène de Rastignac's families live in the country. But de Trailles is alone, completely alone, and without any reasons being given.

He doesn't work, of course, that goes without saying. No one has ever heard of him owning a single acre of land or a single stock, bond or share (*Gobseck*, p.642). In which case, where does he find those "hundred thousand francs" we are told he spends in a year? What a question! God did, after all, create woman as a companion for man, and Maxime quite simply lives off those companions. He completely ruins Esther's mother, the beautiful Dutchwoman so celebrated for her supine activities, and then, opening a second front, he moves in on Delphine's sister, Mme de Restaud, who sacrifices everything for him, right down to her jewels (*Gobseck*). "All the women are mad about him" (*Gobseck*, p.642). Is he handsome then? Yes, but that's not all. He is a lion, a dandy, the most frequently mentioned of all the dandies (*Contrat de Mariage*, p.199; *Cabinet des Antiques*, p.377; *Ursule Mirouët*, pp. 356 and 465; *Fausse Maîtresse*, p.13; *Illusions perdues*, p.810; etc.). "Typical of the knight-errants to be found in our drawing-rooms, in our boudoirs, on our boulevards, a kind of amphibian partaking equally of the characteristics of the man and the woman, the Comte Maxime de Trailles is a singular creature, a Jack of all trades and a master of none, both feared and despised, a know-all who knows nothing, as capable of committing a good deed as he is of performing a crime, at one moment entirely base, the next entirely noble, spattered with mud rather than dripping with blood, suffering more from present difficulties than from remorse over the past, more concerned with his digestion than with the development of his mind, adept at feigning passions and incapable of feeling. He is a glittering link that might serve to unite the convict hulks with high society, a man who belongs to that eminently intelligent class of beings from which there occasionally rises the towering figure of a Mirabeau, a Pitt or a Richelieu, but which more often produces our Comtes de Horn, our Fouquier-Tinvilles and our Coignards" (*Gobseck*, p.642). As familiar a sight at the gaming tables as the cards themselves, a fearless drinker, a great sportsman, a redoutable duellist, such is Maxime de Trailles. But it must be admitted that he has a certain stature, a certain air of style. He leaves the Rubemprés and the Rastignacs a long way behind. Is he even a lion? He seems at times more like a tiger. One of the great cats anyway, and of the same species as Henri de Marsay. Except that de Trailles is less intelligent. He is cunning, of course, but cunning is not the same thing as intelligence. "A man who belongs to that eminently intelligent class of beings . . ." Balzac writes. But nowhere does he quote a single remark by de Trailles that can be compared to the aphorisms he puts in the mouth of Marsay. His intelligence is instinctive and on a lower level than that of Marsay, for Marsay's actions are governed by a conscious philosophy, whereas de Trailles has only a sort of animal cunning on which to rely. I repeat, a tiger, and a tiger who can occasionally deal himself a winning hand, if no one objects to the metaphor. Marsay dies in his prime, but one feels that he would have continued to grow with age, for that is one of the advantages bestowed by intelligence. Maxime de Trailles, on the other hand, deteriorates as he grows older, for that is one of the disadvantages attendant upon instinct. As a young man he was a member of the Thirteen, and probably one of the most active ones. His youth, Balzac tells us, was disfigured "by a series of frightful tragedies" (*Député d'Arcis*, p.726). Later on, he only manages to keep his head above water thanks to Marsay, who entrusts him occasionally "with the sort of secret mission that necessitates a conscience hardened by the hammer of necessity and the kind of undaunted deviousness that will stick at absolutely nothing" (*Député d'Arcis*, p.727). Once Marsay is no longer there, de Trailles begins to stagnate. By 1839, he already has "a fair amount of lines on his face." His amorous activities still continue, but the kind of women with whom we find him involved show how sadly he has slipped: Hortense, then Antonia (whom he keeps—the ultimate fall from grace). In *Un Homme d'affaires*, we see him being very neatly conned. He is clearly uneasy about his position and worrying about his old age. Then, in *le Député d'Arcis*, he persuades Rastignac to entrust him with a secret mission. Since the book was never finished, we shall never know for sure whether he accomplished it successfully; but I doubt it, since only a short while afterwards, in *Béatrix*, we find the Duchesse de Grandlieu entrusting him with the sort of petty task that one would never dare to propose to a man who had really arrived. It is on this occasion too that he announces his impending marriage with a young woman who, despite the fact that he does not disclose her name himself, can be none other than the daughter of Philéas Beauvisage, a parvenu milliner. He has thus at least made certain of having enough to eat during his old age. In 1845, he is a deputy, and votes with the government (*Comédiens sans le savoir*, p.57). One feels justified in supposing that he derives some material advantage from doing so.

Tradition has it that much of Balzac's inspiration for the character of de Trailles was drawn from that of the Comte Casimir de Montrond, whom he had met at the house of his friends the Doumercs. Among other things, this Montrond was also the husband of Aimée de Coigny, the young woman for whom André Chénier wrote *la Jeune Captive*. Such a link between the pure poet who lost his head on the guillotine and the scabrous de Trailles is certainly unexpected.

It is true, however, that de Trailles and Montrond are not exactly the same person. For one thing, the model is much older than the portrait. Balzac only knew Montrond when he was already quite old and, as they say, out to grass; whereas we are shown de Trailles as a young man. Here we have the first transposition. Balzac had to imagine what de Trailles' youth was like, and in doing so he must have based his image not only on direct observation but also on reminiscences, on a legend. On the legend especially. As we learn from the memoirs of his contemporaries, Montrond belonged to that enigmatic race of men around whom there hovers a persistent air of mystery that with the passing of time makes them seem much more mysterious than they ever were in reality. This process becomes clear when we read the passages in which Balzac describes Maxime de Trailles. When he talks about him, the man takes on an epic, legendary quality. When he shows him in action, then de Trailles becomes, if we are to be honest, rather commonplace. Balzac compares him to Pitt and Richelieu. That is a reflection of the Montrond legend. But when it comes to justifying this reputation, all we find is the final intrigue in *Béatrix*, which is not bad, I admit, but which nevertheless does not call for any very extraordinary measure of intelligence, or for "that sang-froid, that aplomb, that gift for immediately grasping a whole situation that are the sure signs of the true Machiavellian in thought and politics" (*Député d'Arcis*, p.727). I have already remarked upon the way in which Maxime de Trailles diminishes in stature with age, the way in which he is gradually reduced to more everyday proportions. This is because Balzac was able to study Montrond as an old man in person. The legend vanishes, it is replaced by direct observation, by the portrait. This is the exact opposite of what happened in the case of Marsay-Morny. Because Balzac knew Morny as a young man, the young Marsay who was modeled on him emerged as a young man-about-town with above-average connections but otherwise normal enough. As he grows older, however, as he gradually detaches himself from his model, so Marsay grows in stature, begins to take on the proportions of a titan and ends up a living legend. Whereas

Maxime de Trailles shrinks as he grows older because he is also growing steadily more like his real-life model. With Balzac, as I shall have occasion to observe again later, there is an almost constant conflict between his observation and his powers of vision. All the strength of his temperament is constantly driving him onwards and upwards to the high peaks of legend, while the lucidity of his perceptions is just as constantly bringing him back to earth. Raphaël de Valentin is the legend, Rastignac the reality. De Trailles as a young man is the vision, de Trailles in old age the reality.

There can be no legend without magnification, no reminiscence without simplification. When I was twenty years old, I once listened to Victor Serge, the revolutionary, telling the story of his life. He had been involved in the Bonnot affair, a typesetter in Barcelona, a soldier in the Red army and an exile in Siberia. He must undoubtedly have had quiet times too, uneventful evenings spent at home; but he didn't tell us about them. Nothing could be more natural, because no one would have been interested, but the result is that whenever I think of him now I can only picture him surrounded by flashes of lightning, bathed in an atmosphere of tragedy, an atmosphere that was in fact the one he lived in, but that was certainly not his constant habitat. That is the first stage of distortion. And if I were to make use of these reminiscences now, in order to create a character in a novel, I should introduce yet another level of distortion. In order to make my hero more striking I should "lay it on thick," as they say: change occasional actions into fixed habits, perhaps, or make some chance happening into the fruit of conscious and deliberate intent. That is the second stage of distortion. Montrond once killed someone in a duel. Once and only once, mark you; but this fact became a part of the legend. He began to be referred to as "a terrible opponent in a duel." That is the first stage of magnification. In Balzac's version, this becomes: "His youth was disfigured by a series of frightful tragedies." That is the second stage of magnification—the novelist's. After all, Balzac never claimed to be giving us Montrond's biography. He was simply trying to create the character of an adventurer, and in order to do this he dipped into the fund of raw material represented by Montrond, picked out certain characteristics while ignoring others, which is the first stage of distortion, then magnified their importance, which is a second stage of distortion. Montrond was an adventurer, it is true, but of a different metal. He was a friend of Louis-Philippe and Talleyrand's confidant for a start. People who knew him spoke of him as a man of education and culture. And there was a certain breadth in his political views. All of these details were not used in the creation of Maxime de Trailles because de Trailles is a simplified Montrond, a fragment of Montrond, just as Rastignac is a fragment of Thiers. And what is more, a fragment seen through a magnifying glass, a fragment that did have its effect on the man as a whole, but nevertheless a fragment, and therefore inferior to the complete original. Rastignac is a Thiers two rungs further down the scale, just as Maxime de Trailles is a slightly lower form of Montrond. Like Montrond, de Trailles ruins a woman; but she is a demi-mondaine, whereas Montrond's victim was his own wife, which, as Coralie would say, makes it good form. Like Montrond, de Trailles is entrusted with missions; but his is in Arcis-sur-Aube, whereas the original's is in London. Like Montrond, de Trailles is a determined lover; but he never rises any higher than the Comtesse de Restaud, whereas Montrond found his way into the bed of Pauline Bonaparte.

I have already mentioned the Doumercs. The *Comédie humaine* owes them a great deal (even its very existence, perhaps, since it was in their house that its author's father first met his future wife). One of these Doumercs, Auguste, had flung himself "into the alchemist's illusion. He frittered away a portion of his father's fortune and the entire dowry of his wife, a Mlle de Chapeaurouge, from Hamburg, in his quest of the absolute . . . Their daughter, Suzanne, fought against this mania of her father's with great energy" (*Balzac mis à nu*). There is no difficulty here in recognizing Balthazar Claës, his foreign wife and their daughter Marguerite. As for Alexandre Doumerc, "after having kept a series of dancers from the Opéra, he then descended to a woman who sold jewels in the Palais-Royal and after that to an acrobat from one of the music-halls . . . Every day saw him sinking further into a hideous physical and moral degradation" (*id.*). Here we recognize the Baron Hulot descending from Josépha to Elodie. And there is another amusing example of Balzac's reminiscences of this family. This same Doumerc's wife had been the viceroy Eugène's mistress, and if we are to believe the author of *Balzac mis à nu* she even attempted to restore the fortunes of her family by making her way into the favors of Napoleon himself. Such behavior could obviously not be used in the portrayal of the Baronne Hulot, who is virtue itself, but some vestiges of these facts nevertheless remain. Mme Hulot, Balzac tells us, "had the honor of refusing the homage of the Emperor" (*Cousine Bette*, p.155), and she is also forced in the end to attempt the seduction of Crevel in an attempt to save her family from ruin.

Before settling down and laying aside the scepter he had borne in his role as Archduke of Bohemia, Maxime de Trailles was to designate his successor himself. "La Palférine!" he exclaims. "You have a bold way of thinking and your daring is only exceeded by the quickness of your wit, You could go very far . . . I'll tell you something . . . out of all those who have launched themselves into the career I am now at the end of, out of all those who have been held up to me as rivals, you are the only one whose chances I have ever fancied" (*Béatrix*, pp. 594-595).

"Gabriel-Jean-Anne-Victor-Benjamin-Georges-Ferdinand-Charles-Edouard Rusticoli, Comte de la Palférine" is the last descendant of a great family. He is also another orphan, completely without relatives and as poor as Job. Nevertheless, he has an air about him. In 1834, he is "the living image of Louis XIII, with the same pale brow, curving gracefully at the temples, the same olive complexion, that Italian skin tint that becomes white in artificial light, the same long dark hair, and the same small black beard" (*Un Prince de la Bohème*, p.832).

Born in 1812, La Palférine belongs to the generation after that of Marsay and de Trailles, and, as I have already mentioned, the lions were disappearing as a social type under Louis-Philippe. La Palférine is already no longer a lion in the full sense of the word. He is still received in Society on account of his name, but his way of life and his careless attitude towards social success place him much nearer to someone like Lousteau and the world of literary Bohemia than to someone like Maxime de Trailles. Not much concerned with personal elegance, lacking all visible attachment to such things as waistcoats, he lives in an attic and is perfectly willing, should the necessity arise, to dine off a piece of bread. Maxime de Trailles, on the other hand, always went to the Café de Paris even when he hadn't a cent to his name. With La Palférine, we are already well on the way to Murger's *Vie de Bohème*. Nor has he the bitter determination of a de Trailles. In *Béatrix*, he agrees to seduce a woman in exchange for a certain sum of money, but in him this trait seems more comic than repulsive. He has somehow retained in his character a childish feeling for mischief, a capricious gaiety that takes the sting out of many of the things he does. One day, while wandering along "following his cane," he meets a woman and gets into conversation with her. "In order to rid herself of his presence, the anonymous lady walked into a dress shop; whereupon Charles-Edouard followed her in, sat down, offered his advice and generally behaved as though he had brought her there in order to buy her a dress. The brazenness of his behavior so bewildered the lady that she was forced to leave the shop again. Out on the staircase, she told him: 'Monsieur, I am going to visit one of my husband's relations, an old lady, Mme de Bonfalot.' 'Oh, Mme de Bonfalot?' the count replied, 'how delightful. I was just going there myself.' So he escorted her to the house in question. And when Charles-Edouard went in with this lady they thought she had brought him with her, so that he was able to join in the conversation as if it were the most ordinary thing in the world . . ." (*Prince de la Bohéme*, p.832). Such behavior is inconceivable in Maxime de Trailles. Genuine lions don't play practical jokes. They are too intent on their prey to waste time amusing themselves.

The anonymous lady in this passage is Claudine, a former actress now married to du Bruel. She becomes La Palférine's mistress. One day, because of an abscess that has formed on her head, she is told she must cut off her hair. "Cut off Claudine's hair!" La Palférine exclaims. "Never! I'd rather lose her altogether" (*id*. p.838). "We laughed over it for half an hour without stopping," comments Nathan, who is the source of the anecdote. For these Bohemians may be more facetious than their predecessors the lions, but they are just as cruel.

We should also note that La Palférine had a short affair with Antonia Chocardelle and that he once attempted to seduce the Comtesse Laginska.

"Count Franchessini, of the Old Guard" (*Père Goriot*, p.1010) is another military lion, but there is the same distance between him and Montriveau, the same shading off as between Marsay and de Trailles. Not that Balzac tells us very much about this Franchessini fellow, mark you, but his name nevertheless suffices to evoke a tall, thin, bony, tanned figure, supple as a rapier, superior to all eventualities, sprung from no one knows where, inscrutable and disturbing. Extremely disturbing, one should perhaps add. Let us not forget that it is he, in *le Père Goriot*, who takes upon himself the task of killing young Taillefer in a duel, and on Vautrin's orders to boot. What is the hidden link between the ex-convict and this elegant young soldier who is mentioned as being one of the leading dandies of his day? We should not, I think, be very far from the mark if we were to identify Franchessini with the young Italian alluded to in *Père Goriot* (p.985) for the love of whom Vautrin had allowed himself to be sent to prison. He must be one of those Corsicans or Italians who served in the armies of Bonaparte's Empire and then, after Napoleon's fall, were reduced to living by their wits, at odds with a society whose laws they could not understand, and trailing behind them a constant feeling of nostalgia for the days when cunning, brutal determination and a saber were all one needed to achieve success.

Charles and Felix de Vandenesse

Lions also are the two Vandenesse brothers. Dandies, men-about-town, lady-killers, lions in fact. But lions, one might say, by divine right, lions who have their paws on what is theirs by right from the very start. Marsay is a bastard, Rastignac a poor cousin, de Trailles an orphan. The Vandenesses, on the other hand, have a whole family to protect them, surround them, support them. Why should they be ravenous? The table is groaning with good fare. Scions of a very noble family in the Touraine, related to both the Grandlieus and the Listomères (*Lys dans la Vallée*, p.846; *Illusions perdues*, p.618), they are accepted as a matter of course by the most exclusive circle of Parisian society in existence at that time, the select group that was referred to as the Petit Château. For though all Balzac's other lions are Orleanists, the Vandenesses, on the contrary, are very strict legitimists. Marsay mentions them as being pillars of reaction (*Contrat de Mariage*, p.200), and they do indeed prove a thousand times more reserved in their behavior than any of the other lions. We know that they keep mistresses, but at no point do we ever find them visiting women like Florine or Suzanne Val Noble. They are also rich; though not to excess, not ostentatiously so. Rich enough to do more or less as they please, but not so rich that it has deprived them of any further ambitions.

Although frequently mentioned together, the two brothers are not fond of one another. The elder occasionally betrays a certain amount of jealousy towards the younger because he proves the more successful of the two. They end up filing suit against one another (*Lys dans la Vallée*, p.1026, and *Un Début dans la Vie*, p.720). Their father dies in 1827, and Balzac tells us very little about him. Their mother is a martinet "a tall, thin, dry woman, fond of gambling, egotistical, and impertinent like all the Listomère women, with whom impertinence is accepted as being an inevitable part of the dowry" (*Lys dans la Vallée*, p.782).

Charles, the Comte and later the Marquis de Vandenesse, must have been born in about 1790. Having taken up a diplomatic career under the Empire, he is "made to see the error of his ways" in time by his father and goes over to the Bourbons. During the Hundred Days he goes to join Louis XVIII in Ghent. Always deliberately formal in his manner, his aim is to be thought of as someone with strength of character. Where is one to look for men with energy in Paris? he exclaims. He is working at making himself cold and calculating, "a dismal role, undertaken for the purpose of achieving what we call today a *good place*" (*Femme de trente ans*, p.755). In keeping with these austere ambitions, he assiduously avoids all contact with women. Such is his attitude when he first meets the Marquise d'Aiglemont. And all his principles crumble into the dust. This forceful character falls in love with an invalid. This man full of ambitions attaches himself to a woman who obliges him, and this at the very outset, to give up a diplomatic mission from which he was expecting a great advancement in his career. His brother, on the other hand, a young man neither forceful nor ambitious, finds a woman who is able to perform wonders for his future. Such are the contradictions that love delights in. However, as a matter of fact, I suspect that Charles de Vandenesse was never a genuinely strong character at any point. One has only to listen to the arguments of the Aiglemont woman, his mistress, for this to become apparent. A man with only the slightest trace of energy in his character would never have put up with her longer than it took to abuse her, whereas Charles de Vandenesse in fact has four children by her and is still seeing her in 1844 (*Femme de trente ans*, p.840) at a time when he has long since been married to Emilie de Fontaine, the Baron de Kergarouët's widow.

One sometimes sees old photographs on which someone has drawn a cross to mark the Pope as a young man, or Arthur Rimbaud as a boy, surrounded by their classmates at college. This is how Félix de Vandenesse appears in the midst of the other lions. There seems to be a cross, a glow that picks him out for our particular attention, some mysterious air about him, an expression on his face perhaps, or a particular kind of grace. Even at the Opéra or in those Parisian drawing-rooms, when he appears one has the impression of a fruit that has still not lost its bloom. What is it that generates this feeling? The delicacy of his physique? The air of reticence that causes the King to refer to him as Mlle de Vandenesse? Or simply the fact that he is the only one of all these lions that we have known while he was still a child? I myself incline to the latter view. For is Félix even a genuine lion? Balzac mentions him along with the Marsays and the Rastignacs, but the principal work devoted to him is concerned only with his pre-lion period, if I may so express myself. One does not become a lion without a period of apprenticeship, without a "sentimental education," but the fact is that in the case of all the other lions this apprenticeship is either not mentioned at all or else accounted for very briefly. Marsay graduates in the arms of Charlotte, his duchess-to-be, but his account of the affair occupies only a very few pages. Rubempré is more inclined to permit others to love him than to fall in love; his apprenticeship is never really completed. As for Rastignac, it is at the dying Goriot's bedside rather than actually in a woman's bed that he does his required reading on the cruel laws of life. With Félix, on the other hand, we are presented with a Sentimental Education already very similar to the one that Flaubert was to envisage later on, which is to say, an education of the heart completed by a revelation of the senses. In Balzac, in Félix's case, Mme Arnoux and the Maréchale are represented by Mme de Mortsauf and Arabella Dudley. The very word education implies patience, development, slow progress. A Sentimental Education is, by definition, a slow-moving book. Marsay and Rubempré go too quickly: the frenzy of their appetites condemns them to life in a hothouse atmosphere. Félix de Vandenesse, on the other hand, alone of the lions, makes us spectators of the slow flowering of his young heart.

We see him first of all as a child, puny, ailing, persecuted by his brother and his sisters, the scapegoat for their misdemeanors, rejected by his mother, abandoned for years on end in a boarding school. By the time he is twenty he has still never been out on his own. He prays, he dreams, he reads; those are his only forms of escape. "I flung myself . . . into the mysterious deeps of prayer," he writes. "I plunged despairingly into my father's library" (*Lys dans la Vallée*, pp.776 and 783). In consequence, he remains a child. "My prolonged adolescence," he says (*id*. p.781). "You're half man, half boy, aren't you?" Mme de Mortsauf says to him (*id*. p. 886). Because of his short and slender physique, people take him for a little boy. Though born in 1794, he is already twenty when he attends his first ball, whereupon, quite suddenly, without our having been given any warning, all those years of privation well up chokingly inside him, and there he is kissing a back as it passes within range! Félix! Who would ever have thought it of him? The back in question escapes, but he manages to find it again. A few days later, while visiting a nearby château, he has a presentiment that he is going to find it again, this back, this all-important back, "this back of love" (*id*. p.786). In fact he is in such an emotional state that I'm not sure he wouldn't have fallen in love with the lady of the house whatever happened, even if it had turned out that she had no connection with that back at all. Hunger for love does produce such effects, after all. This is nothing but hypothesis on my part, however, since the back in question does live there, as it happens, and, what is more, it recognizes Félix too. Seen from the front, the back's name turns out to be the Comtesse de Mortsauf, a lady who lives in seclusion at Clochegourde, near

Tours, together with two ailing children and a husband suffering from neurasthenia.

Love burgeons; or rather there grows up between them a feeling unexpressed in words or gestures, a feeling that is free to grow unhindered either by the city's bustle, the duties of a profession, a husband's jealousy or even desire with its great clumsy clogs and its lightning fencing bouts. Mme de Mortsauf's piety forbids her to betray the fidelity she has sworn to her husband. This leaves only their feeling for one another. Isolated. As solitary as a statue in the middle of a clearing. So that even their slightest gesture, their slightest word sets up endless reverberations. Mme de Mortsauf and Félix are hungry for affection only. They have never had any either of them, since both their mothers were equally sharp-tongued. So there they stand, immobile, frozen in their ecstasy, watching all the tender feelings and impulses that other people experience earlier in life now well up in themselves at last. And because these feelings have come so late they also appear to this couple's wondering gaze in all their richness, displaying their most hidden recesses, their most fleeting savors. Both past twenty, Henriette and Félix are at last discovering their youth. Hence the slowness with which they advance along those delightful paths: they are seeing them for the first time. They are both still children, and everything their eyes light upon is cause for wonder. "Love, like life, has a period of puberty during which it is sufficient unto itself" (*id.* p.807). Mme de Mortsauf is deceived by all this, and sometimes we find her caressing Félix as she might caress one of her own children, with the same candor, but with more pleasure. Her fingers touch him so lightly that the caress might almost have been a dream. Perhaps that is the origin of Félix's peculiar grace: in the midst of all those young men intently calculating their chances, he is not intent, he is not calculating; he is dreaming.

He goes on dreaming until the day when he is claimed by life and the world. Félix is called to Paris. And at this point in *Lys dans la Vallée* we meet with a most extraordinary passage. One moment everything is numb and drowsy. The next, everything is wide awake. The Prince has arrived at the Sleeping Beauty's palace. Ambition was tired of that long doze, and now it is getting up, tightening its belt and speaking out. But the strange thing is, that its voice is the voice of Mme de Mortsauf. In the letter she writes to Félix, tenderness is suddenly replaced by the wide-awake advice of a woman who knows all about the world, its stratagems and ambushes, a woman who now reveals in herself an ambition as vaulting as any Rastignac's, who is transferring this ambition, which has come too late for her husband, too early for her son, onto the young Félix. Does she realize that in doing so she is already beginning to wean him away from her, this Félix she sets so much store by? Perhaps she does. But ambition too has its sacrificial fires.

Félix is appointed secretary to Louis XVIII. The two are in intimate daily contact, and the old king's jejuneness of heart begins to dry up Félix's too. "Who could have remained impervious to the withering influence of Louis XVIII, that monarch who used to say that it is impossible for us to experience true passion before we are middle-aged, because passion cannot be truly beautiful or wild until it is mingled with some measure of impotence?" (*Lys dans la Vallée*, p.986). Félix remains faithful to Mme de Mortsauf; but there is cause to suspect that he is beginning to wear this fidelity in society, in the drawing-rooms that he frequents, like a rosette on his lapel. Everyone talks about it, and for Arabelle Dudley, Henri de Marsay's stepmother, that is challenge enough. She does not rest until she has insinuated herself between Félix's sheets and initiated him into the sublime trifles of love. Mme de Mortsauf learns of this. (As I have already observed, nothing ever remains secret in Balzac's world.) When Félix goes back to see her she receives him coolly, and inserts a few phrases of English into her conversation. The effect is rather comic. Sadly comic. The dream mists fade and vanish. Love shows its teeth. Words can be daggers: Henriette de Mortsauf is sick, and now she must face not only death but also that same abrupt disenchantment that Alissa in *la Porte Etroite* is to experience a hundred years later. She dies. Lady Dudley, now satisfied, breaks with Félix. The Sentimental Education is over. Félix has been made to understand that everything on this earth has its consequences. You think you are dreaming a beautiful dream. Suddenly you are in the midst of death and hatred and disaster. Félix was under the impression that he had been doing nothing except love; but that love was sufficient to cause a woman's death. "You have done me more harm than all the others put together," Henriette tells him (*id.* p.959). I am a murderer, Félix thinks to himself, and he shrinks in terror from the hate that he can read in the eyes of Henriette's daughter. It is a decisive moment, for the discovery of hate is at the same time a final farewell to youth. Like Rastignac at Goriot's bedside, Félix at Henriette's suddenly feels himself in the savage grip of life. In such moments the heart either breaks or turns to bronze. Félix de Vandenesse's heart turns to bronze: he becomes a lion.

For several years after this we only see him from a distance, at the Opéra, on social occasions. He is, Balzac tells us, "a gentle, modest, spiritual young man who achieved success through qualities quite the opposite of those in which de Marsay gloried" (*Illusions perdues*, p.614). This sentence is sufficient explanation of the ever-watchful hatred with which Marsay views Félix. However, Arabelle's influence has some part in it too. "Thanks to her efforts," Félix writes, "I can now count de Marsay as a mortal enemy" (*Lys dans la Vallée*, p.1028). In any case, in 1827 Marsay is still doing his utmost to bring about a duel between Manerville and Félix, by then the lover, or at least the wooer, of Marsay's wife (*Contrat de Mariage*, p.204). It is to Nathalie de Manerville that Félix writes the long letter known to us by the title of *Le Lys dans la Vallée*. In writing it, Félix demonstrates that he has still not lost all his illusions. "That which would anger a vulgar woman," he writes, "will be for you, I am sure, another reason to love me" (*Lys dans la Vallée*, p.1028). Alas, Nathalie is a vulgar woman. This confession does anger her, and it is an understandable reaction. What is less easy to comprehend is her rancor. Several years later, in *Une Fille d'Eve*, we find her still prepared to enter into an alliance with Arabelle Dudley for the purpose of destroying Félix's conjugal happiness. It is odd, this hatred that Félix generates wherever he goes. Henri de Marsay, Nathalie, Lady Dudley, they all hate him. Is it that wicked people are simply unable to tolerate goodness? Can it really be so very offensive to them? Or is it merely, in the latter two, a case of the sort of grudge that women sometimes harbor towards men who have enjoyed them without ever ceasing to despise them? Is Félix perhaps not as nice as he seems? It may be protested that he did nothing, either in the case of Arabelle or that of Nathalie, that could possibly give cause for hatred. After all, it was in both cases the woman who decided to break with him first. What innocence! When people are given to rancor, everything is an excuse for hate.

In 1828, Félix marries one of the Grandville girls. There is a story, told by Taine, that Balzac ran into one of his friends one day and said: "Do you know who is going to marry Félix de Vandenesse? One of the Grandville daughters. He's making an excellent match there too. The Grandvilles are still rich, despite all the money that Mlle de Bellefeuille has cost the family." * In fact, however, it is above all an excellent match for the Grandvilles. "Isn't my eldest daughter the Comtesse de Vandenesse?" the father asked with pride. "And as for the other, her elder sister's marriage is now a guarantee of a fine match for her too" (*Une Double Famille*, p.986). Now a new Sentimental Education begins, and this time the pupil is a woman. People are generally pleased to be able to pass on a lesson well learned, and Félix, once the pupil, is now the teacher. We may even suppose that it was with this purpose in mind that he chose such an extremely

* Taine: *Nouveaux Essais de Critique et d'Histoire.*

ignorant girl, one scarcely untied as yet from her pious mother's apron
strings. He behaves towards her more like a grandfather than a lover. This
does not prevent the young Comtesse from becoming infatuated with Nathan, but her husband, like a kind brother, or a tutor who feels an affectionate indulgence for his pupil's errors, manages to save her from the
follies into which she is preparing to plunge herself. (See *Une Fille
d'Eve*.) The new Sentimental Education is completed, and Félix has displayed his absolute proficiency as a mentor. Under the Restoration he has
been made a peer of the realm. One can picture his brother's fury. Then,
under Louis-Philippe, Félix de Vandenesse fades into obscurity.

Octave de Camps

Octave de Camps is charming, and that's more or less all that can be said
about him. Still, he really is very charming. Also intelligent, open, likeable
and gay. And honest! Honest to such an extent that he restores a fortune
his father has acquired by improper means to its rightful owner. (This
story occurs in the novella entitled *Madame Firmiani*.) He is also elegant,
and is mentioned as being one of the most brilliant young men in Paris. He
marries Mme Firmiani, an exquisite woman. We then continue to glimpse
them from time to time, always happy.

Victurnien d'Esgrignon, Savinien de Portenduère, Paul de Manerville, Godefroid de Beaudenord and August de Maulincour, *or, the lions who fell by the wayside*

After the victors, the vanquished. Here we behold the touching sight of
the lions who were really only lambs in disguise; the dandies who fell by
the wayside; the casualties in that bright theater of war that stretches
from the Chaussée-d'Antin to the Boulevard Saint-Germain. Here are the
ones who failed to get the message.

Victurnien d'Esgrignon is a victim of virtue. Not his own, needless to
say; a victim of other people's virtues. This story, Balzac writes, "will
teach you to what extent the very purest virtues, when intelligence is
lacking, can be harmful" (*Cabinet des Antiques*, p.342). Obviously the
words of a moralist, and nowadays we tend to hold the novel with a purpose in low esteem. Yet *Le Cabinet des Antiques* is, for all that, one of the
most perfect works in the whole *Comédie humaine*. The description of
the d'Esgrignon salon, Chesnel's maneuverings, the artful trickery of Mme
de Maufrigneuse, everything is perfect, exceptionally well brought off.

Yet it is a novel with a purpose all the same, as the author himself indicates: "The story will teach you. . . ." "The final catastrophe proves . . ." It is a moral tale that has been written with the express purpose of demonstrating the sad destiny that awaits a spoiled child.

We have already seen what happened to Lucien de Rubempré, and Victurnien is a second Lucien. Like him, softened by the admiration of his family, he is completely defenseless against the glamour of Paris. Like him again, he is the lover of Mme de Maufrigneuse; like him a forger; like him, he becomes acquainted with the damp straw of a prison cell; like him, he is a weakling, a man-woman, always ready to shed tears or express useless repentance. "I regard periodic repentances as a great hypocrisy," Daniel Arthez says with reference to Lucien (*Illusions perdues*, p.859). "Nothing good is ever to be expected of young men who admit their errors, repent of them, then start committing them again right away," Balzac says when referring to Victurnien. Another example of the parallelism of plots and characters that we meet so frequently in Balzac.

As I was saying, Victurnien is a victim of other people's virtues. A victim of his aunt's self-abnegation, because she sacrifices herself for him and brings him up in exactly the silly way you might expect from a pious old maid who has never set foot outside Alençon. A victim of his father's loyalty, because the old man, like a true champion of the Church and State, refuses all concessions to worldly considerations. A victim of Chesnel, the lawyer, because Chesnel allows his devotion to the family to prevent him from ever trying to check the excesses of that family's heir. And a victim of the Chevalier de Valois, who is another one who thinks he is still living in the days of the Grey Musketeers. The total result of all this is that Victurnien, in the Alençon of 1815, is still living as though it were the reign of Louis XV. The nobility has lost its power. The country is now ruled by money. But how is Victurnien to know this? What sort of people has he to teach him? An aunt for whom money doesn't exist, a father from whom the fact of his dwindling revenues is being carefully hidden, and a man like the Chevalier de Valois who believes that it is impossible to be a true nobleman without debts. At the same time, alas, the world he lives in acts on Victurnien in such a way as to deprive him of that feeling for honor, for personal dignity that tended to preserve the aristocrats of the 18th century from the abysses into which their frivolity might have plunged them. Straddled between two centuries, Victurnien takes from both of them only what will flatter his passions, not what will help him control them.

When he is sent to Paris, in 1822, Victurnien finds himself welcomed with open arms. He is a count; he is handsome. "He had the d'Esgrignons' sparkling blue eyes, their curved and delicately chiseled nose, their oval perfection of face, their ash blond hair, their pale complexion, their elegant bearing." He is not only "skilful and swift in all forms of physical exercise," but has an excellent memory and "a marvelous aptitude for all forms of learning" (*Cabinet des Antiques*, p.355). And on top of all this he also appears to be very rich. Only appears to be so however, for in fact the d'Esgrignons are absolutely ruined. The family lawyer has had to bleed himself white to provide the young man with his allowance of two thousand francs a month. You may perhaps answer that two thousand francs, in 1822 . . . Nevertheless, Balzac seems to imply that the sum was less than munificent. However, it is true that Victurnien begins by taking an apartment with an outhouse and a stable that costs him fifty thousand francs. And he also becomes the lover of Mme de Maufrigneuse. A real crossroads, the Duchesse de Maufrigneuse. And a dangerous one, for she is one of those women who, without ever asking their lovers for a cent, end up by stripping the very shirts off their backs. Félix and she go on a trip together to Italy, after which, Victurnien finds his name at the top of a bill for two hundred thousand francs (*id*. p.394). A painful moment, and one in which the true man is revealed. What is Victurnien's first reaction? "Instead of eating out in restaurants, where each dinner cost him between fifty and sixty francs, he economized by dining at the Duchesse's" (*id*. p.393). Just like Lucien, who after having squandered two thousand francs at his tailor's decides that he must now live on sixty francs a month. It is by just such silly decisions that weaklings always, and with the best will in the world, believe themselves to be affirming their strength of character. Victurnien's second reaction is also an echo of Lucien: he decides to forge a draft that will enable him to go away and live with the Duchesse in Venice. But "he made it a condition of his plan that she should previously have given her consent to their flight" (*id*. p.403). Mme de Maufrigneuse gives her consent. Victurnien commits the forgery. Then Mme de Maufrigneuse goes back on her decision. Run away? But that's so vulgar, she says. Victurnien crumbles, melts away, disappears. As a matter of fact, he has been arrested. The family lawyer arrives in time to save him, and the affair is settled by a duel between Victurnien and his principal persecutor, du Croisier. Victurnien is wounded; but he has all the time in the world in which to recover. He is doomed to seven more years of stagnation in Alençon, champing on the bit, dragging out his days in cafés, until his father's death at last permits him to enter into a misalliance with a young lady named Duval, who is du Croisier's niece and also extremely rich. Victurnien then moves gaily back to Paris in order to spend his wife's fortune. He keeps Josépha, or offers to—Balzac is not quite clear on the point (*Cousine Bette*, p.145)—and if we are to believe all the rumors he is also neatly *cleaned out* by Antonia Chocardelle (*Un Homme d'affaires*). He is mentioned frequently as a member of both Society and the demi-monde (*Béatrix*, pp.579 and 600; *Cousine Bette*, p.200). His misfortunes have done nothing to improve his character. One day, when Mme de Maufrigneuse is being discussed, he says: "She is the one I have to thank for the disgrace of my marriage" (*Secrets de la Princesse de Cadignan*, p.61). That is really killing two birds with one handful of mud. It would be difficult to pack more caddishness than that into so few words.

Savinien de Portenduère is rather more sympathetic as a character. Yet his story is in many ways exactly the same as Victurnien's. He too comes from a ruined aristocratic family, though from Nemours not Alençon; his father is dead, but he is the possessor of a mother quite as proud of her name as old d'Esgrignon was of his, though she is much more petty and sharp-tongued by nature. Savinien himself is a pleasant enough young man without much character. "A boy who dances badly," Emilie de Fontaine calls him (*Bal de Sceaux*, p.91). Several years later, however, Savinien falls in love with the aforesaid Emilie, who has by then become his great-aunt by marriage. When she repulses him he turns to Mme de Sérizy. But instead of confessing to her how poor he is, as Marsay had advised him to do—for Mme de Sérizy is a woman who understands these things—he attempts to stand on his pride and ends up lying in a debtor's prison. Henri de Marsay goes to visit him there. "You have a pair of beautiful, wide, blue eyes," he tells him, "you have a pale, well-modeled forehead, magnificent black hair, a little mustache that looks very well against your white skin, and a slender figure. You have, in short, what I would call a dark elegance . . . Pay off your debts in moderation, so that you still have enough to live on for three years, then go and marry yourself off in the provinces to the first girl you find with an income of thirty thousand *livres* a year" (*Ursule Mirouët*, pp.359 and 360). That is the verdict, and it is certainly no worse than the one Victurnien receives: "Victurnien, marry Mlle Duval" (*Cabinet des Antiques*, p.460). Marsay himself underlines the similarity: "I'm going to tell you what I told young d'Esgrignon . . ."

Back in Nemours, and in the nick of time, Savinien meets Ursule Mirouët, a young orphan with expectations of great wealth. He falls in love

with her on the spot. I can see you smiling. It is not yet a week since
Henri de Marsay, in the debtor's prison, was proposing this toast to her:
"To the girl with money" (*Ursule Mirouët*, p.360). It is scarcely any
longer since Savinien's cousin was writing to his mother about the girls
with money "who would be enchanted to become one of us" (*id*. p.362).
It is not ten hours since he was himself swearing to marry "a young lady
who can give me some social standing" (*id*. p.371). And when he first
looked at Ursule, was she not already framed for him in "those magic
words: seven to eight hundred thousand francs" (*id*. p.374)? So that we
have a great many good reasons for doubting Savinien's sincerity. Well,
we are wrong. This love, though doubtless generated in the first place by
a desire for financial gain, proves with use to be extremely durable. When
Ursule loses her fortune, Savinien remains faithful to her. His mother is
against the marriage, but what does that matter? He will wait. He is
offered a d'Aiglemont as a wife: he refuses her. Then a du Rouvre: he
again declines. Love has made this weakling strong. Or rather, the weakling turns out to have been only a dunderhead. Even during his period of
disappointments in Paris he never descends to the depths of dishonesty
that Victurnien does. He is one of those men whose whole store of energy
seems to be absorbed simply by the effort to exist, and who prove good or
bad according to the environments in which they are placed: involuntary
chameleons. In the company of Henry de Marsay, Savinien lets himself
slide; but confronted with Ursule he becomes an extremely fine young
man. And what is more, his fidelity is finally rewarded. Ursule's fortune is
restored to her, and she marries him, her Savinien. They are happy.
"There aren't two couples like them in all Paris" (*Ursule Mirouët*, p.479).
They set up house in the Rue des-Saint-Pères, near Grasset's. They are
very friendly with the young du Guénic couple (*Béatrix*, p.554), and we
meet them again, still happy, still kind and good, in *les Méfaits d'un Procureur du Roi*, a work that was unhappily scarcely more than begun.

It is Paris that ruins Victurnien, and Paris again that ruins Savinien.
Both of them, in differing degrees, find their salvations only through a
return to their respective provinces, a return that is in both cases followed
by a marriage. Is this some social theory we have stumbled upon perhaps?
Has Balzac some thesis he wishes to expound on this subject, a thesis already foreshadowing the one we find later in *les Déracinés*? Not in the
slightest. For here is Paul de Manerville to demolish any such suspicions.
Having been happy and successful in Paris, he goes under in Bordeaux.
And it is his marriage that proves his ruin.

From Savinien to Paul de Manerville is yet another step down towards nonentity. He exists; that is all that can be said. Who was Noël Bouton de Chamilly, Comte de Saint-Léger? A French army officer whose life, character and tastes are all entirely devoid of interest. Entirely, except for the fact that his existence gave rise to the most beautiful love letters ever written, the *Letters from a Portuguese Nun*. And that existence alone was enough. Enough to provide an object for that love, enough to start that burning chain of words unwinding on its way to us. Men like this, mere hatpegs, as it were, exist. And Manerville is one of them. He exists only in order to provide a hook on which can be hung, on the one side Marsay's advice, on the other his wife's conjugal trickeries.

In *la Fille aux yeux d'Or*, the story in which we meet him first, his role is simple: he is just the confidant. And what does one expect of a confidant? To be there, nothing else. Well, Manerville is there. He is rich, he comes from a good Bordeaux family, he has been attaché to an ambassador. None of which constitutes a character. He is an elegant young man, but nothing more. Balzac is quite clear on this point: he is not a dandy, he is just an elegant young man (*Contrat de Mariage*, p.84). He is mentioned a great deal (*Illusions Perdues*, pp. 786 and 810; *Cabinet des Antiques*, p.377; *Employés*, p.910), but the only detail about him that sticks in the mind, after all this, is that he lisps (*Bal de Sceaux*, p.90).

In 1822, Manerville goes back to Bordeaux and marries a "little crocodile dressed up as a woman," Nathalie Evangelista (*Contrat de Mariage*, p.173). But this marriage still doesn't make him emerge from his nonentity. He remains as much of a hatpeg as ever. The lawyers hang their lawsuits on him, Mme Evangelista her hate, Marsay his letter. When he has been ruined he goes to live abroad, while his wife stays at home being unfaithful to him and writing him letters with little squares in them reserved for kisses. This excess of misfortunes does finally drag him, though only the tiniest fraction, out of his non-existence, and at last we find a phrase in which he becomes a visible human entity: "What? That fat little man in the alpaca topcoat, the one who looks like a coachman?" (*Contrat de Mariage*, p.179.)

Manerville marries a wife who has very little money, and she ruins him. Beaudenord does the same thing, and his wife buries him. In 1822, this Beaudenord was the very flower of dandyism. Ten years later, Blondet and Finot, who know their Paris like the palms of their hands, have never even heard of him (*Maison Nucingen*, p.603). Yet he had held a great many trumps to begin with. "To start with," Bixiou explains, "he was born

Godefroid de Beaudenord. Neither Finot, nor Blondet, nor Couture, nor I myself would ever underestimate such an advantage . . . Furthermore, he was in full enjoyment of all the limbs and organs that God endowed man with, completely sound in wind and limb: no specks on his eyeballs, no false hair or padded calves; he wasn't bow-legged or bandy-legged; his knees weren't knobbly, his spine was straight, his waist was slender, his hands were white and well formed" (*id.* p.603). That is Bixiou's opinion. Emilie de Fontaine is less enthusiastic. She finds Beaudenord fat and unprepossessing (*Bal de Sceaux*, p.90). He is also a sports lover, "orphaned of both father and mother, another piece of good fortune!" and has an income of eighteen thousand *livres*. It is all very well Couture saying that "a young man who makes his début in Society at the age of twenty-one with eighteen thousand *livres* a year income is already ruined," but we know that there are some other young men, like Lucien de Rubempré, who would have been spared a great many errors of judgment by such an advantage.

Beaudenord, like everyone else, begins by being an attaché to an embassy. Back in Paris again, he furnishes the mezzanine apartment on the Quai Malaquais that Lucien de Rubempré is also to rent later on. He becomes a member of the fashionable set and occasionally appears at Suzanne du Val Noble's (*Illusions perdues*, p.785). He has a tiger, "a tiger, not a groom, as some people write when they know nothing at all about Society . . . a little Irish lad . . . ten years old . . . as full of knowledge as a retired lawyer" (*Maison Nucingen*, p.607). And we find this tiger cropping up again constantly. Beaudenord "was known by his tiger in the same way that Couture was always conspicuous because of his waistcoats" (*id.* p.608).

At this point, as though suddenly in the grip of a veritable impatience for misfortune, Beaudenord invests all his capital with Nucingen and falls in love with Isaure d'Aldrigger, a very pretty young person, the offspring of a deceased banker from Strasbourg who had been an honest enough man but a stupid one, if we are to believe Nucingen. This Isaure lives with her mother, a sort of Alpine shepherdess, and her sister, who is in love with du Tillet. There exist certain families that seem to nourish in their communal bosom a veritable vocation for disaster. Beaudenord marries Isaure, the family and the vocation. He is then ruined by Nucingen's financial operations and ends up living in an apartment on the Rue du Mont-Thabor working for his meager living. By the time we see him last, he not only has four children but has also been forced to take in the Alpine shepherdess and the sister. And there is one final misfortune: he realizes that his wife was never anything but a stupid goose.

The Baron Auguste Charbonnon de Maulincour, officer in the Royal Guard, lives with his grandmother, his only living relative. Should we interpret this as being the reason for his appalling character? It is worthy of note, in any case, that except for the Vandenesse brothers all the young men we have discussed up till now are either orphans, like Maxime de Trailles, bastards, like Marsay, lacking one parent, like Victurnien, Savinien and Lucien, or separated from their family like Rastignac. We should not be in too great a hurry to draw conclusions from this fact, however. For all his two thousand characters, Balzac, as I have already said, is in fact very economical in this matter. He does not create characters unless he really needs them. Since he sees no necessity for Savinien to have a father, he eliminates him. Such a course is natural enough. For some of these lions, however, this particular detail is not without its importance. Had he possessed a father of even a slight severity of character, Lucien de Rubempré would have been less soft as a person, and Victurnien's mother would almost certainly have brought him up more sensibly than did his kind-hearted aunt. In Maulincour's case I have my doubts. There is an element of baseness in his nature against which both a father's severity and a mother's tenderness would have been equally powerless. To begin with, he is one of Mme de Sérizy's lovers; that is a pretty poor recommendation to start off with. It means he must be vulgar. And he is: his behavior leaves us in no doubt on that score. One day, he notices Mme de Langeais' carriage drawn up in front of Montriveau's house. He rushes away to pass on this information to everyone he can find (*Duchesse de Langeais*, p.227). A short while later he catches the pretty Mme Desmarets going into a house on the Rue Soly. Without hesitation, he attempts to blackmail her, the price he requires for his silence being only too easy to imagine. He challenges her quite openly. "And the Rue Soly, Madame? What were you doing on the Rue Soly?" The elegance of his approach is quite startling, is it not? And his courage too, for Maulincour imagines that he has no one to cope with but a weak woman. He does not hesitate to follow her, to persecute her. But suddenly there is a huge stone crashing down only a few feet away from him, his vehicle breaks up under him, Ronquerolles challenges him to a duel and wounds him very seriously. The weak woman has strong defences. Mad with rage and fear, Maulincour denounces her to her husband. Another proof of his pretty character. What business is it of his where this woman takes her walks? Yet at least when threatening her in person he could imagine the possibility of her consenting to pay for his silence with her body. But what can he possibly hope to gain by going to her husband? It is useless to look for an answer, it is always useless to try to understand the motives of an informer. Informing is a vice, and vice knows no logic. However, Maulincour is punished. The persecuted woman's father, the ex-convict Ferragus, injects poison into him through his hair (*sic*) and shortly afterwards Maulincour dies, mourned by no one, not even by his grandmother, for the very good reason that she has died several days before him. The details of this story are to be found in *Ferragus*.

VARIETIES OF THE SPECIES

Ajuda-Pinto and Henri Montès *or the exotic lions*

The Marquis d'Ajuda-Pinto (Miguel) is one of the dandies most frequently mentioned in the *Comédie humaine* (*Père Goriot*, p.874; *Illusions perdues*, pp. 794 and 810; *Cabinets des Antiques*, p.337; *Gobseck*, p.645). He is of Portuguese origin, very rich and related to the Grandlieus. Apart from that, we know very little about him. We see him mainly by the light of the love that Mme de Beauséant lavishes upon him with such devotion (see *le Père Goriot*). Is he faithful to her? It seems reasonable to suppose that he is. There is evidence of a brief affair with Mme de Maufrigneuse (*Secrets de la Princesse de Cadignan*, p.27), but none that gives any reason to suppose that this episode did not occur after his liaison with Mme de Beauséant. For, in 1819, Ajuda deserts Mme de Beauséant in order to marry a lady of the Rochefide family who is a millionairess over and over again. And heaven knows that in deserting his mistress Ajuda is still strictly within his rights, but was that any reason to conceal his intentions from her until the very last moment? We can only conclude that he must be another coward, this Portuguese Marquis, and, like a great many cowards, somewhat lacking in powers of decision. "He was perhaps already in despair over his marriage" (*Père Goriot*, p.1060). Left a widower by his Rochefide wife, he then marries a Grandlieu (*Béatrix*, p.589). And that's enough about Ajuda.

After Portugal, Brazil. After Ajuda, the amiable lion of the Chaussée-d'Antin, here is "my beautiful jaguar who has forsaken the virgin forests of Brazil for me" (*Cousine Bette*, p.296), here is the Baron Henri Montès de Montéjanos. This member of the great cat family appears in the second generation of Balzac characters; he is wholly Louis-Philippe in style. With his hundred-thousand-franc diamond pinned into his cravat he makes one think of Valéry Larbaud's Barnabooth. But a Barnabooth without education, without intelligence, without anxiety. Physically, he is a colossus. "That ape," Hulot calls him (*id.* p.294). He makes his appearance in Valérie Marneffe's drawing-room like an elephant, and the moment he is inside it he begins talking about throwing everyone else out of the windows. In fact, this Atlas is a sheep. He has one of those sweet and gentle natures that predestinate their possessors to "the form of exploitation that weak women are able to practice on strong men" (*id.* p.287). He accepts Valérie's explanations without so much as a frown. Yet there is food enough there for one or two suspicions, one would have thought. Leaving her in Paris, he had gone back home to sell his possessions in Brazil only so that he might then return and lay the proceeds at her feet. When he does come back, he finds her being shared by three lovers and the social center of a company of people of unlimited irresponsibility. Before he will become angry with her, it proves necessary to show him the acid Valérie being laced up in a rented lovenest by Steinbock. At this, he waxes as furious as anyone could wish, infects Valérie with an appalling illness and disappears once more to Brazil.

Clément Chardin des Lupeaulx, Sixte du Chatelet, Martial de la Roche-Hugon *or the lions-in-waiting*

Both civil servants, and already more advanced in years than the preceding examples of the species, Chatelet and des Lupeaulx are not genuine lions. However, the former was Montriveau's companion in Egypt, and the latter always seems to enjoy being among the true dandies, so it seemed to me fitting that they should bring up the tail-end of this chapter.

Every form of government needs its charwoman, Balzac tells us more or less (*Employés*, p.886). And in the case of the cabinets under the Restoration, this charwoman is des Lupeaulx. As soon as there appears any shadow of political equivocation, manipulation, secret compromise, under-the-counter bargaining, you can be sure that des Lupeaulx will be there, tucked away in his corner in his little powdered wig, his gray breeches and his short, tight-fitting topcoat. Des Lupeaulx is equivocation incarnate. "To honest people who can only be at ease with the truth, des Lupeaulx's presence was intolerable" (*Employés*, p.891). It is he who negotiates with La Baudraye to achieve the restoration of a dukedom in exchange for a political appointment (*Muse du Département*, p.56). It is he who organizes the trap into which Lucien de Rubempré tumbles in *Illusions perdues* (p.852). It is he who is entrusted with the task of "enlightening" the Attorney General in the Vautrin case (*Splendeurs*, p.1117). And lastly, it is he who manages the shady business of Baudoyer's appointment in *les Employés*. He is used for all the dirty work, for negotiations that cannot be entrusted to anyone honest, for any underhand transaction that a minister must be in a position to disclaim. "He can secure silence from the press on the subject of such and such a loan, or such and such a concession" (*Illusions perdues*, p.831).

This Clément Chardin des Lupeaulx, sprung from heaven knows where, born in about 1785, achieves prominence quite suddenly, in about 1814, by buying up all Louis XVIII's most pressing letters of credit on behalf of Gobseck. "This cleaning-up process" earns him an appointment as an official Receiver of Appeals, another as general secretary to one of the ministries, and a plurality of various other offices that leave him, within a few years, with "thirty thousand francs worth of current and unencumbered debts" (*Employés*, p.888). He is obviously a fellow with a great many needs, and probably vices too. There was a time when he set up an establishment for la Torpille, at that time little more than a child, and a long way from her transformation into Lucien's Esther. He has also been the lover of Mme Colleville, a lady from the middle classes with an innocent enough air who costs twenty-five thousand francs a year. We also meet des Lupeaulx visiting courtesans like Florine and Suzanne du Val Noble (*Illusions perdues*, p.785), and parties like that are only free to young men like Lousteau, whereas des Lupeaulx is certainly well over forty, with a "sixty-four-inch waist, tolerably well-fleshed, a complexion heightened by the effects of good food . . . a pair of delicate little spectacles" (*Employés*, p.891). It is easy to see what sort of man he is. Not at all brilliant, but cunning, "flattering to the point of nausea," insinuating, greedy, friendly towards the press, whom he provides with a little information occasionally, friendly towards Gobseck, to whom he sends clients,* friendly towards everyone he meets, in short, one of those men "that the tide of political events throws into prominence for a few years, then swallows up again one day during a sudden storm" (*id.* p.884). After 1830, we

---

* When Portenduère is in prison for debt, Marsay, Rastignac and Rubempré go and visit him. Whoever put you in touch with an old usurer like Gobseck? Marsay asks. Des Lupeaulx, Portenduère replies. "The three young men looked at one another, each letting the others know that he was thinking the same thought, harboring the same suspicion, even though nothing was expressed" (*Ursule Mirouët*, p.359).

lose sight of him. Meanwhile, he has become a Count, though I have no idea how. (*Splendeurs*, p.1117).

We must be careful not to confuse him with another des Lupeaulx, his nephew, who is sub-prefect of la Ville-aux-Fayes (see *les Paysans*).

The Baron Sixte du Chatelet is cast in much the same mold. Like des Lupeaulx, he is an example of the mediocrity, who is nevertheless cunning enough to make sure his ship comes home with a full hold, however shoddy the actual goods may be. This is a recurring feature in Balzac's world. Chatelet and des Lupeaulx both succeed, whereas Rubempré and Marcas, both a hundred times more gifted than the first pair, are failures. Does this mean that talent is totally unrelated to success? Or is this idea, which we find expressed in Stendhal too, simply a small way of taking revenge on the world for the fact that neither of these men, though both so successful as writers, was able to achieve success in other fields? Was there a single publisher, a single diplomat, in 1830, who had even a quarter of the talent that Balzac and Stendhal possessed? Yet Balzac was a bankrupt and Stendhal never rose higher than consul. Which may perhaps explain the temptation, in both of them, to show that Society, big business, and the upper echelons of the diplomatic corps are not at all full of brilliant people after all.

This Chatelet (for his title is stucco work, not stone, and the "du" is merely on loan), this Chatelet then, born in 1776, was once, under the Empire, secretary to an Imperial Princess. You can imagine what a drain on the intelligence that involved: ordering the flowers, playing piquet with the princess, walking the dog . . . "A good-looking man with a good figure, a good dancer, adept at billiards . . . a mediocre amateur actor, a singer of ballads, an applauder of others' *bon mots* . . . M. du Chatelet was further endowed with a talent for finishing off the flowers that the princess left incomplete in her embroidery; he would hold the skeins of silk with infinite grace while she wound it into balls, and divert her with a flow of frivolous chatter whose scabrous subject matter was concealed beneath a veil not always free from sudden holes" (*Illusions perdues*, p.500). Perhaps he was to some extent the princess's lover too. I say "to some extent" because sleeping with Chatelet must be like sleeping with nothing at all. After the collapse of the Empire, he departs for Egypt, where he spends two long years as "a prisoner of the Arabs, who constantly sold him back and forth amongst themselves without ever being able to find the slightest use for his talents" (*id*. p.501). Can you see

the Arabs doing embroidery?* Because that's the only talent Chatelet possesses. Except, heaven knows, that of lying. His mouth still full of the
calumnies he has just been voicing against Lucien, he turns to the young
man himself and says: "I have defended you everywhere" (*id.* p.626).
Having been appointed excise collector in Angoulême, he insinuates himself into Mme de Bargeton's drawing-room. He is snubbed, but he stands
firm. He has a hardiness often encountered in nonentities. And besides, he
is a civil servant—to the core. When he meets Mme de Bargeton in Paris,
what is the first thing he says? "Even at the price of losing my post!"
(*Illusions perdues*, p.595). None of which prevents him from ending up
married to Mme de Bargeton all the same. He is also made a count and
appointed to the prefecture of the Charente. There are a few further mentions of him (*Interdiction*, p.44; *Employés*, p.910), and we also see him
with Mme d'Espard at the Opéra ball (*Splendeurs*, p.656). I imagine that
his Imperial past enables him to survive the storms of the July Revolution
without suffering much damage, and that he remained prefect of the Charente until the end.

And Martial de la Roche-Hugon, is he too nothing but a mediocrity?
Or is he only pretending to be one in order to please Napoleon, who,
according to Balzac, didn't like people very much if they were too brilliant? I'm not sure. Balzac refuses to allow him anything more than "a
genius for intrigue . . . , the kind of drawing-room eloquence and the
profound knowledge of manners that can so easily usurp the place of the
genuinely superior qualities of a truly able man." That is how Balzac describes him in *la Paix du Ménage* (p.1000), in which Martial appears in the
role of a somewhat asinine fop. He can't be all that stupid, however, since
we later see him surviving not only the fall of the Empire but also that of
the Bourbons, becoming successively a prefect, an ambassador (*Paysans*,
p.151), a peer of the realm (*Contrat de Mariage*, p.205), a cabinet minister
(*Une Fille d'Eve*, p.98) and then an ambassador again (*Député d'Arcis*,
p.725). There is also some question of his being appointed Director General of the War Ministry (*Cousine Bette*, p.423). Earlier on, he married
one of Rastignac's sisters.

---

* It is curious to observe how the same misadventure, recounted so seriously in Montriveau's case, becomes farcical in Chatelet's. The two passages make an interesting
comparison (*Duchesse de Langeais*, 161, and *Illusions perdues*, 501).

Charles Grandet *or the middle-class lion*

The fact that Charles Grandet is never mentioned as being amongst the brilliant band of lions we have already discussed, even though he is a wearer of waistcoats and wields a mean eyeglass, is explained by the fact that he always displays his attractions in an inferior stratum of society. But he is a genuine lion for all that, a young man in whom we can easily discern both the genuine features of the species: foppishness and ruthlessness. He arrives in Saumur with every intention of dazzling that provincial town and of devoting "more time than in Paris to brushing his nails" (*Eugénie Grandet*, p.508). He has "a pale, laughing face" and the prettiest waistcoats in the world. "There were gray ones, white ones, black ones, scarab-colored ones with golden glints, spangled ones, moiré ones, shawl-collared ones, high-collared ones, flat-collared ones and some that buttoned all the way up to the top with golden buttons" (*id*. p.509). To begin with, though a little too soft, he seems a rather nice young man. When he talks about his mother his voice fills with tears. He takes Eugénie, his cousin, to be a reincarnation of Faust's Marguerite, and promises to be faithful to her.

All this, however, is to be effaced by the test to come, the ordeal that sweeps away the waistcoats and reveals this fop's true nature. He discovers that he is ruined, and sets sail for the West Indies. As with Venus once, a new man emerges from the waves on the other side of the Atlantic, a pirate, a slave trader, a smuggler, at once greedy and savage. "The Grandet blood ran true to its destiny. Charles became hard and ruthless in his hunt for prey. He sold Chinamen, Negroes, swallows' nests, children, performers" (*id*. p.632). Performers? Where could he have sold performers? I wonder. But let it pass. The essential fact of the matter is that he is transformed. In Balzac, moving to another country always transforms people in some way. When Charles Grandet comes back to France, in 1828, we perceive that he has left this double of his, so adventurous and so lucid in matters of business, on the other side of the equator. The idiot allows his cousin's seventeen millions to slip though his hands simply so that he can marry a Mlle d'Aubrion who brings him nothing but two bent pennies, a long nose and also, I must admit, the rank of Count and the title of Gentleman of the King's Bedchamber. A very bad bargain, as it turns out. Two years later, the king lost his throne. And Charles Grandet loses his fortune too, in one of Nucingen's crashes.

Amédée de Soulas *or a lion in the country*

Amédée de Soulas is a lion reduced to a scale suitable for life in Besançon. Born in 1809, he is twenty-five when we make his acquaintance in the novella entitled *Albert Savarus*, and one rather tends to take to him on sight because of his "big, ruddy, good-natured face" (*Albert Savarus*, p.758). Since he has an income of four thousand francs a year, he manages to cut a fairly good figure in society, though not without the use of various stratagems that make him into a martyr in the cause of elegance, and a younger brother of Rastignac in his early period. Like Beaudenord, this lion possesses a tiger, in this case named Babylas (short coat with cape, shiny leather belt, gray-blue corduroy breeches, red waistcoat, boots with turned down tops, round hat with black band). He also possesses, Amédée that is, great self-control and a certain breadth of vision. With his eye on the hand of Mlle de Watteville, he decides to pay court to her mother. Not such a bad move either, as it turns out. Mme de Watteville is very much of a churchgoer, but Amédée has sensed that she is not averse to spicy stories for all that, and he proceeds to regale her with them. To cut the story short, she finds him attractive. Everyone finds him attractive, except Mlle de Watteville, who, when the moment comes, sends him packing. Unperturbed, Amédée marries the mother, who has in the meantime become a widow. And it is his freedom from all prejudices, from all embarrassment at this point that makes Amédée the equal of his big brothers in Paris. Except that his fortune costs him dear. Mme de Soulas, it appears, starts to grow younger before everyone's eyes, while her husband begins to age. "To know a pious woman well it is unfortunately necessary to marry her" (*id*. p.857).

The dukes

No matter how young, how elegant, how dissipated a duke may be, for Balzac he is never a lion. This is doubtless because the very eminence of a duke's birth automatically precludes his possession of that minimum of ruthlessness, appetite and ambition without which no one can be a true lion. My reason for mentioning one or two of the young dukes found in the *Comédie humaine* at this point is that we so often glimpse them, whether in Society or in the demi-monde, silhouetted beside characters like Marsay or Rubempré. Though this does not, I insist, make them lions. Besides which, none of them plays a role of any importance. The Duc de

Maufrigneuse, for example, carries no weight in the *Comédie humaine* at all, unless it be that of his name itself. For apart from his name, we know very little about him indeed. Once the lover of Mme d'Uxelles, he later marries her daughter, produces a son by this wife, and then, apparently satisfied with the success of his efforts, turns into an extremely considerate husband of whom his duchess seems to take no notice whatever. He is far more concerned with his regiment than with his wife, as far as one can see. Though appearances may be deceptive, because one day we hear him telling the Duchesse that he has recognized a man in a riot as being someone who stared at her a great deal at the Opéra. Does this mean that he is concerned with his wife's adorers? Is he, perhaps, secretly in love with her, but prevented by his considerateness, by the conventions, by fear of ridicule, from admitting it to her? He keeps a ballet dancer named Mariette Godeschal. But there are also whispered rumors that he has become totally impotent (*Secrets de la Princesse de Cadignan*, p.43). What are we to think? Is Mariette merely a screen to protect him from this imputation against his virility? Or are the rumors rather the result of his reserve in his relations with Mariette? Is it that his ostensible liaison with this ballet dancer is in fact a way of avoiding being made to look ridiculous by the Duchesse's own amorous frolics? Unless, of course, it is his way of giving her an excuse for those frolics. Can it be that Maufrigneuse is a martyr to good form and conjugal solidarity? There is a passage in *les Secrets de la Princesse de Cadignan* (p.44) that might lead one to suppose so: "Whether from pride, from kindness, or from a sense of chivalry, M. de Maufrigneuse had rescued the Duchesse from a great many situations." It is true that Balzac also dismisses him as a fool. But whatever the truth of the matter, it is only very rarely that we find him visiting this Mariette of his, even though he does keep her. In any case, when the Bourbons are deposed, in 1830, he follows them into exile abroad.

This Duc de Maufrigneuse is, of course, the son of the Prince de Cadignan. In 1830 he resumes that title himself, relinquishing that of Maufrigneuse to his eldest son.

The Duc de Rhétoré, first name Alphonse, the eldest son of the Duc de Chaulieu, is a fat young man whose principal way of making himself useful in this world is by keeping Tullia, the famous dancer (*Mémoires de deux jeunes mariées*, p.101). He intends to become a diplomat; he also hunts a great deal. Like everyone else, he was at one time very close to the Princesse de Cadignan. Despite his youth, he is serious, gloomy, boring and pompous. He is willing enough to risk attending the occasional demi-monde supper, but even then he is quick to slip away as soon as things begin to warm up (*Illusions perdues*, p.741). Tullia is unfaithful to him, of course. And Rhétoré is in fact jealous of men who are attractive to women, of Rubempré, for example, whom he slanders whenever the opportunity presents itself. In the end, Rhétoré marries the Duc d'Argaiolo's widow, a brilliant match that he achieves through a misunderstanding (*Albert Savarus*).

The Duc d'Hérouville bears one of the greatest names in France. A great name and a little body. A runt in fact, the duke. A dwarf, Crevel says (*Cousine Bette*, p.145). It runs in his family. As early as the seventeenth century, in *l'Enfant maudit*, there is already mention of a dwarfish Hérouville.

And this little man's fortune is in keeping with his size: the Hérouville finances are in a state of utter ruin. "Today, there are names as illustrious as those of royal houses, like the Foix-Graillys, the Hérouvilles, that for want of money . . . have sunk into an obscurity that is the equivalent of extinction" (*Cabinet des Antiques*, p.376). Hérouville is Master of the Horse and lives on the emoluments he receives from this post with his aunt and his sister, both of them old maids. This sounds likely to finish off the stunting process altogether. But no, Hérouville too has his appetites, his ambitions; but without anything petty or mean about them. Everything Hérouville does or says is impregnated with a rather rare quality: dignity. Though he covets wealth, his main reason for doing so is the desire to restore the family name to greatness (*Modeste Mignon*, p.563). It is with this end in view—and openly admitted—that he asks for Modeste Mignon's hand in marriage. And though he fails in the attempt, still he does so with honor, and thanks to the Mignons' support he is then able to enter into several ingenious business transactions. There are puritan voices raised in complaint: "Is there not something dangerous to public morality in seeing the names of families like the Verneuils, the Maufrigneuses and the Hérouvilles mixed up with those of men like du Tillet and Nucingen in speculations being quoted in the Stock Exchange?" (*Député d'Arcis*, p.712.) Perhaps, but meanwhile the little duke is earning a fortune out of all proportion to his size. Under Louis-Philippe, he is in a position to provide Josépha Mirah with a magnificent establishment and to present her, by way of a house-warming, with an income of thirty thousand *livres* a year disguised as a cornet of sugared almonds (*Cousine Bette*, pp.200 and 201).

The Duc de Langeais is no more than an incidental character in the novel that bears his wife's name. He appears only briefly, but the appearance is a striking one. An ignoble creature, this duke. Though his manners are better, he reminds one of Marneffe. A depraved maniac, as far as one can make out. I shall return to him when discussing his wife. As for the Duc de Béthune, he is a fop of 1842, famous for his hats (*Comédiens sans le savoir*, p.25). And that seems to exhaust the subject.

CHAPTER 4

The Women

*Introductory—women in vogue—Diane de Mau-
frigneuse-Cadignan or cold hands cold heart—Antoinette de Langeais or love's quarry—the Comtesse
Foedora—Jeanne-Clémentine-Athénaïs d'Espard or
intrigue without love—Amélie Camusot or the bargain basement Marquise d'Espard—Virginie de Montcornet or all roads lead to happiness—Delphine de
Nucingen—Léontine de Sérizy—Félicité des Touches,
Dinah de la Baudraye, Naïs de Bargeton Véronique
Graslin and Célestine Rabourdin or the diverse states
of the superior woman—Blanche-Henriette de Mort-
sauf or the bitter Alissa—Renée de l'Estorade or the
industrious Martha—Louise de Chaulieu or love—
Claire de Beauséant or love crushed and avenged—
Mme Firmiani or love gratified—Béatrix de Rochefide
or the thieving magpie—Mesdames Roguin and Ti-
phaine—The Duchesse de Carigliano and the Comtesse
Ferraud or the Empire woman—Sabine du Guénic,
Hortense Steinbock, Honorine de Bauvan, Marie de
Vandenesse, Augustine de Sommervieux and Clémence
Desmarets or the storms of married life—Anastasie de
Restaud—Nathalie de Manerville—Madame de Listo-
mère and Clémentine Laginska or the baffled wives—
Mme de la Chanterie and Lady Brandon or forgotten
tragedies—Julie d'Aiglemont and Vanda de Mergi or
the invalids—Middle-class women, nameless women,
ghosts.*

AFTER HENRI DE MARSAY, Diane de Maufrigneuse. After the lion, the lioness. Put like that, it sounds delightfully simple.

As it is, however, the lion has no exact feminine counterpart. "In Society, the woman does not always prove to be merely the female of the male" (*Avant-Propos*, p.4), and "The *lion* did not give birth to the *lioness* (*Albert Savarus*, p.755). Diane de Maufrigneuse has been Marsay's mistress, and at first glance one might well take her to be his female equivalent: a woman, but of the same species. Marsay, however, is also Paquita Valdès' lover at one point. Except in the most exceptional circumstances, a Duchesse de Maufrigneuse could never be the mistress of Paquita's masculine counterpart. Where would she meet him? For a thousand reasons—mostly to do with the social structure—women in Balzac are much more limited in their development than are men. In 1819, Rastignac is a poor student. Fifteen years later, he is a cabinet minister. His mistress, on the other hand, remains the Baronne de Nucingen from beginning to end. In other words, though she is his mistress she is not his equivalent. A young man like Rubempré can be received by the Grandlieus. A woman in the same position, without money or relations, would not even be received by middle-class families. La Palférine emerges from his attic in order to dine at Mme de Rochefide's. Under the Restoration, no single woman emerging from an attic would be going any further than the sidewalk. For the lions, the field is open; for women, it is closed. The name they are born with, the family they marry into, these two factors restrict them once and for all to one small area from which they stray scarcely at all. It is true that Mme de la Baudraye goes to live with a journalist, and that Mme de Rochefide runs away with a composer; but both of them return to their husbands afterwards.

Should we then look upon women like Tullia, or Mariette, or Malaga, as being the female counterpart of the lion instead? Like Rubempré they are alone. Like Maxime de Trailles they are free. But alas, the field of action open to a woman like Malaga is scarcely less restricted than that open to a Duchesse de Maufrigneuse. The same iron laws hold true for both of them. (I am referring to Balzac's world, of course, not to ours.) A dancer like Mariette can contrive to be kept by someone like the Duc de Maufrigneuse, but this doesn't mean that she has any chance of penetrating his world, or even, more modestly, of being invited into his drawing-room. Short of actually marrying a count, like Rose Chapotel, or a judge, like Mme Schontz, in which case she will simply have moved up into the first category and exchanged one set of restrictions for another. In any case, the two examples just quoted are most exceptional. In the whole of the *Comédie humaine*, Félicité des Touches alone among women enjoys the same freedom of movement as men like Marsay. But she is rich, an orphan and a genius. Not everyone has these advantages. The others, whether they be a Malaga or a Maufrigneuse, are the prisoners of their social positions. They can, like the lions, possess a will to power, but this will to power can never do anything more than temper their characters, emancipate their minds or liberate their senses. Socially, except for the rare exceptions, it can never take them far from their starting point.

Balzac is, of course, obliged to take these social restrictions into account, but it is obvious that he chafes against them. This is another area in which we can sense the presence of the constant conflict, that goes on inside him, between his vision of the world and his observation of reality. His vision tends to make him depict Mme de Maufrigneuse as an adventuress, a female Marsay, and Mme d'Espard as an intriguer on a level with Rastignac. But his observation of the world makes him aware that women like Mmes de Maufrigneuse and d'Espard are always fettered in some way, if not by their families, then by their husbands. So he finds methods of cheating his way out of this impasse. An unmarried girl, if she is a Langeais, is a prisoner of her family. So Balzac gets her out of this prison by marrying her. Marriage is a second prison, but Balzac surreptitiously disposes of this difficulty by sending M. de Langeais away to a garrison. From then on, he ceases to exist. The fact that she has a husband doesn't prevent Mme de Langeais from spending all her time with Montriveau, which is natural enough, or from creating a scandal by her behavior, or even from becoming a nun. What is the point of her husband then? And what is his function? Simply this: to justify his wife's freedom of action, a freedom that (under the Restoration) would be difficult to credit in an unmarried girl.

Moreover, throughout the *Comédie humaine*, these non-existent husbands are legion. Firmiani has disappeared. Dudley is away a great deal. The Comtesse Foedora's husband is simply mysteriously absent. The Marquis d'Espard is separated from his wife, and the Marquis de Rochefide from his, too. Manerville goes abroad. Maufrigneuse pays no attention to his wife and doesn't even live with her. Sérizy is resigned. Aiglemont doesn't give a damn. Beauséant simply smiles. Hence the abundance of conjugal dramas and misunderstandings that have usually preceded the plots of the books themselves: their function is to justify the absence, the elimination of all those husbands. In fact, many of these women live the lives of divorced women today, without relations or husband, with no one to answer to but themselves. Free, in short. And in this respect they can be likened to the lions.

At the same time, Balzac also eliminates adultery. Oh, don't misunderstand me. Mme de Maufrigneuse and Mme de Beauséant do have lovers. And they are married. Therefore they are committing adultery. But we have been made to forget that they are married, so that the idea of adultery fades into the background. Why should we give the matter a second thought? The parties concerned never do! When does one ever hear Mme de Maufrigneuse exclaim: "Heavens! My husband!" When do we ever see Mme d'Espard taking a cab in order to visit some mysterious apartment house? When do we ever find Mme de Beauséant hiding her Ajuda in a closet? By dispensing with the husband, Balzac has also dispensed with adultery. Though I certainly wouldn't say that he is uninterested in the subject. *La Cousine Bette, Ferragus, Une Fille d'Eve, la Paix du Ménage, la Maison du Chat-qui-pelote* and *Une Double Famille* are all works deeply devoted to the examination of conjugal difficulties. But in the case of women like Mme de Maufrigneuse, like Mme de Langeais, like Arabelle Dudley, it is not the adultery that he is interested in; it is their spirit of conquest, their cruelty, their coquetry, or even, quite simply, their love. In these cases, the husband exists only as a social factor, as an accessory imposed upon them by the social structure. Mme de Maufrigneuse is always straining to rise above herself, attempting to enter the same category as Marsay, just as Mme d'Espard is always attempting to enter the same category as Rastignac. I say "attempting," because neither of them, in spite of everything, ever attains to being a genuine counterpart of the two men in question. Their husbands' roles have been curtailed, but they have nevertheless not been cut completely. They are still there, and one of the main consequences of this fact is that their wives can never contemplate further marriages. Rubempré and Marsay, on the other hand, whatever other affairs they may have on hand, never stop thinking about marriage. It is always before their eyes: the possibility of a major change in their fortunes, an event that can still entirely transform their lives. We meet all the lions before their marriages. The Maufrigneuses and the Beauséants, on the other hand, are already married by the time they make their first appearances. The road is closed for them in this direction, all hope of progress exhausted. And this constitutes a difference not only between them and the lions, but also between them and the courtesans. This is why, without prejudice, I felt I should classify the ladies of Society and the ladies of the demi-monde under different headings.

The woman in vogue

"In the farcical battles of High Society," Balzac writes, "the man in vogue is equivalent to a Field-Marshal, whereas the fashionable man ranks merely as a Lieutenant-General" (*Contrat de Mariage*, p.84). This fine distinction holds true amongst the women, too. Mme de Nucingen is a fashionable woman, and the Baronne de Macumer is another. Neither of them is a woman in vogue. In fact, there are only five women in vogue in the whole of the *Comédie humaine:* Mme de Beauséant, Mme de Maufrigneuse, Mme d'Espard, Mme de Langeais and the Comtesse Foedora. What is the difference? As I have already said, it is a subtle one. What makes an athlete a champion? The woman in vogue is a champion. A top performer. Elegance, wealth, a great name, none of these are enough in themselves. It also takes dedication: one must be called. The woman in vogue, that Carmelite of worldly success, Proust writes in his pastiche of Balzac. It also takes a constitution of iron and a heart of steel. A constitution of iron "in order to withstand the rigors of social campaigns" (*Interdiction*, p.14), and a heart of steel in order to avoid being trapped by the temptations of love. From the moment when a woman in vogue begins to care more about a man than about her worldly scepter she loses all right to her title. Sooner or later she will be forced to abdicate. Witness Mme de Beauséant and Mme de Langeais. Whereas Mme de Maufrigneuse never falls in love, and Mme d'Espard even less. They continue triumphant. Their reigns are long ones.

Diane de Maufrigneuse-Cadignan *or cold hands, cold heart*

If we are to believe that kind-hearted gossip Mme d'Espard, the Duchesse de Maufrigneuse has somewhere in the region of ten lovers during her life (*Secrets de la Princesse de Cadignan*, p.14). Of these ten, was there ever one she really loved? Later in her life, she is to say: "I am haunted in my retirement by one frightful regret: I have amused myself, but I have never loved . . . All the men I have known I have found petty, mean-minded and superficial; not one of them ever caused me the slightest surprise; they were without innocence, without greatness, without delicacy" (*id.* pp. 18 and 19). Barren of heart, cold, calculating, Diane de Maufrigneuse is a huntress roaming at will through the drawing-rooms of Parisian Society. There is nothing of the weak woman about her. Nothing, as her first name suggests, of the quivering, hunted quarry.

Born a Uxelles, one of France's greatest families, she was married in 1814 to the Duc de Maufrigneuse.* Her name, as well as that of her husband, her elegance, and her beauty all combine to make her from the very outset one of the queens of Parisian Society (*Interdiction*, p.43; *Bal de Sceaux*, p.126; *Père Goriot*, p.875; *Mémoires de deux Jeunes Mariées*, p.207). Conjugal relations: nil. M. le Duc de Maufrigneuse being, from the age of thirty-six onwards, as impotent as Charles X himself: a punishment "for having, like that monarch, indulged in excessive pleasures during his youth" (*Secrets de la Princesse de Cadignan*, p.43). From the age of thirty-six . . . The Duke had attained that age just before his marriage. He nevertheless manages to achieve "the unexpected happiness of providing himself with an heir," named Georges, after which he goes off to attend to his own affairs, always taking good care to warn his wife a week in advance whenever he returns home from his garrison. Given such a situation, can we really say that his wife is deceiving him by cultivating, either in succession or even at the same time, a certain number of lovers?

Who are these lovers? Later in her life, Diane is to display, with no apparent reluctance, an album containing portraits of "thirty or so intimate friends whom Society had labeled as her lovers" (*id.* p.14). Balzac immediately adds that "this figure was a calumny," but two lines later he himself lists Maxime de Trailles, Henri de Marsay, Rastignac, Montriveau, Victurnien d'Esgrignon, Ronquerolles, Ajuda-Pinto, Prince Galathionne, the young Duc de Grandlieu,† Rhétoré, Lucien de Rubempré and the young Vicomte de Sérizy. At a dinner mentioned later on in *les Secrets*, Mme de Montcornet, referring to Diane, insinuates that "all the guests have been at some time in her good graces" (*id.* p.62). In which case, apart from those already mentioned, we should have to add the names of Blondet, du Tillet, Nathan, Nucingen, the Vandenesse brothers and the Chevalier d'Espard (though the latter, it seems to me, is quite out of the question). Blondet also mentions a famous ambassador and a Russian general.

A strange mixture, and one that leaves the reader somewhat perplexed as to the Duchesse's tastes. Whenever we see her taking the field, it is always she who makes the choice. But what is it she chooses? Youth and

---

* In 1799, in *Les Chouans* (p.994), the future Louis XVIII had promised Montauran that he should marry a Diane d'Uxelles. If it was the future Duchesse de Maufrigneuse he meant, then the future king had considerable powers of forethought, for she was born in approximately 1796 and could hardly have been more than two or three years old at that time.
† I'm not at all sure who this "young" Duc de Grandlieu could have been. Perhaps the Vicomte Juste?

beauty? Nucingen has neither. Money then? Rubempré and Maxime de Trailles, it must in all justice be admitted, usually cost more than they bring in. Intelligence? Victurnian d'Esgrignon is a blockhead, and Ajuda very commonplace. Influence? What good would a Russian general be to her? Or Victurnien and Rubempré either? Is it love then? Maxime de Trailles never loved anyone in his life.

The selection of this group must, in fact, have been determined by two fairly simple principles: the useful and the pleasurable. The Duchesse lives resolutely above her means. Marsay informs us that she is loaded with debts. In one moment of crisis we see her debating with herself: "Go to the king and confess the debt; or seduce someone like du Tillet or Nucingen" (*Cabinet des Antiques*, p.404). So that explains the presence of the two bankers: they are the useful ones. As for the others, they are all good-looking young men or, at the very least, fops, dandies who have made love their career, almost professionals. The Duchesse too has a formidable technique. To begin with, she is blonde. Pierre Abraham, in his curious and fascinating book, *Créatures chez Balzac*, explains that blonde hair, for the author of the *Comédie humaine*, is the ensign of the woman who is more interested in love itself than in the man who enables her to enjoy it. "She was a connoiseur" (*Secrets de la Princesse de Cadignan*, p.49). When d'Arthez kisses her hand, she is aware of the "delicate sensuality" he puts into the gesture, which she feels augurs well for the powers of literature. She hopes to find in him "as much imagination in love as he displays in his style" (*id.* p.49). And to explain Rastignac and the young Sérizy, we should perhaps add to the determining factors in her choice a certain tendency to maliciousness, to spite: Spite towards Delphine in the first case, towards Sérizy's mamma in the second, a delicately administered reminder of her age to the woman who had once filched Rubempré from her.

After contemplating so densely populated a hunting-scene, it can be easily appreciated how far Diane de Maufrigneuse is from being a woman who waits for others to attack. Wait? And lose all that time? She has scarcely set eyes upon the pretty young Victurnien d'Esgrignon before she has arranged for a friend to bring him to see her. The speed with which she draws him into her clutches is a source of amazement even to Marsay. "My dear fellow," he says to Rastignac, "he'll be snapped up, *whup!* like some poor old fool by a cheating cab driver" (*Cabinet des Antiques*, p.383). "And the way she got herself up for him!" Rastignac replies. "That virginal dress, that white neck with its swanlike grace, those chaste madonna glances, those folds of white cloth, that waist in its little girl's belt!" (*id*. p.383). For Mme de Maufrigneuse, after having played the knowledgeable and debauched woman of the world for a time, has just hit upon the notion of transforming herself into an immaculate angel. But under the flickering fringes of those golden lashes, this white dove still retains her expert's eyes. She appraises the innocent Victurnien, weighs him in the balance, and makes her decision. In the twinkling of an eye, we see him caught in a running noose "slipped around his neck with the help of such delicate cajolery as the printed word could never depict. 'You will forget me,' she said. 'You will find so many women eager to flatter and woo you instead of teaching you . . . But you will come back to me when you have been disillusioned . . . Will you come before? No. Just as you wish . . . For my part, I shall tell you, in all simplicity, that it would give me great pleasure if you were to come and visit me. One so rarely meets people with true soul' " (*Cabinet des Antiques*, pp. 386 and 387). People with true soul . . . It makes one think of those classified advertisements in a certain kind of newspaper: Intellectual, refined gentleman seeks affectionate young woman . . .

At the time that she meets Victurnien, in 1822, the Duchesse is twenty-six. Previously, just after the disappointment of her marriage, there has been a period during which she attempted to make up lost ground by pretending to be an emancipated woman, by making jokes with double meanings "that were merely a proof of her ignorance to true connoisseurs" (*id*. p.384). This naïve acerbity is doubtless the cause of her attraction for Marsay, and he takes it upon himself to educate the new bride. Then, by some strange swing of the pendulum, once she has become knowledgeable in fact, this innocent girl who has been playing the knowing woman reverts to an air of innocence. When Victurnien meets her she has all the appearance of an angel, an angel who, before two winters are out, will have cost Victurnien two hundred thousand francs. "That's the price of her wings," as Rastignac puts it (*id*. p.391). She is one of those women who "without one's knowing how, on what, or where, could run through the entire revenues of this earth and the moon as well" (*id*. p.383). And this angel has a taste for the coarsest pleasures. She is constantly to be seen in cabarets and the boxes of burlesque theaters. After their trip to Italy, Victurnien, now sinking under the weight of the debts he has incurred for her, begs her to run away with him. Run away? But of course. To Venice? Certainly. "They told one another the story of their great romance in advance" (*id*. p.406). Like so many liars, Mme de Maufrigneuse wants to squeeze every last drop of juice out of her lies. Though quite determined not to go with him, she nevertheless wants to go as far as possible short of the act itself: she gives her feigned consent to the idea, she encourages him to describe to her what their life would be like there, and she keeps the idea on the boil by continuing to grant him well-timed favors.

As for actually going, that's another matter altogether. While Victurnien is losing his head and committing a forgery, Diane is thinking things over, considering, weighing the pros and the cons. She is blonde and she has blue eyes, as I have already mentioned. For Balzac, this implies "a robustness of spirit, a lucidity of observation, a swiftness of decision and a disregard, or rather a contempt, for certain considerations that would fill a man with the utmost alarm" (*id.* p.403). She has "the faculty of standing outside herself, of considering an impending disaster from a distance instead of allowing herself to be buried beneath it" (*id.* p.404). A new swing of the pendulum makes her forget all about Victurnien and concentrate entirely on her own straits. Should she confess to the King or seduce a banker. Those are the alternatives she is weighing in her mind as she listens to her lover and his gondolas. She would quite like to keep him still, but he is an encumbrance just at that moment. Like a careful general who disposes his supply wagons well back from the fighting, she would like to be able to send him back from the front line for a while, and then, when everything is quiet again, take him back. But try explaining strategy like that to someone like Victurnien! He makes a scene, and she sends him packing. She also keeps the three hundred thousand francs brought in by Victurnien's forgery. Is she intending to use them to settle her own debts? The point is never made clear. Let us do her justice though: when she hears that Victurnien has been arrested she doesn't waste a moment snatching up the three hundred thousand francs and hurrying down to Alençon disguised as a man. Or is it a disguise? Claude-Edmond Magny, in his preface to the *Secrets*, observes that Mme de Cadignan has a character that is in some ways strangely virile. And d'Arthez says of her: "That woman's greatest error is that she tries to compete with men." One has only to see the masterly way in which she circumvents the examining magistrate's wife, the ease with which she gets the better of the magistrate in charge of the case, the detachment with which she draws the moral of the story: "Victurnien, you must marry an heiress. Goodbye!" And she kisses him on the forehead. "Diane!" he cries, driven to despair. "Monsieur, you are forgetting yourself strangely." And once more the angel spreads her wings. The angel? Mme de Maufrigneuse, as Balzac himself points out, has something of Célimène about her too.

The author does not tell us how she sets about the seduction of Lucien de Rubempré several years later. The angel disguise was probably not necessary. Victurnien still had some veils of sacred innocence to protect him, whereas Lucien is merely a gigolo and therefore does not merit such careful handling. Balzac never states the facts of the matter openly, but one can form some idea of their relationship from the letters they write to one another: Lucien's "disturbing" letters, which the Duchesse keeps "because of the flattering hyperboles applied to that part of her less Duchesse than the rest"; Diane's letters in which she celebrates "the poetry of man" (*Splendeurs*, pp. 1091 and 1092). Moreover, when Lucien is arrested in his turn, faced with the danger of seeing these letters made public we find the Duchesse, as she was before at Alençon, swift, energetic, decisive, ready to grasp the bull by the horns, quickly mistress of the situation, perpetually laughing, joking, and scandalizing the respectable Duchesse de Grandlieu who is present at the interviews. I am "an old grenadier who has been under fire before," she says. And again: "There is no forbidden fruit left for me. I've eaten it all" (*Splendeurs*, p.1098). Dear Duchesse!

After 1830, now the Princesse de Cadignan, Mme de Maufrigneuse finds herself with an income reduced to only twelve thousand *livres* a year. Her husband has gone into exile with the Bourbons. She has been forced to sell the beautiful property she had inherited from her mother to La Baudraye (*Muse du Département*, p.58). She is by now thirty-four, and she wants to marry off her son to the pious Mme de Cinq-Cygne's daughter. In order to achieve this it is essential that she should no longer be a subject for gossip, and with this end in view she bravely buries herself away in a little apartment on the Rue Miromesnil. Marsay has come back to her, as Valmont comes back to Mme de Merteuil. She is still unfaithful to him, but in an unexpected way: her house is the headquarters of a conspiracy to overthrow Marsay's government. In the afternoon, she walks in her little garden, sometimes with the Marquise d'Espard. The wistaria must overhear some curious confidences, and it is in their shade that these two hussies decide to make themselves a present of the famous author, Daniel d'Arthez. Blondet, having undertaken the negotiations for them, decides to try keeping his cake as well as eating it and tells d'Arthez quite frankly what is afoot. "Give yourself body and soul; but keep your hand on your wallet" (*Secrets de la Princesse de Cadignan*, p.28). The seduction scene the Princesse puts on in the writer's honor is even more delicately imagined than the one with which she captured Victurnien. I have been so very much maligned, she says. And why? Because my mother was jealous of my husband, because my husband was jealous of me, and because, trapped between these two horrible passions, I attempted to protect myself by giving people to believe that I had indulged in one or two frivolous adventures. A lover, me? I have never done anything more than "behave like a mischievous child. I went on a journey into Italy with a young hothead whom I sent packing the moment he began talking about love" (*id*. p.53). As many untruths as there are words, in fact. And what are we to think of a woman who can trample so light-heartedly on her mother's memory? D'Arthez, however, demands nothing more than to be persuaded. From then on, they spend all their summers together in a villa outside Geneva. D'Arthez more or less stops writing. "Is that a satisfactory ending? For those with the necessary understanding, yes. For those who insist on knowing everything, no" (*id*. p.65). In any case, we know that their liaison was still going on in 1839 (*Député d'Arcis*, p.709).

Antoinette de Langeais *or love's quarry*

Born a Navarreins, in 1794, the Duchesse de Langeais is Mme de Maufrigneuse's equal in birth. Her mother died early on, I'm not quite sure when. Her father is a duke, an egotist, and not much concerned with her. Even when his daughter is struggling against the catastrophe that finally overwhelms her, it is still his own bad luck he laments: "Why put yourself through such endless agonies finding a suitable match for your daughter" (*Duchesse de Langeais*, p.234)? After which, he vanishes from the scene, perfectly happy to leave the task of sorting out the affair to others. In fact, all he had been able to find in the way of suitable matches was Langeais (Marquis of, subsequently Duke). This marriage, one of pure convenience, proved in fact to be a confrontation between "the two most antipathetic natures in the world" (*id*. p.156). At the age of twenty-two, Mme de Langeais is already separated from her husband. She lives alone, like Mme de Maufrigneuse.

Alone with her bitterness. For though it seems safe to assume that the separation between Mme de Maufrigneuse and her husband was agreed upon quite amicably, in the case of Mme de Langeais things are rather different. "There are secret offences," Balzac writes on her account, "that women never forgive." Does this mean that Mme de Langeais has been the victim of some particularly hurtful kind of infidelity? If so, why does she not take her revenge? Because she doesn't. Mme de Langeais is chaste—in her own way. She is one of those women whose "sexual organs are in their heads," as Bianchon crudely puts it (*Interdiction*, p.14). A woman who is "all head," Ronquerolles says . . . "who uses her head to accomplish what other women do more honestly with . . ." (*Duchesse de Langeais*, pp. 199 and 200). We see her at work in her scenes with Montriveau. She permits herself to be loved, she is even provocative at times; but she never goes as far as gestures, or at least not genuine gestures. Montriveau "kissed the hem of the Duchesse's dress, her feet, her knees; but in order to preserve the honor of the Faubourg Saint-Germain it is necessary that we should not reveal the secrets of its boudoirs, those boudoirs whose occupants wanted everything from love except that which would have provided proof of love" (*id.* p.196).

Why this reserve? Surely it cannot be fidelity to a husband whom she loathes. And in any case, can one say that a woman is still faithful if she spends hours allowing herself to be caressed by another man? Religious scruples? Mme de Langeais herself claims as much, but the piety of her phrases rings false. One senses that she is merely using God's name as an expedient. A natural frigidity then? But we all know that a frigid temperament is generally nothing but a temperament that has never encountered an efficient detonator. We begin to glimpse what her husband's "secret offences" must have been. We are confronted with one of those between-the-sheets dramas to which Balzac is so constantly making allusions, with one of those wedding night wounds that can scar a human being forever. In fact, the Duchesse is afraid. She does not dare to let down certain barriers because the first occasion on which she was required to do so was so horrible an experience for her. "For the sake of this woman's honor," Balzac writes, "it is necessary that we should believe her to be a virgin, even in heart; otherwise she would be too horrible" (*id.* p.191). "The Duchesse and Montriveau resembled one another in that they were both far from expert in the matter of love. Of the theory she knew very little, of the practice nothing at all" (*id.* p.195). Things would doubtless have gone on forever like this, if Montriveau had not been a lion, if he had not, in consequence of this fact, been possessed of several rather inconvenient friends. "Has the Duchesse become your mistress?" Ronquerolles asks him. A further example of the indiscreet camaraderie prevalent among the lions. This question is sufficient to awaken Montriveau from his trance. One evening he kidnaps the Duchesse, takes her away to a mysterious apartment, then sends her home again without having laid a finger on her. Whereupon the Duchesse begins to love him. So Ronquerolles was right: she is the sort of woman who will only respond to rough treatment. She shrieks for Montriveau to come back to her till the ceiling almost comes down. But Montriveau will no longer have anything to do with her. She creates a scandal. The scandal falls back on her. She is a creature transformed. The hard, barren-hearted woman becomes a woman genuinely, deeply in love. And she proves as much, when the loss of Montriveau has finally driven her to despair, by entering a convent situated somewhere in Spain, the author does not say where, but in a landscape that bears a staggering resemblance to that of Palma de Mallorca. Montriveau goes there to look for her. Too late. She is dead.

Though not one of Balzac's best works, *la Duchesse de Langeais* is an excellent novel. Yet there is something about it that I find disturbing, something there that seems not quite right. I'm not talking about the occasional slight improbabilities it contains. They are nothing new, after all. It is rather the author's general tone, and the rancor with which he takes sides for and against his characters. "It is essential," he writes of Mme de Langeais, "it is essential that we should believe her to be a virgin; otherwise she would be too horrible." Too horrible! I certainly don't find Mme de Langeais' coldness particularly appealing, and I am not trying to whitewash her, but I must admit that I would be inclined to save the epithet "horrible" for crimes somewhat blacker than hers. But the work, as is well known, owes its origin in large part to Balzac's bitter memories of Mme de Castries, who treated him, it is said, rather in the same way as Mme de Langeais at first treats Montriveau. This bitterness is apparent. It casts a shadow over the whole plot, and sometimes, it seems to me, makes it ring false. Everything is seen from Balzac-Montriveau's point of view, nothing from that of Mme de Castries-Mme de Langeais. I realize that the Duchesse's actions are not such as to inspire sympathy; but that fear we can sense inside her, that terror she cloaks with such bad arguments, all that could have been made moving, could have inspired a little pity, a little understanding for her. Balzac isn't interested. "This cold and cutting woman," he says, "this woman and her pride" (*Duchesse de Langeais*, p.203). And what is more, the Duchesse's arguments aren't always such bad ones at that. What guarantee have I of your love? she asks Montriveau. Tomorrow you may change your mind, then I shall be a ruined woman, and I shall have children who will be my shame. (For the full speech see pages 193 and 194.) There is some truth in that. "Humbug," Balzac comments curtly. Later on, this woman who is "all head" is transformed with a single wave of the wand into a woman who is all heart. This woman who is all pride asks Montriveau if he will "deign" to read her letter, then goes out and "weeps like a Mary Magdalene" outside his door. All this, I must agree, is very convincingly done. But I cannot help wondering whether Balzac wasn't also trying here to achieve what I should call a vicarious revenge. I am well aware, needless to say, that a novelist's intentions are utterly unimportant. Only the result counts. But though personal bitterness may sharpen the powers of observation, it also narrows the vision, and I cannot but wonder whether, if he had been less rancorous, less directly involved, Balzac might not have seen the character of Antoinette de Langeais develop in his pages to a much fuller extent and achieve in the course of this development a much greater truth.

The Comtesse Foedora

Just as Raphaël de Valentin is a simplified and symbolic transposition of Rubempré and Rastignac, so the Comtesse Foedora is a similarly schematic version of Mme de Maufrigneuse, Mme de Langeais and others of their type. Foedora is the symbol of High Society, ravishing and heartless, provoking desires but never satisfying them, ruinous to any man who is fatheaded enough to worship her instead of beating her. Raphaël loses his soul to her without ever raising a jot of feeling in her, and if, one evening, we hear her sigh, it is because she is thinking, not of him, but of her income (*Peau de Chagrin*, p.143). "You want to know whether I ever actually met Foedora," Balzac wrote to Mme Hanska. "There is a woman from icebound Russia, the Princess Bagration, who is thought in Paris to have been the model for her. The total of the women who have had the impertinence to recognize themselves in Foedora now stands, to my knowledge, at seventy-two."

Jeanne-Clémentine-Athénais d'Espard *or intrigue without love*

The Marquise d'Espard: another woman in vogue. More. Of all the women in vogue she is the most in vogue of all, the most perfect embodiment of the type, with all the egoism, the barrenness of heart, the hardness, the powers of strategy and the armor-plating that the role implies. In short, a she-devil.

Born in 1795, daughter of the Prince and Princess de Blamont-Chauvry, she has married, like Antoinette de Langeais, the man least suited to her in the whole world. Mme d'Espard is all self-interest, vanity and intrigue. And the man she chances to marry is of all men the one to whom the idea of intrigue is most foreign; a man who is modest, studious and calm; a man who, not content with honesty according to the letter of the law, insists on going even further than that and restoring to its rightful owner a fortune that he believes to have been wrongfully acquired by one of his distant ancestors. It is not hard to imagine Mme d'Espard's reactions to all that.

It is reasonable to suppose that there never existed between these two so utterly dissimilar beings any greater degree of intimacy than was strictly necessary to achieve the birth of their two sons. They married in 1812, and by 1815 they are already living apart. Mme de Maufrigneuse, Mme de Langeais, Foedora, Mme d'Espard: that makes our fourth woman in vogue so far, and not one of them lives with her husband.

The Marquis goes off to live quietly somewhere on his own, while the Marquise develops into one of the most brilliant women in Parisian Society. We see her everywhere, at the Opéra, at the Grandlieus, at Mme d'Aiglemont's, at Mme de Beauséant's (*Illusions perdues*, p.610; *Splendeurs*, p.730; *Contrat de Mariage*, p.198; *Père Goriot*, p.875). The two sons live with their father. "The woman in vogue is no longer a woman: she is neither a wife, nor a mother, nor a mistress" (*Interdiction*, p.14). Mme d'Espard lives on the Rue du Faubourg-Saint-Honoré. She has an income of twenty-six thousand *livres* a year and a way of life that costs double that amount. She is elegant but not very pretty. Her eyes are bright but cold, her nose is like an eagle's beak, her head is small and her lips are thin. As I have mentioned, she is a she-devil, and what is more she looks like one. In *l'Interdiction*, she is thirty-three, which is the equivalent of being about forty-five today. She owes the preservation of her looks and figure to strict discipline: cold baths and a horsehair mattress. The sharp-eyed Bianchon, however, notices that she has blackheads on her nose.

"Nor a mistress," I quoted this same Bianchon as saying a few lines earlier. Come now! Mme d'Espard must have affairs. I'd risk my life on it. Yet truth obliges me to admit that I can produce no textual evidence on this point. Mme d'Espard is discreet. As the grave. But the really unexpected thing is that her lovers are equally so. Only des Lupeaulx agrees, one day, that . . . (*Employés*, p.1030). But then he's such a liar. And there are allusions in *Une Fille d'Eve* (pp. 83 and 117) that seem to point to Félix de Vandenesse too as being . . . Rastignac possibly, but it could hardly be less certain. And that's all. All? Mme d'Espard? A woman who could make a man a Prefect, just like that! And what is more, a woman so easy to please that she will accept a man like des Lupeaulx. And a woman with so much curiosity that she accepts a rendezvous arranged by anonymous note (*Splendeurs*, p.658). The mystery of all this worries me a great deal. Can there be something behind it all? For my part, I must confess, even though it brands me forever as a malicious gossip, I suspect the Marquise of having a liaison with her husband's own brother. For how else are we to explain the Chevalier d'Espard's presence in a house from which his brother's quasi-divorce ought, by rights, to have kept him away. How else are we to explain that sharp-witted Popinot's comment (*Interdiction*, p.57): "Can't you see that the Marquise is that tall, heartless man's tool?" Or the fact that she employs the Chevalier in her most confidential affairs? (*Splendeurs*, p.938) Later on, however, we find her saying to her friend the Princesse de Cadignan (*Secrets de la Princesse de Cadignan*, p.18): "Can it be that you are like me, my dear, can it be that you have been searching for love all this while and never found it?" But is she telling the truth? With Mme d'Espard one can never be sure of anything. One sees how des Lupeaulx might have been attractive to her. She too, like him, is equivocation incarnate. One has only to hear her talk, with that sanctimonious, plausible, hypocritical tone of hers. "Those exquisite speeches on the subject of charity or religion" (*Splendeurs*, p.939).

Basically, the truth is probably that Mme d'Espard finds her pleasures above all in intrigue. Her drawing-room is one of the political centers of Paris. By birth she is connected to the exclusive legitimist group, but the presence of liberals like Marsay and Ronquerolles in her house (*Interdiction*, p.44) shows that she is not one to choose between hare and hounds. Moreover she is in personal contact with Talleyrand, the creative brain behind the dark conspiracy that is to topple Charles X (*id.* p.43). Through Lupeaulx she has influence in the Civil Service; through Nucingen and du Tillet a finger in the banking pie. She has only to speak one word and Chatelet is appointed Prefect of the Charente (*Illusions perdues*, p.866). On the other hand, she never succeeds in obtaining the injunction she wants against her husband. In this particular affair she runs up against Rubempré, who makes it his business to enlighten the court about the seamier aspects of the case. It must be admitted that in her dealings with Rubempré this past-mistress of intrigue always manages to be on the wrong side of the court. She begins by weaning Mme de Bargeton away from him. It is an error. What business was it of hers? And she realizes her error when Lucien reappears as a journalist with a sharp and unforgiving pen. She tries to make up for her previous mistake. Indeed, one even wonders whether she is not trying to seduce him into a liaison with her. I like ambitious men, she tells him. And a good-looking young fellow like Lucien, so hungry for success, must be attractive to her, even though he is attacking her. But now it is his turn to underestimate her. She revenges herself by having des Lupeaulx dig a little trap for him. He duly falls into it and vanishes from the scene. But alas, he reappears. The people one takes vengeance on always have this disagreeable tendency to reappear. And he reappears in time to have that delightful interdiction she was counting on quashed. Mme d'Espard feels she's had about as much as she can stand. As soon as Lucien has been arrested she does everything she can to see that he is at least guillotined. "Mme d'Espard would like to see that poor young man's head cut off," Mme Camusot says. "I felt a cold shiver go up my back hearing what a beautiful woman's hatred sounds like" (*Splendeurs*, p.939). When Lucien's suicide cuts the ground from under her feet, there is nothing left for the Marquise but to make sure of revenge on his protectors, Grandville and Sérizy. "All those people are going to be very unhappy," is her Sibylline prophecy. And it is an accurate one, though I can perceive no trace of the Marquise's calculating hand in their misfortunes. Perhaps she was clever enough to withdraw it in time to escape detection.

After the upheaval of 1830, Mme d'Espard is one of the first to begin entertaining again. She behaves impeccably towards her friend the Princesse de Cadignan too, now that the latter is ruined. She lends her a carriage whenever she needs one, and also her box at the theater. But the source from which this kindness flows is by no means crystal clear. "There can be no doubt that each knew at least some of the other's important secrets, or that they had each helped the other more than once in dealings with men and other little affairs; for there can be no truly sincere and durable friendship between women that has not been cemented by a few little crimes. When two women who are friends both have the power to kill the other, when they can each see the poisoned dagger in the other's hand, then they must always present a touching and harmonious spectacle to the world, a tableau whose unity will only be disturbed if one of them, in a moment of carelessness, should relinquish her weapon for a moment" (*Secrets de la Princesse de Cadignan*, p.29). You see? I told you there was a mystery in Mme d'Espard's life. I'd have bet anything on it. (Similarly, referring to the Duchesse d'Abrantès and Sophie Gay, two of Balzac's women friends, the author of *Balzac mis à nu* writes: "These two women had amassed such a formidable pile of infamies in their time, had each collected so large a collection of skeletons in their respective closets, that neither of them dared to attack each other any more. Each loathed the other like poison and yet, quite unlike Arsinoé and Célimène, they were never heard to exchange anything but endearments.") Of the fictional pair, Mme d'Espard is the more venomous. Much more. When she sees the Princesse finding happiness again in her liaison with Daniel d'Arthez, she hurriedly invites the new lover to a dinner at which almost all the guests have at some time enjoyed the Princesse's favors (*id.* p.61). If one is already acquainted with the general caddishness and lack of discretion displayed by Balzacian lovers it is not hard to imagine the barrage of epigrams, malicious remarks and slanders that poor d'Arthez has to face. Mme d'Espard herself makes a show of defending the Princesse. But her system of protection calls to mind "the principle of the lightning-conductor, a device intended to attract the lightning" (*id.* p.62). The Marquise's doubtful maneuvers meet with no success, however. Mme d'Espard is never successful when she meddles with matters of love. Besides, she is growing old, and the last we hear of her is that she is on the committee of some charity or other, devoting herself to good works (*Cousine Bette,* p.439).

To be logical, I ought at this point to discuss Mme de Beauséant. She is not only the last of the women in vogue left on our list but also, chronologically, the first, for her reign preceded those of Mme de Maufrigneuse and Mme de Langeais. In fact, however, we do not meet her until what is more or less the moment of her abdication, the moment when she ceases to be a woman in vogue in order to become simply a woman. Well, as excuses go I suppose it's not a bad one. The truth is that I'm rather fond of Mme de Beauséant and I wouldn't feel too happy about lumping her together with women like Mme de Langeais and Mme d'Espard. And I'm also becoming a little tired of High Society drawing-rooms and their stuffy atmosphere. So I'd like to talk about . . .

Amélie Camusot *or the bargain basement Marquise d'Espard*

Take away Mme d'Espard's perfect manners, the insolence bred into her as a Blamont-Chauvry, the refined dissembling of the aristocratic intriguer; add in exchange the small-mindedness of a middle-class housewife, the vulgarity of a servant's daughter, the nagging fidelity of a good wife—and you are left with Mme Camusot, later Camusot de Marville.

Marie-Cécile-Amélie Camusot's maiden name was Thirion. Her father, Louis XVIII's valet de chambre during that monarch's exile, was appointed Privy Usher to the King's person in 1814. And it is easy enough to picture what sort of creature he is. One can almost hear him telling everyone about his duties, about His Majesty and people like us who live at Court, an honest enough fellow probably, but short on brains, swollen with his own importance, more ponderous in his manner than any lawyer, and turning his daughter, naturally enough, into a snob avid for attention, for consideration, for advancement.*

When we first meet her, she is already by nature another harpy. In *la Vendetta*, while still a young girl, an art student working in a painter's studio, she leads a petty persecution campaign against a young girl whose father was a Baron created during the Empire. Amélie is a legitimist. You can imagine, her father's job being what it is! How does she come to marry someone like Camusot, a magistrate and the son of a fairly well-off businessman? I'm not sure. Probably some weight was placed on the fact that her father, in view of his position, might well be able to open a door or two for his son-in-law also. At all events, in 1824 the son-in-law is appointed to a post as examining magistrate in Alençon.

At this period, Mme Camusot presents the appearance of a short, plump, blonde woman with a domed forehead, thin lips and a pointed chin, a combination of features made tolerable by her youth but destined to make her look old quite early on in life. Her eyes are sparkling and intelligent enough, but they are too ready to betray her innocent mania for worldly success, and her fury at not achieving it more quickly (*Cabinet des Antiques*, p.443). She is not really intelligent, or well-educated— twenty years after her apprenticeship in the painter's studio she is still ignorant of Watteau's artistic value (*Cousin Pons*, p.581)—but she is shrewd. She has the sort of mind we have already observed in des Lupeaulx. She is a born intriguer. Her husband, on the other hand, is a fool. A clumsy and rather unscrupulous one, too. A man who is quite prepared to sell his integrity but doesn't quite know how to set about it. Imagine a one-armed burglar; that's what Camusot is like. Luckily for him, however, his wife is very nimble with her hands. In the d'Esgrignon affair it is she who arranges everything with Mme de Maufrigneuse (*Cabinet des Antiques*). Don't forget that she's a snob. The word "duchesse" opens unfathomable prospects of glory before her eyes. Camusot is appointed successively to the posts of acting magistrate in Paris (*id.* p.461), then examining magistrate. From that moment on he follows his wife's instructions blindly. "Mme Camusot dominated her husband entirely" (*Splendeurs*, p.941). "I'm nothing but an empty head, you're the brain," he tells her . . . "I ought to kiss the very ground you walk on" (*id.* pp. 945 and 1023). Mme Camusot is triumphant. She enjoys power over others. And

---

* Where was the young Amélie living while her father was in exile with Louis XVIII? This point is never cleared up. Possibly she went with him, but if so it is odd that her stay abroad should have left no mark whatsoever on either Mme Camusot's character or her mind.

throughout this whole affair she never once utters a single word in which it is possible to discern even the faintest shadow of conjugal affection. She sees her husband only as the instrument of her own success, and the fact that she is not unfaithful to him is solely due, in my belief, to her narrowness of mind, her concern for respectability and, perhaps also, to her lack of imagination.

It goes without saying that no one in the world of the *Comédie humaine* is ignorant of Mme Camusot's dominion over her husband. "If it were only a matter of President Camusot himself," the lawyer Fraisier says, "it would be a trifling matter; but he has, you must realize, a wife" (*Cousin Pons*, p.677). After Lucien's arrest, Mme d'Espard and Mme de Maufrigneuse both send for her to give her their instructions. And just listen to the way they go about it. "My dear, between ourselves, the matter is very simple . . . Lucien de Rubempré has been arrested, your husband is the examining magistrate in the case; I guarantee the poor boy's innocence. See that he's released again within twenty-four hours . . ." And here, again without equivocation, is the ransom: "Monsieur Camusot shall be first to fall promoted to the Court of Appeals, then be made President of it" (*Splendeurs*, p.940). The hypocritical Mme d'Espard is more devious in her way of putting it, but it amounts to much the same thing: "Your husband, madame, has been given a fine opportunity to distinguish himself" (*id*. p.939). Naturally we must make some allowance for the natural insolence of the aristocrat requesting help from an inferior, but neither of them would talk like that unless they were certain of finding Mme Camusot very understanding.

To cut the story short, after several years have passed we meet Camusot again, by now Camusot de Marville and a President of the Court, living in an apartment on the Rue de Hanovre. (Stendhal to Mme Jules: "When are you going to have a cosy little drawing-room, up on the fourth floor, on the Rue de Hanovre?") The Camusots have an investment income of nine thousand francs a year and his eleven thousand francs a year salary. In other words they are by no means spectacularly well off. They have lost their little son, and because her dowry is so small their daughter cannot find a husband. Mme Camusot has not improved with the years. Having arrived in the world, she no longer takes the trouble to feign an amiability that was never in her nature. She even seems to have lost her flair for dealing with people. As a young woman she had vivacity, but that has gone. But though one may lose one's vitality of mind as one grows old, one never loses one's baser feelings: Mme Camusot is still envious, "ruthless, full of hate and naggingly persistent" (*Splendeurs*, p.1090). In the middle-class world of *Cousin Pons* she is the least wealthy, and this is a thorn in her flesh: she has developed a perpetually sullen air, and a hard, disagreeable expression (*Cousin Pons*, p.551). Towards old Pons she behaves quite odiously. One day, when he arrives to dine with her, she tells him that she has to go out. But "the dinner has been ordered," she adds, "you can eat it when we've gone . . ." Yes, just like that, without a thought for his feelings. "The servants would only eat it anyway," she even adds (*id*. p.559). As for scruples, the defense would have no case at all. Still not the slightest shadow of one. In order to lay her hands on Pons' inheritance, Mme Camusot finally enmeshes herself in the kind of maneuvers that would normally lead their originator, not to a place on the judge's bench but to the dock opposite. But Mme Camusot triumphs again, and her husband retains his position. Though one ought to add, in all fairness, that he has never really understood his wife's machinations.

Virginie de Montcornet *or all roads lead to happiness*

Well frequented though it may be, Mme de Montcornet's drawing-room never attains the same importance as that of the Marquise d'Espard. Mme de Montcornet suffers from one slight disadvantage: though her husband is a count, his title only dates back as far as the Empire. She herself, however, is of good birth and was born a Troisville, pronounced Tréville. The Troisvilles are of good stock, a noble Normandy family, and she is the daughter of the Troisville who causes Mlle Cormon such bitter disappointment in *la Vieille Fille*. Her mother is a Sherbellof, a Russian aristocrat who has handed down to her daughter that "excessive pallor found in women from the North" (*Illusions perdues*, p.811). In Alençon, where she spends the latter part of her childhood after returning from exile with the Bourbons, she becomes friendly with the young Blondet. He is her *patito*, her little beau. At this point, Virginie must be about fifteen or sixteen. One imagines the young Emile joining Virginie and her sisters in innocent romps on Sunday afternoons. They laugh, they quarrel, they play at forfeits, they pick cherries for one another.

Then comes the day when a family conclave decides that Virginie is to be married to the Comte de Montcornet, a colonel, the son of a cabinetmaker but also the hero of Essling and very well off. She has never seen him. Nor he her, so the match is an even one. He is simply looking for a girl who is poor but whose family will be influential enough to help him find favor with the Bourbons. Virginie has two uncles who are peers of the realm and two cousins who are deputies (*id*. p.813). She fits the bill perfectly, in fact. The marriage takes place. Perhaps, hidden behind a pillar, Emile wipes away a tear. Perhaps, beneath her orange blossoms, Virginie conceals regrets. I say "perhaps," because neither of them suffers from an excess of sensibility. There is no evidence that Virginie expressed any great aversion to this marriage with a man twenty-five years her senior. But it is not long, in any case, before she brings her Emile to Paris and finds him a job on the *Débats*. She is "frail, delicate and shy" (*Les Paysons*, p.26). But that is purely a matter of appearances, because she always knows exactly what she wants and can, on occasion, prove a formidable opponent in conversational battles (*Secrets de la Princesse de Cadignan*, p.36). Her drawing-room is influential. As for her warrior husband, she soon has the whip hand over him. It's a sight to be seen, Blondet writes to Nathan, "the way that delicate little woman pulls the strings and puts that huge, square, fat general through his paces" (*Paysans*, p.84). During the summer, the Montcornets go out into the country, and while the General is quarreling with his steward the Comtesse and Blondet go picking flowers. She has a good heart and is sensitive to suffering, but her kindness is unfortunately neither lasting nor productive of results. She expresses pity for old Fourchon, but then she suddenly sends him away because he smells (*Paysans*, p.84).

In 1837, when her husband dies, Virginie offers Blondet "her hand in friendship and a considerable fortune" (*id.* p.312). They are neither of them very young any more, but I don't think that Mme de Montcornet has ever been unfaithful to Blondet, or that Blondet ever stayed longer than he ought at those bohemian evenings with actresses that he so delights in. They are married. Doubtless they are happy together. Fidelity can always guarantee at least a certain measure of happiness.

Delphine de Nucingen

Mme de Montcornet and her adulterous fidelity lead us on quite naturally to Delphine de Nucingen, who also traverses more or less the whole of the *Comédie humaine* without losing her Rastignac. We must not be confused by this similarity, however. Delphine is very much inferior to Virginie de Montcornet. From every point of view. Mme de Montcornet is witty. Delphine is stupid. Mme de Montcornet is fairly kindhearted. Kindhearted in a facile, unexceptional kind of way, but nevertheless kindhearted. Delphine has no kindness of heart whatever. Though it's true that in *Une Fille d'Eve* we do find her helping Marie de Vandenesse. From snobbery perhaps? We cannot, however, say that she is positively spiteful.

Spite implies at least some minimal interest in other people, and Delphine never gives other people a single thought. Her world is limited strictly to herself. Though incapable of killing anyone, she commits an even worse crime, to my mind, by letting her father die without sacrificing so much as a single turn around a ballroom to go and visit him. Even socially she is a pigmy beside Mme de Montcornet. Born a Goriot, daughter of a former pasta dealer, Nucingen was as high as she could ever have reached in the way of a husband. Nucingen is a person of considerable importance in the world of the Stock Exchange, but once outside that world he is nothing very much. Under the Restoration, a great fortune in no way constituted a passport to social acceptance. This is a thorn in Delphine's side. It is her tragedy. Her sordid, petty little tragedy. As a means of achieving acceptance, the best she can think of is to become Henri de Marsay's mistress. Snobbery too has its martyrs, for I don't believe she can have loved him for an instant. Like Mme de Maufrigneuse and Mme de Langeais, Delphine is blonde. She is therefore, according to Balzac's private cosmogony, incapable of loving. Marsay does not, in any case, stay with her long (*Père Goriot*, pp. 913 and 950). Does she have other lovers after that? The answer is a mystery. She certainly has debts, and she never stops asking her father for money. At this point she meets Rastignac. He is young, poor and well connected; exactly what she is looking for. He sees to it that she receives invitations from his cousin Mme de Beauséant. She makes him a present of an apartment and has it handsomely furnished for him. Exchange is no robbery. How much love is there involved in all this? Not much. This little woman with her white eyelashes has no need for love. What she wants is a man to carry her *schall* and escort her to the theater. Where she, needless to say, pays for the seats. By the way, it is curious that Delphine, once perpetually at the end of her financial tether, is never heard complaining about lack of money once Goriot is dead. Yet she now has the expense of keeping Rastignac on top of everything else. What is the explanation of this mystery? Did she have some other, more demanding lover before, so that her liaison with Rastignac is in fact an economy? Or has Nucingen become more generous? I don't know. Everything about this affair is rather sordid. Rastignac too can scarcely be particularly enamoured of Delphine. His character was still not entirely spoiled by the time he met her. How could he love a woman whose capacity for baseness he has seen demonstrated at Goriot's bedside? How could he love her with that corpse between them? But perhaps it is the corpse that in fact unites them. So that they are accomplices rather than lovers. He needs her just as she needs him. Yes, accomplices, and accomplices who end up stooping rather low; for Delphine later marries off her daughter to Rastignac. Though if we are to believe what Finot says in *la Maison Nucingen* (p.595), they had in fact ceased being lovers several years before that event.

Léontine de Sérizy*

"Really," Mme de Bargeton exclaims at the Opéra, "not the famous Mme de Sérizy who has had so many affairs and is nevertheless still received by everyone?" (*Illusions perdues*, p.613). Mme de Bargeton has just arrived from the provinces, so we must excuse her for thinking that Mme de Sérizy is received by everyone. Born a Ronquerolles, and therefore not from a family of the very first rank, the widow of General Gaubert, "one of the most illustrious of the Republican generals," then remarried to Sérizy, whose title is by no means an old one, Léontine de Sérizy only reigns, in fact, over a circle somewhat inferior to that of Mme d'Espard. Then why all the astonishment? "It's simply unheard of, my dear," the Marquise d'Espard says in reply (*id.* p.613). Why unheard of? People are all the same, always trying to make things seem more complicated than they are. "No one dares attempt to fathom that mystery," Mme d'Espard adds. What mystery? Balzac doesn't tell us. And yet one senses that there is something hidden there all the same, something murky and not quite right. The Marquise d'Espard is not mistaken. She is like us: she senses it, she is warm, but she can't quite put her finger on it. If I may be permitted to give my opinions frankly, I believe that Mme de Sérizy must be an affiliate of the Thirteen. Or at least she is a helper of theirs. Don't let us forget that her brother, Ronquerolles, is one of this secret society's most active members. Or that the Duchesse de Langeais, when she emerges from the mysterious apartment to which she was carried off, finds herself in Mme de Sérizy's boudoir (*Duchesse de Langeais*, p.219).

Is she intelligent? Intelligent enough, in any case, to have made herself desirable to the Comte de Sérizy, an eminent government official and a member of the Bauvan-Sérizy-Grandville triumvirate of brains. Alas, the dear fellow suffers from a skin disease (*Un Début dans la Vie*, p.688). His wife diligently deceives him with the Marquis d'Aiglemont (*Femme de trente ans*, p.721), with Savinien de Portenduère (*Ursule Mirouët*, p.357) and with Auguste de Maulincour (*Duchesse de Langeais*, p.227). It is evident that she is quite happy to take whatever comes her way. "Mme de

---

* Balzac sometimes spells it Sérisy.

Sérizy," we read in *la Duchesse de Langeais* (p.223), "has never bestowed her favors on any but vulgar men." And it is true that she is no longer in her first youth. She must have been born in about 1785 (*Splendeurs*, p.960), which means that she is already over thirty at the time of her liaison with the first of the gentlemen mentioned above, and over forty when she falls in love with Rubempré. Blonde, thin, slight of build, until this point she has always shown a great deal of coolheadedness in her affairs. With Rubempré, her blood begins to heat. She begins to adore him. When she discovers that he is being unfaithful to her she is mad with jealousy (*Splendeurs*, p.873); when he is arrested she is mad with anxiety; when he dies she is mad with grief. For several days it is feared that she will lose her reason, and her delirium sounds quite terrifying. "Apparently the poor Countess is saying the most frightful things. I'm told it's quite disgusting . . . No respectable woman ought to be susceptible to such attacks" (*Splendeurs*, p.1090). It is the madness of last love. As for poor Sérizy, he sits at her bedside and takes care of her. Can a woman who has inspired an attachment of that sort really be so vulgar after all?

This storm was no doubt the last. For Mme Sérizy's life was further saddened by the death of her son. In *la Fausse Maîtresse*, which takes place in 1835, she is simply a kindhearted aunt concerned about her niece's marriage.

Félicité des Touches, Dinah de la Baudraye, Naïs de Bargeton, Véronique Graslin, Célestine Rabourdin *or the diverse states of the superior woman*

There is a whole world of difference between Mlle des Touches and the ridiculous Dinah de la Baudraye, between the soulless Mme de Bargeton and the charming Mme Rabourdin, yet they all have one thing in common: they are superior women. I use the word in its relative sense. Mme de Bargeton is not very intelligent, but she is, nevertheless, superior to the people around her.

Of these five women, the most remarkable is indisputably Félicité des Touches, better known under the pseudonym of Camille Maupin. To begin with, Camille Maupin is quite simply George Sand. In the novels themselves Balzac resists this identification. "Just as Clara Gazul is the female pseudonym used by a man of genius, and George Sand the masculine pseudonym used by a woman of genius, so Camille Maupin was the mask, etc." Or again: "Camille Maupin, that younger brother to George Sand" (*Béatrix*, pp. 369 and 381). But no one is going to be deceived by that little trick. Camille Maupin writes, she is famous, she smokes, she sometimes dresses like a man, and she bestows her favors on a composer. How can one not think of the author of *Indiana?* Even her pseudonym calls to mind George Sand's *Mauprat*. In private, Balzac is the first to admit it. "Yes, Mlle des Touches is George Sand," he wrote to Mme Hanska.

Transposed, of course. Just as Thiers was transposed into Rastignac and Montrond into Maxime de Trailles. Except that the transposition works in the reverse direction this time. Rastignac and Maxime de Trailles are inferior to Thiers and Montrond. Mlle des Touches, on the other hand, is much superior to George Sand. What? To George Sand? With all her talent? But Mlle des Touches is talented, too. On that score they are equal. In every other way, however, Félicité is far superior. Félicité des Touches is very beautiful. She is also related to the Grandlieus, whereas George Sand's descent from the Maréchal de Saxe was not a legitimate one. And we should also note that whereas George Sand was Sandeau's mistress, Félicité des Touches, unless I am mistaken, never even meets Lousteau, who is Sandeau's Balzacian equivalent. And even if she had, there is every reason to suppose that she could never have tolerated either his baseness of character or his vulgarity.

This "ennobling" of the character may perhaps have been due in the first place to the fact that Balzac was a friend of George Sand's. He may well have been trying to express his admiration or his affection for her in this way. Or perhaps simply making certain he didn't annoy her. It was impossible that his readers should not recognize George Sand in Félicité, and given that fact, Balzac no doubt preferred to offer her a flattering portrait. With Thiers and Morny he did not have to take such precautions, since he scarcely knew them.

The des Touches family are of good aristocratic stock from Brittany. Félicité herself, orphaned at the age of two (again like George Sand), is brought up by an old uncle. The upbringing is in fact quite haphazard, lacking in both guidance and constraints. She reads everything that comes within her grasp, and she has very soon acquired a fund of experience culled entirely from books that forms her character as much as ten years of love affairs and worldly adventures could have done. A book can have the same power to affect a human being as an actual relationship; it can have the same power to sully or enrich the mind and spirit. At the age of eighteen, Félicité is no longer a virgin except in body. Freed of all prejudices, all taboos, she is ruled by intellect alone. Moreover, having been brought up more like a boy than a girl, there is a strong element of virility in her character. At no point do we ever see her dreaming of marriage. She doesn't need anyone else. She has no desire for either domestic life or motherhood. "I find children intolerable," she says. "In that respect I'm not a woman at all" (*Béatrix*, p.397). We should also add that her eighty thousand *livres* a year income (*Illusions perdues*, p.819) permits her to ignore some of the problems that women usually have to face. Even when they have no desire for it, Balzac's other young women are obliged to submit to marriage if they do not wish to spend their lives stagnating in a dark corner. Félicité is the only one who can afford to ignore it.

In 1814, she leaves Brittany for Paris, where she decides to give herself to a gentleman she has met. She decides. No seduction, no vertigo, no romantic mists to obscure her vision. She decides to give herself to him because she has noticed that her chastity is spoiling her complexion. That's the only reason. "She realized that her beauty was bound to be impaired by her stubborn chastity . . . Her intellect notified her of the limitations imposed by nature on its creations, which are equally doomed to deterioration from a failure to recognize its laws as from a deliberate abuse of them" (*Béatrix*, p.374). In the case of Félicité des Touches, morality and prejudice had long since succumbed to the dictates of the intellect. "Ordinarily," Balzac writes, "a woman feels, enjoys, then judges . . . With Mlle des Touches this order was reversed" (*id*. p.379). She therefore enters into her first sexual relationship with an imbecile whom Balzac allows to remain anonymous. "She took some time to recover from her disgust" (*id*. p.379). Having failed at this first attempt, she tries again. There is nothing in Félicité des Touches, as you can see, of Mme de Langeais' tremulousness. Reason is master. Her second lover remains as anonymous as the first, though the description we are given evokes a personality not unlike that of Stendhal: "This man," Balzac writes, "possessed one of the most original minds of our age. He too wrote under a pseudonym, and his first works proclaimed him to be a fervent admirer of Italy . . . Skeptical and ironic . . . that tone, at once original and subtle . . . that lent a special flavor to his talent" (*Béatrix*, p.379).* It was almost certainly due to this man's influence that Félicité herself began to write. She published two volumes of plays and two novels, one of which is entitled *le Nouveau Prométhée* (*Muse du Département*, p.136). She becomes famous. "Ah," says Lucien when he catches sight of her in the Tuileries, "there is

---

* In *Echantillons de Causeries françaises,* an unfinished work, there occurs another figure somewhat reminiscent of Stendhal: "A large, fat man, a fellow with a great deal of wit who was soon to leave for Italy, where there was a diplomatic appointment awaiting him" (*Oeuvres ébauchées*, p.1091).

poetry" (*Illusions perdues*, p.608). Beause of her fame, her wealth and her connection with the Grandlieus, she is received everywhere. She is one of the queens of Paris (*Bal de Sceaux*, p.126; *Fille d'Eve*, p.85). It is in her house that the long conversation we know as *Autre Etude de Femme* takes place, and it is there too that Mme de Maufrigneuse meets Victurnien d'Esgrignon (*Cabinet des Antiques*, p.382). Her talent guarantees her a certain amount of social license. She can, if she so wishes, visit the Nucingens without losing caste (*Splendeurs*, p.718), or invite both duchesses and artists into her drawing-room at the same time with impunity. But there is nothing about her of the lady-novelist who lives in a dressing-gown and is covered with inkstains up to the eyebrows. She is both elegant and a perfect housekeeper. And what is more, very beautiful. Balzac refers to her as "an angel radiant with youth, with hope, with promise" (*Illusions perdues*, p.608). "She was ravishing," he says again in *Béatrix* (p.389). "Her black eyes were as wide as the sky and as ardent as the sun" (*Illusions perdues*, p.608). She has dark hair and a pale complexion. "As black as a raven and as strong as a Turk," old du Guénic comments rather more cavalierly (*Béatrix*, p.368). A regal profile, the shadow of a mustache and magnificent hindquarters (*id.* pp. 376-377).

Having been abandoned by her Stendhal, who has nevertheless left her with an admiration for things Italian, she enters into a relationship with Gennaro Conti, a composer who is an amalgam of Chopin, Liszt and Rossini. This relationship lasts a long time, since she has already entered upon it in 1821 (*Illusions perdues*, p.819), and it does not seem to have come to an end until about 1834 (*Béatrix*). It is reasonable to assume that it was an intermittent one, however. There is a moment when Félicité seems to be entertaining a certain fondness for Lucien de Rubempré. When she first sees him she appears to be "moved by his justly famous good looks" (*id.* p.818). And Lucien too is affected. "If she found me as attractive as I do her, our story would be a short one," he says (*id.* p.818). Yet their feelings never blossom. It becomes another of those relationships that somehow do not happen, and one is never quite sure why. Félicité contents herself with retaining a tender sympathy towards him in her heart, as people with generous souls so often do towards those they have once desired. When the occasion arises, she helps Lucien and lends him two thousand francs.

For she does unquestionably have a generous soul. Though she is amoral, still one might have expected the power of her intellect to shrivel up her heart. Yet nothing could be further from the truth. Though both Conti and Béatrix de Rochefide betray her in the most odious fashion, she bears them not the slightest grudge for it. She even invites them to stay with her at Guérande. Out of generosity, out of disdain for vulgar emotions, and perhaps a little too out of curiosity as a novelist. Mlle des Touches enjoys leading her soul into difficult paths. She is quite willing to experience any emotion, but it must be inventoried first, a tendency in which she is encouraged still further by her new lover, Claude Vignon, a critic whose excess of critical sense has reduced him to a state of genuine moral nihilism. It is during her trip to Italy with him and Léon de Lora that Félicité hears the story we know as *Honorine*. This episode is simply a transposition of George Sand's journey through Italy with Musset, just as the Conti-Rochefide episode is merely a transposition of the complications among George Sand, Liszt and Mme d'Agoult.

After her return from Italy, Félicité goes to stay for a while at Guérande, her château in Brittany. A young neighbor, Calyste du Guénic, falls in love with her with such ardor, such youthful sincerity that she feels her soul refreshed. Still thirsting for lucidity at all costs, she questions all her motives and listens intently to the whispers of her heart. She talks to Vignon about it. Lovers they may be, these two, but one can see that they are alike in their disdain for conventional feelings. You love him, Vignon tells her. Dearly, she replies. And she decides to accept the young man. Here again, a precise knowledge of what she is doing precedes—or at least accompanies—her passion. Enter once more Béatrix de Rochefide, the expert pickpocket in matters of love, who diverts the ardor of Calyste's glances to herself. It is at this point that Félicité shows the full measure of her strange character, at once haughty and brimming with generosity. Stifling her own love, she decides that Calyste shall have Béatrix. She advises him what tactics to adopt to win her. She even pretends to be his mistress in order to make certain that her friend's jealousy shall be aroused. While talking a great deal, it should be added, the whole time. For that is Félicité's weakness: she loves to talk. Finally, she enters a convent, after having made a gift of all her possessions to Calyste so that he shall be able to marry Sabine de Grandlieu.

Mme de la Baudraye is a figure of fun. She is not, however, a mediocrity: Balzac is at pains to point this out in the first few lines of her biography. Born at Bourges into a Calvinist family, Dinah Peidefer becomes a convert to Catholicism for the sole purpose of winning support and protection from the local archbishop. "You may already judge then," Balzac writes, "of Mlle Dinah's superiority, if she was capable, at the age of seventeen, of becoming a religious convert solely from ambition" (*Muse du Départe-*

ment, p.54). Her plan turns out to have been a good one: the excellent archbishop makes it his special business to find Dinah a good husband. All he can find is Milaud de la Baudraye, a man who is rich enough but also excessively delicate. Here we are forced to peep briefly into yet another despair-filled double bed—the tenth, the twentieth?—so common in the *Comédie humaine*. "And there did in fact take place at la Baudraye one of those long, montonous domestic tragedies . . ." (*id.* p.67). A tragedy that Mme de la Baudraye was to bring to the attention of the entire *département* by publishing, under a pseudonym, a poem in which we are regaled with the story of a certain Paquita from Seville.

> *There, the men are different altogether*
> *From ours, in this land of wintry weather.*

And this Paquita found very few men worthy of her, for

> *Their powers were always quite drained*
> *By the urgency of her desire*
> *E'er she, with every sense on fire*
> *To that table groaning with love's rich fare*
> *Could pull up her chair.*

And one can imagine this poor Paquita's fury when, having at last found a soldier more energetic than the rest, he comes back to her from Russia completely frozen. Frozen! M. de la Baudraye alone, Balzac adds, "knew the secrets that lay hidden in this poem" (*id.* p.82).

Second tragedy: Mme de la Baudraye lacks self-knowledge. She is not a mediocrity, as I have already noted. She even has a certain stature. She knows this, she can feel it. But this stature, this quite genuine stature, stems from her character, and the unfortunate woman takes it into her head that it is a product of her intellect. She mistakes her stature in the way that some people mistake their vocation. Ingres, for example, was much prouder of his violin playing than of his paintings. And so it is with Dinah de la Baudraye. She is a woman "whose apparent superiorities were false and whose hidden superiorities were real . . . Dinah, though she made herself ridiculous by the blunders of her intelligence, possessed stature as a woman because of the qualities of her soul" (*id.* p.70).

Is it her fault? Not entirely. According to Balzac, the main culprit is provincial life itself, the narrowness of an existence that banishes all opportunity for comparisons. Had she lived in Paris, Dinah might have met George Sand and Camille Maupin. In which case she would have realized her mistake; for she is by no means blind. When she does finally meet one

of her friends back from Paris she recognizes her own inferiority immediately (*id*. p.75). But meanwhile, she lives in Sancerre surrounded by mediocrities who admire her. "She grew accustomed . . . to hearing the
sound of her own voice, and took pleasure in her own eloquence . . . and
in this way she became a sort of music box that launched into one of its
various tunes as soon as some appropriate turn of conversation activated
the switch" (*id*. p.63).

Until the day when those two Parisians, Lousteau and Bianchon, arrive
in Sancerre. Dinah receives them in a black velvet beret, *à la Raphaël*.
They begin by making fun of her, and it is doubtless purely from a delight in practical jokes that Lousteau conceives "the idea of conquering in
a few moments a castle that had been holding out against the combined
forces of Sancerre for nine years" (*id*. p.117). Dinah is conquered. The
boredom imposed by her stagnant existence, the Parisian glamour of the
visitors, her secret frustration, everything made her fall inevitable. Bianchon too, in his capacity as a doctor, has helped to precipitate it by his
remarks on the disadvantages of chastity (*id*. p.142). There is a curious
comparison to be drawn here between Dinah and Félicité des Touches.
Félicité realizes "that her beauty was bound to be impaired by her stubborn chastity"; Dinah has to listen to Bianchon telling her: "Today, for
you, love has become a necessity." "A necessity?" Dinah exclaims. "Must
I love on doctor's orders then?" "If you go on as you are living now, in
three years you will have deteriorated horribly." And as if that weren't
enough, we must remember that Dinah has just seen her woman friend
from Paris again after all that time. She must have already been feeling
cheated and upset, so that attaching herself to a man surrounded by the
golden haze of Parisian and literary glamour is a means of reversing the
negative verdict she has just been forced to return against herself. What is
astonishing, is that given the choice between two men of equal intelligence she should prefer a despicable roué like Lousteau to the gentlemanly Bianchon. In the first place, however, Bianchon does not pay court
to her, and in the second, he leaves several days before his companion, two
of those "little things that lead to great catastrophes" (*id*. p.138). Besides,
Balzac tells us, "being great-souled herself, Dinah was necessarily more
susceptible to wit than to magnanimity in others. Love usually prefers
contrasts to similarities" (*id*. p. 137). "Farewell, my children, I leave you
my blessing," Bianchon says as he leaves them (*id*. p.137). And this complicity that develops almost immediately among Bianchon, Lousteau and
Dinah is another of the book's curious features, for heaven knows they
could scarcely be more different from one another. And yet, in a way,

they are similar too, for they are all superior beings after their own fashion; Dinah in the realm of character, Lousteau in that of intellect, and Bianchon in both. This shared superiority unites them; they form a league against the petty provincial minds around them. In Paris, Bianchon would doubtless never have consented to abet Lousteau in his love affairs. But in Sancerre, hemmed in by so much mediocrity, Lousteau seems almost like a brother to him. A black sheep, but still a brother. Just as the purest poet, when he is in the army, is delighted with the companionship of a sixth-rate novelist. Besides, Lousteau is only too adept at creating a good impression when he wants to, and he has gone to the trouble, Balzac tells us, of making himself "excessively agreeable" (*id.* p.149). Then, having played his practical joke, he returns to Paris. Dinah follows him. You are a father! she tells him. Bah! Lousteau replies, and prepares to send her back where she came from. But then, having thought it over, he decides to keep her.*

We now see a new Dinah revealed, a woman no longer ridiculous but, believe it or not, sympathetic and touching. "Genuine love, that real need of the great-hearted, was transforming her into an entirely new woman" (*id.* p.149). She acquires lucidity. She discovers at last that Lousteau is nothing but an idler who wastes hour after hour smoking cigars before finally being forced to work like a dog turning out articles written heaven knows how. At this point, a vulgar woman would have left him and gone home, or made the best of things. Dinah neither leaves him nor resigns herself to his failings. She demonstrates that her superiority is genuine. If the man she dreamed of does not exist, then she will create him herself. A truly great soul never shirks the task of remolding the world, or its inhabitants, and Dinah decides to remold Lousteau. She encourages him, backs him up, gives him fresh ideas and helps him to finish his articles. She has always had a strong character, and now, tainted though it may be, Lousteau imparts some of his own intellectual brilliance to her in addition. Dinah becomes in reality the superior woman she once thought herself. It is to her that we owe the novella entitled *Un Prince de la Bohème.* And despite traces of Lousteau's "Parisian" wit we are still a million miles from the saga of Paquita. But as Dinah grows in stature, so Lousteau drifts away from her. Greatness of soul and womanly devotion bore him and cast a gloom over his character. So that Dinah is now subjected to a second domestic tragedy, one quite as tedious as the first. She scrimps and saves while Lousteau goes running after ballet girls. In 1842, Dinah tires of the

---

* There is a "first draft" of Dinah's arrival in Paris to be found in Balzac's short novella *Une Inconséquence*, published in 1830. It has been reprinted in the *Contes et Nouvelles* volume of the Ollendorf edition.

situation, sends her children back to her mother and says to Lousteau: "I shan't be keeping any more suppers warm for you, my friend. Will you come and have dinner on Mme de la Baudraye at the Rocher de Cancale tonight? Come on." Lousteau is taken by surprise: "Is my Didine rebelling?" "Didine doesn't exist any more. You killed her, my friend" (*id.* p.197). She goes back to her husband, who has just taken up residence in Paris, having just that moment been made a peer of the realm. And then, one day, Lousteau comes back to her. To ask for money. One might have expected any trace of love for him still remaining in Dinah's heart to be obliterated by this final revelation. But the body has not said its last word. "The two cheeks touched" (*id.* p.207). Mme de la Baudraye is conquered again. However, after a few days she finds the strength to run away from him once more.

Like Montherlant's Andrée Hacquebaut in *les Jeunes Filles,* Dinah de la Baudraye is one of those women too intelligent not to die of boredom when surrounded by mediocrities, yet not quite intelligent enough to find their own salvation in themselves. Ordinarily, such women end up putting an advertisement in the newspaper. Unless they have a bent for literature, in which case they write to a novelist: a procedure at least equally hazardous. Among the numerous women who wrote to him in this way, Balzac must have known several who resembled Dinah de la Baudraye. There was, in particular, a certain Caroline Marbouty, who was introduced to him by Sandeau, in fact, by that same Sandeau who provided so much of Balzac's raw material for the character of Lousteau. Balzac seems to have found Mlle Marbouty fairly interesting. Sufficiently so to take her to Italy with him at all events. After that we lose sight of her. I seem to remember reading somewhere that she was run over and killed by a hansom cab.

Mme de Baudraye is like an expensive but badly made dress: we laugh at her, but we know she is made of the very best material. Mme Bargeton, on the other hand, is basically a rather flimsy character: no stature, no body to her at all. The compensation for this, however, is that she is less ridiculous than Dinah. Possibly Balzac was unable to divest himself of a last remnant of respect for the woman of high birth when he was describing her. For Mme de Bargeton was born a Nègrepelisse, and her family, the Nègrepelisses of Angoulême, are the junior branch of the d'Espard Nègrepelisses. She has been perfectly brought up and knows Italian, German, counterpoint, literature, Greek and Latin. Not a bad hand to start the game with, you will admit. But for Balzac, intelligence carries no great weight without strength of character, nor a cultured mind without the necessary moral education. Mlle des Touches was an orphan, Dinah de la Baudraye lost her father when still very young and Anaïs de Nègrepelisse has no mother. This is doubtless the cause, in all three, of a certain imbalance in their characters, a lack of proportion and moderation, an excess of certain good qualities that is nevertheless unable to compensate for the lack of certain others. At twenty, Anaïs is a bizarrely excitable creature who is ready to swoon at the slightest thing. "For her, everything was sublime, extraordinary, strange, divine, marvelous." She "felt that there was a certain greatness in being sewn into a sack and thrown into a river" (*Illusions perdues*, p.498).

Born in about 1783, she is therefore about twenty-two when, in 1805, she lights upon another La Baudraye in the person of M. de Bargeton, "a man in his forties much the worse for wear" (*id.* p.496), a chivalrous enough fellow, as we find out when he fights a duel, but a disappointing husband. Anaïs then falls in love with a young colonel who, alas, dies before she has had time to reward his devotion. Under the Empire, with all those battles going on, if you found a good-looking young man for yourself it was as well not to let the grass grow under your feet. Her line of escape thus cut off, Anaïs settles back to life in Angoulême where "her pride preserved her from the boredom of provincial love affairs. Given the choice between nonentity . . . and nothing, a woman of such superior character must of necessity settle for nothing" (*id.* p.499). Mme de Bargeton is not a woman of "such superior character" in any absolute sense. She is simply superior to the environment in which she is obliged to live. Not very intelligent, but a thousand times more so than the blockheads who throng her drawing-room. Not very elegant, but a hundred times better got up than all the old bags clumsily flapping their motheaten feather fans all around her. Like Dinah, she is a prisoner. You may say that she ought to have contented herself with one of those sturdy huntsmen who walk into her house and set the chandeliers aquiver with their thumping tread. But for Mme de Bargeton the small pleasures of conversation are at least as important as those of the body. Moreover, she is vain. What pleasure would she obtain from a liaison that must of necessity remain secret? A liaison that would bring her down to the level of those provincial old cats she so despises. For though she despises them, their good opinion is more important to her than she is willing to admit to herself. After all, has she not a Lucien de Rubempré within her grasp, the very same Rubempré whom a Duchesse de Maufrigneuse is later only too willing to make her official squire? Ought he not to serve as a sufficient distraction? Alas, the handsome young fellow's mother is a midwife, and he lives on the wrong side of the tracks. Mme de Bargeton is hampered by such considerations. Mme de la Baudraye, it will be remembered, is a much bolder woman in such matters: she does not hesitate to escape from Sancerre, impelled simply by her own feelings. Mme de Bargeton does not make up her mind to leave Angoulême until she has been helped to her decision by a scandal that she did nothing to provoke.

Nor is she liberated by her flight. Once in Paris, Mme de la Baudraye becomes a changed woman. Mme de Bargeton limits herself to changing her style of dress. She remains the prisoner of her vanity. Mme de la Baudraye attempts to improve Lousteau's articles; Mme de Bargeton does not even attempt to improve Lucien's taste in waistcoats. Though she blushes when she realizes how badly he is dressed. Already, during the journey, she has been irritated by his naïveté, by his way of behaving like a young rat delighted and grateful to be emerging at last from his hole (*id.* p.594). Her reactions would be natural enough in a young bride, but they are less understandable in a woman of forty who has just kidnapped a young man half her age. One is even inclined to wonder whether she did in fact ever give herself to him. Balzac's text leaves room for doubt. "How fortunate for me that I kept that droll creature at a distance and refused to allow him any favors," she says to herself. But Lucien, in a letter to her, refers to "the favors that you granted me," and one day, when he is angry, Balzac tells us, a few caresses were sufficient to calm him down (*id.* pp. 621 and 599). And besides, what was there to prevent Anaïs from yielding to this young man, once the scandal of their flight had made everyone suppose that she had done so already? Respect for morality would not have done so, for she has none. It therefore seems hard to believe that she did not yield. But, on the other hand, is she capable of any decisive action at all other than those dictated by her vanity? I doubt it. Vanity too is a prison, and a worse one than Angoulême. Mme de Bargeton compares Lucien to Chatelet. One is young and handsome, the other old and plain. In the end, Mme de Bargeton chooses the second. And do you know why? Because he comes to see her in a handsome cabriolet. Where is there room for love in such a mind? Or even for humble, modest desire? She simply deserts Lucien. Later on, she almost beckons him back again. Why? Because he wears such handsome waistcoats. Vain, vain woman, unable to see any further than appearances. A waistcoat! A waistcoat can so easily be taken off! Having become a widow, she marries Chatelet. When Lucien returns to Angoulême, she can still feel the shadow of an emotion for him. But nothing more. Mme de Bargeton enjoys the advantages of vanity too: impeccable behavior, and even a sort of majesty.

Like the three women we have just discussed, Véronique Graslin is at once the victim of provincial life, of her marriage, of what she has read and of a certain natural superiority. Born into a family of wealthy boiler-makers named Sauviat, she has spent a quiet, sheltered childhood tucked away in a side street in Limoges. She has read only one book in her life, *Paul et Virginie*, but that one book has proved quite sufficient to unlock the floodgates of her heart to the flaming tides of love. "For her, that book was worse than a whole volume of obscenities" (*Curé de Village*, p.549). Another prisoner, she accepts the first husband who comes her way, and is as unfortunate in her choice as are Dinah and Anaïs. La Baudraye is impotent, Bargeton is worn out by his youthful excesses and Graslin is old, ugly, and a miser. Mme de la Baudraye is made restive by her disappointment, Mme de Bargeton becomes embittered. Mme Graslin, on the other hand, simply hibernates. She apparently has no other concerns in the world but her household, her at-homes and her good works. Only apparently though, for one day we are to discover that she too has had her moment of escape. Long, long after the execution of a certain murderer, she is to confess that the man in question had been her lover, that she had been an accomplice to his crime, and that, if he had not been arrested, she would have run away with him. Ah, what a long way we are from the shilly-shallying of a Mme de Bargeton! Mme Graslin may be a criminal, but in her we can recognize the greatness of soul, the stature of mind that, although not necessarily upheld in any way by concepts of morality, when the end justifies the effort does not stoop to consider the means that must be employed. That she possesses such greatness of soul Mme Graslin proves, after her lover's death, by becoming the benefactress of her whole canton and a genuine saint, raised by the force of her repentance to heights that a Mme de la Baudraye or a Mme de Bargeton could never know. Of the four superior women that we have examined up till now, there are only two who really deserve that adjective: Mme Graslin and Mlle des Touches. The former dies in the appalling odor of sanctity, the latter ends her life in a convent. Should we interpret these facts as a moral lesson on Balzac's part: that this world is too small for truly great souls?

The novel *les Employés*, in which we encounter Mme Rabourdin, was first published under the title *la Femme Supérieure*. Its heroine therefore has a right to inclusion under this heading. Though there is no high drama in her life, no gloom or tragedy. Her story is a quiet one. She has not even made a bad marriage; her husband is an excellent fellow. At the very most, one sometimes senses that he irritates her occasionally. And that's all. Apart from which, Mme Rabourdin is a charmer. There are some heroines of novels who attract us and others who do not. Why? I don't know. But Mme Rabourdin is one of the attractive ones. It is easy to understand why all the most successful young men in Paris are occasionally to be seen visiting her modest drawing-room on the Rue Duphot. Rubempré, Canalis, Chatelet, des Lupeaulx, Manerville, Bianchon, Finot—she receives them all without making any distinctions. What do they expect to find there? Love? Hardly, since Mme Rabourdin seems quite faithful to her husband. Influence? What influence could she possibly have, little Mme Rabourdin née Célestine Leprince, the daughter of a government surveyor and the wife of an under-secretary at the Ministry of Finance? In short, we are never told why they come. Mme Rabourdin must quite simply be one of those women that people like going to see.

She is a little contemptuous of her husband, as I have already intimated, but in the nicest possible way. She feels that he doesn't know how to make the best of himself. A vulgar woman in this situation would nag at her husband and before long make him envious and embittered. Mme Rabourdin isn't a vulgar woman. Her husband is clumsy when it comes to managing an intrigue? Very well, then she will manage it for him. She embarks upon an intense flirtation with des Lupeaulx. The flirtation fails in its object, but Mme Rabourdin discovers her husband's talents. They are happy together. And we, we are delighted.

Blanche-Henriette de Mortsauf *or the bitter Alissa*

The Princess of Cleves has a daughter, Fromentin's Madeleine a mother, Gide's Alissa a grandmother. She is Blanche-Henriette de Mortsauf, the tender, pure, infuriating heroine of *le Lys dans la Vallée*.

She was born a Lenoncourt, which is an advantage, but she is also the daughter of the Duke and Duchess de Lenoncourt, which is quite the reverse, since the Duke is a mere courtier, more concerned with the King's slightest outbreak of temper than with his own daughter's illnesses, and the Duchess is a hard, heartless, spiteful woman, even to her own daughter. "Even a spy would not have been so dastardly, so treacherous" (*Lys dans la Vallée*, p.803). Lastly, Blanche-Henriette is an only daughter, and her parents hold the fact against her. It is typical of them. Under the Empire, they had been obliged to live in retirement and in a constantly precarious situation. They have become embittered in consequence, and the only occasions on which Henriette experiences any sweetness in life are those when she is with her aunt Verneuil, a very religious old lady who belongs to the same little mystic sect as M. de Saint-Martin (Chateaubriand, in his *Mémoires d'Outre-Tombe*, talks about this Saint-Martin and quotes this truly great remark of his: "Besides, of whom do I have need, except God?" It could stand as the epigraph for *le Lys dans la Vallée*). Then, one day, Henriette finds herself married to Mortsauf, a good-hearted man whose sufferings in exile and "amorous adventures below stairs" have made him into a neurasthenic invalid. Two children are born, Jacques and Madeleine, both of whom inherit their father's precarious health. High birth, unhappy childhood, piety, mystic influence, sad married life, constant worry over her children, such is the sum total of traits that make up Mme de Mortsauf's character.

A happy childhood is necessary to human beings. An unhappy childhood is like a childhood that has not yet happened. It makes you into a child that cannot grow up, like Félix de Vandenesse. It is happiness that brings human beings to maturity, not suffering, so that Mme de Mortsauf, the mother of two children, is in fact still a child herself. At the age of thirty she is still afraid of her mother (*Lys dans la Vallée*, p.844). She is as untouched as a little girl, Balzac tells us (*id*. p.821). "Your childish scruples," her husband says to her (*id*. p.1012). And, "she is as silly as a little girl," he remarks elsewhere (*id*. p.955). She has the unsuspecting ignorance of a child" (*id*. p.1004). And she has sudden impulsive fits of gaiety like a little girl. Inevitably, for her marriage is such a failure that it is as though she were not married at all. M. de Mortsauf, as indiscreet as all Balzac's other characters, does not even try to conceal how little intimacy there really is between himself and his wife. "She uses every trick she knows to remain a little girl," he exclaims. "She has remained a virgin at my expense" (*id*. pp. 873 and 874). She doesn't like happiness. Which is her way of admitting that she has never experienced it. "To me, happiness is like an illness," she says. "I feel crushed by it" (*id*. p.870). The remark of a little girl. The remark of a virgin.

It is this inability of hers to emerge from childhood that draws Henriette to Félix de Vandenesse. "We had the same childhood," she exclaims (*id*. p.870). Even their parents are similar: fathers who take no interest in them, embittered and sharp-tongued mothers. And because the two children, Félix and Henriette, have never been given their fill of the caresses they needed, both have kept buried inside them a great thirst for tenderness, for gentleness, for the childhood they never had. Hearing them talk, one sometimes has the feeling of listening to two children, to two adolescents who are discovering love for the first time, hand in hand, dumb with wonder and delight. While at the same time, in Henriette, this childlike attitude is strangely mingled with motherliness. For this child-woman is also a mother; that is the only sphere of life in which she has escaped from childhood, in which she has achieved maturity. It is from her motherhood that she draws all her strength, as well as that gentle majesty of demeanor from which she never deviates. These two ways of feeling combine in her in such a way that she comes to look upon Félix as a third child. Her maternal feelings absorb her love for the man. So much so that at one point, when Félix returns to her after a period of absence, she is astonished to discover that he is a fully grown man (*id.* p.913). It is the surprise of a mother, not of a woman in love. She even conceives the project of eventually marrying him to her daughter. In other words, since she cannot give up the tenderness she feels for him, she plays with the idea of drowning it, once for all, in her more permissible maternal feelings. Félix helps to maintain this ambiguity in their relationship. He plays with her children, helping her to forget that he is not one of them. One day, during the grape harvest, the children run up to Henriette to show her the baskets of fruit they have picked. Félix runs up to her too. " 'And mine, Mummy?' She replied: 'Dear boy, you mustn't get too hot' then, having run her hand around my neck and through my hair, she gave me a little tap on the cheek, adding: 'You're dripping with perspiration' " (*id.* p.862). That is all that happens. But desire, in the buzzing summer air, has hovered for a moment like an angel. The maternal feelings are still there, but almost like an alibi. Behind them, there is the "joyous stupor of souls that have reached that frontier where exaltation ends and mad ecstasy begins" (*id.* p.884). And let us also add that all this takes place at Saché, in a curve of the Indre, in the midst of ash trees, water lilies and heaven trees, in a climate so gentle that the soul and the passions are easily lulled to sleep there.

And Henriette's piety is there too, spreading its purifying light over Félix's story. Time and again, it holds their relationship back from the brink, poised in disturbing, ambiguous, precarious balance. Until the moment when this piety itself, for a moment or two, yields to the contagion. A strange dialogue begins:

"Is your love for me holy?"

"Holy."

"Like a love for the Virgin Mary? . . ."

"For the Virgin Mary made visible."

"For a sister?"

"For a sister loved too well."

"For a mother?"

"For a mother secretly desired" (*id*. p.914).

It is almost a litany. And let us not forget that Henriette has in fact been under the influence, through her very religious aunt, of one of those mystical societies whose devotions do sometimes take on the strangest verbal forms. Chateaubriand: "M. de Saint-Martin thought he had discovered traces of a certain private cant in *Atala* . . ." and, further on: "M. de Saint-Martin, as he warmed more and more to his subject, began to speak after the fashion of an archangel . . ."

Despite all this, however, Henriette is still a Lenoncourt. We realize this as soon as we begin reading the letter she has handed to Félix as he takes leave of her to go and make a career for himself in Paris. For though it might seem reasonable to imagine that its contents are pure and wistful words of tenderness, anyone who does so is in for a rude shock. To his great surprise, he will find the letter to be a veritable instruction manual for the ambitious young man. Too much so, as a matter of fact. The letter commands our admiration, yes; but it is Balzac who has written it, not Henriette. Admittedly the shock is prepared a long way in advance; we have caught glimpses of the Lenoncourt lurking beneath the surface of the gentle Mme de Mortsauf. "Stay faithful to your own party," we have heard her say one day to Félix. "Especially when it is winning the day" (*id*. p.845). And ambition, in Balzac, is never thought of as detracting from a character's greatness of soul. Quite the reverse. But from there to philosophizing about the origins of society, as Mme de Mortsauf does in her letter; from there to concluding like some old uncle: "I come now to the most serious question, that of your behavior towards women" (*id*. p.895), no, that is really too much. And though Henriette's letter is still far above the level of Marsay's in *le Contrat de Mariage*, it is already too much that we should be able to compare the two. Besides, where could Henriette possibly have aquired such a consummate mastery of the subject? Balzac seems to have foreseen this objection. "The conversations I have had with my aunt," he has Henriette write, ". . . the incidents of his own life recounted to me by M. de Mortsauf, the discourse of my father, who was so familiar with Court life . . ." (*id*. p.886). All of which, I must confess, leaves me still unconvinced.

Meanwhile, the child in Félix is breathing its last. The lion is showing his claws. In Paris, he becomes Lady Dudley's lover. Henriette finds out. When she sees Félix again she is unable to conceal her anger and her jealousy. Little by little, their love is becoming a relationship between adults. "What do you mean?" Félix says to her. "What have you to reproach Lady Dudley with? She, at least, gave me everything." Cruel words, and their cruelty enables us to gauge how far Félix has now left the child behind him. "For the Comtesse," Balzac writes, "the world had been turned upside down . . . Awestruck by the terrible prospect before her, suspecting this martyrdom to be justified by her past happiness, hearing the clamor of her frustrated and protesting flesh, she stood in stupor gazing at the ruin of her life. Yes, she went through a horrible moment of doubt" (*id*. p.960). It is the same disillusion that we find in the last chapter of *la Porte étroite*. "It was like a sudden flood of light stripping all the illusions from my life," Alissa writes. "It seemed to me that I was seeing the bare walls of my room for the very first time." Henriette too looks at the walls of her room. Beyond them, she senses life still going on, and the joys that she will never know again (*id*. p.1005). She has reached that terrible hour when one doubts the value of one's sacrifice, of one's vocation, of one's life. "I no longer know what virtue is," Henriette says, "and whether I have any or not I cannot tell" (*id*. p.963). Her faith begins to fade. Her motherhood is no longer a support. She is nothing but a wretched, mortal woman alone in her struggle. "I am scarcely thirty-five years old yet, I still have some years of beauty left . . . We'll go to Italy together . . . I want to be loved, I'll behave outrageously, like Lady Dudley" (*id*. pp. 1004 and 1005). The last cries of passion. And cries in which, despite the sufferings of the woman, we can still detect the naïveté of the child, of the little girl.

But whereas *la Porte étroite* ends on a cry of despair, *le Lys dans la Vallée* continues on to a new victory, and Henriette de Mortsauf shows herself, in this crisis, infinitely superior to Gide's Alissa. One need only compare the former's last letter to the latter's diary. Between the two there gapes the vast abyss that separates a turbulent and generous soul from a heart that remains, despite all its good impulses, forever without joy. Henriette's faith is victorious. Her death is not a death, it is a resurrection. She was a lost soul, but she has searched and found herself. Her children, who did not recognize her, now recognize her again. Infuriating Henriette, I said at the beginning. The expression is vulgar, cheap, and I offer my apologies for it. Of all the triumphs recounted in the *Comédie humaine* there is none more dazzling than that of Mme de Mortsauf, since on her deathbed she rediscovers the joy, the serenity, the sweetness of God's presence. Everything around her is collapsing into ruins. She has sacrificed herself for her husband and her children. Her husband is unhappy and one of her children is already spitting blood. But the truth is elsewhere. For the Christian, there exists only one truth, only one justification: the soul's salvation. All the rest is mockery. "Woe to any man who should lament at having walked the path of righteousness" (*id*. p.963).

Everyone is aware that the plot and characters of *le Lys dans la Vallée* owe something to Balzac's first love affair, his relationship with Mme Berny. Such information as we have about this lady does not, however, give grounds for believing that she ever displayed either the greatness of soul, the simplicity of heart, or the piety of Mme de Mortsauf. The most that can be said is that she entertained the same maternal feelings towards Balzac that we later find attributed to Mme de Mortsauf, and that their relationship must in the long run have developed the same aura of friendliness and trust that hovers over the first part of *le Lys*. In his biography of Balzac (Volume I, p.51), André Billy quotes a letter from Balzac to Mme de Berny which certainly calls to mind Félix and Henriette's conversations by its tone: "You are unhappy, I know that, but you have stores of wealth in your soul that you yourself are not aware of, and these may yet prove a means of reconciling yourself to life. The very first time I saw you, you were surrounded by that aura of grace that always accompanies human beings whose adversity is a product of their hearts." And here is Balzac-Félix: "Such I am, such I shall always be, timid to excess, in love to the point of madness, and so chaste that I dare not say: I love." Lastly, I should also point out that Mme de Berny, like Mme de Mortsauf with Félix, did at one point think of making Balzac her son-in-law.

It is still, even today, a pleasure to wander through the quiet village of Saché, where Mme de Mortsauf's soul still hovers. There, guarded by three cypress trees, is the graveyard where she lies. There is the church under its gray bell tower. If you have a good face, possibly the village priest will come over to you and tell you, not about Henriette, but about the Blessed Marguerite de Rousselé who lived and died (1608-1628) at Saché, in this selfsame landscape where Henriette de Mortsauf also lived and died. Balzac does not mention her. Should we therefore conclude that the example of the Blessed Marguerite had no bearing at all on the firm piety of Henriette? Is it possible to live in a place where a saint has lived and remained completely unaffected? I don't believe it. Henriette would not have been the same woman had she lived elsewhere. There is a sacred presence always hovering over her. Balzac does not mention the Blessed Marguerite, but it is possible that he was attempting to provide us with a transposition of her influence by referring on several occasions, as he does, to the example and the teachings of the philosopher-mystic Saint-Martin.

In front of the church, there stretches a huge, vaguely outlined square that has probably not changed at all in a hundred years. It is true that when I saw it the center was occupied by a traveling crane left there to rust by the Germans, but I imagine that has been taken away by now. It was there, for the first time, that Félix dared to offer Henriette his arm. She was wearing a straw hat that particular day. She smiled. It was there too, in that little wood just over there, that Félix confessed his intention of going into a seminary. Clochegourde does not exist, never did exist, but there, to the right, is the asymmetrical façade of the château de Saché, in which, after Henriette's funeral, Félix took sanctuary. If you walk down the hill a little way you come to Pont-de-Ruan, where Henriette and Félix came one day and stood in the shade of a *brouillard*, a species of poplar with white bark, to watch the fishermen.

Renèe de l'Estorade *or the industrious Martha*

Like Mme de Mortsauf, Renée de l'Estorade has married a man old before his time. Like Mme de Mortsauf again, she lives in the country, far from the whirl of Society, concerned above all with her estate and her children. And like Henriette she has in her character that mixture of greatness of soul and ambition that is one of the recognizable traits of Balzac's best characters. There, however, the comparison stops. Henriette de Mortsauf is almost a saint. Renée de l'Estorade is a good woman. We are faced here, *mutatis mutandis*, with that same step down in the scale that led us from the lion to the merely elegant young man in a previous chapter. Henriette's virtue obliges her to lift her eyes up to heaven. Renée's makes her look where she's going. Despite her convent upbringing, she does not seem to spend much of her time in prayer. On occasion, she refers to her Christian sentiments, and she is delighted to find that the man she is engaged to shares them (*Mémoires de deux Jeunes Mariées*, p.153). But that is all. She is not religious in an ecstatic way; her piety is of the reasonable kind and produces none of those effusions of the soul we meet with so often in Mme de Mortsauf.

Born in 1805, Renée is the daughter of that same Comte de Maucombe who, under the Terror, was overseer in the Séchard printing works in Angoulême (*Illusions perdues*, p.465). I have been unable to unearth any details about her mother. The Maucombe family is from Provence. Daughters, as far as they are concerned, are an altogether lesser breed.

What fortune they have is kept for the son. This is the first rude shock that reality metes out to Renée. In the convent where she was brought up with Louise de Chaulieu she had grown somewhat excitable and idealistic; but this exaltation ends abruptly. The bubbling vitality of spirit that in Henriette de Mortsauf is never entirely masked by pious serenity seems, in Renée's case, to disappear at her first contact with life. Henriette probably allowed herself to be married off out of ignorance, because it did not occur to her that it was possible to resist. Renée, on the other hand, would have been perfectly capable of resisting. Even at the age of seventeen one feels that she is quite prepared to stand up to anyone. She has a good stance, a quick eye, and can obviously thrust and parry with the best. She is not pushed into her marriage: she accepts it. Coldly and resolutely. Henriette's marriage is entirely arbitrary; Renée's is the product of a principle, of a theory. "Don't worry," she writes to her friend, "I have thought deeply about my consent and did not give it rashly . . . The security that comes from walking a path already laid out and known is something that suits both my mind and my character" (*Mémoires de deux Jeunes Mariées*, p.168). There is nothing of Iphigenia here. Renée is a girl who knows what she is doing; she realizes that this marriage is the best she can hope for. She knows where she is going. So she marries Louis d'Estorade, a man of thirty-seven who looks fifty and is fairly rich. Conscripted in 1813, he was listed as missing after Leipzig and was only able to return to France after a period of wandering that aged him considerably. He is half deaf, has a mean-looking face and suffers from an inferiority complex. Barren ground; but his new wife nevertheless sees enough good in him to conceive the project of making him over into the ideal man of which every woman carries an image in her bosom. At first, it is true, she says that she is resigned. "All's said, all's done" (*id*. p.167). But her greatness lies in the fact that she does not resign herself. Since she has not found a love ready made she proceeds to build one for herself. Like Mme de Baudraye with Lousteau, she goes on to re-create her husband, to give birth not only to children but also, as it were, to a new better half. At the beginning of *Mémoires de deux Jeunes Mariées*, it is Louise de Chaulieu who represents love. Renée seems to be there only to moderate her friend's emotional turmoil with calm advice. Louise makes an inordinately romantic marriage; Renée makes do with a sensible marriage. With the passage of time, everything changes. Weary, no doubt, of waiting to find happiness with Louise, love leaves her, bow and baggage, and takes up residence with Renée. Renée is never going to meet a Spaniard who will risk every bone in his body for a glimpse of her; but what does such derring-do amount to in comparison with the vast labor she herself has embarked upon? "I am undertaking," she says, "to raise this broken character up again, to restore their luster to certain good qualities that I have glimpsed" (*id.* p.184). And she succeeds. "I have seen that face change its expression and become younger again," she writes (*id.* p.185). When she does give herself to her husband at last, it is with a happiness that Louise has never known. "Know . . . that there was nothing lacking of what even the most delicate love could require, or of that unexpectedness that is, in a way, the honor of such a moment; the mysterious graces that our imaginations demand, the impulsiveness that is our excuse, the forced consent, the ideal sensual pleasures that we have glimpsed for so long, and that have already subjugated our souls in imagination before we finally allow ourselves to yield to the reality" (*id.* p. 185). You see what I mean when I say that Renée, of the two, is the one who really knows how to love.

Moreover, questionable though it may be, Balzac's capillary cosmogony ought to have prepared us for this fact already. Renée is a brunette, Louise is blonde. The rules of the *Comédie humaine* admit of almost no exceptions in this matter: blonde women are not good at love. They love love itself too much. And this love of love is inevitably accompanied, according to Balzac, by a certain suppression of the man that inspires it. Brunettes, on the other hand, again according to Balzac, obtain better results because they devote themselves more to the husband or lover himself.

Renée is also ambitious, and her ambition is of the same stamp as her love: steadfast, well considered, and farseeing. Before she is even married she has already asked Louise de Chaulieu to promise lifelong protection to her child (*id.* p.853). Later on, she also asks her to be its godmother. Out of friendship, of course, but also because her friend also happens to be a Chaulieu. And she takes advantage of this fact on occasion. "Do me the kindness of approaching whichever *mamamouchi* this appointment concerns" (*id.* p.266). Living in the depths of Provence, she still manages to keep the strings of the affair in her own hands, and to prevent Louise from wasting her influence. "Above all, don't become involved in the affairs of my most highly esteemed father . . . Such excess of favor might well prove harmful to my husband, so do let him wait a little . . . Keep your favors for me" (*id.* p.266). The letter of a woman with her wits about her. Does she not deserve to succeed? M. de l'Estorade becomes a local councilor, then a deputy. His wife sees to it that he loses no time in going over to Louis-Philippe. She entertains no useless loyalties. Eventually, they move to Paris, and there they remain, apparently moving a great deal in the best society (*Béatrix,* p.590; *Ursule Mirouët,* p.479; *Fausse Maîtresse,* p.15).

Louise de Chaulieu *or love*

Louise de Chaulieu. A name that gives one pause; a name to linger over. For Louise de Chaulieu is love. Love unmindful of all that is not itself, love that looks on tempests and is not moved, all-devouring love, love that is pure passion, love that leaps over every obstacle, that laughs in the face of prejudice, tramples on ambitions, on conventions, on pros and cons, love as a vocation, love the sufficient reason, love in fact, all that we mean when we say love. "Love as I see it is the origin of all the virtues," Louise writes (*Mémoires de deux Jeunes Mariées,* p.191). "Just let the man I deign to love take it into his head to do anything other than love me" (*id.* p.161). "I need do nothing but love, love can become my life, my sole occupation" (*id.* p.164). We see her choosing a husband on two occasions. In neither instance does she give even a moment's thought to the fortunes, the birth, the religion or the professions of the men she chooses. He loves me, she says the first time. And the second time, I love him. She needs no other reason, no other recommendation. What weight can birth, wealth, ambition carry with someone entirely blinded by the dazzle of love! Love alone exists!

The daughter of a duke, Louise must be about eighteen years old at the time she emerges from her convent and begins her correspondence with Renée. Let us look at her first letter. In the sixth line she is already talking about love. That is what she thinks about, that is what she is preparing for. She lists her trumps. "My person is one of the most beautiful in all France" (*id.* p.144). She is blonde, "a blonde from the South, full-blooded not wan." She has blue eyes, a long neck, a rather full mouth and dimples. "My dear little squirrel, if that isn't enough to marry off any girl without a dowry then I don't know the first thing about it" (*id.* pp. 144 and 145). By her fifth letter she is growing impatient. Where has it got to, this love she's expecting? "I've already seen a great many young men, men in their hundreds, and not one of them has stirred anything in me for a moment" (*id.* p.163). She is worried. "I have encountered nothing amongst all those brilliant, avid, wary glances" (*id.* p.164). And this letter is written three months after her first appearance in society. Three months! "I begin to tremble at the fate awaiting us" (*id.* p.163).

Given such favorable predispositions, it may be imagined that love is not long in making its appearance. Louise falls in love with her Spanish teacher. He is short and plain. He has an enormous head and a graceless face. But never mind; his eyes flash fire, and that is enough to make Louise de Chaulieu hurl every objection out of the window. We need not tremble for her, however. There is a God for dukes as well. This particular Spanish teacher is in fact a very respectably born nobleman, temporarily on the official black list, and named Macumer. Like Louise, he loves, he reveres nothing in this world except love. They marry. They are rich and have no money troubles. And since, as we have noted, Macumer is on a political blacklist that for the moment rules ambition out of court, they have nothing to do but love one another. They are free to lock themselves up in love, to lead "the dissipated yet nevertheless full life of people happy together. To us, every day seems too short" (*id.* p.244). It is love in seven-league boots, love that ends up by devouring life itself: "Ten times in the past ten months I have caught myself longing to die at thirty, in all the splendor of life, lying in love's bed of roses, in the soft bosom of pleasure" (*id.* p.244). In short, we see the theme of the love death emerging, of the love that can see nothing beyond itself, that can find nothing else worth talking of besides death, because only death seems to be as eternal, as absolute as itself. No children, of course. To have a child, for Louise, would be to say goodbye to love. It would mean a check to those sensual pleasures to which, in her book, nothing else can possibly be compared. "In reality, what you feel is not love," Renée writes to her. "You will grow weary of your husband's adoration. Sooner or later you are going to despise him because he loves you too much" (*id.* p.259). And over a period of time, it is quite true, we begin to sense in Louise's letters a melancholy that is not always sufficiently explained. She ends up wanting a child, and weeping because her attempts to have one remain unsuccessful. "Each time my hopes are disappointed I am for several days a prey to black grief . . . A woman without children is a monstrosity, the only reason we were created is to be mothers" (*id.* pp. 272 and 273). Only . . . to be mothers . . . This is a far cry from the letter in which she once wrote: "If I never know the joys of motherhood, then you shall describe them to me . . . but there is nothing in my eyes that can be compared with the pleasures of love" (*id.* p.244). Has Macumer let her down? By no means. He remains always as loving, as much in love with her as ever. But the limits of love have been reached: it is no longer sufficient to make them happy. They both grow thinner (*id.* p.272). In Balzac, all moral torments are made visible by physical deterioration of some kind. Macumer dies. Of what? "I killed him," Louise writes. "I killed him with my demands, with my unfounded jealousies, with my ceaseless pestering" (*id*. p.282). In a word, she killed him with love. "Can it be that love, pure and violent as it must be when it is absolute, is as unfruitful in its effects as aversion?" (*id*. p.283). Absolute love, the other face of death. Love against life. Ill-fated love. The love of women with fair hair . . .

After several years of widowhood, Louise falls in love with Marie-Gaston, one of Lady Brandon's adulterine sons. Here again, she does not reflect or calculate for a moment. Marie-Gaston is a bastard, poor, and younger than she. But she loves him. She loves him, that's the only thing that matters. She marries him. She locks herself away once more in love. They go and bury themselves together in the country. Louise has learned nothing. Once more she concentrates all her attention upon love and insists that her husband do the same. Is she happy? Yes, but she is also prey to a constant uneasiness. "When I am forty he will still be young; he will still be young and I shall be old" (*id*. p.308). With this uneasiness in her heart the slightest misunderstanding might kill her. The misunderstanding occurs. And it kills her.

Claire de Beauséant *or love crushed and avenged*

Louise de Chaulieu is eighteen at the time of her first appearance. Mme de Beauséant, born in about 1791, is already at least thirty by the time we make her acquaintance. As a result, Louise displays a vivacity and an impatience in her approach to love that in Claire de Beauséant have already given way to a tender gravity and "a lofty awareness of her own worth" (*Femme abandonnée*, p.219). There is, nevertheless, a close resemblance between the two. They are both women whose lives have been consecrated to love, who only exist for love. And they are both blonde, with the same milky skin typical of fair-haired women, the same warm flesh. They never speak harshly, they never make abrupt or angular movements: love has impregnated their very bones with its languors. The most that can be said is that Mme de Beauséant sometimes displays a touch of aristocratic hauteur that is entirely lacking in the simple, good-hearted Louise. And lastly, love presents itself to both women twice, and in curiously parallel ways: corresponding to the Spanish Macumer there is the Portuguese Ajuda, and to Marie-Gaston another Gaston, Gaston de Nueil. Louise goes from a man who worships her to a man with whom she is madly in love. Mme de Beauséant travels the same road in the opposite direction. But the results are identical: in both cases love is defeated. It is eliminated, ground out of existence every time. By death in the case of

Louise, by a dowry in the case of Mme de Beauséant. In the first case it is God who takes his vengeance, in the second it is society. Mme de Beauséant's love was genuine. She loved strongly and she loved fervently. Yet a dowry is sufficient to defeat her. Ajuda leaves her, not for a rival, but for a Rochefide he scarcely loves at all, and Gaston de Nueil leaves her to marry a La Rodière he doesn't love in the slightest. Such is the vengeance wreaked on love by marriage, on passion by society. Such is the defeat that love must suffer when it aspires to self-sufficiency.

Yet heaven knows that Mme de Beauséant might reasonably have expected to triumph. Beautiful, rich, born Claire de Bourgogne, the last daughter of a quasi-royal house (*Père Goriot*, p.1058), she is one of the queens of Paris. She is a member of the Petit Château circle, the exclusive Bourbon stronghold (*Lys dans la Vallée*, p.911). And to be received by her is tantamount to a patent of nobility (*Gobseck*, p.672; *Père Goriot*, p.874). She has Ajuda at her feet, Ajuda who is one of the handsomest dandies in all Paris, Ajuda who loves her, whom she loves, without restrictions, without subterfuges. M. de Beauséant is aware of their relationship, and Paris accepts it. All that is swept into oblivion by the dizzy prospect of a "sensible marriage," by the few "moneybags" that the Rochefide girl is able to include in the marriage contract. What pain! And all of Parisian Society gossiping about it. All Parisian Society arriving at Mme de Beauséant's ball to see how she is taking it. But, "dressed all in white, without a single ornament in her simply braided hair, she appeared quite calm and made no show of grief, of pride, or of simulated joy. No one could read what was in her heart" (*Père Goriot*, p.1059). Ah, she is a woman worthy of the name. Nothing petty anywhere in her nature. She has greatness. And a kind heart too. In the very midst of her disaster, at a time when everything ought to be a matter of indifference to her, she is still capable of attending to the wretched little needs of her poor cousin, Rastignac. That is a delightful trait.

The day after her ball, Mme de Beauséant leaves Paris and buries herself away in the depths of Lower Normandy. It is not just Ajuda who has deserted her, it is also her reason for living, her vital principle. From that point on, nothing really exists for her any more. Nothing, that is, except young Gaston de Nueil, who falls in love with her, who follows her when she runs away to Geneva in order to escape him. Nine long years of happiness then follow, at the end of which, won round by his mother, young Gaston marries, in his turn, a young lady with a dowry. A fresh defeat for love. Louise de Chaulieu, by insisting on absolute love, killed everything in her husbands other than their love for her. And she brought disaster upon herself. Mme de Beauséant fails in the same way, because she too can offer her men nothing but love. It is not that she is a particularly demanding woman, but being married already she has nothing to give but a happiness outside the bounds of society. A marginal happiness. And she is bound to be defeated. In Balzac, love, love on its own, always brings disaster. And it brings it not only to Mme de Beauséant herself but also to those who abandon her. Ajuda regrets having left her (*Père Goriot*, pp. 1059 and 1060), and his wife dies very soon after their marriage. Gaston de Nueil goes back to her, and when she rejects him he kills himself. So we see Mme de Beauséant avenged. And we also understand the lesson: the same disasters lie in wait for those who aspire to give up everything for love as for those who attempt to mock at it. Love must always compromise, and we must always compromise with it.

Madame Firmiani *or love gratified*

In the midst of all the calculating and treacherous women with which the *Comédie humaine* abounds, Louise de Chaulieu, Claire de Beauséant and Mme Firmiani are, if I may so express myself, like three palm trees marking an oasis. They also constitute the three degrees of reason in love: Louise has almost none, Mme de Beauséant a little, and Mme Firmiani a great deal. But it is a reason without frigidity, without ulterior motives, a reason instinct with tenderness, a reason that does not discount the reasons of the heart. Mme Firmiani is a woman who approached Stendhal's ideal: she is natural. "She has a friendly, laughing approach to life . . . She reduces respect to the status of a gentle shadow; she never tires you, and she leaves you satisfied both with her and with yourself . . . She never strains after effect, never puts on displays, her feelings are always simply expressed, because they are always genuine" (*Madame Firmiani*, p.1036). She is gay and open in her manner. In short, as I have already said, natural. And like all natural people, she is disconcerting. There is nothing more conducive to an air of mystery than utter honesty, and Mme Firmiani stirs up the most contradictory rumors about herself. One thing, however, is certain: she was born a Cadignan. "A woman who was born a Cadignan!" (*les Employés*, p.895). It is something not to be sneezed at. "Even were she entirely without virtues, wealth and youth, she would still be a Cadignan" (*Madame Firmiani*, p.1031). But apart from this fact, "she is a woman who is wholly mysterious" (*id.* p.1031). Originally poor in all probability, born of parents undoubtedly long since dead, in 1813 she marries a Treasury official named Firmiani who disappears during a journey through Greece. Assuming that she was only sixteen at the time of her marriage, Mme Firmiani must be about twenty-eight at the beginning of the novella that bears her name. But "at no period in her life had she been so desirable, or so completely a woman" (*id.* p.1037). Everyone agrees in regarding her as "one of the most charming women in Paris" (*Illusions perdues*, p.609), and even "the most aristocratically beautiful woman in all Paris" (*Madame Firmiani*, p.1037). She is to be seen everywhere, in even the most exclusive of drawing-rooms. She is a friend of Mlle des Touches, of Marie de Vandenesse, of Mme d'Aiglemont, and of little Mme Rabourdin. She is also, I am fairly certain, the most frequently mentioned woman in the *Comédie humaine* (*Autre Etude de Femme*, p.212; *Fille d'Eve*, p.93; *Femme de trente ans*, p.757; *Employés*, p.893; *Splendeurs*, p.730; *Père Goriot*, p.875; *Bal de Sceaux*, p.126; *Interdiction*, p.42; *Illusions perdues*, p.852; *Cabinet des Antiques*, p.377; etc.). All without ever playing a particularly active role. She passes through, she lends distinction, she listens, she enchants. She also sings, for she has a very pretty voice. In 1825, the official notification of her husband's death finally comes through, and Mme Firmiani marries the charming Octave de Camps. There are more brilliant couples in the *Comédie humaine*, but I know of none more difficult not to like.

Béatrix de Rochefide *or the thieving magpie*

Béatrix is an example of the angular blonde. "Slender and straight as a taper." Full face she is pretty. "In profile, her face looks rather as though it has been squashed between two doors." Her complexion varies daily, "today the color of percale, tomorrow sallow and blotchy beneath a grainy skin" (*Béatrix*, pp. 396 and 397). She has green eyes, frequently ringed with dark smudges, thin arms, slender hips and an impertinent nose. To make up for all this, she has the heavy chin of women who are fond of love. "Perhaps I am making a mistake in telling you that women with heavy chins are demanding in matters of love" (*id.* p.396). But note that she is one of the women who love love, not the man. When she takes a man she does so with a gloomy smile; the fury and abandon of the woman who truly loves always remain foreign to her. It is as if, slumbering deep inside her, there is some ancient grudge. "The desolation in my heart," she says at one point, in a moment of abandon (*id.* p.489). There is an habitual bitterness in her mode of speech.

Rich, young, pretty, Béatrix ought to be entirely a stranger to jealousy. Yet she is only too prone to it. "The Marquise conceived the liveliest admiration for me," Mlle des Touches says, "but from admiration to jealousy is only a step" (*id.* p.395). Béatrix loathes other people's happiness instinctively. It distresses her, it weighs painfully upon her heart. And whenever she can, she destroys it. Yet she is not without "superiority of mind" even though it is a superiority devoid of greatness, lacking in generosity, and even further marred by her pride, the grudging, rancorous sort of pride that is only produced in narrow provincial families. Béatrix hails from the Orne. She is a Casteran (pronounced Catéran). "As far as one can tell, the Casterans are of the very best stock," Mlle des Touches says (*id.* p.394). But they are poor. Add beggary to pride and the total, as everyone knows, is always bitterness.

Born in 1808, at the age of twenty Béatrix is married to Arthur de Rochefide, brother of the Rochefide daughter who marries Ajuda, a goodhearted, manly fellow, rather stupid, shy and very eccentric. The marriage, needless to say, is one of convenience, not love. Invited to visit Mlle des Touches, Béatrix finds her hostess surrounded by happiness, holding sway not only over a brilliant *salon* but also over the heart of a socially acceptable lover. Nothing could have distressed Béatrix more. She begins by coaxing away the habitués of Félicité's *salon* and ends up by stealing the lady's lover, with whom she runs away to Italy. The lover, I forgot to mention, is Gennaro Conti. Upon her return to France, she finds Mlle des Touches consoling herself with Calyste du Guénic. What is this? Another scene of happiness? It is more than Béatrix can stand. She sets to work alienating Calyste's affections. Or rather, if we are to be fair, she does nothing to prevent him from falling in love with her. Once he has done so, she departs again, without even taking advantage of the young Breton. For as I told you, she finds her pleasure, not in being happy or loved, but in trampling on the happiness, the loves, the flowerbeds of others.

Several years later she meets Calyste again, married and bringing joy to the heart of a charming young wife. The young man she spurned when he was free suddenly becomes an object of the greatest interest to her. She tries to win him back. Meanwhile, I should add, Conti has abandoned her, she has aged, and she is now "bony and stringy" (*id.* p.542). Doubtless she feels the need to show that she can still triumph at the expense of a married woman, even one much younger than herself and charming into the bargain. How otherwise are we to explain the savage determination with which she approaches the task, not only of winning back Calyste's affections, but also of alienating him completely from his wife? She imposes on him "the horrible ultimatum of giving up Sabine totally and utterly" (*id.* p.549). Another woman would have tried to keep this liaison secret. Béatrix, on the contrary, makes sure that the wife is fully informed of what is going on. She is still possessed by her desire to do harm, to destroy. "Desertion had brought out in her all the ferocity of the Frank, all the cruelty of the Norman" (*id.* p.550). But Béatrix is completely alone in this affair. She is ultimately defeated by the Grandlieus, who work out a complicated plot that first of all throws her into the arms of La Palférine and then, by way of a gentle detour, back into a resumption of conjugal relations with poor Rochefide. I repeat—poor Rochefide. For he was certainly ten times happier without her.

Mesdames Roguin and Tiphaine

Mme Roguin may be considered as a middle-class counterpart of Béatrix de Rochefide in the sense that, like Béatrix, she is the mistress of a man whose wife is a woman very much younger than herself. As to how the two ladies manage this tour de force, I leave the reader to guess, according to his own ideas on the matter.

This Mme Roguin, born Chevrel, closely related to the family of cloth-merchants named Guillaume in *la Maison du Chat-qui-pelote*, is the wife of the notorious lawyer Roguin whose flight brings ruin to so many of the characters in the *Comédie humaine*. Flirtatious, vain, a determined social climber, she plays the lady of fashion, wears diamonds and does not pay her dressmakers (*Maison du Chat-qui-pelote*, pp. 47 and 25; *Une Double Famille*, p.935). She must have some sort of physical attraction, however, or at least a good deal of know-how, for her liaison with du Tillet manages to survive both her own ruin and her lover's marriage to Marie-Eugénie de Grandville. "At her age, and born a Grandville, to have a woman past fifty as a rival!" (*Muse du Département*, p.159); so threatening a state of affairs cannot fail to keep the legal profession of Paris in a state of perpetual alarm. In the end, however, du Tillet does abandon her for other ladies whose virtues are no less easy but whose charms are less withered.

I take this opportunity to mention Mme Roguin's daughter, Mathilde or Mélanie, who marries a magistrate in Provins named Tiphaine. She appears in *Pierrette*, and seems to be a witty, caustic woman who can run a house to perfection.

The Duchess de Carigliano and the Comtesse Ferraud
or the Empire woman

Mme de Carigliano only appears in one scene of *la Maison du Chat-qui-pelote*, but she is often mentioned elsewhere. She is one of Malin de Gondreville's two daughters. I am not at all certain when exactly she was born, and she marries the Maréchal Duc de Carigliano, a character about whom our author gives us no information whatsoever. Obviously the title was created under the Empire. But Mme de Carigliano is enough of an intriguer not to permit the fact to restrict her in any way. The whole Gondreville clan seems to excel in the sphere of devious social maneuvering. The father succeeded in surviving the Revolution, then the Empire, then the Restoration without for a moment ceasing to improve his situation or enlarge his estates. And his daughter has inherited this gift for social survival. Despite her excessively Napoleonic husband, she manages to insinuate herself into the most exclusively legitimist circles. She is even attached to the household of the Duchesse de Berry (*Père Goriot*, p.949). At the same time, through her husband, through her father, and through her sister Cécile Keller, she also keeps in touch with the liberals. This permits her to undertake some useful maneuvers. In particular, it is she who arranges Montcornet's marriage to a Troisville (*Paysans*, p.115). And she is equally adroit when dealing with men. She spins a web for them and they are guled to it in a trice. It is enlightening, in this respect, to read the advice she passes on to Mme de Sommervieux in *la Maison du Chat-qui-pelote*. We know that she engages in a liaison of long duration with the Marquis d'Aiglemont, and she enslaves Sommervieux too, though without ever in fact yielding to his ardors, unless I am much mistaken. She seduces him simply for the pleasure of doing so. Out of sheer flirtatiousness—a flirtatiousness behind which we sometimes glimpse the grimacing face of spite. Nevertheless, despite all her shrewdness, Mme de Carigliano must have experienced occasional bad patches, for at one point she sells her town house to the Lanty family (*Sarrasine*, p.80).

The Comtesse Ferraud, born Rose Chapotel, began her career in a brothel. I can see her now, dragging aimlessly around in her robe and her mules. In 1942 or so, someone made a film based on *le Colonel Chabert*, retaining Balzac's title. The only memorable thing about it was Marie Bell's performance as Rose. That gloomy smile, that listless air, the sagging walk of the brothel prostitute to whom everything is a matter of indifference, that vague aura of disgust—it was Rose Chapotel to the life. Rose Chapotel hearing the assistant madame clap her hands, then trailing down the stairs to greet a customer. Perhaps a regular, perhaps a new one. One day a soldier comes. He finds her attractive. He comes back. He comes back every time he is on leave. "I'll take Rose." Sometimes she is already occupied and he is forced to wait. Rather sordid; but most soldiers are good-hearted sonofaguns. This one especially. Except that he isn't the son of anything; he's a foundling, without any family at all, doubtless raised at the point of a boot, like Captain Coignet, never having known any other women except servant girls and small-time tarts. He isn't hard to please. "I like you, you know." Rose does not alter her plaintive expression. Perhaps it moves him. What a trade! she says. And yawns, her mouth sullen. She is vulgar. Probably this makes the soldier feel at home. Perhaps he gets her to sew on his first bands. She'd be useful to have around all the time. He has a certain frankness in his character, a measure of magnanimity. That poor girl there, in that . . . And also, no doubt, beneath the physical courage, a certain sloppiness. In short, he marries her. She becomes the wife of Captain, then Major, then Colonel Comte Chabert. He is killed at Eylau. His widow is granted a pension by the Emperor.

But how the devil does she manage to hook the Comte Ferraud, a young opportunist who is as poor as Job? I have no idea. Perhaps he happens to have a taste for fat gloomy women. Anyway, she marries him, and Comte Ferraud, a Privy Councilor, gets two children by her. I doubt that the marriage was a particularly happy one. Ferraud must have realized at some point that he could have made a better marriage, and there are doubtless times when he suffers from regrets. Otherwise, why should the Comtesse Ferraud be so very distraught when her first husband returns? (*Colonel Chabert*, p.1124) For that oaf of a Chabert isn't dead at all. Buried, yes; but having escaped from the grave by the skin of his teeth he eventually makes his way back to France. He rushes to see his wife. She refuses to see him. She rushes to see Derville, the lawyer, who suggests a settlement. A settlement? Provide Chabert with an income? The Comtesse's wealth is too close to her heart for her to consent to that. Give money to a man? It's certainly the first time she's heard of such a thing. She carries Chabert off with her, covers him in caresses, lards him with her fleshy favors. The herring barrel always smells of fish, and the former prostitute only knows one method of persuasion. In her arms, Chabert forgets his claims. Until the day comes when he disappears again, sickened to the heart, and leaves the Comtesse in triumphant possession of the field.

In *les Employés* (p.1023), there is mention of a certain Comtesse Féraud who, Balzac informs us, was Louis XVIII's last mistress. One's first reaction is one of delight. Rose Chapotel becoming that impotent old man's mistress! But alas, it is too good to be true. This Comtesse Féraud unfortunately had only one "r" in her name, and did really exist, I believe. But I must confess having immediately thought of Rose Chapotel as I read the following passage in the *Mémoires* of the Comtesse de Boigne: "Chance led Mme du Cayla into the monarch's private apartment. She still had the remains of her beauty, was witty, elegant, and above all possessed a vein of baseness in her nature that would shrink from nothing. The joyless methods she used to seduce the old king were only surpassed by the ignoble wage she received in payment for her efforts." "A vein of baseness in her nature that would shrink from nothing." That is the Comtesse Ferraud in a nutshell.

Sabine du Guénic, Hortense Steinbock, Honorine de Bauvan, Marie de Vandenesse, Augustine de Sommervieux, Clémence Desmarets *or the storms of married life*

Honorine is unfaithful to her husband. Marie de Vandenesse is almost unfaithful to hers. Sabine's and Hortense's husbands are unfaithful to them. Augustine thinks her husband is unfaithful to her. And Mme Desmarets' husband is very suspicious. Adultery on the part of the husband, adultery on the part of the wife, temptation, misunderstanding; these marriages provide us with examples of all four varieties of the conjugal storm.

Sabine du Guénic was born a Grandlieu. The Grandlieus, it will be remembered, are afflicted with five daughters. They must therefore be pardoned for marrying off their fourth to Calyste du Guénic, even though they are aware that he is in love with another woman. Nothing is perfect in this world, after all. Besides, though Calyste is already in love, that love is not returned. And the woman he is in love with is eight years older than Sabine. Such things count in the scales; they diminish the risks. And where would one be if one never took risks? In short, the two young people are married, calmly packed off on the black ship of marital woe. For the storm, needless to say, is not long in coming. Poor Sabine! And she had been so courageous too. On the day the contract was signed she had even pushed self-abnegation to the point of dressing like her rival (*Béatrix*, p.520). And her little ruse succeeds only too well. As her husband takes her in his arms, she realizes that he imagines her to be someone else. Quite soon, he goes back to his Béatrix de Rochefide. Sabine is aware of the fact, and she fights back valiantly with all her little girl's weapons. She finds out that Béatrix loves flowers, so she fills her own house with them. That she likes screens, so she buys herself one "of Hebraic richness" (*id*. p.564). She thinks up "subterfuges that would do credit to a stage farce in order to discover what dishes Mme de Rochefide used to serve Calyste" (*id*. p.565). Finally, thanks to a plot elaborated by her family, Calyste comes back to her. Will she be happy now, brave little Sabine? I hope so, but I doubt it. Calyste is a weakling, and that is the worst kind of husband there is. Look at Wenceslas Steinbock in *la Cousine Bette*. Another weakling. Gutless. And his wife is made to go through the same agonies as Sabine. Yet she has given him everything: love, an easy life, social standing, a child. For him to marry the daughter of Baron Hulot was undreamed-of good fortune. Yet he is unfaithful to her, and unfaithful to her with Mme Marneffe, already the mistress of Hulot, his father-in-law. It must be like a double adultery to be deceived in such a disgusting fashion. It must leave your heart a stony, sandy desert. An old woman like Béatrix, a slut like Mme Marneffe—it must be not only trust in the husband that goes by the board but all esteem as well. After that, a woman must be unable to look at her husband without a shiver, without wondering in anguish what further degradations he may have lurking inside him. Or so I imagine. I have never been a wife.

The same scenes are played out between the du Guénics as between the Steinbocks. The same lies are told too. I dined with the Portenduères, Calyste says. But next day Mme de Portenduère and Sabine meet (*Béatrix*, p.555). I went for a walk with Stidmann, Steinbock says. But next day Stidmann comes to call on Mme Steinbock (*Cousine Bette*, p.342). Hortense Steinbock does not have the stature of a Sabine, however. She is a bourgeoise. She refuses to fight back and goes home to mother. However, like the du Guénics, they are reconciled in the end.

Honorine is not, for my money, a particularly interesting work. The basic story is, nevertheless, rather a curious one. It concerns an orphan, Honorine something or other, rich and very beautiful, who, having been raised by the Bauvans, ends up marrying their son. He is twenty-six and she is nineteen (*Honorine*, p.272). The auspices could scarcely be more favorable. The two young people are perfectly matched as to age and social position, and since they were brought up together they have had plenty of time to get to know each other. Yet we find the husband saying: "I realized later that marriages contracted in the same conditions as ours always conceal a reef on which many affectionate feelings, many prudent plans and many existences are bound to be wrecked" (*id*. p.272). What exactly he means by these Sibylline words he never goes on to explain.

Possibly he couldn't, even if he wanted to. In fact, I think he's fooling himself; deliberately looking for unnecessary complications. All the rest of the story would seem to indicate, more simply, that his wife has a profound physical repugnance for him. A somewhat troublesome truth that no husband is going to admit to willingly. Bauvan does have some inkling of it, however. "Those pleasures," he says, "for which Honorine doubtless had no taste . . ." (*id.* p.273). Had no taste is putting it mildly. Honorine has a downright horror of them. In the end, she runs away with the first man she can lay hands on, who then abandons her in poverty.

It is at this point that the story becomes really interesting. Bauvan, learning of his wife's plight, sets to work, without her knowledge, making sure that she does not lack for any of the necessities of life. He surrounds her with the complications of a full-scale plot, worked out in every detail. When she gives birth, it is the best surgeon in Paris who attends her confinement, but disguised as a local doctor. She finds a cook for two hundred and fifty francs, and a pretty little house for five hundred. The husband pays the difference on the sly. Honorine lives in an enchanted world where everything costs a mere third of its true value. One day, however, she discovers what has been happening. Raging with gratitude, too bighearted not to pay her debts, even though they were incurred involuntarily, she returns to her husband's bed, where she dies of boredom and disgust beneath her benefactor's caresses. She dies of being forced to feign; she dies of prostituting herself to her own husband.

Marie-Angélique de Vandenesse is one of the daughters of Grandville* the Attorney General. Raised by her very pious mother, "a naïve, pure and innocent young girl" (*Fille d'Eve*, p.78), dark-haired, brown-eyed, at the age of twenty she marries Félix de Vandenesse, whose successive love affairs have civilized, refined and polished him to such good effect that he now becomes the kindest, the most attentive, the most lovable of husbands. As a result, after four or five years of happiness, Marie finally rebels. After the failures of so many imperfect husbands, we now see the failure of the perfect husband. Félix is perhaps excessively Félix. His experiences have given him complete control over himself. I am certain that he has never gone into his wife's room without knocking first. Which is charming, but it is scarcely surprising that Marie begins to dream sometimes of a great, rough fellow jumping onto her bed and beating his fists against his chest. Having read Abel Hermant, she now wants a taste of King Kong. So she throws herself at the man as unlike Félix as it is

---

* Balzac sometimes writes it Grandville, sometimes Granville.

possible to imagine. Félix is a gentleman. Nathan is a writer. There is no greater gulf, as we all know. Félix is always clean and smartly dressed; Nathan's fingernails are always black. The one is blond; the other has black, curly hair. The one is from Touraine, born in the very heart of France; the other smacks of the Jew, of the Levant, of Marseille. The one is a Royalist; the other Republican. The one is intelligent; the other is by way of being a genius. The one is respectable and conventional; the other lives a disordered life and is encumbered with debts. In short, it is blindingly apparent that Marie, without knowing it, is looking for an anti-Félix, an antidote to the sweetpoisons administered to her by her husband. At last she is experiencing the storms from which Félix has been sheltering her, at last she knows what it is like to listen to the thunders, the snorts, the throat clearings of a genuinely vulgar but strong nature. Just think! Nathan almost succeeds in killing himself. Such pleasures could never be found with Félix. Marie is able to drink her fill of pathos. But it is at this point that Félix's gentleness triumphs. He has insinuated himself so thoroughly into his wife's mind, he has so thoroughly earned her trust and affection that she tells him everything. Félix prepares a little trap in order to make clear the full extent of Nathan's moral disorder. Marie is saved. Saved by Félix, but saved too by her own inadequacy. She has been more deeply influenced by Félix than she realizes. Even when she is in love with another man, she continues to see things through her husband's eyes. Nathan's vitality attracts her; but the chaos of his life repels her. She does not see that, in fact, the one is a function of the other. Marie-Angélique rather makes one think of a prisoner who dreams of escape but shrinks from the reality because it would mean going through a sewer.

The tragedy of the Sommervieux couple, though more serious in its consequences, is an almost exact counterpart of the Vandenesses'. Augustine is a perfect wife, pretty, sweet and affectionate. But she is only a middle-class girl, originally a Guillaume. Her husband, who is an artist, gets bored with her. It's typical of him. Why did he marry her? Like Marie de Vandenesse, he goes in search of the antipodes. He lays siege to the Duchesse de Carigliano, who is neither young, nor affectionate, nor honest. Augustine, however, does not have the same intellectual resources as Félix. Not knowing how to win her husband back, she dies of grief. The story is to be found in *la Maison du Chat-qui-pelote*. It is also worth noting that Sommervieux did not really ever win the Duchesse's favors. His adultery was one of desire alone. Which is perhaps the worst kind of all. The wife must feel doubly humiliated: for herself in the first place, for her husband in the second.

The exquisite Mme Jules was born Clémence no-name-at-all. It is not known who her father and mother were. She has nothing but a godmother (in reality her mother). She marries Jules Desmarets, a poor clerk who through the influence of some mysterious protector is very quickly made a stockbroker. Like Picasso, Balzac has his periods. His first novels—*Ferragus, la Duchesse de Langeais*, etc.—belong to his mysterious period. He mixes a little mystery into everything. Though there is one thing that remains completely unmysterious, and that is the happiness of the young Desmarets couple. They are rich, and they live in a charming little town house. They are a delight to the eye. Happiness is a thing so rarely encountered in the *Comédie humaine* that it is worth pausing a moment to consider this sentence: "They took one another by the hand without shame, in the middle of a social gathering, like two children, brother and sister, trying to make their way through a crowd while all those around them make way in admiration" (*Ferragus*, p.30). Dear Mme Jules! I see her now as she appeared one evening at the Nucingens': dark-haired, a skin all milk and roses, dressed in white with feathers in her hair (*id.* p.20). Then, one day, she finds her father again, the ex-convict Ferragus. She goes to see him in secret. Desmarets finds out about these visits. With a husband's imagination, he supposes the worst, and his suspicions are sufficient to kill Mme Jules. Fragile, isn't it, this thing called happiness?

Anastasie de Restaud

Delphine de Nucingen is what is generally called a pretty woman. Her sister, Anastasie, is a very pretty woman. We have the testimony of two very discriminating judges on this point: Derville and Gobseck. "I found her attractive," the old Jew comments curtly. Dark-haired (whereas as her sister is blonde), with great black eyes and a certain ardor in her bearing, Anastasie Goriot has "one of the prettiest figures in Paris" (*Père Goriot*, p.874). Moreover, she succeeds in making a much more brilliant marriage than her sister. Delphine was obliged to be content with Nucingen; Anastasie manages to catch the Comte de Restaud, who is young and fairly rich. How? I don't know. Furthermore, before many years have gone by Anastasie is unfaithful to her husband, an incident that would not, it is true, have been particularly worthy of comment if the unfortunate woman had not taken it into her head to choose Maxime de Trailles as the object of her affections. Is Maxime her first lover? Another point on which I am not at all certain. In any case, though she may have been intending only to try her hand, in any case she completely loses her head.

Eventually, we see poor Anastasie reduced to extorting money from her father, who no longer has any, and then to selling her jewels to Gobseck. Her liaison with Maxime must have gone on for some time, however, since of her three children two are by the lover. Fearing that her husband, now on his deathbed, is going to disinherit her, Anastasie establishes a strict guard on him. He has not been dead ten minutes before she is man-handling his corpse in her search for the will. This episode, which occurs in *Gobseck*, is one of the most savage, one of the most harshly depicted in the whole of the *Comédie humaine*. Nor does it save Anastasie de Re-staud from ruin. After her husband's death she retires from society and lives alone with her children, humbly and even, if we are to believe Der-ville, heroically (*Gobseck*, p.667). It goes without saying that Maxime has deserted her.

Nathalie de Manerville

What a charming sight Nathalie Evangelista is in her white cashmere dress with its pink bows, pretty as a picture, full of life, nimble, as fleet of foot "as a Tartar horse coursing across the steppes," grace itself when she chat-ters, apparently so intelligent when silent. Born in 1801 or 1802, she is the daughter of a Spanish merchant from Bordeaux whose wealth had enabled him to marry a Casa-Real. The Spanish father dies in 1813, leaving behind him a wife and a daughter both equally ignorant about money matters. Nathalie is not far from believing that every house has its cooks and its coachmen "the way meadows have their haycrops and trees their fruit" (*Contrat de Mariage*, p.95). Enchanting thoughtlessness. But beware! Such thoughtlessness often suffers a terrible awakening, and Balzac him-self discerns a number of extremely disturbing signs in Nathalie's pretty features. The face is regular, but, says Balzac, such perfect harmony is the harbinger of frigidity. The waist is round, but that is a sign of stubborn-ness. Her hands give warning of a domineering nature, her eyebrows of an inclination to jealousy and her voice of a character like the Duke of Alba's (*id.* pp. 103 and 104). Balzac, as we shall see later, always cherished a lively inclination for the science of physiognomy, but nowhere, I think I am right in saying, did he indulge it to the same extent as in this portrait of Nathalie Evangelista.

The unfortunate thing, however, is that poor Manerville doesn't know anything about physiognomy at all. He falls in love with Nathalie and marries her. The contract that is signed can be advantageous to Manerville only if he has children. That is the prologue. We are then told of the results. But between the two there lies an abyss into which Balzac has scarcely dared do more than glimpse. And one understands his difficulty. He would have been obliged to describe exactly how Nathalie set about making sure she had no children and persuading her husband to let himself be stripped of his possessions. For he knows what's going on, the husband. How did I come to be ruined? he writes: "Deliberately, my dear Henri. I realized the very first day that I could not keep on as I had begun, I knew what the outcome would be, and I willfully closed my eyes to it" (*id.* p.191). Why did he close his eyes to it? How did Nathalie bring him to that state of "perfect obedience" whose nature is made clear to us by a confidence imparted the day after the wedding night (*id.* p.172)? These are things that Balzac does not go into. Though he is generally thought of as the most unstinting of novelists, here he limits himself to mere allusion. The entire drama lies hidden in that blank page between part one and part two. The crux of the novel has been skated over, and it is up to us to imagine it for ourselves. Though we must be careful in doing so not to forget that Nathalie herself is only a tool in the hands of her mother. Indeed, this is perhaps the most curious element in the whole story: the complicity between mother and daughter, a furtive alliance expressed in unfinished phrases, looks and whispers. Nathalie does not exist on her own. She has the brain of a bird, but of a nasty, mean-natured bird, one with a very spiteful beak. She allows Félix de Vandenesse to pay court to her, then writes him the letter at the end of *Lys dans la Vallée* (p.1029). It is a spiteful, odious, cruel letter. Honest, mark you. And just. But odious nevertheless. And later on, in *Une Fille d'Eve*, we see her taking part in a little plot hatched by a group of women for the purpose of destroying Félix's honor. Why this rancor? To avenge herself for having already been forced to treat him badly? To avenge herself for her own cruelty?

Madame de Listomère and Clémentine Laginska
or the baffled wives

It is easy to see that the name Listomère was one that Balzac delighted in, for he uses it several times. First of all, there is an old Comtesse de Listomère-Landon who lives in Tours and dies in 1814 (*Femme de trente ans,* pp 691 and 704). Then, in *le Député d'Arcis,* that is to say in 1839, we are again introduced to an "old Comtesse de Listomère" who attends an evening reception at the Austrian Embassy. Though whether this is an entirely new character, or whether Balzac simply forgot the death in 1814 I am not sure. Then there is a Baronne de Listomère, the widow of a Lieutenant-General, who also lives in Tours and who dies there in 1826 (*Curé de Tours*). Then there is an old Marquise de Listomère, née Grandlieu, who lives in Paris (*Lys dans la Vallée*, p.846). She is the great-aunt of Félix and Charles Vandenesse and their sister, the last of whom also becomes a Marquise de Listomère in her turn by marrying a Listomère who was probably, though his past is not gone into, the son of the old Marquise, and is "a serious man" (*Illusions perdues*, p.619). It is this Marquise de Listomère, née Vandenesse, who is the heroine of the story entitled *Etude de Femme*. In *Lys dans la Vallée* we see her as a child, and her brother Félix complains of her character. After her marriage she plays the prude. One can therefore imagine her astonishment when one day she receives a letter from Rastignac couched in somewhat ardent terms. It is really too much. She can already see herself, delightful vision, putting the insolent fellow in his place. Alas, the insolent fellows calls on her to confess that the letter was intended for someone else. Mme de Listomère is disappointed. She had prepared herself for the exquisite joy of being insulted. There is nothing to be insulted at. She had pictured herself resisting his entreaties. There are no entreaties. She had foreseen the delights of forgiveness. There is no longer anything to forgive. And yet, she says, what a curious piece of absent-mindedness, to write my name on the envelope. She does not dare push the matter any further than that. Rastignac doubtless thinks to himself: What's this? But no, it's quite impossible. Mme de Listomère is the victim of her own excessively good reputation. A very pretty scene. We also meet Mme de Listomère at the Opéra, at the house of a cabinet minister and at Mme Firmiani's (*Illusions perdues*, p.618; *Employés*, p.1019; *Madame Firmiani*, p.1035). She has a certain slight influence in legitimist circles, her own word to add.

Born in 1816, Clémentine Laginska is the daughter of the Marquis and Marquise du Rouvre, her mother, née Ronquerolles, being sister to both the Marquis of that name and also to Mme de Sérizy. Though almost engaged at one point to Savinien de Portendeure (*Ursule Mirouët*, p.434), Clémentine in fact marries the Comte Adam Laginski, a somewhat gutless Pole. This son of the Vistula has a friend, Thaddée Paz, who falls in love with Clémentine and, in order to conceal his passion, pretends to have a liaison with a bareback rider, Malaga. This episode is the subject matter of *la Fausse Maîtresse*.

Why does he remain content with pretending, this Thaddée? I should have preferred Malaga myself. Clémentine is a deadly bore. And with Thaddée she is also petty and spiteful. Malaga is at least a good-hearted girl. Thaddée himself comes around to my view of the matter finally, in fact, and despite all his love there comes a day when, almost unconsciously, as if in a dream, we hear him speak the following words: "There isn't a single one of those Society women with their affected airs who can match her honest young animal's nature." (*Fausse Maîtresse*, p.50). Or could it be that Clémentine is jealous? That she wants Thaddée for herself? But Thaddée goes away. And when he comes back it is just in time to save Clémentine from the arms of La Palférine, into which she had been on the point of falling. A pity! La Palférine might have widened her horizons a bit. True, she is married to a Pole; but geography is not what I had in mind.

Madame de la Chanterie, Lady Brandon *or forgotten tragedies*

There is nothing like a tragedy for fixing characters—in the sense that one says: fix a photograph—or for giving them an air, an appearance, a physiognomy that will always remain with them. Old age may come, and wrinkles, and revenges, but the man remains imprisoned in his tragedy. Could Dreyfus, for example, ever have become anything other than the man condemned to Devil's Island? The same is true of Laurence de Cinq-Cygne, whom I shall discuss elsewhere, and also of Mme de la Chanterie, the heroine of *l'Envers de l'Histoire contemporaine*.

Born a Champignelles (Barbe-Philiberte de), in 1788 she marries Henri de la Chanterie, a good-looking boy who spends money like water, eventually abandons her, probably during the Terror, though it's not quite certain, then dies in 1802 after having been, either in succession or all at the same time, more or less a bigamist, more or less syphilitic, and more or less president of a revolutionary tribunal. Not satisfied with this remarkable achievement, Mme de la Chanterie then decides that it is time she married off her daughter, and the husband she selects is a certain Baron Bryond des Tours-Minières. Where did he come from, this Bryond? No one knows. But he has distinguished himself in the *maquis* of that period and it is this fact that has earned him the laudatory recommendations to which Mme de la Chanterie yields. Such are the errors into which we can be led by judging people by their opinions: Bryond is nothing but a gangster, and as soon as the advantages of being a *Chouan* begin to decline he goes over to the other side, proving his worth by immediately denouncing his mother-in-law, his wife and the latter's lover. And note that the lover was thrown into his wife's arms by Bryond himself. So that the whole story is really very contemporary. The wife is guillotined, Mme de la

Chanterie goes to prison, and the model son-in-law takes up a career in the police under the name of Cotenson.

We meet Mme de la Chanterie again twenty years later. Free once more, of course. Freed from her prison, that is, not from her tragedy. Now an extremely religious woman, she has founded a philanthropic organization, the Brothers of Consolation. And the way in which she runs it is indeed admirable, as is apparent from a speech she makes (*Envers d l'Histoire contemporaine*, p.393) in which her charitable impulses are nicely tempered by a vigorous business sense. But there are certain words that cannot be spoken in her presence. The tragedy of her past is always there, like a fierce beast that has with great difficulty been lulled to sleep but is likely to spring to life again at the slightest shock.

There has been a tragedy in Lady Brandon's life too. What was it? Well, er, I'm afraid no one knows. Félix de Vandenesse (*Lys dans la Vallée*, p.1028) insinuates—and Louise de Chaulieu (*Mémoires de deux Jeunes Marieés*, p.287) confirms—that she has been the victim of a revenge on Lady Dudley's part. But what form did the revenge take and what was it for? Mystery. It is true that Vandenesse, again in *le Lys*, talks about a poisoning and a husband's debts, but the text is an obscure one, and there is no conclusive evidence that Lady Brandon was the person involved. In the first edition of *Père Goriot*, Lady Brandon appears at a ball with Franchessini, to whom, Balzac wrote, "she had sacrificed everything." But in subsequent editions the sentence was removed. The name Willemsens (Augusta-Maria), which Lady Brandon gives in *la Grenadière*, was undoubtedly her maiden name. She has two sons, both adulterine, by an unknown father, possibly Franchessini. Their names are Louis-Gaston and Marie-Gaston, the latter being Louise de Chaulieu's second husband. Lady Brandon dies in 1820, and there we are left, still waiting open-mouthed, still none the wiser.

Julie d'Aiglemont and Vanda de Mergi *or the invalids*

Julie d'Aiglemont is the heroine of *la Femme de trente ans*, a work that has always seemed to me mediocre, despite the phenomenal celebrity achieved by its title. Balzac simply threw the ingredients of the plot together at random, and the fact is apparent. The characters change from chapter to chapter, and for no good reason. Aiglemont is presented to us at first as a clumsy brute, a "garrison seducer" (*Femme de trente ans*, p.726). He then changes, quite inexplicably, into a "fine father" and his physiognomy reveals "an indescribable good nature and honesty" (*id.* pp.

788 and 790). Julie is at one point a "noble woman," at another "a soul withered by evil" (*id.* pp. 767 and 753). And who is going to explain to me the point of all those mysteries that Balzac makes at the beginning of every chapter? "A former army officer . . . to whom we shall refer simply as the Marquis" (*id.* p.787). Why? We've known that the character in question is the Marquis d'Aiglemont for the past hundred pages! Not to mention the chronological errors. Such errors are rare in the *Comédie humaine;* but three-quarters of them are to be found here.* As for the style, what are we to think of this: "The general turned to throw a tear of rage into the sea" (*id.* p.817)?†

Despite these oddities, *la Femme de trente ans* does have its own particular interest. It is a curiously clammy and feverish book, discontinuous in the same way as a high-temperature delirium. You know what strange ideas you get when you are sick, the way certain details will suddenly assume a disproportionate importance while others sink back into the darkness, that feeling of powerlessness that comes in dreams. Well it's rather like that, *la Femme de trente ans.* The incidents occasionally seem to be taking place quite separately from the characters, to loom up uncalled for, almost as though they have a will of their own. Such as the strange passage in which young Hélène pushes her brother into the Bièvre, an incident that seems to be narrated "from a distance," as though it were being seen through a thick pane of glass, and of which the culminating act is hurried over in just a few lines, recounted as though by a narrator who doesn't quite realize the import of what he is saying. Almost like Faulkner a century too soon. Yes, it's a clammy book; I can't think of any other word for it. A book that gives off a mysterious odor as of warm feminine bedrooms. An unhealthy book; perhaps because of a kind of identification with its heroine, who is an invalid. Mme d'Aiglemont is another victim of marriage, a victim of "a single day's, or perhaps a single night's experience" (*id.* p.696). "A husband," she writes to a woman friend, "will make you, in a very few days, what I am already, ugly, ill, and old" (*id.* p.697). And what frightful disillusion there is in this gracefully worded sentence: "As my husband entered, as he searched for me, the muffled laugh he heard me utter from beneath the muslin folds that were enveloping me was the last spark of that sweet gaiety that enlivened all our childhood games . . ." (*id.* p.698).

Only daughter of the Duc de Chastillonet, Julie's mother had died be-

---

* On this subject, see Fernand Lotte's study, *la Chronologie de la Femme de trente ans,* in the *Courrier balzacien* of December 1950.
† Le général se tourna pour jeter à la mer une larme de rage.

fore she knew her, a fact that doubtless explains certain misunderstandings and clumsy mistakes. In 1813, she marries Victor d'Aiglemont, a brutal soldier who refuses to pay the slightest regard to the squeamish susceptibilities of a wife who is probably rather delicate in the first place. It is to his brutality, I imagine, that we should attribute "the female sickness" from which Julie suffers, as well as her repugnance to sensual pleasures. As soon as the word love is mentioned to her, she trembles "like a person in whose mind the memory of some danger is still so much present and alive that the anguish of it is still felt" (*id.* p.696). I should add, however, that the husband's brutality does not seem to me to exempt the wife from a charge of egoism. She had a sort of "*a priori* perverseness," Balzac says (*id.* p.718). She nevertheless finds an Englishman, Lord Grenville, who takes upon himself the task of doctoring her, out of love, and ends up dying on a windowsill in order to avoid compromising her. "These Englishmen are always so intent on attracting attention to themselves" (*id.* p.735). After which, she falls in love with Charles de Vandenesse and embarks upon a long liaison with him that apparently continues even after the lover's marriage. She has four children by this Charles of hers, which, counting the one she has already had, makes five in all.

Like all complicated people, Mme d'Aiglemont attracts complications. To begin with her eldest daughter pushes her little brother into a river. Imagine! Two young children! And ten years later this same Hélène runs away with a murderer whose acquaintance she had made only a quarter of an hour before. Lastly, another of Mme d'Aiglemont's daughters, Moïna, embarks upon a liaison with one of Vandenesse's sons, her half-brother in fact, a disturbing development to which the girl's mother experiences some difficulty in resigning herself.

As for Vandade Mergi, another invalid, I shall do no more than merely mention her name at this point. Her maiden name was Bourlac, and you will find her in the second part of *l'Envers de l'Histoire contemporaine*.

Middle-class women, nameless women, ghosts

The intelligent reader will have observed that this portrait gallery includes rather few women of the middle classes. This fact is not the product of any snobbery on my part, I swear. It is simply that, in Balzac, middle-class women do not in general lead such personal lives. Mme Birotteau, Mme Claës, Mme Grandet, Mme Baudoyer, all these women exist and have their place in the scheme of things, but they exist only in relation to their husbands, in their husbands' shadows. If there is tragedy in their lives, it is their husband's tragedy: Birotteau's bankruptcy, Claës' mania. Let us remember that in order to give the lives of Mme de Langeais, Mme de Maufrigneuse, Mme de Rochefide or Mme d'Espard individual interest, Balzac was in every case obliged to begin by getting rid of the husband. This is not too difficult to manage if the lady in question is a duchess. But what if she is just a middle-class wife like Mme Birotteau? How is one to get her away from her husband? Where would she go? I mean, of course, in 1830. I shall have occasion to discuss some of these ladies later on (Mme Hulot, Mme de Grandville, the epitome of bourgeoise womanhood despite her particle, Mme Marneffe, etc.). Mme Thuillier, in *les Petits Bourgeois*, a good, strong woman, abandoned by her husband and ill-treated by her sister-in-law, is a touching figure. Constance Birotteau too is an excellent woman, livelier, rather gruff in manner, a grumbler at times, tight with her pennies, as they say, but incapable of taking one from anyone else. As for Mme Baudoyer, she is a mean-minded shrew. "Everything about her was petty and mean" (*Employés*, p.899).

There are also several women on whose behalf Balzac has pushed discretion so far as to withhold their names. I have already mentioned Henri de Marsay's Charlotte. At this point let me just quickly list Charles Grandet's Annette (*Eugénie Grandet*, p.575), the blue-stocking who becomes Lousteau's regular mistress for a while (*Muse du Département*, p.154), and the beautiful but vulgar woman who stood in much the same relation to Daniel d'Arthez (*Secrets de la princesse de Cadignan*, p.25).

After the women who have no names, the converse: those who exist as names only. Can a name, a mere name, suffice to create a presence? Balzac can make it do so. What, for example, does he ever tell us about the Princesse Goritza who is so often mentioned in the course of *la Vieille Fille?* Nothing. And yet I can see her even now, nose in the air, roguish face, all curving plumpness, drinking her glass of rusty water at Spa between the Chevalier de Valois and Casanova, who she must certainly have known. And the pretty Moïna de Saint-Héreen, fifty years later, who has such a wicked laugh and is undoubtedly a shameless hussy if we are to go by one of her remarks in *Une Fille d'Eve* (p.85). How much I regret not knowing more about her. Moïna de Saint-Héreen, I never grow tired of that rustling, leafy, mischievous name. And the lively, nimble Mme de Fischtaminel who flashes through *les Petites Misères de la Vie Conjugale*. And the Princesse Galathionne (*Fille d'Eve*, p.45; *Père Goriot*, p.950), tall, no doubt, and blonde, with an ample bosom, and blue eyes like pools of very pure water when you look into them. All those charming ghosts . . .

CHAPTER 5

Young Ladies

Cécile Camusot—Félicie Cardot, Victorine Taillefer, Lydie Peyrade, Françoise de la Haye or the trampled blossoms—Eugénie Grandet—Modeste Mignon, Ursule Mirouët, Marguerite Claës or young love triumphant —Rosalie de Watteville, Clotilde de Grandlieu, Malvina d'Aldrigger, Hélène d'Aiglemont, Marie de Verneuil, Laurence de Cinq-Cygne or energy without judgment—Emilie de Fontaine and Bathilde de Chargeboeuf or the girls who know what they want—Various others.

A FEW GLANCES back to the preceding chapter to begin with. Some of the women discussed there we also meet when they are still young girls: Hortense Hulot in *la Cousine Bette*, Augustine Guillaume in *la Maison du Chat-qui-pelote*, Nathalie Evangelista in *le Contrat de Mariage*. Before their marriages, Louise de Chaulieu and Renée de Maucombe have time to exchange a few girlish letters containing memories of their days in the convent together (*Mémoires de deux Jeunes Mariées*). And I should also mention Laure de Rastignac's charming letter to her brother (*Père Goriot*, p.925).

Then a group photograph: the young students attending the art classes in la Vendetta. Already notable among them is the future Mme Camusot, already a shrew, already an avid social climber, an intriguer and full of humbug. She is to hand this delightful character on to her daughter Cécile, the "girlie" she and her husband have such difficulty marrying off, for she is at the same time stupid, mean-natured and as spiteful as a monkey. When the family is visited by a possible husband who hails from the far side of the Rhine, she takes care to leave the name Goethe lying about carelessly in her conversation. Red-haired and plain, Mlle Camusot, the lawyer Berthier informs us, "leaves the hearts of her *suitors* sufficiently undisturbed for them to keep cool heads on their shoulders" (*Cousin Pons*, p.587). In the end, by disguising her defects behind a large dowry, her parents manage to marry her off to young Vicomte Popinot, a son of the former clerk Birotteau.

Félicie Cardot, Victorine Taillefer, Lydie Peyrade, Françoise de la Haye *or the trampled blossoms*

I shall try to be brief. Félicie Cardot, daughter of Cardot the lawyer and a religious mother, allows herself to be led up the garden path by her papa's head clerk. Except that there is no garden path in fact, and their dismal idyl is conducted in the shade of Cardot's filing cabinets. Where the devil, in what dark corner of that office did they find room for a lovers' bower? But be that as it may, we soon find that Félicie is pregnant. Pregnant by a head clerk who chooses that precise moment to die. In return for the promise of certain advantages, Lousteau agrees to wed the mother-to-be. The poor girl is touched by this. "All my life, Monsieur, shall be devoted to repaying you for your sacrifice," she says. And the ruffian is genuinely moved by her words (*Muse du Département*, p.158). She finally comes to entertain a feeling towards him that is made up mainly of gratitude but also, in part, of amazement at the prospect of anyone pretending to love her. The project is broken off. Félicie is distressed by this. It is generally thought that she has no reason to be. Later on, it is thought that she did in fact have reason to be, for her parents marry her off to Berthier, the second clerk, who regards her simply as a means of stepping into his father-in-law's shoes. In *le Cousin Pons*, we meet her again, still haunted by the memory of her sin, crushed by her husband, modest, reticent, a sadly mousy little creature who can nevertheless still find enough kindness and courage in her heart to speak a good word to poor old Pons (*Cousin Pons*, p.609).

Victorine Taillefer is no luckier. She is the daughter of the same Taillefer who, in *l'Auberge Rouge*, murders a merchant and allows someone else to be shot in his place. Without a mother, rejected by her father, Victorine lives with an old lady in the Pension Vauquer. She is graceful but pale. She is one of those young girls who seem to have lived their whole lives in the shade. Like those mauve flowers you find in the dark corners of a garden. And yet this timid creature is attracted by the frightful, though vigorous, Vautrin. A whim, a delicate moment of feeling that quickly fades; but the trait is there in her character for all that, providing yet one more example of Balzac's extraordinary freedom (*Père Goriot*, p.859). As I have indicated, this curious attraction does not, could not, last. The shy young girl's glances soon desert Vautrin and settle on Rastignac. This time it is genuine love, conscious love; but Eugène is seduced by Delphine, and Victorine goes back to live with her father (*Père Goriot*). In *l'Auberge Rouge*, the narrator—whose name we do not know—summons a meeting of his friends so that they may determine whether or not it is possible for him to marry Victorine. His words do not seem to betray any great love for her. Doubtless she did marry however, and later on, seeing the name of Rastignac in a newspaper, perhaps she mused for a moment on the past, picturing herself back in the little, bare garden of the Pension Vauquer once more.

Like Victorine, Lydie Peyrade has no mamma. Her mother, the actress Beausmesnil, has abandoned her, and Lydie lives in Paris with her father, the police officer Peyrade, and an old woman servant, quietly, peacefully, away from everything. In the evenings, lying in bed, she thinks about Lucien de Rubempré, whom she has seen once in the Tuileries (*Splendeurs*, p.762). One more example of Balzac's parallelism, you will note: Victorine's dreams are haunted by Rastignac, Lydie's by Rubempré.

So Lydie dreams of love. And love is what she gets. In rather greater quantity, doubtless, than she wanted. As a means of revenging himself upon her father, Vautrin has Lydie imprisoned in a brothel, where she is obliged to earn her bed and board in the usual way. The unfortunate girl goes mad. Poor little Lydie. We see her, the evening when she at last escapes from her penal servitude, wandering along the Rue Saint-Honoré in slippers and a white shift (*Splendeurs*, p.896). After her father's death she is taken in by one of his police colleagues, Corentin. This episode occurs in *les Petits Bourgeois*, however, and since Balzac did not finish the work we cannot tell what ultimate fate he had in store for poor Lydie. Charles Rabou, who took upon himself the task of finishing this novel in Balzac's stead, has her marry her cousin, Théodose de la Peyrade. I mention this fact because it does indeed seem likely that this was Balzac's own intention. "Oh, I'd quite forgotten," Peyrade says to his daughter in *Splendeurs et Misères* (p.763), "I must have a whole herd of nephews, and quite possibly one of them may turn out to be good enough for you . . ." "And the odd thing was," Balzac adds, "that at that very moment . . . one of old Canquoëlle's (Peyrade's) nephews was passing through the Porte d'Italie on his way to visit his uncle." Rabou even adds that, at that precise moment, young Peyrade went into a brothel and, without any awareness of her identity, enjoyed his own cousin. A strange coincidence. And a somewhat unbelievable one. The young man, Balzac tells us, was "dying from hunger and fatigue" (*id.* p.763). A strange state in which to visit a brothel. But let it pass.

Here is another crushed bloom: Françoise de la Haye, who appears, rather distantly silhouetted, in *les Illusions perdues*. She is the illegitimate issue of a relationship between Francis du Hautoy, an idiot from Angoulême, and a young lady who was later to become the Comtesse de Senonches. When I say a relationship . . . Provincial life being what it is . . . a young lady of noble family . . . It can't have been very easy. A swift passage of arms behind a bush, in all likelihood, or in a loft. The child must have been considered a catastrophe. She was sent away into the depths of the country, to an old castle. Françoise too falls in love with Rubempré. Without ever having spoken to him, I imagine. She is finally married off to the appalling Petit-Claud, who ill-treats her as unthinkingly as he commits all his other dastardly actions.

I have thought a great deal about these poor girls, about Lydie with her old servant, about Victorine stuck with her old lady companion, about Françoise living with her grandmother, all buried alive in their little Paris streets or their deserted castles, without mothers, without weapons, shut out from life, completely ignorant of its laws, little dreaming girls lost in a Balzacian world so relentless towards all doleful souls. They were waiting for love. But in Balzac's world love is not something you can wait for. It has to be taken. It has to be won by force. It yields only to those with wills of iron.

Eugénie Grandet

Eugénie Grandet is a bigger personality and has more money. Yet she too sees happiness elude her. Like the others, she is a prisoner, a prisoner in that gloomy town of Saumur. I know Saumur quite well. It is not a gloomy town. Yet young girls still complain about it even today. One day, however, there appears in Eugénie's life the pretty young cousin who is to take the same place in her heart as Rastignac and Rubempré in Lydie's, Françoise's and Victorine's. She falls in love with him. All these young girls fall in love with frightening facility. One senses a fund of unattached exaltation in them that cannot help but fix itself upon the first thing that comes to hand, that would be just as likely to hurl itself at a tree if the tree wore a pretty waistcoat and had a pair of bright eyes. Eugénie's cousin is extremely nice to her, goes away to the West Indies and comes back married. Whereupon Eugénie's only recourse is to marry the Président Cruchot de Bonfons. On condition that the President never lays a finger on her. In Saumur it is common gossip that the Grandets and the Bonfons family did really exist. Everyone knows what their real names were. In fact, I have met one of the Bonfons descendants. It was as much as I could do to stop myself asking about his great-aunt Eugénie. He must have thought me very constrained. But, after all, to take tea with a nephew of Grandet, that's a pretty amazing event to me. Perhaps the tea service was one Eugénie herself had bought. Perhaps we were sitting in a room where she had once been, where she had perchance smiled sadly at the thought of her miscarried life. Why did she fail? What was it she lacked? She had had enough strength of character to declare her love to her cousin, enough courage to stand up to her father's fury. That was certainly not nothing. But her energy stopped there, it faded away, and Eugénie allowed events to take the initiative. Woe to her. No energy, no happiness. The law of Balzac's world is implacable.

Modeste Mignon, Ursule Mirouët, Marguerite Claës
or young love triumphant

Modeste Mignon too is imprisoned by her family and by provincial life. But she doesn't rest until she has dug her way out. Instead of dreaming, she spends her time questioning her sister, Bettina, who has been seduced, abandoned and has come back to le Havre to die. One can imagine the conversations they had, the two sisters in their little twin beds, in the evening light, with the murmur of the sea outside. She questions all the books she can find, too. Books play an important role in Balzac's work. They are the source of Félicité des Touches' intellectual immorality. It is reading *Paul et Virginie* that corrupts the future Mme Graslin (*Curé de Village*, p.549). It is in the fact of her having read Schiller's *William Tell* that we should look for an explanation of Hélène d'Aiglemont's flight with her pirate (*Femme de trente ans*, p.792). Modeste Mignon reads a great deal, and ends up by writing to the poet Canalis. The latter, too blasé to bother with it himself, lets one of his friends answer the letter for him, using his name. As it happens, this friend has a beautiful soul, and Modeste is beside herself with delight. After various reversals of fortune, to be found in full in the novel that bears her name, Modeste marries this friend, whose name is Ernest de la Brière, and is then perfectly happy. She attains happiness because she is strong willed, because she knew what she wanted, and because she was intelligent enough not to shrink from the necessary means of getting it. Can you imagine Eugénie Grandet writing to Canalis? Some people may say that there's nothing very daring about that. But they would be wrong. Given the conditions in which Modeste lives, her letter to Canalis is as striking a proof of strength of character as Mme de la Baudraye's departure for Paris. Moreover, Modeste also possesses what Mme de la Baudraye lacks: foresight and intelligence. Modeste has a choice of three suitors: a girl with more emotion than sense would have chosen Canalis, a vulgar woman would have taken the Duc d'Hérouville. Modeste is intelligent enough to pick La Brière, the least brilliant of the three, but the most reliable.

The reader may perhaps remember the contrast between the behavior of Sabine du Guénic and that of Hortense Steinbock. Confronted with identical marital difficulties, the former fought back, the latter fled. The aristocrat accepted the struggle; the middle-class wife decided that it would be more dignified to retreat. The one draws her sword, the other hands in her resignation.* We now find the same contrast expressed in the behavior of Modeste Mignon and Ursule Mirouët. The former is descended from the counts Mignon de la Bastie. Hence, I suppose, her boldness and her contempt for the conventions. Ursule Mirouët, on the other hand, is entirely non-aristocratic by birth, being the daughter of a musician and a middle-class woman from Hamburg. In Balzac, Germans are always tranquil, soft-hearted sheep, and it is from her mother that Ursule has inherited her sweetness, her timidity and a slight air of the plaster saint. But she has will-power too, a will-power quite as firm and resolute as Modeste's. The difference is, that whereas Modeste's expresses itself in the form of sudden capricious decisions, Ursule's emerges as steady, determined progress towards a given goal. An orphan, taken in by her uncle Minoret and brought up in Nemours in a household consisting of four old people, she eventually falls in love with Savinien de Portenduère, her neighbor. She falls in love with him in the same way as Victorine Taillefer falls in love with Rastignac, only instead of just dreaming about him, instead of falling asleep, she acts. Gently. Patiently. Savinien hasn't even noticed her existence. What does that matter? It doesn't stop her from managing to convince her uncle that he should pay off the young man's debts. She makes Savinien love her. Her beloved's mother is against the match. It makes no difference; Ursule will wait. She has the kind of patience that can move mountains. Her uncle is an atheist; she converts him. Her inheritance is stolen from her; she remains unmoved. She prays. Quietly, determinedly, she besieges God in much the same way as she has already besieged her uncle. And once more she succeeds. Her inheritance is restored to her.

* A great deal could be written about the handing in of one's resignation as the very last word in middle-class dignity.

She marries her Savinien. They go to live in Paris. They are very friendly with the du Guénic couple (*Béatrix*, p.555) and with the de l'Estorades (*Oeuvres ébauchées*, p.1071). There is little doubt that they were destined to play an important role in a work, unhappily little more than begun, entitled *les Méfaits d'un Procureur du Roi*. In the few pages that were actually written, we perceive that Ursule still continues to exercise her relentless but gentle influence on other people's lives. It is she who marries young Bongrand to Derville's daughter (*Oeuvres ébauchées*, p.1074).

Marguerite Claës, in *la Recherche de l'Absolu*, has a somewhat similar character. A little colorless to begin with, despite her charm, Marguerite's true strength of character does not become apparent until after her mother's death. Then she becomes the true head of her family. Eugénie Grandet, after her initial moments of courage, becomes apathetic. She allows her father to do as he pleases with her life. Marguerite, on the other hand, fights against hers and prevents him from ruining the family fortunes. Marguerite is one of the wise virgins. She thinks about other people and brings her influence to bear on their lives. Her father is a prodigal; but she keeps him in check. Ursule's uncle is an atheist; but Ursule makes it her business to convert him. Eugénie, on the other hand, makes not the slightest attempt to prevent her father indulging his avarice to the full. She allows him to crush her. Marguerite fights back. And what is more, she knows where she's going and she has a good head on her shoulders. In consequence, she succeeds. Among other things, she marries the man she loves, the charming Emmanuel de Solis.

Rosalie de Watteville, Clotilde de Grandlieu, Malvina d'Aldrigger, Hélène d'Aiglemont, Marie de Verneuil, Laurence de Cinq-Cygne
or energy without judgment

Ursule, Modeste and Marguerite are all victorious. This is partly because they all three have will-power of course; but also because, in all three cases, this will-power has a firm foundation to rest on: intelligence in Modeste's case, a sense of duty in Marguerite's, probity and trust in God in Ursule's. Where such a foundation is lacking, then the will becomes confused and force of character is misapplied.

Rosalie de Watteville is a heroine out of Julien Green. Had she married, she would have been Thérèse Desqueyroux. "I know her," her mother says. "There's more than one Beelzebub inside that skin of hers" (*Albert Savarus*, p.763). Eighteen years old, of good family, "frail, slender, blonde, pale-skinned and of utterly insignificant appearance . . . a few freckles" (*id*. p.762), Rosalie feels like a prisoner in Besançon. Searching for a way of escape, her eyes fall upon her neighbor, Albert Savarus. The will-power is there: Rosalie is prepared to take the initiative with life. And her choice is a good one: Savarus is a remarkable man. But this will-power and this intelligence are pressed into the service of a dishonest heart and a perverted judgment. Rosalie does not shrink from employing abominable means to gain her ends. She intercepts Savarus' correspondence with Mme d'Argaiolo. Worse, she imitates his handwriting and sends the Duchesse forged letters couched in terms of cruel indifference. It is one of those actions that you only find in tranquil, cozy provincial towns, those places where fine souls decay while the opposite kind flower into perfection. The old priest to whom Rosalie finally shows her first drafts is stupefied by the "infernal intelligence" with which they were written. Where did Rosalie acquire this "genius for evil"? "Rosalie knew absolutely nothing . . . No newspaper had ever sullied her eyes" (*id*. p.761 and p.762).* Is wickedness a sufficient substitute for experience then? Mme de Watteville was not mistaken when she spoke of Beelzebub.

Rosalie succeeds in parting Savarus and his duchesse, but she does not succeed in marrying him herself. Savarus takes holy orders and makes no attempt to seek revenge. That is left to God, and there would be no sin in seeing his hand in the explosion that later makes Rosalie a lifelong cripple. The old priest had predicted this outcome: "Purely moral crimes . . . are the most infamous, the most odious of all. God often punishes them in this world, and there lies the cause of many appalling misfortunes that in our eyes appear inexplicable" (*id*. p.850).

As for Clotilde de Grandlieu . . . But it is high time, I think, to go into rather more detail on the subject of this covey of Grandlieus that we're forever running into. The Duc de Grandlieu and his wife, née Ajuda, have five daughters. The eldest goes into a convent (*Splendeurs*, p.729). The second is Clotilde. The third, Joséphine, marries the widowed Ajuda and is never mentioned except in passing. The fourth, Sabine, marries du Guénic and plays an important part in *Béatrix*. The last, Marie-Athénaïs, is engaged to marry her cousin Juste, Vicomte de Grandlieu. This Juste de Grandlieu, whose father is dead and whose mother appears in *Gobseck*, has a sister, Camille, who later marries Ernest de Restaud. There is also another Grandlieu girl whose relationship with the main branch remains a

---

* According to Balzac, a well-brought-up girl never reads newspapers. "My wife-to-be had never so much as set eyes on those sheets," Benassis says in *Médecin de Campagne* (p.492). "What, do you think my daughter reads the newspaper then?" the Vicomtesse de Grandlieu asks (*Gobseck*, p.656).

mystery to me and who is married to the Prefect of the Orne (*Cabinet des Antiques*).

This Clotilde then, when we first meet her (in *Splendeurs et Misères*), is well on the way to thirty. Not pretty, with no breasts to speak of and an equally deficient dowry, she too is beginning to feel herself a prisoner. She wants to escape. And for young ladies living under the Restoration, escape means a man, a man to marry. Clotilde makes the acquaintance of Lucien de Rubempré. Has she been making advances to him? I have no idea, but she responds to his, that I can swear to. There is nothing lackadaisical about her behavior. She knows what she wants and she concentrates all her energy on getting it. She harries her parents until they invite him to their house, this very unlikely suitor, then makes their lives misery until they agree to give their consent to a marriage the idea of which they don't like at all. She ought to have emerged victorious. But she lacked judgment. Had she been more intelligent, she would have realized that Lucien was a rogue horse, that he would shy at the very first obstacle. The first obstacle appears, Lucien loses his head, finally he kills himself. In *Béatrix*, Clotilde has already taken on the guise of an old maid. When she speaks, her words are resigned but bitter.

We find the same lack of judgment in Malvina d'Aldrigger. She has picked du Tillet as the object of her passion, and nothing could be sillier than that. Can you see du Tillet marrying a girl who has no money? Malvina is a brunette, an Andalusian type, sallow complexioned, eaten up with the idea of marriage, plagued with black shadows around her eyes, and in the end a little mad. You see piano teachers sometimes who look much the same. And indeed, Malvina does end up giving lessons (*Maison Nucingen*).

Hélène d'Aiglemont is the eldest daughter of the Marquise d'Aiglemont I have already discussed. While still a child, she provides us with a fair indication of her character by pushing her little brother into the Bièvre. Why? It's never clearly explained. *La Femme de trente ans* is possibly the most obscure work in the whole of the *Comédie humaine*. I imagine that Mme d'Aiglemont was unable to conceal her preference for the little boy, who was the product of her liaison with Vandenesse, whereas Hélène is legitimate. Jealousy in other words. Unless Hélène has guessed at her mother's liaison and can't forgive her for it. "Between those two and God there certainly yawned some sinister mystery," Balzac writes later (*Femme de trente ans*, p.793). Hélène grows up to be a tall, beautiful girl; but she is taciturn, hard, closed in on herself. Even so, she cannot conceal the seething, passionate nature beneath. Is it her mother's adultery that weighs so heavily upon her? Is it remorse for killing her little brother? Nothing in this story is made quite clear. But whatever the truth of the matter, Hélène ends up by running away with a mysterious murderer who takes her to live with him on a pirate ship and gives her four children. He dies. She dies too.

Marie de Verneuil is the illegitimate issue of a liaison between the Duc de Verneuil (Victor-Amédée) and a Casteran who later becomes a nun. Brought up I'm not sure where, taken in by an old Duc de Lenoncourt who deserts her during the Terror, she marries Danton. What? *The* Danton? Robespierre's Danton? Daring, more daring, and yet more daring! That Danton? The fat man with the black all round his eyes? Exactly. It makes Hélène d'Aiglemont's pirate seem rather tame by comparison, doesn't it? Danton's head once off, Marie finds herself reduced to poverty and becomes more or less a member of the police force. In 1799, she is sent by Fouché "down Fougères way" to seduce one of the leaders of the Chouans. She is a tall, beautiful girl, more spirited than Hélène d'Aiglemont, bright as a new penny, impossible to discourage, and always ready to deploy her charms. Bold and forceful as she is, she seduces Montauran in a twinkling. But the trouble is that he's such a good-looking young fellow, and Marie isn't at all eager to betray him. She hates waste, and it seems too cruel to send so pretty a piece of flesh to be riddled by a firing squad. She hesitates, wavers, changes her mind, then gives him up and tries to save him at the same time. She lacks that marriage of will-power and good judgment that makes Modeste Mignon such a forceful character. Her intelligence pulls her one way and her heart the other. This conflict is her undoing. Montauran is killed and so is Marie. The details are to be found in *les Chouans*.

Laurence de Cinq-Cygne, in *Une Ténébreuse Affaire*, has three men in love with her. She ends up by marrying the one she cared least for. The other two are killed. As might have been expected. Complicated people always attract complications, and tragic people tragedies. Laurence is essentially a tragic character. Forceful but incapable of the slightest compromise, as deficient in judgment as a village pump, utterly tireless, always on the go, taking food to émigrés in hiding, bluffing the police, or rushing off all the way to Germany to obtain a pardon for her cousins. Finally, she marries Adrien de Hauteserre, not because she loves him, but because he has been one of her underground companions, as it were, and because he is therefore one of her memories. Tragic women adore their memories. She gives him her name, because the Cinq-Cygne title can descend through the female line. In our day she would have been a female politician, and her husband would have been one of those unfortunate men always referred to as Mrs. ———'s husband. Twenty years later, when we meet her again, she is still exactly the same, walking out of a drawing-room as soon as a Republican walks into it, without weaknesses, without feelings, without anything but the same icy fire burning away inside. She had become an orphan at a very young age; perhaps that explains the ruggedness of her character. A great many of Balzac's young girls lack a father, or a mother, or both. I'm not sure that we should be too quick to draw conclusions from this. Balzac, as I have already said, disliked superfluous characters. He would have preferred a dead father to a useless one every time.

Emilie de Fontaine and Bathilde de Chargeboeuf *or the girls who know what they want*

Emilie de Fontaine, though I hardly need say it, is not a very sympathetic character. She often behaves arrogantly and odiously. One only needs to catch a glimpse of her at the Birotteaus' ball (*César Birotteau*, p.459), making no attempt to conceal her utter contempt for the good people all around her. Yet there is a certain firmness, a dignity in her character that inspires respect all the same. The Comte de Fontaine, her father, is a man who has understood his age, has understood that it is no good relying too much on the nobility or on kings any more, and though he does still make use of Louis XVIII, it is only in order to get his children settled in life. And he knows just where to settle them too: among the wealthy middle classes. His sons have married into the Grossetêtes and the Mongenods; both families without a "de" before their names but with a great deal of money in the bank. One of his daughters has married a highly placed internal revenue official, another a man who has made a fortune as a wood merchant. And rich though they are, all these sons and sons-in-law work, have a job to do. The Fontaine family is already a family of today. There is a freedom in their behavior and in their speech that we find in none of their contemporaries. Among all the young girls in the *Comédie humaine*, all of them more or less sequestered, practically behind bars, Emilie alone enjoys a total liberty. It is true that she is the little girl of the family, the youngest, the prettiest, the spoiled one. And though there is a certain amount of teasing, none of them tries to stop her indulging her caprice, which is to marry a peer of the realm. After one setback, which is re- counted in *le Bal de Sceaux*, she marries her old uncle, Kergarouët. A vul- gar woman would have been unfaithful to him. Emilie is not. She rebuffs Portenduère's advances (*Ursule Mirouët*). She possesses herself in patience and waits for her old husband to die. It is even possible that she is quite fond of him. She coddles him, she prevents him from indulging in rash acts of generosity (*id.* p.361). Once widowed, she remarries with Charles de Vandenesse and continues firmly on her way through a life that is never illuminated for a moment, as far as one can see, with the slightest spark of love.

Bathilde de Chargeboeuf is cast in much the same mold. A noble name, no money, very beautiful. Buried away in Provins, she is intelligent enough to marry old Rogron. While waiting for him to die, she accepts the attentions of Montriveau. Everything leads one to believe that she will succeed in marrying him (*Pierrette*).

We have now examined the biographies of about fifteen young women. However, if we are to consider them as a group we must immediately exclude Laurence de Cinq-Cygne. When a girl has three suitors and two of them are killed it is difficult to draw much of a conclusion from the fact that she marries the third. It was tragic, and there you are. Explanations seem a little superfluous. And besides, in Laurence de Cinq-Cygne's life marriage is the merest detail. For the others, on the contrary, marriage is an end. Once they have succeeded in marrying, or failed, they fade away, they disappear.

In this respect, as we have noted, these young girls fall quite naturally into four categories: those who get trampled on, the failures, the ones who know just what they want, and the ones whose marriages are triumphs. And the reasons for these various outcomes are clear and obvious. Those in the first category lack both will-power and daring. They dream, they leave fate, or chance, or their parents to decide what shall happen to them. They are beaten without ever having fought. But a Rosalie de Watteville, or a Clotilde de Grandlieu, these are made of sterner stuff. They make their own choices. In this category, however, it is judgment that is lacking. One chooses the wrong horse, the other the wrong kind of lasso. Rubempré, that is, and forged letters. Both choices lead to disaster. Rubempré escapes from Clotilde into death, Savarus from Rosalie into a monastery. Eugénie partakes of both categories: she chooses badly and she is also insufficiently forceful; she gives up the fight too soon. Emilie de Fontaine and Bathilde de Chargeboeuf both have their heads rather better screwed on. They have will-power and judgment too. Only their judgment is of an inferior kind, and the will-power is directed towards lower goals. They both, very sensibly, elect to marry old men, then wait for the whirligig of time to bring compensation in the form of a second marriage.

Lastly, in Modeste Mignon, in Ursule Mirouët, in Marguerite Claës, we find will-power, judgment and also probity. Their probity prevents them from marrying any man they do not love. Their judgment enables them to bestow their love on men worthy of them. Their will-power enables them to choose for themselves and to act upon that choice. They alone truly succeed.

Adélaide de Rouville, Pauline de Witschnau, Césarine Birotteau, Céleste Colleville, Charlotte de Kergarouët, Madeleine de Mortsauf, la Fosseuse

Adélaide de Rouville, the heroine of *la Bourse*, is a good-hearted young girl about whom there is not much one can say. In the end, she marries the painter Schinner.

Dipping into the same barrel we also find: the charming Pauline de Witschnau of *la Peau Chagrin*, the good-hearted Césarine Birotteau who marries Anselme Popinot, the pious little Céleste Colleville who quarrels so prettily with her husband-to-be in *les Petits Bourgeois*.

I have a personal weakness for Charlotte de Kergarouët in *Béatrix*. There is so much candor, so much good nature in her love for Calyste du Guénic. He spurns her in favor of Mme de Rochefide. The oaf! Myself, I'd have preferred Charlotte a thousand times, with her little plaid merino coat and her bright, bright lawn dress with the little pleated collar. She is only sixteen at the time, a round face, black eyes, and "the curt, decisive way of talking that girls in the provinces affect in order not to be taken for little ninnies" (*Béatrix*, p.441). She isn't exactly overflowing with ideas, I admit, but those she does have come out with such an air of freshness about them. It's true, it's refreshing to feel all that space between her ideas, it gives a feeling of airiness to her personality. She's exactly like the young girls one meets today.

There is not a great deal to be said about Madeleine de Mortsauf either. She is Henriette's daughter; but during most of *le Lys dans la Vallée* she is still only a child. She does assert her personality towards the end of the book, however. When she meets Félix at her dying mother's bedside she is unable to conceal the hatred that she feels for him. We have already encountered a somewhat similar reaction in Hélène d'Aiglemont. But where the latter is unable to forgive her mother, Madeleine de Mortsauf reserves all her bitterness for the lover. Hélène loves her father, and she hates her mother for having betrayed him. Madeleine, on the other hand, feels something more like contempt for her father, and if she hates Félix it is not, I think, because he was Henriette's lover but because he wasn't, because he did not make her happy. I think, I'm not sure. It is not always easy to see what goes on inside young girls. "The tone of her voice," Félix says, "betrayed a considered hatred . . . as implacable as people's verdicts always are when they have no experience of life, when they are unable to accept any extenuation for crimes committed against the laws of the heart" (*Lys dans la Vallée*, p.1011). And note that he says the laws of the heart, not the laws of honor or morality. Later, Madeleine de Mortsauf marries the third Chaulieu son, who takes the title of Lenoncourt-Chaulieu. It is she, in *Splendeurs* (p.914), who is present during Clotilde de Grandlieu's last meeting with Rubempré on the road to Fontainebleau.

Pierrette Lorrain, the heroine of *Pierrette*, is still only a little girl, like Péchina in *les Paysans*. In this latter work there are also several country girls; though Balzac doesn't have much to say about them. He does, on the other hand, attach a certain importance to another peasant girl, la Fosseuse in *Médecin de Campagne*, a child-woman, at once slightly comic and rather touching, burdened by the weight of her own soul, so full of sensibility it is practically an illness, so changeable that a break in the weather, a cloud, a bird flying by is enough to alter her mood completely. She is also a person without roots. Born into the humblest possible surroundings, an orphan at the age of one, a beggar by the time she is nine, she is then taken in by a countess who completes the malformation of her soul by developing the extremist kind of sensitivity in her without giving her the means to lead an existence protected from the harsher aspects of life.

CHAPTER 6

Old Maids

*Mesdemoiselles d'Esgrignon, de Pen-Hoël, du Guénic,
Cormon, Fischer (known as Cousine Bette), Gamard,
Rogron and Michonneau.*

WHEN WE FIRST make her acquaintance, in *le Cabinet des Antiques*, Armande d'Esgrignon is still fairly young. Nevertheless, she has given up all idea of marriage, devoted her life to her brother and her nephew and presents all the characteristics of the old maid. She does inspire one passion, nevertheless, but it is in the heart of a child, in the little Emile Blondet, who pretends to be rolling on the grass so that he can better admire her darling little feet (*Cabinet des Antiques*, p.341). She had, he tells us, tawny blonde hair, emerald eyes, and a fine bloom of down upon her cheeks. One might have expected such a combination to find a taker without too much difficulty. But Armande was born in 1755, and therefore came of age at a time when everyone's chances of happiness were being given rather rough treatment. She was forced to lay everything else aside and give all her time to saving the possessions of her half-brother, the Marquis, who was away being a *chouan*. Later on, she devotes herself entirely to bringing up her nephew, Victurnien. Such sacrifices are not rare. What is less usual, however, is to find them being made with such smiling good grace, lit up by so imperturbable a sweetness of soul. But love still, now and then, flutters a gentle wing in that rejected heart. "An old maid's facticious motherhood implies . . . adorations too blindly lavished for her to have the power of admonishing a handsome boy" (*id.* p.354). Mlle d'Esgrignon also appears in *la Vieille Fille*.

Jacqueline de Pen-Hoël, in *Béatrix*, has reached her majority thirty-six years before we meet her. The last descendant of "the illustrious Pen-Hoël family of Brittany" (*Béatrix*, p.346), she is a dried-up, wrinkled, slightly hunchbacked old lady who wears a green sarsenet hat and walks with a small-handled cane. Slightly ridiculous, but probity personified.

[162]

Though she never spends more than a thousand francs a year herself, she does not hesitate to send the Duchesse de Berry ten thousand at the time of that great lady's expedition in the Vendée (*id*. p.347). She is miserly, but miserly for a specific purpose, and that is not genuine miserliness at all. She wants to see her nieces make suitable marriages, and in order to guarantee them dowries she displays in her business affairs "a Dutchman's sense of order, a catlike caution and the persistence of a priest" (*id*. p.348). Every morning, despite her age, she straddles a horse and rides out to inspect her estate. Every evening, escorted by a little serving-boy, she goes to play her hand of *mouche* with the du Guénics, who are her neighbors in Guérande. In this household, she enjoys the company of another old maid, Zéphirine du Guénic, her senior in fact, already over eighty, blind, never without her brown, quilted calico headwarmer that looks like a piece of an eiderdown, always knitting, occasionally stopping to rake at her hair with one of her needles, straight as a church spire, merry as a grig. And also, despite her blindness, aided and abetted by her young sister-in-law who tells her what cards have been played, an incorrigible card-player. But one has to read, in *Béatrix* (pp. 350 to 353), the account that Balzac gives us of one of these evenings. It is at once so droll and so charming. After so many drawing-rooms in which treachery and self-interest go constantly hand in hand, how refreshing it is to find ourselves in one where, out of the five or six people present, there is not one that has ever committed a crime against the laws of generosity and honor. Like her friend Jacqueline de Pen-Hoël, and like Armande d'Esgrignon too, Zéphirine du Guénic, despite her piety, still retains the robust, broad-minded attitude of the women of the Ancien Régime towards matters of sexual morality. When someone complains of Calyste's assiduous attentions to Mlle des Touches, Zéphirine good-humoredly replies: "Oh, if the child is enjoying himself" (*id*. p.364). There is nothing narrow about her. Quite the contrary. She is all simplicity, all grandeur. And she has a keener mind than appears at first glance. "Calyste," she says to her nephew, "your father never opened a book, he speaks Breton, he fought at the risk of his life for his king and for God. The educated people had started the trouble, and the learned nobles all left their country to fend for itself. There's a lesson there if you care to learn it" (id. p.367). There is some pith in the old lady's words.

These three old maids all gave up the idea of marriage. Mlle Cormon, on the other hand, rages against her unmarried state. She wants to be married, and this desire occupies her, obsesses her almost to the point of paralysis.

Sometimes, in my young days, when I had five francs to spend, I would run down to the bookstalls along the Seine in order to buy a book. A second-hand book at that time cost more or less five francs. I could therefore buy only one. One and no more. You can imagine how carefully I set about making my choice. I left no book unturned. Beginning at the Gare d'Orsay, I would find a Gide that tempted me sorely, then a Montherlant that fascinated me, then a Reverdy, a Ramuz. I would end up in front of the Halle aux Vins, worn out, still not having made a purchase. And that's how it is with Mlle Cormon. After all, you can only get married once, and the importance she attaches to this matter always makes her shrink from a decision. She is looking for perfection. She wants nothing but the best. And an excess of desire tends always to produce inhibition. At the age of forty-two, Rose-Marie-Victoire is still unmarried. Yet she represents a good match. Admittedly she is "as ignorant as a fish and just a little bit *simple*" (*Vieille Fille*, p.268). And also not pretty. Fresh-complexioned, but flat-footed, bow legs like a sailor, the figure of a wet nurse, protruding eyes and a general air of being perpetually astonished and not too bright. Moreover, with age, she has become somewhat lumpy (*id*. p.255). But she is rich and her own mistress. She belongs to the very highest middle-class society in Alençon. She is practically an aristocrat. And her drawing-room is not without influence. "To marry Mlle Cormon," Balzac tells us, "meant to reign over all Alençon" (*id*. p.251). And there are some men who are attracted by ample charms.

In short, despite her age, Mlle Cormon still has three suitors: little Granson, the Chevalier de Valois and the Sire du Bousquier. Valois is an extremely dissolute old royalist who nevertheless passes for being respectable. Du Bousquier is a republican, very much the worse for wear but with the reputation of being a great womanizer. Mlle Cormon, who is religious and much concerned with the matter of social status, ought not to hesitate for a moment. But her plump little soul isn't quite as simple as that. She is religious, yes, but she also has her regrets. "Nature had destined her for all the pleasures, for all the joys, for all the burdens of motherhood" (*id*. p.254). She finds Valois attractive, but, she says to herself, "what a pity he isn't just a little dissolute" (*id*. p.273). What a pity indeed! If she only knew how the Chevalier spends his mornings, among all those laundry-girls. But on the other hand, how can she marry a republican, even one with a torso on him like the Farnese Hercules? "The poor maiden groaned at finding her election urn thus split in two" (*id*. p.273). As for Granson, he is like Mlle Cormon herself; the very force of his desire neutralizes it, paralyzes it. Since he cannot even bring himself to make an offer, he is beaten in advance. But the real cream of the joke comes when Valois, in his attempts to discourage Mlle Cormon from favoring his two rivals, spreads exactly those slanders about them best calculated to increase their attractions in her aging eyes. He insinuates that Granson is given to certain bad habits, and that du Bousquier has got a girl with child. This last is more than Mlle Cormon can resist, and she proffers du Bousquier her "nice, fat hand dripping with crowns" (*id*. p.305). Her awakening is a cruel one. Du Bousquier announces that he is incapable of begetting a child. He is "entirely devoid of conjugal love" (*id*. p.325). "I wish," Rose says, "that he would take less trouble in public and that he would . . ." (*id*. p.326). And as if that weren't enough, she has her husband's liberalism perpetually searing her soul like a red-hot iron. In short, misfortune has entered into her being "like a drop of oil that will not leave a piece of cloth until it has slowly soaked its way into every thread" (*id*. p.327). We meet Rose du Bousquier again in *le Cabinet des Antiques,* in which she is from then on known as Mme du Croisier. Balzac gives a long explanation for this change of name that is of no interest to us here. Rose du Bousquier has not, in any case, changed: still unhappy, still religious, still rather stupid. She provides us with another example of the disasters to which a strong will can lead when it is not accompanied by a healthy power of judgment about people and things. Mlle Cormon had all the energy necessary to find happiness, but she misapplied it by marrying precisely the one of her three suitors who was least suited to her. And she was punished for her mistake.

Lisbeth Fischer, better known as Cousine Bette, is Envy. "Jealousy formed the very foundation of this character" (*Cousine Bette*, p.160). She is jealous of her pretty cousin who married the Baron Hulot. Lisbeth, you see, is plain, "skinny, dark-complexioned . . . thick eyebrows . . . several warts" (*id*. p.160). And the only husbands she has ever been offered were a clerk, a major, an army supply contractor, a retired captain and a passementerie dealer (*id*. pp. 164-165). At first, this jealousy appears somewhat vague. There is simply a seething reservoir of still-undirected energy, a desire for revenge, a will to power as yet unharnessed. Then, one day, Lisbeth gets her hands on a young Pole, and this chance event unleashes in her an incredible desire for domination. She has soon established "an absolute sway" (*id*. p.195) over this protégé. She gives herself up with frantic joy to "the happiness of possessing a man who is all hers" (*id*. p.197), to the happiness of knowing that this man lives off her money, that he depends upon her, that he is her thing and her property. She is not his mistress. No, that word confuses the issue here: she doesn't sleep with him, but she is in fact his mistress, in the primary sense of the word. "I'll be your slave," Wenceslas says to her. "You belong to me," she replies (*id.* pp. 191 and 195). It is one of the most disturbing episodes in the whole of the *Comédie humaine*. Lisbeth's words have a disordered, frenzied ring to them that suggests a woman in orgasm. Even Mme Marneffe herself can't make head nor tail of what her friend is saying, and God knows her own language offends against modesty often enough. "All that . . . ," she says, "is even more incomprehensible to me than what goes on in my husband's heart" (*id.* p.224).

The fury that this already half-mad woman feels can therefore be imagined when her Pole is taken away from her, and moreover by the daughter of that same Hulot couple of whom she already has a thousand reasons to be jealous. "Water! My head is on fire! I'm going mad" (*id.* p.225). For there are no half measures with Cousine Bette. She has "that savage streak found in people of the peasant class" (*id.* p.165), that tendency towards frantic obsession that, in Balzac, is one of the characteristics of the uneducated. And, like all people completely without education, she pursues only one passion at a time. Suddenly, her love subsides. And all that remains is the desire for revenge. "Adéline, I'll see you down in the mud," she cries (*id.* p.225). Hate now occupies her wholly "like a plague germ that can breed and ravage a whole town once someone has opened the fatal bundle of wool in which it was contained" (*id.* p.162). In Mme Marneffe, Lisbeth finds a tool that she then uses, over a period of time, to ruin Hulot, destroy the happiness of his daughter, drag down Crevel and, through Crevel, attempt to ruin Hulot's son. Nor is the mere fact of vengeance sufficient for her. She must also be a spectator of the disasters she achieves. She manages things so that she can remain intimate with both Mme Marneffe and the Hulot family at the same time. She goes to Mme Marneffe's to watch Hulot being duped, then to the Hulots' to watch her cousin weep, to lap up her tears "like a cat drinking milk" (*id.* p.317). The Devil does not remain indifferent to his tools. Between Lisbeth and Mme Marneffe there grows up a complicity that smacks of love, that smacks "of those friendships between women so strong and so unlikely that the Parisians, always too prone to wit, immediately slander" (*id.* p.272). "She had made her into her daughter, her friend, her love" (*id.* p.277). "There is no pleasure that I do not enjoy," she says to Valérie . . . "I didn't begin to live until the day when we decided to become sisters" (*id.* p.315). She experiences once again with Mme Marneffe the disturbing pleasures that she had originally found with Wenceslas Steinbock. In both cases, it is a matter of dominating beings who possess "the beauty that she worshipped" (*id.* p.278). In both cases, we see "a powerful will acting . . . on a weak character" (*id.* p.187). On the one hand the apathy of the young Pole, on the other, the kept woman's fatalism. And both are unaware of what is happening to them. Indeed, they even make fun of Lisbeth and her fits of fury. "She's mad," Steinbock says (*id.* p.245). "She'll be in the asylum at Charenton tomorrow," says Mme Marneffe (*id.* p.225). That's one of the Devil's tricks: he allows his victims to make fun of him. In fact, Wenceslas and Valérie are this imperious creature's slaves, her toys. Mme Marneffe imagines that she is free. Yet she never does anything but what her tyrant wishes her to do. "Lisbeth planned, Mme Marneffe acted" (*id.* p.278). It has long been Lisbeth's dream to marry the old Comte Hulot and so make the entire family dependent upon her. And she would have succeeded if her hatred had not made her strike too hard. The old Maréchal dies of grief and Lisbeth remains a spinster.

Mlle Gamard, in *le Curé de Tours*, is more restricted in her field of operations. We should not allow ourselves to be deceived by this smallness of scale, however: Mlle Gamard is another Cousine Bette, though a provincial Cousine Bette, and consequently reduced to provincial proportions, as well as to the proportions of the novella. But we see in her the selfsame "despotism" (*Curé de Tours*, p.800) which, at the first sign of opposition changes into hate. Like Bette, Sophie Gamard wants dominion over others. She wants to hold absolute sway over the two priests who lodge with her. One of them, like Wenceslas, evades her edicts. He abandons her for other pious ladies, already the object of Mlle Gamard's jealousy, and the latter avenges herself with the same savagery as Lisbeth Fischer. It is true that the story hinges on the pettiest of motives; but spite, envy and hatred are not dependent on the magnitude of their causes, and Mlle Gamard succeeds in driving the poor Abbé Birotteau to the gates of death itself.

The same spitefulness, the same despotism are displayed by Sylvie Rogron in *Pierrette*. Everyone must have seen, in big stores, those head saleswomen, those counter commanders, those tartan tyrants, harsh-tongued, overweening, domineering, speaking through disdainful noses, perpetually persecuting the little salesgirls who, when the harpies' backs are turned, roll their eyes up expressively to the ceiling. Sylvie is a head saleswoman. The daughter of an innkeeper in Provins, she is sent to Paris, where she goes into business with her brother, a cretin of the storekeeper variety. When they return to Provins, these "two surreptitiously baptized automota" (*Pierrette*, p.665), they are engulfed by the most profound boredom. Just think! No more clerks to nag the life out of. "They dawdled about all morning, lay about in bed when it was time to get up, dressed slowly" (*id*. p.684). Their attempts to cut a figure in the social life of Provins have failed, and this failure has left a terrible deposit of rancor and envy in their hearts. The Devil finally sends them a great-niece whom they are at liberty to mistreat to their hearts' desire. Sylvie and her brother are the sort of creatures for whom the phrase *bene amat bene castigat* was invented. They express the opinion that children should be brought up the hard way, that this forms their characters, and other idiocies of that sort. In fact, they are a pair of savage beasts. That this description is no exaggeration is proved by the tortures they proceed to inflict on little Pierrette, tortures of which the little girl eventually dies. At least the murders committed by Lisbeth and by Sophie Gamard were only moral murders; Sylvie's murder of Pierrette is just murder pure and simple. "You could be tried in the criminal courts," a lawyer tells her (*id*. p.765). However, there is no case, and Sylvie is allowed to die in her bed, in her cold, empty old maid's bed.

The same desire for dominating others is also to be found in Marie-Jeanne-Brigitte Thuillier, another old maid, whom we meet in *les Petits Bourgeois*. "The instinct for domination" was a leading characteristic of this "despotic nature" (*Petits Bourgeois*, pp. 81 and 85).

I should like to emphasize here the distinction that Balzac makes between his aristocratic old maids and his middle-class ones. Though they all have their various defects, Mlles d'Esgrignon, de Pen-Hoël and du Guénic all have intelligence, generous natures and upright characters. We cannot but feel sympathetic towards them. Mlle Cormon is a middle-class woman, but her mother was an aristocrat, and she herself is so preoccupied with things aristocratic that she almost appears to be one herself. She is ridiculous, but she is a good, respectable woman. The four representatives of middle-class female celibacy, on the other hand, are odious. They all display the same characteristics: envy, despotism and a petty but terrifying spitefulness. They are killers. *La Cousine Bette* ends with a veritable massacre. Mlle Gamard kills the Abbé Birotteau. Sylvie kills Pierrette. And we should also note not only that the three aristocratic old maids, as well as Mlle Cormon, are all religious, but also that their religion has in no way dried up their hearts. Though very strict with themselves, though completely virtuous, they are indulgent towards others. The middle-class examples, on the contrary, are narrow-minded. Of the four, Mlle Gamard alone is religious, or at any rate a churchgoer. Lisbeth is a republican and Mlle Thuillier a liberal. Sylvie Rogron sometimes sees a priest, but her house is a haunt of liberals. As for Mlle Michonneau, it goes without saying that she has never displayed the slightest flicker of religious sentiments.

This Mlle Michonneau (Christine-Michelle, born in 1779) is only an old maid by virtue of her age, since her eventful past life, which Balzac does not go into but which we may easily imagine, has long since deprived her of the right to be called a maid. One day, in the Pension Vauquer, Vautrin gets on to the subject of men who are controlled by their passions. "At these words," Balzac tells us, "Mlle Michonneau looked at Vautrin with understanding eyes. Like an old warhorse, you might have thought to yourself, an old warhorse hearing the sound of the trumpet" (*Père Goriot*, pp. 884-885). She also lives on a small allowance, her right to which "is periodically disputed by the heirs to whose slanders she was being constantly subjected" (*id.* p.855). She may perhaps have been pretty. "Though her face had been ravaged by the play of passions, there were still certain vestiges of whiteness to be observed in it, as well as a delicacy of texture, that gave reason to suppose that the body still retained some remains of physical beauty" (*id.* p.855). At the Pension Vauquer, she has moved in with a retired civil servant named Poiret, whom she refers to as her "dear darling" and who obeys her "like a dog whose master has just given it a good kick" (*id.* p.986 and p.1010). This latter phrase should be considered side by side with the little incident of the men controlled by their passions. "What did she do to him, that man, to attach him to her like that and make him follow her around like a little bow-bow?" Mme Vauquer wonders. Big Sylvie voices the reply of sturdy, lower-class common sense to this question: "Oh, heavens, those old maids, they know every dodge there is" (*id.* p.1028). It is this "Ninon in decay," this "tattered Pompadour" (*id.* p.1028) who betrays Vautrin to the police. This exploit earns her excommunication from the Pension Vauquer. People still felt that way about such things in those days. She marries Poiret. In 1830, the poor old fellow is obliged to take to his bed (*Splendeurs*, p.973). Possibly his wife has been taking advantage of his docility. She has taken up an occupation that suits her to a T: she lets out furnished rooms. Her establishment is situated on the Rue aux Poules. Cérizet, the poor man's moneylender, has moved into the ground floor apartment (*Petits Bourgeois*). By about 1840, the former Mlle Michonneau is a widow. Poiret couldn't take it.

CHAPTER 7

The Young Men

Gaston de Nueil, Arthur Grenville, Maurice de l'Hostal, Ernest de la Brière or the hatpegs—Albert Savarus, Z. Marcas and David Séchard or genius at work—Goupil, Petit-Claud, Vinet, Fraisier and Poulain or the slugs—Théodose de la Peyrade or the young Tartuffe—Oscar Husson, Georges and Frédéric Marest, Jean Butscha and Sébastien de la Roche or the young clerks.

Gaston de Nueil, Arthur Grenville, Maurice de l'Hostal, Ernest de la Brière *or the hatpegs*

THE DISTINCTION that I am drawing between the lions and the young men may appear arbitrary to some people. Well, that can't be helped. As well as the great natural frontiers provided by mountain ranges and Bidassoas, there are also smaller, artificial ones that can effectively separate the two halves of a single lawn, of a meadow that is all the same green, of a field that is all planted with the same crop. On the surface, Gaston de Nueil looks much like Ajuda. Moreover, they both have the same woman as their mistress. Yet I cannot find it in me to lump them together. There is at least a certain impressiveness about Ajuda; whereas there is nothing impressive at all about Gaston de Nueil. Yes, I know, he does go to visit Mme de Beauséant when she has forbidden all visitors (*Femme abandonnée*). But this action inspires me with no more than a limited sympathy for him. What does he want with Mme de Beauséant after all? With this woman he has never set eyes on? To console her? To take advantage of her despair? Or is there, perhaps, in the impulse that motivates his action, something akin to the emotion that makes an adolescent boy's heart beat a little faster as he walks past a house of ill-fame? Ah well, taking into account the particular weakness I have for Mme de Beauséant, let us at least enter on Gaston's credit sheet the fact that he gives her nine years of fidelity and happiness. After which, the lease having expired, he marries a Mlle la Rodière, whom he does not love, in order to please his mamma. A weakling, in short, a prey to the first strong personality he encounters. Mme de Beauséant accepts his advances: he falls in with all her wishes. His mother wants him to marry: he obeys. But, like all weaklings, he only half obeys. Once married, he returns to throw himself at Mme de Beauséant's feet. She rejects him. He kills himself. And so ends this gutless life that love alone was able to raise, for a while, to any height. Gaston de Nueil's only reason for living was to provide an object for Mme de Beauséant's love. He is a hatpeg. When nothing is hanging on a hatpeg you don't notice it. When someone hangs a hat on it, you see only the hat.

Some years ago, Hollywood made a film of *la Dame aux Camélias*. The part of Armand Duval was played by Robert Taylor. I trust that no one will hold it against me if I say that he is one of the least attention-riveting gods of the American Olympus. He was, in fact, an excellent choice. In this particular story the lover doesn't count. He exists only in order to provide an object, a justification for Marguerite Gauthier's passion, for her cries, her tears, her coughing fits. Without her, he immediately ceases to exist. The same is true of Gaston de Nueil. Mme de Beauséant's passion plays over him like a searchlight, and it gives him highlights and shadows that, without her, he in fact does not have.

The same thing is true of Arthur Ormond, Lord Grenville, whom we meet in *la Femme de trente ans*. He is one of those Englishmen who, happening for some reason to be in France during the Empire period, were interned on Napoleon's orders. An internee, that is the first fact we register about his existence, and it is a circumstance entirely external to his character. If only he would escape! But that would mean he was affirming his own existence, taking fate into his own hands, and that is something Lord Grenville would never think of doing. Then love comes on the scene. He falls in love with Mme d'Aiglemont, an invalid, just as Gaston fell in love with a woman who had been abandoned. The inherent negation of misfortune seems to attract these negative men. Grenville nurses his delicate mistress. Again, a variant of Gaston offering Mme de Beauséant consolation. He cures her, but dies at the very moment when he is about to receive his reward, at the very moment when he is about to affirm his existence at last. In Charles du Bos' diary, we find the following rather involved sentence: "The *raison d'être*, as well as the value of *l'Education sentimentale* are to be found above all in the picture this work offers us of the inevitable final state to which any human being must come who is inhabited only by feelings, and in whom, because he does not secrete, as it

were, so much as a single iota of will, the unthinking acceptance of self
and a total resignation to external events result in a life so entirely flaccid
that it loses even the little worth it originally had." This sentence applies
exactly to these young men of Balzac's too, and it is this fact that, in the
final analysis, puts them in a different category from the lions.

Maurice de l'Hostal, despite the fact that he is "the living image of Lord
Byron" (*Honorine*, p.250), carries scarcely any more weight than de
Nueil and Ormond. Here again, we have a man who drifts wherever events
take him, aimless, directionless, falling in love with precisely the one
woman who is forbidden to him, the wife of the Comte de Bauvan, by
whom he is employed as a secretary, making no effort to get what he
wants, unable to risk a single gesture, allowing himself to be parted from
her without saying a word. He is left with only his memories. Men of this
sort are very fond of memories. Perhaps they feel that their memories
dispense them from the necessity of living. Later, when he recounts this
episode in his life, Maurice de l'Hostal still quivers at the thought of it. It
in his great adventure, the moment when the golden gates almost, but not
quite, opened up for him. Having been appointed Consul in Genoa, he
marries, and, like a great many men who have experienced a great but
thwarted love, he marries a woman with a large fortune.

Ernest de la Brière has rather more stature, but not a great deal more.
"He is one of those ordinary men with positive virtues and dependable
morals who appeal to parents" (*Modeste Mignon*, p.493). Related to one
of Charles X's premiers, he begins his career as secretary to an excellency
and appears in *les Employés* in this role. After his patron's downfall,
Ernest is put out to grass in the quiet pastures of the audit office. At the
same time, he constitutes himself honorary secretary to the poet Canalis.
He is evidently a secretary by nature: it's in his blood. And what is a
secretary, if not someone who is prepared to mold his mind on that of
another? Someone who exists only as a reflection, a double of someone
else. Even when it comes to love, Ernest needs to shelter behind someone else. He would never dream of taking the initiative himself. But one
day, Canalis allows him to answer in his stead a letter written to him by
one of his female readers. Ernest writes back. And the letters he writes are
really quite pretty pieces of work. But he signs them Canalis. He is still
the secretary, and it is only because he is being protected by that illustrious name that he is at last expressing himself, at last displaying his own
little personality. And he ends up marrying this lady correspondent, his
Modeste Mignon and her eight millions. That's the way it is: there are
some hands in which timidity turns out to be the ace of trumps.

One last observation. Of these four young men, three fall in love with women they have never seen. And this is a trait we have already encountered in Calyste du Guénic, another weakling, another drifter.

Albert Savarus, Z. Marcas, David Séchard *or genius at work*

When first introduced to us, Albert Savarus is nearing his thirty-fifth year. Marcas is almost as old, and David Séchard is one of those men who are thirty at three days old. Yet all three men appear to have all the characteristics of youth. All three are still on the threshold of what is to be the most important event of their life. They are still in the stage of preparation. Marcas is preparing himself for his assumption of power. Savarus is preparing himself for marriage. Séchard is preparing to rock the foundations of the paper industry with his invention. They are all three waiting. And waiting is the occupation of youth.

Savarus is a Fleming, descended from the Savarons de Savarus, a good Douai family mentioned in *la Recherche de l'Absolu* (p.524). Having fallen in love with the Duchesse d'Argaiolo, who is unfortunately encumbered with a husband, he has placed all his hopes in Providence and is waiting for the Duke to die. Why has he chosen to live in Besançon while he waits? Why doesn't he live tied to his mistress's apron strings on the banks of that Lago di Garda so auspicious for love affairs? For the same reason, no doubt, that led Balzac to live thousands of kilometers from Mme Hanska. For Savarus, as for Balzac, the world—society—exists. For Savarus, as for Balzac, love has no meaning unless marriage has cemented it into a harmoniously constructed life that contains all the essential elements: career, wealth, social position. Like the busy traveler who catches up with his correspondence between two trains, Balzac and Savarus work while they are waiting for happiness to arrive. They work, not as a means of escape, not to pass the time, but in order to increase that happiness when it comes. They are filling their bottom drawers, if I may so put it, so that when the happy day arrives they will be able to kneel before their beloved and offer her, not just a man no better than the next one, but Balzac the famous author, or Savarus the successful politician.

So, while he waits, Savarus works and writes his Duchesse twenty-page letters. Alas, they are intercepted by the perfidious Rosalie de Watteville, who substitutes other and, one imagines, rather curter messages. Beside herself with anger, the Duchesse marries Rhétoré. Without warning! Which is stupid of her. Never do that. I mean, allow a quarrel by letter to become definitive. Better one scene of explanation too many than none at all. After the Duchesse's marriage, Savarus enters a monastery. But he had already been leading a monk's life during his stay in Besançon, locked up in his love, secluded by his passion, lonely as a lighthouse.

Recluses are rare in the *Comédie humaine*. Savarus is one, and Marcas is another. Not that their seclusion brings them much success. And the same thing might be said to be true of their biographer, to a lesser degree. For interesting though it is, a story like Z. *Marcas* offers neither the life, nor the vitality, nor the teeming truth of *Illusions perdues* or *Père Goriot*. One is even inclined to wonder whether Balzac did not look upon stories of this sort as preliminary studies, as it were, that enabled him to advance later with increased confidence through his great novels. Marcas is ambition in its pure state, a concentrate of ambition, without any admixture, without any secondary characteristics. This being so, the story has somewhat the appearance of those drawings by Leonardo da Vinci consisting of twenty or thirty feet or hands, perfectly drawn in themselves, but whose *raison d'être* lies rather in the fact they will enable the artist to address himself later on to much vaster compositions, in which such hands and feet will assume their true placement and importance. We shall find the traits gathered together in the character of Marcas—though more scattered, mingled with others, scaled down to less overwhelming proportions —in Rastignac or Marsay, whose characters are less of a piece but more true to life. Marcas, on the other hand, is less a character than a moral example.

Though we should immediately add that the example does not correspond exactly with what it is intended to illustrate. This Marcas is offered to us as a man in every way superior, a man who has meditated on life, a man who is also a wise observer of the human heart. But, in fact, all he seems to have done is to attach himself to a wealthy, ambitious, but also stupid man and then wait for that man to repay him out of gratitude. For a sagacious observer, that's not very impressive. He is, Balzac tells us, "a true statesman . . . a talented politician" (Z. *Marcus*, p.753). And I'm afraid we shall have to take Balzac's word for it, since at the age of thirty-three this virtuoso careerist is still living off liver sausage in a garret. There is nothing incompatible between a garret and genius certainly, but here we are concerned, not with a genius for painting or a genius for sonnets, but with a genius for success. And what sort of a genius for success is it that ends up with its possessor living in a garret? The careerist without power may be likened, not to the violinist who has not found success, but to the violinist without a violin. So the genius still remains to be proved. In reality—and this, I think, is the most interesting aspect of the story—Marcas's ambition appears to be a passion so strong that it can dispense with its own gratification. Its very excess blunts it. Marcas's ambition seems to achieve its own satisfaction in a dream world. His gaze, Balzac tells us, "was contemplating a world beyond that which appears to the eyes of ordinary men" (*id*. p.756). This Breton with the great, leonine head is a long way from being the realist that Balzac claims he is.

With David Séchard, we are back within earshot of the heart's and society's distant thunder. Séchard does not live alone and his passion is not locked up inside him. The big thing in his life is his invention of a new process for making better and cheaper paper; but this invention does not cut him off from the rest of the world. He does sometimes think about other things. About friendship, as his relationship with Rubempré shows. About love, as his marriage to Eve Chardon proves. Hence the element of human warmth in him that seems almost completely lacking in Marcas, and even in Savarus. In Balzac, preoccupation with a single passion always leads to a certain callosity of the heart.

David Séchard is big and fat. He looks like a jolly monk. He is generous by nature but rather vague. Talented though he may be, this does not prevent him from being cheated by a group of tricksters who aren't fit to to clean his shoes. And this kind of error in judgment is met with frequently in *la Comédie humaine*. "The man with intelligence never lowers himself to examine the bourgeois creatures around him, with the result that this inattention allows them to dance rings around him, and then, while he is still scornfully ignoring them, garrotte him at their leisure" (*Muse du Département*, p.160). David does, however, manage to salvage sufficient money to take his little family and retire into the country (*Splendeurs*, p.886). Indeed, he would probably be very happy there were it not for the troubles brought on him by his brother-in-law Rubempré.

It seems almost unnecessary to underline how much all these three characters owe to Balzac himself. Marcas is the Balzac who pondered deeply on the subject of worldly ambition and considered, for a moment, undertaking a political career. Savarus is Balzac waiting for Mme Hanska. Séchard is the product of the period Balzac spent in the printing business. And Séchard also resembles his creator physically. He has a "large chest . . . ," a "swarthy, highly colored, well-fleshed face supported by a thick neck . . . a square nose, and a deeply cleft chin" (*Illusions perdues*, p.485). As for Savarus and Marcas, they even push the resemblance as far as adopting Balzac's own timetable. Savarus "rises every night between one and two in the morning, works until eight, breakfasts, then works some more. He goes out . . . comes back, eats dinner, and goes to bed be-tween six and seven in the evening" (*Albert Savarus*, p.766). Marcas too works half the night, goes to bed between six and ten in the morning, spends the remainder of the day working, then goes back to bed at six in the evening (Z. *Marcas*, p.744).

Goupil, Petit-Claud, Vinet, Fraisier and Poulain *or the slugs*

I did attempt to find another description, but no other phrase gives a bet-ter idea of these creatures who, though they have the outward appear-ances of men, are in fact a much lower form of life, beings that crawl through the world like slugs, coating everything they touch with their slimy traces. They are wicked men, but their wickedness is of a particular kind, one that oozes with envy, with poverty, with inadmissible passions. It cannot be denied that Rastignac is no paragon of virtue, or that Philippe Bridau is a brute. But they are not slugs. The slug is never a brute. He is a weakling reduced to a state of sly and furtive spitefulness. As a general rule he is also physically sick. His complexion is muddy, his hands clammy, his hair ratty or moth-eaten. For Balzac, the body and the soul are intimately connected. Vice produces pimples. A healthy conscience makes its possessor put on weight. Unhappiness makes people ill (Mme de Mortsauf, Mme Graslin).* The slug is also, by definition, poor. The rich man may be odious, vile or cruel; but he can never suffer from the afflic-tion that is the essential ingredient of the slug's sliminess: envy, a gnawing, corrosive envy. The slug is the scum of the earth who has nothing, who rages against this fact, who gnaws his own heart out, and who turns his blood to poisonous slime in the process.

Our first specimen of the slug species is Jean-Sébastien-Marie Goupil, a solicitor's clerk in Nemours, a little man as defective physically as he is in the moral sphere, with very thin legs, a gray complexion, and sparse, sandy hair. He gives the impression of a hunchback "whose hump is in-side" (*Ursule Mirouët*, p.273). Beneath this repulsive exterior is concealed —though not very well—an even more repulsive soul. And Goupil knows it. For that is one of the slugs' peculiar characteristics: they are aware of their own ignominy. I might even say that they make use of it. They

---

* "So that people with strong feelings die of bad stomachs?"
   "Don't laugh, Félix," Mortsauf replied, "nothing could be more true . . . Such states of exalted sensibility maintain the stomach lining in a constant state of irritation," etc.
. . . (*Lys dans la Vallée*, p. 955).

employ their own repulsiveness as a factor in their calculations. "What use would my blood be to you?" Goupil asks Portenduère. "Would you drink it? It would poison you" (*id.* p.444). Total lack of pride. Their line is humility. Their shield is the disgust they inspire. Their weapon is the anonymous letter. It is the weapon that Goupil uses, and the ones he sends to Ursule Mirouët are very nasty examples indeed. And if he subsequently chooses to defect and go over to her side, it is only because he has been insufficiently rewarded for his villainy. The slugs have no intrinsic preferences: they simply crawl towards the largest source of money. Can they be affected by anything other than money? One wonders. Certainly love plays no part in these slime-coated lives. The French word for love, as Victor Hugo pointed out, also contains the word for soul, and the poet's conclusion was that there can be no love without soul. But Balzac's slugs, in a manner of speaking, have no souls. One perceives in them that same elimination of the soul by which the Devil's most proficient agents may always be recognized. The most that can be said of the slugs is that they have desires. Ignoble ones, I need scarcely add. For his sexual gratification, Goupil is quite content to take over the tarts tossed aside by his friend Désiré Minoret.

We should note, however, that Goupil does improve to some extent during the course of his existence. Once married to Mlle Massin-Levrault, who is plain but rich, once a solicitor himself, he takes to wearing clean shirts and white cravats. Cleanliness, he says, is a product of wealth. "In the moral sphere as well as the physical sphere," Judge Bongrand replies (*id.* p.473). As I have said, the slug is a creation of envy. Once his envy has disappeared, once his jealousy has been appeased, the slug becomes simply a blackguard, like everyone else.

Pierre Petit-Claud, in *les Illusions perdues*, provides us with a counterpart of Goupil. Like him he is a member of the legal profession: a solicitor in Angoulême. Like him, he is low-born: one is a farmer's son, the other a tailor's. And like Goupil too, he is physically repulsive. "His face presented the observer with one of those complexions whose muddied, dirty tones testify to former illnesses, to sleepless, wretched nights, and almost always to bad thoughts" (*Illusions perdues*, p.913). Skinny, almost bald, scarred by smallpox, "weighed down by the world's contempt, devoured by a corrosive desire to become somebody," he has been forced, like Goupil, to swallow so many affronts that he oozes spite at every pore. And like Goupil again, Petit-Claud will sell himself at the first opportunity. He marries Françoise de la Haye, a piece of good luck, despite the bride's illegitimacy, that he could scarcely have hoped for, and one that he repays with a pretty series of betrayals. An account of them is to be found in the second part of *Illusions perdues*.

Third sample: the lawyer Vinet, in Provins. The same vileness of character, the same poverty, the same effect on his health. And the same unprepossessing exterior. Vinet has "a flat-headed, viper's face," a "wide, thin mouth," and a "sharp, persistent little voice." "His muddy complexion, consisting mainly of sickly tones, with occasional patches of green and yellow, spoke clearly of his repressed ambition, his endless failures, and his hidden wretchedness" (*Pierrette*, p.692). This Apollo, supposing himself to be bringing off a stroke of genius, interferes with an aristocratic young girl, a Chargeboeuf, and forces her parents to let him marry her. Though the plan is in fact a failure, since the parents, once having given their consent to the marriage, make all possible haste to abandon this injudicious daughter and her pimply husband to their own devices.

Though he is as much of a blackguard as the preceding examples—and perhaps even more of one, for he is more intelligent—this Vinet nevertheless seems to me to be rather less slug-like. He is more closely allied to the simple adventurer, in the style of Nucingen or Maxime de Trailles. Perhaps he owes this fact to the love in his life. Goupil and Petit-Claud both marry, but no one has ever loved them. Vinet is beloved, and however badly it is received, however unattractive it may be, a woman's love never passes over a man without insinuating some measure of unction, of blandness into his character. The tiniest quantity, an almost invisible speck sometimes, but enough to warm up the blood of even the most reptilian creature a degree or two. Moreover, we soon see Vinet progressing quite rapidly on the path towards success, and consequently losing his original sliminess. "Instead of the Vinet of old, pale and skinny, irritable and gloomy, he presented, in his new form, a Vinet with the bearing of a successful politician . . . His cunning little head was so well combed, and his well-shaven chin gave him such a dainty air, that he made a distinctly pleasant, though cold, impression, rather in the style of Roberspierre" * (*Pierrette*, p.739). Having started life rather higher in the social scale than Goupil, Vinet also manages to get further. He becomes a deputy and Attorney General. In view of Balzac's clear-cut preferences in such matters, is it necessary for me to add that Vinet, Goupil and Petit-Claud all belong to the Liberal party?

This Vinet should not be confused with his son Olivier, also a member

---

* For reasons I am unable to fathom, Balzac almost always spelled Roberspierre with one more r than is customary.

of the legal profession, whom we meet in *le Député d'Arcis,* in *les Petits Bourgeois* and also in *le Cousin Pons.*

Our fourth specimen of the species slug is the Sieur Fraisier, a Paris lawyer. (A notary, a solicitor, two lawyers, there is evidently no doubt . . .) Like those specimens we have already observed, Fraisier is a man still youthful in years but in a wretched state of health. "A little, dried-up, sickly man," Balzac writes, "with a red face covered in eruptions that were a clear indication of the serious taint in his blood" (*Cousin Pons,* p.673). "That jar of poisons," he also adds later (*id.* p.683). Of the four, he is easily the one in worst shape. Fraisier suffers from "appalling diseases" (*id.* p.700). He gives off a pestilential odor. He drink the juices of herbs. The other three all have at least some hair left; Fraisier, on the other hand, wears a wig. And needless to say, he is poor, envious and full of spite. Balzac compares him first to a toad, then to a snake rearing up on its tail (*id.* pp. 683 and 720). However, these comparisons are not new. They have already been used for Vinet ("viper's face") and for Goupil, who also gives one "the sensation caused by a toad" and whose voice was similar to that of a "viper's hiss" (*Ursule Mirouët,* p.381 and p.443).

And, like Goupil again, as soon as he achieves his first success Fraisier begins to improve. At the moment when he feels himself to be on the verge of success, this creature upon whom no sudorific has ever had the slightest effect begins, if only slightly, to sweat. "I'm saved," he says to himself, "for Poulain promised me I should become healthy as soon as I was able to perspire again" (*id.* p.700). It is human warmth flowing back into him. And knowing the intimate interrelation that Balzac posits between the moral and the physical spheres, we may justifiably suppose that physical improvement in Fraisier's condition denotes some imminent improvement in his character.

Like the preceding examples in this section, Fraisier is a member of the lowest ranks of the middle class. He is a lawyer, but a poor man's lawyer, a creature even more wretched than his clients, reduced to eating an unappetizing diet of hash and sleeping with the help. I admit that this last statement is no more than inference; I have no definite proof. But it seems reasonable to wonder, all the same, why Mme Sauvage eavesdrops when her employer receives a visit from Mme Cibot, who is an extremely handsome woman, and why she throws this intruder a "murderous glance" (*id.* pp. 673 and 685).

We should also note that the slugs, as a class, are also capable of momentary good feelings. Goupil is touched for an instant by Ursule Mirouët's greatness of soul (*Ursule Mirouët,* p.445). Petit-Claud has "a flash of generous feeling" (*Illusions perdues*, p.983). And Fraisier has the saving grace of his friendship for Docteur Poulain. He "would let himself be chopped to bits for him" (*Cousin Pons*, p.706).

Alas, this Poulain is a slug too. Less so than Fraisier himself perhaps, but it's a close contest. He is another poor bachelor eaten up with envy. The son of a breeches-maker, he has become a doctor. "The young lawyer without clients and the young doctor without patients are the two greatest expressions of that respectable Despair so peculiar to the city of Paris . . . These two black suits of clothes, always on foot, worn by two professions for whom the world is one great wound, to whom humanity displays only its most squalid aspects; these two men, crushed beneath the difficulty of making a start in life, express themselves in the gloomiest, most defiant of phrases, while the concentrated hate and ambition pent up in them flashes out in glances that resemble the first flickering efforts of a long smoldering fire" (*Cousin Pons*, p.664). Again the gnawing fury of covetousness. Though Poulain, despite his moments of impatience and anger, is only a latent blackguard. He does not create opportunities for his evil intentions. But as soon as one presents itself, he pounces. No, that's not true. He doesn't pounce: he reaches out a cautious paw. When Mme Cibot tries to involve him in her devious schemes, he extricates himself by referring to his "professional conscience." But at the same time this does not stop him sending the aforesaid Mme Cibot on to Fraisier, whom he knows to be an unscrupulous wretch, or from going to see Fraisier himself afterwards and fertilizing the ground with a few forkfuls of pertinent advice (*id*. pp. 666 and 678). Yet there is one ray of light in his character too. He venerates his old mother, and the tenderness he feels for her is "sublime" (*id*. p.660). It is rare, in the *Comédie humaine*, to come across a man who does not have some little corner of his being in which we recognize, sometimes with stupefaction, the trace of God's hand. Though even this vestigial touch of grace is lacking, totally lacking, in the two slugs I shall return to in a later section: Cérizet and Marneffe.

Théodose de la Peyrade *or the young Tartuffe*

La Peyrade is a lawyer like Fraisier, poverty-stricken like Petit-Claud, young like Goupil and a blackguard like Vinet. Yet he isn't a slug. Antipathetic though he may be, at least he excites no physical revulsion in the reader. Nor, for that matter, does he suffer from envy. Ambitious, yes, avid for success; but that's not the same thing. He will stop at nothing, but he never does harm unless it will bring him some definite advantage. Like all fair-haired people from Provence, Balzac says, he is capable of "savage deeds"; but in Peyrade these are the "product of an inner intoxication" (*Petits Bourgeois*, p.108) and not of a gloomy delight in such things, of spitefulness on principle, as with the true slug. He is ambitious, but his ambition is of the elevating, not the inwardly gnawing kind. And in consequence, La Peyrade enjoys perfect health. He shows no outward traces of a poisoned bloodstream such as we have observed in Goupil. Nor has God been too unkind to him as far as looks are concerned. Théodose is a little fat, a little gelatinous, I admit; but the mouth is pleasant, and the brow noble. And he has a nose like a hunting dog: thick at the tip and with a groove in it. He is dishonest, as dishonest as it is possible to be if one is a determined careerist prepared to stoop to even the lowest of means. That apart, he stands closer to Rastignac than to Petit-Claud. He is a Rastignac making his way to the top by using, not women, but his virtues. Théodose is hypocrisy incarnate. Balzac himself tells us so. "A few scraps of the clay left by Molière at the foot of his colossal statue of Tartuffe have been worked up here by a hand more daring than able" (*Petits Bourgeois*, preface).

There are rather few hypocrites in the *Comédie humaine*, a face that makes it difficult to reconcile oneself to this one's appearing in a novel that was left incomplete. Nevertheless, La Peyrade has some excellent scenes. He insinuates himself into the Thuillier household, as Tartuffe did into Orgon's, by a great show of religious and philanthropic feeling, and he is certainly a sight worth seeing when he pauses for a moment in the middle of some rascality or other "one knee on the ground, his hands crossed on his chest, his eyes raised to heaven in a religious ecstasy as he recited a prayer . . ." "It was as moving," Balzac says, "as 'Saint Jerome Communing with God' " (*id*. p.199).

Oscar Husson, Georges and Frédéric Marest, Jean Butscha and Sébastien de la Roche *or the young clerks*

Oscar Husson is the personification of youth, real youth, the callow, ungrateful age at which young men are hovering on the brink of the nest, irritated at feeling themselves still the object of a maternal solicitude that they are nevertheless totally incapable of doing without. Oscar's mamma goes to see him off on the stagecoach and slips some chocolate into his hand for the journey. Oscar is beside himself with vexation. He would like to see the ground open and swallow her up, chocolate and all. When another passenger makes a joke, Oscar protests: "My mother, sir! That was our housekeeper, if you please" (*Un Début dans la Vie*, pp. 630 and 665). Isn't that youth all over? The scene, with its hidden comedy, is very like certain chapters of Jules Vallès' *l'Enfant*. Oscar Husson is already the same character as Jacques Vingtras before his disappointments.

Wearing his caped, olive topcoat, Oscar is on his way to the home of his protector, M. Moreau, once the lover of his mother, the widow Husson, now remarried to an insignificant clerk named Clapart. This Moreau has got into the habit of dropping in from time to time to say hello to his former mistress. He brings her baskets of game, then they sit and chat of this and that. Moreau tells her all the little domestic secrets of the Comte de Sérizy, who employs him as his agent. Oscar, hunched over his homework in one corner, listens. These Parisian apartments are so minute. And on this particular day in the stagecoach, what do the other passengers start talking about but the Count. Oscar can't wait to put his word in. Sérizy? There's no one in the world I know better, he informs them. Isn't that a nineteen-year-old to the life? Just the age when one is so insecure about one's position in the world that lying is the only way to give oneself some sort of real existence. Though in this case there is more than just Oscar's age to be considered. It seems likely that heredity enters into it too. His mother, once a kept woman on a fairly large scale, has known her days of glory. There is nothing like someone who's once been rich for refusing to accept more restricted circumstances. She had also been Mme Laetitia's chambermaid into the bargain. Another reason for taking her at her word. One can imagine Mme Husson's bouts of nostalgia, the stories with which she regaled her son, her connections, the duchesses she has seen . . . And doubtless from time to time, she embellishes the truth a little. Oscar takes after her. The Comte de Sérizy? "I'm a friend of his son," he says. "We ride together almost every day" (*id*. p.667). He doesn't know how close to the truth he is coming. The day will come, in fact, when he does ride with the Vicomte de Sérizy; but it will be in the army, and under the Vicomte's orders. In such ways, slowly but surely, does God make the lies of liars come true. Seeing the interest that his words have aroused, Oscar pursues his advantage. He tells his fellow travelers that Sérizy is constantly being cuckolded by his wife because of a skin disease to which the Comtesse is unable to reconcile herself. Unfortunately, Sérizy himself is in the stagecoach. Oscar's subsequent discomfiture can therefore be imagined.

Having been taken on by Desroches as a clerk, Oscar works zealously at his job. We must give him his due, he is by no means a ne'er-do-well. Quite the contrary. But he is still plagued by that vanity of his. One day, piqued because a woman has made fun of him, he gambles away five hundred francs that his employer had entrusted him with. There is nothing left for him but to become a soldier, a course which, in Balzac, represents the lowest degradation to which a man can fall. Being both courageous and disciplined, he rises to the rank of Lieutenant-Colonel, loses an arm and is appointed to the post of revenue collector. You think it sounds as though he has got rid of his vanity at last? But wait a moment! He assumes a patronizing attitude towards the good Pierrotin, and shortly afterwards Heaven repays him for this piece of arrogance by making him Pierrotin's son-in-law.

Surrounding Oscar, in *Un Début dans la Vie*, we meet a whole flock of other young clerks. There are also some in *le Colonel Chabert*. These are charming episodes, in which a genuine feeling of youth glows through the dust of the lawyers' files. Since he always took such a lively interest in the mechanics of society, Balzac sees a marriage above all as a contract, and a death above all as a will. Hence all the solicitors and lawyers in his work, and, as a result, all these clerks and various small fry of the legal profession. Besides, he had some personal reminiscences in this sphere to use up, having himself been a clerk to Maître Guyonnet-Merville. Apart from Oscar, we ought to mention Georges Marest, a clerk employed by Crottat and later by Hannequin, though a rich clerk, a clerk with a yearly income of thirty thousand francs who is probably only working in order to please his hardware merchant father. He dresses like a captain of industry: tight trousers, fitted cashmere waistcoat, frogged topcoat. He likes *to have his fun*. When traveling in the stagecoach with Oscar he passes himself off as an ex-colonel in the Turkish army. His stories are partly the product of natural blarney, partly inspired by the books he has read. He is Florentine's fancy man, and leads young Lupin and Desroches' clerks into bad ways (*Un Début dans la Vie, Paysans*). He is one of those good-natured young fellows whose natural gaiety and good humor end up bringing misfortune not only to others but to himself as well. He reminds me very much indeed of the character of the big cousin in Zénaïde Fleuriot's *Petit Chef de Famille*. We meet Georges Marest again at the end of *Un Début dans la Vie*, ruined by this time, in pretty bad shape, but still with something in his manner of the man who wants to *put on a good show*.

A more serious-minded young man, his cousin Frédéric is successively a clerk in the employ of Desroches, an examining magistrate in Paris, then Prosecutor for the Crown in Arcis (*Début dans la vie*, p.712; *Envers de l'Histoire contemporaine*, p.416; *Député d'Arcis*, p.640).

Jean Butscha lives modestly in a world a thousand miles removed from the one inhabited by these brilliant Parisian figures. He is an obscure clerk, as he says himself, poor, hunchbacked, the illegitimate son of a le Havre girl seduced by a Swedish sailor. But where legal procedure is concerned he need defer to no one. "Find me a single hunchback who isn't endowed with an exceptional talent in some particular field" (*Modeste Mignon*, p.455). Butscha's gaze is far-ranging beneath those heavy, screwed-up eyelids. He is the first to divine Modeste Mignon's secret. Though it's true that he loves her, and with one of those loves that, far from blinding the lover, lends his gaze a singular perspicacity. Moreover he loves Modeste without hope. "I love all on my own, at a distance, almost the same distance as from here to the stars" (*id.* p.455). It is a conception of love we do not meet with very often in the *Comédie humaine:* love for love's sake, the love of the young Werther. "And if I love you, what is that to you?" it seems to say. It is love considered as a personal enrichment rather than as a means of self-affirmation. Though timid at first, Butscha's love makes him progressively more assured, so that later on we find him taking on the responsibility for Modeste's happiness with as much aplomb as though he were her guardian, and then, in the end, completely bamboozling the glamorous Canalis.

Another timid clerk: Sébastien de la Roche, who fills a minor and non-established post in the civil service. We glimpse his rather misty silhouette in *les Employés.* His dream is to find a post that will pay twelve hundred francs and provide him with a certain amount of social standing. Rabourdin finally uproots him from the civil service and gives him a chance in business. Alas, I'm not at all sure that Sébastien doesn't regret the tranquil pleasures of government administration.

CHAPTER 8

The Literary, Artistic and Pleasure-Seeking Worlds

A supper at Coralie's, or the world of pleasure in 1821:
Etienne Lousteau, Raoul Nathan, Florine, Andoche
Finot, Florentine, Mariette, Tullia, Jean-François du
Bruel, Suzanne du Val Noble, Hector Merlin, Théo-
dore Gaillard, Emile Blondet, Claude Vignon, Félicien
Vernou and Jean-Jacques Bixiou—The Cénacle: Mey-
raux, Léon Giraud, Fulgence Ridal, Michel Chrestien,
Joseph Bridau, Horace Bianchon and Daniel d'Arthez.
—Painting and sculpture: Pierre Grassou, Hippolyte
Schinner, Théodore de Sommervieux, Léon de Lora,
Dubourdieu, Ernest-Jean Sarrasine and Stidmann. Mel-
chior de Canalis or the Rastignac of poetry—Music:
Gennaro Conti and Gambara—The world of pleasure
in 1821 (continued)—The homebodies: Caroline
Crochard de Bellefeuille, Jenny Courand and Aquilina
—The world of pleasure in 1840 (approx.): Jenny
Cadine, Olympe Cardinal, Josépha Mirah, Héloïse
Brisetout, Malaga, Mme Schontz, Arthur de Rochefide,
Carabine, Cydalise, Antonia Chocardelle, Olympe
Bijou, Elodie Chardin, Victor de Vernisset, Verman-
ton, Massol—The anonymous poet—The procuresses.

IT MAY CAUSE some astonishment that I have included a blameless writer
like Daniel d'Arthez under the same heading as a kept woman like the
good-natured Carabine. I might well allege, in my defense, that venal love-

making is an art like any other. ("I am an artiste," Mme Schontz says.) Or I could say, as so many others have done before me, that literature is a form of prostitution. "A man of letters, a public whore," Paul Claudel has written. In fact, my reasons are rather more superficial. Quite simply, it is impossible for me to discuss the blameless writer without comparing him to others who are not blameless, or to speak of Nathan and Lousteau without bringing in the Florines and the Mariettes who are their usual companions, the Florines and the Mariettes who are, taken all together, both the cause and the symbol of the two men's corruption. Indeed, Balzac himself writes of Nathan: "That pen soaks up its ink in an actress's boudoir, you can sense it" (*Fille d'Eve*, p.92).

Apart from its author, the *Comédie humaine* contains four important writers: Mlle des Touches under her pseudonym Camille Maupin, Daniel d'Arthez, Canalis and Nathan. Canalis, however, is scarcely presented to us in any light except that of his social activities. And Mlle des Touches' tragedy in *Béatrix* is more the tragedy of a woman plain and simple than that of a writer. In *Une Fille d'Eve*, on the other hand, we see Nathan fully immersed in his professional activities, and the second part of *Illusions perdues* gives us a picture of a d'Arthez entirely devoted to his calling. So that we have two writers whose words and actions are a direct product of their professional functions. Each is the leader of one of the two currents that Balzac distinguishes in the literary world. On the one hand, the honest members of the Cénacle; on the other, the good-time scribblers who appear at rowdy suppers with actresses. Two opposing conceptions of life. Opposing but contiguous. Nathan's frivolous world is not merely the reverse side of Daniel's serious world; it also constitutes its temptation. Rubempré moves from the one into the other without even being aware that he has done so. D'Arthez is a friend of Bianchon's, who is a friend of Lousteau's, who is Florine's lover. If we discuss the first member of this chain we are inevitably led, by imperceptible degrees, to a consideration of the fourth also.

A SUPPER AT CORALIE'S *or*
THE WORLD OF PLEASURE IN 1821

Etienne Lousteau, Raoul Nathan, Florine, Andoche Finot,
Florentine, Mariette, Tullia, Jean-François du Bruel, Suzanne
du Val Noble, Hector Merlin, Théodore Gaillard, Emile Blondet,
Claude Vignon, Félicien Vernou and Jean-Jacques Bixiou

Oh, the number of suppers there are in the *Comédie humaine!* The number of parties that go on until dawn! Where would you like to go? To see Florine, in her drawing-room with its yellow silk walls and brown trimmings? (*Illusions perdues*, p.727). Or would you rather visit Coralie on the Rue de Vendôme? There's a party at her place tonight (*id*. pp. 801 and 809). It's on Lucien. We shall meet Dauriat the bookseller there, Matifat the pharmacist with Florine, whom he keeps, as well as Lousteau whom Florine keeps; Papa Cardot, his Florentine and his son-in-law Camusot, Finot, Nathan, Merlin and Suzanne du Val Noble, Philippe Bridau who is Joseph's brother, Tullia and Bixiou, du Bruel and Mariette. And, extraordinarily enough, three members of the Cénacle.

Étienne Lousteau

This Lousteau is one of the most odious characters in the whole of the *Comédie humaine*. Not that he has ever killed anyone. It's even worse than that. Lousteau is one of those men who kill people's souls. "There is no Didine any more. You killed her, my friend," his mistress Dinah de la Baudraye says to him (*Muse du Département*, p.197).

Born in 1799, this Etienne Lousteau is the son of the subdelegate Lousteau who was forced to leave Issoudun after a quarrel with Docteur Rouget (*Rabouilleuse*). Having settled in Sancerre, the subdelegate married someone or other and died in 1800. Lousteau is therefore yet another orphan.

Do you remember Lucien de Rubempré? Lousteau, in the beginning, was another Lucien. "I see myself in you as I used to be," he says to the hero of *les Illusions perdues* (p.681). "Like Lucien, Etienne had come up to the capital from his country town . . . his tragedy in his pocket, drawn there by the same baits as Lucien: fame, power, money" (*id*. p.634). But he soon sinks into the bog of journalism. When Lucien meets him, his "handsome face was already withered, and one could see how the death of his hopes had wearied his brow" (*id*. p.634). He has become the journalist who can serve up his copy in any sauce you like, able to write anything required of him quickly, but with an equal lack of conviction and competence, indispensable because he always has a little paragraph up his sleeve that he can produce at the last moment. "Such paragraphs are committed like crimes, in the middle of the night" (*Monographie de la Presse*). He will turn anything into a commodity for financial gain; sells his free theater tickets and his privileges as a member of the press; writes fliers for beauty products; and in this way makes fifty crowns a month. One only has to listen to the lecture he gives Lucien on the subject of writing in general. Everything is corruption! exclaims this St. John Chrysostom of the cheap prospectus. Literature is a hell, and I am one of the damned. For he is still capable of such despairing cries. A lament still rises occasionally from the depths of this dishonor into which he has fallen. Though even these soon cease. Lousteau has already sold his soul. He has already reached that point when a man is no longer content to be corrupt himself, when he must drag others down with him. From the convert to the apostle, from the damned soul to the demon is but one short step. Lousteau's words, Balzac tells us, "Fell like an avalanche of snow into Lucien's heart and froze it with an icy cold" (*Illusions perdues*, p.682). It is the cold produced in human beings by the proximity of Satan. Lousteau takes on the role of Lucien's Mephistopheles. And indeed, he has all that spirit's characteristics, including his willingness to please. He conceives a sort of friendship for Lucien and constitutes himself the young man's guide through the labyrinth of literary corruption. At this period he is the fancy-man of Florine, who is being kept in her turn by "a druggist who gives himself the airs of a lord" (*id*. p.679). When he isn't sleeping at Florine's apartment he camps out in a wretched little room on the Rue de la Harpe.

As he grows older, Lousteau merely sinks deeper and deeper into this life of unresisting corruption so pleasing to the Evil One. The narrow-minded devil, as Sologoub puts it. In about 1830, for a consideration of one thousand francs, Lousteau also takes on the job of continuing the process of corruption in Philippe de Bridau's wife (*Rabouilleuse*, p.1110). A more ignoble task would be hard to imagine; but as I have said, Lousteau is a man who kills people's souls. In 1836, he is managing to earn seven or eight hundred francs a month "a sum that the prodigality so often found in poor people rendered insufficient. So that Lousteau still found himself as poverty-stricken then as at the time of his arrival in Paris" (*Muse du Département*, p.152). During this period, we find him living on the Rue des Martyrs, the preferred neighborhood of the courtesans who are still his daily companions. Florine has been stolen from him by Nathan, but he has fallen back on Mme Schontz, "a woman pretty enough to be able to sell the usufruct of her beauty at a very high price while still keeping the unencumbered property for Lousteau's use" (*id.* p.153). At thirty-seven he is still the fancy-man, the preferred lover. But what does age have to do with the matter? What else does a woman like that want from her chosen lover except the knowledge that with him at least she need not pretend? She simply wants someone with whom she can be herself. The gentleman's apathy is all part of the pleasure. When he has nothing better to do, Lousteau also pays his attentions to a marquise, "a woman somewhat free of her person" (*id.* p.154). He does work for three or four newspapers "but don't worry, there was no artistic conscience in any of his work for them" (*id.* p.151). His pen is still on hire to anyone who will pay for it. And not only his pen. He does not turn a hair, he does not so much as raise an eyebrow when Mme Schontz suggests that he should marry a certain lawyer's daughter, a girl with a good dowry but also somewhat pregnant. "Having at first attempted to deceive himself with an inward display of scruples, by next morning Lousteau had reached the stage of feeling apprehensive lest this marriage should fall through" (*id.* p.157). You see what sort of a creature he is. A villain without the courage of his crimes, a debauchee without the stature to carry it off, a criminal with the mentality of a petty pickpocket. As it turns out, the marriage is prevented by the sudden arrival in Paris of Mme de la Baudraye, whom Lousteau has seduced in the course of a visit to Sancerre. You are a father, she tells him. Bah! Lousteau replies. (I never grow tired of quoting that "bah!" There, in one word, and one that could hardly be shorter, we have the whole character, the whole man with his hidden recesses, his winding corridors, his murky depths.) At first, he tries to get rid of Dinah with a series of farcical tricks. Lousteau adores practical jokes. And he is also a born liar. "Your cousin is *the author of the manuscript farce,*" he says to young Boirouge (*Muse du Département*, p.146). An utter lie. And what admirable italics. I have long considered the use of italics an unjustly neglected stylistic device. Vallès often puts it to very happy use. Balzac too. Another writer would have taken up ten lines explaining Lousteau's lie. Balzac accomplishes all that simply by using italics.

Bogged down in a morass of lies, his marriage plans gone by the board, Lousteau finally perceives that it might prove to his advantage to keep Mme de la Baudraye. So he keeps her, makes their liaison as public as possible and even pushes the scandal as far as personally sending out announcements of their child's birth. Needless to say, he doesn't take long to grow tired of his Didine. He is unfaithful to her, or at any rate neglects her. She leaves him. Later on he seeks her out again to ask her for money. She gives him some. And extends her generosity to other spheres.

What happens then? *La Muse du Département* ends in a flurry of panic, excellently done, swift, staccato, but in which everything is nevertheless not quite clear. Didine goes back to Sancerre. A sudden fit of pride? Strong-arm measures on the part of her mother? Some new piece of villainy committed by Lousteau? And why, despite the spare, swift tone of the narrative, does Balzac bother to mention the tutor that Didine takes with her? It seems very unlikely that this tutor could be Lousteau.

We meet Lousteau once again in *les Comédiens sans le savoir*. He has become co-manager of a theater.

The incident of Lousteau's announcing his child's birth is borrowed from the biography of Jules Janin. For the rest, he owes a great many of his character traits to Jules Sandeau, a second-rate writer whose fame rests mainly on the fact that Georges Sand loved him enough to pay him the tribute of borrowing the first half of his name—whereas Balzac, on Lousteau's behalf, borrowed the last half. Well, that's how it is: fame can't always come all at once. Balzac knew Sandeau well and indeed employed him, for a time, as his secretary. Moreover, in reading Sandeau's work one discovers a certain kinship with that of his great employer. The kinship is a distant one, needless to say, about as distant as the one between my pipe and Vesuvius. It was through Sandeau that Balzac came to know Mme Marbouty, the provincial blue-stocking who was probably the inspiration for Mme de la Baudraye. And I should also like to quote here a passage from one of Sandeau's stories entitled *Hélène Vaillant*. It is about a village poetess who comes up to Paris to seek literary fame. "I explained literary life to her," the narrator tells us. "I pointed out the reefs and shallows lying in wait, I attempted to prove to her that she was living in a fool's paradise in every respect; I was hard with her, pitiless . . . The future betrays us (I told her), fame escapes us; we can count ourselves fortunate if our talents do not lead us into poverty and hunger." Wouldn't you believe that was Lousteau talking to Lucien?

Raoul Nathan

Lousteau has talent, but it is a talent without breadth, a talent that is never applied, one that could only have come to anything by means of hard work and probity. Idle and dishonest, Lousteau becomes completely worthless. Nathan is made of sterner stuff. He too is a failure, as Balzac points out, in the sense that he does not give the full measure of which he is capable. But what he does give has its worth. The disorder of his life lays waste his character, but there are some beautiful fragments left standing. In 1821, Lucien is already talking of Nathan as a god. And Balzac tells us that he had just published a magnificent novel (*Illusions perdues*, p.698 and p.699). "If this man is a genius . . ." (*Fille d'Eve*, p.96). The clause is conditional, but the fact remains that people don't go around asking questions like that about just anyone. Lousteau is an idler. Nathan is a worker. A worker without perseverance and without method, needless to say, but nevertheless capable of spending six nights in a row slaving away at a novel. In *Une Fille d'Eve*, we see him killing himself at his work. And his output is considerable. He collaborates with du Bruel on one play, with Marie-Gaston on another and has a third put on that is all his own work (*Illusions perdues*, p.724; *Mémoires de deux Jeunes Mariées*, p.317; *Muse du Département*, p.171). He writes the theater column for *La Gazette* (*Illusions perdues*, p.707). And besides the novel mentioned in *Illusions perdues*, he also publishes another entitled *la Perle de Dol* (*Envers de l'Histoire contemporaine*, p.386). I repeat, he is an entirely different kettle of fish from Lousteau. The latter is never offered anything more than the editorship of a rather insignificant little paper. Nathan, on the other hand, is offered control of one of the large dailies. He also visits Mme d'Espard and Mme de Rochefide in their homes; whereas Lousteau would never be allowed to set foot in them. And Nathan is on friendly terms with Canalis and Blondet, both of whom occupy positions of some eminence (*Béatrix*, p.540; *Paysans*, p.13).

And all this Nathan has achieved by means of hard work, by the strength of his own right arm, without outside help, without patrons, without family connections. For Nathan is the son of a Jewish second-hand dealer who died bankrupt (*Fille d'Eve*, p.118). There boils in his veins the adulterated but genuine power of those exotic immigrants, those Jews from Tangiers, those refugees from the Levant who pour into Paris trailing behind them the violence of some Moroccan grandfather, the sober mental habits of an uncle steeped in the Talmud, the rudimentary cunning of an aged Syrian great-great-grandmother. He is a man perpetually on the brink of starting a newspaper, his head bursting with ideas, his pockets bursting with paper, always in a hurry, always late, excitable, vehement, mocking, tossing off works as he goes that are always gripping at the moment and almost always ephemeral. Bernstein must have been rather like that. And Nathan, like Bernstein, is above all a man of the theater. Of all the literary genres, the drama, it seems to me, is the one least conducive to spiritual composure. Once the play has been written, there are the actors to be chosen, contracts to be signed, sets to be made, a whole brouhaha. And Nathan loves excitement of this sort. He is one of those writers who are excited by such distractions rather than put off by them, whose best lines come to them in the excitement of rehearsals, surrounded by the noise of other people talking. In society, he is dazzling. Listen to him telling the story of La Palférine's life in *Un Prince de la Bohème*. The brilliance of it is enough to make your head spin. It doesn't do to dig too deeply though. Because there's nothing underneath. This, according to Balzac, is the man's defect, his limitation: Nathan works, but he has never thought out what it is he is writing. He works, but without any particular goal in view, without a sense of direction. Let us complete the sentence I half quoted above: "If this man is a genius, he has neither the constancy nor the patience that should accompany genius" (*Fille d'Eve*, p.96). "Neither the constancy nor the patience that should accompany genius." These words should be underlined. Genius is tireless patience. If it is too swift, then it dissipates itself, crumbles and becomes something dangerously close to dishonesty. Nathan is dishonest. There are rumors that he employs ghost writers (*Peau de Chagrin*, p.56). And he ends up living wholly in the world of pleasure, where he is surrounded by the same fecklessness, the same disorder and lack of restraint that form the foundations of his own character. In 1823, he steals Florine from Lousteau. This relationship is still going on in 1836. And everything seems to indicate that in the interim Florine has continued to be kept by a succession of assorted noblemen. We ought not to blame Nathan too much for this. Principles, passions—all that sort of thing is just tossed about pell mell on the surface of his agitated soul. Given a certain fundamental disorder in a life, the notions of good and bad soon lose any definition of outline. Nathan, I am quite sure, has never stopped to balance his books in this respect. How then can he be expected to start auditing his mistress's? He is an honest charlatan, Mlle des Touches tells us. One of those men who "lie to themselves" and who "practice their dishonest trade with a sort of innocence" (*Béatrix*, p.399). It is the innocence of the man who has absolutely no grasp on life, the innocence of the man who is unable to see any further than the end of his own nose. And if Nathan ends up living more at Florine's than in his own apartment, that too is simply a matter of feck-lessness, simply a product of the fundamental disorder of his life. He is a member of a nomadic race. Tent or caravan, Escurial or Florine, it doesn't matter to him. As long as he has a warm fire and his ream of paper, he cares very little about anything else. Soap and a towel? What for? Nathan doesn't go in very much for washing. If you want to see him wash his hands you'll have to wait until he falls in love with his comtesse (*Une Fille d'Eve*, p.117).

The comtesse is Marie de Vandenesse. Nathan falls in love with her because he "has absolutely no idea what a comtesse's love looks like" (*id.* p.95). And she falls in love with him because she is tired of her husband Félix's relentless perfection. There is nothing perfect about Nathan. His hair is greasy and badly combed, his clothes are always frayed, he has legs like a heron, he is barrel-chested, and his hands are like the pincers of a crab. "His ravaged, dilapidated face gives him an air of having been de-feated in a struggle against angels or devils" (*id.* p.86). And note that this relationship, despite the oddness of the motives on both sides, has nothing base about it. The incidents described are sometimes very touching, and there is no point at which Nathan does not inspire our sympathy. Never-theless, the relationship does not develop into an affair. Nathan marries Florine, goes over to the Establishment, and takes refuge in a sinecure "like any mediocrity" (*id.* p.168).

Tradition has it that Nathan is derived to a large extent from Léon Gozlan, also a native of la Canebière, a successful novelist of the day of whose work nothing is ever read now but his two little volumes of mem-oirs relating to Balzac. They are purely anecdotal works, without preten-sions but not without significance. I have read one of his other works: *la Clef de Cristal*. It's not very good. The plot is rather complicated and the writing heavy-handed.

Florine

This Florine, who provides the link between Lousteau and Nathan, is one of the great demi-mondaines of that time. "In those days, Florine, Floren-tine, Tullia, Coralie and Mariette were like the thumb and four fingers of a hand" (*Muse du Département*, p.157).

Born in 1805 and registered under the name of Sophie Grignoult, Flo-rine began her career as a walk-on at the Gaîté. She then moved on to the

Théâtre Madame (*Eugénie Grandet*, p.596) and was eventually offered an engagement at the Panorama Dramatique. It is at this point that she becomes the mistress of both the druggist Matifat and Lousteau, the latter being, so Balzac informs us, her seventh lover. And she's only seventeen! The list of lovers imputed to her includes: a banker from Saumur, M. des Grassins, the Marquis du Rouvre, du Bruel, Lord Dudley and Désiré Minoret (*Eugénie Grandet*, p.596; *Fausse Maîtresse*, p.11; *Rabouilleuse*, p.1093; *Ursule Mirouët*, p.306). Moreover, Florine has a good bite on her. Des Grassins and du Rouvre have both completely ruined themselves trying to keep her. As for Matifat, she costs him sixty thousand francs over a period of eleven months. As a result, if you go to visit her on the Rue de Hauteville you will think you're at the Rothschilds': yellow drawing-room, violet bedroom, a ceiling hung in white cashmere . . .

At the time of our supper at Coralie's, Florine is a thin, tantalizing, tart-tongued girl. Since she is completely devoid of all scruples, she does not hesitate to become an accomplice to a little blackmail plot being hatched against her Matifat. And since she is also very shrewd, despite her ignorance, since her calculations are always correct to the last centime despite the fact that she can only count on her fingers, it does not take her long to see that Nathan can do more for her than Lousteau. So she takes him. And as usual her calculations are correct. Thanks to Nathan, she becomes a star, and it is apropos of her that Balzac paints us a picture of the life of a star that is still true today (*Une Fille d'Eve*, pp. 106 and 107). By this time she has thickened physically; but it suits her. A magnificent neck, Balzac comments after 1830, a round, willful head, eyes like a gazelle's, but glinting with the cold, malicious mockery of the courtesan. The chin is a shade heavy, an indication of "amorous violence" (*id.* p.104). In the end, she marries Nathan.

Andoche Finot

Andoche Finot is one of those journalists who never actually write anything, who get others to do the writing, the manager of a newspaper, an exploiter of others' thoughts, the man who launches things, who gets things going, who has his nose always to the wind. It's a profession there's something to be said for; whether you end up a creator or a pimp depends on the way you set about it. Finot belongs to the pimp variety. The son of a hatter, he runs his newspaper as though it's a hatshop. His stupidity is stupefying. One only has to watch him, in *la Maison Nucingen*, when confronted with opponents of any wit. They all laugh him to scorn. But

Finot lets them mock on. Once they've run out of puns, these witty people, they'll offer him articles for a hundred francs that will bring him in a thousand. That's his particular talent. An expert at moral blackmail, "prepared to crawl to anyone who could be of use to him . . . arrogant with those he no longer needed" (*Maison Nucingen*, p.593), occasionally grateful, but only out of self-interest, as deficient in scruples as he is in the ability to spell, he has a finger in every pie there is, in Society as well as in the demi-monde, in the ministries as well as in the theaters. "I've sent the Opéra my ultimatum," he says (*Illusions perdues*, p.714). He has some mysterious bond with des Lupeaulx, the secretary to the Treasury. In *les Illusions perdues*, (p.852), they join forces to bring down Lucien. In *les Employés* (p.1019), des Lupeaulx passes on some secret information to him, and Finot wittily replies: "Hi, hi, hi." There are some secret funds somewhere that Finot is able to nibble at, that I'd stake my last cent on. In 1820 or so, he was on his uppers (*Illusions perdues*, p.718). Shortly after 1830 he has an income of thirty thousand *livres,* and there is some question of his being made a peer (*Illustre Gaudissart*, p.20). In 1840, he is referred to as "an extremely rich man" (*Béatrix*, p.582). There was a short period when he had his eyes on Mme Schontz.

It should be noted that, in his youth, Finot had literary ambitions. He wrote a "one-act comedy" that Gaudissart thinks is superb (*César Birotteau*, p.423). He also covered the little theaters for *le Courrier des Spectacles*. And he is the author of one very fine piece: the prospectus for César Birotteau's "cephalic oil." In those days he was "a heavily built, rather chubby young man," with a "Kalmuk" face, usually pompous in his manner. "He was beginning at that time to recognize the fact that he possessed no literary talent whatever; but it occurred to him that he could remain in the literary world as an exploiter, climb up on the shoulders of the fellows who had the wit and turn to signing profitable business contracts rather than continuing to write badly paid copy or books" (*id.* p.438).

It is by Finot's newspaper that Lucien is engaged when he first enters journalism. And it is Finot's paper again that provides employment for Giroudeau and Philippe Bridau, two ex-officers of Napoleon's army whom I shall discuss later on. As for Cardot and Camusot, the latter being Finot's son-in-law (and also, in his turn, the father-in-law of Mme Camusot de Marville), they are both silk merchants, the former retired, the latter still in business. The son-in-law keeps Coralie, who is unfaithful to him with Lucien. The old man keeps Florentine, who is unfaithful to him with Giroudeau. The wild life does rather lack variety.

Florentine

We must take care not to confuse Florentine with Florine. She is one stage lower in the social scale: merely a dancer at the Gaîté (*Un Début dans la Vie*, p.729). To make up for this, she has a mother whom she trails around with her as a chaperone. Florentine's maiden name is Cabirolles, and Georges Marest refers to her as the Marquise de los Cabirollos (*id.* p.720). She is as common as it's possible to be and what she really loves is a good belly laugh. *Maie Laurt Querdotte* she says when referring to her aging lover (my Lord Cardot). And in exchange for her facetiousness Cardot gives her five hundred francs a month and buys up all Coralie's furnishings for her (*Illusions perdues*, pp. 726 and 841). This liaison has been going on for a long time, and Florentine eases the tedium of it by sleeping concurrently with Giroudeau, Finot's uncle. She also enjoys the company of Georges Marest. They both have a humorous turn of phrase and must have had some good times together occasionally. She's a good-hearted girl too, and generous. When young Husson loses the five hundred francs his employer has entrusted to him, she does her best to get him out of the scrape (*Un Début dans la Vie*, p.731). In 1840, she is still being mentioned as a well-known courtesan (*Béatrix*, p.575).

Mariette

Florentine is the dancer who does the splits and wears ostrich feathers. Mariette Godeschal, on the other hand, is a virtuoso of the *entrechat* and the *jeté-battu*. Trained by Vestris (*Rabouilleuse*, p.887), she is a serious girl, and kept by the Duc de Maufrigneuse, who is not much of a joker either. She is unfaithful to him with Philippe Bridau, but without losing her head about it. "I'm more fortunate than your brother Philippe, who doesn't know how to manage Mariette," Lucien says (*Illusions perdues*, p.803). She does occasionally appear at Florine's, or at one of the other demi-mondaine's, but I very much suspect that she prefers the nice quiet evenings she spends in the company of her brother, the upright Godeschal, the model clerk. They live together, in a little apartment on the Rue Vieille-du-Temple. In the evening, she knits, I imagine, while he smokes his pipe. She tells him about her duke. He tells him about his boss. They are both honest, hard-working folk. And they do well for themselves. Godeschal becomes a solicitor, and Mariette one of "the most celebrated *premier sujets* at the Opéra" (*Cousin Pons*, p.737).

Tullia and du Bruel

Tullia is another *premier sujet* at the Opéra (*Rabouilleuse*, p.893). As early as 1822, she has already become a star. One can sense it. Her entrances, her way of speaking, everything about her indicates a woman who knows that her name is always at the top of the bill. Her real name is Claudine Chaffaroux. She is known to have an uncle, a big contractor who is mentioned in *les Petits Bourgeois*. Official lover: the Duc de Rhétoré. Preferred lover: du Bruel, whom she eventually marries. There are no flies on Tullia. What has Rhétoré to offer her? Furniture? That's not enough. Du Bruel brings her social standing and comfortable respectability. Tullia senses in him the same power that Florine perceived in Nathan. The power itself is of a strictly limited kind, but she feels that it is within hers to urge it into action. Du Bruel is a hard worker. And one who knows how to organize his life. He is a civil servant employed at one of the ministries (*Employés*, p.927), but all he does when he goes in to the office is write his vaudevilles. His work suffers, but on the other hand, thanks to him, the head of his office and *his lady* are always provided with a box on opening nights: an arrangement that makes everyone happy. He also writes criticism, which does him no harm as a playwright, and from time to time he comes out with an article that is of use to his ministry. As for his spare time—for he also has spare time—he spends that writing a novel dedicated to the Duc de Chaulieu, the father of the Duc de Rhétoré with whom he has a relationship . . . How shall I put it, what does one call the relationship that exists between two men who are both lovers to the same woman? We ought to have a word for it. To love the same body is not nothing, after all. But be that as it may, all this explains the patronage that du Bruel enjoys. Apart from his royalties and his salary, he receives "a Civil List pension of twelve hundred francs and eight hundred francs from the hundred thousand crowns voted by Parliament as an encouragement to the Arts" (*Employés*, p.929). Wasn't Tullia right to discern intelligence and resourcefulness there? Originally, he was Florine's lover, but later on swapped her for Tullia, who lives in the same house. He's not a fellow who's fond of big upsets in his life; just the sort to make a good husband. So Tullia marries him, and it is a move that turns out well for both of them. Tullia likes men who keep their eyes strictly ahead of them. And du Bruel never wavers in this respect. He is heavily built, fat and round (*id.* p.929). In appearance he is "partly bureaucrat, partly landowner and partly stockbroker" (*Illusions perdues*, p.710). They make a

perfect couple. One day, however, Tullia falls in love with La Palférine.
But such is the grace that surrounds this serious-minded couple that even
this affair turns to their greater glory. As a joke, La Palférine assures Tullia that he could never love any woman who was not a countess. Tullia
does not give up hope. She simply goes back home and without a moment's hesitation sets about the task of having du Bruel made a peer.
Moreover, she succeeds (see *Un Prince de la Bohème*).

Suzanne du Val Noble

With Suzanne du Val Noble we are entering the world of the whores
proper. Both Florine and Tullia still had alibis. The fact that they employ
their charms as a commodity of trade is at least partly concealed by the
tarlatan of the tutu, or by the froufrous of light comedy. Suzanne has no
alibi. She earns her living with her body, quite simply.

Charming Suzanne! I have a weakness for this tall, beautiful young
creature. There is something so open, so spontaneous about her. I can see
her still, walking through the streets of Alençon, in 1816, when she was
still a laundry-girl. It's a pretty profession, and one that leads naturally to
thoughts of pleasure. Do you remember Lantier, in *l'Assommoir*, languish-
ing in Gervaise's shop? How the girls laughed, how they held the hot
irons up to their cheeks, how they joked about Mme la Présidente's un-
mentionables? And occasionally one of them would go out into the town,
her basket under her arm, laughing at the old men who ogled her. That's
Suzanne; gay, bold, easy, lingering for a while sometimes to visit the Chevalier de Valois or du Bousquier. Pretty scenes. With just a hint of something repugnant in them too. Du Bousquier is worn out by past excesses; it
can't be a very pretty sight, watching him fondle our laundry-girl. Suzanne bears him some sort of grudge for it too, and convinces him that
one of his hard-won successes has made her pregnant. She is no more
pregnant than I am, needless to say. She simply wants to get a little nest-
egg together so that she can go and try her luck in Paris. "We're patriotic
folk," the Chevalier de Valois says to her, "we want to help France get her
money back out of our guests' pockets" (*Vieille Fille*, p.223). "Our
guests" being the Russians, the English and the Austrians occupying
France at that time. How little our expressions have changed. "Our
guests . . ." It might almost be 1940.

While on fire at the idea of leaving, in the very middle of all her preparations, Suzanne meets Athanase Granson and falls in love with him. But
this love is to have no sequel. Suzanne and Athanase are both already

caught up in their separate destinies. Paris is waiting for her. Suicide is lying in wait for him. On the surface, this little episode seems to serve no purpose. But it gives off that melancholy scent of loves that might have been. The tiniest tip of the scales, and everything might have been different. Athanase might have found something in that tall, fresh body to dissolve his despair. Perhaps Suzanne might not have left. The eagerness with which she falls in love reveals a tender heart, one little suited to a life of venal coquetry. There is justification for musing on what might have been.

Once in Paris—where she takes the name of Val Noble—Suzanne has several strings to her bow in no time at all. She has been endowed by nature with a "fresh, dazzling, well-fleshed," Norman beauty (*Vieille Fille*, p.220). The chin is a little common, but that kind of beauty has its admirers. A stockbroker, Jacques Falleix, sets her up in a superb apartment on the Rue Saint-Georges. "Behold the entails of a thousand and one nights," she comments when showing it off (*Illusions perdues*, p.823). For she has wit. "A touch of the mischievous malice of a monkey" (*Vieille Fille*, p.235). It is she who originates the charming herring joke, forerunner of all our present-day jokes about madmen. "Ah, there you are," Mme du Val Noble said, "it's the story of the herring, which is the most intriguing of all the fish."—"Why?"—"Ah, no one's ever been able to find out" (*Splendeurs*, p.903).

Apart from this M. Falleix—who lasts only a rather short while—I am not at all sure who can be keeping Suzanne. Balzac does tell us that she has influence with bankers and with some very high-born gentlemen, but he never mentions any names (*Illusions perdues*, p.823). She also looks very favorably upon two journalists, Merlin and Gaillard. And moreover she has her ups and downs. I told you she hadn't the requisite coolness of head to succeed in such a profession, didn't I? In *les Illusions perdues* (p.785) she gives a superb dinner. In *les Splendeurs* (p.902), she is on foot, and we hear her lament: "If only I had at least a hundred louis a year coming in! With a sum like that, my dear, one can retire to some little village or other and find someone to marry." You see, the girl's got no vocation at all. She is then reduced to "raising" a phony Englishman who turns out to be none other than the policeman Peyrade, and who only allows her five hundred francs a month. This episode takes place in 1830. Apart from this, Suzanne is also frequently mentioned simply by name (*Un Début dans la Vie*, p.729; *Rabouilleuse*, p.1110; *Fille d'Eve*, p.105; *Béatrix*, p.575; etc.). Apart from such glimpses, we don't meet her again until 1845. True to her genuine vocation, she has married in the meantime, and is now the wife of her former lover Théodore Gaillard. Despite her forty-five years she is still beautiful. We learn this from an exclamation made by Gazonal (*Comédiens sans le savoir*, p.20).

Hector Merlin

The law of compensation does exist. There is a period during which Suzanne du Val Noble, who is good through and through, has as her lover a man who is absolutely wicked. Hector Merlin is "a little dried-up man with pinched lips, possessed by a brooding, limitless ambition, overjoyed at all the evils occurring round about him, taking advantage of the quarrels he fomented, extremely witty, lacking in will-power, but compensated for this lack by the possession of that instinct which leads social climbers unerringly towards places lit by the dazzle of gold and power" (*Illusions perdues*, p.749). In this respect he is akin to Finot. He will stoop to anything. "I've seen him get down and pick up an editor's hat when it had fallen to the floor," Lousteau recounts (*id.* p.681). But all the affronts he has been forced to swallow have soured his stomach. Merlin is rancorous without reason, spiteful on principle. "If you are good-natured," he tells Lucien, "make yourself ill-natured . . . To make yourself loved, never leave your mistress without having made her cry a little" (*id.* p.750). One day, he learns, at the same time, that Lucien is ill and that his book isn't selling. "It was impossible to prevent Hector Merlin from going in to visit his dying friend; and he made him drain this bitter cup of *broth* drop by drop" (*id.* p.870). Unreasoning jealousy. Merlin is a political columnist. Lucien's successes cannot harm him in any way. But he likes to make people suffer. I can find no references to his subsequent career. Politically he is of the right wing.

Théodore Gaillard

Théodore Gaillard, who succeeds Merlin in the favors of Suzanne du Val Noble, is a less wicked man. He is not the kind to make a woman cry. Quite the contrary. One day, while walking on the Champs-Elysées with his mistress, he notices a stranger eyeing the latter's charms with great interest. He immediately does his best to facilitate their meeting (*Splendeurs*, p.847). A heart of gold, as you see. Yet it is not poverty that drives him to such excesses of understanding. For Gaillard is the editor of a government-controlled newspaper and undoubtedly has hidden sources of income. In *la Vieille Fille* (p.331), allusion is made to a protector of Suzanne's who, apprehensive of the vengeance of the Liberal party, comes to hide himself away, after the 1830 rising, in a village of the Orne. I imagine that this fugitive is our Théodore. When next we meet him, fifteen years or so later, he is the owner "of one of the most important political newspapers" (*Cousine Bette*, p.481) and happily married to Suzanne. "Théodore Gaillard, once a man of wit, had developed over the years into a stupid one as a result of always staying in the same circle . . . His principal amusement now consisted of larding his conversation with phrases borrowed from successful plays, which he pronounced with the intonations given to them by the famous actors who had originally spoken them. *What can I do for your lordships*, he would say, imitating Frédérick Lemaître. We've come *for some fun*, Léon would reply. *Whaaat, young felloooh* (Odry in *les Saltimabanques*)" (*Comédiens sans le savoir*, p.20).

Emile Blondet

Emile Blondet is the son of the Alençon magistrate who intervenes in *le Cabinet des Antiques*. The official son, that is. In fact, he is the issue of a long and touching relationship between Mme Blondet and a prefect. "Born in Alençon of an old judge and a prefect," as he puts it himself (*Paysans*, p.27). The judge-father is aware of the facts. "You, you were born a prefect," he says to his son (*Cabinet des Antiques*, p.463). There seems little doubt that this detail was taken by Balzac from the biography of his friend, the journalist Emile de Girardin, bastard son of the General Comte de Girardin and Mme Dupuy, the wife of a judge in the department of the Seine. Though the resemblance should not be pushed any further. There is nothing in common between the idle, frivolous Blondet and the hard-working, cold Girardin.

Having come up to Paris, where he enjoys the patronage not only of his real father but also that of Mme de Montcornet, his childhood sweetheart, Blondet, who is moreover extremely gifted, enters journalism very much through the front door. At the time of his debut he is already looked upon as "a master in the literary world" (*id*. p.435). In about 1820, he is already "one of the princes of criticism" (*Illusions perdues*, p.697). He is paid a hundred francs a column. Among the Lousteaus and the Merlins, he makes one think of those young princes who are made colonels at the age of thirty, then generals when they are only thirty-five. His manner suggests the same thing. He is pleasant enough, but inclined to be patronizing. He is always saying: "my dear fellow" or "my dear child." But we must not ignore the fact that there is more to this rapid rise to fame than influence.

Blondet has talent, a thousand times more talent than Lousteau. His mind is lively, brilliant, sensitive. To appreciate this, one need only read his letter to Nathan in *les Paysans*, or listen to his interpolations in *le Cabinet des Antiques*.

But this intelligence does not rest on a sound character; it is sapped, drained, limited by two serious defects. To begin with, Blondet is idle. "The idlest pen of our age" (*Paysans*, p.27). Secondly, he himself does not respect his intelligence. He has no vocation. You only have to hear him explaining to Lucien how it is possible to produce three different articles on the same subject all of which contradict the other two (*Illusions perdues*, pp. 790 to 792). It's a dazzling display. And as hollow as a conjuror's wand. "My dear fellow, in literature, every idea has its obverse side and its reverse side . . . Everything in the realm of thought is two-sided" (*id.* p.788 and p.789). He has no convictions. Blondet is a rhetorician, a juggler with words, a prostitute of the mind who sells his intelligence in much the same way as a Val Noble sells her body. His speeches sometimes remind one of Anatole France's M. Bergeret, or Proust's Brichot. There is a cultivated mind there, and ingenious ideas, but also an irony, a skepticism that robs the words of all substance. There is a difference, though: Brichot and Bergeret have their intellectual honesty to redeem them, whereas Blondet's intellect has become rotten. Though, curiously enough, this rottenness remains always confined to his mind and is never apparent in any of his actions. Though a veritable Regius Professor of rogueries, Blondet never indulges in any himself. In fact, he almost never manages to translate this dazzling intelligence, so miraculously trained to grasp the best as well as the worst, into action of any kind. He is one of those men whose astuteness is only applicable to others, who can give you a brilliant demonstration of how any given member of a government has come to make his mistakes, but who as soon as he becomes a member of the government himself makes even more mistakes than his colleagues. One of those men "whose ability to plan another man's success is limitless but who can do nothing to achieve it for themselves. An Aladdin who allows others to borrow his lamp" (*Splendeurs*, p.661). Intelligent as he is, Blondet still allows himself to be exploited by Finot. In *les Paysans* he even allows himself to be swindled by an old drunkard.

Pleasure-seeking, frivolous, inconsistent, a faithful disciple of Proust's all-powerful god Whogivesadam, Blondet has a need for the excitements provided by frivolous conversation, champagne and good food. And in consequence we meet him at all the suppers given for the Florines and Coralies. Though the company of these young ladies themselves does not interest him: Blondet is the faithful lover of Mme de Montcornet. But this idler takes pleasure in the emptiness of these festivities, in their languorous struggles to dissipate the encroaching darkness of remorse. Himself a prostitute of the mind, he finds his natural companions in those who prostitute their bodies.

Gifted, but without character or strength of will, Blondet is doomed to stagnation. In 1820, we see him as a young prince of journalism. He stands out from all the others. By 1830, he has already ceased to stand out. The others have caught up with him. In *les Illusions*, he is cited to Lucien as a model to emulate. In *Splendeurs*, it is Lucien who occupies the superior position, and Blondet who is the hanger-on. "But I'm not going to leave you," he said, "until you have paid off a sacred debt towards me. What about that little supper, eh?" (*Splendeurs*, p.663). He is on the way to becoming a sponger. "Why don't we have supper together!" (*Une Fille d' Eve*, p.94). It is usually Finot who pays the bill. Blondet has constituted himself his councilor, his toady, almost his fool. This is the role we see him in at the big supper in *la Maison Nucingen*. During the summer he goes away to rest (from what?) on the Montcornets' country estate (see *les Paysans*). Eventually he sinks into poverty, and since he is incapable of getting out of this hole himself, once again he has to wait until someone comes to his rescue. Montcornet dies in 1837 and his widow marries Blondet, who is appointed prefect. Fame, farewell!

Claude Vignon

What saves Blondet from despair is his fecklessness, his frivolity. Claude Vignon lacks these qualities. He is a tragic version of Blondet. Tragic because he is so lucid. Like Blondet, Vignon is an excessively gifted and excessively idle critic. But in one case this idleness is inborn; in the other it is the result of a profession. Vignon is more serious than Blondet, and there is a measure of respect in the portrait that Balzac gives us of him. Vignon believes in what he is doing, but Balzac, on the other hand, doesn't believe in it at all. Because Balzac just doesn't believe in criticism. For him, it is a literary genre of no interest, and certainly with no relation whatsoever to creative genius. It is an idea he comes back to quite often. For example, the painter Pierre Grassou can give excellent advice, but he will never paint anything but mediocre pictures. He resembles, Balzac tells us, "those newspaper critics who are incapable of writing books themselves but who know exactly what is wrong with other people's books" (*Pierre Grassou*, p.122). Steinbock gives up sculpture to become a critic "like all ineffective artists who have concealed their impotence at first" (*Cousine Bette*, p.522). "Inside every critic," Balzac also writes, "there is a failed author. Since he hasn't the power to create himself, the critic stays on in the harem as a eunuch" (*Monographie de la Presse Parisienne*). As we know, Balzac was not unduly favored by the critics of his own time. Hence the tone of bitterness perhaps. In *Splendeurs* (p.680), he even goes so far as to draw a parallel between the critic and the prostitute, both of whom, according to Balzac, have reached a state of indifference, the one to books and the other to men, engendered by excessive familiarity. It is the trade, he writes in *la Muse du Département* (p.178), "best suited to idle minds, to those who lack the sublime faculty of imagination, or who, if they do possess it, do not also have the courage to cultivate it." I know that he is referring to Lousteau here, and that he makes a distinction in this very same passage between two sorts of critics. But who is it he cites as his example of the better sort? Why Vignon! And what is Vignon? An honest, good man. A man not only intelligent but also high-minded. Yet ineffectual all the same. Made impotent by his pursuit of the critic's profession, because he is not a critic. "Criticism is fatal to the critic" (*Muse du Département*, p.177).

Yet Claude Vignon was gifted, he is highly educated, he is even a university man (and there are very few of them in the *Comédie humaine*) and has been a teacher of Greek. But what vitiates all this, according to Balzac, is the man's excess of critical sense. Just as Louise de Chaulieu annihilates herself by the absoluteness of her love, so Claude Vignon annihilates himself with the absoluteness of his own critical faculty. "Attacked by doubt as soon as there is any question of creating anything, he sees all the obstacles without being ravished by the possible beauties, and having expended all his energy discussing the means, he is left exhausted and empty-handed . . . He is the Turk of intellect . . . Criticism is his opium . . . He dissects the thought of others without purpose, without method; his criticism is a pickaxe capable only of perpetual demolition, never of construction" (*Béatrix*, p.404 and p.403). And he too, drawn by some mysterious sympathetic vibration, finds his natural environment in the world of debauchery. He is taken out of it by Mlle des Touches, who makes him her lover and carries him off with her, first to Italy (*Honorine*), and later to her home in Guérande (*Béatrix*). But even in the sphere of love, Vignon is destroyed, sapped, eroded by his critical sense. Because he is afraid of being made to look a fool, he expends his energy in sarcasm. He applies the same scorched-earth policy to his personal happiness as he does to his mind. Intelligence, when it is not harnessed to a useful purpose, can lay its possessor's life waste. When Vignon sees that his mistress is attracted to Calyste, far from opposing this attraction he encourages it. Yet he loves her. But hovering above that love, ever present, are his intelligence, his fear of being made to look a fool, his contempt for the blindness of passion, his thirst for lucidity and his curiosity, intellect's eldest daughter. He must be able to see things clearly. He is walking into an abyss, but he is aware of the fact. That is the difference between him and Blondet. He insists on knowing, on understanding. Even though he knows he will suffer for it.

For he does suffer. There is a note of bitterness in every word he speaks. Though he is not jealous, or envious, or spiteful. Vignon is incapable of a base sentiment. No, he suffers from never being able to escape from himself, from not being able to experience any emotion without immediately being aware of its true nature and its limits. He has been swallowed, gulped down alive by his own critical faculty. He watches himself living, passes judgment on what he sees, and in doing so stops himself living. Once he has lost Mlle des Touches, Vignon goes back to the life of debauchery and drunken parties. It is his only means of ridding himself at last of this abominable self-awareness. He often dines at Mme Schontz's (*Béatrix*, p.581). In about 1840, he is still only the Prince de Wissembourg's secretary (*Cousine Bette*, p.427). And he is one of the witnesses at Crevel's wedding to Valérie Marneffe. Men like this do exist, men who are perpetually fated to be witnesses of the world's vileness, and who use this fact as an excuse for entrenching themselves ever more firmly behind their ironic vision of the world. In 1845, Claude Vignon is a teacher, a librarian and a clerk of appeals. These occupations bring him in twenty thousand francs a year, which is not bad, but he's still a long way from Rastignac's three hundred thousand (*Comédiens sans le savoir*, p.26). I forgot to mention that he is tall, stoops slightly, has blue eyes and was modeled to a great extent on Gustave Planche.

Félicien Vernou

Félicien Vernou has become a critic in much the same way as some men become executioners: out of bitterness and hate. Look at him. Look at that "arrogant, disdainful" manner (*Illusions perdues*, p.756). What a surprise, after watching him in public, to visit his home and find him "in a dining room of the utmost vulgarity, hung with nasty, cheap, imitation brickwork wallpaper . . . decorated with aquatint engravings . . . sitting at a table opposite a woman too plain not to be his wife" (*id.* p.756). This is

Vernou's tragedy. The suppers at Coralie's, and then, waiting at home, this wife with the blotchy mauve cheeks. "That poor Vernou can't forgive us for his wife," Lousteau says (*id*. p.758). It is she who has turned him into this envious critic, this harsh-tongued, bitter journalist, seething with resentment, gnawed by inner rage. "If he were a bachelor . . . he'd be an optimist" (*id*. p.759). Unlike Blondet, he is a hard worker. But his talents are limited, his vision narrow. He can only write articles, nothing but articles. He is "incapable of conceiving a large-scale work" (*id*. p.759).

Jean-Jacques Bixiou

"Small of stature, but well proportioned, a delicate face that attracts attention because of a vague resemblance to Napoleon's, thin lips, straight, flat chin, auburn sidewhiskers, twenty-seven years old, fair complexion, piercing voice, sparkling eyes, there you have Bixiou" (*Employés*, p.940). Bixiou, pronounced Bisiou, Jean-Jacques Bixiou the caricaturist, the life and soul of every party, the joker without whom no celebration is complete.

He is the son of a soldier who was killed at Dresden and the grandson of old Mme Descoings in *la Rabouilleuse*. This makes him, though somewhat unofficially, a cousin of the two Bridau brothers. At a very early age he begins to cultivate the acquaintance of young ladies in the dancing profession, who obtain a post for him in one of the ministries. Little of his time there seems to be spent working. He plays practical jokes on his colleagues, alarms them with his idiotic behavior, batters them over the head with his witticisms, smears lard inside young Poiret's hat, and thereby reduces the poor fellow to a terrible state of anxiety lest he should have caught *the greasy fever, an illness peculiar to the province of Champagne* (*Employés*, p.950). Bixiou's wit is much like a mischievous monkey's, entirely without significance, inconsequential, dazzling when he is aroused, but fading at other times and leaving him "gloomy and sad in his own company, like most great comics" (*id*. p.941). This gloomy streak explains his assiduity in attending all the demi-monde suppers. Bixiou is another of those men who are afraid of solitude, who have a horror of calm and meditation, who never offer up an orison, as Maurras puts it, and who, in consequence, are incapable of creating anything. Bixiou is, in fact, a caricaturist. And caricature, in a way, is simply another form of criticism. Certainly Balzac views it with identical antipathy. But as a raconteur Bixiou is inimitable. Nothing of his subjects escapes him: voice, gestures, character, he captures it all. He is at his best in *la Maison Nucingen*. The act we see him do there is dazzling. But once again, his is an intelligence employed more for the purpose of tearing apart than for that of creation. His nature is of a corrosive, negative kind, and it eventually begins to corrode the man himself. " '*If that is what will make him happy, then so be it,*' he said in that plummy bass voice and with that middle-class pomposity that he imitates so well" (*Illusions perdues*, p.991). The model is easily recognized. It is Henri Monnier, the creator of Joseph Prudhomme gradually being devoured by his own creation, ending up by becoming as Prudhomme as his own character, unable to fight free of it, devoured by his own parody. Like Vignon, like Blondet, Bixiou is a prisoner. He can no longer escape from the farcical world he has created. This is a source of suffering to him, and in the long run his nature becomes soured. He is "furious at having expended so much wit without the slightest profit" (*Maison Nucingen*, p.593). "A hidden discontent sometimes became apparent in his speech" (*Employés*, p.941). His jokes become cruel and ill-tempered. A born actor, Bixiou loves to dress up in disguises; but whenever he does so it is always in order to play some unpleasant trick. In *la Rabouilleuse* (p.1113), he disguises himself as an old gentleman, pays a call on the Comte de Soulanges, and by dint of judicious slanders manages to break off Philippe Bridau's intended marriage. In *la Muse du Département* (p.164), he plays the role of the friend who tries to prevent Lousteau from ruining his future. And of all his disguises, this is the most far-fetched: Bixiou is nobody's friend. Even when he does a good deed he manages to do it spitefully. While he is rescuing Philippe Bridau's wife, he thinks of the annoyance this good deed will cause her bad husband, and this makes him exultant. "How delightful," he said, "to think up a good deed that will cause so much unpleasantness" (*Rabouilleuse*, p.1112). Later on, we find him still bringing pleasure to the nights of Héloïse Brisetout (*Cousin Pons*, p.737). Brisetout. The name is well chosen. Bixiou too breaks everything.

Also present at this supper at Coralie's are three delegates from the Cénacle: Michel Chrestien, Joseph Bridau and Fulgence Ridal. Not that they are in the habit of passing their evenings in such company. Far from it. They have come tonight with the intention of attempting to rescue Lucien. None of them is in any way prudish; though we notice that they silently disappear at the first opportunity. They have realized that their presence is serving no useful purpose, that Lucien is already lost. "They behave very oddly for Christians," Merlin comments. "They looked as

gloomy as men who've been condemned to death," Coralie adds later.
"No, as gloomy as judges condemning others," Lucien corrects her. (*Illusions perdues*, p.809). Judges, not of the courtesans, but of those frivolous
and dishonest writers, those mountebanks careless of the poisons they are
handling, those self-evaders, those pimps of Parnassus, those men who prefer the champagne that drags you down under the table to the bitter
sweets of the coffeepot that enables a man to keep on his feet. Lousteau,
Nathan, Vignon are so many anti-Arthez's, so many impure souls, so
many idlers, so many vocations destroyed by riotous living and now hur-
tling towards the abyss. For we must be careful to note that the antithesis
between these men and d'Arthez does not hinge on the matter of talent or
intelligence, but primarily on that of character. Nathan is in his way a
genius, Blondet and Vignon are both intelligent. But none of them has any
character or principles. Therefore they go to the wall. The only ones in
this group who succeed are the ones with least talent of all: Finot and du
Bruel. But even so, their success is only of the pettiest kind. Neither of
them is a creator. The only sense in which they can be called successful is
that they become rich. They leave no mark upon their age. Nathan and
Blondet could have left their mark. But the disorder of the one and the
idleness of the other cause them to fail even in the lower spheres of
achievement where the two mediocrities achieve success. Instead of the
fertile but slow creative process of literature, they opt for the swift successes of the journalist. And Balzac hates journalism. He has expressed his
opinions on the subject in a little work entitled *Monographie de la Presse
parisienne*. It should be read. For one thing, it contains some excellent
pieces of pastiche. Then, in the second part of *Illusions perdues*, Balzac
has provided us with illustrations for this *Monographie*. We are presented
with a cross-section of a newspaper. There is Finot the manager, Nathan
and Gaillard the directors, Lousteau the editor. Then the heads of the
various sections: Merlin for politics, Vignon and Blondet for literature,
Lucien for the theater. Then there is the caricaturist Bixiou. We even
have the treasurer (Philippe Bridau) and the head of publicity (Giroudeau). All of them rogues or buffoons. And it's not even a question of the
views they hold. As a general rule, these journalists are liberals. But Gaillard runs a royalist broadsheet and Merlin is center right. But as far as
Balzac's concerned, they're all tarred with the same brush. It's their profession he's got it in for. "Journalists fill me with horror," Fulgence Ridal
exclaims. "Journalism is a hell, an abyss of iniquities, of lies, of treachery"
(*Illusions perdues*, p.663). "Anyone who has ever dabbled in journalism,
or is still dabbling in it at the moment, is under the cruel necessity of

greeting men he despises, smiling at his worst enemy, coming to terms with the most putrid baseness . . . One grows accustomed to seeing people do wrong, to accepting it as part of life; then one begins to approve of it, and ends up doing wrong oneself" (*Splendeurs*, p.661). There can be no journalism, according to Balzac, without cliquishness, and being part of a clique "corrodes even the noblest souls: it eats away their pride, dries up the wellspring of great works and encourages spiritual laxity . . . This apparent goodfellowship that wins over the newcomers and is proof against no form of treachery, that stops at nothing and justifies everything, that cries out in indignation at a wound and then forgives it, is one of the distinctive characteristics of journalists" (*Fille d'Eve*, p.91).

In *Illusions perdues*, Balzac does, it is true, allude to a "serious and worthy" newspaper staffed by the members of the Cénacle (just as, in *la Muse du Département*, he spoke of a form of criticism that would be at once a science and a form of priesthood); but ought we to see anything more in this than a rhetorical precaution? Or is it that Balzac, like almost all novelists, never found much inspiration in perfection? Whatever the truth of the matter, this honest newspaper and this priestly criticism neither have more than a few lines allotted to them, whereas the deadly form of criticism and the dishonest newspaper occupy a hundred or so pages.

THE CENACLE

After the negative, the positive. After the shysters, the honest men, the studious men who work, who meditate on things, who concentrate their powers instead of dissipating them like the journalists. After the frivolous group, the serious group—the Cénacle.

It was visibly Balzac's intention to set these two groups one against the other, just as Jesus, in the parable, contrasts the behavior of the wise and foolish virgins. They are meant to counterbalance one another. Has he succeeded in this intention? That is another matter. For there is no denying the fact that the Nathan-Lousteau-Blondet group has a much greater role in the *Comédie humaine*, and is in itself much more interesting, than the seven members of the Cénacle. Eight if we include Louis Lambert, who very soon disappears from the scene. Numerically the balance seems even enough, since Nathan's gang is scarcely any larger. But Nathan has a whole novel devoted to him (*Une Fille d'Eve*), and Lousteau another (*La Muse du Département*). Rubempré the journalist takes up a good third of *les Illusions*. Bixiou, Vignon and Blondet all play important roles in *les Employés*, *Béatrix* and *les Paysans*. And what have we to set in the other scale? Of the seven members of the Cénacle, three are more or less non-existent. Collect together all the passages that concern Meyraux, Ridal and Giraud. You'll find that they barely make up four pages. Bianchon and Joseph Bridau are more important; but the first is a doctor and the second a painter. Michel Chrestien is principally a politician and does not, in any case, occupy a great deal of space. Louis Lambert sinks from view into insanity. Which leaves us with Daniel d'Arthez. A single writer with whom to confront, to counterbalance, Nathan, Blondet, Lousteau, Vignon, Vernou and their ilk. It seems rather inadequate.

Even without taking into account another factor, one that has nothing to do with numbers and is rather more difficult to define. Suppose that in one and the same novel we have stuck in a saint and a crook, a great man and a fool, a cabinet minister and a tinker. Their relative weight, for the reader, will depend not on their virtues, not on their intelligence, not on their social situation, but solely on what effect their actions have on the plot and on their success as fictional creations. In this respect, the meetings of the Cénacle, much more briefly described, and occasionally in rather too vague and idyllic a way, are less striking than the suppers in the demi-monde. It is the old, old argument—vice versus virtue. And no matter what one may say, there is much less to be said about virtue. D'Arthez is perfect. And he suffers from the disadvantage that must attend perfection: we know all there is to know about him very quickly. "Lovelace has a thousand forms," Balzac writes in his *Avant-Propos*. "For social corruption takes its colors from the different environments in which it develops. Clarisse, on the other hand, that beautiful portrait of passionate virtue, has a line of heartbreaking purity." Heartbreaking . . . The despairing cry of the novelist. In real life, and for the history of their age, the members of the Cénacle are without doubt a hundred times more interesting than all the Lousteaus of this world. In the *Comédie humaine* they are a hundred times less so.

Meyraux, Giraud and Ridal

In *Louis Lambert*, Meyraux appears as a young man interested in the unity of zoological forms. Having become a doctor, despite his chronic ill health, he dies in about 1832 "after having stirred up the celebrated argument between Cuvier and Geoffroy Saint-Hilaire" (*Illusions perdues*, p.653). This detail has been inserted as a means of lending the character importance. It does not suffice, nevertheless, to provide him with any real existence.

Although he is mentioned more often (*Rabouilleuse, Splendeurs, Cousine Bette*), Léon Giraud has scarcely any more reality. He is a very significant political philosopher, Balzac tells us. But he offers hardly any further details. We meet Giraud again in 1845, by which time he has become a deputy of the center left (*Comédiens sans le savoir*, p.55).

As for Fulgence Ridal, Balzac sees him as "one of the writers of our age most gifted with comic flair, a poet careless of fame, tossing only his most vulgar creations to the theatrical profession and keeping his best scenes hidden away in the seraglio of his brain for himself and for his friends" (*Illusions perdues*, p.653). He is a lover of good food, a skeptic, "as prolific and as idle as Rossini." Despite his membership in the Cénacle, he is not really pure. I can scent the seeds of corruption in him. So that we should not be astonished when we find him, twenty years later, sharing the managership of a theater with Lousteau (*Comédiens sans le savoir*, p.36).

Michel Chrestien

Michel Chrestien has more stature. Like Giraud, he is a politician. A politician with the energy of a Saint-Just, Balzac tells us (*Illusions perdues*, p.654). He is a republican, but we must take care, as d'Arthez makes clear, "not to take him for one of those republicans whose ideas are so limited that they would like to begin the Convention and the delights of the Committee of Public Safety all over again; no, Michel's dream was the principle of the Swiss Federation applied to the whole of Europe" (*Secrets de la Princesse de Cadignan*, p.31). He loves to sing. His voice is tuneful. And his remarks often to the point. "You know," he says to Rubempré, "you could be a great writer, but you'll never be anything but a petty trifler" (*Illusions perdues*, p.754). Of a generous nature, he is indulgent towards everything except the despicable kind of behavior that indicates baseness of soul. "If you were so unfortunate as to kill your mistress," he said, again to Rubempré, "I should help you cover up your crime and not feel obliged to withdraw my esteem; but if you became a spy, then I should shrink from you with horror" (*id.* p.664). And later on, when Rubempré writes his article about d'Arthez, Chrestien does in fact challenge him to a duel and wound him rather seriously (*id.* p.867).

"Michel Chrestien was an angel," d'Arthez says (*Secrets de la Princesse de Cadignan*, p.31). And everything fated him to fall in love with that mock angel, the Duchesse de Maufrigneuse. Though the love is platonic— that goes without saying. Michel never sees the Duchesse other than at a distance; but during the riots of 1830 he pushes aside a gun that has been sighted on the beloved's husband. He dies in 1832, killed in the riot at the monastery of Saint-Merry.

Joseph Bridau

The painter Joseph Bridau is known above all for his fine *Méphisto*, to which he alludes in *Ursule Mirouët* (p.433). He has also done a pretty portrait of Josépha (*Cousine Bette*, p.452) and a canvas depicting a young Venetian lady being introduced to a senator by a procuress.* His model for the young Venetian lady was Coralie. Coralie? Josépha? What's this? Is the upright Bridau a frequenter of courtesans? No. Though he does seem to lack the high-minded purity of a Daniel d'Arthez on this point. Bridau's youth was spent in painters' studios, and something of that world is still sometimes apparent in his manner. He sometimes uses slang, for example. (*Pierre Grassou*, p.128). He enjoys making a show of robust cynicism and is even prepared to go as far as playing practical jokes. On one occasion, while on a journey, he passes himself off as Schinner (*Un Début dans la Vie*).

All this is subordinated in Bridau to his talent, however, to the relentless sway exercised by his vocation. Though it is true that even here, for all his talent, we can discern some warning signs of that spiritual disorder which, in its extreme form, is the ruin of Nathan. Bridau never measures up to his full capabilities. In this sense he is to some extent a failure. Though a failure of considerable stature. "Were it not for the secret unhappiness to which he has been condemned by the excessive impressionability of his nature," Balzac tells us, "Joseph . . . could have continued the work of the great Italian masters . . . , but love kills him . . . shoots its arrows into his brain, upsets his life and causes him to make strange zigzags from his true course. If his mistress of the moment makes him either too happy or too wretched, Joseph will set before the public either sketches in which the drawing is coarsened and obliterated by the colors, or paintings . . . in which he has been so preoccupied with the drawing that color, having been left to take care of itself, is entirely lacking" (*Illusions perdues*, p.652). This disorder of mind is mirrored in his physiognomy. When Bridau arrives in Issodun his face makes a sensation. He looks like a macaw, people say. "He has the face of a brigand and the eyes of a basilisk . . . They say he has a curious appearance, frightening . . . He has deep eye-

---

* This painting does in fact exist. It is by Xavier Sigalon and is at present in the Louvre.

sockets like a horse and waves his arms about like a madman" (*Rabouil-leuse*, p.1001). Mme Hochon, more kindly disposed, exclaims: "He looks ill" (*id.* p.1000). In *Pierre Grassou*, he appalls the respectable Vervelles. "His hair was in the wildest disorder; he displayed his great ravaged face, darted his lightning gaze into every corner of the studio, then suddenly came back over to Grassou, bunching his topcoat up over his stomach" (*Pierre Grassou*, p.127). If it is true that Delacroix was in part the model for this character, then we should probably be right to picture Bridau as looking like the fine Delacroix self-portrait now in the Louvre. Also, I should add that this disorder I have mentioned is never revealed except in passing allusions. In *la Rabouilleuse*, a work in which he plays a leading role, Bridau appears on the contrary as a model son and man who leads a rather quiet life, despite all his liveliness of manner and his imaginative flights. His mistress of the moment . . . , Balzac writes in *les Illusions*. But I am totally incapable of giving you the name of a single one of them.

Joseph is the second son of Agathe Bridau, the widow of a highly placed civil servant under the Empire. Though somewhat neglected by his mother, who prefers her elder son, Joseph nevertheless stays with her, taking care of her and coddling her. He has a heart of gold. He could very easily reveal to his mother what a scoundrel her favorite really is: he does not do so. His brother steals his little savings from him: he does not tell. An ignorant cousin gives him some pictures without realizing how valuable they are: Joseph gives them back. Being honest, he is unsuccessful when it comes to intrigue. In *la Rabouilleuse* we see him fail where his brute of a brother succeeds triumphantly. In *Un Début dans la Vie* we see him at the beginning of his career as an artist, painting a dining room for the Comte de Sérizy. He is hard-working and demands a lot of himself. His reputation steadily increases. By 1840 he is famous. He has married a Mlle Léger, the daughter of a rich farmer, and he inherits the fine town house that his brother had acquired by dint of so much dishonesty (*Comédiens sans le savoir*, p.11).

Horace Bianchon

Horace Bianchon is another example of the curious optical illusions created by the recurrence of characters technique. At first glance, Bianchon seems to be one of the principal figures in the *Comédie humaine*. He is certainly one of the most well known. We have the feeling that we know every corner of his character intimately, that we have followed every step of his career, from the dining table at the Pension Vauquer where he eats

214] *THE CHARACTERS*

as a student, to the seat in the Institut that he occupies in middle age. But this is, in fact, purely an effect of perspective. Because we meet Bianchon so often we end up taking him for an old friend. In fact, we know rather little about him. Has he a relationship with a woman? I don't know. Has he ever been in love? Mystery. In *Autre Etude de Femme* (p.256), he confesses briefly to some vague affair with a girl who worked at an inn. As far as Bianchon's love life goes, that is all we are ever told. An allusion to Mme Rabourdin, in *l'Interdiction* . . . But even that is very vague.

Though very often mentioned (Bianchon appears or is named in twenty-four of the works in the *Comédie humaine*), he is never a principal character. Though we are always running into him, he is always overshadowed by someone else. By Desplein (*Messe de l'Athée*), by Rastignac (*Père Goriot, Etude de Femme, Interdiction*), by Lousteau (*Muse du Département*), by Daniel d'Arthez (*Illusions perdues*). He is to be found at every sickbed. He attends old Goriot, Lucien, Coralie, Mme Bridau, La Billardière in *les Employés*, Pierrette, Mme de Listomère in *Etude de Femme*, Nucingen, Lydie Peyrade and Mme de Sérizy in *les Splendeurs*, Honorine, Vanda de Mergi in *l'Envers de l'Histoire contemporaine*, Valentin in *la Peau de Chagrin*, Caroline Crochard in *Une Double Famille*, Mme du Bruel in *Un Prince de la Bohème*, Mme Graslin in *le Curé de Village*, Mme de la Baudraye in *la Muse du Département*, Laginski in *la Fausse Maîtresse*, Crevel and his wife in *la Cousine Bette*. But when we stand beside a sickbed it is the tortured face of the invalid that we look at, not the impassive, rather fat face of Bianchon. In fact, Bianchon is a bit-player. The most important, the number-one bit-player, but a bit-player all the same. He is the onlooker. The philosopher who comments on events. The confidant of classical tragedy. "The Pylades of more than one Orestes" (*Messe de l'Athée*, p.1152).

Born in Sancerre, the son of a doctor, Bianchon is introduced to us for the first time in *le Père Goriot*, at the Pension Vauquer where he takes his meals. At this period he is an intern in a hospital. When we meet him again, in *les Illusions perdues*, he is a member of the Cénacle and very friendly with Daniel d'Arthez. Bianchon is serious and hard-working. "As sober as a camel, as alert as a stag" (*Messe de l'Athée*, p.1152). He becomes a first-class doctor. But that is all. He never displays the extraordinary intuition of his teacher Desplein. Nor, on the other hand, does he have d'Arthez's frowning puritanism. "Neither a puritan nor a sermonizer" (*id*. p.1151). Bianchon is a good-hearted chap. In this respect he rather resembles Joseph Bridau. Perhaps there is something in the air of hospital wards, as in that of painters' studios, that has a relaxing effect on the principles, that makes a man somewhat more indulgent. Like Bridau again, Bianchon is by no means averse to a good joke. We see him indulging this weakness in *la Muse du Département*, and also in *César Birotteau* when, in all seriousness, he assures the perfume-maker that he puts hazelnut oil on his sidewhiskers. He's not starchy either. It's difficult to imagine d'Arthez taking even a modicum of pleasure in talking to Rastignac or Lousteau; but Bianchon is perfectly prepared to enjoy their company. It's probably a matter of curiosity. The spectacle offered by society interests him. Though modest in his own expectations, and perfectly disinterested, he nevertheless listens attentively to Rastignac's ambitious schemes and even pushes this complaisant attitude as far as giving him advice (see the beginning of *Interdiction*). Though honest, he nevertheless helps Lousteau in the latter's seduction of Mme de la Baudraye (*Muse du Département*). Bianchon is one of those men who will help perpetrate a shameful action rather than break the laws of comradeship. Unless there is also a sour streak in him somewhere that enables him to extract amusement from the sight of a Lousteau or a Rastignac doing violence to a society that he despises. There is a remark of his in *Interdiction* (p.16) that seems to give some grounds for this suspicion: "I hate those kinds of people," he says. "I long for a revolution that will free us of them forever."

In general, however, Bianchon appears to be just a good-hearted fellow, honest with himself, skeptical with others. "Ideas are something you can cure yourself of," he tells Rastignac. "How?" "By acting on them." (*Père Goriot*, p.960). In this same spirit, when consulted by Nucingen, he advises the banker to stop making such a song and dance and to sleep with Esther (*Splendeurs*). Lousteau amuses him; so he sees him. D'Arthez impresses him; so he is friendly with him. But it should be duly noted that he never dreams of trying to bring all his different friends together. This division of his relationships into watertight compartments—which is also to be found, for example, in the life of Proust—indicates that his choice of friends proceeds more from the intelligence than from the heart, that it is dictated by curiosity rather than by feeling. Perhaps one should not even use the term friendship. Bianchon is a spectator. And a spectator in a theater does not need to feel any esteem for the actors he goes to see. Bianchon does not need to feel esteem for Lousteau; it is enough that Lousteau should amuse him. And it is similarly noticeable that though, in his own words, he hates Society, he is constantly present at all its meetings. He loves big dinners and brilliant conversations over the port and the nuts. And he pays his own way with a little store of anecdotes, which he tells well. "The doctor had recounted this story in such gripping tones, his

gestures had been so picturesque and his diction so realistic . . ."
(*Oeuvres ébauchées*, p.1090). It is to him that we owe the famous anecdote about la Grande Bretèche, which he tells first in *Autre Etude de
Femme* and then again in *la Muse du Département*. And it is he too who
tells the little story that Balzac published under the title *Etude de Femme*.

Bianchon is "big and fat," he has "a patriarchal air, a great deal of long
hair, and a domed forehead" (*Muse du Département*, p.86). Through a
sister of his father's, who married the judge Popinot, he is connected to
the vast Parisian tribe of the Popinots, Camusots and Cardots. With the
exception of the judge, he does not frequent these connections, however. I
imagine he finds very little to amuse him in those middle-class homes.

Daniel d'Arthez

Born in 1794, Daniel d'Arthez is the product of a Picardy family about
which I know nothing whatever. All we ever hear about it is one allusion
to an uncle in *les Secrets de la Princesse de Cadignan* (p.24).

Entirely without wealth, but studious, Daniel d'Arthez spends his days
in the library of Sainte-Geneviève. He is "short, thin and pale" (*Illusions
perdues*, p.654), with black hair and a resemblance to the young Bonaparte. He drinks water and has a noble bearing. He is chaste and serious-
minded. Ambitious but good. Profoundly, actively good. He guesses what
straits Lucien de Rubempré is in and procures him two hundred francs (*id.*
p.658). He also takes the trouble to read his novel in manuscript, to revise
it for him and to provide it with a fine preface. Moreover, when he himself publishes a book in his turn and Lucien is called upon to tear it to
pieces, it is d'Arthez himself who writes the article. A saint in fact. He
presents us, as Balzac himself says, with "the perfect harmony of a fine
talent and a beautiful character" (*id.* p.647). Despite all Lucien's treachery, Daniel rushes to Coralie's deathbed (*id.* p.877). Then, for several
years, Balzac does not mention him again. All we know is that his fame is
growing, that he is working, that he is a deputy, that he is a right-winger,
that he has become slightly fat and that he is living with a woman who is
beautiful but vulgar. Then he enters into a liaison with the Princesse de
Cadignan (*Secrets de la Princesse de Cadignan*). And the last we hear is
that this liaison is still going on. Is d'Arthez a simpleton? I think not. At no
point do we ever hear him say anything stupid or naïve. But the generosity and elevation of his soul enable him to rise above certain ugly aspects
of the world. Such men do exist, men who are strong enough to eliminate,
at least from their own lives, the petty effects of fate. Yet all the same,

that so much virtue, so much seriousness, so much unswerving probity should all end up at the feet of the same mistress as Rubempré, and when she is ten years older too! It is an outcome that gives food for thought.

D'Arthez is to a large extent an idealized Balzac. He is undoubtedly a reflection of that image which every man holds in front of him. It is also probable that he owes a great deal to a friend of Balzac's named Jean Thomassy, a future magistrate and a serious-minded man.* But I believe he owes even more to Alfred de Vigny, whom Balzac knew very well early on in his career when, in his capacity as a printer, he was involved in the republication of *Cinq-Mars*. The conversations the two men had together at that time were doubtless similar to the ones between d'Arthez and Lucien. In an article in the *Correspondant* (July, 1931), M. Baldensperger gives us some very strange details on this subject. For example, in *les Secrets de la Princesse de Cadignan*, which was published in 1839, Balzac writes that d'Arthez has inherited his uncle's estate. And Vigny, the previous year, had inherited his father-in-law's fortune. Vigny, as is well known, was the lover of Marie Dorval, an actress famous above all for her parts in popular melodramas. In Balzac, she becomes D'Arthez's vulgar mistress. But this vulgar mistress is abandoned in favor of Mme de Cadignan. And M. Baldensperger quotes a letter in which there is mention of a mistress of de Vigny's who is described as being "a woman who moves in the best and highest society." Lastly, the author of the article makes an apposite comparison between a passage from Vigny's *Journal d'un poète* and another from the words of d'Arthez. "I give thanks to heaven," Vigny writes, "that this year has gone by like the others without any change in the independence of my character and the sylvan happiness of my life. I have done no man ill, and I have not written a single line against my own conscience or against any living being." And d'Arthez: "Is it not a viaticum to fortify the spirit, the knowledge that one can lay one's head on one's pillow at night and say: I have not passed judgment on the work of others, I have caused no man affliction, and my mind, like an unsullied dagger, has been plunged into no innocent soul?" (*Illusions perdues*, p.752). The words are different, but not the inspiration.

In creating the Cénacle, Balzac was obeying a belief in the value of conspiracy that, as I shall demonstrate elsewhere, is a constant factor in his work. In *la Comédie humaine*, the man who acts alone always fails. The only ones who succeed are those who have the backing of a group. Mar-

* J. L. Arrigon. *Les Débuts littéraires de Honoré de Balzac.*

say has his clique. D'Arthez has his Cénacle. But it still remains to be asked why Balzac decided to make this Cénacle such a patchwork of opposing personalities. It consists of seven young men. What is the bond that unites them? We have all known groups, coteries, societies and so on. But they were coteries of writers, groups of politicians, societies of doctors. Here, we have one writer, one farce writer, two politicians, one doctor, one naturalist and one painter. Odd. But perhaps they are linked by some political or religious conviction they all hold? No, that's not true either. "Daniel d'Arthez, a nobleman from Picardy, was equally as staunch in his support of the monarchy as Michel Chrestien in his advocacy of a European federation. Fulgence Ridal used to make fun of the philosophic beliefs held by Léon Giraud, who in his turn liked to predict the death of Christianity and family life to d'Arthez. While Michel Chrestien, who believed in the religion taught by Christ, the divine legislator of Equality, was forced to defend the immortality of the soul against Bianchon's scalpel" (*Illusions perdues*, p.654). As for Bridau, none of all that is of the slightest interest to him: "What does it matter whether it's Louis XVIII's bedbugs or Napoleon's cuckoo we have on our flags?" he asks (*Rabouilleuse*, p.908). Could it be mere chance that brought them together? Or the poverty they all share? I don't think so. Balzac intended this group as an example, a model. Which means that its odd composition was deliberate and purposeful. It means that for Balzac there exists a value superior to men's opinions and vocations, a value that is in itself sufficient to bring all these young men together. And this value is character, seriousness, self-respect. Each of these young men has a different vocation, but they all respect that vocation. None of them is prepared to use it for dishonest profit or prostitute it. That is the bond that unites them, and that is what makes them different from the Nathans and the Lousteaus. You would only have to introduce the smallest suggestion of baseness into each of their characters for the Cénacle to collapse. Each of its members would then go off to join those to whom he felt bound by the most commonplace ties of opinion or profession. The royalist d'Arthez would consort with the royalists Gaillard and Merlin. The painter Bridau would prefer the company of the caricaturist Bixiou to that of the doctor Bianchon. And the reason this does not in fact happen is precisely because, for them as for Balzac, it is character that matters above everything else. Opinions don't matter. At a certain level, all opinions look much alike. Nothing resembles a right-wing extremist quite so much as a left-wing extremist, and there will always be much more in common between an extremely able priest and an eminent atheist than between that same atheist and some backstreet freemason. This is an elementary truth that it has taken all the savagery of our age to make us forget. We have become barbarians. We allow opinions to divide us. Balzac, on the other hand, belonged to an epoch still civilized enough to be able to say: "It is from the conflict of characters and not from the collision of ideas that antipathies arise" (*Ursule Mirouët*, p. 287).

This disparity of vocations also has another justification and meaning. I shall demonstrate, when the occasions arises, how for Balzac friendship is a complementary sentiment that ought, at every turn, to provide an illustration for the fable of the cripple and the blind man. People in Balzac's world seek friends who will complement them, not reflect them. Look at Séchard and Lucien, Vautrin and Lucien, Louise de Chaulieu and Renée de l'Estorade. In each case we see a pair of beings each of whom tends to complete the other. D'Arthez, instead of frequenting other men of letters in whose company he could find echoes of his own thoughts, prefers to enrich his mind by seeing only scientists and politicians. And his world becomes that much larger. He does exactly the opposite of Théodore Gaillard who, Balzac tells us "became stupid in the end as a result of remaining always in the same circle" (*Comédiens sans le savoir*, p.20). There is an esthetic theory here: the writer, according to Balzac, should be, not someone in an ivory tower, not a bellelettriste, but a mind reaching out to take in the whole world. Hence the hours that d'Arthez spends studying in libraries. He "could not admit the existence of any exceptional talent without the possession of profound metaphysical knowledge . . . He wanted, like Molière, to be a profound philosopher before writing comedies" (*Illusions perdues*, p.650). Hence his tendency to surround himself with men who can replace these library studies with their conversation, who can initiate him into disciplines apparently quite unrelated to literature. He wants friends who will be a library in themselves. "That living encyclopedia," Balzac writes of the Cénacle. And d'Arthez uses this encyclopedia. When he revises Lucien's novel, he adds some "physiological observations no doubt provided by Bianchon" (*id.* p.751). This attitude is obviously Balzac's own, since he too inserts into his work remarks and comments on such subjects as medicine, architecture, art and town-planning, something that writers today almost never do, since literature has now become "pure," a mandarin art. For Balzac, a mind that does not strive to be universal lacks a sense of mission. For him, even the most eminent specialist cannot be a truly great man. As witness the celebrated Desplein. He is acknowledged to be the greatest surgeon of his day. But has he "that universality of knowledge that makes a man the *voice* or **the** *image* of his age? . . . Has he summed up the whole of science in his person as Hippocrates, Galen and Aristotle did? . . ." (*Messe de l'Athée*, p.1149). No, Balzac answers. And as a result his name has already been almost forgotten (*id.* p.1148).

PAINTING AND SCULPTURE

Pierre Grassou, Hippolyte Schinner, Théodore de Sommervieux, Léon de Lora, Dubourdieu, Ernest-Jean Sarrasine, Stidmann

Having just discussed Bridau, let me take this opportunity to say a few words about the other painters who occur in the *Comédie humaine*.

The difference between the writers of the Nathan type and Daniel d'Arthez resides above all, as I have pointed out, in character, not in talent. At the outset, Nathan is as gifted as d'Arthez. When Lucien moves on from Daniel to Lousteau, it is not a matter of exchanging intelligence for stupidity but of abandoning the belief in work for the cult of facility. In giving us the character of Pierre Grassou, Balzac immediately corrects the somewhat too summary character of that distinction. Pierre Grassou believes in work. He has courage and will-power. He shuts himself up in his studio for two months on end to paint. He lives on bread and nuts. He studies the great masters. He is willing to accept advice. He loves his trade. And one cannot help but love him for this perseverance. "The sufferings it cost him, and how he managed to live while he was studying, God only knows" (*Pierre Grassou*, p.117). Only, there it is, Grassou has no talent. And he never gets anywhere. So you see, a belief in hard work is not enough. "There is no such thing as a great talent without great will-power" Balzac writes in *la Muse du Département* (p.177). But the will-power on its own is not enough, and Grassou is there as a living proof of this fact. When Bridau goes to see Grassou in the latter's studio, we are at last shown mediocrity and genius in conflict, and this example is the only one in the entire *Comédie humaine*, since, I repeat, this particular conflict is never allowed to arise when Balzac confronts Bridau with Bixiou, or d'Arthez with Blondet. However, thanks to all his hard work, Grassou does manage to achieve a sort of success. His paintings sell. Though not for very high prices. He marries Virginie Vervelle, who is stupid but has a good heart and a lot of money. He paints portraits for the upper middle classes. Louis-Philippe commissions a battle picture from him for the museum at Versailles. And since Grassou has a most discerning taste, he also acquires a very good little private collection of excellent paintings. Other people's paintings, of course.

Hippolyte Schinner, on the other hand, is a great painter. Less fiery than Bridau, he is described as "a gentle, patient artist" (*Pierre Grassou*, p.117), whose paintings are highly thought of and who is always willing to give good advice. The illegitimate son of an Alsatian mother, in 1819 he marries Adélaïde de Rouville. This charming idyll is to be found in *la Bourse*. Schinner has a great many commissions. Among others, he decorates Esther's house on the Rue Saint-Georges and also the Laginskis' (*Splendeurs*, p.838; *Fausse Maîtresse*, p.16). In *les Petites Misères de la Vie conjugale*, we hear of a Baronne Schinner who is a hostess "famed for her wit, her influence and her wealth." I find it difficult to picture the timid Adélaïde holding sway over a salon, but twenty years can do quite a lot to change a woman.

Théodore de Sommervieux must be about the same age as Schinner. He is successful. And talented. But his talent is of a very quiet, very patient kind. He is the great specialist in chiaroscuro, famous for the sort of little paintings in which one admires the curtains, or the cat playing in one corner. He also does book illustration, and the vignettes in Canalis's volumes of poetry are his work (*Modeste Mignon*, p.400). Sommervieux is to be found in *la Maison du Chat-qui-pelote*. He marries the daughter of a cloth-merchant, Mlle Guillaume, a girl he adores, who adores him, and who soon bores him to such an extent that he turns to the Duchesse de Carigliano in the hope of a little distraction. He formerly lived on the Rue Taitbout. A noisy neighborhood for a painter.

Born of an old, noble, but poor Spanish family settled in Roussillon, Léon de Lora belongs to the next Balzacian generation. In *Un Début dans la Vie*, he is still no more than a little apprentice who accompanies Bridau and assists him in his work. He is referred to at that time as Mistigris. He has something nimble and lively about him that justifies this nickname. He adores puns. All of which does not prevent him from achieving success. Twenty years later, he has an income of twenty thousand francs a year. He still hasn't lost his sense of humor, and in *les Comédiens sans le savoir* we find him playing a practical joke on his cousin Gazonal. He is known as the white wolf. He is to be observed in the houses of Jenny Cadine (*id.*), Héloïse Brisetout (*Cousine Bette*) and Mme Schontz (*Béatrix*). In other words, we are a long way from the serious young men of the Cénacle. From Bridau to Léon de Lora there is more or less the same step down as from Maxime de Trailles to La Palférine. The new generation doesn't measure up to the old one. Is this an effect of the times? Is it that Louis-Philippe's reign was more commonplace than that of Charles X? Or is it that Balzac looks back on the characters he knew in his youth with more respect? Does he lend them a glamour that he refuses to the characters created in his maturity? I don't know. Though I am not, in any case, saying that Lora's paintings are mediocre. I've never seen any. But one does discern a frivolity, a hail-fellow-well-met quality in him that is, in general, incompatible with a very great talent. One could wish him just a touch of divine madness. He must be one of those painters who can turn their brushes to any use, the complete technician who takes advantage of people's snobberies and secretly pokes fun at the pearl-hung women whose portraits he paints. Before taking leave of him, I should add that in 1836 he accompanies Mlle des Touches and Vignon on their trip to Italy (*Honorine*).

Dubourdieu is the painter with ideas. He believes in things. There's always a symbol stuck in his compositions somewhere. He's a philosopher, you see, and he wants to explain his philosophy through his painting. He is the sort of painter that Cultural Societies would dote on. Though mark you, all of this in perfectly good faith. "But," Léon de Lora says, "even though opinions cannot give a man talent, they always ruin any talent he already has . . . The only opinion an artist ought to have is faith in his work" (*Comédiens sans le savoir*, p.47).

To visit Ernest-Jean Sarrasine we have to go back in time, practically, indeed, to the flood. Born in Besançon in 1736, Sarrasine is a great worker, a sculptor with a future, but alas! one fine day he falls in love with a Roman *cantatrice*. Delightful misfortune! you will say. Roman or not, a beautiful singer is always worth any man's taking. Innocents that you are! Didn't you know that all Roman sopranos at that time were castrati? Sarrasine is bewildered, the castrato's patron has the sculptor done away with, and that's the last we ever hear of him (*Sarrasine*).

Wenceslas Steinbock, who is more Pole than sculptor, I shall deal with in another section. His friend Stidmann has talent, but his work is mostly on a smallish scale: statuettes, seals, clockcases. "An ornamenter," Bubourdieu scornfully remarks (*Comédiens sans le savoir*, p.45). He can turn you out a monument for a tomb, though, on occasion. As witness those for Charles Keller and Henri de Marsay in Père Lachaise (*Cousin Pons*, pp. 776 and 777). He is not insensible to the eternal feminine and is known to have had an affair with Mme Schontz (*Cousine Bette*, p.324), as well as entertaining warm feelings towards Steinbock's wife (*id.* p.356). Moreover, he is "a very handsome young man" (*Béatrix*, p.583).

Melchior de Canalis *or the Rastignac of poetry*

Oh heavens, how I detest this Canalis! He is one great bag of pomposity and conceit. And one wonders how far he is aware of this himself. Gide, in his *Ecole des Femmes*, gives us the portrait of a man who, by following his principles and prejudices blindly to the end, manages to end up living, not according to his own true nature any more, but according to an ideal image of himself he holds up in front of him. And this without lying to himself. Without hypocrisy. Because the hypocrite knows that his virtue is only a mask, and Gide's Robert believes in his virtue. In the same way, Canalis has become so identified with the part he is playing that the role has now become the real man. "He has made his behavior into a second nature" (*Modeste Mignon*, p.403). Is his life a lie nevertheless? Hardly, I think. For the liar is above all flexible. He changes according to his listener. "The exquisite flexibility of the liar . . ." Canalis has no flexibility. And he never talks to anyone but himself. Consequently his lie never changes. Whether he is talking to his secretary, to Dumay, or to a social gathering in le Havre, he is always the same (*Modeste Mignon*, pp. 408, 479, 514). The world is a theater to him, and he is on stage from morning till night. He plays his part, and it is always the same; like the actor who never varies his performance one iota from day to day. Canalis' lie is based, not on motives of self-interest, but on self-infatuation. He is, in a way, a dreamer. He does not listen to the other actors' lines. And why should he listen to them? Other people don't interest him.

Does Canalis at least have some valid foundation for this infatuation with himself? Is he really talented? Judging from the way in which Balzac so often mentions him in the same breath as the very greatest poets, we might well think so. "Byron, Lamartine, Hugo, Delavigne, Canalis and Béranger" (*Illusions perdues*, p.702). "Lamartine and Victor Hugo, Casimir Delavigne and Canalis" (*id.* p.492). "Moore, Byron . . . Canalis" (*Splendeurs*, p.1029). But he is also referred to as a "churner out of ballads," as a "poet created by newspaper articles," as a "sacristy Dorat" (*Peau de Chagrin*, p.53; *Illusions perdues*, p.703; *Modeste Mignon*, p.402).

Canalis is a specialist in the elegiac mode, and there is some reason to believe that he is based to a certain extent on Lamartine. To begin with, Balzac arouses this suspicion by the care he has taken to differentiate between the two. "Canalis can be distinguished from Lamartine . . . by his coaxing bedside manner, by a certain treacherous sweetness, by a delicious correctness of style . . . Women see in him the friend they are looking

for, a discreet masculine confidant . . . Canalis does not possess the gift
of breathing real life into his creations; but he does have the power to
calm vague sufferings . . . He speaks to young girls in their own language . . . Come to me (he says to them), let us weep together on the
bank of this stream, under the willow trees. And they go! They sit and
listen to his empty and mellifluous poetry" (*Modeste Mignon*, p.401). Imagine Lamartine crossed with Géraldy, and then just a touch of Marcel
Prévost. Or, simpler still, imagine Lamartine without the excuse of genius.
Not the Lamartine of *Harmonies poétiques*, but the Lamartine of the
often ridiculous commentaries that he tacks on to his poems. The Lamartine who wrote, after a visit to Reboul: "I spoke my name, he did not
blush." Or again: "I wrote on, weeping and dreaming, until nearly six
o'clock. Just then, two eminent literary and political figures I used to see
something of in those days were shown in: M. Thiers and M. Mignet.
They asked what I was working on. On a sad memory, I told them, and
read them some of the lines I had written. They seemed moved by them"
(*Secondes Harmonies poétiques*). We can no longer see Lamartine without his halo around his head. But his contemporaries could. And if you
take his halo away, what remains? "A man made up, not even of ambitions,
but of childish vanities," Vieil-Castel writes in his *Mémoires*. "Lamartine,"
he tells us further on, "appeared before us clad in the most vainglorious
of his vainglories and played his role of monarch with noble con-
descension." I know that Vieil-Castel's opinions should be handled with
care, but for his detestation of Lamartine to have translated itself into
terms so perfectly suited to describe Canalis there must undoubtedly have
been some points of resemblance between the two. Lamartine, a royalist
and religious poet, supplemented his poetic career with a political one.
Canalis does the same. Lamartine was an embassy secretary, a deputy, then
a cabinet minister. This description also applies to Canalis.

One can love a woman for her breasts, for her virtue, for her wit, for
her fortune. One can love a woman despite the fact that she is married.
Constant-Cyr-Melchoir de Canalis goes one step further. He loves the
Duchesse de Chaulieu *because* she is married, and because she is married to
that particular husband. Unusual, but by no means stupid. Canalis wants
to be made an embassy attaché. The Duc de Chaulieu is an ambassador.
Therefore Canalis becomes the Duchesse's lover. Who can fail to admire
the pure logic of this syllogism? And the end certainly makes it worth-
while to ignore the various minor snags involved, one of them being the
fact that the Duchesse already has children who are at least as old as the
lover. (All the birth dates are not available, but Canalis was born in 1800,

and in 1821, Rhétoré, one of the Duchesse's sons, is already keeping Tullia. We are therefore justified in supposing that he is no twelve-year-old.) Does this disturb Canalis? Hoping to throw a smokescreen over the facts, he attempts to pass himself off as an *admirer* of Mme d'Espard (*Illusions perdues*, p.615). To no effect whatsoever, though. No one is unaware of his liaison with the Duchesse, and certainly not the Duc or his children. Louise de Chaulieu, scarcely out of her convent school, writes to her friend: "My mother would go with my father to Madrid if he would agree to take M. Canalis on as embassy secretary; but these appointments are made by the King, and the Duc does not wish either to go against the wishes of the King, who is very despotic, or annoy my mother." Meanwhile "M. Canalis . . . is with her from three o'clock until five every day, no doubt studying diplomacy" (*Mémoires de deux Jeunes Mariées*, p.161). Quite how much pleasure the great poet is able to extract from this liaison it would be difficult to say. The Duchesse has a rather nasty temper, the Duc makes fun of him, and the children all despise him. It's terrifying, what can be read in the gaze of a young girl as she contemplates her mother's lover. And it wouldn't be so bad if he were an older man, serious about the relationship and therefore necessarily in a different world. But a lover who is the same age as the daughter, and therefore keeps the realities of the liaison odiously present in the imagination! But such nuances are completely lost on Canalis. His self-infatuation blinds him, his ambition encases him in an invulnerable shell. The dogs bark as he goes by them, but the gigolo pays no heed. Canalis is the perfect gigolo. Even physically. He is a short, dry, swarthy man with a calflike face and a rather small head (*Modeste Mignon*, p.403). "His almost dainty good looks and his caressing smiles were unable to disguise the profound egoism and the constant calculations of an existence still precarious in those days" (*Illusions perdues*, p.615). For he is calculating endlessly. And, like other calculating people, he comes up with the wrong answer twice as often as people who don't calculate. Act at random. Take life as it comes, heads or tails. That way at least the odds are equal; you should succeed once in every two throws. But the man who calculates spoils the odds, and he fails more often than he succeeds. Modeste Mignon writes to Canalis. She offers him her heart, more or less. Canalis makes inquiries and discovers that she is poor. Canalis the farsighted therefore backs out. But it turns out that Modeste has eight million. "If you play by the rules you only lose!" Canalis exclaims . . . "Ah, I am the biggest Nicodemus that ever fell out of the moon" (*Modeste Mignon*, p.575). There is nothing left for him but to go back to the Duchesse. After all, she's bound to marry me, he tells himself. In *Un Début dans la Vie*, we find him married to the Moreau girl, who has brought him a dowry of two million. True, the father is a former steward and the mother an ex-chambermaid, but that is at least one thing in favor of gigolos: they're rarely given to snobbery. Canalis becomes a deputy, a peer and a cabinet minister. He is elected to the Académie Française. "He is hollow, and produces a great deal of sound," Léon Giraud says . . . "He believes himself indispensable to France; but in no circumstances could he ever be *the man in command of the situation*" (*Comédiens sans le savoir*, p.58).

MUSIC

Gennaro Conti and Gambara

Gennaro Conti, whom we meet mostly in *Béatrix*, derives some of his characteristics from Rossini, some from Chopin and some from Liszt. He is Italian like the first, Mlle des Touches' lover like the second and Mme d'Agoult's lover like the third, since we have Balzac's own admission that Mme d'Agoult was at least in part his inspiration for Béatrix de Rochefide.

Born in Marseille, though of Italian extraction, Conti, like Nathan, is a charlatan. He has talent, intelligence and a heavenly voice; but he is envious and treacherous. Possibly without being aware of it. He is another of those men who are so deceitful that they even deceive themselves. "His vanity is of a kind that perpetually leads him to express those feelings that are furthest from his heart," Mlle des Touches says. "He gives himself out to be an artist who receives his inspirations from heaven" when he is in fact "as cold as a wet well-rope" (*Béatrix*, p.399). Telling lies comes as naturally to him as breathing. Having become Mlle des Touches' lover, Conti later runs away to Italy with Béatrix de Rochefide. Shortly afterwards, he abandons her too.

With Conti, we enter the world of treble clefs and diminished sevenths. Was Balzac a genuine music lover? Works such as *Gambara* and *Massimila Doni* certainly indicate that he did at least have a fair knowledge of the subject—or that he had done a good deal of research into it. But whatever the truth of the matter, music does play a definite part in the *Comédie humaine*. It is at the piano that Mlle des Touches expresses her despair, and at the piano too that Mme de Langeais reveals her frigidity. Modeste Mignon sets a poem by Canalis to music. Ursule Mirouët sets the ears of her provincial neighbors agog with her Beethoven recital. Vanda de Mergi plays the accordion (*Envers de l'Histoire contemporaine*, p.383). Facino

Cane is a clarinetist. Schmucke is a music teacher. Pons is a conductor, and much of his sad story is played out to the noisy accompaniment of instruments tuning up. A novel like *Massimila Doni* is incomprehensible unless one remembers all the time that its characters are people for whom trills and tessituras are as important as money and appointments to the Camusots. And this panorama of the musical world even has its example of excess, of the quest for the absolute and eventual bankruptcy that all such infatuation for the absolute, in Balzac's world, must inevitably bring in its train. Paolo Gambara is determined to discover the physical laws that govern music. He attempts to achieve the absolute in music just as Louise de Chaulieu attempts to achieve the absolute in love or Frenhofer in the field of painting. And Gambara's attempt, like theirs, ends in total failure. He goes mad.

THE WORLD OF PLEASURE IN 1821 (*continued*)

The supper at Coralie's provides us with a more or less complete picture of the courtesans' world during the first half of the Restoration period. Esther is not present because she has not yet appeared on the scene, but on the other hand we hear a great deal about her mother, Sara Van Gobseck, "one of the most magnificent creatures of that age, known in the sumptuous world of prostitution by the nickname of la belle Hollandaise" (*César Birotteau*, p.371). Originally from Bruges, she keeps Maxime de Trailles (*Député d'Arcis*, p.726), ruins the lawyer Roguin and dies "without a farthing" in 1819, murdered by a captain in the army (*César Birotteau*, p.471; *Splendeurs*, p.676).

Then a few more prostitutes: the pretty English girl in *Splendeurs* who is given the job of fooling Nucingen. She has a sense of fun. "*Vot are you den?* my big, tame viol d'amore?" she asks the fat banker in an imitation of his own accent. One day indeed, when slightly tipsy, she carried this talent for repartee so far as to kill her lover. Fair-haired and pale skinned, she also has the pleasure of spending a night with Rubempré (*Splendeurs*, p.768).

Little Euphrasie is a blonde too. She has big blue eyes, and is obviously incapable of even the most venial misdemeanor. But don't count on that. She sleeps with a young clerk and gives him a disease so frightful that he dies with a face as black as your boots. Though it's true that the Devil himself takes a hand in the affair (*Melmoth réconcilié*).

THE HOMEBODIES

Caroline Crochard de Bellefeuille, Jenny Courand, Aquilina

With Caroline Crochard, known as de Bellefeuille, we move into rather more middle-class surroundings. We are now in the world of the ladies whose gentlemen provide them with comfortable nests of mahogany and rosewood. This Caroline is the daughter of a male dancer who, after the taking of the Bastille, becomes a colonel and fails to survive the rigors of army life. His daughter is an honest little dressmaker, and would doubtless have remained so had it not been for her mamma. Mme Crochard, you see, can't get used to living in poverty. And since her views are somewhat less restricted than her daughter's she sees nothing wrong in calling the latter to the attention of Attorney General Granville, who eventually provides the young girl with a little establishment. Caroline now spends her whole day doing nothing. She grows plump. She has two children. And a dog too, I wouldn't be surprised. She is stupid and soft. Then she is unfaithful to Granville with a certain Solvet who reduces her to beggary. The Attorney General is really very cross (*Une Double Famille*).

Jenny Courand is a florist who lives with Gaudissart the traveling salesman. She is his "little friend" in the full sense of the term. Ignorant, a trifle stupid, but refreshing. "Ah! When one loves a man," she says, "if we knew in advance what we're letting ourselves in for, on my word of honor we'd leave you all to manage on your own, you men." (*Illustre Gaudissart*, p.19). Her lover simply laughs at her. But he's very fond of her all the same. When he's away on his trips he writes to her every day. And he signs off: "Who kisses you on your eyes? Your FELIX, for ever" (*id.* p.25).

Though kept by the cashier Castanier, Aquilina is unfaithful to him with one of the four sergeants of la Rochelle, a certain Léon. When the latter is executed, and Castanier gone, Aquilina becomes an ordinary prostitute, a role in which she appears in *la Peau de Chagrin* (p.67). She is a handsome woman, though tending somewhat to the gigantic (*Melmoth réconcilié*).

THE WORLD OF PLEASURE IN 1840 (*approx.*)

Jenny Cadine, Olympe Cardinal, Josépha Mirah, Héloïse Brisetout,
Malaga, Madame Schontz, Arthur de Rochefide, Carabine, Cydalise,
Antonia Chocardelle, Olympe Bijou, Elodie Chardin, Victor
de Vernisset, Vermanton, Massol

Corresponding to the supper at Coralie's, twenty years later, we have the
dinner at Mme Schontz's in *Béatrix*, the supper at Malaga's in *Un Homme
d'Affaires* and the party at Carabine's in *les Comédiens sans le savoir*. On
the masculine side, we meet a few old friends. On the female side, however, the cast is an entirely new one. We should never lose sight of the
fact that the *Comédie humaine*, or the essential part of it at least, covers
two generations. I have already pointed this out, but I make no apologies
for repeating a fact that is of such indisputable importance. And especially where the ladies of easy virtue dealt with in this chapter are concerned. A character like Rastignac, who is about twenty years old in *Père
Goriot*, is still under fifty in *les Comédiens sans le savoir:* he is still active
and still influential. Whereas a courtesan who appeared in *Illusions* can
scarcely expect to appear again in *la Cousine Bette*. Twenty years have
gone by. Whether married, dead or simply retired, she will certainly not
still be exercising her old profession. Florine, Florentine, Tullia, Coralie,
Suzanne du Val Noble, these were the first generation. Now we move on
to the second.

Jenny Cadine

I don't know what Jenny Cadine's real name is. She was born in 1814 and
she is an actress. But at the age of thirteen, under the patronage of the
Baron Hulot, she also enters upon a career as a courtesan. This pseudo-
conjugal arrangement seems to have lasted for about seven or eight years,
at the end of which the Baron finally tired of spending up to thirty thousand francs a year on keeping a woman who was being unfaithful to him
not only with a young state councilor but also with an artist (*Cousine
Bette*). Hulot therefore moves on to Josépha, leaving Jenny to fall back on
Couture, a businessman whose business is of the most precarious nature.
He furnishes a charming ground-floor apartment for her on the Rue
Blanche. In the garden, there is a little smoking kiosk to which one gains
access via "a rustic wooden gallery hung with Indian mats and decorated

with pieces of pottery" (*Béatrix*, p.586). Once Couture is ruined, the kiosk, the mats and Jenny Cadine are all taken over by Fabien du Ronceret, who adds a conservatory to the collection. Later on, we are to meet Couture and Ronceret again, disputing the favors of Mme Schontz. As I have already pointed out, sharing a mistress creates a definite bond between two men.

Slim, pretty, witty, blonde (I think), Jenny Cadine is held, in 1840, to be one of the very best actresses then working in the non-classical theaters. "All Paris," Balzac says, "knows the beauty of this leading young actress . . . sole rival to the celebrated Déjazet" (*Comédiens sans le savoir*, pp. 63 and 66). But she is also a whore and a bloodsucker. When she is introduced to a "new girl," the first thing she asks is: "What's her price?" (*Cousine Bette*, p.480). Quite straightforwardly, without any beating about the bush. In 1845, she is the mistress of a young lawyer in the Court of Appeals named Massol. Though whether he is keeping her or whether he is her fancy-man I'm afraid I don't know. Whatever the truth of the matter, however, Massol certainly does not restrict her movements in any way, since we see her taking home Léon de Lora's cousin from the South, Gazonal, and gorging him with such irresistible delights that the kindhearted fellow ends up writing out banker's drafts in her name for more money than he in fact possesses. However, she gives them back to him. Which is proof, all at the same time, of her savoir-faire, her kindness of heart and her partiality for playing jokes. She's a rather likable girl on the whole.

Olympe Cardinal

Olympe Cardinal is an actress too. But on a lower level. She is a juvenile lead at the Bobino (*Petits bourgeois*, p.219). She gets the costumes that have gone a bit under the arms, the dirty dressing rooms with one dim and guttering lamp, and also the tomatoes with which the cheerful Bobino audience bombards the actors it doesn't care for. A heavily built girl, I imagine, with heavy hindquarters. She is the daughter of a porter in les Halles, now dead, and a fishwife whom she abandoned at the age of fourteen in order to *go into the profession*. She cannot be particularly well known, since it is only by chance that her mother happens to see her at the Bobino. "You'll be hearing from me, you little mother-murderer!" she shrieks from the auditorium (*id*. p.220). At that time Olympe is the mistress of the company comic. *Les Petits Bourgeois* was, alas, never finished. Alas for us, that is. Fortunately, from Olympe's point of view, since the way things were going it looks as though she would have ended up married to the disgusting Cérizet.

Josépha Mirah

With Josépha, we are in the presence of a star of the first magnitude. Josépha Mirah is a Jewess. She is a foundling, the illegitimate daughter of a Jewish banker. When Crevel came upon her, though where I don't know, she was fifteen. Hulot and Crevel both have the collector's mentality in this matter. They cannot rest content with the girls already on the open market. They're constantly ferreting around, looking for something new. So Crevel finds Josépha and sets her up in an establishment. But he's no fool! He brings in his own aunt, "my mother's sister!" to keep an eye on the girl. Josépha has a beautiful voice, so Crevel arranges for her to have lessons. And before many years have passed she becomes a famous singer. "Slim and highly strung," she has "the golden skin tints of the Andalucian . . . black hair as shiny as satin, eyes with long, dark lashes" (*Cousine Bette*, p.146). At about this time, Hulot steps in and carries her off. Crevel laments his misfortune. Bad examples, he says, have developed in this young creature "the instinct of the early Hebrews for gold and jewels, for the Golden Calf!" She has become nothing but "a wolf-trap, a cat-trap for gold pieces . . . And she's become full of *tricks* . . . my little girl who was once so innocent" (*id.* pp. 145 and 146). It is the lament of the collector who now sees other art lovers rushing to buy up the canvases of a painter whose pictures he has been able to buy for nothing up till now. Josépha has profited from the lessons to be learned from this former tradesman. Even while she is ruining Hulot, she finds time to cause serious depredations in the fortune of Victurnien d'Esgrignon, now married, and also in that of one of the Kellers. Then she moves on to a palace of silk and gold provided by the Duc d'Hérouville. For the Duc offers her not only the house but also an income of thirty thousand francs a year. You can imagine with what scant ceremony Hulot, a mere government official, is handed his dismissal.

She's an odd girl, this Josépha. Her jokes are often shockingly cruel. For instance, her remark about sending back Hulot's belt and nightcap (*Cousine Bette*, p.201). That's really savage. At the very moment when she's kicking him out, does she really need to . . . But on the other hand, when she sees Hulot reduced to poverty, she is sorry for him, and she finds him not only somewhere to live but also a pretty little companion. Now that really is very nice of her. Only . . . is it really kindness? Is she not, perhaps, secretly taking pleasure in the sight of her former protector sinking further and further into the mire? "Listen, my old blunderbuss," she says (*Cousine Bette*, p.434). And though I know that this is simply the language of her profession, though I know that kindness can often be expressed in the strangest of language, still I also know that there can be no genuine kindness without a little respect for those one is helping. Hulot wants to redeem himself, to leave for America. Josépha persuades him not to. "Oh, leave all that morality to the grocers, to the simple-minded soldier lads, to the good Frrrench citizens" (*id*. p.436). "Aren't I nice?" she ends up. Seriously, I wonder. Isn't she, in reality, taking a fundamentally cruel, spiteful delight in the situation? And yet, when Mme Hulot comes to see her, Josépha displays kindness, sympathy, even compassion. Mme Marneffe in an almost identical situation merely sneers. "What has she done to melt your heart, that old thing? What did she let you catch a glimpse of? Her . . . her religion!" (*id*. p.408). Whereas Josépha does everything within her power to help. She is intelligent, of course. More intelligent than Mme Marneffe. And that makes a difference. No one who is intelligent is ever really base. Josépha "had the nobility of her talent" (*id*. p.445). In the same way, even a more or less dishonest artist like Nathan is sometimes affected, and precisely because he is an artist, by "moral beauty" (*Fille d'Eve*, p.128).

Héloïse Brisetout

From the world of song to the world of dance. Now let us turn to Héloïse Brisetout, who emerges onto the stage of the *Comédie humaine* on page 198 of *la Cousine Bette*. There, we learn that she has moved into the apartment vacated by Josépha on the Rue Chauchat and that she is in the process of warming her new house with the help of M. Bixiou, M. Léon de Lora, M. Lousteau, M. de Vernisset, M. Stidmann and some women reeking of patchouli" (*Cousine Bette*, p.198). But who keeps her? No answer. None of the guests listed above is in any position to keep anyone. Perhaps it is already Isidore Baudoyer, the office superintendent in *les Employés* who later becomes mayor of a Paris *arrondissement* (*Cousin Pons*, pp. 739-740). Héloïse has also been Crevel's mistress, though I'm not at all sure when (*id*. p.740). Her preferred lover is Bixiou. He is no longer in the first flush of youth of course, but Héloïse likes a good laugh, and Bixiou, you will remember, is a jester. She also bestows her favors upon Gaudissart. Needless to say—he's the manager of her theater. "I'll show people the children I've had by you," she says. "I'll go out and borrow some"

(*Cousin Pons*, p.693). All Balzac's young ladies of pleasure seem to have a quip always ready on their lips. And Héloïse Brisetout is altogether a charmer. Elegant, delicate, graceful, she also shows "more wit than is ordinarily met with in the soloists of ballet companies" (*id.* p.692). Though excessively literary, she has nevertheless lost none of her spontaneity. She is "one of those natures that remain genuine even in a false position, capable of every possible sort of joke at the expense of paying worshipers . . . but a true comrade, and in awe of no human power on earth" (*id.* p.735).

Malaga

Actress, dancer, singer. To complete our panorama of the performing arts all we need now is an acrobat. Ladies and gentlemen, here she is: Marguerite Turquet, known as Malaga, bareback rider at the Cirque Olympique. And a rather odd story it is, Malaga's. There she was, quietly leading her little bareback rider's life, jumping through her hoops every evening, waving her flags, prancing about, knitting stockings or whipping up omelettes on the back of her galloping horse, when suddenly in walks this Polish fellow. And this respectable stranger assures her that she looks just like his daughter, for which good reason he rents her an apartment on the Rue Saint-Lazare, hires two servants for her and comes to see her now and again. And apparently he is a man who knows what's right and proper, since after every visit he leaves "two forty-franc pieces on the mantelpiece." And that's it. Not once does he so much as walk into the bareback rider's bedroom. "Work that one out!" says Malaga (*Fausse Maîtresse*, p.41).

This Polish fellow, as we of course know, is Thaddée Paz who, in order to prevent himself from attempting to sin with the Comtesse Laginska, wishes to spread the rumor that he has *"une habitude"*—as they say in the priestly world of Mauriac. But Malaga is a simple girl. She can't make it out at all. And she gazes into her mirror with great anxiety. What? Can she really not be desirable with "her black hair held in place with a bandeau of blue satin ribbon fluttering down onto her bare, olive-tinted shoulders, dressed in a white tunic with a golden edging and a leotard of tight silk interlock" (*id.* p.37)? After a while, the Pole gets on her nerves. After all, people are beginning to say she's some sort of a zombie, and that Paz is a magnetizer who's searching for the philosopher's stone (*id.* p.42). So she sends him back to his complications, while at the same time, her appetite having been aroused, deciding not to turn her back on this new way of life. Ronquerolles comes to see her, and Laginski too. "Malaga received all these gentlemen very cordially" (*id*. p.48). Oh great and sublime lesson! Paz tried to save the Laginski marriage by rejecting all thoughts of romance with the Comtesse. And all he succeeded in doing was pushing the husband into bed with a bareback rider. Such is the punishment that lies in store for those who employ impure means.

Several years later, Malaga is the mistress of the lawyer Cardot, whom she deceives with "a little eighteen-year-old snip of a musician" (*Muse du Département*, p.156). In 1845, she still appears in all the procuress's books (*Comédiens sans le savoir*, p.31). She is tall, strong enough to take on three men, vulgar to the nth degree, but a good-hearted girl, without affectations, who does not hesitate to refer to "my *colleagues* who walk up and down the boulevard" (*Un Homme d'Affaires*, p.806).*

All these women, as we have seen, pitched their tents on the borderlands between Art and Prostitution. Kept women, yes, but all with an alibi. No matter how wretched their early years, there are still certain gutters through which they have never splashed. Now here are the others, the women who live resolutely on the far side of the border, the scarlet women, the cocottes, the dyed-in-the-wool professionals, and, at their head, the queen of them all, the only one who is never referred to other than as Madame.

Madame Schontz

Madame Schontz was born Joséphine Schiltz. She is the daughter of a colonel, "the eternal colonel who is always to be found blooming in the dawns of these female existences, whether as a father or as a seducer" (*Béatrix*, p.576). It's true, too. How is one to explain this superabundance of colonels in the careers of cocottes? What is the connection between the brigade of guards and the sinful couch? Mme Schontz's father is nevertheless authentic, I should add, and his daughter, a godchild of the Empress, was brought up at Saint-Denis. Having become an orphan, she remained there a long while, until 1827 in fact, first of all as a pupil, later as an assistant mistress. She is well educated. She speaks four languages (*id*. p.578).

Then suddenly, having tired of Saint-Denis—or having been expelled—

---

* There was a real Malaga, though a long time before ours, somewhere about 1790. She was a tightrope walker who finally married a student nicknamed l'Huguet. He became Luguet, and is an ancestor of the actor André Luguet.

she took up a career as a cocotte. She was twenty-two at the time, which means of course that she had a lot of catching up to do. Jenny Cadine and Josépha began at thirteen and fifteen. However, since she is older than they, and more educated, perhaps Joséphine Schiltz will manage her career more adroitly than they do. By no means. In the *Comédie humaine* it is an almost invariable rule that intelligent people make more mistakes than uneducated ones. "Lively, witty, well educated, she made more errors than those of her stupid companions whose misjudgments were always based on self-interest" (*Béatrix*, p.577). Like a good schoolteacher dazzled by all things artistic, Aurélie—for that is her new name—cultivates several "poor but dishonest" writers. She then attempts to make up for lost time with a few rich men, but she always picks the thrifty ones. In short, she gets nowhere. What is more, she is still being referred to as la Petite Aurélie, to distinguish her from a "colleague" who is known simply as Aurélie. Though she is petite, as a matter of fact. And somewhat swarthy.

One day, at last, while dancing—not, needless to say, at a Society ball— she meets Arthur de Rochefide, Béatrix's husband, who has just been deserted by his wife. Since he is a cautious person, and also slightly ratlike by nature, Rochefide begins by allowing Mme Schontz only five hundred francs a month. Poor innocent! Two or three years later, Mme Schontz owns a house on the Rue La Bruyère and several hundreds of thousands of francs invested in her name. And as a consequence she begins to demand a certain amount of respect. The former pupil of Saint-Denis begins to peep out from behind the cocotte. I'm not a tart, she says, I'm an artiste (*Béatrix*, p.598). (Artiste in what? One is reminded of the reply made by another kept woman, in Colette's *Chéri:* "An artiste? My lovers must be very indiscreet.") Though it is true that Mme Schontz's education and intelligence render her infinitely superior to the other demi-mondaines of her time. The law of compensations again: Rochefide, who is an imbecile, has as his mistress and his wife two of the most intelligent women in all the *Comédie humaine*.

Now that her ship has come in, Mme Schontz sets herself up in a pretty house. Her servants know how to behave. She insists on that sort of thing. She likes order. She is conscious of what she takes to be her duties. She takes an interest in Rochefide's son, whom his mother, to Aurélie's way of thinking, neglects. It is in her house that the boy spends his days off from school. He calls her his little mummy. She is unfaithful to Rochefide, of course, but as tactfully as possible. Among others, she bestows her favors upon Lousteau, even though she is at the same time occupying herself with the problem of marrying him off (*Muse du Département*, p.155). She is a planner, a manager. In this respect she resembles Tullia a little. She knows what she wants. And just as Tullia lets go of her Rhétoré in order to marry a man less well-born, less rich, but likely to assure her of more durable profits, so Mme Schontz finally dismisses Rochefide in order to marry Fabien du Ronceret, to whom, by virtue of her connections, she brings a dowry consisting of the presidency of a court, the title of Baron and the Légion d'honneur. On the debit side, this decision means she is forced to spend several years in Alençon, than which there are a great many gayer places to be. But Mme Schontz is a woman who takes life seriously. She knows what is expected of her. Besides, she arrives with the warmest recommendations to the local nobility. I can picture her very easily in Alençon, occupying herself with good works, receiving the Dean. Mme Schontz is not one of those shameless creatures of whom there are really far too many about.

Arthur de Rochefide

I have deliberately omitted the men who do the keeping from this picture of the demi-monde up till this point. However important he may be, the keeper remains a foreign element, like the tourist disembarking on Capri or Madeira; the coachdrivers and the guides may welcome him with open arms, but he remains, nonetheless, a stranger. All these bankers and lawyers have lives of their own, family and social existences in which they are generally much more interesting to observe than at these suppers given at their expense. I am making an exception of Arthur de Rochefide, however, because he has no life except as a keeper, and because away from Mme Schontz he hardly has any existence at all. Of far from ancient nobility but extremely rich, in 1828 this Rochefide marries Béatrix de Casteran, who quickly deserts him in order to run away to Italy with Conti. Arthur seeks consolation in the company of various Society women and finally comes across Mme Schontz. He is a physically frail little man, eccentric, calculating but weak, the worst kind of calculator, the most deplorable variety of weaklings, since they are duped no less than the others but only allow themselves to be taken in with a great deal of groaning and cannot abandon themselves to their fate without a show of regret, like plaintive calves bellowing as they are dragged to the slaughter.

Like all timid people, Rochefide sets great store by what he thinks he possesses. Mme Schontz tries to get rid of him. He hangs on all the harder. Who was it who came to see you? he asks. No one, she replies, when there is a man's hat in full view on the piano. "Arthur lowered his head" (*Béatrix*, p.606). Another day, he surprises her with Ronceret and "withdraws on tiptoe" (*id*. p.611). He is eventually reconciled with his wife, but we see him attending a supper at Josépha's in *Cousine Bette* all the same (p.200).

Carabine and Cydalise

The celebrated Carabine is younger than the others. Carabine is, of course, only a nickname, and one that may possibly have originated in a reputation for having "always brought down her pigeon" (*Comédiens sans le savoir*, p.64). Her real name is Séraphine Sinet. She achieves eminence in about 1838, when she is set up in an establishment by du Tillet, who must by that time have grown tired of the aged Mme Roguin. Born in 1820, Carabine is only eighteen at this time. Du Tillet sets her up on the Rue Saint-Georges, almost next door to Thiers, in a house that has been occupied successively by Suzanne du Val Noble, Esther, Florine and Mme Schontz. (In Balzac, the houses recur too.) The furnishings are sumptuous. It's even more magnificent than the Tuileries, says Gazonal. Though it's true that Gazonal has never set foot in the Tuileries, or even, before this moment, in the house of a cocotte.

Carabine seems to have been a tall, well-fleshed girl, with bold eyes, quick reflexes, and a thoroughly vulgar tongue in her head. When Léon de Lora suggests that she shouldn't allow his cousin to drink too much, she replies: "Just as Monsieur pleases. Wine's not cheap" (*id*. p.65). She's one of those women who treat men like horses. Du Tillet must enjoy being with her because she reminds him of the ignominy of his early years. The liveliness of her language indicates a woman who is no stranger to the gutter. In *la Cousine Bette* we see her in tandem with the old procuress Mme Nourrisson. It is a remarkable scene. The night when I saw Valérie again, Montès says. "Saw her again! What a delicate way of putting it," Carabine comments. "I must remember it." But Mme Nourrisson is vexed. "That's enough fooling about, Carabine" (*Cousine Bette*, pp. 480 to 492). It is in the course of this scene that Montès learns of the way he has been betrayed by Valérie Marneffe, whom he then goes on to surprise in a rented love-nest, with Cydalise trailing behind him.

This Cydalise, a sixteen-year-old from Normandy, is a member of la Nourrisson's stable. Her particular attractions, Balzac tells us, are "a maddening freshness, and an air of candor that would stir up desire in a dying man" (*id*. p.480). This particular day she is wearing a little dress of white cashmere with blue passementerie trimmings. It is Cydalise whom Montès uses in order to impregnate Valérie with the disease that kills her. After which, this young and candid creature goes back with him to the pampas.

Antonia Chocardelle

Antonia Chocardelle is a young woman who was, for a time, kept by Maxime de Trailles. Yes, you have the right to be astonished. Where Maxime de Trailles is concerned, all the giving is usually in the opposite direction. Yet in the same story we also see him paying off a creditor. He's getting older is Maxime. Though it should be added that he keeps Antonia on only a very modest footing. He has set her up in a little bookstore-cum-rental library which she runs with her aunt, Ida Bonamy. Later, Antonia makes a name for herself as a cocotte. She must be strikingly beautiful, despite the fact that Malaga claims she has rough skin (*Un Homme d'Affaires*, p.816). She is also known to have had a short liaison with La Palférine and another with Victurnien d'Esgrignon. She has a ready wit (*Un Homme d'Affaires* and *Un Prince de la Bohème*).

Olympe Bijou and Elodie Chardin

Continuing our descent in this private hierarchy, we come to Olympe Bijou, an embroidery worker, sixteen years old, who is stagnating in a family circle where they drink canal water out of the town pipes because water from the Seine is too dear (*Cousine Bette*, p.435). For a consideration of one hundred and fifty francs a month, the family hands little Olympe over to old Hulot. She continues to co-habit with the baron until the day when she falls in love with a professional *claqueur* who wears earrings and glories in the name of Idamore. This dilettante takes Olympe away, but provides Hulot with consolation in the form of his own sister, Elodie Chardin, a lace and shawl mender by profession (*id*. p.465). After which he moves on to a juvenile lead at the Funambules, and Olympe, finding herself deserted, marries M. Grenouville, the most respectable match in the world and owner of a large novelty store (*id*. pp. 455 and 457).

Vernisset, Vermanton and Massol

As I have already noted, it is above all the female personnel that has changed in this motley and ephemeral world. On the masculine side, we still meet the Bixious and Lousteaus who were already flourishing in 1820. At Mme Schontz's, however, we do meet a few newcomers, among whom are Vernisset and Vermanton. Victor de Vernisset is a "poet of the Canalis school" (*Béatrix*, p.583). This means, presumably, that his verses are for the most part doleful. On the other hand, his interest in Mme Schontz's wealth could scarcely be more lively. Cast your mind back to Canalis. In *l'Envers de l'Histoire contemporaine* (p.267), we see Vernisset at the feet of the venerable Mme de la Chanterie, kissing the hem of her robe, swearing that he will never write a word against the true religion, and successfully borrowing a small sum of money. When one thinks what an assiduous visitor he is at the houses of kept women like Mme Schontz and Valérie Marneffe (*Cousine Bette*, p.348 and *Béatrix*, p.583), the scene is not without its savor. Even from here I can catch the snickers it would draw from Vermanton, another frequent visitor at Mme Schontz's, but one who does at least have the honesty to describe himself as a "cynical philosopher" (*Béatrix*, p.584).

Léon Massol is one of those walk-ons over whom Balzac, though not disdaining to use them, never lingers. A lawyer, this Massol also has a finger in the journalistic pie, firstly as editor of *La Gazette des Tribunaux* (*Splendeurs*), secondly as managing director of Nathan's paper (*Fille d'Eve*). He is also a right-hand man to Nucingen and du Tillet, becomes a councilor of state, and is eventually rich enough to keep a woman like Jenny Cadine (*Comédiens sans le savoir*).

The unknown poet

I really don't know what heading to put him under, this "man of high intelligence" whose name Balzac does not tell us, but whom we see in about 1820 at Samanon the pawnbroker's "wearing a short topcoat so much stiffened by accretions of various foreign substances that it seemed to have been cut from a zinc bar-top" (*Illusions perdues*, p.838). He intrigues me, I confess. He reminds me of someone, but who? Baudelaire perhaps? "In the grip of opium . . . a captive in enchanted palaces of contemplation," Balzac writes, he "would not or could not create" (*id.* p.872). He has a "divine mistress" (*id.* p.872). But one day, when all he has is ten francs, he spends them all "in a vile house of ill-fame" (*id.* p.872).

THE PROCURESSES

Madame Nourrisson, Jacqueline Collin, Madame Meynardie

Having begun her career as a confidential agent to the Prince d'Ysembourg (*Comédiens sans le savoir*, p.31), Mme Nourrisson later left this post in order to set up on her own as a pawnbroker and secondhand-clothes dealer. These convenient trades enable her to wriggle her way in anywhere she chooses with her witchlike appearance, her faded and feathered hat, her vast handbag, and her propositions. She will sell you anything: dresses, shawls, historical souvenirs, banker's drafts, a night with Malaga, two hours with Carabine (*id.* pp. 29-31). An old ostrich, Montès calls her to her face (*Cousine Bette*, p.489). But Mme Nourrisson isn't upset. She's seen and heard everything before. Nothing stops her making her deals, spying, poking her nose in anywhere she chooses, always insinuating, always insisting, pulling what the customer wants out of her great bag. She has a finger in a great many pies. She runs a store on the Rue Saint-Marc, a brothel on the Place Boieldieu, a house of rented love-nests on the Rue Sainte-Barbe (*Splendeurs, Cousine Bette*). She does a great deal of business with her old friend Jacqueline Collin, former mistress of Marat, a counterfeiter, Vautrin's aunt, and a generally enigmatic old witch of whom I shall have occasion to say more later. On occasion, this Collin will also act as a go-between for her shyer clients. It is she who organizes the meeting between Esther and Nucingen in *Splendeurs*. (When it becomes known that the rich Nucingen is hooked, there is a frightful slump in the market price of breasts. A similar panic on the same market is also to be found in Alphonse Daudet's *l'Evangéliste*.) As for Mme Meynardie, she is only mentioned by the way. She is the manageress of the brothel where Esther works (*Splendeurs*, p.676). Apparently she also has a store (*Ferragus*, p.42).

Out of this teeming and seemingly chaotic mass of characters, there has gradually emerged a complete and almost systematic picture of the literary, artistic and pleasure-seeking world. Literature is represented in all its forms: poetry by Canalis and Vernisset, the novel by d'Arthez and Rubempré, criticism by Vignon and Blondet, the theater by du Bruel, Ridal and Nathan. Then we have the more material aspects of the literary world: the publisher Doguereau, the printer Séchard, the bookseller Dauriat, all three in *les Illusions perdues*. Then the various levels of vocation:

the upright and hardworking genius (d'Arthez and Mlle des Touches), the temptations (Rubempré), work without talent (Vernou), talent without application (Blondet), talent destroyed by disorder (Nathan), talent destroyed by lack of character (Lousteau), intellect as an opium (Vignon). Then, as I have already pointed out, a complete survey of a journalistic world: Finot the manager, Nathan and Gaillard the directors, Lousteau the editor, Merlin the leader-writer, Blondet the literary critic, Lucien the theater critic, Bixiou the cartoonist, Giroudeau the publicity and subscription manager, Bridau the accountant, Coloquinte the distribution manager, and not forgetting the Protean Cérizet, all of them in *les Illusions*.

Music too is fully represented, from the great composer Gennaro Conti, down through the honest bandleader Pons, the piano teacher Schmucke, the street musician Gambara, to the flautist Schwab. Nor should we forget the public: the boxes at the Opéra, the music enthusiasts of *Massimila Doni*. Sculpture is represented by Steinbock, Sarrasine and Stidmann, and we are given glimpses of paintings produced by genius (Bridau), respectable run-of-the-mill painting (Schinner), painting of ideas (Dubourdieu), easel painting (Sommervieux) and the society painter (Léon de Lora). In the story entitled *Pierre Grassou* we also see a failed artist, a picture dealer and a collector, to say nothing of a to-do about forged paintings. In *le Cousin Pons* there is another art lover. In *la Vendetta* an art teacher and his pupils.

Balzac was prevented by death from continuing with his novel entitled *le Théâtre comme il est*, which was to have had as its principal character an actor, Robert Médal. But this is the only character lacking to complete his panorama of the backstage world, since it already comprises playwrights (Nathan and du Bruel), a great star (Florine), a supporting actress (Olympe Cardinal), classical dancers (Tullia and Mariette) a befeathered vaudeville dancer (Florentine), an opera singer (Josépha), a music-hall singer (Héloïse Brisetout) and a bareback rider (Malaga). Another facet of this world is examined in *le Cousin Pons*, where we meet the manager (Gaudissart), the bandleader (Pons), several musicians, a spear-carrier and a dresser (Topinard and his wife). To which we should also add the *claque* leader Braulard in *les Illusions perdues* and the simple *claqueur* Idamore in *la Cousine Bette*.

The world of venal love is also represented in all its varieties: the actress who is kept, the kept woman who is that and nothing else (Mme Schontz), the simple prostitute (Esther), the pseudo-marriage (Caroline de Bellefeuille), the conniving mother (Mmes Crochard and Cabirolles), the obliging husband (Marneffe and Colleville, to whom I shall return later), the procuress (Jacqueline Collin), the hotel owner (Mme Nourrisson), the brothel keeper (Mme Meynardie), the gentleman who does the paying (Grandville, Crevel, Hulot, Rochefide), the lover on the side (Lousteau, Rubempré) and the eventual husband (Ronceret). We even have examples of that particular sub-species, the courtesan's personal maid: Bérénice in *les Illusions*, Asie in *Splendeurs*, and not forgetting the variety that is attempting to step into her employer's shoes: Jenny in *Melmoth réconcilié*.

I should like to linger just a little longer over this review of the courtesans who urge their graceful arguments throughout the pages of the *Comédie humaine*. As I have said, their presence is necessary to demonstrate to us the dissipation to which men like Nathan and Blondet have abandoned themselves; they are symbols, as it were, of these men's spiritual prostitution. Agreed. And that would explain the presence of, say, five or six. But from Florine to Malaga, if you take a quick count, you will see that there are in fact almost thirty of them. Even more courtesans than lawyers. The lawyers, of course, present no difficulty. In Balzac, money plays an extremely important part, and in those days where there was money there had to be a lawyer. That's simple enough. But what about all these courtesans? Are they simply there to balance out the lawyers? The formers' task being to preserve wealth and the latters' being to eat it up? It's a nice idea. But in fact, in the whole of the *Comédie humaine* there are scarcely three or four men who are ruined by such women: Roguin, the Marquis du Rouvre and Hulot. And even then, Hulot only ruins himself definitively for Mme Marneffe, who is not strictly a professional. Camusot, Crevel, Dudley and Rhétoré all devote themselves assiduously to women of pleasure; but there is no evidence that any of their fortunes are seriously jeopardized by this. Victurnien d'Esgrignon ruins himself for women, but with him it is a habit, and one he indulges in equally successfully with Mme de Maufrigneuse, who is a duchess. Manerville ruins himself too, but the woman in that case is his own wife. Gazonal gives Jenny Cadine everything he has, and more, but she gives it back. And this is not all: far from ruining du Bruel and du Ronceret, Tullia and Mme Schontz actually bring them wealth and titles. We should also note that these women are shown to us much more frequently in the company of their non-paying lovers than with the men who keep them: Florine more often with Nathan than with Matifat, Coralie more often with Lucien than with Camusot. In short, our attention is called far more to the moral ravages of their lives than to their functions as devourers of patrimonies. What should we conclude from this? Should we simply assume that the social importance of cocottes at that time was such that Balzac was forced to allot them so large a role if he wanted his picture to be complete? Or was it perhaps that he had a great many personal memories of this particular world that he wanted to use? The answer to this second question is quite definitely no. If we are to believe his biographers, Balzac only knew one courtesan during the whole course of his life: a certain Olympe Descuiller. He made good use of this solitary contact, however. This Olympe was a *petit rat* at the Opéra. That's Esther. She was sold by her mother. That's Coralie. To a young duke. That's Tullia. Then to an Englishman. That's Suzanne du Val Noble and her nabob. She posed for Vernet's *Judith*. Again that's Coralie, who it will be remembered poses for Bridau. Successively the mistress of Vernet, Eugène Sue and Rossini, she finally married the last of these. That's Suzanne marrying Gaillard.

Well, perhaps it's precisely because he had so little experience of the world of debauchery that Balzac felt impelled to depict it. In other words, should we think of him as repressed, and using his creative abilities as a form of compensation? This doesn't seem tenable to me. After all, where do we meet these young ladies? In their bedrooms? Rarely. As a general rule, Balzac shows them to us in their drawing-rooms. They appear much more as mistresses of households than as mistresses period. And that, I think, is the clue. Before all else, Balzac is a painter of society, of groups. Think of his characters. How often are they alone? Very rarely. Their most revealing thoughts spring from them, not in moments of quiet meditation, but in the give and take of conversation. When a Balzac character examines his conscience, he usually does so in public. Though in the *Comédie humaine*, generally speaking, it is other people who examine your conscience for you. Balzac's heroes and heroines scarcely ever question their hearts. The explanation of their behavior, the verdict on their conduct, these are usually left for the other characters to formulate. Hence Balzac's constant need to assemble his characters into groups, to confront them with one another. And hence, too, his need for suitable places in which to assemble them. How, for instance, is Balzac to bring together a poor journalist like Lousteau, a young duke like Rhétoré and a successful writer like Nathan? Where would they meet? In a little middle-class salon? What would Nathan be doing there? In an editor's office? The atmosphere would lack that special softness that only the presence of women can provide. At Mme d'Espard's? Lousteau and Vernou would never be allowed up the front steps. Besides, in those upper-class drawing-rooms the atmosphere is always stiff and formal, no matter how hard one tries. But at Coralie's, on the other hand, one can be at ease, let oneself go, enjoy oneself. There's wine to drink. And then a song or two perhaps. Everyone is so much more relaxed. And that, in my opinion, is the point, the real reason for this abundance of demi-monde suppers. "The house of a sensible girl like Florine was neutral territory" (*Fille d'Eve*, p.132). Neutral territory where everyone can meet, a crossroads that makes every imaginable confrontation possible.

NOTE

Fictional distance

As may be seen from the list at the beginning of this book, Balzac's works may be arranged in two different chronological sequences: the first according to the order in which the books were written, the second according to the date at which the stories of the works take place. A single glance is enough to tell us that the time difference between these two different chronologies tends, generally speaking, to become steadily smaller. In a curious work entitled *Créatures chez Balzac*, Pierre Abraham has established the following table:

Time Difference

Less than 5 years	13 works, of which 10 in the last ten years of Balzac's working life.
5 to 10 years	20 of which 15 in the last ten years
10 to 15 years	26 of which 21 in the ten middle years
15 to 20 years	20 of which 11 in the ten middle years
20 to 25 years	12 of which 7 in the first ten years
More than 25 years	9 equally distributed.

Since the matter being examined is one so delicate and so resistant to expression in numerical terms as the composition of a novel, obviously these statistics must be taken as no more than approximations. Especially since, in some cases, it is difficult to know how to classify the works. *La Rabouilleuse*, for instance, begins in 1792, but the essential action does not really begin until the two Bridau brothers have come of age, which is to say after 1815. Should we say that the time difference is thirty years or fifty? It is an open question. Nevertheless, this statistical table, taken as a whole, is substantially correct. And Pierre Abraham draws the following conclusions from it: "As Balzac advanced in age, so the stories he wrote moved forward in time too (and at an even faster rate). As history continued to be made, he abandoned first the Revolutionary period, then the Empire period, then the Restoration period as sources of material. And towards the end, his plots came to be chosen more and more exclusively from the period of the July Monarchy. Why? Because Balzac, a contemporary novelist who used material drawn from his own experience, needed to deal with events situated at the right *fictional distance*. Whether this is for reasons to do with memory or determined by even more secret motives . . . this *fictional distance* is based upon a certain "average distance" that is as real in time as the Frenchman's "average height" is in space. . . . We should point out that the number of events he has dealt with that took place less than fifteen years before the time of writing is slightly more (52%) than half of the total number of fictional events. Further, the fifteenth year taken by itself provides more (8%) of the total events of the *Comédie humaine* than any other year. We are therefore justified in saying that for Balzac, a novelist dealing with contemporary material, the *average fictional distance* separating the actions of the novels from the date at which they are treated by the author is fifteen years . . ." "These fifteen years," Pierre Abraham continues, "should doubtless be looked upon as the average period of maturation within an organism that is necessary to any experience before it can be expressed . . . The important thing here is to note the fact that this period, though relatively long at the beginning of Balzac's creative life, tends to grow progressively shorter as the constant demands made upon the maturing process render it steadily more flexible and efficient."

II

THE THEMES

CHAPTER 9

The Use of
General Ideas

INFLUENCED BY Mallarmé (one doesn't write with ideas, one writes with words) and also by a curious form of puritanism, we have generally come to believe in these days that ideas have no value for a novelist, that they are an encumbrance to him, that they don't mix well with the passions, and that they are inimical to the enchantments expected of a novel.

Balzac was obviously of a different opinion. When he criticizes Nathan as a novelist it is precisely for his lack of ideas: "Instead of awakening ideas in the reader, his principal characters are nothing but large-scale individual portraits that excite only ephemeral sympathies; they are not tied in with the great interests of life, and in consequence they do not represent anything" (*Fille d'Eve*, p.91). Balzac, on the other hand, does have ideas. A great many, in fact. To use his own terms: his characters are tied in with the great interests of life—and even with the little ones. They are tied in to them, not only by the presence of these interests in their own lives, in everything that they do and everything they experience, but also in an even more immediately palpable manner, by the innumerable observations, comments and considerations that Balzac does not hesitate to insert into his narrative. In *les Employés* (p.1022), during the course of a toilette, he points out the advantages of woolen muslin. In *le Cousin Pons* (p.634), we find a few observations on gilding, and further on (p.669) a brief gloss on the word *monsieur*. In *la Rabouilleuse* (p.939), we are given, in black and white, the reasons for the decadence of Issoudun, preceded (p.902) by a short comment on the lottery. In *la Fille aux yeux d'Or*, we are given a duly motivated verdict on Jean-Jacques Rousseau right in the middle of a love scene. In *les Employés*, there is an entire plan for the reorganization of the Civil Service; in *le Cousin Pons*, some remarks on the running of museums; in *la Cousine Bette*, a passage on the subject of town-planning. From behind the novelist, we constantly see emerging the man with ideas, constructive ideas, who wants not only to

[249]

express them but also to have them put into practice: "Oughtn't a little law of some sort be worked out that . . ." (*Illusions perdues*, p.938). "This is a matter for legislation" (*Physiologie du Mariage*, p.637).

Of course, these are cases in which it would be possible to argue that the ideas expressed are mere parentheses, more or less external to the narrative proper. But more often the idea is closely linked to the character or to the plot. It is either a product of them or a controlling factor in their existence. Sometimes it is the character who leads us into the general idea, as in *le Cousin Pons* (p.529) when, after a description of the character, Balzac adds: "This last spencer-wearer . . . provided a free demonstration of what can happen to the innumerable victims of the fatal and deadly system known as competitive examination, which still reigns supreme in France even after having been practiced for a full century without results"; sometimes it is the general idea which leads us to the character (*l'Illustre Gaudissart* begins with a hundred lines describing the profession of the traveling salesman. Then: "You know the Species: here is the individual specimen." Or the beginning of *Melmoth réconcilié*: "There is a kind of men whose natures Civilization . . ."); sometimes again, we find the general idea and the character constantly relaying one another throughout the length of the work, as in *le Médecin de Campagne*, which is at the same time a handbook and an illustration of good government.

On the other hand, we find frequent examples in which the operation is split up into separate compartments. The fictional part becomes more strictly fictional, more strictly an illustration, but it is preceded, accompanied or followed by another work that provides us with the theory, as it were. In *les Illusions perdues*, Balzac gives us a picture of the journalistic world. He shows us Blondet, Finot, Lousteau, etc., at work. They can be considered as merely illustrations for his *Monographie de la Presse parisienne* in which he classifies this same journalistic fauna more rigorously according to family and species. Here is the manager: "He is part proprietor, part grocer, part speculator . . . Since he is always rubbing elbows with his editors, their ideas rub off on him." Here is the critic: "He dines out, he sups out, he is a guest at every party . . . You have seen him young, elegant . . . You meet him again withered, finished, his eyes as dead as his intelligence; he goes out to look for a job and, strange to say, he finds one." All these traits ring a bell immediately: they are precisely those we find in *les Illusions perdues* illustrated by the manager Finot and by the critic Blondet, the brilliant journalist who slowly decays into a sponger and ends up a prefect. Between the *Monographie* and *les Illusions* the ideas have turned into flesh and blood. And the same thing is true of

the novel *les Petits Bourgeois* and the *Monographie du Rentier* that preceded it, in which the stockholder is described as "anthropomorphous according to Linnaeus, mammiferous according to Cuvier." And similarly
too with the novel *les Employés*, written in 1836 then followed, in 1841,
by a *Physiologie de l'Employé* in which we find descriptions of the various species: the cashier, the private secretary, the clerk-cum-man of letters, the moonlighter, the poor clerk, the temporary, the incompetent, the
collector, the office supervisor—in short, precisely those same species that
we have already seen illustrated, that have been already exemplified in the
characters of Saillard, la Brière, du Bruel, Colleville, Minard, la Roche,
Phellion, Dutocq and Rabourdin. And then, of course, there is the *Physiologie du Mariage*, the illustrations for which are to be found scattered
throughout the whole of the *Comédie humaine*.

I am perfectly well aware that these *Physiologies* are intended as amusing trifles rather than imposing tomes, but in writing them Balzac is nevertheless conforming to the program that he attributes to the serious-
minded Daniel d'Arthez, who "wanted, like Molière, to be a profound
philosopher before writing comedies" (*Illusions perdues*, p.650).

It is in his almost constant reliance upon the science of physiognomy
that Balzac betrays most ingenuously his tendency to look to some general
system of ideas for the governing factors and justification of his plots. Not
content with simply describing a character's face and appearance, he also
insists on each of the features described revealing some aspect of the person's psychology and character. Here is Roguin: "To the eye of the astute
observer, his face betrayed the pangs, the fatigues of the hunt for pleasure.
When a man plunges into the muddy streams of excess, it is difficult for
his face not to have some traces of that mud left upon it" (*César Birotteau*, p.370). Or Mlle Gamard: "Her aquiline nose was of all her facial
characteristics the one that did most to express the despotism of her ideas,
just as the flattened angle of her forehead betrayed the narrowness of her
mind" (*Curé de Tours*, p.810). Or M. Guillaume: "That wan face spoke
of his patience and his good business sense" (*Maison du Chat-qui-pelote*,
p.22). In *le Contrat de Mariage* (pp. 103-104), the portrait of Nathalie
Evangelista constitutes a veritable demonstration of this science: "Nathalie was round-waisted, a mark of strength, but also the invariable sign of a
will-power that may often go as far as blind stubbornness . . . The
hands, which were like those of a Greek statue, confirmed the predictions
of the face and the waist in giving warning of an unreasoning spirit of
domination, willfulness for willfulness's sake . . . Her rather thin-lipped

mouth expressed a scarlet pride." After that, can anyone still be astonished at seeing Balzac use the term "diagnostic"? For him, physiognomy is a genuine scientific system, and every now and then he will throw in one of its general principles for our edification. "It is rare for a tall man to have any great abilities . . ." he writes in le Député d'Arcis (p.650). "For a man to be both tall and witty is exceptional" (Modeste Mignon, p.526). "All tall men have a touch of the horse in their brains" (l'Illustre Gaudissart, p.39). A large nose, according to Balzac, is an infallible mark of a vigorous temperament. When Pons confesses that he has led a very chaste life, Mme Cibot exclaims: "With a nose like that, for you have a noble nose, how did you manage it, my cherubim?" (Cousin Pons, p.647).* No, don't laugh. Unless you keep that remark firmly engraved in your memory, you risk completely missing the point of la Vieille Fille. The entire plot of that novel is in fact based on a series of allusions to the anthropological science, allusions that are intended at the same time to make the action clear to us and also to veil its scabrous nature. The author of Balzac mis à nu recounts that when the novel was first brought out, in serial form, it caused a scandal. "The provincial subscribers refused to accept the installments that were sent to them through the mails." What is this hidden drama? The fact that Mlle Cormon cannot achieve a state of conjugal bliss unless she picks a husband who is excessively well endowed. She has two suitors. And what does she go and do but pick the impotent du Bousquier at the expense of the sprightly Chevalier de Valois? How does she come to make this fatal error? Because she is ignorant of the principles of anthropology. "If there had been a professor of anthropology in the department of the Orne . . . would the appalling miseries of her conjugal life ever have occurred?" (Vieille Fille, p.332). For lack of this professor, the innocent lady let her choice fall upon du Bousquier, who has "a torso on him like the Farnese Hercules," whereas the Chevalier is blond and slender. But what are fair hair and large pectoral muscles to the experienced anthropologist? Meaningless externals. What she should have taken note of was du Bousquier's voice, the "voice of a broken-backed speculator," as compared with the Chevalier's fine organ with its "cor anglais tone." What she should have noted was that du Bousquier wears false hair, whereas Valois has a large nose and one cheek that goes red after he has eaten. "According to some doctors, this sign of heat on the left side denotes a prodigal heart. The Chevalier's love life confirmed these scientific assertions . . . Though his face was wrinkled to some extent . . . an ed-

---

* Similarly, Mme Vauquer entertains certain hopes where Goriot is concerned because of his "long square nose" (Père Goriot, 862).

ucated observer would have recognized these lines as the stigmata of passion and the furrows dug by pleasure. And indeed, the *crow's feet* and the *palace steps* to be observed on his face are the most elegant of wrinkles, highly prized at the court of Cytherea" (*id.* p.211). But Mlle Cormon is entirely ignorant of all this. Hence her misfortunes. And Balzac draws his conclusion: "Does this story not demonstrate the necessity for a new kind of instruction? Does it not invoke . . . the creation of a Chair of Anthropology?" (*id.* p.332).*

Physiognomy is not the only scientific system upon which Balzac relies. He also, on occasion, invokes the aid of cognomology and graphology. In *les Employés* (p.1026), he reproduces Gobseck's signature for the reader's benefit. It "should prove precious for those who like to search for people's characters in the physiognomy of their signatures. If ever there was a hieroglyphic image that truly expressed some animal, then assuredly it is this name in which the initial and the final letter depict the voracious maw of an insatiable shark, forever gaping, grasping and devouring everything." As for the names of his characters, the care with which Balzac chose those is famous. "Should we not agree with Sterne in recognizing the occult power in names, which sometimes mock and sometimes define the characters of their possessors?" (*Ursule Mirouët*, p.268). Or again, apropos of Z. Marcas: "That Z . . . suggested some indefinable quality of fatality to the mind. Marcas. Repeat that name to yourself . . . Do you not feel some sinister significance in it? . . . Between men's names and the facts of their lives there exist secret and inexpressible harmonies, or else visible and astonishing disharmonies" (*Z. Marcas*, p.736). Or again: "Even those people to whom the systematic cognomology of Sterne is unknown could not pronounce those three words MADAME DE LISTOMÈRE! without creating a picture of her in their minds, noble, worthy, tempering the rigors of piety with the aging elegance of monarchic and classic courtesy and manners; kindly but a little formal; slightly nasal of speech; permitting herself to read *la Nouvelle Héloïse* and visit the theater; still refusing to hide her hair under a cap." (*Curé de Tours*, p.817).

All this physiognomy and cognomology may well cause a few smiles, and there is some justification for thinking that it does not represent what is best in Balzac's work. But it is a writer's eccentricities and ties that

---

* It is perhaps worth noting that we find this idea in Tolstoy's work as well. He writes, for example: "For me, the back is an important physiognomical sign; particularly the point at which the neck connects into it. In no other part of the body can lack of self-confidence and insincere feelings be so easily sensed." He held these beliefs so strongly that Drughinin once wrote to him: "Sometimes one has the impression that you are

reveal him to us. This concern with physiology is in fact no more than the most visible aspect, almost indeed amounting to caricature, of a profound tendency that is found throughout the whole of the *Comédie humaine*. I mean the profound tendency to see (and to depict) the world not as a collection of individuals but as a structure, as an organization obeying certain fixed laws. A social structure, as we have seen, but over and above that a moral, or at least a mental structure. Balzac's characters do not wander around in a void. They are all linked to laws, to principles, to what Balzac has termed the great interests of life. These laws produce different results in his novels according to the various temperaments and circumstances to which and in which they are applied; but this variety does not mean they exist any the less. They are to be found all together both at the beginning and at the end of the character. They constitute the wellspring of his actions and also, in many cases, the conclusion of his story, the moral. "Balzac," Thibaudet writes, "is the only one of the great novelists whose novels are governed by a positive philosophy, by a total conception of the world." I'm not at all sure myself that he is the only one, but it is in his novels that such a conception of the world is strongest.

And it is certainly in Balzac too that such a vision of the world has been best incorporated into the novel form. The writer of the "problem novel" starts from a thesis to which his plot and all his characters are subjected in advance. Worse still, he eliminates these characters and turns them into principles. Because he believes in those principles, because he attributes to them an absolute and absolutely unchanging value. Whereas with Balzac, though the principle exists, its value remains relative, perpetually dependent upon the variables to which it is applied, in other words the particular combination of character and circumstances. There can be no novel without a certain modesty on the part of the novelist, without a certain self-effacement, a certain degree of identification of the novelist with his character. The "problem novelist" is incapable of such identification; whereas it is a constant factor in all Balzac's work. It is apparent even in the fundamental tone of the narrative. *Un Prince de la Bohème* is written in a lively, ironic, mocking tone that bears no relation to that used in *le Lys dans la Vallée*. But nevertheless, both this *Prince* and this *Lys* must pass through an already rigorously organized mind, through a man who has his own vision of the world and who, even if he so wished, could no longer prevent himself from imparting something of that mind's particular coloring

---

prepared to write: such and such a man's buttocks made it clear that he longed to take a trip to India." (Quoted by Henri Troyat, *Tolstoi*, pp. 193-194.)

to everything it creates. So that, different though they may be, there are fundamental lines of force that run through both these works.

Lines of force, nothing more. This is not a moral question. Not, that is, except in the very widest sense of the term. In the sense that one says: the moral of this story. But such a moral must be deliberately imposed on a work, just as a thesis in a "problem novel" is deliberately imposed. With Balzac, it is a question of something that has soaked deep into his whole being, something that mingles with the creative stream inside in exactly the same way as the dreams, the memories, the longings with which all novelists nourish their characters. I don't believe in the "Catholic novelist" or, indeed, in the "Communist novelist." I mean, in the sense that I find it hard to imagine a genuine novelist saying to himself: I'm going to write a Catholic novel, or a Communist novel. But if he is truly a Catholic or a Communist, if such a faith or such a doctrine is genuinely the daily bread without which he could not exist, then there is nothing he could do to prevent his novel from taking on a certain coloration from his beliefs. And so it is with Balzac's conception of the world. It is part of him, it is embodied in his very flesh. Instead of being, as it is with the writer of "problem novels," a foreign body introduced into the work by main force and preventing the character from breathing, the general idea becomes a raw material for the novelist to work on, and even a mode of apprehension.

Raw material. Though the general idea is sometimes directly expressed, more often it is integrated into the plot or into a character. Which is to say that it is not presented here in the rigorous form that a moralist would give it. Balzac is not a moralist. Before all else, he is a storyteller. We may even be justified in thinking that, quite often, the general idea is present without his being clearly aware of the fact, or without his having expressly intended it, as an obsession rather than as a principle. Furthermore, as in all novels, it is not always easy to determine who is speaking, the novelist or his character. Lastly, I hope you will not lose sight of the fact that between *les Chouans* and *le Cousin Pons* there lie twenty long years. A man changes in twenty years. To everything that I say it will be possible to find exceptions. After twenty years of saying that something is white, Balzac will suddenly turn around and say that it's black. This does not mean that it is not worth pointing out that the white occurs more often than the black. "Where the passions are concerned, everything is true," Balzac wrote, "but it is the task of genius to go searching through all the random chances of these truths for what should seem probable to everyone" (*Fille d'Eve*, p.91). And it is this probability that is finally apparent in the *Comédie humaine*. In other words, not a rigorous philosophic system, not theses to be proved, but themes, tendencies, and obsessions.

CHAPTER 10

Love

Love defeated or love the scourge—Béatrix—Ces Plaisirs . . . —The Anti-Dame aux Camélias: les Mémoires de deux jeune Mariées—Angélique de Sommervieux—Love as a product of the will—Love as a driving force or love as an end—Athanase Granson—the Duc d'Hérouville—Love must come to terms, and we must come to terms with love—Marriage—The marriage compact—The married life of the artist.

As WE WATCH the parade of the *Comédie humaine*, as we observe so many foolish men so preoccupied with their persons, so many women so concerned with being attractive, we are attempted to believe that of all the forces depicted in this great work love must be the most fully represented. But this is by no means so. There is certainly a great deal of love in the *Comédie humaine;* but generally speaking it appears in an unfortunate light, often defeated, or else, even when it triumphs, crushing the lovers. Defeat or disaster, such are the two most frequent guises of Eros in the *Comédie humaine*. Emilie de Fontaine renounces love in order to marry an old gentleman. Louise de Chaulieu refuses to renounce love and dies of it. Those are the two ways out.

You may say: Oh goodness, Balzac is a novelist, and all novelists are alike in this respect; they are obliged to put obstacles in the way of love, for otherwise where would the interest be? But in Balzac it is not a matter of obstacles; it is a question of dead ends. Thwarted love is not the same as defeated love. In *la Dame aux Camélias*, the course of true love is blocked by old Duval's hat. But it is only an obstacle: love does not die. Indeed, it still has sufficient strength left to kill Marguerite. When Emilie de Fontaine marries her old uncle, on the other hand, there is nothing forcing her to do so. It is just that when faced with the ritual conflict between love and reason, she sees to it that reason triumphs. Love is conquered, trampled, eliminated. It has disappeared.

[257]

We also find examples of ordinary thwarted love in Balzac, of course. In
la Duchesse de Langeais, the heroine's piety is only an obstacle. Love as-
saults this obstacle; and it proves strong enough to drive Mme de Langeais
into a convent and her lover onto the deck of a brig. In *Une Double
Famille*, on the other hand, this piety becomes something more than a
mere obstacle: it actively kills love. Granville parts from his wife. Love is
conquered. Just as, in *la Maison du Chat-qui-pelote*, it is conquered by the
boredom of marriage. Just as, in *le Contrat de Mariage*, it is conquered by
the hatred of a mother-in-law. You will find, in fact, that the adversary
often appears far from threatening at first glance. In *la Fausse Maîtresse*,
love is defeated by friendship. In *le Bal de Sceaux*, it is defeated by vanity.
In *Eugénie Grandet*, it is defeated by money. In *Adieu*, it is defeated quite
simply by cold. "Love had succumbed to the cold" (*Adieu*, p.770). Mme
de Beauséant loves twice. And both her lovers leave her to make marriages
of convenience.

What? Are there no examples at all then of love proving stronger than
self-interest, than the conventions, than vanity? Yes, there are some. But
in those cases we generally find that it is the lover who succumbs: crushed
by love, led by his love into ruin or disaster. Either love or the lover; a
victim there must be. *Nisi paret imperat*. The moment love ceases to obey,
it assumes full command. And once it is in command it becomes a tyrant,
it shows its claws. "Love is hard and terrible as hell," wrote Saint Theresa
of Avila. Balzac, echoing her, exclaims: "Love, real love, is pitiless as
everyone knows" (*Splendeurs*, p.962). In *la Comédie humaine*, this is
only too apparent. Look at Lucien de Rubempré. Coralie loves him: she
dies. Esther loves him: it kills her. Clotilde de Grandlieu loves him: this
time it is Lucien who kills himself. Then there is the beautiful love of
Montauran and Marie de Verneuil in *les Chouans:* he dies because she
betrays him to the enemy, and she dies of having betrayed him. In *le Curé
de Village*, Tascheron loves Mme Graslin: his love takes him to the
scaffold. The Girl with the Golden Eyes falls in love: she dies of it. Mme
Jules, in *Ferragus*, loves her husband: she dies of it. Mme d'Aiglemont
falls in love: her lover dies on her windowsill. Mme de Merret loves: her
love causes her lover's death. Athanase Granson loves: he commits suicide.
Mme de Mortsauf loves: she dies of her struggle against that love. If she
had given way to it she would have died of remorse. Each time, one can
almost hear the first words of Tristan ringing in one's ears: "My lords, if
you would hear a high tale of love and of death . . ."

And even when it isn't death . . . Facino Cane, in payment for having
loved, is doomed to prison and exile. In *la Muse du Département*, Mme de

la Baudraye takes a lover: he reduces her to the status of a fallen woman and to a state of disgust. In *le Cabinet des Antiques,* Victurnien d'Esgrignon is in love; he just misses a prison sentence. Sarrasine falls in love: he's out of luck, the beloved turns out to be a castrato. Mme de Cadignan has had between ten and twenty lovers: she admits that none of them ever brought her happiness. In *Béatrix,* there are two women in love, Félicité des Touches and Sabine du Guénic: Calyste deserts them both for Mme de Rochefide who does not love him. And when it is this same Mme de Rochefide's turn to love, she fares no better: Conti makes her life thoroughly unhappy. "There had been several examples among the upper classes recently of these escapades whose uncertain pleasures must be paid for by the remorse and social discredit attendant upon false positions, and Eugénie now recalled their frightful results" (*Fille d'Eve,* p.157). "Their frightful results." "Uncertain pleasures!" Where are the delights of love in all this?

These are all guilty loves, though, or, at least, loves not sanctified by the marriage tie. Will such sanctification remedy matters perhaps? Not much. The Langeais marriage is a disaster. The Maufrigneuse, Restaud, La Baudraye, Mortsauf, Aiglemont and d'Espard couples are all equally legitimate and equally unhappy. Sommervieux is unfaithful to his wife (*Maison du Chat-qui-pelote*). Granville is unfaithful to his (*Double Famille*). Louise de Chaulieu takes the trouble to marry twice, and twice the bridal bouquet becomes a funeral wreath (*Mémoires de deux Jeunes Mariées*). Beaudenord marries: the marriage ruins him (*Maison Nucingen*). Manerville follows suit, with the same result (*Contrat de Mariage*). Laurence de Cinq-Cygne has three suitors: two are killed, and she marries the one she never loved (*Une Ténébreuse Affaire*). Mlle Cormon makes up her mind to marry: the husband she picks is impotent (*Vieille Fille*). Mme de la Chanterie marries: the husband she picks is a bandit. Her daughter marries: her husband is a member of the police who informs on her (*Envers de l'Histoire contemporaine*). Mme Hulot is ceaselessly being deceived by her husband, and her daughter is betrayed by hers. Nor do the more unusual forms of love produce any better results. Vautrin and Rubempré, Paquita and the Marquise de San-Real, the soldier and his panther, love between two men, love between two women or bestial love, in each case these less generally acceptable bonds are severed by violent death or suicide. It is as though the devil himself is savagely determined to destroy everything that has to do with love. "How strange and ruthless it is, this power that always throws the angel to a madman, the tainted woman to the man who is sincerely and poetically in love, the tall women to the short man, a beautiful and sublime creature to an ape; to the noble Juana her Capitaine Diard, whose story you have heard, to Mme de Beauséant an Ajuda, to Mme d'Aiglemont her husband, to the Marquis d'Espard his wife" (*Lys dans la Vallée*, p.880). Ill-matched love, love doomed to defeat, love as a scourge. "My love is a mortal sickness," Esther cries (*Splendeurs*, p.791). Where are our usual dogmas in all this: Love stronger than Death, Love the only source of happiness, Love the universal remedy?

"Since I have no love, why should I not seek for happiness?" Renée de l'Estorade writes in *Mémoires de deux Jeunes Mariées* (p.181). Clearly, for her, they are two distinctly different things. And for Balzac too. *Le Lys dans la Vallée* brims over with love; but the happiness in that book is never anything but ephemeral, precarious and dearly paid for. You may say that this doesn't count, because Mme Mortsauf rejects love. But Mme Graslin doesn't. She yields to it, and what does it lead to? Remorse and the scaffold. Then perhaps is it because, in both these cases, love comes too late, when the women in question are already married? Very well, take *Béatrix*. Here, there are no obstacles, no marriage ties. Vignon, Conti and Félicité des Touches are all single people. So too, during the first part of the book, is Calyste du Guénic. And Béatrix de Rochefide, who is separated from her husband, lives more or less the same life as a divorced woman of today. Nor are they under any moral constraints. These are intellectual circles, without prejudices, without very many principles and almost entirely devoid of religious beliefs. Of the five characters before us, four at least are very intelligent and live according to the dictates of their intelligence alone. No social terrors, no taboos. And among these five completely free beings Balzac creates all the possible situations imaginable. In this respect *Béatrix* is a sort of compendium, a catalogue. To begin with, Conti is Félicité's lover. It is a liaison between two artists: first situation. A woman friend of Félicité's, Béatrix de Rochefide, alienates the affection of this lover and runs away with him to Italy, deserting her husband in order to do so: second situation. Calyste falls in love with Félicité. First love of a young man for a woman older than himself: a new situation. Félicité rejects his advances at first, but her new lover, Claude Vignon, enlightens her as to her true feelings. Another new situation: the lovers who refuse to be hoodwinked by love. Félicité agrees that she loves Calyste, yet it is she who introduces him to Béatrix and who talks about Béatrix to him in such a way that he falls in love with her before he has even seen her. Another situation: the crystallization of love around an idea, around a phrase. Balzac has already given us a glimpse of the same phenomenon in *la Femme abandonnée*, with Gaston de Neueil and Mme de

Beauséant; but here everything is made clear, explained in detail: it is a laboratory demonstration. Béatrix arrives. Relationship of two women one of whom has taken the other's lover. New situation. Béatrix scorns Calyste's love. Félicité takes the affair into her hands. She explains to Calyste —to the Calyste she loves—how he should set about seducing Béatrix. Knowing her friend's jealous character, Félicité behaves as though she is Calyste's mistress. She has him spend hours on end in her bedroom. It's farcical. But isn't that what love is? A farce that is occasionally no laughing matter? The scheme succeeds. Béatrix, stung by what she sees, shows Félicité the letters that Calyste has been writing to her. And Vignon is there all the time too. He observes and comments. Like Mme de Merteuil in *les Liaisons Dangereuses*. And as in *les Liaisons too*, everything is explained, taken apart before our eyes. The characters treat their emotions as if they were the parts of a clock. For we are indeed being taken on a guided tour of love's workshop, and here are the mechanics to show us all the blueprints. Calyste asks Félicité's advice. He also asks for that of his mother, who is the young wife of an old husband. New situation. It's like a hand of bridge being played with all the cards down on the table. Everyone knows everyone else's hand. There are no surprises. As I have said, it is a mechanism that we are being shown. The characters are all nerved up together in the château where the affair takes place, locked in with their passions, undisturbed by the outside world, living in a vacuum like the characters of Sartre's *Huis Clos*, tearing each other to pieces. At last a door opens: Conti has come back. And with him a little common sense. Conti has come from the outside world and is therefore free from these obsessive follies. He leaves with Béatrix. Whereupon Félicité immediately gives up Calyste. Yet another situation: the woman accepting her age. She gives Calyste her entire fortune so that he shall be able to marry Sabine de Grandlieu. Sabine is only a very young girl still, but it is with a full awareness of what she is about that she enters the game. She knows that Calyste has not ceased to love Béatrix. A new piece of marivaudage—cruel marivaudage—which Sabine recounts in detail to her mother. Here again, all the cards are laid on the table. And we have another new situation: the wife fighting against the ghost. Calyste sees Béatrix again. When he was free, she spurned him. Now that he is married she tries to take him back. Further emotional complication. Béatrix is older than Sabine it should be noted, so that we now have yet another situation—only the twentieth or so: the old mistress.* What is to be done? The problem is hammered out

---

* In fact, the age difference between Béatrix and Sabine is only eight years. But Balzac insists on this difference all through the novel as though it were much greater.

among five or six people: the wife, her mother, one of her brothers, her confessor, de Trailles and La Palférine. All the possible points of view are represented: love, family, religion, society and the effect of gossip.

There then begins a further ring-around-the-rosy, a new and equally gloomy farce of which the stages are as follows: seduction of Béatrix by La Palférine leading to quarrel between aforesaid Béatrix and Calyste; precautions taken against possible relapse by reconciling Béatrix with her husband; marriage of the husband's mistress in order to facilitate the aforementioned reconciliation; lastly, reconciliation of Calyste with his faithful wife. Home at last! And what a journey we've had! Yes, but to what purpose? Where has it got us? None. Nowhere. Love on its own never leads anywhere. It leaves nothing in the hand but dust and ashes. We have seen a certain number of beings excite themselves a great deal, put themselves to infinite trouble, place themselves in all the situations it is possible to imagine, yet not one of them is happy. In all this novel, which is entirely devoted to love, there is not a single moment's happiness. Not even the precarious happiness of two bodies in ephemeral harmony. In the midst of all this emotional to-ing and fro-ing, was there not even a single occasion when a moment's pleasure was able, however briefly, to obliterate all the rest? Perhaps. But Balzac does not give us to understand so.

Neither in *Béatrix* nor in any other work. And this is another point that seems to me worth highlighting. A novelist who likes love cannot prevent himself from occasionally evoking the sensual pleasures that it can bring. These warmer moments are more or less entirely absent in Balzac's work. His lovers and his mistresses meet in drawing-rooms, at the theater, rarely elsewhere.

There are admittedly two little scenes of adultery in *la Cousine Bette*, a pretty glimpse of Coralie *en déshabillé* in *les Illusions perdues*, another of Mme Rabourdin in *les Employés*, the curious passage dealing with the Duc Cataneo's sensual gratifications in *Massimila Doni*, the transvestite episode in *la Fille aux Yeux d'Or* in which we find one of the rare sentences in the *Comédie humaine* containing an element of sensuousness: "He encircled her whole body with his arm, sat her upon his knees, and felt an inexpressible intoxication at the sensuous pressure of this girl whose amply and softly developed charms were enveloping him so gently" (*Fille aux Yeux d'Or*, p.303). And we should also add this singular remark made by Rémonecq in *le Cousin Pons* (p.654): "Oh, your arms," he said to Mme Cibot, "I dreamed last night that they were bread and that I was made of butter and that I was spreading myself all over them." But the entire list wouldn't take up ten pages. What? So many lovers and so little tenderness? Precisely. But all those evocative titles: *la Fausse Maîtresse, Une Fille d'Eve, les Mémoires de deux Jeunes Mariées.* Yes, they are evocative. But that's all. "The bed is missing," as Rastignac says in *le Père Goriot* (p.1023). Very rarely do we find a scene that quivers, even slightly, with tenderness, with sensuality or with any momentary happiness. Or with happiness—the word has been spoken. It is not one that is spoken very often in the *Comédie humaine.*

I have already had cause to mention *la Dame aux Camélias.* It is the story of what happens to love when it refuses to respect social taboos. And our sympathy in this affair goes, as did the author's, to love. All the unhappiness in that book comes from society, from old Duval and his hat. In Balzac's work, on the contrary, the unhappiness is a product of love itself. He gave the world an anti-*Dame aux Camélias* even before that lady had appeared on the scene. There is an Armand Duval in the *Comédie humaine:* Louise de Chaulieu. For, like Armand, she represents the love that will not come to terms. And Balzac condemns her. "Courtesan," her friend Renée de l'Estorade writes to her. And she herself confesses: "I am worse than a little kept girl from the Opéra" (*Mémoires de deux Jeunes Mariées,* p.271). Already there are shades of Marguerite Gauthier. In *Béatrix,* Balzac shows us the failure that attends love when reduced to itself. In *les Mémoires de deux Jeunes Mariées* he shows us the failure of marriage when it is reduced to love. And in order to make his proof more startling, he runs through the experiment twice. The book is constructed like Maurois' *Climats.* The first time through, it is the husband who loves more than the wife; the second time, the situation is reversed. But the end result in both cases is bankruptcy. Because in both cases the man and the woman have relied exclusively upon their love. There is only one suit in Louise de Chaulieu's pack: hearts. Love, absolute love, love that refuses ever to come to terms, holy love, a love that little by little disqualifies all other passions. "Love is, in my eyes, the origin of all the virtues," Louise de Chaulieu writes (*Mémoires de deux Jeunes Mariées,* p.191). "Pleasure has no need of religion . . . it is everything all by itself" (*id.* p.237). " 'In my eyes,' her future husband said, 'your actions are sanctified simply by the fact that you yourself have allowed them' " (*id,* p.212). This is already Dumas *fils,* love as a vocation, love the only happiness, love as sufficient excuse for everything done in its name. And to this love, Louise's husband will sacrifice everything. Isn't that sublime? No, Balzac replies. "Before two years are out, you will grow weary of this adoration," writes the wise Renée de l'Estorade . . . "Sooner or later you will come to despise him (your husband) for loving you too much." And the husband "who glimpses this future, feels diminished by his love" (*id.* pp. 259-260). Diminished, because he is no longer anything else but a man in love, and because he has renounced everything that, according to Balzac, constitutes a man's true life and worth: ambition, money, power, vocation.

And indeed, Louise's letters do soon begin to reflect a certain disenchantment. She who once did not want to have children now expresses her regret at not being a mother. What? Is that fine and noble love no longer sufficient to fill a whole life? And note that it is not by chance that Balzac refuses Louise the joys of motherhood. For him, that kind of love is barren in all the ways there are. "Excessive passion is infertile and deadly," says the Duchesse de Grandlieu (*Béatrix*, p.568). "The cold produced by egoism and the excessive heat of a continual ecstasy must certainly produce a void in the heart of any woman" (*Modeste Mignon*, p.548). Macumer, the husband who is too much in love, finally dies, killed by his love, killed, his wife admits, "by my demands, by my unreasonable jealousies, by my continual provocations" (*Mémoires de deux Jeunes Mariées*, p.282).

Having become a widow, Louise marries again. This time too, she does so without consulting any other code of beliefs than that of pure love. In fact, she goes further this time. Her first husband was at least a man from the same social stratum as she. The second is a bastard. He is also poor. Louise doesn't care at all. It's a lover she's looking for. Bastards are not intrinsically inferior as lovers to the rest of the world. Love mocks at caste and prejudices. And what does money matter, since they're going to live in the country? It's true that Louise did perhaps grow a little tired of her first husband's adoration. Never mind, she will alter the experiment slightly: this time it is she who will do the adoring. Is there more joy in loving than in being loved? Evidently not. By dint of living on love and on nothing but love, these two married lovers end up creating a misunderstanding between them that would have been of almost no importance at all between two reasonable married people, but which in this case takes on enormous proportions because of Louise's jealousy. She kills herself.

Dare I make the comment, however, that the proof is not as conclusive as it might be? The event that leads to Louise's death is not an inevitable outcome of her love. It could quite well not have occurred. The important thing here, however, is not to decide whether Balzac was right or wrong but to see what his ideas and the habitual tendencies of his mind are in such a matter. They are expressed quite clearly. In *la Maison du Chat-qui-pelote*, a painter, Théodore de Sommervieux, falls in love with a little middle-class girl and marries her. Here again we are confronted with a passion that has deliberately refused to take into account either the class prejudices or the other objections that the sensible Guillaume family have suggested to this artistic son-in-law. "What, my child," exclaims the good Mme Guillaume, "your husband shuts himself up with naked women and you are simple enough to believe he's drawing them!" (*Maison du Chat-qui-pelote*, p.58). We may laugh at this reaction. But the good woman is nonetheless right. She is right for the wrong reasons, but still she is right. For the painter very soon becomes bored with the company of this wife who is all love, who knows nothing else but love, who is simple enough to believe that love is enough to fill a person's life. So he is unfaithful to her. And she dies of grief. Where is the triumph? In the beautiful love of Théodore and Augustine? No, the real victors are the brother-in-law and his wife, Joseph Lebas and Virginie, who married without a great love, who accepted a match arranged by their parents, who make "a well-suited couple" (*id*. p.56), and who, because they approach life reasonably, finally discover a love for each other more productive of happiness and more durable than the kind we hear of in romantic serenades. "Not encountering any excessive love for her on her husband's part, the wife had applied herself to the task of fostering it. And since he had been led to respect and cherish Virginie by such imperceptible degrees, the time that this happiness took to flower was for Joseph Lebas, and for his wife, a guarantee of its duration" (*id*. p.56).

For Balzac does not hate love. He does not present it as an enemy to happiness. On the contrary, for him there is no happiness without love. But this love, in his eyes, is no more than one element of happiness. It cannot lead to happiness if it takes over the entire personality: it must be kept in its proper place. Renée de l'Estorade is another character who experiences happiness, and in particular the happiness brought by love. "Know," she writes to Louise, "that there was nothing lacking of what even the most discriminating love could require" (*Mémoires de deux Jeunes Mariées*, p.185). But there were no moans of pleasure on the honeymoon. Directly after her marriage, Renée wrote: "The necessary provisions for the journey of marriage are to be found in these words: resignation and devotion" (*id*. p.228). Not for an instant did she cease to think about her husband's career, about her family's fortunes, about her children's futures. She never let herself be taken over by love. She always had other things to think about. That is the key to happiness in Balzac. For there are happy couples in the *Comédie humaine*. There are the l'Estorades, there is the Lebas couple, there are the Camusots, the Birotteaus and their daughter, who marries Anselme Popinot, there are the Rabourdins in *les Employés*, the Séchards, Ursule Mirouët and her Savinien, Modeste Mignon and her La Brière, Mme Firmiani and her Octave de Camps, Massimila Doni and her Prince de Varèse and Emile Blondet and Mme de Montcornet. Let us examine these couples more closely. In every case we shall see that there is an element in this happiness exterior to love, an element of reason, an element, in short, that enables love to avoid the dangerous regions of the absolute and link itself firmly to society. Lebas and his wife are happy, as we have seen, but theirs is a match concluded according to the principles of their social class, desired by their parents and lauded by the neighbors, who, Balzac tells us, approved of "the good sense shown by Mlle Virginie in making, as they put it, such a solid marriage and remaining faithful to the neighborhood" (*Maison du Chat-qui-pelote*, p.49). Modeste Mignon, though with rather more of a to-do, behaves in exactly the same way. She rejects the Duc d'Hérouville, who would have taken her out of the class in which she was born; she rejects Canalis despite his halo of literary glamour; and she marries the suitor preferred by her father, the good, honest La Brière, "one of those ordinary men with positive virtues and dependable morals that appeal to parents" (*Modeste Mignon*, p.493). Mme Firmiani, née Cadignan, marries Octave de Camps. Same social stratum, sensible marriage, happy couple. The clerk Birotteau marries a young lady who works in a store. Popinot asks for the hand of his employer's daughter. The judge Camusot marries the daughter of the King's usher. All unions contracted according to the principles of society. All sensible matches. All happy marriages. Happy because sensible. "I cannot think of one Balzac novel," Alain wrote, "in which love manages to attain happiness without bending to the laws of society." The daughter of a duke, Louise de Chaulieu marries a Gaston, which is scarcely a name at all: disaster. Sommervieux marries the daughter of a cloth-merchant: disaster. Mme de la Baudraye goes to live with Lousteau: disaster. Marie de Vandenesse falls in love with Nathan, though he is a writer, and God knows writers have had a bad press in literature: the affair comes to nothing. In this respect, Balzac remains a classic. In Marivaux's plays, we see serving-maids and Marquises forever dressing up as their superiors or inferiors. But Marivaux never goes so far as to make a marquise fall in love with a genuine valet, or a maidservant with a real marquis. Beneath the periwigs and the aprons, the social categories remain unchanged. If they did not, then the comedy would become a drama. And in Balzac we have that drama. We are shown what happens to characters who smash the social barriers and ignore the laws of their class. The duchess marries the bastard, the artist a tradesman's daughter. Quietly, sitting on his milestone, confident of his prey, Misfortune waits for them on the road ahead. Marivaux's characters emerge unscathed because they respect the social barriers; Balzac's are destroyed because they do not. We are a long way from the Prince and the Shepherdess, a far cry from the kind of romantic love that pays no heed to anything outside itself.

But Savinien, I hear someone protesting. Savinien de Portenduère who marries the middle-class Ursule Mirouët. Isn't theirs a happy love? True. But Savinien falls in love with Ursule at precisely that moment when, having emerged from the prison where his debts had landed him, he has understood that "money is the pivot, the sole effective agent, the sole motive force" in society; at the moment when he has just announced that he intends to marry a young lady who will provide him with social standing. He falls in love with her, in short, because "some inexplicable presentiment" causes him to see in Ursule "the woman whose portrait the doctor had limned for him, setting her in a golden frame with these magic words: seven to eight hundred thousand francs" (Ursule Mirouët, pp. 371 and 373). However sincere and passionate that love later becomes, it first sprang from considerations totally alien to love. Savinien's love is not like Armand Duval's but like that of young Fenton in *The Merry Wives of Windsor*:

> Albeit I will confess thy father's wealth
> Was the first motive that I woo'd thee, Anne;
> Yet, wooing thee, I found thee of more value
> Than stamps in gold or sums in sealed bags;
> And 'tis the very riches of thyself
> That now I aim at.

A perfect compatibility of social situations is not the only foreign element that Balzac introduces into love, however. The Lebas couple, the Camusots and the Popinots are happy not only because their choice of partner was governed by the right reason but also because they hardly ever have the time to think about love. They have other things to occupy their minds: their businesses, their finances, their careers. Birotteau has his perfume to think about, Renée de l'Estorade her children, Rabourdin his projected administrative reforms, Emile Blondet his articles, Mme de Montcornet her salon. Not one of them permits love to take over his or her life entirely. Not one of them follows the example of Louise de Chaulieu and her two husbands. David Séchard marries Eve Chardon whose social status is inferior to his own. And they are happy together. But again for the same reason: because he is not only a man in love, he is also an inventor. And perhaps it is worth noting that the only misfortune that does overtake him is in fact, though indirectly, the result of his love, since it is a matter of some banker's drafts that he has endorsed on behalf of his wife's brother. And it is his invention that rescues him from the abyss into which his love almost hurls him. But let us not quibble. Eve and David provide us with an image of love so touching that it would be churlish for us to find fault. Listen to them as they go for a walk together. What is it they are talking about? Their love? Naturally. But also: "In order to give you some idea of the extent of this trade, I should tell you, mademoiselle, that in 1814 the banker Cardon, etc . . . In another ten years, Holland paper, that is, paper made of linen rags, will be quite unobtainable" (*Illusions perdues*, pp. 558 and 561). There is another charming love scene, this time in *la Recherche de l'Absolu*, between Marguerite Claës and Emmanuel de Solis. They blush, their hands brush against one another, but, at the same time, they are discussing the legal means available to them for salvaging the Claës family fortune. For Balzac, there is more love in that linen rag paper and in those legal pros and cons than in all the cooings of any Coralie. It is for love that young Emmanuel has delved into those law books, for love that Savarus has buried himself away in Besançon in order to achieve election as a deputy, for love that Popinot slaves away like a member of a chain-gang in his pharmacy. "He could see Césarine sitting on all the packing cases, lying on every way-bill, printed on every invoice; he said to himself, as with shirtsleeves rolled up to his elbows and jacket off he hammered nails furiously into a packing-case: she shall be my wife" (*César Birotteau*, p.489). "The power and the glory, that immense moral fortune I am seeking to acquire," Savarus writes, "is only secondary in itself: these things are for me a means to bliss, the pedestal on which to set my idol" (*Albert Savarus*, p.814).

Nothing could therefore be more erroneous than to suppose that the conception we find of love in these works is a weak one. We all know men and women who have loved or who have married out of interest or ambition. But they did not love one another. They were feigning love. Shriveled hearts accepting without a qualm the prospect of a life without love, or minds with the necessary duplicity to marry a woman while already planning in advance to seek their pleasures elsewhere. There is nothing of that sort in the happy couples I have just dealt with. Though I should except from that claim the Camusots de Marville, both of whom are out and out social climbers. The others are good-hearted, disinterested, sincere people who love one another sincerely. But whose love does not make them lose sight of the world around them. Who know that happiness is a thing that must be built, and that it takes more than one kind of material to build it. A man loves a woman. Is the best method of proving this to curl up at her feet with a guitar? Would it not be better to sally forth into the world, to storm the antechambers of success, then to bring back and pile up at her feet the fame, the Golden Fleeces, and the entries in the Grand-Livre that you have won for her sake? A woman loves a man. What better way of proving it to him than by urging on, by guiding his natural energies, as Renée de l'Estorade does? What better way to serve him than by making one's body his stepping-stone to glory, as Suzanne dreams of doing for Athanase Granson (*Vieille Fille*). This is still the classical conception of love, of love not as a weak passion but as a passion that, like all passions, has its limits. Forestalling Proust, Balzac has revealed the discontinuities of the human heart. In *la Dame aux Camélias*, the lovers go to live in the country. It's charming. A cottage and a loving heart, what does anything else matter? When Armand's father arrives, we become angry, we're ready to rush up onto the stage and stamp on that fateful hat of his. But we forget to ask ourselves what would have happened if this sequestered life had gone on for ten years, what would have happened on that day when young Duval read in the newspaper (for there is no lover who does not eventually go back to reading newspapers), on that day, I repeat, when he learned that his brother had been appointed a state councilor, and his cousin made a cabinet minister? For Duval, Marguerite Gauthier could never be either a stepping-stone or a source of energy. She can never be anything but an obstacle between him and society, between him and fame, between him and his work.

Aside from Louise de Chaulieu and Macumer, there is another lover in the *Comédie humaine* who allows himself to be taken over entirely by his love; who instead of using it as a lever sees it as a god to which he must sacrifice his ambition, his vocation. "Farewell glory, farewell future, farewell the life I dreamed of! For now, my dearly dearly beloved, my glory is to belong to you . . . To sit at your feet, is that not my whole life now? Would it not be stealing joys from our love, precious moments from our happiness, feelings that are the due of your divine soul, if I were to give up my time to study?" Alas, it is a madman speaking: that unfortunate Louis Lambert. And this idolatrous love has helped contribute to his madness. Balzac's thumb is turned firmly down. "The sight of Louis had exercised an indescribably sinister influence upon me" (*Louis Lambert*, pp. 433 and 455). He never departs from his classical attitude. Louis

Lambert with Pauline, Macumer with Louise, both are Hercules languish-
ing at the feet of Omphale. Balzac's verdict is the same as that of the
Greeks.

But we cannot choose whom we love, you may say. "One loves because
one loves," says Bianchon, for the doctor does have these moments of
simplicity. But Rastignac replies: "Possibly, but I love her for a great
many other reasons. She is the Marquise d'Espard, she was born a
Blamont-Chauvry, she is in vogue, she has soul, she has a foot as well-
turned as the Duchesse de Berry's, she has perhaps a hundred thousand
francs of yearly income" (*Interdiction*, p.12). Rastignac is, of course, an
ambitious young man who refuses to allow himself even a moment's spontaneity. But in Balzac, even when love is at its most disinterested, there is
always a choice, a preliminary deliberation, that is to say, on the part of
the intelligence and the will. The notion of love not controlled by the will
is absurd, he declares curtly. In which he is of the same opinion as Cor-
neille: "The love of an *honnête homme* should always be controlled by
the will." And of the same opinion as Racine: "I call the love he (Hippolyte) feels for Aricie despite himself a weakness." For Balzac, as for the
classic writers, the love that does not choose, the love that is not controlled by will, fatal love, the love-that-brooks-no-resistance, can lead
only to disaster. For Armand Duval, as for us too, generally speaking, love
is a strictly individual matter, one that begins with the individual, with the
man stripped, if I may hazard the term, of all externals. In those conditions, what does the past matter? Or parents, or money, or social bounda-
ries? How could Marguerite Gauthier possibly be an ex-cocotte, since she
did not begin to live until the day I fell in love with her? "There are
moments," Marguerite Gauthier says, "when I forget what I have been,
when the me I used to be becomes so detached from the me I am today
that the result is two quite separate women."

For Balzac, on the other hand, a past cannot be interred, a family cannot
be dispensed with, an upbringing cannot be abolished. The individual does
not exist. It is not Clotilde that I love, or Ernestine or Emma. It is Mlle
Clotilde de Grandlieu, the daughter of a duke, and nothing on earth can
ever change the fact that she is the daughter of a duke. Her family connections and her fortune are as much an integral part of her as the color of
her eyes and the goodness of her character. For Balzac, such characteristics are not accidentals but essentials. And they are things that one has the
right to love or not love in exactly the same way as the curve of a hip, the
weight of a breast, or a quality of soul. Anyone who forgets this is

doomed to make the direst mistakes. Théodore de Sommervieux marries Angélique Guillaume because she is pretty and affectionate. He deliberately closes his eyes to the fact that she is also a shopkeeper's daughter, that she has spent twenty years in a shop, that the shop has necessarily left an indelible mark on her soul, and that nothing in her upbringing has prepared her for becoming the wife of a society painter. And before long he is neglecting her in order to go looking for the wit and sparkle he needs in the company of a woman like Mme de Carigliano. Today, in an age when society is no longer so rigidly structured, we may well find these principles outmoded or excessive. But that is no reason to refuse this conception of love its great strength and its great sincerity. Balzac's biographers often speak rather slightingly of his love for Mme Hanska. They are not averse from insinuating that the lady's château and title were not without their effect on Balzac's passion. And they are right. Yet his love was nevertheless profound, sincere and lasting. Mme Hanska's château was included in it, that is all.

With all the reservations that ought to be made when discussing a man who has expressed himself through the creation of characters and not in the form of axioms, it therefore seems to be true that, for Balzac, love has no value unless, far from laying a man's life to waste, it provides him, on the contrary, with a source of energy. Unless it creates energy, or at least permits him to deploy the energies he already has. Love as a driving force, or love as a means. A driving force as it is for Savarus and Popinot, who only work as much as they do because they are in love. Or a means as it is for some of the other characters, for example young Athanase Granson in *la Vieille Fille*. Perhaps the example is badly chosen, because Athanase fails in what he attempts. But this failure is only an accident. There is little doubt that he had only to declare his love in order to see it rewarded. His failure is not a product of the nature of his love but of his shyness, of that demon of heaviness, of that absent-mindedness that he displays in everything he does, and of which one rather fears the explanation is to be found in the insinuations made by the Chevalier de Valois (*Vieille Fille*, p.275): "The morals of those Imperial lycées were truly appalling."

Balzac presents this Athanese to us as the Arabian bird of those parts, as "genius in disguise," as "a man of imprisoned talent" (*id*. p.236). He has, we are told, an exalted sensibility and an untamed pride. He is "a man capable of becoming one of France's most noble and illustrious examples" (*id*. p.237). After such a fanfare to announce his entrance, Athanase must certainly be going to provide us with an example of true love as Balzac sees it. And whom does he love? He loves Mlle Cormon, who is twenty years older than he is, who is fat, not at all beautiful and not at all intelligent. Is he blinded by love then? Not at all. Athanase has fallen in love with her quite simply because she is rich. Balzac admits this frankly. "This love," he says, "was engendered by calculation" (*id.* p.237). And let us not be too quick to protest. Savinien de Portenduère's noble sentiments were not originally engendered otherwise. Athanase is led to love Mlle Cormon "by a desire for material happiness, by a wish . . . to gild his mother's declining years" (*id.* p.237). This touching filial concern notwithstanding, such motives are, in our eyes, sufficient to disqualify both the lover and his love. But Balzac takes a different attitude. "What? When it is customary in the provinces to arrange matches on actuarial principles in order to guarantee oneself a comfortable future, should the poor artist or man of science be forbidden to make marriage serve a double purpose, and to serve as a safeguard for his thought by assuring him of the means to live?" (*id.* p.239)

Very well. We accept that reasoning. But the result is surely going to be a very dismal union. A man who has married out of material self-interest, a woman wedded without love . . . Once more, not at all. Originating in this first and purely interested motive, crystallizing around it, we now see appearing in Athanase both desire and tender feelings. Everything, in short, that goes to make a happy marriage. Desire: Mlle Cormon's ample breasts eventually come to excite our young lover as much as the extent of her acres. "That plump body was offering (him) . . . the sort of charms that were fated to attract him" (*id.* p.255). The astute Chevalier de Valois catches him casting glances at Rose-Marie-Victoire's corsage (*id.* p.272). Tender feelings: "She certainly has no idea, he said to himself, that there is a young man walking past her house at this moment who would love her dearly, who would be faithful to her, who would never cause her any grief" (*id.* p.242). This is a far cry from the cold and calculating adventurer, from the vulgar dowry hunter.

Despite the infinite social gap between them, we find Athanase's sentiments in the Duc d'Hérouville as well.

Here is another man who is presented to us by Balzac as being totally sympathetic. Insipid but honest. The comments put into his mouth have considerable astuteness. He is modest. He is not fond either of Society, of the Court or of Paris generally (*Modeste Mignon*, p.563). I repeat, sympathetic. Yet it is quite obvious that though he appreciates Modeste Mignon's personal qualities, it is above all for her dowry that he wishes to marry her. He is poor. He wants to regild his coat-of-arms, as the Camusots say. But he's not hypocritical about it and he doesn't beat about the bush. "Ah, believe me, mademoiselle," he says, "it is a great humiliation for me to have to bring financial considerations into the matter of our marriage" (*id.* p.563). Try putting a remark like that into a modern novel: your hero is now a complete bounder and that's that. But in Balzac he isn't, not in the slightest. Hérouville remains as sympathetic as ever. "The simplicity of this confession touched Modeste," Balzac writes. And Modeste's father goes further: "For those who are highly born, to employ wealth in the restoration of old and historic houses suffering from the ravages of time is a noble thing." Modeste agrees. "Yes, papa" (*id.* p.563). She speaks to the duke of "the profound esteem that I have conceived for your character, and the friendship that is inspired by a heart such as yours" (*id.* p.592).

Yet I do not wish anyone to accuse me of saying that Balzac condemns love, or that he preaches the doctrine of marrying solely for money or social suitability. Hérouville is looking for a girl with a dowry. Balzac presents him in a sympathetic light. But that sympathy does not extend as far as allowing him to bring off this marriage. Marsay, Rastignac and Victurnien d'Esgrignon all marry for money. Not one of those marriages is shown to be a happy one. And similarly with the marriages of pure convenience. "My parents," Mme d'Espard says, "married me off to M. d'Espard, because his name, his fortune and his way of life were exactly those required by my family in the man who was to be my husband" (*Interdiction*, p.50). In this case, the marriage is a thoroughly bad one. The Duchesse de Langeais and Mme de Maufrigneuse also married men chosen by their families on the basis of social suitability. And the same is true of Mme de Mortsauf, Mme de Bargeton, Mme de La Baudraye and Mme Graslin. All these marriages result in disasters even worse than those produced by love. Because every one of them has spurned and neglected love exactly as Louise de Chaulieu's two marriages spurned and neglected society. Both love and society take their revenge. There is nothing more significant in this respect than the example of Mme de Beauséant in *le Père Goriot* and in *la Femme abandonnée*. Twice she loves against the laws of society. And twice she is punished by the sufferings that her two lovers inflict upon her by leaving her. She is punished for dedicating herself exclusively to love, punished for having dedicated herself to fundamentally antisocial forms of love. But her two lovers are later punished in their turn for having married without love, punished for having sacrificed everything to society. One is punished by the death of his wife (Ajuda), the other by his own suicide (Gaston) and both by their regrets. According to Balzac, we must come to terms. "Marriage of reason," yes, provided the reasonableness applies equally in the social and in the emotional sphere, provided you do not forget that there is no worse unreason than to rely exclusively upon reason. Love is indispensable. But it cannot rule alone.

"To explain society according to the theory of individual happiness skillfully acquired at the expense of that society as a whole is a fatal doctrine" (*Lys dans la Vallée*, p.887). "The society in which you are to live," Mlle des Touches writes, "could not exist without the religion of duty, and you would be failing to appreciate this, as I failed to appreciate it, in allowing yourself to be governed by passion, by caprice, as I in fact did" (*Béatrix*, p.521). Love-for-love, love based exclusively upon the notion of individual happiness is precarious and dangerous. It is a challenge that the powers, society in general, sometimes even God himself, will take up and avenge. "It has seemed to me," Renée de l'Estorade writes to Louise de Chaulieu; "it has seemed to me that this splendid love was a defiance of God. Are you at least making some effort to redeem this defiance, to propitiate this threat? You do go to church together, don't you? And do good in secret?" (*Mémoires de deux Jeunes Mariées*, p.241).

For Balzac, true love is not the sort of passion that grips hold of a man and shakes him by the scruff of the neck, that ruins his sleep and makes him neglect his own interests or his vocation. On the contrary, true love should be yet another reason for a man to devote himself to his vocation, one more reason for writing his books or for becoming a peer of the realm. Instead of cutting him off from society (a cottage and a loving heart), it should plunge him deeper into it (a palace for my beloved!).

This love that has been integrated into society has a name. It is called marriage. Has the reader noticed, I wonder, that this chapter on the subject of love has by imperceptible degrees become a chapter about marriage. I have given a list of the happy couples in the *Comédie humaine* already. They are almost all legitimately married. Of all Balzac's lovers, I think it's true to say that the most in love is Albert Savarus. Alas, the woman he loves is already married. This need not, of course, prevent him from indulging in the compromises of adultery. But he does not do so. Far from his beloved, hard at work, he waits for the moment when the husband's death will permit him to give his love the only form he finds acceptable: marriage. And if he spends his time working, that too is with a view to that marriage. Balzac himself did the same thing with Mme Hanska. He could have organized his life perfectly well so as to include that love, found the means to live with his head in beloved's lap. But he preferred to love away from her, and to occupy himself solely with the marriage that was still so far in the distance. And so it is in his work: marriage —with or without love—occupies a much greater place than love. Marriage is Balzac's great concern. His tournament field, as Taine put it. Marriage is love being integrated into religion by the sacrament, being integrated into society by the mayor, being integrated into life by the birth of children. The husband and wife are still two lovers, but they are lovers who sign a contract, who make themselves legal partners, who have set about building something together. And that, in fact, is what really interests our indefatigable creator. Not the sacrament (there are very few wedding ceremonies in the *Comédie humaine*), but the civil contract, the integration into society, the formation of a new social cell.

So that in fact it is marriage that is the true subject matter of all the Balzac novels that have been too hastily labeled love stories. *Le Bal de Sceaux* is the story of a father who wants to find suitable matches for his children. *Le Père Goriot* is (also) the tragedy of a man who has married his daughters badly (there is one theme that runs throughout *le Père Goriot*: hatred of the son-in-law). *Modeste Mignon* is the story of a courtship by correspondence, a prefiguration of marriage via the classified advertisement. *Gobseck* is a pre-marital consultation (can the young Grandlieu girl marry young Restaud?). *Madame Firmiani* is the story of a clandestine marriage. *Le Contrat de Mariage, la Paix du Ménage, Mémoires de deux Jeunes Mariées, Une Double Famille, Petites Misères de la Vie Conjugale, Physiologie du Mariage*, all these titles speak for themselves. *La Maison du Chat-qui-Pelote, Ferragus, Une Fille d'Eve, la Fausse Maîtresse*, all these are stories of married life, of adultery, of jealousy. *Le Colonel Chabert* deals with bigamy. *Le Lys dans la Vallée* is an epic of marital fidelity. *Béatrix*, though its characters are all single to begin with, also ends as a story of married life. *Eugénie Grandet* is the story of a marriage that fell through. *Honorine* is the story of the husband who remains faithful despite his wife's misconduct. *La Vieille Fille* is a steeplechase with Mlle Cormon's plump hand as the prize. And even now I haven't mentioned innumerable other marriages or projected marriages, for they are everywhere in the *Comédie humaine*, and every one of them is a major plot development. We stumble through orange blossoms at every step. The wedding march never ceases to sound.

It is unnecessary at this point to comment at length on Balzac's conception of a good marriage. I think the reader must already have a sufficient notion of what it is. All that I have said about his conception of love applies to an even greater extent to marriage. It is worth pointing out, though, that apart from the happy couples already mentioned, Balzac also presents us with a certain number of couples that I should hesitate to call happy but that nevertheless achieve the social form of happiness: success. The Nucingens, the du Bruels, the Félix de Vandenesses, the Grassous, all these couples have one thing in common: the possession, by one of the partners, of a strong will, of a precise plan to which the other partner consents. A source of energy and complete marital agreement. Agreement, not fidelity. The Nucingens are both unfaithful to each other, but they both know it, and neither of them cares. They are successful. With the Mortsaufs—a marriage in which both partners are very much superior to either Nucingen or Delphine—there is fidelity but no agreement, so that their relationship stagnates, thereby leading to suffering. Nucingen is able to impose his vocation on his wife. That vocation is to earn a great deal of money, and his wife is prepared to aid and abet him. Her being unfaithful to him does not worry him in the slightest. On the contrary, Nucingen is delighted to see her find a young man who will relieve him of his obligation to express marital affection. Valérie Marneffe is another married character with a fixed determination: to be kept. She is unfaithful to her husband, but he is aware of it, he gives his consent to it, and he profits by it. In short, they are a successful couple. And the relationship of the Colle-villes in *les Petits Bourgeois* is much the same, allowing for the fact that they are much pleasanter people. Tullia du Bruel is unfaithful to her husband, but that does not prevent her from seeing to it that he remains energetic enough to become a count and a peer of the realm. Again, as a couple they succeed. The Diards in *Marana*, on the other hand, end up in disaster. Because the source of energy was lacking. "You have never loved me," Diard says to his wife. "If you had wanted it, I could have conquered kingdoms for your sake" (*Marana*, p.835). Félix de Vandenesse, in *Une Fille d'Eve*, sets about molding his young wife according to his own ideas. And it is the will-power with which he approaches this task that enables him to overcome the love that his wife conceives for Nathan.

This sense of vocation, and this strength of will, are particularly all-pervading, according to Balzac, in the artist, the creator, the inventor. Consequently it is more difficult for them than it is for other men to find the marriage that will not call upon them to sacrifice that vocation in any way. When torn between love and the distractions that he needs, Sommervieux sacrifices his wife. The sculptor Steinbock chooses his wife: he becomes one of "those charming eunuchs" (*Cousine Bette*, p. 321) who talk instead of creating. D'Arthez finds happiness with the Princesse de Cadignan: he never writes another line. As for the painter Schinner, "his happiness made him stupid" (*Bourse*, p.345).

Indeed, Balzac comes very near to saying that it is better for the artist not to marry at all. "Those talented people should all stay at home and not go getting married," Mme Guillaume declares roundly (*Maison du Chat-qui-pelote*, p.60). Of course Mme Guillaume has a middle-class mind. But Mme de Carigliano, who is a duchess, shares her feelings in this matter: "We women, you know, should admire men who have talent, enjoy them as one does a play, but live with them! Never" (*id.* p.66). And here is Louise de Chaulieu's opinion on the subject: "When men with talent are in love, they should stop writing, otherwise they are not in love. There is something in their brain that is taking precedence over their mistress" (*Mémoires de deux Jeunes Mariées*, p.149). And Massimila Doni's opinion: "When an artist has the misfortune to be full of the passion that he wishes to express he can never depict it, for he is the thing itself instead of being its image" (*Massimila Doni*, p.381). Which is quite a good definition of fictional perspective, be it said in passing. And also an effective side-swipe at romanticism. For Balzac, as we shall see, was much given to passionate protests against the age he lived in. According to Mme Claës: "A great man can have neither wife nor children . . . Your virtues are different from those of ordinary people . . . You dry up the earth all around you the way great trees do!" (*Recherche de l'Absolu*, p.573). "Those who have married," Mme de Carigliano also says, "have with very few exceptions married women who were nonentities" (*Maison du Chat-qui-pelote*, p.67). But Mme de Carigliano is a martinet, of course. What she means by a woman who is a nonentity is a woman who gives up all thought of herself in order to serve her husband's imperious vocation, a woman like the ones that the painters Bridau and Schinner marry, loving, devoted wives who, far from attempting to take over their husbands' minds, are content to offer them a "humble, discreet love . . . always smiling" (*Cousine Bette*, p.323). "The poet's wife . . . must resign herself to the necessity of possessing the charity of an angel, an angel's indulgence, and all the maternal virtues" (*Modeste Mignon*, p.412).

For such is, for Balzac, the true greatness of the wife: submission to her husband's vocation. Even if she is obliged to create that vocation in him herself, as Renée de l'Estorade does. "Sacrifice everything to the man whose name you bear" (*Mémoires de deux Jeunes Mariées*, p.231).

CHAPTER 11

A Digression on the Darker Aspects of Love

La Rabouilleuse—Baron Hulot—the Marneffes—the Collevilles—Vices—the Duchesse de Langeais—the Duc Cataneo—Vagaries—Une Passion dans le Désert —Sarrasine—Paquita.

I HAVE SAID that Balzac, generally speaking, shows great reticence in his manner of depicting love. It would be a mistake, however, to infer from this that he is a timid novelist. A great mistake. For though Balzac does not often describe the pleasures of the senses, he does evoke them. We have already seen that he does not shrink from scenes of cruelty. Nor does he hesitate to wade into the turbid stream of sensuality. It flows throughout his work. Underground much of the time. But always present. It is present in Lucien's advances, and in the sighs of Coralie. What is the dark secret between Calyste and Béatrix? How is it that this already aging woman is in a position to alienate that young husband from his young wife? Again, what are the hidden talents that enable Mme Roguin, who is frankly old, to retain all her power over a man like du Tillet, who not only has a charming wife but is also rich enough to provide a love nest for the prettiest legs in Paris? Balzac is silent on these points. We are reduced to suppositions.

In *la Rabouilleuse*, the allusions are more precise. I don't know if *la Rabouilleuse* is read very much these days, but read or not, it is certainly an excellent novel. The animation and the veracity of its narrative are admirably sustained. It contains misers, ex-soldiers, a provincial town, old ladies who play at lotto, in short all the things at which Balzac particularly excels. There is an element of mystery, there is a complicated web of kin-

[278]

ships in which one loses oneself with pleasure. The author insinuates that little Agathe Rouget is the daughter of the subdelegate Lousteau, which would make Etienne Lousteau into Bridau's uncle. It is true that later on Balzac denies this, but the idea is there and its presence is sufficient to titillate the mind. Then there is Max Gilet, whom both Lousteau and Rouget claim is their son, though in fact the honor of being Max's father belongs to a third party. There is all the heavy-footed blundering of provincial philandering. It's quite charming. But the novel also merits our attention because of a daring and a savagery in its situations that were never, in my opinion, surpassed elsewhere. First of all, we are shown a depraved old doctor taking in a little twelve-year-old girl to provide a little pleasure during his evenings at home. Alas, his strength is not adequate to the demands he had intended to make upon it. He does not even mention the little girl in his will, and the lawyer claims to have discerned in him "the concentrated hatred of a man in whom nature had disappointed the calculations of vice" (*Rabouilleuse*, p.969). "Your father . . . was such a laugh," the innocent young creature confides to young Rouget. "Poor old fellow, it certainly wasn't that he didn't want to . . . Oh yes, he certainly wanted me to be his wife all right . . . but . . ." (*id.* p.974).

For Rouget the younger would be perfectly happy to take over where his father left off. He questions her. "What do you mean? Are you the same now as when you stood there, barefooted, just brought in by your uncle?" "A fine question, I must say," Flore replies with a blush. "The crestfallen heir lowered his head" (*id.* p.973). That "crestfallen" is unexpected. Can it really mean that he is crestfallen because this girl he wants for himself hasn't been his father's mistress? It can, and it does. "Far from being jealous of his father, he was enchanted to see Flore receiving such an education" (*id.* p.972). For this young Rouget (Jean-Jacques) is mentally retarded, a feeble-minded creature who is filled with a cretinous, violent, and by no means vague feeling of concupiscence towards women that he has never dared to express. (Balzac even alludes to his "bad habits.") In consequence "was that not the kind of woman he needed, one already made easy, one with whom there was no necessity for polite preliminaries?" (*id.* p.972).

As may be imagined, Flore makes a quick mouthful of this feeble-minded creature. Jean-Jacques' concupiscence is gratified. And his pimples disappear. No, I'm not embroidering. It's in the text: Her master's face, until then "wan and livid, defaced by clusters of pimples at the temples and across the brow, became clean and clear of skin, then suffused with pinkish tints" (*id*. p.975). And further on: "La Rabouilleuse no doubt obliged her master to perform some of those scenes, usually played out unseen in the dark recesses of private life, for which Otway has given us the model in the activities of Aquilina and the senator in his *Venice Preserved*" (*id*. p.979). This evidently refers to the scene in which Aquilina makes the senator crawl around on the floor imitating animals. Note, however, the reticence with which the facts are expressed. Balzac has told us everything; yet he has described nothing. (Zola was to be less reticent in this respect. He actually shows us Nana making Muffat caper around on his Chamberlain's uniform. On a Chamberlain's uniform! Where is the pleasure in that? But then . . .)

However, though Jean-Jacques is now in his seventh heaven, Flore is understandably less content with this state of affairs. She therefore introduces another, and rather more robust, young man into the household. The *ménage à trois* thus constituted may be imagined: Flore performing her expected duties with Jean-Jacques, whom she rapidly transforms into "the most decrepit of old men" (*id*. p.1094), and then, those duties once accomplished, turning to Max Gilet for her reward. But now the hand of God intervenes, in the person of Philippe Bridau, Rouget's nephew. In the twinkling of an eye, Bridau has completely destroyed this nest of bliss, exterminated the gigolo, married Flore to the cretin, taken them off to Paris, and sent Rouget off to expire with pleasure in the arms of a certain Lolotte. "Giroudeau took on the task of procuring old Rouget the pleasant death, etc." (*id*. p.1096). After which, Philippe marries Flore, the old fellow's widow and heir, then immediately sets about trying to get rid of her by a series of measures as masterly as they are criminal. First of all, he gives Lousteau a thousand francs a month to acquaint his wife with the corruptions of the demi-monde. Once his wife has acquired the habit of this easy life, he cuts off her supplies, counting on the fact that she will obtain others "you know how." Since it is better to be safe than sorry, he also sends her a "young non-commissioned officer" who has been given express instructions to develop her taste for drink. And eventually Flore dies of a frightful disease. Well, there you are. And now tell me, quite honestly, do you know many modern novels, for all their iconoclastic airs, that have ventured so deep into the lower depths?

Lust, in *la Rabouilleuse*, is still only one of the elements in the drama. In *la Cousine Bette*, it grows bolder, it wells up on every side, it overflows. The Baron Hulot is eaten up with lust. He is no longer a man but a robot, an automaton, a skeleton. Yet in his youth he had been "one of the most active and upright workers in his corps" (*Cousine Bette*, p.155). For twelve years he was a faithful husband. He is a good father, indulgent to his daughter, always ready with good advice for his son, pleasant to his daughter-in-law who finds him "charming" (*id*. p.176). But all this is slowly to be gnawed away, destroyed. Family, government post, fortune, everything vanishes. Because of Mme Marneffe? No, Valérie Marneffe only represents one of the stages in this disaster. Hulot is on his way to ruin long before he meets her. Jenny Cadine has already cost him thirty thousand francs a year at one point (*id*. p.145). As for Josépha, if we are to believe Crevel, "that little canary costs him more than a hundred thousand francs a year" (*id*. p.149). Valérie Marneffe is simply the Waterloo that turns this decline into a disaster. Before, Hulot was merely prodigal; for her, he becomes a rogue. But even when he has lost Valérie, he still continues. He sinks ever deeper and deeper. He goes to live with a bit-player like Olympe Bijou, with a working-girl like Elodie Chardin and finally with a little girl, the young Atala Judici. His family rescues him once again, shuts him away, keeps him in illegal confinement, deprives him of the means to indulge himself. Poor innocent creatures! When the devil has his hooks into a man, what need has he of money, what need of liberty? Hulot still manages to visit the cook up in her attic and buy her favors with this bloodcurdling promise: "My wife hasn't much longer to live, and if you like you can be a baroness" (*id*. p.524). Those words are lust's crowning achievement. It is useless to attempt any more detailed analysis of Hulot's character. Is he good, is he wicked, is he intelligent, is he vain? Irrelevant questions. He is no longer anything but lust. You are no longer a man but a humor, the Prince de Wissembourg tells him (*id*. p.421). His character has been wiped out. "You're like a corpse that even the crows have abandoned," Josépha tells him . . . "One can see right through you!" (*id*. p.432) The father and the husband have disappeared. So has the man himself, and all his pride. Having been tricked and betrayed by Crevel, he walks away with him arm in arm. When Josépha drops him, he complains about it to his wife (*id*. p.202). When Valérie deserts him, he does the same thing. He weeps "like a child whose toy has been taken away" (*id*. p.384). He had respected his wife once; but even that respect has been destroyed by his lust, like all the rest.

Alas, if that were all that lust destroyed! But it has reached the point in Baron Hulot where it has become contagious. Over a period of time, it infects the whole family. God only knows the Baronne Hulot is a saintly woman. Her sufferings, her piety, her resignation, all these compel our admiration. And yet there is something inside her that slowly begins to spoil, to become degraded. Her very devotion to her husband tends to pull her down to his ignominious level. "If you absolutely must have mistresses," she says to him, "why don't you find women who aren't expensive, the way Crevel does?" (*id.* p.202). Finally, she attempts to beat the devil at his own game: "Tell me what it is they do, these women, to get such a hold on you. I'll try my best . . . Why did you never teach me what it is you want?" (*id.* p.385). Worse still, she eventually contemplates the idea of giving herself to Crevel in exchange for a certain sum of money. We are given a frightful scene in which this virtuous woman attempts to behave as she thinks courtesans do. All of this, needless to say, stems from the most excellent intentions. But would such expedients ever have entered Mme Hulot's head if she had been married to a different husband? She has been contaminated. And her son Victorin, once so respectful towards his father, ends up expressing a hope that the old man won't leave Mme Marneffe. He "might move on to some other woman, and there at least the initial outlay, the most expensive part, has already been made" (*id.* p.286). So that he too has been attacked by the contagion. No one can continue to live in close contact with lust and escape its effects. The son-in-law too finds this out. He hears Mme Marneffe talked about so incessantly that he eventually ends up in bed with her. In Balzac, hearing accounts of a woman's erotic attachment to a certain man, far from keeping other men away from her, only serves to heighten the interest she inspires in them. As witness: Steinbock and Valérie, Rouget and Flore, Calyste du Guénic, who falls in love with Béatrix while listening to the story of her affairs with other men, and Gaston de Nueil, who falls in love with Mme de Beauséant at a time when she has just been abandoned. Curiously enough, we find this theme again, though more brutally treated, in some of Simenon's recent books. The theme, if I may so express it, of the shared belly: the woman whose ability to inspire desire is directly proportionate to the extent to which she has already inspired it in others. See, in particular, *Lettre à mon juge* and *le Ventre d'Anaïs*.

In Hulot, we still perceive, very occasionally, a feeble fluttering of wings, a last twitch from his dying soul, a suspicion of remorse, a shadow of regret, a final semblance of a struggle. In Valérie Marneffe, there is nothing of that sort. From the word go, she is at home with her lust, she wallows in it, rolls in it, delights in it. To her, it is like a familiar weapon, like a mount she has grown accustomed to. Indeed, seeing her so assured, one might even be inclined to suspect her of feigning lust, of being a woman who merely uses her lust as Marsay uses his waistcoats, without believing in it, without ever for a moment being excited by it herself. She sometimes uses the phraseology of an overworked charwoman with reference to it: "Lisbeth, my love, I've got two hours of Crevel to get through this morning. It'll be the death of me." But Valérie's strength really lies, it seems to me, in the fact that she has become totally identified with her demon. Despite those ten or twenty lovers, Mme de Maufrigneuse still retains a sort of purity, the sort of purity that, as Laclos says, is sometimes actually engendered by the very excesses of pleasure. It is, in fact, a direct product of pleasure. And a life that involves pleasure, real pleasure, can never be entirely sordid. With Valérie, everything is sordid. What we hear from behind the lemon-yellow curtains of her bed is not the light laughter of pleasure but the snorts of the animal poking its muzzle into a soiled patch of earth. Lust, sullied, gummy—these are words whose very sound bodes some ill. Whereas pleasure, on the other hand, is an open, attractive word.* We may sometimes find ourselves smiling at the pleasantries of a Malaga. Valérie Marneffe never makes us smile. There reigns around her that particular kind of gloominess that is always produced in their vicinity by beings who have lost their souls, the joylessness of beings for whom evil has become a second nature, the same joylessness that we have already observed surrounding Lousteau, and that is the sign of the Evil One. Since lust is her livelihood, Valérie might be expected to despise it or to despise herself. But no: she is quite happy to be damned. Everything in her is rotten. She spreads decay to everything she touches. Even her friendship for Lisbeth becomes in the long run a murky, equivocal thing.

Everything in her is rotten. There are no qualifications. Everything. From her birth to her death. Valérie is the daughter of an unmarried lady named Fortin, Montcornet's kept woman. So there she is living in a world of lust from the very outset, like Colette's Chéri. She could have attempted to escape from it, of course, but she does nothing of the kind. She chooses as a husband Jean-Paul-Stanislas Marneffe, who is possibly, out of all the characters in the entire *Comédie humaine*, the most repulsive, the most slug-like, the most vile.

This Marneffe is a modest office-worker (in the Ministry for War) but endowed with "the kind of power bestowed by depravity" (*Cousine Bette*, p.181). He is "as corrupt as a prison hulk" (*id.* p.227), "destroyed

---

* *Translator's note.* The French words of which the author is so suspicious are: *luxure, souillure, bavure.* And the particular sound he is concerned with is the closed u of their final syllables. Since this sound does not exist in English the translation is obviously only approximate. Also, the word *pleasure* occurs in one very famous line of English literature only too heavily laden with precisely those connotations that the author here denies it in French. I mean Antony's "For i' the East my pleasure lies." However, since the author is, I suspect, somewhat less than deadly serious about the matter, these discrepancies need not be taken too much to heart.

by those debauches particular to great capitals, described by the Roman poets, and for which our modern sense of decency has no name" (*id.* p.271). In passing, I should like to observe that this is another good example of Balzac's reticence in the matter of language. Everything is conveyed; nothing is directly expressed. Marneffe's vices have ravaged him utterly. He is like "a corpse that someone has forgotten to bury" (*id.* p.277). Poor Valérie! you will say. Perhaps. Why did she marry him? Marneffe isn't rich. If she accepted him, then she must have liked him for what he was. Perhaps he didn't reveal his true nature until after they were actually married? But in that case his wife ought to hate him. And she doesn't, not in the slightest. On the contrary. One senses an understanding, a sort of friendship between them. Valérie talks to him in a way she never does to her lovers. He wants to become head of his department; so she uses her influence to see that his wish is fulfilled. Why? Need for money? But some of Hulot's presents are equal to two years of Marneffe's salary. Ambition on his behalf? But everyone agrees that Marneffe is at death's door. There is no way out: it has to be faced that Valérie loves her husband. But again, why? Because he leaves her in peace? "By preferring the dirty sluts he finds on street corners he leaves me free" (*id.* p.227). All right. But what still continues to astonish me is Valérie's coldness, and the self-possession she retains even in her wildest moments of extravagance. We see her surrounded by four or five lovers, with Montès whom she loves, with Steinbock whom she finds attractive, yet she never loses her head. Lucien never lost his head when in the arms of Mme de Sérizy either; but that was because he was concurrently finding his real satisfaction with Esther. Why should the same explanation not be true for Valérie? She possessed, her creator tells us, "special and tender talents that rendered her indispensable to Crevel as well as to the Baron" (*id.* p.270). Since she is willing to accommodate the caprices of two old men, why should we suppose that she would refuse to accommodate her husband's? Is it possible to imagine anything from which Valérie Marneffe would shrink? Hardly. And if I am to say what is really in my mind, then to be honest, I suspect that the bond between Valérie and her husband may in fact lie precisely in that gentleman's vices, and that it is their equal partnership in those vices which explains both the friendship that this obedient helpmeet feels for her husband and the cool head that she is always able to retain with her lovers.

Sexual passion has its horrors, but at least it sometimes has its flames as well. Pleasure may often be a source of shame, but at least it sometimes has its bright side too. In the Marneffe household, we never see either flames or brightness. Lust always has something lusterless about it, something chill. You only have to walk into the Marneffes' apartment on the Rue du Doyenné to realize this. The threadbare carpet, the socks lying about, the dinner that is always late, the veal coated in its ginger-colored sauce, the German silver cutlery, everything betrays "a poverty without dignity, the complete lack of concern of both husband and wife for family life" (*Cousine Bette*, p.183). Valérie is already deceiving her husband. Except that that is a very bad way of putting it. When a professional prostitute hooks a customer, who is it that's being deceived: the pimp sitting over his coffee nearby, or the customer painfully shelling out a thousand francs more than he'd counted on? No, Valérie does not deceive her husband. She has extra-marital relationships, which is not necessarily the same thing at all. Relationships of no particular consequence apparently, without any definite end in view. Enter Hulot, Baron Hulot, permanent under-secretary to the ministry in which her husband is employed. Valérie lets herself off the leash. She ruins Hulot and then, having worked up an appetite, adds Crevel to her stable. She is pregnant. The child is yours, she tells Hulot. Yours, she says to Crevel; Yours, she informs her lover Montès, who has meanwhile returned from Brazil. The whole thing threatens to become a farce. But a very dismal farce. In order to find a single gleam of light in all this sordid story, we are forced to wait for the moment when Valérie, dying her horrible death, is converted. Having herself become a putrefying, nameless object, she rediscovers her soul.

As you doubtless know, after becoming a widow in 1842, Valérie remarries with Célestin Crevel then dies shortly afterwards of an unknown disease that is passed on to her by Montès, whom she has still not relinquished the idea of eventually marrying. Montès, who never travels without an escort of Negroes, pays a young courtesan named Cydalise to allow one of these Negro servants to impregnate her with a disease that is completely unknown in Europe. After which, Montès undertakes the pleasurable task of contracting this disease from Cydalise in his turn so that he can pass it on to Valérie, who then gives it to Crevel. An amazing relay race, I think you will agree. And one of which we find an echo in *Béatrix*, though in this case it is a matter of a venereal disease (or, according to Docteur Lotte, of growths of a venereal origin). It is amusing to see how cautiously Balzac deals with this matter. Open *Béatrix* at page 618. You've been told what to expect. You follow what is meant. But I must confess that the first time I read *Béatrix* I had no idea what was going on. The second time through, however, one realizes that Mme Schontz, in order to avenge herself on Mme de Rochefide, has asked du Ronceret to pass on to her the indisposition (whatever its exact nature) in question. She has then generously shared it with Rochefide, who has passed it on to his wife, who has passed it on to Calyste du Guénic. It is true that there is some justification for wondering whether perhaps the whole thing is not a fabrication on the part of La Palférine for the purpose of leading Calyste back into the path of virtue. The last lines of the novel seem to suggest this. But the idea is there at any rate.

Balzac, as I have had occasion to observe elsewhere, does not like limiting himself to a single specimen. And in the case of this species we have Flavie Colleville to complete, to correct Valérie Marneffe. Flavie is another Valérie, only a gay, good-hearted Valérie, a Valérie without the cruelty. Born a Minoret, she is, like Valérie, the daughter of an unmarried mother. Of a lady who was kept, among others, by du Bousquier. Then, having reached the age of consent, Flavie also marries a government employee.

You were a government employee!
You earned two hundred francs a month.

And she is unfaithful to him. She is unfaithful to him with everyone. And for money. And he knows it. And he is quite happy about it. He likes his comfort, this Colleville. And thanks to his wife he has a comfortable home and sits down to a good table. He also has a numerous family. For the sentimental Flavie insists on keeping a souvenir of each one of her lovers. And in order to keep the books quite straight she gives each child its father's first name. Her first child, a daughter, was a gift from her husband. After that, Charles Gondreville comes up with a fine bouncing boy that is christened Charles. Then François Keller offers her a little François. Then Thuillier adds his little Céleste to the household. And finally there is a little Théodore who, if his name is anything to go by, was the product of good works on the part of an ecclesiastic. And indeed, I can produce textual references in support of this hypothesis. "What a pity that Monseigneur is dead," Flavie says to her husband (*Petits Bourgeois*, p.119). Where did he spring from suddenly, this Monseigneur that no one has ever mentioned before? Ought we not to identify him perhaps with the young Abbé who, several years earlier (*les Employés*, p.999) was showing such an interest in the future of this happy household? For the Collevilles are happy, that is the big difference between them and the Marneffes. The Marneffes are successful, but never, as one reads the story of their successes, does the idea of happiness spring to mind. The Collevilles, on the other hand, are as happy as larks. And yet, discounting the children, their activities are identical. The two couples are both tarred with the same brush. But, according to the characters of those committing them, the same acts can take on a quite different aspect. "Certain characters have the power to sterilize a vile action, certain others can distill infection and gangrene into acts which, according to the book, ought to be considered virtuous" (Aldous Huxley). Though both launched on the same profession, the Marneffes are odious and the Collevilles make us laugh. The difference between tragedy and farce can often hinge on a single line, on just a pair of underpants.

Rouget and Marneffe have already led us down somewhat risqué paths. Now, without wishing to compare her with those two in any way, I feel some mention must be made of the Duchesse de Langeais, for her tastes in the sexual sphere certainly give one pause. "She immersed herself," her creator tells us, "in those intoxicating sensations of pleasure that are the fruit of ceaselessly repressed desires. Armand and Mme de Langeais were like those Indian fakirs who are rewarded for their chastity by the temptations that it procures them. It is even possible that the Duchesse had finally come to the stage of being able to resolve her love in these brotherly caresses, caresses that would no doubt have appeared quite innocent to the world at large, but which the power of her imagination was able to transform, for her, into the most extravagant depravities" (*Duchesse de Langeais*, p.184). Here again, everything is allusion. We see the abyss yawn for an instant. But we don't fall into it.

In *la Rabouilleuse*, it will be remembered, rather than actually describe a scene perhaps too shocking for his age, Balzac made use of a literary allusion: he referred us to a certain scene in *Venice Preserved*. Then, for Marneffe's vices, he referred us to the Roman poets. In other places, he makes use of transposition. At least, I suppose that is what he is doing, and it seems to me the only way of explaining the behavior of, for example, the Duc Cataneo in *Massimila Doni*. This Cataneo is, at first glance, an innocent music lover. But his enthusiasm for music has some strange undertones to it. This man, la Tinti explains, "this man, who is a hundred and eighteen if you count from his baptism into the church of Vice and forty-seven if you look him up in the real church register, now has only one last avenue to pleasure left open to him" which is to catch "a perfect harmony between two voices or between a voice and the highest note of his violin. The old monkey sits himself down on me," she continues, "takes up his violin, which he plays quite well, draws notes out of it, then I try to reproduce them and when the long-awaited moment comes when it is impossible for him to distinguish in the total sound which is the sound of the violin and which is the note emerging from my throat, then the old creature falls into an ecstasy, his dead old eyes flicker with a final flame, he is filled with joy, he rolls on the ground like a man who is drunk" (*Massimila Doni*, p.329). Is it really the music that is important here? Or is it that Balzac has used music as a means of alluding to one of those erotic mechanisms that novelists generally shrink from describing? A little later on, this Cataneo and Capraja fall to discussing the pleasures that can be derived from music. They are surrounded by music-lovers. Why, then, does Balzac add: "The Duke and Capraja were playing a game whose rules were not known to all those listening" (*id*. p.351)? Why does he say that the only ones who do understand these rules are Vendramin and a doctor? Is it because Vendramin is an opium eater and the doctor a doctor? Because the vice of the one and the profession of the other are the only two possible keys to an understanding of a "game" that is doubtless more akin to vice than to matters of major and minor keys?

And then there are the notorious Thirteen, to whom Balzac devoted three novels. "There came together, under the Empire and in the city of Paris, thirteen men . . . all fatalists, men of soul and poetry, but weary of the tedious life they were living, drawn towards asiatic pleasures by forces all the more active for having lain long asleep, and therefore wild and raging when at last awakened." Taking careful note of the terms used, we are bound to recognize these Thirteen as a counterpart of the secret societies of debauchees to be found in the novels of Nerciat or Sade. When Montriveau kidnaps the Duchesse de Langeais, he takes her into a room that contains certain instruments of torture. Where have they come from? Have they never been used for anything other than the exaction of vengeance? And then, the second time the Duchesse is carried off, what are we to think of that? Of that nun? Of that corpse? Here again, should we not take these things as a transportation of the sacrilegious or macabre sexual activities of the Marquis de Sade? At least you will admit that there are some grounds for thinking so.

Till now, this chapter has remained, more or less, in the domain of the kind of love that is allowed to speak its name. We must now venture beyond those frontiers. *Une Passion dans le Désert* shows us a French soldier, lost in the Sahara, who is led by his loneliness, by his boredom, and by a certain eccentricity of mind, to love a panther. No, there's no need to look flustered: it's all couched in the nicest possible terms. In *Sarrasine*, we see the sculptor of that name fall in love with an actress and then discover that she is a castrato. He is given no time to brood over this disappointment, however, since he is promptly and very efficiently murdered by the patron of this sexually ambiguous person. The amusing part of it is that this castrato later becomes a little old man whom we see wandering through the receptions given by the Comte de Lanty, his nephew and heir. Finally, there is Paquita Valdès who, like Proust's *Prisonnière*, leads a life of total confinement, shut away by the Marquise de San-Real, a lady who does not like young men and is determined that her little Paquita shall remain forever ignorant of such dangerous rivals. Nevertheless, Paquita manages to give herself to Henri de Marsay, and this revelation of what a man can mean fills her with the utmost delight. There are several pages to be found on this subject in *la Fille aux Yeux d'Or* whose somewhat ardent sensuality, especially since it is complicated by a little matter of transvestitism, cannot be considered entirely Catholic. Having discovered her betrayal, the Marquise murders Paquita, though not until after a scene in which, Balzac says, "the eye of a man whose life was dependent upon his amorous adventures was forced to recognize that there are kinds of madness common to all the passions" (*Fille aux Yeux d'Or*, p.320).

Paquita and her mistress, Zambinella and his patron are all foreigners. This is doubtless a rhetorical precaution intended to make the boldness of the subject matter more acceptable; unless it is simply a literary device intended to reinforce the exotic nature of these unusual forms of love by the use of exotic foreign characters. Vautrin, however, is not foreign. He is French.

CHAPTER 12

Vautrin

His life—The enemy of the laws—The homosexual—
Vicarious pleasure—The will to power—The use of
Satan—The myth—Vautrin in the theater—The world
of crime.

JACQUES COLLIN, alias Vautrin, alias Trompe-la-Mort, was born in 1779. All he apparently possesses in the way of a family is one aunt, Jacqueline Collin, former mistress to Marat, a receiver of stolen goods by profession and once convicted on a charge of corrupting underage girls. As for Vautrin, his antecedents are not at all clear. Only one thing is certain: while still a young man he was convicted on a charge of forgery. But everything about him, his behavior as well as his reputation, indicates that he is not the sort of man to have limited his career to that one crime. At all events, he escapes from his prison and comes to live quietly in Paris, at the Pension Vauquer.

At this period, Vautrin is forty years old. He is a short, squarely built man with wide shoulders, bulging muscles, heavy square hands and fingers with very noticeable tufts of bright red hair on each joint. Ravaged face, yellow eyes, basso profundo voice, chest as hairy as a bear's back. What does he live on? The inhabitants of the Pension Vauquer can't answer that question, but there is certainly some mystery in his life. At night, men come to visit him wearing list slippers (*Père Goriot*, p.876). In fact, we find out the truth about this later on: some thieves, temporarily prevented from enjoying their worldly goods by prison sentences, have entrusted Vautrin with the management of their affairs. A singular enough occupation; but one that Vautrin masks behind a jovial appearance. He is kind and good-natured. He is free with his money. He takes Mme Vauquer around the waist and carries her off to the theater humming: *Oh I have been in many lands* . . . "Oh Lord," she says, "what a lovely man he is . . . I could be happy with him even in a hovel" (*id*. pp. 964 and 999).

It is at the Pension Vauquer that Vautrin meets Rastignac and attempts

[290]

to make him his associate. But the police catch up with him. He goes back to prison, where he enters into an intimate relationship with a pretty convict named Théodore Calvi, whose gracefulness of manner has earned him the nickname of Madeleine. Escaping once again, Vautrin then slaughters the Abbé Carlos Herrera, one of the King of Spain's secret agents, seizes his papers, dons his cassock and applies a small quantity of vitriol to his own face in order to make himself unrecognizable. It is at this point that he meets Lucien de Rubempré and falls in love with him. (Last pages of *Illusions perdues*.) He takes the young man back to Paris and sets up housekeeping with him. Esther's suicide causes them both to be arrested. Lucien kills himself. Vautrin is appointed Chief of Police, a post he continues to hold from 1830 until 1845, in which year he goes into retirement.

Such, briefly, the man. Such his career. Both were obviously suggested to Balzac by two real-life characters: Vidocq and Cogniard. Vidocq, as is well known, was a convict who turned policeman and ended up as Chief of Police. As for Pierre Cogniard, born, by a notable coincidence, in Langeais, he was an escaped convict who seized the personal papers of a French nobleman, the Comte de Saint-Hélène Pontis, who had fled to Spain. Returning to France under this assumed name, Cogniard then made a fine career for himself in Napoleon's army, went over to the Bourbons at an opportune moment, was made a colonel in the constabulary and then assumed leadership of a gang of burglars. He was unmasked in 1817. In *le Père Goriot* (p.987) we even find an allusion made to him, and in *Splendeurs* we also find another Chief of Police, this one named Bibi-Lupin, who is also a former convict. Obviously Vautrin's story was one very much in the air at that time. Victor Hugo too, it seems hardly necessary to add, tells us the story in his *les Misérables* of Jean Valjean, another escaped convict who builds a new life for himself disguised as the gentle M. Madeleine.

These reference points are useful. But they still leave us a long way from the real Vautrin. Cogniard was merely a particularly audacious impostor. Vidocq is the Bibi-Lupin of *Splendeurs:* the man who, either because he is disgusted with his life of crime or else because it has brought him no success, decides that the grass is greener on the other side of the fence. As for Valjean, he is the honest man who has been misunderstood, whom chance and necessity alone have led to commit what is, in fact, a rather harmless crime. In reality, he is not disguised as M. Madeleine at all: the good M. Madeleine is his true self. All these men are quite simple cases. Just as Vautrin is a simple case in the play that is named after him. Indeed, it is curious to observe how entirely Balzac has limited himself to the outward aspect, to the surface of the character, when translating him to the stage. The Vautrin of the play is simply the escaped convict, period. Intelligent, but without much significance, without any hidden depths. And the same is true of Ferragus in the novel of that name: he is an escaped convict who lives as an outlaw only because his situation forces him to, not because it is an essential part of his character to do so.

The Vautrin of *la Comédie humaine* is not merely a criminal, he is crime itself, the very embodiment of crime. He becomes a myth, a symbol. When describing the ex-convict's interview with Grandville, the Attorney General, Balzac writes: "These two men, CRIME and JUSTICE, were facing one another" (*Splendeurs*, p.1112). He is "no longer a man," Balzac also writes, "but the archetype of a whole degenerate tribe, a savage and logical, brutal and devious people . . . An infernal poem . . . The fallen archangel" (*Père Goriot*, p.1015). Vautrin is not a criminal created by circumstances. He is a criminal by vocation. He lives outside the law not only from necessity and because he is an escaped convict but by nature, because crime is his natural element. And far from complaining of the fact that he lives in a state of war with society, he draws all his pride from it. "I am alone against the government with all its courts and its police and its budgets, and I fool them all" (*id.* 1016). An outlaw, but happy to be so, delighting in "the sovereignty conferred upon him by the cynicism of his thoughts and actions, by the strength of a constitution inured to everything" (*id.* p.1013). Never a hint of remorse, of hesitation, of scruples in this untamable spirit.

There is the sinner who hates his sin and there is the sinner who hates morality. Gide, if you like, is an example of the first. But Vautrin is of the second kind. He is an enemy of the laws. And Balzac is careful to indicate this when the ex-convict first appears. "He seemed to take pleasure in flouting the laws, in scourging high society, in convincing it that it was being illogical with itself" (*Père Goriot*, p.859). Vautrin adds: "For every million of these two-legged cattle you will find ten stalwart fellows who place themselves above everything, even the laws: I am one of those" (*id.* p.937). He loves crime so much that he constitutes himself its apostle, its apologist. Even at the risk of self-betrayal, he never ceases to let slip remarks, observations, axioms that are so many criticisms of the social contract. He insists at every turn on offering proofs of the injustice and absurdity of the laws and of morality. "That's your laws for you," he says, "there's not a single one of them that doesn't lead to an absurdity" (*id.* p.941). First with Rastignac, in *le Père Goriot*, then with Rubempré at the end of *Illusions perdues*, he plays the part of the Professor of Crime, he mounts the dais, he expounds his theories. As we say "the Antichrist," so Vautrin is "the Anti-Social Contract."

Little by little, the shape that Balzac wishes to give this particular creation begins to emerge. In the context of the *Comédie humaine*, Vautrin represents a fundamental protest against society. Marsay is a rogue too, and also a Professor Emeritus of roguery. But Marsay respects the laws; or at least appears to respect them. For Marsay is very underhand in this particular respect. Vautrin, on the other hand, carries on the struggle openly, being forced to do so by the very fact of his situation in the world, which also obliges him "to live outside a society of which the doors had been closed to him forever by the law" (*Splendeurs*, p.725). Faced with a Marsay, society can still continue to deceive itself. But with Vautrin such a thing is impossible. Vautrin uses no wiles, he makes no attempt to come to terms. Even his passions, even his weaknesses are still protests against the social order. Victor Hugo's Valjean has one weakness: he loves Cosette. Ferragus loves his daughter. Le Biffon, another convict in *Splendeurs*, loves his wife. Such sentiments are links between these outlaws and ordinary people, bonds that keep them still attached to the social order. But Vautrin is a homosexual. Even in the sphere of love he is an outlaw.

Though there may of course be other reasons to be taken into account here. Though Balzac doubtless felt the need to include homosexuality in the picture he was painting of society, I imagine that in those days one still had to take certain precautions if one wished to deal with such a subject. In consequence, rather than blotting, say, the Duc de Grandlieu's escutcheon with this passion, it was doubtless wiser to have it represented by a convict, which is to say by a man who, for the ordinary reader, remained a fairly exotic creature, and one whom he rarely had the opportunity to encounter. Similarly, when dealing with the subject of love between women, Balzac made use of two foreigners: Paquita and Euphemia Porraberil.

I have read somewhere, though I'm no longer sure where, that the readers of Balzac's day never came within a mile of guessing the true nature of Vautrin's affections. This seems to me hardly believable. Doubtless we are particularly well trained to spot these things nowadays, but all the same, even in Vautrin's first tentative advances to Rastignac, in that hodge podge of verbiage with which he tries to enmesh him, it seems to me that the homosexual is clearly revealed. "But I, I love you," he says . . . "A man is a god when he looks like you" (*Père Goriot*, p.982). A little further on (*id.* p.985), are we not told that he once allowed himself to be imprisoned in the place of a very good-looking young man? And besides, there is also the policeman who takes the trouble to spell it out for us: "Let me tell you a secret, he feels no love for women" (*id.* p.987). And when he is arrested, in the midst of all the hate-filled remarks that escape him, he can still find a smile for Rastignac. "Farewell, Eugène, he said in a sad and gentle voice" (*id.* p.1016). It is the gentle sadness of loves that might have been.

In the play *Vautrin*, despite the simplification imposed upon the character, there is one trait that remains: his hatred of women. "Women don't know how to do anything but scream." Or again: "It's inconceivable, all that women manage to destroy." And the matter is made even clearer still in this remark from *Splendeurs* (p.1115): "For me, a woman can only be beautiful when she looks like a man." True to this esthetic, when he goes back to prison Vautrin falls in love with a young convict whose nickname, la belle Madeleine, is an explanation in itself. "His queen," as Fil-de-Soie puts it. Though doubtless this word (*tante* in French) had not at that time become part of the everyday vocabulary, for Balzac feels the need to make it quite clear that he is concerned here with "the third sex" (*id.* p.1055).

Then comes the day when, on a country road, Vautrin sees Lucien de Rubempré wandering along clutching his bunch of yellow flowers. On the spot, all thoughts of la belle Madeleine and Rastignac are erased from his mind. Yet where should chance lead them as they journey on together but to the Rastignac family's château. As they pass in front of it, Vautrin stops the carriage, alights and goes for a walk along the avenue that leads up to it. In *A la Recherche du Temps perdu*, the Baron de Charlus recalls this scene. To him, it is redolent of all the melancholy inherent in love between two men. In reality, if you reread the scene (*Illusions perdues*, p.1017), there is little enough to go on. But this is a trait common to a great many homosexuals: they see homosexuality everywhere. Give them a few trees or some birds and before long they'll be telling you about shepherds or sailors. It is a trait that Balzac too is well aware of. Three minutes after having met Lucien, Vautrin is already telling him about a cabinet minister who engaged a good-looking young secretary (*id.* p.1017. He once more delivers, this time for Lucien's benefit, the lecture on ambition that he has already given to Rastignac. And here again, it is not long before his expressions take on a highly equivocal turn. "My child, have you ever thought at all deeply about Otway's *Venice Preserved?* Have you understood that profound friendship, between man and man, that binds Pierre and Jaffier together, that makes a woman the merest trifle to them, and that changes the meaning of all social terms between them?" (*id.* p.1031) Here, in one sentence, is Vautrin in his entirety: the lover of men, the scorner of women, the negator of social terms.

So he carries Lucien off with him. And in order to give the young man the kind of life he likes, Vautrin is obliged to dip into the money that has been entrusted to him by his fellow prisoners. Just as Roguin dips into his clients' funds on behalf of la belle Hollandaise. "Despite all his strength, he was so weak when it came to opposing his minion's caprices" (*Splendeurs*, p.725). They live together. Needless to say, Balzac does not depart from his usual reticence. But we know Vautrin and Lucien well enough to use our imaginations. Vautrin is accustomed to shrinking from nothing, and Lucien, as we know, possesses neither energy nor scruples. The man who has lived off Coralie's money, the man who has accepted the few francs that Coralie's maid earned for him on the sidewalk is certainly capable of accepting his bed and board and his pocket money from the hands of a male lover too. Lucien has very little strength of character. We have seen him dominated successively by Mme de Bargeton, by d'Arthez, by Lousteau. What defense could he possibly put up against a will as strong as Vautrin's? Besides, and Balzac has told us this often enough, Lucien is a man-woman. Is it likely that this description applies only in the moral sphere? Should we not rather believe that it implies an ambiguity that runs through his whole being, an ambiguity that will allow him to accommodate himself just as easily to a Vautrin as to a Coralie? Certainly the bond between them must be very strong for Lucien to accept sharing his life in this way with a man whom he knows to be an impostor, an ex-convict and a grave social risk.

If only Rubempré felt some friendship for Vautrin, some feeling of gratitude; but there is not the slightest sign that he does. Given the opportunity, Lucien is perfectly prepared to hurl things at his protector's head (*Splendeurs*, p.701). The day before his death, he writes to him: "My contempt for you was equal to my admiration" (*id.* p.1007). Why should he feel contempt? Hatred would be more understandable. It is customary to hate one's demon. But Vautrin is not only Lucien's demon, he is also his lover. This contempt gives us a further insight into their relationship. Lucien feels the contempt of the prostitute for the man whose weakness has been revealed to him because he has gratified his desires. In this couple, all the love is on one side. When he learns of Lucien's death, Vautrin becomes desperate. "No tiger finding its little ones gone has ever filled the jungles of India with so appalling a cry" (*id.* p.1032). "This thing is worse for me than even death could be, but you have no way of knowing what it is I mean . . . You are none of you fathers, if you are fathers, except in one way . . . I am a mother too! . . . I . . . I am mad . . . I can feel it." He is taken to see the corpse. "He fell onto that body and clung to it in a despairing embrace so violent and passionate as to make all three spectators of the scene shudder as they watched." For hour after hour, Vautrin stays there holding Lucien's hand. And after this funereal vigil, the bold and ruthless Trompe-la-Mort is "as weak as a child" (*id*. pp. 1034, 1035 and 1037).

All these passages are quite clear. Despite one or two precautions, Balzac has not shrunk from a subject that in his day, I imagine, it still took a great deal of daring to approach. And Balzac pushes this daring to the point of demonstrating that this passion, reputedly so unnatural, is not, in its manifestations, any different from any other passion. Another example of the moral imperturbability to which we shall have occasion to return later. Vautrin's behavior when faced with Lucien's corpse is no different from that of Mme de Sérizy. And when Lucien was still alive, his concern for him was expressed no differently from that of David Séchard. Vautrin takes pleasure in seeing Lucien riding in a handsome tilbury just as David takes pleasure in seeing him invited to Mme de Bargeton's. Yet there is a world of difference all the same between Vautrin and the kindhearted Séchard, between Vautrin and the upright Michel Chrestien, between Vautrin and the chaste Mlle d'Esgrignon. In all of these, nevertheless, affection takes the same form. "I'll be driving with you in your tilbury, my boy," Vautrin exclaims. And in exactly the same way, Mlle d'Esgrignon sees herself floating with her nephew in a gondola along the Grand Canal (*Cabinet des Antiques*, p.397). Fearing the effect that the temptations of journalism will have upon Lucien, Chrestien offers to "penetrate into one of those intellectual brothels" in Lucien's stead (*Illusions perdues*, p.664). In the same way, Vautrin says, first of all to Rastignac: "I'm just a kind-hearted fellow who is willing to get dirty instead of you, so that you can keep out of the mud" (*Père Goriot*, p.981). And then to Rubempré: "You shall shine, you shall walk in glory while I, crouching in the mud of the foundations, carry the brilliant edifice of your great fortune on my back" (*Illusions perdues*, p.1028).

But it is in Vautrin that this process of identification is most forcefully apparent. When he talks to Rastignac we see him really getting inside the skin of that ambitious young man. He becomes part of Rastignac's own awareness. He can sense what Rastignac is thinking even before the latter has properly formulated his thoughts even to himself. "I know you as if I had made you" (*Père Goriot*, p.931). "I breathe through his mouth, I live his life, I feel his passions as my own" (*Vautrin*, the play). He becomes the other. When Lucien is arrested, Vautrin lives his life for him literally. He can sense the younger man's anguish. He makes a reality, Balzac writes, of "the German superstition of the *Double* by a phenomenon of moral paternity that will be understood by women . . . who have truly loved" (*Splendeurs,* p.1030).

For Balzac, to love is to identify oneself with the beloved and to project oneself into that person. Vautrin is in love with Lucien. He therefore projects himself into him; but since he is a criminal he can project nothing into Lucien that is not criminal also. And this tendency is made even stronger by the fact that his own corruption creates in him a need to corrupt. When he meets Lucien, he passes himself off as a man of some standing, as a Canon carrying out a diplomatic mission. He could have gone on playing this role. Why does he not? Why does he reveal the fact that he is an escaped convict? Why, when such a revelation might well have alarmed Lucien and caused him to run away? Why, when this confession gives Lucien a weapon that can be turned against him? Because he is a criminal to the depths of his soul, down to the last tiny convolution of his brain; because, like all profoundly wicked people, he has the desire to corrupt; because that desire is stronger in him than even his instinct for self-preservation; because, given his need to identify himself with Lucien, he must first render Lucien as corrupt as he is himself; because he must have the intellectual pleasure of Lucien's awareness that he is not the minion of a diplomat but an ex-convict's *queen.* The presence of the beloved is not enough: he also has to "mold him to (his) use" (*Illusions perdues,* p.1032), "strip him one by one of his beautiful illusions and wrap him in the shroud of experience" (*Vautrin,* the play). For this is another of Vautrin's traits: the spirit of domination. He is one of the ancestors of Nietzsche's superman. The active principle in him, the force that Balzac is trying to make us see in him, through him, is the will to power. Everything in Vautrin is a function of power. Physically, he is as strong as Hercules. "And then the observer was able to admire a hairy torso of cyclopean strength. The Farnese Hercules in Naples come to life" (*Splendeurs,* p.969). Given a pistol, he can hit the bull at twenty paces. He possesses the kind of skill, peculiar to convicts, that enables him to make a knife out of a fork or a ladder out of three pieces of wood. He also has the gift of second sight, another sign of power. He has a "magnetic," "divining," "fascinating," "profound gaze." "His eyes seemed to pierce to the depths . . . of everyone's conscience" (*Père Goriot,* p.858). He is rich. He has all the funds entrusted to him by the convicts at his disposal. He has spies everywhere. No sooner is he back in prison than he has found a set of accomplices to do his bidding. He lords it over all the Fil-de-Soies, the Arrache-laines and the Biffons. In fact he is treated like a king. He is the *dab*, the *caid*, the big boss. Through his helpers, he can reach any branch of society. He has his aunt Jacqueline, alias Asie, alias Mme de Saint-Estève; Prudence Servien, alias Europe; Paccard; Mme Nourrisson, and a whole society of hoods and thugs, informers and go-betweens. Not to mention several rather more highly placed accomplices, such as Colonel Franchessini. It is to the latter that Vautrin applies when he wants young Taillefer murdered. At first, we are shocked and refuse to believe it. What link could there possibly be between a convict and this highly regarded colonel? Then we remember the young Italian soldier for whose sake Vautrin allowed himself to be condemned (*Père Goriot*, p.985).

It is, in any case, of little consequence how Vautrin has managed to recruit all these accomplices. The important thing is that, through them, he stands at the head of a veritable conspiracy. And for Balzac, conspiracy is another name for power. This is another theme that we shall return to later. In the *Comédie humaine*, there are certain artists who succeed: the Cénacle; there are pleasure seekers who achieve their pleasures: the Thirteen; there are philanthropists who succeed in their aims: the Brothers of Consolation; there are usurers who grow rich: the Gobseck-Webrust-Gigonnet group; there are politicians who reach positions of power: Marsay and the clique of which he describes the formation in *Contrat de Mariage*. In the same way, Vautrin is powerful thanks to his conspiracy of rogues. And he enjoys his power. " 'Is there even one among you who is rich, as I am, with the knowledge that he has ten thousand brothers ready to do no matter what for him?' he asked with pride" (*Père Goriot*, p.1016).

Has he never sought accomplices in other directions? Has he never invoked the dark Prince whose power is evoked in *la Peau de Chagrin* and *Melmoth réconcilié?* Vautrin's motive forces are the desire for corruption and the will to power. These are also the distinguishing features of the Prince of Darkness. Is Vautrin a man possessed by the Devil? Or is he even, in *la Comédie humaine*, the Devil himself incarnate? If we turn back and read the speeches that he makes to Rastignac and Rubempré, we shall see that they are paraphrases of Satan's words to Jesus on the mountain. And then his claim to be a replacement for destiny: "I intend to be his providence," Vautrin says in the play. "Monsieur is a replacement for Destiny. A nice job," his accomplices remark in the same work. "I have taken on myself the role of Providence," he says to Rastignac (*Père Go-*

riot, p.940). "We have been replacing Providence now for forty years, Monsieur," Vautrin's aunt says in *la Cousine Bette* (p.462). In each case, it is an echo of the Devil's phrase in *Jerusalem Delivered*: "Let my will be Fate." "Is he the Devil?" Esther asks (*Splendeurs*, p.706). "The fallen arch-angel," Balzac himself says at another point. And let us not forget that, in his disguise as a priest, Vautrin celebrates the Mass every day (*id.* p.706). He is therefore living a permanent blasphemy.

Nevertheless, there is no textural reference that permits us to conclude that Vautrin is possessed by the Devil in the real sense of that term. We have already observed two or three cases in the *Comédie humaine* of pairs of characters that are outwardly very much alike but of which one is given a supernatural or symbolic explanation, the other a purely psycho-logical and natural one. Foedora, in *la Peau de Chagrin*, is a symbol whose counterpart on the more realistic plane is Delphine de Nucingen, or Clo-tilde de Grandlieu. In the same way, Vautrin constitutes the "realistic" aspect of the dark power that we meet in its supernatural aspect in *la Peau de Chagrin* or *Melmoth réconcilié*. The only thing that makes us wonder for a moment whether Vautrin is in fact the Devil himself is the phrase-ology Balzac uses when referring to him. There is something in his power, in the immutability of his power, in the absoluteness of his character, that removes us from the domain of observation into a visionary world. The Manervilles, the Nucingens, the Maxime de Trailles are all of merely hu-man stature. Vautrin is on a larger scale than they are. Balzac never speaks of him without a shudder. He even goes so far as to compare him to Molière, to Cuvier (*Splendeurs*, p.951). There is so vast a flow of energy in this mock priest that he eventually becomes a myth more than a mere character. If he must be put in a category, then it is not between Mme Bovary and Dominique that he should be placed but rather with Judex, with Fantômas, with Buffalo Bill, with the Vicomte Andréa in *Rocam-bole;* amongst all those who carry the vast dream of invincible power on their giants' shoulders. All these heroes belong to a branch of literature that is not generally considered as such. This is because literature thinks of its essential purpose as being a psychological rather than a mythological one. It is concerned with men, not with gods. Fantômas and Judex are gods, and so, to a certain extent, is Vautrin. Balzac is the only author who has introduced a god into a story in which all the other characters exist on a more normal psychological plane. After Balzac, we find no more Vau-trins in literature proper. Or at least, only in the work of those authors who do quite frankly adopt the theory of demoniacal possession.

I have referred to the play that Balzac had performed under the title of *Vautrin*. It is the story of another Lucien who has been picked up "on the highroad preparing to knock himself off" and who, with Vautrin's support, attempts to marry a girl from the aristocracy. With the difference that he does genuinely love this aristocratic girl, and with the difference too that, thanks to a providential recognition scene, he turns out to be the son of a duke himself. The plot lacks the fascination to be found in *Splendeurs* and the characters are not really very interesting. Balzac must have felt uncomfortable in the theater. There are far too many *coups de théâtre*, too many tricks, too many asides. Nor does he always avoid being ridiculous. Seeing the police enter for the sixth or seventh time, Vautrin remarks: "Anyone else would get tired of this." And what are we to think of this stage direction: "There is a noise of prrrrr." There is one very nice line that's worth remembering, though. "You have nothing but faults," Vautrin says, "and that's halfway to virtue."

The world of crime—the prisons

The world of the prisons does have a certain importance in *la Comédie humaine*. Balzac, as is well known, had himself experienced the damp straw of the prison cell. The debtor's prison still existed in his day, and in order to avoid being thrown into it Balzac was often obliged to go into hiding, frequently in the house of the Comtesse Guidoboni-Visconti. The young Bonapartist officer who is hidden by the painter Servin in *la Vendetta* may well be a reminiscence of this period in the author's life. And the same situation occurs again in *Un Episode sous la Terreur*. On the other hand, Balzac never accepted what was the equivalent in those days of our military service. His refusal to bow to the demands of the Garde Nationale earned him several days in *the jug*. Not a long stay, certainly, but one that has left its mark on his work. Savinien de Portenduère in *Ursule Mirouët*, David Séchard in *les Illusions perdues*, Steinbock in *Cousine Bette*, Victurnien d'Esgrignon in *le Cabinet des Antiques*, all four spend a few days in the lock-up. Facino Cane, on the other hand, is a connoisseur of the Venetian prisons. In *Melmoth réconcilié*, the young non-commissioned officer Léon is involved in the notorious plot of the four sergeants of La Rochelle. He is executed. Philippe Bridau too is implicated in a Bonapartist conspiracy, but he manages to get out of it with no more than a few years of probation (*Rabouilleuse*). In *Une Ténébreuse Affaire*, we are shown the trial of the Simeuses, of the Hauteserres, of the guard Michu, and also the latter's execution. In *l'Envers de l'Histoire contempo-*

raine, we are spectators at an awesome trial during which the sentences rain down like hailstones. In *le Curé de Village*, Tascheron dies on the scaffold. In *la Cousine Bette*, Johann Fischer, Hulot's uncle, commits suicide in his prison cell.

All those things are merely peripheral trifles, however. It is only with Vautrin that we really begin to penetrate the world of crime. A large part of *les Splendeurs* takes place in prison, either in the cells or in the yard of the Conciergerie. There, the petty thieves rub shoulders with the great aristocrats of crime, the Grands Fanandels or the Ten Thou', so called because they never bother themselves unless there are at least ten bags involved in a job. Here is Sélérier, for example, Sélérier alias l'Auvergnat, alias le Père Ralleau, alias le Rouleur, alias Fil-de-Soie. He is a fine figure of a man, built like an oak cupboard, with the face of a wolf and eyes covered with gray, lusterless, leathery eyelids like those of a vulture (*Splendeurs*, p.1052). He is a philosopher, he has a taste for expressing himself in waggish aphorisms. Le Biffon, his friend, is short and fat. He has a prospect of twenty years in prison stretching before him. And he's upset about it. He's afraid his wife will take advantage of the situation in order to be unfaithful to him. He therefore arranges for her to be sentenced to a year in jail too, which he feels will prevent her from going out on the loose while he sets about deciding how best to escape. Dannepont, alias la Pouraille, is one stage lower in the hierarchy. He has murdered several vaguely human beings, among them some relatives of the lawyer Crottat. He has some good qualities, he doesn't inform on his accomplices, but he's stupid. Vautrin only has to offer him the vaguest flicker of hope for him to reveal where he has hidden his hoard immediately. He lives with la Gonore, a pretty woman and a most accomplished thief who is the widow of a certain Moïse, "that Jew who was at the head of the Midi gang" (*Splendeurs*, p.1082). These three stalwarts also have several cronies, about whom we know little more than their names; among them, Goddet and Ruffard, alias Arrachelaine.

Théodore Calvi has rather more substance. Though still young, he has eighteen murders on his conscience. He is the charming rascal type, with blond hair, blue eyes and a low forehead. He wins people's hearts. Vautrin's for one, but also Manon la Blonde's and that of Ginetta, the little Corsican girl, "as big as your thumb, as slender as an eel, as clever as a monkey" (*Splendeurs*, p.1075). Théodore too becomes a policeman later on.

CHAPTER 13

The Will to Power

*The builders—The devourers—The will to power
among the lesser species—Virginity.*

THAT VAUTRIN, in the *Comédie humaine*, assumes such formidable proportions must be attributed to the fact that he represents in its completest
and, if I may so express it, in its purest form what is fundamentally, in my
opinion, the principal theme of Balzac's novels: the will to power.

In differing degrees, and for the most part mingled with other sentiments, this will to power is to be found in almost all of Balzac's characters.
There are weaklings, tender-hearted characters, characters that allow
themselves to be stepped on, but their role is minimal. The others, the
ones we meet time and time again throughout the length of the work, the
ones who are obviously the author's favorites, are all conquerors. Valiant
or devious, termites or lions, rodents or princes of the jungle, but all of
them conquerors. Emigrés determined to make up for their twenty years
of privations, colonels of the Empire champing at the bit, lions prowling
in search of some rich mistress, usurers with claws out ready to grasp their
prey, courtesans casting their perfumed nets, peasants with their noses to
the wind, industrialists with their noses to the ground, these are the stars
of the Balzacian parade.

There is no need for me to prove that this spirit of conquest is the
motive force behind characters like Nucingen, Graslin, Rastignac or
Henri de Marsay. But we also find it in what at first sight appear to be the
most frivolous and the most disinterested of characters. The Princesse de
Cadignan has had fifteen or twenty lovers. No one can deny that this
indicates a spirit of conquest. Mme Rabourdin is invited to the house of a
cabinet minister. There first of all, she says, and one day the Tuileries!
(*Employés*, p.1020). Pons is apparently nothing but a harmless old eccentric. Yet he too has his will to power; he wants to create, without money,
a collection worthy of the Louvre. Grassou is only a mediocre painter, yet
for two years he eats less than it would take to keep a mouse alive just in

order to paint a few canvases. There is something of the Spartan in Amédée de Soulas (*Albert Savarus*) or in a character like the Chevalier de Valois (*Cabinet des Antiques*), for both of them manage to cut a considerable figure in Society without two pennies to rub together. They both spin their webs, the one in Besançon the other in Alençon, in much the same way as Magus spins his web of correspondents across the whole of Europe in order to be sure that not a single one of the pictures he covets shall escape him.

Balzac himself, need I say it, is a builder. He has his own will to power: to construct his work. And this work is in itself, more than any other man's, a construction, a re-creation of the world, or rather the creation of a new world, of a whole kingdom with "its geography . . . its genealogy and its families, its places and its things, its characters and its deeds . . . its heraldry, its aristocrats and its middle class, it artisans and its peasants, its politicians and its dandies" (*Avant-Propos*, p.14). This passion for construction is such that inside this vast building itself Balzac even finds a place for what is in fact a builder's manual, by showing us, in *le Médecin de Campagne*, how to set about creating a harmonious city. It is not, I must admit, one of his best works. Yet it is significant that it was one of those to which he himself attached most importance. "I have done a great thing for my country. To my way of thinking, this book is worth more than many laws and victories in war." * In the same way, the principal characters to whom he returns most eagerly are the constructive ones. Nucingen and Rastignac build their fortunes. Birotteau launches a new cosmetic. David Séchard changes the paper industry. Rabourdin attempts to reform the Civil Service. Mme Graslin changes the economy of an entire region. Renée de l'Estorade makes a success and a father out of her timid husband. Félix de Vandenesse, in *Une Fille d'Eve*, works at his happiness like an industrious architect.

It is instructive to compare the *Comédie humaine* with the *Rougon-Macquart* novels in this respect. In Zola, nine times out of ten the plots end in a disaster, in bankruptcy, in a rout. (I once read, possibly in the Goncourts, though I'm not certain, that in order to form an opinion of a writer it is essential to decide which is the word he most frequently used. This may be true or it may not. But it does apply rather well to Zola. His favorite word is rout—*débandade*.) More often than not, his main characters are worse off at the end of the novel than at the beginning. With Balzac, the reverse is true. Generally speaking, his characters move up-

---

* From a letter quoted in André Billy's *Vie de Balzac* (I, 181).

wards. Rastignac was poor, Popinot was just a clerk, Marsay never did anything but try on waistcoats, Canalis was an embassy attaché. All four of them end up as cabinet ministers.

And even when the father doesn't succeed, the son does. It is only necessary to glance through the index of characters at the end of this book to perceive that the immense majority of Balzacian families develop in obedience to an upward drive. In *le Curé de Village*, Sauviat is a boilermaker: his daughter becomes a rich banker's wife. The Hauteserres, in *Une Ténébreuse Affaire*, are nothing but obscure country gentry: their granddaughter marries a Cadignan. In *Un Début dans la Vie*, Mme Moreau is an ex-chambermaid: she becomes the mother-in-law of a cabinet minister. Old du Bruel is a civil servant: his son becomes a count. There are bankruptcies and downfalls too, of course, but the curious thing is that even these individual disasters never serve to do more than slow down the upward movement of the family as a whole. After a while, they begin to continue their rise once more. Goriot dies on his straw bed. But the old pasta merchant's grandson marries a Grandlieu, thereby allying himself with the Bragances, a royal house. Birotteau goes bankrupt; but this does not prevent his daughter from becoming the Comtesse Popinot. One of the Tascherons dies on the scaffold: at first, his family seems to have been dragged down into disaster with him, and they emigrate. But after several years in America, they emerge triumphant, and the name of the condemned man becomes the name of a town. Hulot and Balthazar Claës both ruin their families. Yet none of their children end up in the gutter.

Besides, let us look a little more closely into these various failures. In most cases they are the result, not of idleness or apathy but of an ill-regulated will to power. Birotteau only goes bankrupt because he has aimed too high. It is the strength of his character that ruins him, not its weakness. In *la Recherche de l'Absolu*, Claës only ends up in disaster because he has undertaken researches that are beyond his strength. Had he been a less active, a less inventive, a less energetic man, he would never have ruined anyone. Moreover, it is worth noting that as he lies dying he discovers the formula he has been looking for; so that, in another sense, he is victorious. Even the disaster in *la Cousine Bette* itself is caused by the conflict between two positive sources of energy: Bette's jealousy and Baron Hulot's lust. The Baron's lust is abominable but it is strong, it is a will to power that has been misapplied, not a lack in his character. In his way, even Hulot is a builder. He drowns himself, it's true, but what efforts to keep his head above the water just for one last moment, what inventiveness, what lavish expenditure of energy. His lust may make him into a dishonest official, but it certainly doesn't make him into a lackadaisical one. In Zola, vice saps the energies. In Balzac, it unleashes them. In *l'Assommoir*, Gervaise takes to drink and lets her laundry go downhill. Hulot, on the other hand, is never even a minute late arriving at the ministry. He begins robbing the State as soon as he does arrive, that I must admit; but nevertheless his misappropriations are still the product of an excess of energy, not of a lack of it. Far from rendering him apathetic, Hulot's vice fills him with new energy. And this is another of Balzac's favorite notions. He talks about "the singular power imparted by the vices," about "the energy of vice," about that "kind of power produced by depravity" (*Cousine Bette*, pp. 253, 287 and 181).

For the jealousy that is the source of both Lisbeth Fischer's frenzy and her activity is also a vice. Lisbeth is a creature of fire and brimstone (*id.* p.226). Her fits of anger are so violent that she has to plunge her head into cold water (*id.* p.225). She has "the ferocious streak of the peasant class" (*id.* p.165). The attic she shuts Steinbock up in is the darkened theater of a will to power and a consumption of energy so enormous as to make one shudder. It smacks of black magic. "Will you do everything that I tell you to do?" "I will be your slave," Steinbock replies. "Mlle Fischer thus assumed over this soul an absolute sway. The love of domination, till then lying like a dormant seed in her old maid's heart, now began to develop at lightning pace" (*id.* p.195). With the result that when Steinbock escapes she behaves like a madwoman. "She kissed him on the forehead . . . with all the frenzy that a condemned man must feel as he savors his last morning . . . This word fell like an avalanche of snow into that flaming crater . . . This final effort . . . was made with such violence that it can only be compared to the frenzied clutching of a dying man in a shipwreck" (*id.* pp. 224 and 245).

In *Ferragus*, there is talk of a sect called the Devourers. Almost all Balzac's characters are devourers. "I don't like looking at anything I can't have," the young Sébastien de la Roche says in *les Employés* (p.990). The amazement we feel when reading this remark, and the sensation it gives us of a sudden gust of fresh air, are a good measure of how rarely this calm and sensible attitude is met with in the *Comédie humaine*. Sébastien is almost the sole representative of his species in fact. The rest all look, as hard as they possibly can, and their hands are already held out preparing to take. As soon as anything passes within their reach that is worth the having, we are treated to the spectacle of a veritable earthquake. Sarrasine falls in love with Zambinella. He experiences "a stirring of madness, the kind of frenzy that can only shake our being at that age when desire has something mysteriously terrible and hellish mixed with it . . . To be loved by her, or to die, such was the sentence that Sarrasine passed on himself" (*Sarrasine*, p.96). The good Abbé Birotteau limits himself to yearning after an apartment. "This trivial emotion . . . had been for him a vast passion, a passion fraught with obstacles, and fraught also, like all the great criminal passions, with hopes, with pleasures, and with remorse" (*Curé de Tours*, p.785). A passion so strong that the frustration of it is enough to kill him.

And what a will to power, what a consumption of energy in all those shopkeepers determined to make themselves rich, all those moneylenders up before the dawn, all those painters burning the midnight oil in their studies. The clerk Minard gets up at dawn, goes to the market and makes sure that his wife, who is a florist, has everything she needs for her day's work. Then he goes to the ministry, where, even while he is working, he never for a moment gives up his search for the idea that will make him rich (*Employés*). Colleville is a clerk in a government department too. But every morning, before going to the office, he does the bookkeeping for a private business firm. In the evening, he is the first oboist at the Opéra-Comique, and even then he can still find time to make up anagrams (*Employés*, p.945). If you also think that while he is doing all those things his wife is busy being unfaithful to him, you really can't accuse the Collevilles of letting the grass grow under their feet.

The will to power, as we saw in the case of Balthazar Claës, can sometimes aim too high, can fail because it tries to bite off more than it can chew. But it can also find itself with nothing to get its teeth into at all, if it occurs in a mediocrity. In that case, it degenerates into a narrow, petty, nagging kind of despotism. Even the will to power can produce its caricatures. The small-minded, lower middle-class Molineux for instance. "Like all Parisians, Molineux felt the need to dominate" (*César Birotteau*, p.391). Having been appointed a public trustee after Birotteau's bankruptcy, he is "as delighted to have Birotteau to order about as a child finding an insect it can torment" (*id*. p.559). Sylvie Rogron and her brother are similarly delighted to take in their little cousin Pierrette, because it means they will have someone to tyrannize. "Small minds feel a need to be despotic" (*Pierrette*. p.702). Old maids "mostly have a mania for making people around them do as they are told. In Mlle Gamard's case this tendency had degenerated into out-and-out tyranny" (*Curé de Tours*, p.800).

Characters from the lower classes, generally speaking, play only a very restricted role in the *Comédie humaine*. There are a few exceptions however, and all of them are the result of exceptional energy. The workman Tascheron pushes energy of character as far as seducing a woman of the upper middle classes; then as far as murdering a rich old man. As for Mme Cibot, Pons' concierge, she has the soul of an empress. She is Théodora, she is Catherine de Médicis. She dreams of being "waited on like a queen" (*Cousin Pons*, p.617); "I shall 'ave me own waiting woman" (*id*. p.623). She orders her tenants about: "Got to do as I say" (*id*. p.619). She completely dominates her husband, whom she holds with her physical charms. "He still loves me like the first day. I don't know what's the matter with 'im. Hates to let me out of 'is sight. There we are, always beside one another, always!" (*id*. p.619). When Rémonencq falls in love with her, she has him under her thumb immediately. "Now then, lad, you just let me paddle the canoe" (*id*. p.623). We perceive in her "the mysterious reservoir of the will" (*id*. p.707). "With women of this stamp, to wish is to act" (*id*. p.618). Jacquotte, Benassis' cook, rules the whole house according to her whim. She reigns over it, she is all-powerful. "Jacquotte was without doubt the happiest cook in the whole kingdom" (*Médecin de campagne*, p.343).

So you see, even the tiniest of creatures have their will to power. And on several occasions Balzac goes out of his way to prove to us that they are not necessarily the least formidable. Beware of little people! This cry of warning echoes again and again throughout the *Comédie humaine*. "There is no danger except with little, rancorous minds that have nothing better to do than seek for revenge" (*Employés*, p.1021). "It takes a nonentity to think of everything" (*Pierre Grassou*, p.123). Butscha is nothing but a little hunchbacked clerk. "You have no idea the amount of audacity there is in that little runt" (*Modeste Mignon*, p.458). Their very littleness can become a weapon or a means of defense. "You can't crush the little people, they're too flat against the ground" (*Employés*, p.1016). "We must make like woodlice," Contenson decides. "Let's crawl into the woodwork," Peyrade adds (*Splendeurs*, p.782). Balzac gives us several demonstrations of how intelligent or powerful people can be defeated by the termites whose maneuvers they have never even deigned to notice. The intelligent Lousteau is defeated by the imbecile Mme Cardot (*Muse du Département*), the remarkable Rabourdins are left standing by the mediocre Baudoyers (*Employés*), the famous poet Canalis is bamboozled by the obscure Butscha (*Modeste Mignon*), the brilliant deputy public prosecutor Vinet by the Thuilliers: "Like all men of superior intellect, for he did not lack such superiority, the deputy public prosecutor had never stooped low enough to be able to perceive these middle-class webs, and now he had rushed headlong into the trap like any foolish fly" (*Petits Bourgeois*, p.110). "You see, Madame," Crevel says, "an imbecile of a perfume maker (retired!) without an idea in his head is stronger than a clever man who has thousands of them" (*Cousine Bette*, p.147). "In order to conceal one's thoughts," Balzac also writes, "one should never have more than one. Any complex man is easily seen through. And in consequence, all great men are tricked by beings who are inferior to them" (*Traité de la Démarche*).

For power, to Balzac's way of thinking, is directly proportionate to the economy with which it is used, and above all to the economy with which one's intelligence is used. Claude Vignon is intelligent. Too intelligent. His critical faculty destroys him. Whereas on the other hand, as Crevel points out, the imbecile may have only one idea at a time but it's important to him. It becomes an obsession. On several separate occasions, Balzac underlines "the phenomenon . . . of the concentration of moral energies (that occurs) in all coarse-grained people who, since they do not constantly expend their intellectual faculties day after day, like people in the higher reaches of society, find them still fresh and vigorous at that moment when they conceive in their minds one of those formidable weapons called *idées fixes*" (*Cousin Pons*, p.632). "Perhaps it is the same with the peasant as it is with the prisoner," Benassis says. "Since he does not scatter the energies of his soul, he is able to concentrate them all onto a single idea and thus produce a very strong emotional charge" (*Médecin de Campagne*, p.388). Rémonencq, for example, is a brute, but he comes to feel "by degrees one of those passions such as can only be conceived by people without learning who come up to Paris from the depths of the country, with all the obsessions that are produced by an isolated country existence, with the complicated ignorance of primitive natures and the brutalities of their desires so easily transformed into *idées fixes*" (*Cousin Pons*, p.694). And so it is that in *les Paysans* we see the intelligent Blondet being fooled by an old peasant and Général Montcornet defeated by the lower middle-class people and the peasants who surround him. Power, according to Balzac, is a function of virginity. The spiritual virginity possessed by Rémonencq or by Montcornet's peasants. The physical virginity of all those old maids whose hates and plots and rancors we see festering on every side, women like Mlle Gamard in *le Curé de Tours*, like Sylvie Rogron in *Pierrette*, like Cousine Bette. "Constitutions that have escaped the ravages of passion have a great abundance of vital fluid at their disposal," Balzac tells us in *Pierrette* (p.732). And in *la Cousine Bette* (p.230): "Virginity . . . has special stores of wealth, a self-contained stature. The life of the virgin human being, since its strength has all been stored away, has acquired an incalculable fund of resistance and durability . . . When chaste individuals eventually need to use their bodies or their souls . . . they find they have muscles of steel at their disposal, or knowledge lying latent in their minds, a diabolical strength or the black magic of the Will." And we should note that although Balzac talks of viriginity in *la Cousine Bette* as a monstrosity, he is also emphatic that there can be no great work without chastity. "A woman's caresses," he writes, "cause the Muse to languish" (*id*. p.319). Chastity, he believes, is inherent in "the tyranny of ideas" (*Recherche de l'Absolu*, p.488).

CHAPTER 14

The Theme
of the Group

*First form: love, marriage—Second form: friendship
or vicarious power—Malin and Grévin—The Keller
brothers—David Séchard and Lucien de Rubempré—
Louise de Chaulieu and Renée de l'Estorade—Armande d'Esgrignon—Schucke and Pons—Digression
on terrors—Third form: the conspiracy—Mystique of
mystery, mystique of secret power—The Ten Thousand—The Thirteen—Marsay's clique—The usurers
—Les Paysans—The Knights of Idleness—The brothers of Consolation—Practical jokes—Disguises—A feature of the age—Fourth form: the family—The family
cell—Nobility and Middle classes—Your father and
mother . . . —Goriot—Agathe Bridau—Fifth form:
help from Satan—Valentin and Castanier—The Parisian captain—Occult powers—fortune-tellers—Ursule
Mirouët.*

THE WILL to power makes the Nietzschean superman into a hermit. He is
a hermit because he is exercising that will power on himself. Other people
would only bother and disturb him. Balzac, on the other hand, has no
interest at all in the individual on his own or in individual ecstasies. For
him, man is a social animal who can only exist as a function of at least one
other person. His hero will therefore seek, not to go beyond himself, but
to outstrip his competitors. The Balzacian man is deeply embedded in society, and it is in society that he seeks his goals, his weapons and his victories. The Balzacian man is never alone, or, if he tries to be, then he fails in
life. Z. Marcas has just as much talent as Marsay and probably more. Yet

he is beaten by life and Marsay triumphs. Because Marcas is alone. *Vae soli!* Louis Lambert is another who chooses a solitary path towards success. And he too is defeated. Marsay isn't alone. Vautrin isn't alone. He has his accomplices, his aunt, his visitors in their list slippers. Cousine Bette is jealous. One would have thought that jealousy was the solitary passion par excellence; yet this passion does not really become active in Bette until she has found an accomplice in the person of Mme Marneffe. "It's between the two of us!" Rastignac shouts down at Paris. But that is mere braggadoccio. Rastignac is not confronting his Babylon alone. At the beginning of *Père Goriot* yes, he is alone then. But his solitary struggle, his nights of study have got him nowhere. At the moment when he makes his famous exclamation he has already turned to his cousin Mme de Beauséant for help, he has already formed an alliance with his mistress Delphine. In short, he has already inserted himself into a network of family connections and also into a network of social connections. He is no longer alone.

You may answer: but look here, Rastignac has deliberately chosen the social road to success. How could he be alone? But he could just as well have chosen to stick to his law studies, and in that case he might have achieved his success without his cousin, without his mistress. Very well, I accept that. We will take Desplein in *la Messe de l'Athée* instead. Desplein is Rastignac without society. He is a student and he thinks of nothing else besides his studies. Yet even he is obliged to turn to someone else for help. As it happens, this someone else turns out to be the humble water carrier who takes on the responsibility of Desplein's material existence. But alone, alone Desplein was going under. And d'Arthez? The fame that d'Arthez seeks is of a very pure kind. Yet even he makes himself part of a group: the Cénacle. Wherever we turn in the *Comédie humaine*, we find this need for outside help, for the group, for the clan, for association.

Love and marriage

The basic cell, the most primitive form of the group: the couple. Whether legitimate or illegitimate is of little importance here. In a previous chapter I have already demonstrated that, for Balzac, love and marriage should be before anything else sources of energy, the combining of two individuals' total resources. All their resources, mark you, from the most commonplace to the most sublime. Delphine brings Rastignac the money and the connections he lacks: together they triumph. Marsay's wife brings him the fortune that he needs: he becomes Premier. Mme de Bargeton brings her second husband the support of her cousin, Mme d'Espard: with the help of the latter's influence they succeed. Mme Camusot brings her husband her shrewdness and her ability for dealing with people. Mme Birotteau brings hers a good head for business. Mme de l'Estorade inspires hers with the ambition he himself lacks. In every case, a unit of energy is formed. Without his wife, Camusot would have remained on his provincial circuit; without his, l'Estorade would have just gone on weeding his flowerbeds.

A mistress! all the young lions in the *Comédie Humaine* cry. And desire has very little to do with this eagerness (besides which, it is very rarely that we catch these young men in their effusive moments). Often indeed, we ought to take the word in its other sense—rather as one says "a geography mistress." Someone who teaches you all about the world. Benassis—who is an intelligent man, mark you—expresses regret at never having met "a woman who would have devoted herself to pointing out the various reefs that threatened me, to providing me with an excellent social manner, to advising me without ever hurting my pride, and to seeing that I was received in all the places where I might have found useful connections" (*Médecin de Campagne*, p.478). Monsieur de Rastignac "is looking for an instructress," Mme de Beauséant says (*Père Goriot*, p.908).

Moving up a degree in the scale, we find that love alone can also be a source of energy, provided it is stimulated by the existence of a beloved for whom it is worth the trouble to work and struggle. This is the relation in which Lucien stands to Vautrin, Césarine Birotteau to Popinot, and the Duchesse d'Argaiolo to Savarus. If she had been a man, Célestine Rabourdin thinks to herself, she would certainly have had the energy to make herself rich in order to make the woman she loved happy (*Employés*, p.869). Sometimes the energy flows into strangely devious channels: Tullia du Bruel falls in love with La Palférine, who for his part claims that he can only love a countess. Whereupon Tullia makes her husband a count. If it is true that adultery is one of the forms of marriage, then here we have a model social unit, one in which, to the general satisfaction, we find concentrated not merely two, but three sources of energy: the lover's snobbery, the wife's energy and the husband's talent. "Love," Blondet concludes, "is the only chance that fools have of advancement" (*Maison Nucingen*, p.624).

Friendship or vicarious power

When two beings pool their ambitions and their resources, the name of their state may be love. But it could also be friendship. In Balzac, both of these, friendship as well as love, stem from the same principle of association. Grévin and Malin are to be looked upon as a social unit quite as much as Camusot and his wife, as Rastignac and his Delphine, as Blondet and Mme de Montcornet.

These two men, Malin and Grévin, appear in two novels: *Une Ténébreuse Affaire* first, and later in *le Député d'Arcis*, which was unfortunately never finished. Equally concerned with worldly goods, but the one endowed with a talent for politics and the other with a talent for business, Malin and Grévin distribute their labors accordingly. Malin goes up to Paris in order to give his attention not only to his own career but also to Grévin's, while Grévin remains in Arcis in order to watch over both his and Malin's financial affairs. In this way, each of them is relieved of an important source of worry and thereby enabled to apply himself more fruitfully to the specialized task that has been left to him.

The same distribution of labor is employed by the Kellers, the famous bankers on the Rue Taitbout. "The two brothers had divided up their roles. Above, there was François . . . behaving like a king, handing out graces and promises, making himself agreeable to everybody . . . Below, Adolphe would explain that his brother was so very preoccupied with political questions, and then nimbly dart his rake across the baize; he was the one who had been compromised by his trade, the difficult brother . . . Quite often the gracious *yes* in François' luxurious office became a curt *no* in Adolphe's. This deliberately indecisive maneuver gave them time to think, and also served quite often to bemuse less skillful competitors" (*César Birotteau*, p.495).

In both cases, as you see, the principle is the same: both pairs of men have found a method of harnessing radically different talents to a common end. What a man looks for in his friend, in his associate, is not a double, not a reflection of himself, not a spiritual twin, but precisely those things he lacks himself. The cripple on the blind man's shoulders, that is Balzac's notion of friendship. Not two blind men commiserating over their common misfortune.

Even so, in the case of the Kellers, or in that of Malin and Grévin, it might be possible to interpret their relationship as being no more than good business tactics, the product of pure self-interest. But in fact, this complementary principle is also to be found in the most disinterested friendships we meet in *la Comédie humaine*, such as that between Lucien and David Séchard in *les Illusions perdues*, or that between Louise de Chaulieu and Renée de l'Estorade in *Mémoires de deux Jeunes Mariées*. "The bonds of their friendship," Balzac writes of the first two, "were soon tightened by the similarities of their lives and *by the differences in their characters*" (*Illusions perdues* p.482—the italics are mine). And the same is true of the two friends in the story that Albert Savarus writes: "The character of his companion . . . offered such a contrast to his own that it was doubtless the conflict thus produced that had eventually tightened the bonds that united them" (*Albert Savarus*, p.778). And the same is true again of Renée de l'Estorade. Since she is married to a country gentleman, one might expect her to look for a friend in one of the surrounding châteaux, a woman who keeps rabbits just as she does. But no: her friend is precisely the opposite kind of woman; for in the beginning, Louise de Chaulieu leads an excessively social existence. "You, my dear Louise, shall be the romantic part of my existence. So be sure to tell me all your adventures" (*Mémoires de deux Jeunes Mariées*, p.154). Lastly, this same principle is also embodied in the Cénacle. Since he is a writer and a royalist, it would have been understandable for Daniel d'Arthez to spend his leisure hours in the company of other writers and other royalists. Not at all. His Cénacle includes a little of everything: a farce writer, a painter, a doctor, a liberal, a republican and an abstainer.

This conception of friendship is yet another manifestation of the ubiquitous will to power. A will to power so determined that it cannot resign itself to losing even the tiniest contributory trickle. Others may see friendship—or love—as a relaxation, a form of self-abandonment, as a reward. But for the Balzacian man there is never any relaxation, never any rest. He is forever straining towards his goal. And everything that comes within his grasp he seizes and uses. Friendship—like love—becomes a tool.

The will to power is discernible in another fact too: each one of these characters is filled with a vast and disproportionate ambition that it is beyond his powers to achieve alone. Malin wants to be a senator; but he also wants to be a millionaire. Keller is a banker; but he also wants to be a deputy. Renée de l'Estorade has not resigned herself to being merely the mistress of a country house forever. She also wants to cut a figure, even if only vicariously, in those Parisian salons. Has not resigned herself . . . That is a key phrase to the understanding of Balzac's characters. They do not resign themselves to being only what they are. They always want more. And since they cannot be everywhere at the same time, since they cannot do everything themselves, they appoint delegates. But these delegates are still only different manifestations of the persons doing the delegating, extensions of the original self. "You, my dear Louise, shall be the romantic part of my existence . . ." The most striking thing about these friendships is that they do in fact appear to be veritable fusions of two beings into one. "An uninterrupted devotion that enables two men to say to one another, at any moment: in me, you have another yourself" (*Cousin Pons*, p.568).

In unfeeling beings like the Kellers, or Malin and Grévin, this fusion takes an unfeeling form. In passionate and generous natures like Renée de l'Estorade's or David Séchard's, this fusion becomes a total gift, a constant effusion. As in *les Illusions perdues* (p.482), for example: "Although expected to undertake a career of the most elevated speculation in the natural sciences, Lucien felt himself ardently impelled towards the achievement of literary fame; whereas David, whose meditative natural genius seemed to mark him out as a poet, was inclined by his tastes towards the exact sciences . . . Lucien . . . explained to David the high views he had acquired from his father on the applications of science to industry, and David pointed out to Lucien the new paths ready to be opened up in the field of literature." The result is not a Lucien-writer and a David-inventor, but a David-Lucien, in whom, because of this mingling of tastes, of inclinations, of vocations, of advice, it becomes almost impossible to decide how much David's inventions owe to Lucien and how much Lucien's books owe to David. Each of them invests his resources in the common account, thus producing a sort of man with two heads who is able to enjoy a writer's fame (the Lucien head) and an inventor's success (the David head) at one and the same time. Just as the two-headed Malin-Grévin man is able to enjoy the ecstasy of power and the joys of landed property at one and the same time. Just as the Kellers have two voices, one to say *aye* (thereby ensuring re-election) and one to say *no* (thus avoiding all infringement of the laws of financial prudence). Just as, if I may so express it, Renée de l'Estorade has two dresses: one of wool (which she wears while attending to her rabbits) and another of satin or lamé (in which to attend balls in Paris).

As you can see, mere self-interest is no longer a sufficient reason for all these fusions. There is something else: the desire both to lead a double life and to live inside another being, to be fused with another being. This desire is, for Balzac, so spontaneous that he shows it occurring even in the childish friendship he describes to us in *Louis Lambert* (p.382): "We both learned to imitate the other's writing, so that one of us could always do the homework for both of us all on his own."

There is probably a desire for compensation involved too. Just as Vautrin revenges himself on society by sending Lucien to visit at the Grandlieus, so Renée de l'Estorade is compensated for her rustic life by delegating her friend to appear at the balls of the Faubourg Saint-Germain. For

that friend is a part of herself, the part of her that has not entirely accepted the rabbits. "There will be two of you there, dancing, listening,
feeling the tips of your fingers being squeezed" (*Mémoires de deux Jeunes
Mariées*, p.154). And when her friend has let her down, Renée turns to
her husband and pumps this same energy and will to enjoy life into him.

For that is their great discovery: that power and happiness are things it
is possible to enjoy through and in another person, things one can enjoy
vicariously. The fusion is so complete that every pleasure felt, every acquisition made by the one becomes a pleasure and an acquisition for the
other—and even more so when it is to the other that the first owes that
pleasure or that acquisition. It is the feeling we have already heard expressed by Vautrin: "I'll be driving with you in that tilbury, my lad."
And by Renée: "There will be two of you . . ." And by David: "I shall
enjoy your successes with you" (*Illusions perdues*, p.523). It is the feeling
that Grévin expresses when Malin becomes Comte de Gondreville: "All
Grévin's pride was in the Comte de Gondreville. Grévin was as much the
Comte de Gondreville as the Comte de Gondreville himself" (*Député
d'Arcis*, p.690). The feeling Macumer expresses as he gives up his fiancée
to his brother: "Think, Fernand, how happy I am to live again in you and
in Marie" (*Mémoires de deux Jeunes Mariées*, p.159).

In varying degrees, we find this feeling throughout the whole of the
Comédie humaine. Mme de Mortsauf too, like Renée, is buried away in
the country. And the only way she can resign herself to this fact is by
transferring her ambitions to her children. Those children are "my other
selves," she says (*Lys dans la Vallée*, p.938). Out of love for her, Félix de
Vandenesse is ready to sacrifice his career; but not without creating a
possibility of vicarious compensation. I will be your son's tutor, he tells
Mme de Mortsauf. "Your Jacques shall be like another me; political ideas,
thought, energy, patience, I will give him everything" (*id*. p.843). God
knows, no woman could less resemble Mme de Mortsauf than Mme Evangelista, yet we find a very similar sentiment being expressed by her too. It
is her aim "to employ the resources of her talent and her knowledge of the
world on her son-in-law's behalf, so that she will be able to taste the pleasure of power in his name. Many men act as screens for anonymous female
ambitions in this way" (*Contrat de Mariage*, p.99). In the same way, Mme
de Vaudremont loves Martial de la Roche-Hugon because she thinks she
has met in him "a man of talent on whose support she (could count) to
embellish her life with all the enchantments of power" (*Paix du Ménage*,
p.1011).

Nor is it a question only of power. "I enjoy every kind of pleasure now," Lisbeth Fischer says to Valérie Marneffe. "I was not really living until the day we became sisters." (*Cousine Bette*, p.315). One day, Armande d'Esgrignon receives a letter from her nephew in which he tells her about his liaison with Mme de Maufrigneuse. "Mlle Armande," Balzac writes, "savored this letter in long draughts." She seemed "to be a half-sharer in Mme de Maufrigneuse's pleasures" (*Cabinet des Antiques*, pp. 397 and 398). True, there is a slight difference here, in that for Mlle Armande the person beloved is her nephew and not Mme de Maufrigneuse, whom she has never seen. Yet why, that being the case, does Balzac write: she seemed to be a half-sharer in Mme de Maufrigneuse's pleasures, and not: . . . in Victurnien's pleasures? Should we seek the reason for this nuance of meaning in that other sentence: "The factitious motherhood of a maiden aunt is in any case too much influenced by blind adoration to be able to reprimand a handsome young boy" (*id.* p.354). Another excellent example of Balzac's reticence in the matter of language.

This fusion can also take even more astonishing forms. One day, old Schmucke finds Pons dying. "He took that moist, cold brow between his hands," Balzac writes, "and summoned life into it with a power of will worthy of Apollonius of Thyanus. He kissed his friend on the eyes . . . These godlike efforts, this outpouring of one life into another, these maternal and loving attentions were crowned with complete success. At the end of half an hour, the warmth had returned to Pons' body and he resumed a human appearance" (*Cousin Pons*, p.723). This outpouring of one life into another . . . It would be impossible to express it any better. That is the form that friendship takes in Balzac. And it is also the will to power, a will to power so strong that it enables human beings to go beyond the boundaries of their own souls and to breathe life into others. Just as Bette, one day when Steinbock is feeling particularly low, cries out: "Oh! I shan't let you die. I have enough life for two, and I would transfuse my blood into your veins if necessary" (*Cousine Bette*, p.187).

Digression on terrors

All that said, and this will to power duly noted, we are now justified in asking ourselves whether there is not something else here, something deeper still. It is true that in most cases the use of other people can be explained either by the excess of a character's ambitions or by a desire for compensation, a refusal to be limited to what he or she is. But we have also seen that, in Balzac, the man alone is automatically defeated. Everything seems to indicate, therefore, that this use of other people is not only possible, not only desirable, but also indispensable. Everything seems to make it clear that it is quite impossible to struggle alone. Malin perhaps asks too much of life. David Séchard too, perhaps, expects too much in asking for both literary glory and the inventor's fame at the same time. But what about Marcas? Or Savarus? Marcas wants to achieve a position of power. Savarus simply wants to make himself a respectable career. Not a great deal to ask. Yet it is too much, apparently. Too much for a man on his own. Both fail. I have already referred to the fable of the blind man and the cripple. They manage very well, of course; but let us no forget that the blind man is blind, and the cripple paralyzed. One begins to wonder whether, for Balzac, a man on his own is not a sort of cripple too, incapable of coping with life on his own; one begins to wonder whether this principle of using others does not betray a hidden distress, a terror, the anxiety of a man who has, on occasions, sunk beneath the burden of life.

Terror? Faced with a life's work that seems to have been created with such measured assurance one hesitates to use the word. Perhaps one is simply falling victim to the errors of one's own age. And yet this condemnation of solitude, this perpetual need for another person, this longing to find someone else who will share one's burdens, this constant failure of all solitary efforts . . . And in a man who worked alone all his life! But isn't that the very reason? Is that condemnation of solitude not simply the lament of the man who is alone? In a later chapter I shall discuss Balzac's mistrust of the masses. And there again, is there not some admixture of terror? Is there not a hint of terror in Mme Claës' words: "A great man can have neither a wife nor children . . . Your virtues are not the same as those of ordinary people . . . You dry up the earth all around you as great trees do" (*Recherche de l'Absolu*, p.573). It is the terror of the man facing an artistic vocation, just as it was expressed by Paul Claudel more recently in his *Mémoires improvisées*. And lastly, is there not an element of terror too in Balzac's conception of love? A love that is forever being obliged to come to terms, to lean on something other than itself, a thing of bars, precautions, parapets, never an instant of abandon. Balzac, as is well known, really loved only two women, one of whom was more like a mother to him than a mistress, and the second of whom was never there. What better defense could he have erected! For to love a woman who is not there is to escape almost all the dangers that love has to offer. The dangers presented by the beloved, since she is not there, and the dangers presented by other women because one is in love already.

The conspiracy

It is possible for two people to join forces in order to succeed. It is also possible to extend this principle and join a group of three, or thirteen, or a hundred. One is then part of the group, the clan, the trust, the syndicate, the coterie, the clique, the Cénacle, the conspiracy. In short, any form of association. But whatever the size of the group, the principle has not changed: the group is victorious where the individual is defeated. The individual is too weak to struggle against society. He can therefore assuage his will to power only by insinuating himself into a group. "Association is a way to win worlds," Balzac writes in *l'Envers de l'Histoire contemporaine* (p.341). "It is one of the greatest of all social forces." The future, he assures us, lies in a return to organizations such as the Hanseatic League and great federations. Let us not forget that it was Balzac who launched the idea of the *Société des Gens de Lettres*. "We are our own salvation," he wrote on that occasion, "for that salvation lies in an agreement as to our rights, in a mutual recognition of our strengths. It is therefore to the greatest interest of all of us that we should meet together." * Léon Gozlan recounts how Balzac founded a sort of Cénacle which called itself the Cheval Rouge. Notable amongst its members were Théophile Gautier, Granier de Cassagne, Alphonse Karr, Gozlan and, of course, Balzac himself. Aim and method: mutual aid.

So far, nothing could be more natural, more reasonable. But this taste for association, this belief in concerted action and this technique of distributing labor are allied in Balzac's case with a curious taste for secrecy and mystery. The Cheval Rouge group, for instance, which was a purely literary association with nothing subversive about it, always met in a different place "so as to avoid arousing suspicions." Arousing whose suspicions? you ask yourself. You try to work it out. There is nothing to work out. A character trait of that sort can't be explained. It just exists, and that's all there is to it. Balzac likes secrecy, the clandestine. True power, in his eyes, is invisible power. Balzac is in many ways a very simple creature, and simple people like secrecy. He loves silence, too. One might almost say that there is a *mystique* of silence in the *Comédie humaine*. The strong man is a man who keeps his own counsel. Tascheron goes to the scaffold without revealing his mystery. Arthur Grenville and Mme de Merret's lover die rather than call for help. The Brothers of Consolation

---

* Cf. *Le Président Balzac*, by Pierre Descaves (p. 39).

are—to say the very least—taciturn. Whereas Rubempré, on the other hand, and Oscar Husson in *Un Début*, both bring about their own downfall by chattering too much. "Between the time of his capture and his death, Toussaint-Louverture did not utter a single word. Napoleon, once he had set foot on his rock, began chattering like a magpie" (Z. *Marcas*, p.747).

In fact, Balzac himself (as far as one can judge from the facts and the anecdotes we possess) displayed several of the symptoms of persecution mania in his own life. Ceaselessly hounded by his creditors, by his publishers, by bores, by recruiters for the National Guard, he ended up taking the most incredible precautions against such threats. If ever you are passing near the Rue Raynouard, go and look at his house. It has two exits, and Balzac lived there under the name of his governess, Mme de Bougniol. On the Rue des Batailles, he became metamorphosed into Mme Dubois, and you had to know a password to get in. Sometimes he would go and lie low at Sandeau's, sometimes at the Comtesse Guidoboni's. The author of *Balzac mis à nu* claims that he once hid himself on account of a laundry-girl who happened to be passing. "She's a spy who's been sent to watch me." When a play of his was put on, he insisted that someone from the theater should deliver the tickets to him, not at his home, but in front of the twentieth tree along the Champs-Elysées. With a password, of course. "This mysterious family had all the attraction of a poem by Lord Byron," he writes in *Sarrasine* (p.82). Mystery, for him, is an attraction in itself. But let us not forget Balzac's literary origins. He emerged from a school of literature in which mystery had been all the rage.*

It is this taste for mystery, combined with his belief in the value of the group, that explains the abundance of conspiracies in Balzac's work. With the one exception of the Cénacle, all the groups that we encounter in the *Comédie humaine*, all the clans, all the coteries, are in the nature of conspiracies: more or less clandestine, secret, invisible associations whose methods are much more those of the political conspiracy than those of the limited company.

Vautrin immediately springs to mind here. He is a member, and even the treasurer, of two secret societies: the Grands Fanandels and also the Ten Thou'. He is thus at the head of a permanent conspiracy which leaves nothing to be desired in the way of assumed names, hideouts and secret passwords. "You will go to the Rue Oblin, number 6, fourth floor. You will knock seven times, slowly. You will ask for old M. Giroflée. The

---

* See *Balzac romancier*, by Maurice Bardèche.

answer will be: where have you come from? You will reply: from the seacoast of Bohemia. You will then be allowed to enter" (*Vautrin*, the play). And then there are all the complicated maneuvers he sets afoot in *Splendeurs et Misères des Courtisanes* as soon as he is arrested. A veritable labyrinth of schemes, passwords, disguised noblewomen, dungeons and dark corridors.

Then there are the Thirteen. Another conspiracy, and one to which Balzac devoted three whole novels: *Ferragus, la Duchesse de Langeais* and *la Fille aux Yeux d'Or*. "There came together, under the Empire and in the city of Paris," he writes, "thirteen men all equally gripped by the same feeling, all endowed with sufficient energy of character to be faithful to the same thought, honest enough among themselves not to betray one another, even when their interests came into conflict, sufficiently politic to dissimulate the sacred bonds that bound them together . . . audacious enough to undertake anything . . . having all accepted each other, just as they were, without any account being taken of social prejudices; criminal doubtless, but certainly possessed to a remarkable degree of some of those qualities that go to make great men . . . Finally, in order that nothing should be lacking in the somber and mysterious poetry of this story, these thirteen men have all remained anonymous" (*Histoire de Treize*, p.11). Mystery, will to power, mystique of the group, everything is there. And what is the aim of these thirteen fine fellows? Political supremacy? Wealth? Less and more than that: pleasure. They were "men of heart and poetry . . . drawn towards Asiatic pleasures by forces all the more violent for having lain long asleep, and raging in fury now they were aroused" (*id*. p.14). "The certainty of being able to make everything yield to a caprice . . . this religion of pleasure and egoism turned these thirteen men into fanatics who started another Society of Jesus on the Devil's behalf" (*id*. p.15). Though more frenetic, more self-aware, the spirit behind this organization is no different from that giving strength to the David-Lucien or the Delphine-Rastignac units. "I do not belong to myself," Henri de Marsay says. "I am bound by an oath to the destinies of several other persons, who all belong to me just as I do to them" (*Fille aux Yeux d'Or*, p.313). For Marsay is a member of the Thirteen, and along with him, Ronquerolles, Montriveau, Maxime de Trailles and the escaped convict Bourignard, better known under the name of Ferragus. We don't know who the others were. Balzac has remained discreet on this point. Though he could have told us if he had wanted to, since the Thirteen turn out to a man for the interment of Mme Jules at Saint-Roch (*Ferragus*, p.112).

The group seems to have dissolved more or less after Napoleon's death. Why? Balzac doesn't tell us. Having been caught up in the game, he plays the conspirator himself. "A chance event that the author is not yet free to divulge . . ." (*Histoire des Treize*, p.11). What is the link between the Thirteen and the Little Corporal on St. Helena? A simple association of ideas, I imagine. Although it was founded under the Empire, the Thirteen is probably no more than a transposition of those conspiracies of former soldiers who were planning to carry Napoleon off in a submarine and bring him back to France. In *la Rabouilleuse* (p.865), Balzac alludes directly to these Bonapartist submarinists. In any case, there is certainly an analogy to be drawn with the kidnapping of the Duchesse de Langeais.

The Thirteen may dissolve, but Marsay does not give up conspiring for all that. Only now he conspires toward different ends. Girls with Golden Eyes no longer interest him. What he wants now is power. "There comes an age," he writes, "when the most beautiful mistress a man can serve is his country" (*Contrat de Mariage*, p.200). But though the conspiracy's aim may have changed, its principles and its methods remain exactly the same. We find the same profound belief in the efficacy of united effort, the same distribution of specialized tasks, the same secrecy. "Let us review our situation," he writes to his friend Manerville. "My real father is a member of the British government. We shall receive secret information from Spain through the Evangelistas . . . Montriveau, my dear fellow, is a Lieutenant-General now and will certainly be the Minister of War one day, for his gift as an orator gives him a great deal of influence in the Chambre. Then there is Ronquerolles who is Secretary of State and a member of the Privy Council. Martial de La Roche-Hugon has been appointed Ambassador to Germany, is now a peer, and has brought us the Maréchal-Duc de Carigliano as a dowry, together will all the rest of the Empire tail that's still wagging . . . Sérizy heads the Council of State and is indispensable to it. Granville is the leader of the magistracy and has both his sons well placed in it; the Grandlieus are in an excellent position at Court; Ferraud is the very heart of the Gondreville clique, a group of low intriguers who are always on top, heavens knows why. With that sort of support what have we to fear? We have a foot in every capital, an eye in every cabinet and we have the entire administration surrounded without its knowledge" (*id.* p.205). And shortly afterwards, in 1830, we see Henri de Marsay become Premier and his whole clique seize every position of power in the country.

We find exactly the same organization, the same distribution of roles among the usurers. "Since we are all bound together by the same interest," Gobseck explains, "we all meet together on certain days of the week at the Café Thémis near the Pont-Neuf. There, we divulge to one another all the mysteries of the financial world . . . We have a kind of *black book* in which we enter up the most important bills against the public credit, against the Bank, against the Board of Trade . . . This one keeps an eye on the financial dealings of the judiciary, that one on the state of the financiers; that one on how the civil servants are doing; and another on the businessmen's affairs. My particular job is to keep my eye on the young men of good family, the artists, and the Society lot generally" (*Gobseck*, p.636). Then there is the same organization once again in *les Paysans*, where we see a single and immense family splitting up all the public functions of the entire canton between its various members. Suppose you've had a difference of opinion with the mortgage registrar. Who should you apply to for aid? To the president of the civil court? He's the registrar's father. To the mayor? He's the registrar's uncle. Very well, you consult a lawyer. Alas, the lawyer is your adversary's first cousin. You rush to see the sub-prefect. He is engaged to be married to the mayor's daughter, that is, to another cousin of your nightmare registrar. It is a singular foreshadowing—in purely social terms—of Kafka's hermetic world.

If you scale the Thirteen down to the provincial proportions of Issoudun you are left with the Knights of Idleness, a secret society whose exploits we are given an account of in *la Rabouilleuse*. At first glance, there seems to be no possible comparison between the formidable group that aids and abets Ferragus and the wretched set of young men who make up the Knights of Idleness, no possible comparison between the kidnapping of the Duchesse de Langeais and the cruel but unintelligent practical jokes that constitute the usual activity of the Issoudun group. But this pettiness is simply due to the exiguity of the sphere in which the young men in question are obliged to operate. The methods are the same: it is a conspiracy in every sense of the word. In fact, these young fellows even walk around in list slippers, like Vautrin's accomplices (*Rabouilleuse*, p.961). And it is in this same book, *la Rabouilleuse*, that we see, albeit from a distance, the Bonapartist plot in which Philippe Bridau is implicated. Later, we see yet another in *Melmoth réconciliée*.

A conspiracy of thieves, a conspiracy of sensualists, a conspiracy of politicians, a conspiracy of practical jokers, Bonapartist conspiracies—all we need is a conspiracy of philanthropists and the list will be complete. Needless to say, there is one. Balzac has even made good works into a matter for conspiracy. In *l'Envers de l'Histoire contemporaine*, Mme de la

Chanterie and her friends found a sort of Society of Saint-Vincent de Paul. Nothing could be more innocent. Yet these honest folk have assumed false names, live in a secluded house, and work with such an air of mystery that Godefroid, during his first few days, thinks he has become involved in a political plot (*Envers de l'Histoire contemporaine*, p.251). And heaven knows he has reason to. "If you ever meet me elsewhere," M. Alain says, "you are never to show that you know me (just as Marsay and Ronquerolles pretend that they're no more than acquaintances), you are never to show that you know me, unless you see me rubbing my hands together in the way that people do when they're pleased about something. That's one of our signs" (*id.* p.337). You'd think it was Vautrin talking, wouldn't you? Yet, I repeat, this association is made up of none but the most virtuous and honorable folk. There is Mme de la Chanterie; there was at one time the Judge Popinot; there is the good country doctor, who is a corresponding member (*id.* p.340); there is the Abbé de Vèze; there is M. Nicolas, a former colonel of the constabulary; and there is M. Alain, a former accountant whom Mme de la Chanterie refers to as her lamb (*id.* p.334), which is really rather nice of her because, if we are to believe Balzac, Alain has "a face like a calf" (*id.* p.256). Well, he may be a calf or he may be a lamb, but M. Alain is without any possible dispute a very gentle creature, and his friends, like him, are all most sedate. In which case, why do they feel impelled to make such a mystery of their activities?

First, let us take note of something that strikes me as rather curious: every one of these conspiracies is the work of a former prisoner. Vautrin and Ferragus have both been convicts. The founder of the Knights of Idleness, Max Gilet, has spent a long period as a prisoner of war. And lastly, Mme de la Chanterie has spent several years in jail. Possibly it is rather libellous of me to lump a political prisoner and a prisoner of war together in this way with two old jailbirds. But political prison or criminal prison, a jail is a jail, and it seems likely to me that it will leave much the same mark on whoever is shut up in it. As for the Spanish prison ships that Max Gilet lived in, they were, Balzac tells us, "the same as penal servitude without the crime and without the shame" (*Rabouilleuse*, p.945). I think we are justified in supposing, therefore, that in Balzac's opinion a stay in prison always leaves one with a taste for mystery, for secrecy. Here again, perhaps we are stumbling against a vague feeling of terror. A terror of liberty, of daylight, and an inability to re-adapt to them.

But that explanation will only suffice for Mme de La Chanterie. It doesn't help us with M. Alain, and even less with Colonel Nicolas and the court president M. Joseph, both of whom, far from ever having been in prison, have spent most of their time sending others there. There is there-fore some other reason. Some other reason that quite possibly doesn't exit in the candid soul of M. Alain but which certainly exists in Balzac's. This other reason is the feeling that the only true power is one that no one is aware of, the feeling that power increases in proportion to its degree of incognito. Let us not forget that the novel is called *l'Envers de l'Histoire contemporaine:* Balzac is attempting to show us what goes on behind the scenes. You may say that we are concerned here with good works, not with politics. That's as it may be. But M. Alain says very clearly: "Re-member the omnipotence at your disposal. The Brothers are with you" (*Envers de l'Histoire contemporaine*, p.339). A conspiracy. Why should we be afraid of the word in this context? Didn't Christ, in his parable about the bad steward, advise us to borrow the methods of the worldly on occasion? And "is it not our task to outwit the permanent conspiracy of evil?" (*id.* p.336) Elsewhere, Alain also speaks of "the exquisite delights afforded by the pleasure of playing the role of Providence on a small scale" (*id.* p.288). The intention expressed is a good one, but the language is no different from that of Vautrin's aunt when she says: "Why it's forty years now, Monsieur, since we took over from fate" (*Cousine Bette*, p.462). And in any case, even if there is no will to power to be found in Alain, it is certainly present in his disciple Godefroid. "The observer able to penetrate into his heart would have been filled with wonder at that curious phenomenon, the transference of collective power. He was no longer just one man but a being with the strength of ten, aware that he was the representative of five other people whose combined forces were behind his every action . . . Carrying this power in his heart, he experi-enced a plenitude of vitality, a noble inner strength that carried him to the heights" (*id.* p.341). You see? You thought it was Saint-Vincent de Paul under that cassock, didn't you? And it's Fantômas!

The conspiracies we have examined so far have all been models of their kind, hatched according to the best available techniques, complete in every detail. But if we are willing to settle for a less rigorous definition of the conspiracy, then it is a theme that we shall find exemplified through-out the *Comédie humaine*. Under Balzac's pen, almost everything takes on an air of conspiracy, and the most honest of people the manner of conspirators. In *le Cabinet des Antiques*, the liberals of Alençon machi-nate the downfall of Victurnien d'Esgrignon. The affair is managed just like a real conspiracy. And the royalists riposte in similar fashion: the lawyer Chesnel hides his client, Mme de Maufrigneuse disguises herself as a man and travels with a forged passport. In the first part of *les Illusions perdues* there is also the little plot hatched by Mme de Bargeton's friends. "That stupid conspiracy," "the little conspiracy," the word is used ceaselessly (*Illusions perdues*, pp. 544 and 796). In the second part of the same book there is the plot to get rid of Rubempré. In the third, a third plot, this time hatched by the Cointets against David Séchard. People hiding, people forging letters, people buying other people's consciences. In *Splendeurs et Misères*, first of all we have Mme d'Espard arriving at the Opéra in response to a mysterious letter, then Esther living under an assumed name, then Vautrin kidnapping Peyrade's daughter, whose father, moreover, is disguised as an Englishman. We find more forged letters in both *Albert Savarus* and *Modeste Mignon*. And there are conspiracies to subvert people's emotions on every side. There is the one in *Béatrix*, for example, to make Calyste du Guénic break off with his mistress; the one in *Une Fille d'Eve* to make Marie de Vandenesse stumble into the arms of Nathan; the one in *les Secrets de la Princesse de Cadignan* to procure for the said Princesse the usufruct and unencumbered enjoyment of Daniel d'Arthez. Yet another occasion, by the way, on which we observe the small strong hand of Mme la Marquise d'Espard. Mme d'Espard is a born intriguer. The intriguer is the civilized, the social form of the conspirator. The simple Birotteau finds himself in a royalist conspiracy, and his employer, the stalwart Ragon, is a plotter of note. *Les Chouans* is a story about civil war. Any civil war, needless to say, includes plots, double-crosses, disguises, whispered conversations. In *Honorine*, the Comte de Bauvan involves himself in a series of conspiratorial ruses in order to ensure that his wife is supplied with all the comforts of life without being aware of their source. Here again, there is nothing missing in the way of assumed names and bought silences. In *Une Ténébreuse Affaire* the plot is so thick that it takes a quarter of an hour of explanations at the end of the book before we know what has actually happened. And it is in this work that Malin, when he wants to talk to his friend Grévin on one occasion, not only takes him out into a field but insists on standing right out in the middle of it so that no one can hear them. And what about the machinations of Minoret's heirs? "In the dining room . . . there was a respectable plot being hatched" (*Ursule Mirouët*, p.336). And Dumay's ruses-when he's trying to find out if Modeste Mignon has a suitor or not? And Cérizet's maneuvers in *Un Homme d'Affaires* to make sure a debt is repaid? And Baudoyer's appointment in *les Employés*? Everywhere you look you find nothing but clandestine meetings, secret conclaves and characters huddling together with, as the saying goes, intent.

We have already met the Knights of Idleness, an association of mischief-makers; and the practical joke, which is really a good-humored form of conspiracy, is also abundantly represented in the *Comédie humaine*. Need I recall the charming humor of the scene in *la Muse du Département* during which Bianchon and Lousteau offer their grave glosses on a burlesque novel? Then, in *les Comédiens sans le savior*, Léon de Lora and Bixiou lead Lora's poor cousin Gazonal up the garden path. In *l'Illustre Gaudissart* the inhabitants of Vouvray get together to do the same thing to that celebrated traveling salesman. In *Un Début dans la Vie*, the upright Joseph Bridau passes himself off as Schinner and Georges Marest poses as a Turkish colonel. In *la Rabouilleuse*, Bixiou dresses up as an old gentleman. In fact, disguises in Balzac are the most ordinary thing in the world. Even discounting the disguises that the three policemen, Corentin, Peyrade and Contenson, are obliged to don professionally. And they are no slouches either: in *Splendeurs et Misères* alone we see them successively as the head of an office, a little old man, a diplomat, a nabob back from India, a mulatto, a costermonger and a porter in les Halles (*Splendeurs*, pp. 881, 896, 770, 846, 764, 850). But apart from these three, there is also Vautrin, who spends most of his time disguised as a Spanish priest but also appears on occasion, in disguises-within-a-disguise, as a soldier, a traveling salesman, a civil servant and an Englishman (*id.* pp. 694, 864, 852, 786). Like Fantômas, he is always ready for anything; he has writing paper in his wig, and a pencil in his real hair under it. Cérizet disguises himself either as an old gentleman or as a doctor (*Un Homme d'Affaires* and *Petits Bourgeois*). Mme de Maufrigneuse disguises herself as a man (*Cabinet des Antiques*), Marsay's manservant transforms himself into a commissionaire (*Fille aux Yeux d'Or*). When he arrives to visit the doctor in *Médecin de Campagne*, the entirely honest Genestas introduces himself under an assumed name. Why? Only God can answer that question, the God who also created Balzac and gave him this passion for mysteries, for false doors and for secrets. Take that upright civil servant Rabourdin. Every morning he goes to his office in the ministry. Every evening he comes home again. What could be more straightforward? But don't be taken in. "This man's life," Balzac writes, "was not without certain mysterious circumstances" (*Employés*, p.865). "He is the man of hidden power," des Lupeaulx also exclaims (*id.* p.1043). Here again, one has the impression that, for Balzac, man unadorned is really rather inadequate, that he has to be given some adventitious resource, a crutch of some sort. Lady Brandon has a tragedy in her life. What tragedy? Heaven knows! I certainly don't (*Grenadière*). In Nemours, it is M. de Jordy who is "concealing the painful mystery of his past beneath a philosophic gaiety" (*Ursule Mirouët*, p.290). What painful mystery? Balzac does not say. Though it is not of course impossible that he intended to return to the subject in a later novel. Meanwhile, for us, the mystery remains totally unresolved. Any yet, like a well-calculated smudge of charcoal, it gives the character a certain relief, it conveys a hint of perspective.

It is also, I assume, to this passion for mystery and secrecy that we owe all the "asides" and "in his ear's" that occur so frequently in Balzac's work. These devices are particularly noticeable in his plays, where we are constantly finding ourselves in the presence of three or four characters adjuring one another to the utmost secrecy. I am aware that this is a device much honored in the use by Molière, but in Balzac's plays, which are written with a pretense at realism, it tends to stand out like the proverbial sore thumb. See in particular Act IV, scene vi of *Vautrin*. The remarks made "in his/her ear" in the novels are often similarly improbable. In *Gobseck* (p.645), Derville visits the old usurer in the company of Maxime de Trailles: "Monsieur Gobseck, I said to him, I have brought one of my closest friends to see you (a fellow I trust as I would the Devil, I added in the old man's ear)." How did he prevent Maxime from hearing? In *Melmoth réconcilié* (p.285), Aquilina takes Castanier "by the neck in order to push his head down into her corsage" then seizes this opportunity to whisper a speech of four lines into the maid's ear. It is a maneuver that I certainly hope some of my lady readers will at least try.

This taste for mystery and conspiracy is paralleled, as we have seen, by a similar trait, or by several traits, in Balzac's own character. But it is also a characteristic feature of the age he lived in. We also find conspiracies, false passports and mysterious meetings in *le Rouge et le Noir*, in *Lucien Leuwen*, and in *la Chartreuse de Parme*. Whether they were royalists during the Revolution or Bonapartists under Louis XVIII, there were a great many people then alive who had been real conspirators. In particular, Balzac knew a certain Chevalier de Jarjaye, a relative of Mme de Berny's, who had in his time served as an intermediary between Marie-Antoinette and Barnave, and who had even attempted, later on, to help the Queen escape. Balzac also knew Caron, who was to become Ragon in *César Birotteau*. Caron's shop had been a meeting place for royalist conspirators.

Furthermore, Balzac had only to read the newspapers of his day to find fresh details every week about the thousand and one plots that were actually hatched between 1815 and 1821. Until this latter date indeed, the liberal opposition could scarcely have undertaken any activity at all that was not clandestine in nature. Hence all the great scandals and outbreaks of the early Restoration years: the Bazar Français plot, the Belfort plot, the conspiracy in the Midi, the plots in Saumur and Nantes, and the affair of the four sergeants of La Rochelle, which forms part of the background of *Melmoth réconciliée*. It was an age when everything tended to take on the appearance of a plot. Just a moment ago I was leafing through a book by Comte Lefebvre de Béhaine on the return of the Comte d'Artois in 1814. It is a tissue of plots, secret parleys, Machiavellian schemes. "Strange things used to happen under the Empire," the author of *Balzac mis à nu* tells us. "Men of both the very highest society and the most humble birth used to disappear without one ever knowing why or how. When the Empire fell, none of these individuals was ever found in the State prisons. Others were found dead in their beds or outside their houses, and the police always religiously kept the secret of how they died . . . It was above all at the time of the Empire's fall that certain dangerous and mysterious associations came into being, secret societies as ruthless and vengeful as the courts of the *Franc Juges*. The insolence of the returning *émigrés*, the stupidity and cruelty of certain nobles, especially the would-be nobles, were sufficient to justify all kinds of undertakings and the darkest of plots . . . Even after 1830 one scarcely dared to speak openly of the secret societies formed under the Restoration and possibly still in existence. So that it is only from the Duchesse d'Abrantès, so indiscreet, so imprudent, that we know the few facts we do about well-known personages. It is notorious, for instance, that had Marshal Ney escaped the justice of Louis XVIII there were Bonapartists ready and waiting to punish him for his betrayal of the Emperor . . . Another incident the truth of which was revealed to M. de Balzac by the Duchesse d'Abrantès was the death of Berthier, Prince de Wagram, de Neuchâtel, de Valengin. Crushed by the universal contempt he had earned, terrified at the fate that was threatening him, he had taken refuge in Bavaria, in Bamberg, under the protection of the royal house to which Napoleon had allied him. His precautions were useless: a mysterious avenger found his way into Berthier's hiding place, strangled him and threw him out of a window. Who was this avenger? It has always been thought that it was Caulaincourt, the Duke of Vicenza." In an age when people are prepared to attribute such vagaries of conduct to a former ambassador like Caulaincourt, is it surprising that Balzac felt free to attribute a few—and less extraordinary ones too, be it said—to a future Premier like Henri de Marsay? In an account of his stay in Paris during 1843-1844, the German Hebbel mentions a secret society that was unmasked at that time. It had been presided over by two women who had taken the names of Marguerite de Bourgogne and the Marquise de Brinvilliers. Among the less serious misdeeds of this association there was a matter of certain little girls who had been stolen, put to sleep with narcotics, raped and then exposed in backstreets. It is exactly the story of Lydie Peyrade in *Splendeurs et Misères*, a novel that was composed, I would point out, between 1839 and 1847. Forty or fifty years before *l'Histoire des Treize*, Andréa de Nerciat and Sade were already describing secret societies formed for the purpose of debauchery. Thirty years after it, we shall find yet another in Dostoevski's *The Possessed*. "Is it true," Shatov asks Stavrogin, "that you were a member of a bestial and sensual secret society in St. Petersburg?" So there is nothing so very startling about the existence of the Thirteen.

Similarly, though there is some reason to protest at the dark and obscure plot in *Une Ténébreuse Affaire*, we must remember while doing so that it was inspired by an historical fact no less confused than the novel it produced. The organization of the clique assembled by Marsay in order to seize political power may perhaps seem childish. But in 1851, only twenty years later, a little group whose organization was not so very different managed to seize power in France with the greatest of ease, and held on to it until 1870. If you like, however, we will be more modest in our comparisons. Here is another group, described for us by Viel-Castel in his *Mémoires* in an entry headed February 4, 1851: "What really commands my admiration," he writes, "is the very clever fashion in which they have distributed the various tasks. My brother occupies the diplomatic post and answers for all foreign powers. Flavigny conducts home affairs through the National Assembly. Bois le Comte is an insurance policy . . . in case the legitimist party come back in. And Gabriac, that leader of saints, guarantees the support of the Congregationists. Though almost unknown, these four men make up a council rather like that of the Ten in Venice once upon a time. They all move a great deal in Society, and are always on the lookout for some new plunder . . . Their method is rather like that of a gang of pickpockets at a fair; they are always careful to see that one of their group is in the government, so that they are always informed of what's going on and always have a door half-open ready for a quick escape if necessary." The organization is exactly the same as that of Marsay's group.

The family

There is another group too, the simplest, the most natural of all, the one we become part of automatically at birth: the family. A new social unit. The family, that social cell, as Bourget used to say. There is a particularly good example of the family in action in *La Duchesse de Langeais*, where we are shown an actual family council discussing means of rescuing the Duchesse from the situation she has got herself into. There is another such council in *Béatrix*, where the object is to rescue Calyste du Guénic from a harmful liaison; another in *Cousin Pons* to spare the Camusots the shame of a broken engagement; another in *les Employés* to make sure of Baudoyer's appointment; another in *Ursule Mirouët* to strip poor Ursule of her inheritance. In all these cases we see the family closing its ranks in order to face a common enemy. On occasion, it will go so far as to cut off an offending member, to reject a kinsman who is a liability—or as in the case of old Pons, who is sacrificed to the greater glory of the Camusots, as in the case of the Piombo family in *la Vendetta*. These cases are rare, however. The family unit in the *Comédie humaine*, though implacable towards the enemy, usually has untold stories of indulgence for its own members. And though Balzac is very strict in the amount of tenderness he will allow to love, in the case of the family he is much more generous. There are several really charming family scenes to be found here and there. I myself have a weakness for the rather humble drawing-room of the du Guénic family in Guérande. It is presided over by Mme du Guénic, an exquisite mother, one of those very young mothers just a little in love with their sons, and about whom their sons feel rather the same way. There is also a pleasant family dinner at the Fontaine house in *Bal de Sceaux*, during which her brothers and sisters make fun of Emilie in the nicest possible way.

Honest or dishonest, tender or cruel, the family group in Balzac operates exactly like all the other groups. It is a natural and permanent conspiracy. This being so, Balzac is naturally very much in favor of it. "Consequently," he tells us, "I took the family and not the individual as the real social unit" (*Avant-Propos*, p.9). "The family will always be the foundation of all societies" (*Curé de Village*, p.617). And the Duc de Chaulieu has this to add: "Every animal has its particular instinct, and man's is family feeling." He then elucidates his point of view in terms that leave very little room for the Christian or sentimental conceptions of home life: "A country is strong when it is made up of rich families all of whose members have a personal stake in the defense of the common wealth" (*Mémoires de deux Jeunes Mariées*, p.174).

Moreover, family feeling (and particularly the awareness of the family's collective and unlimited responsibility) constitutes one of the essential springs of action in several of the novels. In *Cousine Bette*, the Hulots might well have grown tired of the Baron's persistent misbehavior; they don't. In *les Illusions perdues*, David Séchard could easily have allowed his brother-in-law's drafts to be bounced: the idea doesn't even cross his mind. Mme Bridau and Joseph could leave Philippe to his fate: they only do so after being discouraged by a piling up of vile actions that would have made Saint-Vincent de Paul turn back. The only one who hesitates is Grandet. He resists the idea of paying his brother's debts. Mark you, he has scarcely seen the brother for a very long time. But this does not prevent his hesitation being severely condemned. In *Interdiction* and in *Madame Firmiani*, the Marquis d'Espard and Octave de Camps both push this family feeling to the point of holding themselves responsible for thefts committed by distant ancestors and long since covered by all kinds of legal dispensations.

It is a feeling that is not confined only to legitimate members of a family. Dudley provides his illegitimate son with a very sizable income. Blondet is protected by his natural father. Montcornet finds an appointment for Marneffe, who is only his son-out-of-law, as it were. Nor is it confined to purely material obligations: Mlle Cormon blames herself for having married a man whose opinions had once wounded her late great-uncle (*Cabinet des Antiques*, p.426). Juana Mancini sees all her misfortunes as an expiation of all her ancestresses' amorous frolics. "I have suffered for you all," she says to her mother (*Marana*, p.849). Vanda de Mergi, in *l'Envers de l'Histoire contemporaine* (p.585), wonders whether her illness is not perhaps a punishment sent from heaven because her grandfather had a hand in the partition of Poland.

Here it should be noted, however, that although the family group does often play an important role in the *Comédie humaine*, it does so in a rather different manner according to the social stratum involved. Among the higher aristocracy, the family ties are often vague. Balzac tells us, of course, that all his Chaulieus, Grandlieus and Navarreins are related, but he usually omits to tell us exactly how; whereas we know down to the last detail exactly how the middle-class Cardot is related to the middle-class Camusot. Let us take a look at the Chaulieus. Louise de Chaulieu has just finished school. She goes back home from her convent. Her mother has written to her twice during the eight years she has been away (*Mémoires de deux Jeunes Mariées*, p.136). You're a good girl, this slightly uncommunicative mother tells her. I hope that we are going to be good friends (*id*. p.137). Such is the extent of her welcome. "As for my father," Louise writes, "he played the role of father so well that I really believed he meant it" (*id*. p.138). But in fact he was preparing to bury his daughter away in a convent in order to avoid paying out a dowry, thus sparing himself the necessity of giving up the three hundred thousand francs' worth of improvements he wants to make to his house. A brother arrives. "Here is your sister," the father says. "My brother came over in his own good time, took my hand and squeezed it a little. 'Kiss her then,' the Duke said. And he kissed me on both cheeks" (*id*. p.138). "I then withdrew, apprehensive lest any strangers should arrive," Louise then adds. Strangers? Can she really not be joking?

I should immediately add, however, that the Chaulieus are fairly exceptional in this respect. There is more affection shown among the Grandlieus. Though even so, we are still a thousand miles from the middle-class family as exemplified in *Cousin Pons*. Old Pons is invited out regularly to dine, and without anyone questioning the fact, simply because he is a cousin. Invited by whom? Well, to begin with by old Camusot, the reason being that this Camusot once married a cousin of Pons, a lady who is in any case deceased. Secondly, by Camusot de Marville, old Camusot's son. Fair enough. The relationship is even vaguer but it does exist. Old Camusot has remarried with a Mlle Cardot whose brother is a lawyer. This is considered sufficient grounds for Pons to be treated as a relation of the lawyer too. But in fact there is no kinship between them at all. The lawyer's wife was born a Chiffreville. To Pons, she's part of the family too. And there is a place set for him at the Chiffrevilles' table. A daughter of the lawyer Cardot has married Berthier. My cousins the Berthiers, Pons says. Lastly, there is some talk of marrying Camusot's daughter off to a Popinot. So Pons is a cousin of this Popinot too. Clearly we are moving in a world where even the most tenuous links of kinship have their importance.

There are various possible reasons for all this, but one in particular springs to mind first: in a novelist, family awareness is someting that reaches right back to his very earliest childhood. Balzac's childhood was a middle-class one. Though he knew dukes and duchesses, his acquaintance with them was as individuals in society and did not, I imagine, include the possibility of being allowed to soak up their family atmosphere. His auntie Jeanne and his uncle Oscar must have resembled Bette and Pons much more than they did the Duchesse de Chaulieu or the Duc de Navarreins.

Then again: for Balzac, quite obviously, the aristocracy, or at least its higher reaches, takes the outward form, not of a series of families but of one immense family, within the boundaries of which the more detailed family relationships appear to be merely accessory. The dear old papa of this family is the King, at whose feet the Duchesse de Maufrigneuse and the Comte de Fontaine can always throw themselves in order to ask for help of a strictly family nature: the one for help in paying her debts, the other in marrying his daughters. The unit here is the aristocracy, not the family. Whereas the middle class, since it is too numerous not to become rather confused if left as a single body, has to be subdivided into a series of castes, the castes being naturally based on the various families. These families are used at the same time as a source of aid (thus replacing the aristocrats' King) and as references (thus replacing the aristocrats' titles). The Duc de Navarreins has no possible use for references: his name is enough. Whereas Mme Clapart, in *Un Début dans la Vie*, has only one reference: her uncle Cardot. And only one source of aid: her uncle Cardot. The millionaire uncle and the cousin who is a deputy thus take on an immense importance, and their prestige is used and appealed to by relations whose kinship to them may be distant in the extreme. Hence the immense tribal communities, all of them middle class, that we find swarming throughout the *Comédie humaine:* the Cardot-Camusot-Popinot tribe in Paris, the Guénée-Auffray tribe in Provins, the Minoret-Massin-Levrault-Crémière tribe in Nemours, the Mouchon-Gaubertin-Sarcus tribe in Soulanges. So many social units, so many permanent conspiracies.

Furthermore, as proof of the fact that the basic unit of the middle classes is the family, one can point to the way in which the novel, after Balzac, became more and more essentially middle class and more and more essentially concerned with families. There are fifty titles that one could quote between the *Rougon-Macquart* series and *les Thibault.* Though I admit that one would be forced to ignore the fact that in some of them the family is only the framework of the novel, not its subject. This is particularly the case with *les Rougon-Macquart*, in which the links between the various individual lives is often extremely tenuous. (In what way can Nana's fate possibly be said to be affected by the fact that her cousin is a cabinet minister?) But nevertheless, from all the imaginable frameworks possible, Zola did choose that one, and that fact remains significant.

Your father and mother . . .

In the *Comédie humaine*, the father par excellence, the father made flesh, if I may so put it, the Christ of paternity, is Goriot, Jean-Joachim Goriot, former manufacturer of vermicelli, Italian pastas and starch. To the very end he goes on despoiling himself for his daughters' sakes. His sacrifice is sublime; the results, as we shall see, are less so.

True, there is nothing left to be desired from the social aspect. Thanks to his wealth, this tradesman has brought off brilliant marriages for his daughters. One of them is Comtesse de Restaud, the other Baronne de Nucingen. One of his granddaughters will marry a cabinet minister, one of his grandsons a Grandlieu girl allied to the house of Braganza. Up there in his paradise, Goriot will find himself kin, even though somewhat distantly, to more than one crowned head.

But happiness? Where is the happiness in all this? Delphine has found nothing in marriage but "the most horrible of disappointments." "I should throw myself out of the window if it were necessary to live with Nucingen without us both having our separate rooms" (*Père Goriot*, p.968). As for Anastasie, we are given an account of the disaster that overtakes her married life in the story entitled *Gobseck*. Yes, I know that Goriot isn't to be blamed for this. His daughters both married "just as they pleased" (even though Goriot does seem to have spoiled them outrageously—"at the age of fifteen, they had their own carriages"—but let is pass). Having failed to advise them on their choice of husbands, their father might at least have done something to warn these women away from the reefs of adultery onto which, with a full head of sail, they both so quickly and so gaily run aground. It doesn't even occur to him. Indeed, he abets them in their adulteries. It is he who acts as go-between for Delphine and Rastignac, and it is he who sets them up in their love-nest. Yet he himself has been a model husband. It seems that the very thought of his daughters is sufficient to drive all ideas of morality from his mind. A husband like Nucingen, it must be admitted, is justification for a great deal. But the other son-in-law, Restaud, is apparently a quite passable husband. And the lover in this case is not an agreeable young man like Rastignac but the appalling Maxime de Trailles. This would seem to be grounds for Goriot to give his daughter a good talking to. But in fact, far from doing any such thing, he attacks her husband. "Ah, ah, Monsieur de Restaud, you don't know what it is to make a woman happy, she goes off to find happiness where she can, and you punish her for your own weak-minded impotence" (*id*. p.1042). The old man seems to lose all his common sense over this business. His daughter confesses to him that her lover has been taking her money, that he has made her sell her jewels. "Let me kill him!" Goriot cries. Who? This cruel gigolo who is making his Nasie weep? No. The man who has revealed the sale of the jewels. What is he thinking of? Have all those years of selling pasta turned his brains to macaroni pudding? Surely he must know what disasters a fellow like Maxime de Trailles can bring on a woman!

Probably he does know; but it is as though he doesn't really care. It is here that his true character appears. A real father would make it his business to lead his daughter back into safer paths. Because true love is far-sighted, because real love looks to the future. Goriot doesn't give the future a thought. He is entirely concerned with the here and now. And that is one of the traits by which we recognize a passion. Paternal love in Goriot's case, by its own excess, has become corrupted into a passion; into an all-excluding, all-devouring, deadly passion. This so-called model father must be looked upon as a further example of the invariable verdict that Balzac always brings in against any passion when it becomes absolute, uncontrollable, no longer contained within some limit. Goriot, you might say, is the absolute of fatherly love. And Balzac condemns him, exactly as he condemns absolute love in Louise de Chaulieu, absolute lust in the Baron Hulot and the absolute spirit of inquiry in Claës. In *la Rabouilleuse*, we meet Mme Bridau, also a too-doting parent. But in her, this passion is kept within limits by the almost religious feeling she still retains for her dead husband. There is nothing of this sort to be found in Goriot. Balzac does tell us that he adored his wife while she was alive (*id*. p.920). But no trace of this adoration now remains. He has more than one heart-rending scene with his daughters; but at no point does he ever ask them to remember their mother. During the whole course of his long death struggle he does not mention her once. Father love has destroyed everything else inside him. There is nothing left there but his passion. And the disturbing effects that such passions bring in their wake. For this father's love, so pure in its origin, becomes strangely equivocal in its manifestations. Goriot corrupts chambermaids in order to find out at what time his daughters go out, then lurks in the Champs-Elysées to watch them drive by; just as, later on, the young Proust was to wait for a glimpse of Odette de Crécy. After a while, this sort of thing begins to have a deleterious effect on all three of them. Re-read the scenes between Goriot and his daughters. The two women sound like tarts extorting money from some aged customer. You think the comparison exaggerated? Yet it springs to mind only too naturally: "They were living lives such as the mistresses of some rich old lord might have lived." Or again: "The old man was like a lover" (*id.* pp. 921 and 943). When Goriot takes Delphine and Rastignac to see their lovenest, he indulges in the most incredible effusions. "He knelt down at his daughter's feet in order to kiss them; he gazed for a long while into her eyes; he rubbed his head against her dress" (*id.* p.1027). Ratignac is eventually moved to "feelings of jealousy." Dare we say, mistakenly? And doesn't old Goriot on his side seem curiously jealous of his sons-in-law? On his deathbed, it is to them that his insults are directed. "The son-in-law is a rogue who spoils everything in one's daughter, he dirties everything . . . Death to Restaud! Death to that Alsatian!" (*id.* p.1073). And let us remember this remark of Restaud's: "He has compromised his character" (*id.* p.1075).

In fact, however moving, however sublime it may be, and despite the tears it draws from us, this paternal love has come to display all the characteristics of vice. Goriot says to himself: "My daughters were my vice" (*id.* p.1069). Goriot's degeneracy is scarcely any different in kind from Hulot's. Away from his daughters, he fails and fades. "Deprived of his passion, as you see, he is merely a brute beast" (*id.* p.885). He is an opium addict deprived of opium, an alcoholic without his whiskey. Goriot is not a blind father. He knows when his daughters are unhappy, he knows when they behave abominably. But the knowledge cannot affect his passion. He has the stubbornness, the indifference of a man in the grip of vice. There can be no vice without a certain negation of the soul, both in the vicious person and in the object of his desire. The man truly in the grip of the smoking habit will smoke anything he can lay hands on if reduced to extremities. During Prohibition, American alcoholics drank cleaning fluid if there was nothing else. The sexual eccentric who makes women dress up as nuns or bullfighters is thereby, in a sense, eliminating those women. When deprived of his actresses, Hulot turns to music-hall chorus girls. In the same way, Goriot no longer asks for affection from his daughters. Their presence is enough. "No, they won't come," he says on his deathbed, "I've known that for ten years" (*id.* p.1068). He has suspected for a long while that his passion is out of all proportion to its objects. And yet he clings to it. He demands that they be brought to him by trickery, by force, by the police (*id.* p.1072). But what could his daughters bring him if they came between two policemen? Nothing but a simulacrum, a smile that he would know to be false, a kiss that he would know to be compulsory. Yet it is just this simulacrum that he clamors for. Again like the sexual deviate, who has little interest in being loved, who asks only for a certain physcial gesture, always the same. Like Hulot, Goriot is annihilated by his passion. "What am I? A loathsome corpse whose soul is wherever my daughters are" (*id*. p.945). His body lies dying on the pallet; but he said goodbye to his soul a long, long while before.

Agathe Bridau has two sons, Philippe and Joseph, one good and one bad. Her preference goes to the rotter. A grave error. And a double error. For the error does not lie only in having misplaced her preference. Her essential error is to have a preference at all. In *la Femme de Trente Ans*, Mme d'Aiglemont also prefers one of her children to another. The result is an appalling crime, for the neglected child goes to the length of killing the favorite. It is this same error that Mme Bridau falls into. "Your whole life, my daughter, has been one long error," the Abbé Loraux tells her, even though she has sacrificed herself for her childrens' sake (*Rabouilleuse*, p.1103). "Poor Agathe," Balzac insists, "despite her virtues, was the innocent cause of a great many misfortunes" (*id*. p.859).

To tell you the truth, I find this condemnation somewhat severe. Mme. Bridau seems to me to be simply a good, kind mother with the best of intentions but "limited intelligence" (*id*. p.864) who, having been widowed, simply does not possess the necessary qualities in herself to replace the influence of the departed father. Balzac indicates as much: "We shall see later on perhaps what effects can be produced by the diminution of parental authority . . . However affectionate and kind the mother may be, she cannot replace . . . that patriarchal sovereignty" (*id*. p.848). Agathe Bridau had worshipped her husband, who was one of the Emperor's assistants. Is it astonishing then that she sees him reflected in her son Philippe, who fought at Waterloo, rather than in her son Joseph, who is a painter? Is she wrong in thinking that her husband would have preferred the battalion commander to the artist? Even her Hochon cousins, who haven't the excuse of her maternal feelings, are inclined to look upon Philippe as a somewhat hotheaded but fundamentally estimable young man. "If your son can remain away from the temptations of Paris for a while, he will eventually make you very pleased with him indeed" (*id*. p.1088). When he goes to the dogs, she finds excuses for him, the sort of exquisite excuses that only mothers can think up: "If I had found a wife for him he would never have got mixed up with that dancer. He has such a passionate constitution! . . ." (*id*. p.899). As she passes by his prison, she sighs: "And to think, if it weren't for the Allies he wouldn't be in there!" (*id*. p.933). We may smile at this, and think to ourselves that she will always be just "a foolish mother" (*id*. p.933). But after all, doesn't

Balzac himself tell us that, if it hadn't been for Waterloo, Bridau had the makings of a good general? What in Goriot is conscious permissiveness is in Mme Bridau the result of an illusion. The former loves his daughters just as they are, materialistic, selfish, abominable—and in so doing lowers himself to their level. Mme Bridau loves her son as she herself sees him, hounded by ill luck—and she remains pure. The day when she does finally see her son as he is, her love for him does not vanish, because mother love never disappears entirely, but it diminishes, it fades to a steady but small glow. But her love never degrades her. Because she is blind she is never an accomplice. What saves her, in Balzac's eyes, is precisely the fact that this love of hers is less exclusive, less absolute than Goriot's. The latter is a father and nothing else. Agathe Bridau is a widow as well as a mother, and we are never allowed to forget it. There is always another presence, another intelligence hovering beside her. And that is what prevents her love from becoming, as it does with Goriot, a passion, a poison, a cancer.

Glancing quickly around, I cannot see any other particularly remarkable fathers or mothers in the *Comédie humaine*. I have already given the Baronne du Guénic a brief mention. We are already quite familiar with Mme de Mortsauf and Mme de l'Estorade, both charming, affectionate and attentive young mothers. In *l'Envers de l'Histoire contemporaine*, we meet the most unfortunate and devoted of fathers in the person of the Baron Bourlac. And at the other extreme, in *les Illusions perdues*, there is old Séchard who exploits his own son and sells him the family business for three times what it is worth. Between these two we find a whole series of fathers, some affectionate and concerned for their childrens' futures, like the Comte de Fontaine in *le Bal des Sceaux;* others indifferent to such matters like the Vandenesses' father, or the Duc de Lenoncourt, Mme de Mortsauf's father, who is above all a courtier and takes good care not to leave his post beside the King just so that he can go gadding off to be beside his dying daughter (*Lys dans la Vallée*, p.993). It appears, generally speaking, that parental feeling is not a thing that the militant, high-society aristocracy goes in for very much. According to Balzac, of course. Mme d'Espard has nothing but scornful indifference for her offspring, Mme de Lenoncourt has no affection for hers, and Mme de Vandenesse, the two Vandenesse brothers' mother, is an out and out harpy. As for Mme de Chaulieu, she is much more interested in her lover Canalis than she is in her children. In order to find any pretty scenes of motherhood we have to go out into the provinces, into the countryside, and visit Mme de Mortsauf, or Mme du Guénic, or Mme Granson, who is a member of the lower and rather needier middle classes. Mme Granson is really a commonplace enough woman. But her love for her son clothes her in a singularly touching kind of grace. "You're beautiful this evening, I love to look at you," her son says to her. "She got up from her armchair, took a little chair over beside him and pressed herself against Athanase in a position that enabled her to place her head on her son's chest. True motherhood always lends a woman something of the grace of a woman in love. Athanase kissed his mother's eyes, her gray hairs, her brow, with the holy desire to press his soul wherever he pressed his lips" (*Vieille Fille*, p.313).

Hatred of the son-in-law is one of the themes of *le Père Goriot*. "The tragedy of the son-in-law is a frightening one," Balzac has Mme de Langeais say in the same work (p.910). Yet in his other novels he scarcely ever returns to this subject again. All these fathers and mothers are very rarely shown to us in the light of their relations with either their sons-in-law or their daughters-in-law. There is Mme Guillaume of course, whom we have already observed, a quick sketch of a mother-in-law appalled by the behavior of her son-in-law the artist. And Mme Evangelista, a specimen of the mother-in-law who takes advantage of her position, full of hatred towards her son-in-law Manerville and interfering in even the most intimate activities of the young couple.

Another specimen of the mother-in-law, or rather mother-out-of-law: Mme Crochard, in *Une Double Famille*. As soon as Mme Crochard perceives that a respectable gentleman is seriously interested in her little girl, who is however a virtuous working-girl, she very neatly arranges for them to meet. And then, in the carriage that comes to take them away, the respectable and serious gentleman, the little girl and herself, she soon falls into a very timely slumber. She eggs things on. When the gentleman proves to be a little timid, despite his seriousness, she becomes quite roguish and wags her finger at him from a distance. Really quite charming. I feel sorry for men who have never encountered such an accommodating mother.

Help from Satan

Rastignac turns for help to Delphine de Nucingen; Rubempré turns to Vautrin; Marsay to the Thirteen. Each of them is given the help he needs at the price of a certain corruption, at the price of his soul: Rastignac becomes a gigolo, Rubempré becomes a convict's minion, Marsay becomes the accomplice of a criminal like Ferragus. In each case there is a moment when we catch a glimpse of the devil. Of the devil who can take on any shape, that of Delphine as well as that of Vautrin or Ferragus, as well as that of the tailor in the film *Sunset Boulevard* (when the hero agrees to let the aging movie star buy him a coat). Delphine and Vautrin in these cases are merely the devil's intermediaries. But Raphaël in *la Peau de Chagrin* and Castanier in *Melmoth réconcilié* dispense with these intermediaries: they address themselves directly to the devil himself. The result is a new form of association that is nevertheless fundamentally identical to all the ones we have already discussed. Castanier sees the devil appear at the exact moment when he commits a theft. His sin has simply materialized, and the devil becomes a visible character. But because he is not visible, because he is not described, does not mean that he is not also there, in exactly the same way, when Rastignac accepts an apartment from Delphine, or when Rubempré agrees to go with Vautrin, or when Marsay enters into contact with Ferragus. In short, at that moment when each of them accepts evil into his life.

Delphine, for Rastignac, is power, the means of becoming rich. Vautrin, for Rubempré, is power. The Thirteen, for Marsay, are power. And so too is the devil himself for Raphaël and Castanier. But the associate in the latter two cases is of rather more standing, so the power involved is not merely power but omnipotence, with all its varied attributes: the gift of second sight, since Castanier guesses where his rival is hidden; knowledge of the future, since he knows that his rival will perish on the scaffold; and finally, the power of life and death. "I no longer need to fight," he says, "I can kill any man I wish with a look . . . You know well enough that steel no longer has any power to do me harm" (*Melmoth réconcilié*, pp. 293 and 294). And Raphaël de Valentin, at the moment when he is about to fight a duel, can say: "I possess a terrible power . . . In order to kill you, I have only to wish it" (*Peau de Chagrin*, p.229).

These attributes are not entirely new to us. In a less absolute form we have already observed them in Vautrin. He too is possessed of Herculean strength. He too can put five bullets in a row through the ace of spades. He too has a sort of gift of second sight, one that permits him to penetrate into Rastignac's most secret thoughts. In his case, of course, these attributes are presented to us as being natural gifts. In Castanier's case, and in Raphaël's, they are the gifts of the devil. But they are the same gifts. After Lucien's death, Vautrin collapses. Castanier, when the pact is dissolved, crumbles. His "body found itself alone, exhausted, deserted" (*Melmoth réconcilié*, p.307). It is the disintegration of Dorian Gray.

In *la Femme de Trente Ans*, there is another presence with a whiff of brimstone about it: that of the unknown figure who appears one night at the Aiglemonts' house covered in blood. He too, like Castanier and Vautrin, is a figure of mystery and power, and like them he possesses all the attributes of the devil. His glance is "a jet of intelligence and will . . . with the blasting power of lightning" (*Femme de Trente Ans*, p.796). Everything about him reveals "an incredible daring," "tumultuous thoughts," an "untamed genius," a "superior spirituality," "an indefinable air of command" of which he is "both the source and the effect" and which floods out from him "with all the progressive rapidity of an inundation" (*id*. p.802). Hélène d'Aiglemont is immediately "*enchanted*" by him (the italics are Balzac's). She is "overwhelmed, enslaved." She can no longer find "the strength to defend herself against the magnetic power of that gaze" (*id*. p.803). Général d'Aiglemont snatches up a pistol but, gripped in the stranger's gaze, he feels himself overwhelmed by an inexplicable lethargy, and his arm falls to his side "relaxed by an irresistible softening of the muscles" (*id*. p.809). "My dear," his wife cries out, "it is the devil. He can guess everything" (*id*. pp. 809-807). Is this mysterious stranger the devil? Balzac does not say so. It seems rather to be a case of magnetism, of a sort of enchantment or numbing of the household's collective will. Only such an explanation can account for the rapidity with which Hélène decides to go away with the stranger, or the inconceivable facility with which her parents allow her to leave. The whole scene takes place as though in a dream, one of those dreams in which you want to cry out or run away but are powerless to move. Scarcely has the "Parisian captain" disappeared when everyone wakes up again. "As though with a counter-spell, the General broke the enchantment in which some diabolical power had imprisoned him" (*id*. p.810).

La Femme de Trente Ans is a work begun in 1828. *La Peau de Chagrin* is dated 1830, and *Melmoth réconcilié* 1835. They are works from the early part of Balzac's career. It is in the period 1834-35 also, that Balzac writes of Marsay that he was a "soldier in the service of the devil, to whom he owed his charmed life" (*Fille aux yeux d'Or*, p.360). But not once, despite the great number of times that he has occasion to refer to Marsay again during the *Comédie humaine*, and despite the fact that it would seem to be a fairly remarkable attribute, does Balzac ever refer to this "charmed life" again. In the novels written after 1835, Balzac abandons such supernatural explanations, he renounces the devil—or rather, he employs him only in human disguise (Vautrin, Delphine). When one reads the novels in the order in which Balzac wrote them, one notices immediately that he constantly tended towards greater and greater simplicity. And this is true both for the plots and for the language. One has only to compare the *Duchesse de Langeais* (1834) to *Cousin Pons* (1847), for example, to see that both matter and style have become much simpler in the interim. Even in *Melmoth réconcilié*, which was written after *la Peau de Chagrin*, we can see Balzac's tendency to concentrate on the real world. The devil still appears in that work, but his victim is a very commonplace cashier, married as a result of a lower middle-class seduction of the most drearily ordinary kind. Balzac has already realized that the devil is not Mephisto.

Halfway between the devil and the stale, flat facts of real life, between the supernatural and the natural, there is a vague no-man's-land that Balzac felt drawn to explore. There are still all those mental and nervous phenomena that we understand so little of, all those manifestations of a will whose possibilities and resources are still so little known, and all those things commonly referred to by the names of magnetism, spiritualism or telepathy. Balzac makes frequent allusions to all these things. The word magnetic, for example, recurs constantly throughout his work. Sarrasine's glance, he writes, "has a sort of magnetic influence." Vautrin has magnetic eyes, so have Ferragus and the innocent little Pierrette. This magnetic gaze is the result, in the case of the two convicts, of their will to power and the constant danger in which they live. In Sarrasine, it comes from an excess of passion. In Pierrette, from an excess of suffering. It is also an excess, this time of mother love, that gives la Marana the gift of second sight (*Les Marana*). And it is an excess of despair that gives Mme de Sérizy, in *Splendeurs et Misères*, the strength to rip away the bars in the Conciergerie. A doctor who happens to be nearby explains the incident by emphasizing "all the nervous strength available to a human being excited by passion" . . . "This little lady," he says, "under the pressure of her despair, had sent all her vital powers into her wrists . . . Moreover, it is in much the same way that mothers, in order to rescue their children, magnetize lions, or climb out, when houses are on fire, along ledges that would scarcely provide foothold for a cat" (*Splendeurs*, pp. 1012, 1026 and 1028). Even a woman who is ordinarily rather insignificant, like Marie de Vandenesse, can become magnetic in this way through an excess of passion. "She fixed upon him (Nathan) that violent and fixed gaze by means of which the will is projected from the eye . . . and which, according to the magnetizers, penetrates the person at whom it is directed. It was as though Raoul had been struck by a magic wand: he raised his head" (*Fille d'Eve*, p.148). In *le Cousin Pons*, when Schmucke finds Pons unconscious, he proceeds to project his own energy into his friend and succeeds in bringing him back to life. For Balzac, this is a kind of magnetism that is scarcely even worth exclaiming over. "A sick person surrounded by affectionate attention . . . will survive when another, nursed by paid strangers, will succumb . . . There is many a mother that knows the strength of such ardent projections of an unflagging desire" (*Cousin Pons*, p.723). "Whatever people may do, whatever people may say," he also writes in *la Recherche de l'Absolu* (p.581), "there does exist a kind of magnetism that is admirable in itself and whose effects are never illusory."

These magnetic influences and powers of projection are not attributes restricted to human beings only. Places or houses can also be endowed with them. The Descoings' house, for example, brings misfortune. "The solution of this problem," Balzac writes, "is a matter for the occult sciences" (*Rabouilleuse*, p.853). For there does exist a science of such things for him, "the ancient science of Magnetism" (*Messe de l'Athée*, p.1149), and it is this science in fact, according to Balzac, that makes Desplein a great surgeon. In *l'Envers de l'Histoire contemporaine* (pp. 352 and 353), it is again to magnetism, and to possession, that Bourlac turns for an explanation of his daughter's nervous ailments.

Premonitory dreams are an everyday occurrence in *la Comédie humaine*. In *la Rabouilleuse*, Mme Descoings sees in a dream the numbers that she is going to need in order to win a fortune in the lottery. Here again Balzac's conviction is so strong that it succeeds in infecting us with old Mme Descoing's own belief. If we shudder with horror as we watch Philippe Bridau stealing the stake money, it is because we feel that this is no ordinary draw; it is because, thanks to that dream, we know that the money being stolen was destined to make that old lady's fortune. Before our very eyes, Philippe Bridau steals, not ten or twenty francs, which is how a judge would estimate it, but the first prize, Mme Descoing's certainty of the first prize. Mme Birotteau, who is an extremely ordinary woman, sees her husband's ruin in a dream. Her fear, in that half-waking state, gives her "the monstrous power of conceiving more ideas, of bringing back more memories than in the ordinary state of her faculties she would have had during the course of a whole day . . . Fear is an emotion . . . that puts the human machine under such violent stress that its faculties are immediately driven either to their highest possible peak of power or else down into a state of complete disorganization. This explanation will become commonplace on the day when scientists recognize the immense role played by electricity in human thought" (*César Birotteau*, p.325). Emmanuel de Solis and Marguerite Claës meet for the first time,

yet they recognize one another . . . They "had doubtless seen one another already in their dreams," Balzac writes (*Recherche de l'Absolu*,
p.558). In *la Cousine Bette*, Mme Hulot justifies a certain course of action
on the grounds that she has had a dream, and she does so, what is more, as
though it were the most ordinary thing in the world. Louis Lambert, during the course of a country walk, recognizes a place that he has already
visited in a dream (*Louis Lambert*, p.384).

This use of mysterious forces sometimes appears in its most commonplace form: the visit to the fortune-teller. In *le Cousin Pons*, Mme Cibot
goes to consult the famous Mme Fontaine. Not that there is anything odd,
in all conscience, in a concierge going to have her fortune told. But what
is odd is the trouble Balzac takes to justify this visit. "The people," he
writes, "have indelible instincts. Among these instincts, the one that is so
stupidly referred to as *superstition* has as deep a hold in the blood of the
people as it does on the minds of better educated people. There is more
than one statesman in Paris who consults the fortune-tellers" (*Cousin
Pons*, p.624). Is that absurd? Very well, if you like. "But it was on the
grounds of its absurdity that people dismissed the steamboat, and it is on
the same grounds that they are still dismissing the possibility of manned
flight . . . To predict the events of a man's life from the appearance of
his hand is no more extraordinary a feat for someone endowed with the
faculties of clairvoyance than it would be for an ordinary person to tell a
soldier that he is going to be in a battle, or a lawyer that he is going to do a
lot of talking . . . Today, so many authenticated results have been produced by the occult sciences that one day those sciences will be taught
officially in exactly the same way as chemistry and astronomy." Moreover, guessing the past or predicting the future, it all amounts to the same
thing. "If past events have left traces behind them, then it seems reasonable to imagine that the roots of future events can also be observed." Magnetism, phrenology, physiognomy, "the illustrious creators of these sciences . . . have made only one mistake, the one made by all innovators,
which is to try and construct an absolute system out of isolated facts
. . . One day, the Catholic Church and Modern Philosophy entered into
an alliance with Justice in order to proscribe, persecute, and laugh to scorn
the mysteries of the cabala as well as its adepts, and the result has been a
regrettable gap of a hundred years in the influence and in the study of
occult science." Sometimes, alas! Balzac admits, there is a certain amount
of charlatanry involved in "the practice of this sublime faculty." This is
because, still according to Balzac, this gift is for the most part only
granted to brutish and uncultivated minds (*Cousin Pons*, pp. 625 to 628).

But, as we have seen, it is also to brutish and uneducated people that Balzac attributes the greatest power of radiating energy.

It is in *Ursule Mirouët* that we find the most systematic use of psychic forces. Mme Sérizy's sudden access of strength and Mme Cibot's visit to Mme Fontaine are only isolated incidents; they could be removed from their respective contexts without affecting the plots of the two novels to any extent. In *Ursule Mirouët*, on the other hand, the phenomena mentioned are indispensable to the story. First of all, we see Doctor Minoret watching an experiment involving hypnotically induced sleep accompanied by second sight. It is in this way that he learns of Ursule's love for Savinien. That is the first development essential to the plot. It is also because of this experiment that Minoret is converted. Second plot development. Though for Balzac himself, be it said, a belief in psychic forces has nothing intrinsically religious about it. In the same book, the Abbé Chaperon tells how St. Alfonso di Liguori was forewarned of the Pope's death at the very moment when it occurred. And the Abbé, far from treating this occurrence as a scientific phenomenon, regards it as a miracle, a miracle just like the multiplication of the loaves and the fishes, a proof that God's power is infinite (*Ursule Mirouët*, p.333). For Balzac, on the contrary, God has nothing to do with it. These phenomena, little known they may be, are to his way of thinking perfectly natural, and no more odd than "those of sleep, sight, or light" (*id*. p.332). Though the doctor is converted as a result of an experiment in hypnotism, it is only because of the complete intellectual chaos that this experience creates within him. "His way of life was based on two solid supports: his indifference in religious matters and his rejection of magnetism" (*id*. p.332). When one of these supports is destroyed the other crumbles too, by sympathetic vibration as it were, and without it being properly speaking a matter of cause and effect. It is simply that the doctor feels he is too old to build a new philosophical system for himself in which religious unbelief could co-exist with a belief in magnetism after having consorted for so many years with his rejection of it.

The doctor is merely a spectator of these magnetic phenomena, however. Ursule, on the other hand, is the theater of them: it is within her that they take place. Balzac has prepared us for this development well in advance. For a start, Ursule is introduced to us early on in the novel as a being of "excessive sensitivity" (*id*. p.313). A hostile glance is painful for her, a caress makes her swoon. And on top of this, it is during her convalescence, "in (a) state of bodily prostration that left her soul and mind quite free" (*id*. p.450), that she experiences the magnetic phenomena. Her godfather appears to her in a dream and informs her of how she has been despoiled of her inheritance. And it is worth noting, by the way, that these revelations have to do with a number of facts, among others, that Ursule could not know of. But this is by no means all. The doctor discloses an event—the death of Désiré—that has not yet occurred. In the same way, the hypnotized sleeper at the beginning of the book reveals facts that she could not herself know and that are equally outside the knowledge of the doctor, whose hand she is holding. The phenomena in question are therefore extremely remarkable ones. But the whole story goes to show that Balzac found them quite natural. There is nothing miraculous in all this for him. All these things are the province of a science that is, in his opinion, deplorably neglected. "It is sad . . . to be forced to recognize that a science as old as society itself should have experienced the same fate in mid-eighteenth-century Paris as the truth was forced to undergo in the person of Galileo during the seventeenth . . . Magnetism," he continues, "the favorite science of Jesus and one of the divine powers handed on to the apostles" (*id.* pp. 3136-3137). Even the Abbé Chaperon eventually finds a non-miraculous explanation. There is a world of ideas, he says, and ideas "must have forms that cannot be grasped by our external senses but that are nevertheless perceptible to our inner senses when they are in certain conditions" (*id.* p.453). If your thief has really "committed these actions, then they can be resolved into ideas; for any action is the result of several ideas. So that, if these ideas are able to move about in the spiritual world, your mind was able to perceive them by penetrating into it. Such phenomena are no more to be wondered at than those of memory" (*id.* p.453). But the Abbé Chaperon nevertheless continues to believe that, however natural these phenomena may be, the intervention of God is necessary before they can be set into motion. This power emanates from God, says the mysterious disciple of Swedenborg whom we hear about at the beginning of *Ursule Mirouët* (p.322).

Especially in the early years of his career, Balzac took a great deal of interest in mysticism and the occult sciences. In both *Lys dans la Vallée* (p.811) and *Ursule Mirouët* he makes allusions to M. de Saint-Martin, a philosopher whose disciples "practiced the virtues counseled by the sublime speculations of mystic illuminism." The Duchesse de Verneuil, Mme de Mortsauf's aunt, was actually one of the disciples, and Mme de Mortsauf herself receives visits from this "man of peace and virtuous knowledge" on more than one occasion (*Lys dans la Vallée*, p.812). Even though Balzac himself was never an initiate of this sect, he was certainly very well acquainted with Henri de Latouche, who was one of Saint-Martin's real-life disciples. There is also another doctrine of a very similar nature referred to in *les Proscrits*. There was also another mystic in Balzac's life: Mme Hanska herself. And it was to her that he dedicated his great mystical work *Séraphita*.

As for spiritualists, Balzac also knew several of those. His own mother and his mistress, the Comtesse Guidoboni-Visconti, for a start. Moreover, he himself regularly consulted fortune-tellers. Though I can't help wondering what about. Do you think he used to ask them who was going to marry Marie de Grandville and other questions of that kind?

I'm afraid spiritualism, mysticism and magnetism have all become a little jumbled up here. I hope I shall be excused. I understand nothing about these matters; and I tend to think that Balzac's mind was not too clear about them either. I once talked to an expert occultist about it. He smiled. Rather than provoke smiles on my account as well, I would refer the reader to André Billy's chapters on this question in his *Vie de Balzac* (vol. I, pp. 99 and 209). The important thing for us here is to note that Balzac had some knowledge of occultism and that he looked upon it from his characters' point of view as one of the attributes of power as well as one of the methods of acquiring that power.*

---

* It is perhaps worth remarking here on the frequency with which his contemporaries made use of "magic" terms when referring to Balzac. Théophile Gautier wrote that he had second sight. Saint-Beuve wrote that he was a magnetizer, also adding: "In former times he could have been tried on charges of black magic" (*Mes Poisons*). "In everyday life," Gavarni wrote, "he was brutish and ignorant. But some strange phenomenon seemed to take place inside him when he worked, so that he was able, when concentrated to a fine point, to recall everything by means of some intuition, even the things furthest from his awareness." His eyes "had a life, a light, an inconceivable magnetism in them," wrote Jules Sandeau. "A visionary rather than an observer," said Philarèt Chasles. And Balzac himself: "To what do I owe this gift? Is it a form of second sight?" (*Facino Cane*, p. 67).

CHAPTER 15

The Theme of
the Absolute

*Repugnance for types—Parallelism of plots—Con-
demnation of the absolute—leveling of values—breaking of the link between cause and effect—moral imperturbability—man and his environment.*

THIBAUDET has already pointed out that in the whole of the *Comédie
Humaine,* teeming with characters though it is, there are only two of
Balzac's creations that can be called types: Gobseck and Gaudissart. And
even then, he has added, they are only types because the reader simplifies
them a great deal.

Nothing could be more true. Gobseck simplified into a type is the Jewish moneylender in all his uncomplicated horror. Shylock. But Balzac's
Gobseck is much more complex than that. A moneylender he is, true, but
he is also capable of feeling affection for Derville, or of rescuing young
Restaud's fortune. There is some reason to suppose that, as things turned
out, Balzac has here been the victim of his own care in choosing his characters' names. Gobseck, to a French-speaking reader, immediately conjures up something rapacious and evil: a pike gulping down its prey. (Fr.
gober, to gulp). Gaudissart derives from the Latin *gaudere, gaudeamus
igitur:* he has to be a jolly kind of fellow. Both characters have been made
famous by their names but also devoured by them.

One could, it is true, quibble over Thibaudet's dictum. One could ask
why he is willing to accept Gobseck and Gaudissart as types and not
Hulot, or Nucingen, or Rastignac, all of whom are striking, clearly de-
fined figures. But no sooner has one formed this objection in one's mind
than one sees it to be invalid. Hulot and Rastignac are both characters, not
types. The type is an assemblage of all the characteristics of his species.
And Hulot and Rastignac do not present all the possible characteristics of

[349]

lust and ambition. The best proof of this is that Balzac was able to set Hulot beside another lustful character, Crevel; that he was able to set Nucingen beside another banker, du Tillet; that he surrounded Rastignac with at least half a dozen other ambitious young men. Those are things that a creator of types would never do. On the contrary, in order to render his Harpagon and his Tartuffe more immediately striking, Molière sets them against backdrops of prodigality and honesty. Tartuffe is shown beside Mme Pernelle and Dorine, both very outspoken women. Harpagon has two particularly spendthrift children. Don Quixote is accompanied by Sancho Panza, who is his exact opposite. We are given the type, his ruling passion, and then, all around him, people for whom this passion is not merely excessive in this particular case but also an absurdity in itself. There is no shading. Whereas there is almost always a degree of shading in Balzac. If Hulot had been content to keep a little friend quietly on the side, no one would have turned a hair. The people around him are not Puritans. It is the excess that is in question, not the passion itself.

Furthermore, Balzac almost always presents his characters to us in the contexts of novels that have already, if I may so express it, been colored by the passion in question. Rastignac and Nucingen live in environments where, even without their presence, money and ambition are the central interest, where their particular passions are already present. Similarly, in *la Cousine Bette*, every sofa we see is a potential scene of lust, even when Hulot isn't there. The miserly Grandet is shown living in a petty-minded environment where his avarice is only considered shocking because of its excess.

In so far as it is possible to penetrate so mysterious a region as the realm of artistic creation, I think it is possible to say that Molière and Balzac employ completely different creative procedures or mechanisms. In order to create his Tartuffe, his Harpagon, his Jourdain, I imagine that Molière collected together all the characteristics he had ever observed in hypocrites, misers or snobs. In his one Tartuffe he seems to have crammed together ten hypocrites; in Harpagon ten misers (so that we, the spectators, are always able to recognize our particular hypocrite or miser in these two characters). This process of amalgamation is in direct contrast to Balzac's method, which is one of dispersion, of proliferation. It is a process we have encountered whenever we have attempted to delve into the sources of his characters. Out of one ambitious acquaintance Balzac makes ten ambitious characters. Out of one real cocotte twenty imaginary ones. And there was nothing to stop him going on to create an eleventh or a twenty-first. Whereas Molière, once he had created Tartuffe, had exhausted all the possibilities of hypocrisy. The type always, and by definition, exhausts the possibilities of the passion. He is a concentrate of it, a résumé of the whole question. Molière never attempted to create another Tartuffe. Balzac, on the other hand, does create other Hulots, and one of them even occurs in the same novel. Behind Hulot there is Crevel; behind Crevel, Steinbock. Harpagon stands alone. Alone with his passion. Alone in a world entirely hostile to him. "Nothing but jibes and mockery . . ." But neither Hulot nor Rastignac is alone in that way. They are surrounded by other sensualists, other ambitious climbers. They are able to find accomplices. Their passion may be stronger in them than it is in the others, more all-pervading; but it is not different. It is almost as though Balzac creates in groups, in bundles, in series. Where Molière presents us with his one Harpagon, his one Tartuffe, his one Jourdain, Balzac hands us a whole bundle of sensualists, a whole bundle of social climbers. Hulot and Crevel and Steinbock and Montès and Roguin: all sensualists, all possessed by the same passion, yet all different, each complementing the other, each presenting us with a new image of the one passion. A different image because everything else is different from character to character: temperament, circumstances, social position. What interests Molière is the passion, the passion in itself, exacerbated even further by being solitary and misunderstood. What interests Balzac is the effect of that passion on such and such a temperament and in such and such a set of circumstances.

That Balzac has a repugnance for creating types and that any given passion interests him only in its effects on individuals seems to me to be indicated also by the lack of concern he displays over avoiding parallelism in his plots. Mme de Bargeton in *les Illusions perdues* and Mme de La Baudraye in *la Muse du Département*, for example, have almost identical careers. Both are in love with literature and feel themselves to be superior to their provincial milieu; both run away to Paris with a writer; both are disappointed and take refuge in marriage, one by going back to her husband, the other by marrying a second one. And the same is true of Victurnien in *Cabinet des Antiques* and Savinien in *Ursule Mirouët*. They are both spoiled children brought up in the provinces, one without a mother, the other without a father. Both go up to Paris, sleep with countesses, get into debt, are arrested, crawl back into their burrows and marry. If Balzac was able to tell us these stories and make us interested in them twice in succession, then it must be that these same passions and these same misadventures acted upon us in each case in a completely different manner. It is also because Balzac never looked upon any of these characters, even for an instant, as a type, whether the "provincial in Paris" type or the "blue-stocking disappointed in a man of letters" type.

While I am on the subject of parallel plots, I shall take the opportunity of mentioning a few even more disconcerting examples. In *Une Ténébreuse Affaire*, for instance, there are the two Simeuse boys and the two Hauteserre boys. Except for a few trifling details, these four young men are all absolutely identical, as healthy as it's possible to be, as good as gold, with no more wit than the horses on which they spend half their time, emigrating at the same time, coming home together, implicated in the same plot. The two Simeuse boys, Paul-Marie and Marie-Paul, are almost indistinguishable by their first names, equal in age, since they are twins, equal in love, since they both fall in love with the one Laurence, and remain equal even in death, since they both disappear in the same battle. Another example: Charles Keller and Charles Gondreville. These two Charleses are both literally cast in the same mold. They are even members of the same family, since one is the other's nephew. Both are rich, both have influence behind them, both have powerful fathers, both are destined for the same triumphs, and both are cut down in the first flush of youth by the same death, one being killed in Spain the other in Algeria. And even then I have omitted a more mysterious kinship, for Gondreville and Charles Keller's father each fathered one of Mme Colle-ville's illegitimate children.

The style is the man. Or, as Sartre puts it, "the novelist's technique always refers back to a set of metaphysical beliefs." If Balzac has an es-thetic aversion to the type, it's because he has an ethical revulsion from the absolute. Harpagon, Tartuffe, Jourdain, Don Quixote, or even Al-phonse Daudet's Tartarin and Delobelle, all these types have at least one thing in common, which is that they all have only one passion, one mania that fills their lives. They are types only because their creator has kept them rigidly within the bounds of that passion, because he has imprisoned them in an absolute.

Balzac condemns the absolute. "All absolutism is bad," he writes in his *Avant-Propos*. It is not merely by chance that one of the worst and most total disasters in the *Comédie humaine* occurs in a work called *la Re-cherche de l'Absolu*. The absolute in this case is only the philosopher's stone of course, but the choice of terms is nevertheless significant. The philosopher's stone can be taken here as a symbol or as an equivalent of the absolutes that constitute the various goals of Goriot, Hulot, Louise de

Chaulieu, Gobseck, Louis Lambert and Z. Marcas. In each case we are dealing with a solitary passion that rejects any form of compromise, that takes over the being in question entirely, and that obliges him or her to seek for the absolute inherent in that passion, for its quintessence: the quintessence of fatherhood, of lust, of love, of money, of will-power, of power. And to this list we must also add the search for absolute strength undertaken by Castanier and Raphaël de Valentin, the search for the absolute of beauty as exemplified in *le Chef-d'Oeuvre inconnu* with regard to painting and in *Gambara* with regard to music.

In every case, this search for the absolute, this submission of the being to a passion totally incapable of compromise, this search for a quintessence, results in disaster. Claës ruins himself. Frenhofer, the hero of *le Chef-d'Oeuvre inconnu*, dies after burning his paintings. Louis Lambert goes mad. Hulot ruins his family. Louise de Chaulieu commits suicide. Goriot dies deserted by his daughters. Gobseck dies half mad. Castanier dies. Valentin dies. Is the lesson to be drawn that there is only one absolute: death? And for Balzac death is a kind of failure. The miser Grandet is the only exception. Does this mean that money is a less dangerous absolute to meddle with than the others? No, because though Grandet does succeed in a certain sense, he nevertheless destroys the lives of his wife and daughter in the process. Grandet's disaster comes after his death: it is Eugénie's ruined happiness. Not one of these searchers after the absolute builds anything during his or her life. They leave nothing behind them but ruins. And they reduce themselves to ruins. All of them are reduced to states of incapacity and inhibition that demonstrate quite clearly how deeply their inmost beings have been ravaged. Frenhofer is reduced to a state of "stupor" (*Chef-d'Oeuvre inconnu*, p.401). Hulot is attacked by senile decay. Goriot is practically raving. Louise de Chaulieu is sapped of all energy. Gobseck and Louis Lambert both go mad. Claës lives in perpetual oblivion of the present. (At his dying wife's bedside he thinks only of how to break down nitrogen. The impression he gives, Balzac tells us, is that of "the cold melancholy of the idiot.") Castanier and Valentin both live on the verge of the madness to which they are being inevitably drawn by the "horrible melancholy of absolute power" (*Melmoth réconcilié*, p.298).

The same principle also applies in less serious cases. Balzac frequently shows us how a very strongly felt passion can produce exactly the same result as the absence of that passion, how a passion's very excess can render it, as it were, useless and inefficacious, or cancel it out altogether. The more her love urged Mme Claës to approach her husband, "the less she dared to tell him of her feelings" (*Recherche de l'Absolu*, p.494). In the same work, Balzac refers to "those sudden impulses to speak and act that are repressed by their very violence" (*id.* p.493). In *la Vieille Fille*, it is the excess of Athanase Granson's desire that renders him stupid and incapable of expressing it. "Because I felt so strongly," Raphaël de Valentin says, "my words were insignificant and my silence suggested stupidity" (*Peau de Chagrin*, p.83). Even study, taken to extremes, can defeat its own object. By dint of studying woman so hard, d'Arthez ends up knowing nothing about women at all (*Secrets de la Princesse de Cadignan*, p.24).

A father's love for his children is generally considered to be praiseworthy; the desire for money base. Yet Gobseck and Goriot achieve strictly identical results. The one dies betrayed by his rotting supplies; the other lies on his deathbed deserted by two daughters who are out having a good time.

This is because, for Balzac, there is no such thing as a noble passion or a base passion. He has no moral preconceptions whatsoever in this respect. You may say that it is not Goriot's love for his children that Balzac condemns but the excess of that love, its disproportion, and that all excess is fundamentally the same. But there is no such disproportion in Mlle d'Esgrignon's feelings in *Cabinet des Antiques*, nor any all-devouring passion. Mlle d'Esgrignon has all the virtues: uprightness, modesty, virtue, in short —the kind of virtue that includes all the others. Yet this very virtue is one of the causes of Victurnien's downfall. We are in the presence of a kind of moral impartiality or imperturbability of which the final development is to be found in a writer like Gide.

However, we should not push this comparison too far. For Gide, every passion is natural and should therefore be allowed to express itself, to translate itself into acts, without being judged. Balzac, on the other hand, judges a great deal. He will praise or condemn. He will deplore or admire. But he is perfectly capable of praising a virtue in one place and then condemning it in another. He is quite likely to show us the same action, here in a sympathetic light, there in a thoroughly odious one. Or the same passion leading one man to victory and another to utter defeat. D'Arthez reads a great deal: he becomes one of the glories of his age. Louis Lambert also reads a great deal: he goes mad. Rubempré, a provincial in Paris, goes under. Rastignac, another provincial in Paris (and from the same province what's more) succeeds triumphantly. Victurnien d'Esgrignon becomes the lover of a woman much richer than he is and ruins himself. Rastignac seduces a banker's wife and she makes him rich. Sommervieux marries a middle-class girl, becomes bored with her and is unfaithful to her. Savinien de Portenduère marries a middle-class girl too; yet Savinien and Ursule make one of the handsomest and happiest couples in Paris. Desplein is an atheist: Balzac never speaks of him other than reverently. Crevel is an atheist too: he is a grotesque.

In every case, it will be seen, it is not the act, the principle, the method that is being judged, it is the man. Devotion to her religion turns Mme de La Chanterie into a saint, Mme de Granville into a harpy and Mlle Cormon into an imbecile. Everyone since Jesus Christ is aware, of course, that good seed can sometimes fall onto barren ground. But it remains good seed for all that. In Balzac, the seed itself can change its nature, and that which becomes a source of excellence in Mme de La Chanterie can equally well become a source of the opposite in Mme de Granville. Mme de La Chanterie was already a woman of stature: her religion merely increases that stature. Mme de Granville has a mean and petty nature: instead of correcting this defect, her religion simply makes it worse. Mlle Cormon is rather simple-minded: the "moral ophthalmia" produced by her religion only serves to make her more idiotic still. So that religious feeling here loses its status as a virtue and becomes simply a source of energy that does no more than intensify the qualities that existed in each of these characters in the first place. It is no more than a force, a coefficient that produces very good results when matched to a plus quantity and very bad ones when applied to a negative quantity. It therefore has no absolute moral value in itself. So that Balzac is unable either to praise it (look at Mme de Granville) or condemn it (look at Mme de La Chanterie). He therefore contents himself with praising the combination "religious feeling-Mme de La Chanterie" and condemning the combination "religious feeling-Mme de Granville." Just as he has the combination Rastignac-Delphine succeed and the combination Victurnien-Mme de Maufrigneuse end in disaster, even though their constituent elements are so similar (young provincial and rich mistress). All possibility of absolutes is thus destroyed. What is good in one context becomes bad in another. Everything is relative. A book as innocent as *Paul et Virginie* becomes a source of corruption for the young Véronique Graslin. Principles are no longer principles. Methods are no longer methods. There remain only tools that can either be used or else not used; chemicals that can produce absolutely different precipitates according to the solutions with which they are mixed. Poisons for some, cordial to others, lined up in front of us, as though in a pharmacy, in their identical jars: hellebore, henbane and deadly nightshade, also known as belladonna. No drug can be called beneficial in any absolute sense. It depends on the patient. Such and such a substance, deadly to the diabetic, may cure a consumption and remain absolutely without effect on a person suffering from catarrh. "Events are never absolute. Their results depend entirely on the individuals concerned: misfortune may be a step-ping stone for the genius, a baptism for the Christian, a treasure for an able man, an abyss for the weak" (*César Birotteau,* p.341).

Given these conditions, it is obvious that there can be no absolute rules. In any sphere. Should one be religious or not religious? Ought one to read *Paul et Virginie?* Is it wise to sleep with countesses, or should one restrict oneself to laundry-girls? Everything depends on the man. Are you d'Ar-thez or Louis Lambert? Are you Rastignac or Victurnien? That is the important question. It is from the man himself that his acts and passions derive their color and meaning. "As they occur in each man (emotions) so they combine with the elements personal to him and change their aspect accordingly" (*Vieille Fille,* p.317).

From which it follows that emotions, passions, virtues, methods, princi-ples, since they are all no more than chemical elements, can be neither good nor bad, and can only be recommended or the opposite in accord-ance with the individuals and the individual temperaments concerned. We are only a step away from the morality of the superman. "At bottom," François Mauriac writes (in his preface to *Aimer Balzac* by Claude Mau-riac), "Balzac, like almost all his peers, lays claim to the indefeasible right of superior individuals to be judged only according to a morality cut to their measure."

"At bottom . . ." The doctrine is by no means clearly formulated in Balzac's work, but it does rise to the surface from time to time. "Do you believe," Modeste Mignon asks, "that one should judge the genius by the same standards as ordinary men?" (*Modeste Mignon,* p.528). And Balzac adds: "For kings, and for statesmen, there is, as Napoleon put it, a lesser and a greater morality" (*Avant-Propos,* p.11).

If the passions are only what men make of them; if the same causes can, according to the man, produce differing results, then it follows that, again according to the man, absolutely different causes can also produce identi-cal effects. I have already mentioned the example of Gobseck and Goriot, both of whom, the one through avarice and the other through love of his daughters, come to die identical deaths. In *les Employés* (p.966), Bixiou is amazed to see that Dutocq is capable of arranging a plot: "Can it be that violent emotions are able to produce the same results as talent?" In *la Rabouilleuse* (p.864), talking of Mme Descoing and Mme Bridau, Balzac writes: "So that these two widows had both passed from an illusory opulence to deliberate poverty, the one under the influence of a vice, the other guided by the very purest of virtue." The virtuous Popinot practices good works and the loathsome Cérizet usury. Socially, Balzac remarks, the result is identical (*Petits Bourgeois*, p.168). In *la Cousine Bette* (p.508), the grotesque Crevel dies a courageous death. His son-in-law watches him sadly "wondering to himself whether stupidity and vanity did not perhaps possess a strength equal to that of true greatness of soul. The causes that set in motion the mechanisms of the soul seem to be entirely unrelated to the results. Could it be that the strength deployed by a great criminal is identical with that so proudly displayed by a Champcenetz on his way to the scaffold?" Again in *la Rabouilleuse*, as though this moral indifference had been deliberately expressed in action, we see the good Mme Hochon and the appalling Bridau employ in one case prayers and in the other crimes to reach the same result. "Avarice and charity are revealed by similar effects," Balzac also writes. "The Abbé Chaperon argued with his housekeeper on the subject of household expenses even more sternly than Gobseck with his" (*Ursule Mirouët*, p.287). Or: "If he was unable to save more than eight thousand francs a year, the doctor must have had a great many vices or a great many virtues to satisfy" (*id.* p.284). Vices or virtues. Charity or avarice. Good works or usury. The causes are different, but the results, at least in one respect, can be the same. "It seemed difficult to ascertain whether this poverty was the product of vices or of an extreme probity" (*Bourse*, p.340). "Noble sentiments pushed to the absolute produce results similar to those of the greatest vices" (*Cousine Bette*, p.202). "Too often, vice and genius produce effects so similar that ordinary people confuse them" (*Recherche de l'Absolu*, p.489).

In all these quotations, it will be noted, the same words constantly recur: effects, results. Because Balzac is much more interested in results then he is in motives. Passion is reduced in the *Comédie humaine* to little more than a lever. All that one asks of a lever is that it be strong enough to do its job: it is not moral and it is not immoral. When contemplating a passion, Balzac is much more concerned with the amount of strength it can exert than with its moral value; much more concerned, if I may so put it, with its quantity than with its quality. He himself was a man of quantity. I know, of course, that it is possible to write sixty volumes of fiction and all of them bad; but when the work is not bad, then it is not a matter of indifference whether it has ten thousand pages rather than two hundred. There is a certain amount of rubbish in the *Comédie humaine*. But one must consider just how far this rubbish is indispensable to the work as a whole, how far it contributes to its breadth, to its vitality, to that Mississippi-like flow that carries us irresistibly with it, how far it may be considered as a compost that enables the excellences to flourish. Just as Mme de La Chanterie's stature and Mlle Cormon's silliness are multiplied by their religious feelings, so in my opinion is the quality of Balzac's work multiplied by its quantity. He has been criticized for his bad taste. That is to judge the *Comédie humaine* by the standards of *Dominique*. The notions of good taste and bad taste are left far behind. And good taste is in a way the esthetic equivalent of morality. Because they are both notions that precede and are exterior to a work, the great creators have always found it difficult to bow to them. Have you ever encountered one of those business men whose ventures are on a really gigantic scale, who have one foot in the Chilean phosphate business, another on the Rio Tinto, their right hand in the Mecca pilgrim trade and their left in the tramways of Point-à-Pitre? It's immoral, people say. Maybe it is. But by what standards? Where exactly is the line beyond which things suddenly become immoral? Because morality is affected by quantity, and beyond a certain point, when things become big enough, morality becomes confusing and confused. And when a passion goes beyond a certain "quantity," that passion's quality disappears. It is this fact that enables Balzac to make the connection between a Gobseck and a Goriot, or even between a Claës and a Louise de Chaulieu. It is this fact too that enables him, on a lesser scale, to make a similar connection between Mme Descoings and Joseph Bridau. The old lady has a passion for lotteries. It is an absurd passion but it is a strong one. Everyone makes fun of her. Only one person understands her—Bridau. He understands her because he too has a strong passion, in his case for painting. The fact that one of the passions is petty and the other great has no bearing on the matter. What brings them together is not the quality of their passions but the strength of them, the quantity. "All great talents understand and respect true passions" (*Rabouilleuse*, p.902). "All titanic passions have the same aspect" (*Honorine*, p.274).

We are faced here with a veritable bulldozing of all moral values, virtues, passion, vices, and emotions down to the same level. As both dukes and construction workers are lined up for a medical examination when they have been drafted, side by side, naked, without any adventitious tokens left to differentiate one from another, so Balzac has no hesitation in lining up in a single sentence, without benefit of any rhetorical frippery or precautions, values ordinarily thought of as being utterly different. "The spy has the Christian humility of priests" (*Ténébreuse Affaire*, p.525). "Mothers and gamblers are insatiable" (*Marana*, p.833). "Only a man of genius or an intriguer says to himself: I was wrong there" (*Curé de Tours*, p.794). "Like Jesuits and pirates, like Abbés and white-slavers . . ." That's how one sentence begins in *la Vieille Fille* (p.221). And there are a thousand others like it elsewhere; there are so many that one is justified in regarding them as one of those tics that reveal some strong underlying tendency in the writer who uses them. Here that tendency is towards a leveling down of values, a rejection of all à priori moral notions. The priesthood, mother love and genius are things that we think of as possessing higher values. We are accustomed to placing them a long way above such base things as spying, gambling, plotting or piracy. Balzac pushes them brutally back down to the same level. He will allow no levels but the one. His sacrilegious hand strips our noble values of their halo and our baser values of their infamy. He makes us see that, in one respect at least, they are alike; that, in one respect at least, their results are identical.

In short, Balzac proceeds before our very eyes to set about systematically destroying the link between cause and effect. Or rather, he makes it clear that, for him, this link only exists in relation to the individual and in relation to that individual's circumstances. It is a rejection of all moral absolutes. For the moralist, good is good and evil is evil. The one cannot, by definition, have anything but excellent results; the other must always produce deplorable results. And it is certain that the two can never produce the same results. For Balzac, on the contrary, their results can be very much alike. Popinot is charitable and Cérizet is a bloodsucker: identical results. As far as their effects on society are concerned there is nothing to choose between them. (This is a point I shall return to.) The priest will say: religious practices lead to saintliness. The Freemason will say: religious practices produce pettiness and stupidity. Because they both believe in the absolute value of those practices, in a value that is always the same, that always acts in the same manner, and that must therefore always produce either a saint or a fool. For Balzac, this is not so at all. Religious beliefs can lead to saintliness but only in the case of a Mme de La Chanterie. Religious beliefs can lead to petty-mindedness or idiocy—but only in the case of a woman like Mme de Granville or one like Mlle Cormon.

All of which, added to the idea of a separate morality for the superior being, adds up to a fairly relative notion of morality. "*Happiness*, like *Virtue* and *Evil*, is a word that expresses a relative thing" (*Maison Nucingen*, p.604). It is Blondet who says this, I admit, just as it is Vautrin and not Balzac who exclaims: "Do you believe there is anything fixed in this world of ours?" (*Père Goriot*, p.942). But it is Balzac himself, in his dedi-

catory preface to *les Parents* Pauvres, who says: "Everything has two
faces, even virtue." It is Balzac who says: "Morally speaking, good is almost always backed with a corresponding evil" (*Muse du Département*,
p.51). It is Balzac who says: "The laws are a function of morality, and
morality varies" (*Physiologie du Mariage*, p.593). It is Balzac who says:
"The ideas suitable for one country can be fatal to another" (*Médecin de
Campagne*, p.363). And how could he think he was illustrating anything
but a very relative morality by showing us differing moral values producing identical results, and morally similar values producing utterly diver-
gent ones?

Moreover, we might note in passing that this moral (or immoral) tendency is also a very useful adjunct to the novelist's art, which includes,
among other things, the necessity of making any situation dramatic, even
when what is at stake is, both in our eyes and in an absolute sense, ab-
surdly petty. In *le Curé de Tours*, for example, the whole tragedy re-
volves around an apartment. But it is a tragedy all the same. And the
tragedy depends upon the extent to which Balzac can manage to convince
us that so tiny a cause can produce an effect on the Abbé Birotteau as
deadly and fatal as that of bankruptcy on his brother or that of his daughters' ingratitude on Goriot. The cause is nothing in itself. But multiplied
by passion, multiplied, that is, by the man himself, it becomes immense. It
goes without saying too, that if Balzac eliminates the link between cause
and effect, the vertical connection, as it were, between motive and result,
he likewise eliminates the horizontal link that we are accustomed to think
of as existing between the various virtues and the various vices. Pons is a
good old man, one with a heart of gold and "a tender, dreaming, delicate
soul" (*Cousin Pons*, p.536), but he is also a parasite whose gluttony makes
him stoop to a great many base actions. Nor, needless to say, is there any
correlation for Balzac between moral and intellectual values. Birotteau is
both a saint and a fool. Phellion, in *les Petits Bourgeois*, is an imbecile and
at the same time the best of men. As for Pierre Grassou, the epithets that
Balzac applies to him are a startling measure of what this moral impartiality can lead to: That "honest artist, that infamous mediocrity . . . that
utterly upright being, that stupid illustrator" (*Pierre Grassou*, p.129).

The preceding section requires some qualifications. It may perhaps have
given the impression that Balzac's work leads directly on into that of
Nietzsche and Gide. I am not the first to mention Nietzsche in connection
with the author of the *Comédie humaine*. This idea is in the public domain, and I have found it even in a straightforward manual of philosophy

such as Will Durant's *Lives and Teachings of the Great Philosophers*. Nor is the notion of making such a connection erroneous. And yet it is not entirely accurate either. In both Nietzsche and Gide there is a rejection of moral values that cannot be found in Balzac unless one pushes his thoughts very much further than he himself ever did. It is true that by tampering with the link between causes and effects he was impairing the integrity of the causes themselves, and thereby undermining the mental constructions that two thousand years of moral beliefs had led us to erect around the notion of values. And from there to rejecting them entirely is only a step. "Results are what profit society," Balzac wrote in *Modeste Mignon* (p.407); "motives are a matter for God." That is a key sentence.

Needless to say, there is nothing of the Catholic novelist in Balzac. But he is a novelist for whom God exists, for whom the life everlasting exists. I am even tempted to add that if we forget this we are in danger of failing to understand certain aspects of his work. Claude Roy, for example, in his book *Commerce des Classiques*, rebels against the injustice and the horror of Balzac's world. And he is right. He is right in so far as, being a Marxist himself, he does not realize that, for Balzac, all his characters are going to be called to account by their Maker, and that quite often the novelist himself calls them to account here below: Birotteau is destroyed by rogues, but he dies in an apotheosis, he goes to heaven; Rosalie de Watteville is never brought to court, but she is crippled by an explosion. (This is another point to which I shall return.) God exists. But the novelist does not infringe on God's rights; he is consciously operating in a different territory. In this respect, one might almost say that Balzac is the opposite of the Catholic novelists. God exists . . . but that is not what Balzac is talking about. "Results are what profit society." Since he is a painter of social relationships, of man as a social animal, Balzac does not judge vices, or virtues, or passions, except according to their social results. He presents these results to us as being sometimes harmful, sometimes profitable. That does not mean that he is necessarily passing the same judgment on the causes and the motives for them. "Motives are a matter for God." When Balzac shows us a gigolo like Rastignac succeeding in life, that does not mean that he finds the profession in itself particularly praiseworthy—or particularly blameworthy either. It simply means that society is so constituted that it can sometimes prove profitable to be a gigolo. Nothing more than that. Socially, he tells us, Popinot's good works and Cérizet's usury produce identical results. The assertion is subversive enough. But note that Balzac has limited it. "Socially . . ." he says. In other words, he is not putting the two men themselves on an equal plane. He speaks of the one with reverence and of the other with disgust. His refusal to be swayed by moral values exists (and it is also accompanied by admiration when the value, even if it is criminal, is a strong one: Vautrin) but it in no way impairs the judgment of God—or that of the reader. Despite the purely social verdict that momentarily places them side by side, we are perfectly well aware that Popinot is a good man and Cérizet a rotten crook, that the one is destined to end up in heaven and the other in hell. It is simply that, for Balzac, heaven and hell are no business of the novelist's. They are God's business. Every man to his own trade. What interests Balzac is not the salvation of a character's soul, or the purity of his motives, or the extent of his virtues, but the effect of those virtues in social terms. Let God fathom men's hearts and loins. Balzac judges them only in so far as they are firmly rooted in society.

This is another difference—and a capital one—between Balzac and both Nietzsche and Gide. They all three place man at the center of the universe, but the word man does not have the same meaning in all three cases. Nietzsche's man and Gide's man is man on his own, naked man, man reduced to nothing but himself. For Balzac, man is never just man: the term also includes his circumstances, his family, his children, his wealth, his occupation, his town or province, everything, in short, that Zarathustra refers to as chains, everything from which the Immoralist is striving to liberate himself. Balzac's man is not striving to liberate himself in the slightest. A job: he leaps upon it. A rich woman: he hurls himself in pursuit. An ambition: he makes it his. Zarathustra and the Immoralist fight their way out of society. Balzac's man is always fighting his way in. Even Vautrin expends all his efforts on acheiving—even though it is through another person—a magnificent social position. Balzac's man is not trying to establish the individual's right to a personal code of law. Indeed, he is seeking exactly the opposite: to fit himself into the law of society, to learn the rules of the game, the technique of how to live successfully in society. An "environmental" morality, it could be called. In *le Lys dans la Vallée,* Vandenesse woos Mme de Mortsauf. She does not yield to him. Balzac respects her for this. In *la Duchesse de Langeais*, Montriveau woos the Duchesse of the title. She does not yield to him. Balzac condemns her for it. His attitude seems to be that by accepting the social role of a woman in vogue, by not having children, by being separated from her husband, in other words by putting herself in entirely different circumstances from those surrounding Mme de Mortsauf, Mme de Langeais has committed herself to the obligations of a different morality. By not yielding to her lover she is breaking, not the general law of morality, but the rules of the game, the moral law of her particular environment. She is not being "straight."

That man exists for Balzac, generally speaking, only as a social entity, only insofar as he is rooted in society, mortised and tenoned into it by all his attendant circumstances, seems to me to be further proved by another tic that is to be observed in his style. I mean by all those notorious formulas that Proust imitated to such happy effect in his Balzac pastiche. Du Bousquier, "that Cromwell of the Val-Noble" (*Vieille Fille*, p.326); Vautrin, "that Machiavelli of the prison hulks" (*Splendeurs*, p.921); Rigou, "that Louis XV without a throne" (*Paysans*, p.210); Troubert, "that Louis XI in a cassock" (*Curé de Tours*, p.843); Mme Matifat, "that store counter Catherine II" (*César Birotteau*, p.458); Gaudissart, "that travelers' Murat" (*id.* p.489); Mme de Blamont-Chauvry, "that female Talleyrand" (*Duchesse de Langeais*, p.228); Madeleine Vivet, "that Dido of the antechamber" (*Cousin Pons*, p.458); or even: "the Vistula, that Loire of the North" (*Muse du Département*, p.49).

Comic though it often is, and mechanical though it may have become, the significance of the formula is nevertheless quite clear: everything is a matter of circumstances. Faced with results as different as Cromwell's life in London and Bousquier's in Alençon, one might be excused for thinking that there is no possible resemblance between the causes and the forces that determined their actions. But one would be mistaken. If we are to take this formula literally, the only thing that du Bousquier lacked to make him Cromwell was an England to govern. Take Catherine II off her throne and you have Mme Matifat. Put Mme Matifat on that throne and you have Catherine II. I repeat, the formula must be taken with a smile. There are occasions, however, when it takes on a more serious tone. Troubert is merely the vicar-general of a province, but: "There is no doubt that in another age Troubert would have been a Hildebrandt or an Alexander VI" (*Curé de Tours*, p.854). Mme Rabourdin is merely a charming middle-class woman, but: "Possibly she would have achieved greatness in greater circumstances" (*Employés*, p.896). Max Gilet lives by sponging off a servant-girl, but he could have done "great things if he had remained in an environment that was favorable to him" (*Rabouilleuse*, p.1085). Again, it is a matter of the man plus his circumstances. "Isn't it true that society can produce as many different kinds of men, according to the environments in which their energies are deployed, as there are zoological varieties?" (*Avant-Propos*, p.4). If Mme de Langeais is condemned while Mme de Mortsauf is acclaimed, if Mme de La Chanterie is great where Mme de Granville is petty, it is not only because they are different by nature, but also, and even more, because their environments, their circumstances are fundamentally different (Mme de Granville has a husband, Mme de La Chanterie does not; Mme de Granville is young, Mme de La Chanterie is old). "There is no absolute virtue," Rastignac thinks, "but only circumstances" (*Maison Nucingen*, p.599). "There are no principles," Vautrin adds, "there are only events; there are no laws, there are only circumstances" (*Père Goriot*, p.940). And Balzac, rather more curtly, adds: "Everything is modified by events" (*César Birotteau*, p.492).

There is one passage, in *Splendeurs et Misères des Courtisanes*, that is particularly curious in this respect. Esther, it will be remembered, is a prostitute who chances to meet Lucien de Rubempré one day and falls in love with him. This new love makes her loathe her former life. She gives up her trade, attempts to make a living by sewing and prays every evening in front of a statue of the Virgin Mary. Her prayers are answered, Fate is kind to her, and she is given the opportunity to slake this thirst for purity to the full. In order to make her worthy of Lucien, Vautrin places Esther in a convent. Esther can at last say farewell to the life that she hated. She can become converted, she can purify herself. She is happy, she is in her seventh heaven—almost literally you might say. But then she begins to pine away. She is sapped by an invisible fever. She wanted to pray and now she is praying; she wanted to be educated and now she is being educated. She was poor and despised. Now she is leading the same life as all those rich young girls that she had always envied. But she goes into a decline. She is eating the healthiest of diets, she is enjoying untroubled nights instead of the "crushing fatigues" imposed on her by her former trade. But she is fading away. "She grew pale, she changed, she grew thin . . . Her vitality was being sapped at its very source." Perhaps she is grieving because she is away from Lucien? No, Balzac is quite clear on this point: she is dying because she has been transplanted. It is not her evenings with Lucien she sees again in her dreams but "those lascivious laughter-filled nights . . . maenadic, wild and brutal." "The muddy gutters of Paris that she had abjured" are summoning her back to them. The environment from which she has been too violently uprooted is taking its revenge. Having been born and brought up in the midst of corruption, Esther has grown accustomed to it, and even though she despises it, even though she hates it, she also longs for it, and she is dying because she can no longer breathe its poisoned air. Vautrin tells her brutally: "You're a whore, and you always will be a whore. Because despite all the attractive theories of the cattle breeders, one can never become anything in this world except what one is." Heavens knows that will-power can accomplish amazing things in Balzac's world. But in Esther's case it is defeated by the powerful pressures of environment. "The infernal region that had been her home still exercised its dominion over her despite the sovereign orders of an absolute will." According to Balzac, nothing is more difficult to accomplish than the transplantation of a human being from one environment to another. "Perhaps it is the same with men's minds as it is with those animals that lose the power to reproduce when they are transplanted from the climate in which they were born" (*Eugénie Grandet*, p.562).

CHAPTER 16

Place

The descriptions—man's influence on his surroundings —influence of his surroundings on man—rootless characters and transplanted characters—Paris and the provinces—foreigners—the exotic works—foreigners in France—the Poles: Steinbock, Laginski and Halpersohn—the Germans: Schmucke—the English: Arabelle Dudley, Lord Dudley, Marsay and Miss Stevens, Melmoth and Toby—the Italians—the Spaniards—Various —Absence and racism—the Jews—Magus.

THEIR ENVIRONMENT is the governing factor in men's lives. They themselves, their passions and their values are all modified by their circumstances. "There are environments," Canalis says, "in which moral truths, like animals, can change their outward aspect to the point where they become unrecognizable" (*Modeste Mignon,* p.533). This truth is observable in Balzac's work even in his style of writing. There is a distinct difference of tone between those novels that take place in 1820 and those that take place in 1840. There is also a similar difference between those that take place in an aristocratic world and those that take place in a middle-class world. In the former, the style is tight, ornamented, and rather dashing. In the latter it becomes jovial, good-natured, more like the storytelling style of the traveling salesman. When Balzac says of a character's conversation that it is "pluvial," when he writes: "Whereupon the masons began wielding their picks with an energy that made both the house and Constance groan," when he tells me that Pons and Schmucke clean their apartment "with the ability of two sailors scrubbing the decks of a flagship," then I don't need to be told that these phrases are taken from *César Birotteau* (pp. 429 and 426) and *Cousin Pons* (p.592) in order to sense that they can only refer to middle-class people. When confronted with a marquise, Balzac talks in a quite different way. Armande d'Esgrignon and Rose Cormon are both old maids, but Balzac is all pirouettes when refer-

[366]

ring to the one and all hearty slaps on the back when talking about the second. Both women still have sufficient charms for a man to muse upon. But whereas the middle-class lady's corsage "is not unlike two kettledrums being carried in a military parade," the most that Balzac permits himself to say of the aristocrat is that men "used to watch the play of her long, brown dress" (*Vieille Fille*, p.272; *Cabinet des Antiques*, p.341). Possibly there is a little snobbery in this; but what is snobbery after all except, by definition, a recognition of the august laws of social environment?

All this is rather self-evident and need not detain us long. What I should like to do, however, is to merely underline the importance that Balzac attaches to two essential circumstances of any life, the two principal elements of any environment: place and time.

People are sometimes amazed and irritated by the way in which Balzac will spend such enormous amounts of time describing a street, or a drawing-room or a house. The number of inventories there are in the *Comédie humaine!* In *César Birotteau* alone, for example, Balzac successively describes for us, and in detail, Birotteau's own apartment, that of Molineux, Popinot's store, Ragon's house, Claparon's office, the Kellers' office, du Tillet's apartment and Gigonnet's house. He has been criticized for these inventories often enough, and it appears that his readers, or his critics, were already complaining about them in his own day. "The Saint-Jean turnpike," Balzac writes, "of which the description appeared so tedious at one time" (*Petits Bourgeois*, p.68). Or again, in *la Recherche de l'Absolu* (p.474): "Perhaps it is in the interests of writers to establish the necessity for these didactic preparations against which certain ignorant and voracious persons see fit to protest." Upon which, there follows a description of three or four pages. In other words, Balzac is aware of the objection. And if he ignores it that means he has good reasons for doing so.

Mark you, there is no denying that these inventories do stem partly from a veritable mania for bric-à-brac on the author's part. I don't need to excuse myself for the term because Balzac used it himself. He adored furniture and pictures.* And he loved to talk about them. Every writer has certain subjects that he can't broach without a quivering of the pen. Balzac's is attacked by this particular kind of quiver whenever he begins to deal with any kind of interior decorations that are at all worthy of note, or any collection of pictures that has anything at all to recommend it. One

---

* See André Billy's *Vie de Balzac* on this subject (II, 130).

only has to read *Cousin Pons* in order to realize that only a man who has himself dreamed of having a collection as fine as the old man's could possibly write about it in that way. He spreads himself, he returns to it with such joy, he takes pleasure in emphasizing that such satisfactions are not within the grasp of the first nouveau-riche merchant who comes along, he shows that he has the genuine feelings of the bargain-hunter. "One cannot gaze at a Ruysdaël or a Hobbema with real pleasure," he writes, "unless one knows that it cost only fifty francs" (*Cousin Pons*, p.531). That, needless to say, is the remark of a collector, not of a connoisseur. "Each pane of the two casements in the old man's room was a sheet of stained glass from Switzerland. The least of these was worth a thousand francs, and there were sixteen of these masterpieces altogether . . . In 1815, these pieces of stained glass were being sold for between six and ten francs" (*id.* p.594). One senses that this was written by a man who has been dreaming all his life of stumbling upon just such a bargain, who has not done so, and who is now compensating himself for this disappointment by making it happen to one of his creations instead. Balzac has his vicarious pleasures too, you see. Mme Rabourdin, when decorating her drawing-room, makes use of "some ravishing Turkish rugs, a bargain snapped up by her father, hung around the walls in old ebony frames now only to be bought at the most exorbitant prices. Some admirable Boulle buffets . . . had been used to decorate the periphery of the room, while in its center there glistened the inlaid brass arabesques set in a great tortoise-shell clock, the first pedestal clock to reappear from the seventeenth century, a herald of the movement that was to bring the masterpieces of that age back into general esteem" (*Employés*, p.892). Doesn't it make your mouth water? Balzac writes about those buffets and that clock in the same tone as the aging Casanova recalling the brilliant conquests of his youth, in the same tone as Sade in his cell evoking the savage delights of past debauches. When, in *la Rabouilleuse*, Balzac shows us Rouget giving his nephew Bridau a collection of Tintorettos and Poussins of whose value he has absolutely no idea, one can sense that the writer is enchanted by this detail, that he is exultant at the very idea. His passion for these things is such that it sometimes causes him to lose all contact with reality. At one point, we find him hanging a Raphaël and a Gerard Dow in a pirate's cabin (*Femme de Trente Ans*, p.822). And in the Claës house we find ourselves, literally, up to our knees in paintings. Elsewhere, we are able to admire "two paintings by Greuze and two by Watteau, two Van Dyck heads, two Ruysdaël landscapes, two more by le Guaspre, a Rembrandt and a Holbein, a Murillo and a Titian, two Teniers and two Metzus, a Van

Huysum and an Abraham Mignon" (*Cousine Bette*, p.200). Where are we? In the Salon Carré of the Louvre? By no means. It is merely the drawing-room of a kept woman whose lover has just had the place redecorated for her.

Only the description is often just as lengthy when the decorations in question are frankly bad. Neither Molineux's apartment in *César Birotteau* nor Schmucke's room in *Une Fille d'Eve* has anything to offer the collector in the way of Holbeins or Boulle furniture; but the inventory is made none the less meticulously for all that. In other words there is more involved here than just a mania for bric-à-brac. It is a question of a literary device, a principle of literary esthetics. And indeed Balzac does actually express this principle through the mouth of d'Arthez in *les Illusions perdues* (p.649): "Replace all those diffuse digressions, so magnificent in Scott but so colorless in your work, with the kind of descriptions to which our language is so perfectly suited." In matters of painting, Balzac was a determined admirer of the Dutch masters, of all precise and detailed painters. In certain of his descriptions he is aiming at giving us the written equivalent of a Vermeer or a Teniers. For example, the description of the Guillaume house in *le Chat-qui-pelote*. The house, its old beams, the russet muslin curtains, the sign over it, the merchant himself coming out onto the step for a breath of fresh air, all that is the exact equivalent of a genre painting. Moreover, there are direct references to painting throughout. This "picture," Balzac writes, "would have made any painter in the world stop to look at it. The store . . . formed a dark background beyond which the merchant's dining room could be glimpsed. Inside, there stood an oil lamp casting all around it the same golden light that brings so much grace to the paintings of the Dutch school" (*Maison du Chat-qui-pelote*, p.30). Or elsewhere: "During the last days of August, one Sunday after the evening service, a woman was seated in her low armchair in front of one of the windows looking out onto the garden. The rays of the sun . . . were enveloping this woman in the brightly glowing zone of light reflected by the curtain of draped damask hanging down one side of the window" (*Recherche de l'Absolu*, p.484). Doesn't it sound like a description of a painting? And the author is the first to underline this resemblance. "A painter," he says, "who . . . tried to copy this woman . . ." Or again, this scene in the Tascherons' house at Montégnac: "The two old men . . . were sitting huddled in one corner on their sacks . . . Denise was leaning against the bread-bin, watching the lawyer as he used this piece of domestic furniture as a writing table . . . The buyer was seated on a chair beside the scrivener . . . The men were half seated on a large bed covered in green serge. The mother was busy over by the fireplace beating eggs for an omelette" (*Curé de Village*, p.618). Every detail there is seen with a painter's eye. "This painting," Balzac himself says. And he is not mistaken.

Balzac did not consider himself to be only a novelist. It was also his intention to leave a portrait of the age in which he lived. He is trying to give us a complete inventory of his times. And why should the houses and the streets be excluded from that inventory? "Will our nephews not be enchanted to have an account of all the physical aspects of an age that they will refer to as the good old days?" (*Début dans la Vie*, p.600). Is it not the novelist's function to preserve in his works all these houses, these physical specimens of an age, "these curious expressions of the past" that disappear with "a terrifying rapidity" (*Petits Bourgeois*, p.69)?

But no esthetic principle is ever anything but the obverse of a principle, period. The principle here is that man is a function of his environment and the environment a function of man. They act upon one another reciprocally. The man reveals himself to us through the street that he has chosen to live on (when he was able to choose), through the furniture with which he surrounds himself, through the order or the disorder in which he chooses or allows himself to live. And on the other hand, the environment too has its effect: no one is exactly the same man in a fine apartment as he is in an attic, in Paris as in Mende. Hence the necessity for describing them, these streets and these attics.

The principle needs no elaboration. A hundred years of more or less naturalistic novels have accustomed us to it only too well. But for Balzac the idea was still new. In all the novels of Crébillon fils I am fairly certain that you will find only two pieces of furniture: a sofa and a ladle. And even then they are both enchanted. Nor did it ever occur to Laclos to let us know whether the château in *les Liaisons dangereuses* was a Renaissance one or one with battlements.

Who would dream of trying to explain Napoleon without giving some account of the disturbances he created all over Europe? Yet the energy that Napoleon employed in his rearrangement of duchies and kingdoms was in no way intrinsically different from that expended by a woman in furnishing her house. In both cases there is a projection of energy into the world, a projection of the personality into space. Schmucke's room, as described in *Une Fille d'Eve*, is strictly a portrait of the old musician painted "in furniture," a portrait in mahogany and rosewood. Even if he himself were not there when we walked into it for the first time, an attentive examination of its contents would be sufficient to give us a fair idea of the man who lives in it, and of his complete indifference to the things of this world. Neither Molineux nor Birotteau could possibly live in such disorder. The room becomes, as it were, something that Schmucke himself has secreted. In order to know the man himself, a description of this place is as indispensable to us as a description of its shell would be in the case of a snail or a hermit crab. And this analogy is not of my invention: it is one that we find springing constantly from Balzac's own pen. "You would have said an oyster clinging to its rock" (*Gobseck*, p.625). And speaking of concierges: "Their little lodge has become to them what its shell is to an oyster" (*Cousin Pons*, p.561). "After thirty years of stagnation, every individual has completed the shell into which he can retire" (*Monographie du Rentier*). In *Une Double Famille*, Mme de Granville's house is quite literally her shell. Her "self-righteous and petty spirit revived inside her house, beneath the concave, circular ceiling panels ornamented with those motifs whose trailing and contorted arabesques are in such bad taste" (*Une Double Famille*, p.966). The Pension Vauquer too is a shell for its owner: "Her whole person explains the pension, just as the pension implies her person . . . That little woman's fleshy pallor is the product of her life here in exactly the same way as typhus is a product of the bad air in a hospital" (*Père Goriot*, p.852). Mme Vauquer is a product of the house and, reciprocally, the house derives its essence from Mme Vauquer. They influence one another mutually, and it would be impossible to give any accurate account of the one without the other. The Rogrons' dining room has a definite character, and "it gives a very good picture of the owners' character too . . . An observer would have immediately sensed the petty ideas and the absolute self-satisfaction of the retired shop-keeper." (*Pierrette*, pp. 680 and 651). "The furnishings of the offices," Balzac also writes in *les Employés* (p.321), "would have indicated to any observer in need of such information what the quality of those who worked in them was." "In accordance with some strange law, everything in a house imitates the master of it, his spirit is always hovering there" (*Curé de Village*, p.653). "The first glance thrown into a house tells us whether it is love or despair that rules in it" (*Cousine Bette*, p.279). And, in *la Recherche de l'Absolu* (p.474); "The events of human life, whether public or private, are so intimately linked to the products of architecture that most observers can reconstruct nations or individuals in all the reality of their daily habits simply from the ruins of their public monuments or from an examination of their domestic remains."

It goes without saying that clothes too can furnish precious information. Balzac writes of a character—I can't at the moment recall which particular one—in *Une Ténébreuse Affaire* (p.489): "His costume, at once the envelope and the expression of his character, was a portrait of both the man and the age." Or, in *la Bourse* (p.342); "Two men whose costumes, physiognomies and aspects had a whole story to tell." Here again, Balzac is starting from a general idea, from a theory that he has explained in detail in a little work entitled *Physiologie de la Toilette*. "The cravat is the man . . . That starched, stiff, straight cravat without a single ruffle . . . tells you that you are in the presence of a man who is precise, unfeeling, egotistical. That light muslin cravat there, flowing, without starch . . . that means a man whose conversation will be elegant, diffuse, colorless."

The influence is reciprocal. While the man may impose his order on the environment in which he lives, this environment in its turn leaves a mark on the man. Physical surroundings have an influence on people's souls, scruples may be left behind when one moves house, the passions may change when one changes one's address. Granville is driven out of his home as much by the frigidity of its furnishings as by that of his wife. "The influence exercised on the soul by physical locations is a thing worthy of remark" (*Femme de Trente Ans*, p.721). In *la Physiologie du Mariage*, Balzac does not hesitate for a moment to make conjugal happiness a function of the way apartments are arranged. The heart of this work is a theory about the role of the bed that takes up a good twenty pages. And I don't mean the bed metaphorically. I mean the bed as a physical object, the bed with its mattress and its pillow. "The bed is one of these decisive pieces of furniture," Balzac says (*Physiologie du Mariage*, p.730). "Messieurs," someone says in this same work (p.752), "I once passed through a little town near Orléans where the entire population was made up of hunchbacks, of people with sullen or unhappy faces . . . Well . . . all the beds there were in a frightful state and . . . the bedrooms of the married couples were in every case an affront to the eye." Love, Balzac also writes (*Ferragus*, p.60), is "a basic element of life that can only develop its full grace on Savonnerie carpets, in the glow from an opaline shaded lamp, between sympathetic, silk-hung walls . . . there must be mirrors . . . very low divans . . . furs on the floor for bare feet, candles under glass surrounded by muslin drapes." Mme Rabourdin's apartment, he tells us in *les Employés* (p.892), "was extremely well appointed, an advantage that is of the greatest importance in ensuring the nobility of home life." Sometimes, I am fairly certain, this influence makes itself felt without the author's knowledge. In *Etude de Femme*, we see Rastignac occupying a spacious and pleasantly furnished apartment. His manner of speech is kindly, his character sunny. In *la Peau de Chagrin*, there are some old socks left hanging over his divan. His remarks are decidedly more bitter in tone. He has his claws out all the time. He is "without pity" and indulges in "biting sallies" (*Peau de Chagrin*, p.134).

This influence is not, I need hardly add, confined merely to apartments. Everything, according to Balzac, has its effect on a man: wealth or poverty, upbringing, example, even his diet. "The destiny of nations is dependent upon the food they eat, upon their daily diet. Cereals led to the creation of artistic nations . . . Brandy killed off the Indians . . . Tobacco has already meted out justice to the Turks, to the Dutch and is now threatening Germany . . . Wherever women drink tea, love has been tainted at its very source . . . I dare say that the tranquillity of the Germans is in large measure due to their practice of smoking pipes" (*Traité des Excitants modernes*). I know of course that these little treatises of Balzac's are intentionally light-hearted works, and that it would be absurd to treat them too seriously; but after all, a man can reveal himself just as easily through the jokes he makes as through his more serious remarks. And Balzac's thought, whether he is in his light-hearted vein or his serious vein, always tends in the same direction.

Towns and landscapes also affect human temperaments. Provincial towns lull a man's energies to sleep, whereas living out in the country gives the character a certain limpidity. "The purity of the air contributes a great deal to an innocent way of life," Benassis says in *le Médecin de Campagne* (p.380). In *le Curé de Village* (p.601), Balzac explains the character of the inhabitants of Montégnac with reference to the appearance of the soil. The inhabitant of a village, he says, identifies himself with nature. "But for the office-worker," he writes elsewhere, "Nature means Offices. His horizon is closed in on every side by green cardboard boxes. His weather, his meteorological situation, is always the same: the close air of corridors, the masculine smells exhaled and imprisoned in unventilated cubicles . . . Several distinguished doctors have expressed alarm at the influence of this natural habitat . . . on the moral being enclosed within those frightful compartments" (*Employés*, p.954). As for the streets of Paris, they have "human qualities, and their own physiognomies, by means of which they impress upon our souls certain ideas against which we have no defenses" (*Ferragus*, p.17). There are "murderous streets that can kill with impunity; Justice today takes no account of them; but once upon a time the High Court might well have sent for the lieutenant of police and reprimanded him *for the reasons aforesaid*, and would at least have issued some sort of writ against the offending thoroughfare" (*id.* p.18). More-over, the Parisian is a distinct species whose physiognomy, character and ambitions have nothing in common with the thoughts and preoccupations of the provincial. This is a subject you will find dealt with both at the beginning of *Ferragus* and in the first few pages of *la Fille aux Yeux d'Or*.

There are also substantial differences between the inhabitants of the various provinces. There is a scene between Mme de Rochefide and Ca-lyste du Guénic that is a good example of this. They have both been living in Paris for quite a while when it takes place, it should be noted. And furthermore, the kind of paroxysm it deals with is one that we should expect to provoke exactly the same reaction in a German or a Portuguese. Yet Balzac feels the need to remind us of both characters' origins. "Calyste fell back into an armchair and turned as pale as a corpse. But the inhabi-tants of Brittany possess a courageous nature that impels them to become stubborn when faced with any difficulty. The young Baron pulled himself up again, etc. . . . He cut such a superb figure that a woman from the North or from the Midi would have fallen at his feet saying: 'Take me!' But Béatrix, born on the borders of Normandy and Brittany, was a mem-ber of the tribe of Casteran, and desertion had developed in her nature all the ferocity of the Frank and the cruelty of the Norman" (*Béatrix*, p.550).

Since man is so much influenced by his environment, it follows that any change of environment will produce a corresponding change in the man. This, too, is an idea to which we have become accustomed. But before Balzac it had scarcely existed at all. The complications of Marivaux's plots remain the same whether the characters are in Paris or in the country. In *les Liaisons dangereuses*, we see Valmont and Mme de Tourvel in the heart of the country. But when they go back to Paris their characters remain exactly the same. This is because Marivaux and Laclos were writ-ing in an age ruled by the intellect. And intellect is the same wherever it goes. Reason does not change with longitude. In order to win the object of his desires, the Venetian Casanova propounds exactly the same rational arguments as the Frenchman Valmont or the Englishman Lovelace. With Balzac, on the other hand, we are already in the realm of our own kind of sensibility, one governed by the heart and the nerves, which are sensitive to everything, to the color of the sky on a particular day as to the style of the furniture in a given room. In *l'Envers de l'Histoire contemporaine*, Godefroid goes off to live in an old, silent, secluded house. His character is affected immediately. "It is a fact that there are certain people who no longer present the same appearance or have the same value once they are separated from the faces, the things and the places that make up the framework of their lives" (*Illusions perdues*, p.595). Mme de Bargeton and Lucien de Rubempré are both perfectly contented with one another as long as they stay in Angoulême; but as soon as they arrive in la Ville-Lumière it is a different story altogether. The theaters and the boulevards act on them like some chemical solution and give both of them an entirely new appearance. Balzac gave us his versions of what happens to people who are uprooted long before Barrès wrote his *Déracinés*. We have Rubempré (the second part of *Illusions perdues* is entitled *Un grand Homme de Province à Paris*), old Schmucke ("Paris *iss not gut* for Germans"), and Victurnien d'Esgrignon, who leaves Alençon, goes to Paris and is corrupted there just as Racadot is corrupted in the Barrès book. The Rogrons in Provins are uprooted creatures too, though in reverse. "No small shopkeeper can pass with impunity from the continual chatter of his business to a world of silence, from Parisian activity to provincial stagnation" (*Pierrette*, p.671). The Parisian Gaudissart is as completely at sea in Vouvray as the provincial Gazonal is in Paris. "To be someone who is somebody in one's hometown and to be nobody at all in Paris are two distinct states that require certain transitions between them, and those who move too abruptly from one to the other suffer a kind of moral annihilation" (*Illusions perdues*, p.602).

Moreover, by grouping his works under such headings as *Scènes de la vie parisienne*, *Scènes de la vie de province*, *Les Parisiens en province*, Balzac makes it fairly clear what importance he attaches to this factor, and how ridiculous it would be to imagine that *la Fausse Maîtresse* could ever take place in Poitiers or *la Vieille Fille* in the eighth arrondissement. "Let us never forget it! France in the nineteenth century is divided into two great zones: Paris and the provinces" (*Muse du Département*, p.70).

Here again we find the style mirroring the thoughts. In the novels that take place in Paris, the style—generally speaking—is all a matter of nerves: sometimes as lively as a sparrow, sometimes languid, with sudden caprices, yielding moments, something that does in the end seem to resemble the description that Saint-Beuve gave of it: "this style so often coaxing and melting, languorous, pink and veined with all the colors of the rainbow." In the novels set in the provinces, Balzac's tread is heavier, and he moves much more slowly. There is less stucco and more masonry. In the Parisian novels the style is a woman. In the provincial ones it is a lawyer. In *la Muse du Département*, we are witnesses of a confrontation between the inhabitants of Sancerre and the two Parisians, Lousteau and Bianchon.

The two sides can barely understand one another. It is as though they talk different languages. One looks around for the interpreter. Lousteau and Bianchon appear to be two foreigners. And this fact is not without its repercussions on the plot. Why does Mme de la Baudraye yield to Lousteau so swiftly? Why does the honest Bianchon abet him in his designs? Is it not because both of them have been affected by that feeling of "demoralization," that forgetfulness of the notion of "consequences" that invades us so much more easily in a foreign country, or in the presence of foreigners?

Balzac took a great deal of his material from provincial life. *Ursule Mirouët* takes place in Nemours, *Pierrette* in Provins, *le Cabinet des Antiques* and *la Vieille Fille* in Alençon, part of *les Illusions perdues* in Angoulême, part of *la Rabouilleuse* in Issoudun, *le Curé de Village* in Limoges, *le Réquisitionnaire* in Carentan, *Modeste Mignon* in le Havre, *les Chouans* in Fougères, part of *Béatrix* in Guérande, *Eugénie Grandet* in Saumur, *Une Ténébreuse Affaire* in and around Troyes, *la Recherche de l'Absolu* in Douai, *la Muse du Département* in Sancerre, *Albert Savarus* in Besançon, *le Contrat de Mariage* in Bordeaux, *le Lys dans la Vallée* in Touraine, *les Paysans* in Burgundy, *le Médecin de Campagne* in Savoy (these last three novels are about rural life rather than provincial life, properly speaking), *Un Drame au bord de la Mer* in le Croisic, *le Curé de Tours* and *le Député d'Arcis* in, as you may perhaps have guessed, Tours and Arcis respectively.

In other words, the provinces provided Balzac with almost half his subjects and almost half his settings. However, ingrate that he is, this does not prevent him from talking about them, on the whole, in very denigrating tones. There is some respect, admittedly, even a measure of affection, in the manner he adopts towards the du Guénic family in Guérande, or towards old d'Esgrignon in Alençon. But neither young du Guénic nor young d'Esgrignon manages to cut much of a figure when he goes up to Paris. And provincial life, in Balzac's eyes, must take part of the responsibility for this. Had they lived in Paris, the two fathers would have been aware of the sweeping changes occurring in the sphere of morals and manners, and they would have altered their way of thinking accordingly. But the provinces in which they live, "the enervating, gentle lives that people habitually lead there" (*Cabinet des Antiques*, p.347) have lulled them to sleep and made them entirely unaware of the real laws of existence.

These real laws being, for Balzac, those obtaining in Paris. For him,

Paris constitutes an environment not only different from that of the provinces but also infinitely superior. Though a provincial cannot even venture into the neighborhood of the Opéra without risking total ruin, Balzac's Parisians on the other hand can go anywhere they choose and emerge victorious every time. Gaudissart is an exception in this respect, an exception due, perhaps, to the author's patriotic feelings for his native Touraine (and there are the Rogrons too, if you like; but the Rogrons aren't really human beings at all). Lousteau, for example, goes to Sancerre. In the twinkling of an eye, he has stormed the battlements of a virtue around which several of the most outstanding examples of the native population had been prowling for years. Manerville is really just a fool. Yet he can go to Bordeaux and triumphantly carry off the prettiest girl in the place. And though he is made a fool of later, it is not by the inhabitants of Bordeaux but by his wife. Charles Grandet dazzles the whole of Saumur. Savarus is only a step away from becoming the most important man in Besançon. Philippe Bridau, spewed up by Paris, is entirely successful in Issoudun. It is as though Balzac looked upon life in Paris as a sort of initiation, a university of life. There are as many fools inside universities as there are outside them; yet somehow or other it is rarely that anyone who passes through such an institution does not acquire, and retain, a certain superiority over his fellows. And so it is with Balzac's Parisians. On occasion, it is true, he will refer to them as "ignorant and clannish" (*Cousin Pons*, p.552), and make fun of their love of conformity (*Cousine Bette*, p.135), but nevertheless, throughout his work the Parisians always keep their position of pre-eminence. And though we do find several superior men in the provinces (David Séchard, Docteur Minoret, Claës, Benassis), it should be noted that they have all spent some time in Paris. For Balzac, Paris is not only a different environment, it is a superior one, it is a melting-pot, a crucible in which men's souls are purified and turned into fine bronze.

Many of the criticisms that Balzac makes of the provinces are, needless to say, the old, time-honored ones: the tittle-tattle, the gossip, the inquisitiveness, the pettiness of both minds and customs. In Angoulême "tea was still sold in apothecaries' shops as a medicine to cure indigestion" (*Illusions perdues*, p.513). In Saumur "a housewife can't buy a partridge without her neighbors asking the husband if it was well cooked" (*Eugénie Grandet*, p.482). In Carentan, everyone knows that Mme de Dey dislikes game, and the whole place is in a fever of curiosity when her cook is seen buying a hare (*Réquisitionnaire*, p.855). Everywhere, the conversations are "stupid, empty, or filled only with matters of local or personal interest" (*Curé de Village*, p.564). Take a look at the provincial evening receptions described in *les Illusions perdues* (pp. 531 to 550) or in *le Député d'Arcis* (pp. 705 to 711). In each case, what you will find is a festival of silliness, stupidity and pretentiousness.

All these things, however, are merely the outward signs of the provinces' inferiority. We know our Balzac well enough to be fairly sure that he will want to dig down to the underlying causes. And the main one, according to him, is that any man who wants to make a brilliant career for himself must of necessity go to Paris. "The men with talent, the artists, the educated men, all the cocks with the brightest plumage fly away to Paris" (*Muse du Département*, p.71). The only ones left behind are the mediocrities—and the women, who have to make do with the mediocrities. The Parisienne too, of course, may well end up married to an imbecile. But she can remedy her situation by cultivating intelligent friends, or by taking a lover. In the provinces, the lover is never anything but "a so-called handsome man, a local dandy, a platitude in more or less elegant attire" (*id*. p.71). In consequence, as long as she continues to live in Sancerre, Mme de la Baudraye remains well-behaved, and Mme de Bargeton too, in her Angoulême. Not out of virtue, but for lack of even one man capable of inspiring in them that minimum of admiration that an intelligent woman needs to feel. "Her pride preserved her from dismal provincial love affairs," Balzac tells us of Mme de Bargeton. "There was not one of the men around her who was capable of inspiring, etc." (*Illusions perdues*, pp. 498 and 499). And of Mme de la Baudraye: "During the space of six years, amongst all the men that were presented to her, who came from twenty miles on either side, there was not a single one at the sight of whom Dinah experienced the inner disturbance caused by beauty, by a belief in the possibility of happiness, by collision with a superior spirit" (*Muse du Département*, p.72). In the same way, Véronique Graslin "has requirements that nothing in the limited provincial fare available was able to meet" (*Curé de Village*, p.564).

Lacking either a husband or a lover of reasonable intelligence, a woman needs some means of making comparisons, a buoy to guide her, a milestone to tell her whether she is making progress or retrogressing. This is what Paris can provide and the provinces cannot. And it is as true in the realm of clothes as it is in that of ideas. Mme de la Baudraye ends up having her dresses made by a local dressmaker. "Her gentlemen friends found her charming" (*Muse du Département*, p.73). In reality, she is an absolute fright; but since she has no one really well-dressed with whom to compare herself, how could she possibly know? She has two or three ideas that she repeats constantly. But where is she to find fresh ones? She mocks the other inhabitants of Sancerre; but just as Monnier was eventually trapped in the voice and manner of Joseph Prudhomme because he had imitated him so much, so Mme de la Baudraye is gradually infected by the petty thinking of all the people around her. The environment is doing its work. Having obtained their superiority cheaply, for want of competition, such superior women end up by losing all capacity for self-criticism. Or if they can still perceive a defect, a lack in themselves, then they just accept it— so hard is it to put ourselves out for an audience we despise. They have had their passions of course, their enthusiasms; but where is all that energy to be directed in the provinces, other than into the pettiest of channels? For want of proper exercise, the passions are shriveled up by a continual effort to make the insignificant seem important. That is the reason for all the avarice and tittle-tattle that infect provincial life" (*Illusions perdues*, p.497).

FOREIGNERS

Having visited the provinces, it is now time for us to venture abroad. *Facino Cane* (or part of it) and *Massimila Doni* take place in Venice, *Sarrasine* in Rome, *les Marana* and *El Verdugo* in Spain, *Séraphita* in Norway, part of *Albert Savarus* in Switzerland, *l'Auberge Rouge* in Germany. The titles of both *Jésus-Christ en Flandre* and *Une Passion dans le Désert* are self-explanatory. To these we should also add several excursions to other countries made during the course of various works mainly set in France (*Adieu, Autre Etude de Femme, le Médecin de Campagne*), and also *Gambara*, which takes place in Paris, but in the Italian colony.

There is one observation that forces itself upon our attention here from the very start: this list does not include any of the truly great works comprised in the *Comédie humaine*. *Massimila Doni* has its fervent admirers, and deserves them. The description of Venice to be found in it is far and away the best of Balzac's exotic descriptions. But it still does not possess either the life or the truth of the picture of Saumur in *Eugénie Grandet*, or that of Paris in *les Petits Bourgeois*. Was Balzac aware of this? It is at any rate worthy of note that in these tales set abroad, or in most of them, he does not address the reader directly himself but uses a third person, a narrator, to tell the story for him. It is a German businessman, not Balzac, who is telling us the story of *l'Auberge Rouge*; it is a soldier who tells us the story of *Une Passion dans le Désert*; another soldier who tells the story of *Adieu*. It is Facino Cane himself, not Balzac, who tells the story that bears his name. It is to Bianchon and Savarus, not to Balzac, that we owe the Spanish anecdote in *Autre Etude de Femme* and the Swiss story in *Albert Savarus*.

I can see you're going to laugh at me for what I've just said. Who actually did the writing: Balzac or Savarus? Bianchon is one of Balzac's creations; therefore whenever Bianchon speaks it is Balzac who is speaking through him. Of course. But it does seem curious to me, all the same, that Balzac has resorted to this fiction of someone other than himself telling these stories in almost every case. I feel there is some justification for believing that he experienced a certain timidity when faced with these foreign settings. A timidity that led him to seek support from an imaginary third person.

That being so, it still remains to be asked why Balzac chose to encumber himself with these palm trees and these fjords at all. In some cases, admittedly, he was forced into it by his subject. It is difficult to imagine the panther from *Une Passion* pacing the Rue Rambuteau, or the gondoliers from *Massimila Doni* gliding along the Bièvre. Nor is it impossible to see these things also as a concession to the taste of an age which, as is well known, was particularly partial to castanets and guitars. But the essential reason, it seems to me, must again be sought in the principle of strict conformity between man and his environment. No doubt Balzac is hampered by having to set one of his plots in Tarragona, but he would be even more hampered by an attempt to transplant characters like Perez de Lagounia or Juana Mancini to the Rue Fortuny. He is much too deeply aware of the disharmony that would always subsist between such characters and the setting, the way of life, the whole color of the seventeenth arrondissement or of Brives-la-Gaillarde. Spanish reality is different from French reality. And this, of course, is yet another new principle. As far as Racine was concerned, the Turkish Bajazet need not reason any differently from the Roman Britannicus, nor the Jewish Athalie any differently from the Cretan Phèdre. Molière's *Dom Juan* takes place in Sicily, but the peasants who appear in it say "jarguienne," not "porca miseria." Had he been cast up on the shores of Brittany, this Don Juan would have encountered natives no different from the ones we are shown. Nor is Beaumarchais' Spanish Figaro any different in kind from Molière's Neapolitan Scapin. I have read both *Dom Juan* and *les Fourberies de Scapin* at least two or three times. Yet before making the point here that one of them takes place—partly—in Sicily and the other in Naples, I was forced to check. Which goes to show that it is a matter of absolutely no importance.

For the classical writer, as I have already pointed out, man remains the same whatever latitude he is in.

Balzac is not a classical writer in this respect. For him, the Pyrenees exist, and their existence is sufficient to transform a truth, a passion, a character. Their existence is sufficient to render certain reactions believable that would not be so between Carentan and Maners. Did Balzac succeed in catching this Spanish reality, or this Italian reality? That is another story. As I have already said, Balzac's exotic works are not among his best. The foreign setting always seems to be an excuse, an alibi, rather than a genuine setting. But the criminal who is trying to establish an alibi, who is claiming to have been in Bordeaux on the day when he is accused of killing a rich old woman in Chatou, that criminal doesn't care one way or the other about Bordeaux. It might just as well have been Cahors he said he was in, or Clermont-Ferrand. The only important thing is that it should be somewhere else. Anywhere else. Anywhere except Chatou, that is the principle he works on. And it is also the principle Balzac works on sometimes. *Séraphita* would seem very improbable set in Paris. Very well, let's set it somewhere else. And note that these stories, or these fragments of stories, that Balzac has set in foreign countries are precisely those of his works that have the most unusual plots and characters. The gondoliers in *Massimila Doni* are merely accessories; Balzac could have transposed them easily enough. But that would not have eliminated the strangeness of the leading characters. The Duc Cataneo is a rare, a curious and motley bird. There may be such creatures in the Jardin d'Acclimatation, but to make us accept him as a denizen of this country would have required a supplementary effort, a process of preparation on the author's part. Whereas by setting the story in Venice he spares himself this preparation. The exotic setting serves both to justify and to intensify the exoticism of the character. A traveler's tales are always true.

This use of foreignness as an alibi is also to be found in certain characters who live in France but whom Balzac has cannily taken care to establish as foreigners. There is Henri Montès, for example, the lover who takes such cruel vengeance on Valérie Crevel in *la Cousine Bette*. Has anyone ever seen such a savage creature? His behavior would certainly be thought astonishing in a young man born, let us say, at Nogent. But Montès is a Brazilian, you see. He has come straight from the jungle. And since everyone knows that the sun can make a man's brain boil, everyone is prepared to accept these equatorial frenzies. Which is fortunate, because without this obliging Brazilian, Balzac would have been forced to waste a great deal of time on explaining the whys and wherefores of such furies to us, on giving us some credible account of the slowly building anger inside this necessary avenger of his. The confinement of Paquita Valdès in *la Fille aux Yeux d'Or* also verges on the hard to take. But it is, after all, a Spanish woman who shuts her away like that, and Paquita Valdès herself comes from . . . Where? No one quite knows. All of which enables the author to make us accept all those violent scenes and those daggers without having to waste too much energy on psychological explanations. And much the same might be said of the young Englishman in *la Femme de Trente Ans* who devotes himself to nursing a woman back to health without being her lover, and of the young Spaniard in *Autre Etude de Femme* who allows himself to be walled up alive rather than compromise his mistress. If attributed to a young man from, let us say, Poitou, such an excess of devotion or such an excess of chivalry might well have appeared rather less than believable.

It should be added immediately, however, that though there may sometimes be a certain amount of jobbery in Balzac's "foreign" stories, this disappears when it comes to the foreign characters that Balzac introduces into his French works. The German Schmucke is just as real as the French Pons, the Polish Steinbock as the French Marneffe. Though here again, it is a reality strictly linked to the characters' circumstances, and in particular to their nationalities. Schmucke is real, but his reality is one in which his country of origin has its part. He is a German. Had he been English or Italian he would have been different. Balzac emphasizes this. When Félix de Vandenesse introduces Lady Dudley to us, in *le Lys dans la Vallée*, he begins with three pages of observations about England in general. And when he leaves her, he exclaims: "I have come to hate England" (*Lys dans la Vallée*, p.997).

Wenceslas Steinbock is a Pole by profession. In order to explain his character to us, Balzac begins by giving us a summary of Polish history. "What Poland was politically, most Poles are in their private lives" (*Cousine Bette*, p.332). It is one more example of the general idea preceding the particular case, the theory preceding the example. For Balzac, Steinbock is a character whose nationality alone already renders him inevitably and fundamentally different from a Rastignac or a Rubempré. He is the product of a certain climate, of a certain upbringing, of particular customs. The psychological explanation that is deduced elsewhere from a family or from an upbringing is here deduced from the characteristics of a nation. Steinbock's behavior is made intelligible to us not only by means of traits particular to him as an individual but also by means of general remarks on his country and his compatriots. "The Pole," Balzac writes, "has . . . in his character the childishness and the fickleness of the beardless nations. He possesses courage, spirit, and strength; but being flawed by a lack of stability, this courage, this strength and this spirit are devoid of all method and order, for the Pole is as changeable as the wind that reigns over that vast plain." Bravery, certainly, "an heroic courage on the field of battle," but "an incredible inconsistency of conduct," "a moral slackness," and a deplorable tendency to overconfidence. "Show a Pole a precipice and he will hurl himself over it on the spot" (*id*. pp. 187, 331 and 333).

All these characteristics are also to be found in Steinbock. This ethographic introduction serves here as a psychological preparation for the individual Pole we are to meet. Steinbock is a spineless character. He has talent but no perseverance. Courage and spirit, but no method, no character. All through *Cousine Bette* we see him constantly under the sway of characters with stronger wills than his. True to the image of his homeland, Steinbock is ceaselessly being invaded and overrun. First of all, he falls under the domination of Lisbeth Fischer. One is sometimes amazed to see young men no less well endowed physically than the next being kept in tow for years by mistresses that even a hunchback wouldn't look at. This is because there are the men who choose and the others who are chosen. Steinbock is one of the second sort. And he would have stayed with Lisbeth till doomsday if he had not met Hortense Hulot, who snaps him up and marries him. For it is she, not Steinbock, who manages the whole affair. And after they are married he is unfaithful to Hortense with Valérie Marneffe. There again, it is the woman who is the aggressor. Wenceslas for his part would have been quite happy to go on staring at her from a distance.

As far as indecisiveness goes, Adam Laginski in *la Fausse Maîtresse* is cut to the same pattern. There seems reason to suppose that he loves his wife. Yet he does nothing to make her happy. Although he has all the time in the world at his disposal, he leaves the task of furnishing and running his house to a friend. In *la Fausse Maîtresse*, it is the lover, not the husband, who defends the citadel of marital bliss. Except that the lover, Thaddée Paz, is a Pole too, and contents himself with loving the Comtesse Laginska in secret and never taking her. Which is praiseworthy behavior certainly, and does something to rehabilitate the Polish character. But it would have been preferable, all the same, if Paz had not attempted to attain his ends by resorting to a lie in which one recognizes something of the tortuousness already observed in Steinbock. Once the lover has de-

parted, the marriage begins to go bad. The Comtesse is not a little tempted
by the thought of La Palférine, while the husband begins prowling around
his friend's putative mistress, the celebrated Malaga. Does he sleep with
her? Worse, he wants to. Like Steinbock, he woos when what he really
wants is rape. I don't imagine he had to go on wooing long. In *la Cousine
Bette* (p.200), we find him a welcome visitor in the demi-monde.

But Poland, according to Balzac, has also "often produced singular and
mysterious beings" (*Envers de l'Histoire contemporaine*, p.397). He gives
us two examples of this species in the persons of Adam de Wierzchownia,
the alchemist in *la Recherche de l'Absolu*, and Moïse Halpersohn, the doctor in *l'Envers de l'Histoire contemporaine*. This latter is also a Jew, but
Balzac presents him above all as a product of Poland. Though he has a
"long, Hebraic nose, curved like a Damascus scimitar," he also has "a truly
Polish brow, wide and noble." "Great national disturbances always produce a species of truncated giants" (*id.* pp. 387 and 397). He is the kind of
doctor who is a genius at his profession, but quite unfeeling, certain of his
diagnoses, never listening to anyone else. When people raise objections he
simply says no. No, nothing else. But he asks for his fees in advance.

In *le Cousin Pons*, there is a whole German colony, and there is one
point in particular when we are taken to a little family reunion at the
Graffs', where a great deal of eating and drinking gets done. "No one
knows," Balzac comments, "the amount of such liquids the Germans can
absorb without losing their tranquillity and calm." They drink a great
deal "but the atmosphere remains harmonious, and there is none of the
usual French rowdiness; their faces become flushed in the same way as the
faces of young brides-to-be in frescoes by Cornelius or Schnorr, which is
to say imperceptibly, and the reminiscences spread through the air like the
smoke from their pipes, gently and slowly" (*Cousin Pons*, p.588). "This
Teutonic appetite so famous throughout Europe," he also says in *l'Auberge Rouge*. The pipe, a large appetite, calmness, gentleness, sentimentality, such are the essential characteristics of the early nineteenth-century
German for Balzac. Not one of his Germans is violent or excitable. "That
pure and noble land of the Teutons," Balzac writes, "so fertile in honorable characteristics, and whose peaceful way of life has never been belied
(*Auberge Rouge*, p.955). They are gentle, simple, sentimental, oh heavens! sentimental is hardly the word for it, with "those childish effusions of
sentimentality . . . such as their passion for flowers, such as their adoration of nature and its effects, which leads them to plant out great bottles in
their gardens so that they can see the view already before them a second

time, reflected on a tiny scale . . . such as . . . their need to lend a psychic significance to the tiniest trifles of the creation, a need that has produced the unfathomable works of Jean-Paul Richter, the drunken ecstasies published by Hoffmann, and the parapets of piled-up folio tomes with which Germans always surround even the simplest questions" (*Cousin Pons*, p.539). "The soft-hearted sentimentality of the Germans," he also writes (*Ferragus*, p.26). "You whose simple-hearted goodness . . . ," he writes when dedicating *le Cabinet des Antiques* to a German friend. "A Germanic passion": that is the pure love felt by David Séchard (*Illusions perdues*, p.519). And lastly, they are a nation of musicians. All of them are musicians. "This pianist, like all pianists, was a German" (*Cousin Pons*, p.538).

The pianist in question is Wilhelm Schmucke, one of the central characters of *le Cousin Pons*, a German who has remained German to such an extent that Balzac felt it necessary to attempt some representation of his accent. "*Monsir, mône hâmi Bons relèfe d'eine malatie et fu ne l'afez sans tude pas regonni*" * (*id.* p.607). This is a device that Balzac employs not only with Schmucke but also for conveying the accents of the Alsatians Kolb and Nucingen, that of Monistrol, who comes from the Auvergne, and also that of the Englishwoman in *Gaudissart II*. Which is already far too much, if I may be permitted to say *vot I tink*.

Despite his age, this Schmucke has preserved the soul of a sweet and simple child. He distrusts nothing and no one. Mme de Vandenesse asks him to sign some letters of exchange that could well put him in prison: he signs without even looking at them (*Fille d'Eve*, p.152). In *le Cousin Pons*, he lets himself be fleeced like a lamb. It takes a great many such impositions to make him finally utter a complaint. And such a little complaint. "*Paris iss not gut for Chermanss, vee are mate fooiss off.*" And as he says this he makes a "little gesture with his head as of a man who thinks he sees clearly into all the recesses of this vile world" (*Cousin Pons*, p.793). When we first meet him he is living on the Rue de Nevers surrounded by unbelievable chaos, for "this divine man" (*Fille d'Eve*, p.151) is as blind to the disorder of things as he is to the wickedness of men. To him, this smoky room is "a temple inhabited by two divinities," which is to say: music and the memory of his three pupils, Marie de Vandenesse, her sister Marie-Eugénie, who is married to du Tillet, and Ursule Mirouët. He was

---

* *Monsieur, mon ami Pons relève d'une maladie et vous ne l'avez sans doute pas reconnu.*
Monsieur, my friend Pons is recovering from an illness, and you doubtless did not recognize him.

also Lydie Peyrade's music teacher (*Splendeurs*, p.760). He lives in a perpetual dream, in an enchanted world in which there is room for only the
joys of music, the delights of friendship and the one companion incapable
of ever letting him down, his "nice, big German pipe." Later on he goes to
live with Pons, and it is then that we find ourselves confronted by the
purest and most deeply moving image of friendship that Balzac has created for us. Pons is a goodhearted creature himself, but how coarse, how
egotistical, how brutal he appears beside his gentle companion Schmucke,
beside this soul that "sparkles like a sun," beside that smile, "so open, so
ingenuous," beside those eyes brimming with "celestial beams" (*Fille
d'Eve*, p.151).

Schmucke dies several days after Pons. He allows himself to be stripped
of his entire inheritance and makes only one condition: that a sum of three
thousand francs shall be set aside for little Olga Topinard, because she
looks like "*a little Cherman girl*" and because her father once did him a
service, "an unimportant trifle in the eyes of the world, but which, in the
eyes of this celestial lamb weighed more, like Bossuet's glass of water, than
all the victories of earthly conquerors" (*Cousin Pons*, p.794).

We are accustomed to think of the Germans somewhat differently
today. But that does not mean that Balzac's picture is false. The characteristics of a nation may change in a hundred years. The other day, I was
reading the diary kept by the German Hebbel while he was living in Paris
during the year 1844. He was evidently a real-life Schmucke. He watches
little girls playing in the Tuileries. He is moved. Their governess buys
them a bottle of beer but is unable to open it. Hebbel offers his services,
and with the help of the lady's parasol succeeds in opening the bottle, a
deed "that earned me a kindly smile," he notes with joy. He finds a letter
that someone has dropped. Perhaps it is a love letter, he says to himself,
and rushes off to mail it—though not without having first added a friendly
message on the back. Another day, he is approached by an old lady. "She
appeared to be a member of the highest class of society," he writes. In fact,
she is a bawd.

Innocent Schmucke. Candid Hebbel. But we must be on our guard all
the same. According to Balzac, although all Germans inevitably go
through a stage of being naïve, some of them lose that naïveté and then go
on to simulate it "in order to fertilize their success . . . by dispelling
other people's suspicions" (*Cousin Pons*, p.538). "When, under that surface appearance of kindliness and honesty, they start to become cunning
and double-dealing, then they are even worse than the rest" (*Père Goriot*,
p.1036). Take Nucingen. (I know that Nucingen was born in Strasbourg

and is not therefore a true German, but by making him talk in the same accent as Schmucke Balzac forces me to classify them together. I hope that explanation will suffice.) He uses his blundering manner to lull his opponents to sleep. But as soon as he leaves the business world, then his fundamental and genuine naïveté reappears. "The naïveté of this old man" (*Splendeurs*, p.721). "You have become as innocent as a child," Esther tells him (*id.* p.905).

Other Germans: the businessman who tells us the story of the *Auberge Rouge*, the tailor Wolfgang Graff and his brother Johann, a hotelkeeper whose daughter marries Wilhelm Schwab. They are all to be found in *le Cousin Pons*. There is nothing much to be said about them. They are simply your average *Comédie humaine* Germans, if I may so express it: quiet folk who like their pleasures, pipe-smokers, naïve and cunning at the same time, good people, extremely respectful of the status quo and the established social hierarchies. "Everyone knows how much the Germans respect social distinctions!" Balzac writes. "In Germany, a married woman is always referred to by her husband's title as well as his name, for this is important in establishing her social status" * (*Cousin Pons*, pp. 591-592). Because of this, Schwab and Graff are very insistent that their friend Brunner should marry the daughter of the Président Camusot de Marville. But Brunner is a somewhat individualistic kind of German. A great libertine, extremely dissipated, having been brought up (I must confess) "according to French principles," worn out before his time, he has preserved no more of his native German naïveté than is necessary to make him adhere firmly to his principles with regard to marriage. He has sworn to himself that he will never marry an only daughter. He does not marry Cécile Camusot.

Another German: the Baronne d'Aldrigger. She is from Mannheim. That is to say, she has "a tender heart." Easily moved to tears, she is also easily consoled. Her husband's death almost causes her to die of grief, but next day she is already consoling herself with some delicious green peas. She has the soul of a shepherdess, and also, alas, the clothes. Though a mother with two daughters to find husbands for, she allows herself to dress in "pink, with a short skirt and a bow to finish off the long, pointed bodice" (*Maison Nucingen*, pp. 167 and 616).

There are two or three characters with German ancestors; though none of them have anything in common. It is possible that Ursule Mirouët has inherited her gentleness and her dreamy tendencies from her German

---

* Translator's note. This is a free translation. There is no English equivalent of the examples Balzac gives: *Madame la générale, Madame la conseillère, Madame l'avocate.*

mother, but there is nothing very gentle or dreamy about Mme Schontz, or about young Giguet, though both of these had German mothers too.

Now let us cross the Channel. Here are Lord Dudley and his wife. Also their daughter-in-law, Dinah Stevens, the happy wife of Henri de Marsay. Also Lord Grenville, Melmoth, the groom John Barry, Lady Barimore, Miss Griffith, the groom Toby, and not forgetting the young English girl in *Splendeurs*.

It had best be stated at the very outset that the overall estimate is not a favorable one. In fact, to be blunt about the matter, Balzac doesn't much care for the English. Some of his characters even go so far as to hate them. Certainly it would go hard with any Englishman who happened to meet Goguelat and Gondrin from *le Médecin de Campagne* on a dark night. Or Genestas either. "Death to the English!" Carpentier cries during the course of a banquet. And this toast, Balzac tells us, is prodigiously well received (*Rabouilleuse*, p.1081).

But all these characters have been soldiers in Napoleon's army. They have a specific reason for disliking the English. Balzac does not share their bitterness himself; but that is almost as far as his sympathy goes. The very most he seems to be prepared to allow the English is a certain whiteness of skin (*Femme de Trente Ans*, p.690), and a feeling for "comfort" (*Maison Nucingen*, p.643), "that science of everyday existence . . . which ensures that your slippers will be the most exquisite slippers in the world . . . which transforms matter into a soft and nourishing, clean and shining pulp, in the depths of which the souls can swoon away with sheer pleasure, which produces the frightful monotony of perpetual well-being, enables you to lead a life without obstacles, devoid of spontaneity, and which, in sum, turns you into a machine" (*Lys dans la Vallée*, p.947). But Balzac also refers to the Englishman's arrogance (*Femme de Trente Ans*, p.689), to his mania for being different from other people (*id.* p.735), and to the "solemnity with which (they) approach their idiotic patriotic displays, which is so inane that it cannot even be called positively stupid" (*Vieille Fille*, p.269), and above all to their "atrocious hypocrisy" (*Muse du Département*, p.90). In *la Maison Nucingen*, Bixiou delivers a whole lecture on this subject: "An English lady . . . will get up to the most amazing things in her bedroom without feeling that she is being what she calls 'improper,' but if a gentleman were to come into that same bedroom on a friendly visit she would consider her reputation utterly lost . . ." "When you think," Blondet adds, "that there are nincompoops here in France who would like to import all the solemn sillinesses that the English practice at home with that sublime aplomb of theirs, one can only shudder with apprehension" (*Maison Nucingen,* p.606).

This hypocrisy, Félix de Vandenesse explains, makes the Englishwoman into a "poor creature who is virtuous because she is forced to be . . . condemned to continual lies . . ." which sometimes, seized by a sudden rebelliousness, she throws aside, then plunges into a life of wickedness in search, not of pleasure, but of a cruel revenge. "A cruel kind of love that resembles English politics." The hypocrisy is then thrown off in a great unleashing of the emotions, but a cruel unleashing "that laughs over the corpses of those it kills." Cruel in the same way as English humor, "an acid so corrosive . . . that it leaves them like washed and scrubbed skeletons" (*Lys dans la Vallée,* pp. 944, 948 and 980).

Here again, as with Steinbock, these ethnological observations serve as a psychological introduction. If the reader is unaware of these national characteristics, then he runs the risk—according to Balzac—of entirely failing to understand Dudley and his wife, Arabelle, since they are both examples of precisely this unleashed hypocrisy, which has turned, in the one case, to lust, in the other, to cruelty.

This Arabelle Dudley is red-haired, beautiful and can manage a horse as well as any bareback rider in a circus. Of mysterious origins, married to Lord Dudley, who must be quite a lot older than she is, she arrives in Paris and is scarcely out of her traveling clothes before she is pricking up her ears at the latest piece of gossip: Félix de Vandenesse's faithful attachment to Henriette de Mortsauf. Aha, she thinks, here is a quarry worth the chase. What quarry? Félix? Not at all. For her, the thing worth going after is that noble love just waiting to be destroyed, that sublime constancy ripe for her to play havoc with. Félix, who is an upright young man, resists valiantly. One evening, when he comes home, he finds Arabelle waiting for him. The shock is immense, and the subsequent pleasure no less so. "Arabelle," says the victim of this rape, "took pleasure . . . in displaying to me all the richest regions of her ardent kingdom" (*Lys dans la Vallée,* p.946).

There is no love involved. Once Henriette is dead, Arabelle breaks with Félix immediately. As soon as the liaison can no longer do any possible harm to anyone she loses interest in it. So that now we perceive her true character, one for which the introductory digressions about England have prepared us: Arabelle Dudley is wicked and cruel. Everything, for her, is always a means of revenge. In *Une Fille d'Eve,* she arranges a whole complicated plot simply to ensure that Félix's wife shall be unfaithful to him. And not only unfaithful to him either, but unfaithful to him with someone best calculated to cause Félix the maximum possible distress: the son of a Jewish second-hand dealer who died bankrupt. (We have to look at these things from the point of view of those involved, even though we do not share their prejudices.) "She savored in advance the pleasure she would take in turning some savage epigram on the subject with which to taunt Vandenesse" (*Fille d'Eve*, p.118). Yet it was she who broke with Félix, not he with her. In which case, why should she hate him so? Because all executioners hate their victims? Because during their moments of intimacy earlier she had always felt he despised her to some extent? With Lady Dudley, anything is possible. In *les Mémoires de deux Jeunes Mariées* (p.287), allusion is made to a terrible vengeance she once wreaked on Lady Brandon. Though I have no idea what it was all about. Lady Dudley is a woman of secret corridors and unplumbed mysteries. Like Marsay, she takes pleasure in evil, and it is this common trait that no doubt finally brings them together. Between these two godless creatures the bond had perforce to be ungodly: Lady Dudley becomes the mistress of her husband's son. To be quite honest, I have to admit that I cannot produce any quotation to support this assertion. I am just certain about it, and that's that. It's one of those things you can feel. For one thing, how could a woman like Arabelle Dudley have resisted the idea of becoming her stepson's mistress? And why does Vandenesse, in *le Lys dans la Vallée* (p.1027), takes such pains to stress the resemblance between Marsay and Lady Dudley's children? Though it's true that the least they can be to one another is half-brothers. And why, in *le Contrat de Mariage* (p.204), does Marsay display such jealousy towards Vandenesse? Posthumous jealousy? The matter is far from clear. The only absolute certainty is the perfect understanding that indubitably exists between this Lancashire Phaedra and her Hippolytus on the Rue Taitbout.

According to André Billy (*Vie de Balzac*, I, p.239), Lady Dudley was suggested to Balzac in part by the Comtesse de Venningen, née Ellenborough. On the whole, however, it must be said that she leaves one with the impression of being to some extent a literary convention. Arabelle is first cousin to Dumas's Milady, grandmother to Gide's Lady Griffith in *les Faux-Monnayeurs*, and great-grandmother to *la Madone des Sleepings*. Though even if it is a literary convention we are dealing with, who knows whether it was not Balzac who created it? And it is also worth noting that Aldous Huxley, an Englishman himself, has given us a portrait of a young English lady in his *Point Counterpoint* who is really not so very different from either Balzac's Lady Dudley or Gide's Lady Griffith.

As for this jade's husband, he too is a recognizable English character.

Lord Dudley is Byron, or Sheridan, or Oscar Wilde, or the Lord Alfred Douglas we meet in Gide's *Si le Grain ne meurt*. He is the conquering hero who finds himself hampered by the moral rigidity of his own country and who moves to the continent in order to find some spot where he can at last be free to lead the life of a man of pleasure. Like both Byron and Wilde, Dudley has known brilliant social success: he has been a member of the government. Again like Byron and Wilde, he then finds himself rejected by his country. His first visits to Paris are made entirely for pleasure. The last one, Balzac tells us, is made "to avoid the reprisals of British Justice, which permits the importation of merchandise from the East but nothing else" (*Fille aux Yeux d'Or*, p.273). In my innocence, I find that the meaning of this metaphor eludes me. Should we take it to mean that Lord Dudley, as he advances in years, has become overfond of young men? Is he even more like Wilde than we had originally supposed? For how, otherwise, are we to interpret the exclamation that escapes from him in the presence of a certain handsome young man: "Ah, it's my son. How unfortunate!" (*id*. p.273). Decidedly a mysterious family altogether.

At all events, whether he likes young men or not, Dudley has not given up women. Later we find him keeping, first Florine (*Rabouilleuse*, p.1093), then a certain Hortense who is unfaithful to him with Cérizet (*Homme d'Affaires*, p.820). This liaison occurs in 1833, approximately. More than thirty years beforehand, Dudley had had a son, Henri, by a young girl who subsequently married old Marsay. After that, Dudley seduced another young girl. The child this time was a girl, Euphémia Porraberil, who marries the Marquis de San Real and is the lesbian in *la Fille aux Yeux d'Or*. We also know that he had another daughter, Lady Barimore, who appears briefly in *Autre Etude de Femme*. And lastly, from his marriage with Arabelle, there are two children who are to be found, should anyone be anxious to find them, at the end of *le Lys dans la Vallée*.

Some of Henri de Marsay's character traits are obviously inherited from his father: his imperturbability, his lust for pleasure and his capacity for cold frenzy. "The ferocity of the northerner, of which the Englishman's blood has a fairly strong admixture, had been handed on to him by his father" (*Fille aux Yeux d'Or*, p.318). It is from Dudley too, perhaps, that he has inherited his apparent futility, as well as what one might call his donjuanist conception of politics, according to which the best initiation into the problems of power is the seduction of women. "Politics in the heart of Society's drawing-rooms" (*id*. p.271). And lastly, it is also to Dudley perhaps that he owes his taste for sport. Marsay is one of the very few sportsmen in the *Comédie humaine*. Moreover, not content with having inherited all these English traits, he also ends up with an English wife. The bride, it will be remembered, is Miss Dinah Stevens, the perfect English lady, "an irrefutable proof of the English genius . . . English engineering brought to its absolute pitch of perfection . . . A red nose, eyes like a dead goat's, and a waist that makes me afraid she'll break into three pieces if she falls over." Completely stupid. "If there were another more stupid in existence, then I would set out in search of her." On this point, Marsay is of the same school as his grandfather Talleyrand, who also married a very stupid woman. "But she is delightfully thrifty . . . And it plays the woman so well that you would almost believe it was one . . . And moreover, white enough not to be too disagreeable as a wife, provided marriage has become an absolute necessity anyway" (*Contrat de Mariage*, p.202). If one keeps in mind that it is the lady's husband-to-be who is composing this portrait, it is impossible not to admire the delicacy of the execution.

John Melmoth too, is an Englishman. "The man reeked of Englishness" (*Melmoth réconcilié*, p.272). And as if that weren't enough in itself, he also has a pact with the Devil, which takes him a little out of the common rut to begin with. There is already something of Mr. Hyde about him. He is the Englishman who prowls through London fogs, that rather disturbing fellow whose ghost still haunts our detective novels today. He dies in a wretched furnished room near Saint-Sulpice, another prefiguration of Wilde, who was to come to Paris, fifty years later, and die in a modest little hotel in the same neighborhood. Wilde before Reading Gaol: Dudley. Wilde after Reading Gaol: Melmoth. Did this occur to Wilde too? Or was it simply a coincidence that when he came out of prison he changed his name to Melmoth?

I have already spoken elsewhere of Lord Grenville and of the English prostitute in *Splendeurs et Misères*, that delicious young creature who one day, "drunk with gin," killed her lover. Gin also has its part to play in the character of Toby (or Paddy or Joby), a little chap about ten years old "three feet tall, twenty inches wide, face like a ferret, nerves of steel tempered in gin . . . a seat on a horse like old Franconi . . . a true flower of perversity, gambling and swearing, fond of both jam and punch, as vituperative as any broadsheet, as tough and light-fingered as any Paris guttersnipe" (*Maison Nucingen*, p.607). Originally tiger to a London Lord, Toby then passes into the service of Beaudenord, in which capacity he is mentioned frequently in various works. One step above Toby, there is John Barry, the English groom who occurs in *Modeste Mignon*.

As you can see, they are not a particularly sympathetic bunch, these English. There is Lady Brandon too, of course, but then there is nothing in any of the texts to justify the assumption that she is English other than by marriage. There is Miss Griffith, the English governess in *Mémoires de deux Jeunes Mariées:* she is merely insignificant. And then, then there is the Baronne du Guénic in *Béatrix*. But she is Irish. Well, no matter, Emerald Isle or Perfidious Albion here at last is a really charming woman. Married to an old man, the mother of a grown son, she still has all the grace of a young girl. Lastly, in *Gaudissart II*, there is a caricature of the Englishwoman traveling abroad. "Englishwomen . . . don't know what they want," a Parisian businessman comments on this occasion.

There are a great many Italians and Spaniards in the *Comédie Humaine*, but generally speaking they occur only in the stories that take place in their own countries. In their own homes, not transplanted to another country, they fail to stand out from their environment in the way that Schmucke does from the backdrop of Parisian life. And the same is also true of the Italians in *Gambara*, for though the novel is set in Paris it takes place entirely within the Italian colony there. Here is a comment on the Italian way of life that has a faint flavor of Stendhal: "That's the way the Italians live their lives: in the morning, love; in the evening, music; at night, sleep. How much preferable such an existence is to life in countries where everyone uses his lungs and his energy in politics the whole time, without any more being able to change the march of events all on his own than a grain of sand can make a cloud of dust . . . In this, the country of passion, every passion carries its own excuse with it, and there exists an adorable indulgence for every kind of moral eccentricity" (*Massimila Doni*, pp. 335 and 341). Though there are also times when we meet passion wearing its agonized face in Italy too: the opium addict Vendramin, the music addict Cataneo.

It also seems to be true, for Balzac at least, that when Italians leave their own country they forfeit some of their good qualities. Franchessini is a low cad. So is Montefiore, one of the characters in *les Marana*. And Bianchi is a brute. Balzac also makes frequent allusions to the Légion Italienne recruited by Napoleon. Always in unsympathetic terms.

If the Italians live in a world of pleasure, the Spaniards live in a world of passion. "The Spaniards have more greatness in their souls than we" (*Mémoires de deux Jeunes Mariées*, p.285). In Balzac, they all have a grave, frenzied quality that almost always impels them towards a confrontation with the only genuine absolute: death. In *El Verdugo*, we see the

Leganès family doing everything in their power to kill a number of Frenchmen, then dying, once they have been tried, without a murmur. In *Autre Etude de Femme*, a Spaniard accepts a frightful death rather than compromise his mistress. In *les Marana*, Perez de Lagounia surprises a man in his ward's room: he immediately talks of killing him. Even the honest Fario in *la Rabouilleuse* ends up trying to commit murder. As for Macumer, in *les Mémoires de deux Jeunes Mariées* (a character not a little reminiscent of the Spanish conspirator in *le Rouge et le Noir*), both Balzac's Spanish themes are to be found united in him: death, since he has been condemned to death for desertion, and the frenzied passion that impels him to climb trees and risk breaking his neck in order to catch a glimpse of the woman he loves.

I have already dealt with Mme Evangelista. Then there is an example of the influence of Spanish heredity. Euphémia Porraberil, presumably the daughter of a Spanish mother, is literally driven mad by passion and stabs Paquita Valdès to death in a fit of jealousy.

Portugal is represented only by the Duchesse de Grandlieu and by her cousin and son-in-law the Marquis d'Ajuda-Pinto. There is little that one can say about the latter; he is very ordinary. Probably his nationality is no more than a clever device on Balzac's part, since its only function appears to be that of helping us to distinguish him from all the other young men-about-town in the *Comédie humaine*.

No other countries have any important representatives. There are a few Belgians in *la Recherche de l'Absolu*. The Peyrades' old maid, Katt, is also Belgian. So are Magus and Gobseck, but I shall return to them later. Here is one national characteristic: "Since they were Belgians, their powers of calculation were as swift as their eyes were sharp" (*Physiologie du Mariage*, p.598). There is a brief breath of Swiss air to be had in the story-within-the-story of *Albert Savarus*, but nothing very memorable, apart from this one unkind cut: "You only have to rub a Swiss and he'll turn into a usurer" (*Albert Savarus*, p.780). The Baron de Watteville is Swiss; but there's nothing much that can be said about him. As for the Russians, they have the defect, according to Balzac, of always thinking that they're in Russia. And they are "so given to imitating others that every disease of civilization eventually has its repercussions in their homeland" (*Cousin Pons*, pp. 580 and 802).* These general remarks are not illustrated how-

---

* "The Russians copy French manners, but they are always fifty years behindhand," was Stendhal's comment on this same question.

ever, since Russia is represented only by such episodic figures as the Prince and Princess Galathionne.

North America is represented by Mme Dumay (Modeste Mignon), South America by Henri Montès. There is one mulatto: Christemio, in *la Fille aux Yeux d'Or*.

It is apparent, then, that although the nationality of Balzac's characters is occasionally no more than a picturesque addition intended to add color to otherwise somewhat colorless figures, it much more often constitutes an important element without which those characters would have been fundamentally different. It is impossible to imagine an Italian Schmucke or a Dutch Macumer: each of these men is a product of his particular country, of its society, of its customs, of everything that makes it a distinctive and active environment.

Note, however, that this influence is exclusively an environmental one. There is not the slightest trace of nationalism or racism to be found in it. The homelands that have left their marks upon these characters are strictly a matter of physical environment, climate, social hierarchies, prevailing customs and modes of thought. Schmucke is different, not because he is German, but because he grew up in Germany. If this were not so, then Balzac would have given us illustrations of the effects of heredity. But he does not do so. Several of these foreigners have children that are born or brought up in France. In dealing with them individually, I have attempted to uncover specific traits in their characters that may be attributed to their having a foreign parent. With the single exception of Marsay, I was unable to find anything of any importance. Nathalie de Manerville, the daughter of Spanish parents but brought up in France, has nothing Iberian about her at all. "I am French," she writes about herself at one point. And not once does Balzac resort to the mystique of the castanet to explain her behavior, though he does so frequently in the case of her mother. Ursule Mirouët and Mme Schontz both have German mothers, yet they have nothing in common. Mme de Montcornet has a Russian mother, yet no trace of this fact is apparent in her character. It is true that Sabine de Grandlieu says at one point: "I am practically Portuguese" (*Béatrix*, p.528). But nothing is ever made of this fact. For in Balzac, the nation is much like the family in this respect: neither has much importance in his eyes unless it is a concrete environment, unless it entails specific circumstances. Blood has no part to play in the matter at all. Having been brought up away from her brothers, Louise de Chaulieu has nothing in

common with them. Having been brought up in France, Nathalie de Manerville has nothing Spanish about her.

We also find a fairly striking proof of the fact that nationality only
counts for Balzac if it entails a set of concrete circumstances in the way in
which he writes about his Jewish characters. For while the pictures we are
given in the *Comédie humaine* of the Englishman and the German are
quite strikingly clearcut, that of the Jew is vague in the extreme.

This is because the Jews, with certain exceptions, excluding those in
ghettoes, live scattered amongst the Gentiles of whatever country they
happen to be in, and therefore do not constitute a nation in the concrete
sense of the term (for we cannot expect Balzac to have foreseen the State
of Israel). And it is for this reason, I assume, that Balzac displays an almost
total indifference to the race of his Jewish characters. For though there
are a fair number of them in the *Comédie humaine* it is by no means easy
to perceive any common denominators in them. The avarice of Magus and
Gobseck? That won't do, because Nucingen is munificent and Nathan a
spendthrift. Lust for gold? Esther and Coralie are both completely disinterested. A certain will to power? A certain possessiveness in the realm of
passion? Pauline Salomon displays admirable resignation, and Coralie is
always ready to move on to the next. A certain impulse towards destruc-
tion, and that delight in baseness for its own sake that Gide thought he
could discern in Jewish writers? There is a vague echo of this in one
remark of Gobseck's: "I like dirtying rich men's carpets. Not from any
pettiness, but in order to make them feel the claws of Necessity" (*Gobseck*, p.631). And Josépha Mirah, in *la Cousine Bette* (pp. 432-437), displays a strange joy in seeing Hulot ravaged by his vices. But there is no
hint of this feeling to be found in any of the other Jews in the *Comédie
humaine*. Even Josépha and Gobseck end up making quite admirable gestures. And Balzac himself does not give any indication at any point that he
sees this as a racial characteristic. If Coralie and Josépha are Jewesses, the
reason is, above all, I suspect, in order to endow them with particular
physical characteristics, in order to make us immediately picture to ourselves a certain physical type, a certain glossiness of the hair, a certain
matte texture of skin. It is true that when speaking of Josépha, Balzac has
Crevel refer to "the instinct of the early Israelites for gold and jewels"
(*Cousine Bette*, p.145). But of Magus, who is another who loves gold, he
writes: "Magus, a sort of Hollando-Belgo-Fleming, thus had three reasons
for being what he became: miserly and rich" (*Pierre Grassou*, p.118)

The fact that he is a Jew isn't even mentioned. Balzac does, I admit, say at one point that the Jews are grasping. But he doesn't allow them a monopoly of this minor defect: "The Jews, people from Normandy, people from the Auvergne and people from Savoy, all these four races of men have the same instincts and obtain their wealth by the same means" (*Cousin Pons*, p.615).

Docteur Halpersohn receives his patients in a sordid office, Magus is in rags, Gobseck lives just any way and Nathan settles down for the night wherever he happens to be. "Those people," Genestas also remarks of a Jewish family, "they live in filth" (*Médecin de Campagne*, p.511). Should we take this to be a racial characteristic? Hardly. Josépha has the most beautifully appointed drawing-rooms in Paris, and Nucingen's place is very nicely furnished too.

Many of these Jews have a fairly pronounced exotic streak in their natures, that I must admit. But then, with the exception of Coralie and Pauline Salomon (who are French and therefore can't be exotic) they are all foreigners. Their exotic character is a result of their having grown up elsewhere, not of their racial affiliations. Nucingen speaks with a German accent, but there is not the slightest hint of Yiddish. And his naïveté is entirely German too; there is nothing Jewish about that.

In other words, we are forced to conclude that. Jewishness is never in itself more than an accessory characteristic of the Jews who appear in the *Comédie humaine*. I myself would only make one exception in this respect, and not for Gobseck, though he is the one usually chosen, but for Magus. In the cases of Nucingen and Coralie, Balzac contents himself with mentioning that they are Jewish when he introduces them, then never returns to the subject again. With Magus, on the other hand, he does return to it. "This Jew," he calls him on several occasions. And if he dresses like a beggar, that too is a racial characteristic, because, as Balzac explains, "in the middle ages, the persecution they underwent obliged Jews to dress in tatters in order to turn away suspicion, as well as to lament and whimper and complain about their poverty all the time" (*Cousin Pons*, p.633). Magus is a passionate collector. There is a real will to power working inside him. But in his case this will to power makes use of his race. It is on his co-religionists that he relies to give him information about any beautiful works of art that might be coming onto the market. Again, we have the theme of the conspiracy. Only here the conspiracy is a Jewish one. A new variety. We meet Magus successively as an expert on precious stones in Bordeaux (*Contrat de Mariage*), as a picture dealer on the Rue Bonne-Nouvelle in Paris (*Pierre Grassou*) and as a collector in *le Cousin Pons*. I'm not sure where he came from. Hollando-Belgo-Flemish, Balzac calls him in *Pierre Grassou* (p.118), but three pages earlier he was referring to him as being made of "old German wood . . ."

CHAPTER 17

Time

*The survivors—Ancien Régime: the Princesse de Bla-
mont-Chauvry, the Vidame de Pamiers, the Chevalier
de Valois, Kergarouët, Chesnel—the émigrés: the Mar-
quis d'Esgrignon, the Baron du Guénic, the Comte de
Mortsauf—the Revolution: du Bousquier—the Empire:
Baron Hulot, Maréchal Cottin, Philippe Bridau, Max
Gilet, Giroudeau, Hyacinthe Chabert, Gouraud,
Montcornet, Genestas, Gondrin, Goguelat, the Comte
Hulot—the prisoners of time.*

ANOTHER circumstance: time.

Balzac's characters are deeply affected by their physical environments.
They are even more deeply affected by the age they live in. Immortal
though a Hulot or a Pons may be, they are both colored by their times.
Even if the texts of the two books included no dates (and it is striking to
see what care Balzac almost always takes to place his stories in time), we
should still be able to discern with a fair amount of ease that *la Cousine
Bette* and *le Cousin Pons* both take place during the reign of Louis-Philippe.

Another rejection of the absolute. Classical man, the man we meet in
classical literature, is always the same: he is not affected by place or by
time. Even when geographical or historical references occur in a classical
work they are merely accessory. Britannicus and Bajazet, Roxane and
Bérénice think and argue in exactly the same way, even though their respective stories are separated by an interval of about fifteen hundred
years. This, I imagine, is the reason for those approximations in the matter
of costumes and décor that Racine and his audience found so easy to accept. With Phèdre, a few centuries here or there are of no consequence.
Whereas with Balzac even a twenty-year time lapse makes a great deal of
difference. I have already had occasion to remark on the fact that his
novels set in 1820 have a quite different color from those set in 1840. Man

is not simply man, he is also what his time and his place have made him. Like chairs or hats, Balzac's characters all have a precise style, the style of their particular epoch.

Moreover, Balzac has also taken care to emphasize the influence of time on his characters by much the same means as he used to emphasize the effect of place: by contrast. Corresponding to the characters who have been uprooted, transplanted into a different environment, the provincials in Paris, the foreigners in France, we also find what might be called the survivors, all those characters so frequently met with in the *Comédie humaine* who have outlived their own epoch, who have carried over the customs, the manners, the principles, the habits of thought of their own generation into the generation that has now superseded it.

For there comes a moment when a man ceases to change. Health, passions, education, vices, virtues, tastes, eccentricities, these are all so many raw materials from which men little by little construct their personas, masks that are still vague at first, still capable of change, but which suddenly, at a certain point in their lives, harden into precisely recognizable contours. A character's characteristics have set. And from that time on they will remain unchanged. The man begins to petrify, to become a fossil. His die is cast.

At what age does this petrifaction in time take place? It is something of a moot point. Generally speaking, it seems to coincide with a man's first successes, his first triumphs, the first blaze of glory. At that point, having affirmed himself, the man's sense of satisfaction seems to work like a fixing agent on his character. If, after that point, History continues to advance at a normal pace, the man will not ordinarily begin to lose contact with his age until he becomes old, until he retires, takes to seclusion, slippers, and literal or metaphorical gardening; in short, until he gives up the idea of action. But if history suddenly accelerates, then the man is overtaken by events and eventually left behind. He becomes a living ghost. And since one cannot yet give life up, hand in one's resignation, leave one's profession, at the age of forty, we are left with a man who is still trying to impose on his age, on his family, on all those around him, a set of principles no longer valid.

And it so happens that the years from which Balzac took most of his material were, more than any other period, particularly rich in examples of premature aging and precipitate comings of age. In 1821—the year in which, for instance, the story of *Illusions perdues* begins—a man of sixty could well have danced in his youth at the Court of Louis XVI; a man of fifty could have known the wars in the Vendée, the meetings of the Convention, the prisons of the Terror, and the bitter exile of the émigré; a man of thirty, or even twenty-five, could have been decorated by le Tondu, his Emperor. But in 1822, Terror, Trianon, Tondu, those are so many worlds already gone into the dark backward and abysm of time. The Bastille, the imperial bees, the young colonels galloping across Europe brandishing their sabers—gone, all gone. Except that those years have left behind them many men who, having reached the stage of self-awareness at the first night of *Figaro*, or in the field at Austerlitz, find it difficult to adapt themselves to a world without Beaumarchais or without gold epaulettes. Many of these, needless to say, do eventually adapt. But there are others who are unable to, who will never be able to.

It is worthy noting at this point, by the way, that political loyalty plays only a subsidiary role in this matter. The former Commandant, Genestas, in *Médecin de Campagne*, regrets the passing of Napoleon much more sincerely than Bridau in *la Rabouilleuse*. Yet it is Bridau, not Genestas, who is living in the past. The old Marquis d'Esgrignon, in *le Cabinet des Antiques*, is a royalist. Yet when the King returns the Marquis still remains an outsider, a man out of his time. Because his loyalty is not only to a principle but also to a conception of life, to modes of thought that were more those of an age than of a political regime. It is not the King that people like the Vidame de Pamiers and the Princesse de Blamont-Chauvry yearn for, because there he is, back on the throne. It is a way of life they are regretting. Of Pons, Balzac does not say: he was a Bonapartist (Pons is not one to pay any attention to such trifling matters). He says: he was an Empire-man. As one says: an Empire sideboard. The survivals I intend to discuss here are above all survivals of style.

THE ANCIEN REGIME

The Princesse de Blamont-Chauvry, the Vidame de Pamiers, the Chevalier de Valois, the Amiral de Kergarouët, the lawyer Chesnel

The débris of the Ancien Régime first of all. The débris of those easy years before '89, of the good old days when one still had good manners instead of principles, gaiety instead of gravity. "My jewel," the Princesse de Blamont-Chauvry says to the Duchesse de Langeais, "my jewel, I know of nothing that is the object of more calumny in this vile world than God and the eighteenth century." Already the exquisite tone of a bygone age. "The novelists and the scribblers have dishonored the reign of Louis XV, but don't believe them. La Dubarry, my dear, was every bit as good as the widow Scarron before her, and as to looks, why there was no comparison. In my day, a woman knew how to keep her dignity even in her amours. It was the indiscretions of others that lost us our reputations." One of these indiscretions was, needless to say, *les Liaisons dangereuses*. Without Laclos, "without that rabble of poetasters and rhymesters and moralists, who took to keeping our chambermaids and writing down all the slanders they squeezed out of them, our age would have appeared in literature as a rather moral one" (*Duchesse de Langeais*, pp. 237 and 238).

This Mme Blamont-Chauvry who talks so prettily is, at the time we first make her acquaintance, an extremely old lady and the proud possessor of a nose as hooked "as a Turkish scimitar" and of a face resembling "an old white glove" (*id*. p.228). She is also the possessor of an infrequently mentioned husband and has one daughter: Mme d'Espard. Despite her great age, the Princess is one of the oracles of the aristocratic Faubourg, and it is difficult to make any sort of career in Society without her approval. "No old woman knew how to close and pocket the snuffbox with such an air; and the movements of her skirt as she sat down, or as she crossed her legs, were so precisely controlled, so full of grace, that she was the despair of even the most elegant younger women" (*id*. p.228).

This "female Talleyrand" has a masculine counterpart in the person of the Vidame de Pamiers, an old bachelor, a former Commander of the Knights of Malta, whose entire person presents "a perfect model of aristocratic grace, small and delicate lines, supple and pleasing; lines that, like those of the serpent, could at the will of their possessor either curve or rear up, become flowing or stiff" (*Duchesse de Langeais*, p.229). We find all the same traits in him that we have already met in the Princesse de Blamont-Chauvry: frivolity, indulgence, kindly scorn, perfect manners. And no principles: he lends his services to Mme de Langeais and Montriveau, to Mme de Maufrigneuse and Victurnien, without for an instant asking himself whether these liaisons he is aiding and abetting may not be pregnant with disasters. Because he is the product of an age when amorous liaisons simply didn't end in disaster, an age when one worshipped women and love without taking either of them very seriously. "Their honor, their feelings? Nonsense, fiddle-faddle, play-acting! When in their company he believed in them, this ci-devant *monster*, he never contradicted them and he always made them appear to advantage. But when talking about them with friends, then the Vidame laid it down as a principle that to deceive women, to carry on several amorous intrigues at the same time, should be the whole occupation of young men, and that such young fellows would only be wasting their time if they tried to meddle with such things as affairs of State" (*Ferragus*, p.25). This is much the same advice that old Mme de Blamont-Chauvry gives, in more ceremonious terms, to Mme de Langeais; the same advice that we find the old Chevalier de Valois giving, in rather more veiled terms, to Victurnien d'Esgrignon.

Where did he spring from, this Chevalier with the resounding name? There is no authentic Valois known to have left male issue in real life. Is he simply an impostor? Is he no more a Chevalier or a Valois than Casanova was a knight or a Seingalt? Balzac is too discreet to say so; but he lets it be understood. Moreover, it is noteworthy that although he calls him by his name in *la Vieille Fille*, in *le Cabinet des Antiques* he no longer refers to him except by his title. "A certain Chevalier whose illustrious name, etc." (*Cabinet des Antiques*, p.348). Admittedly, at the time of the Restoration the Chevalier is given the rank of a retired colonel in recognition of his services to the Crown during his days as a chouan. But that can scarcely be considered as a certificate of authenticity. After all, say Casanova had been a chouan. Would anyone in 1815 have started quibbling about his claims to being a Seingalt if he had brought honor to the name by his underground exploits? Nor are the Chevalier de Valois' financial resources any less mysterious than his origins. He claims to live on an income of six hundred francs. And indeed he does receive this sum every year, in regular quarterly installments. But there have been kindly souls only too ready to point out that six hundred francs is exactly the figure of this redoubtable whist-player's profits at the card table every year. Later on, Valois justifies the disappearance of his tiny income by claiming that he made it over to Charles X when that monarch was driven into exile. But do not all serious historians and all the eye witnesses assure us that Charles X refused to accept any such offerings from his faithful followers? No, the more I think about it, the more I am inclined to regard the Chevalier de Valois as simply an impostor. A charming impostor, the kind of impostor one is quite happy to see around, but still an impostor. In fact, as I have implied, he is Casanova. A more discreet, a more sedate Casanova. Perhaps they had even met at one time? At Spa, say; for we know that Valois traveled there in 1788 as the escort of the Princess Goritza, a lady of whom he still retains a dazzled memory. Too dazzled. He talks about her too much for us not to suspect that this Princess must have represented something rather exceptional in his eyes, and that he himself cannot therefore have been a very important personage. He too regrets the old days. "The reigns of Louis XIV and Louis XV, remember this my boy, were our farewells to the noblest way of life in the world" (*Vieille Fille*, p.222). Though he cannot in fact be talking except from hearsay, since he

was born in 1759 and was therefore only fifteen at the time of Louis le
Bien-Aimé's death. A fact that has nevertheless not prevented him from
retaining not only the spirit and the manners of that age but also something of its style in clothes. He wears a maroon coat with gilt buttons,
rather tight-fitting silk breeches with gold buckles, a white waistcoat
without embroidery, a tight cravat without a shirt collar, and shoes with
square gold buckles on them.

Not intelligent, but witty, adroit, well-mannered, egotistical, but with
an egotism so kindly in its effects that it "was as valuable as devoted
friendship" (*Vieille Fille*, p.215), such is the Chevalier de Valois when we
meet him again in *la Vieille Fille* and *le Cabinet des Antiques* after our first
glimpse of him in *les Chouans*. He has retained not only the good manners
of the eighteenth century but also its loose morals. He boards with a laundress and is by no means averse to tearing the little collars of the laundry-
girls she employs. But nicely, like a genuine old libertine who knows better than to treat anyone roughly. And they are grateful to him for this.
They "all kept their home and private lives strictly secret from him . . .
but in the house, they would quite willingly have perched on his shoulders like parakeets" (*Vieille Fille*, p.220). Through them, he knows all the
gossip of the town. And true champion of the eighteenth century that he
is, he takes an inordinate delight in the pleasures of conversation. He likes
to slip into the language of the peasants, as the members of ducal households still do today, as Oriane de Guermantes does in Proust, or as the
people in the novels of La Varende do. "This town is a hole," he says . . .
"All that he (Victurnien) will ever meet in it is some Miss from *here-
abouts*. And what will she be like? *Er'll be thick*, probably. A girl that
knows *nowt fra' nowt. So what good'll 'er be to the lad?* (*Cabinet des
Antiques*, p.362).* He has also retained the frivolous principles of his past
with regard to money. Though this does not stop him making a play for
Mlle Cormon's acres and wealth. And his failure in this attempt deals him
a blow from which he never recovers. He no longer pays attention to his
personal appearance. "One day, he came to see Mlle Armande with one
calf round in front of his shinbone" (*Vieille Fille*, p.319). A false calf,
needless to say. He dies in 1830, after having married, according to hearsay, a laundress.

We find the same good-natured frivolity, the same kindly immorality in

---

* Translator's note. Since the social hierarchy involved here can be paralleled in English social history, whereas the United States has always suffered from a chronic short-
age of dukes, I have used a British dialect in the translation of these quotations. I
hope American readers will accept this explanation—gladly.

the old Admiral de Kergarouët. His niece, Emilie, has only to take notice of a young man and the admiral gaily pushes her into his arms (*Bal de Sceaux*). In *la Bourse*, he wants to be of financial assistance to a certain old lady. Instead of solemnly making over Government stocks to her, or something of that sort—as any of the Camusots would have done were it possible for a Camusot to be charitable at all—he goes to the trouble of visiting her every day and losing to her at cards. A sunny kind of goodness, delicate and lightly born. And his absence of principles even allows him to go so far in the end as to marry his niece, Emilie de Fontaine, who is thirty years younger than he is.

At first glance, one might think that these are merely picturesque secondary figures; that their "survival" is simply a detail slipped in to add a little depth, to liven up one corner of the picture. But this is not true. With the exception of Valois, it is true, I admit, that these old ruins do not take up very much space. Almost nothing actually happens to them personally. Yet their role is one of the first importance. Let us look again, more closely: the Princesse, the Chevalier and the Vidame are, to a certain extent, directly responsible for the catastrophes of which we are given accounts in *la Duchesse de Langeais*, in *le Cabinet des Antiques*, and in *Ferragus*.

For these ruins have great prestige. To the young people around them they are models to be copied, oracles of the truth. They themselves take on the role of teachers. Secure in their own past triumphs, they feel they have the right to preach. The Princess de Blamont-Chauvry dispenses advice to Antoinette de Langeais, Valois does the same to Victurnien d'Esgrignon, and Pamiers to Maulincour. Let us listen to this advice. It all contains the same fundamental recommendations: frivolity, heedlessness, good manners, no tragedies, you can't die from lack of money. These are the principles of their own age. But they are forty years out of date. As so often happens, these advisers are advising no one but themselves. They are rectifying their own pasts without really being aware that it is the present they are supposed to be dealing with—and someone else's present, what's more. Mme de Blamont-Chauvry talks to Antoinette de Langeais as though she were a young Blamont-Chauvry, Pamiers talks to Maulincour as though he were Pamiers himself at the age of twenty. They forget that everything is different, the character as well as the circumstances. They too have imprisoned themselves in an absolute. Pamiers presents Victurnien to Mme de Maufrigneuse. It's really very kind of him, and no doubt when he was twenty he would have been delighted to find an old gentleman to do the same for him. But he has lost sight of the fact that Victurnien isn't Pamiers, that he has neither honor nor money, that he is living in an age when this second article has taken on a great deal of importance, that the King is no longer willing to pay his nobles' debts. He also attempts to reconcile Mme de Langeais with Montriveau. Here again, he forgets that Montriveau is not just a social butterfly like himself, that he is rather a tragic figure, that he is not a gray musketeer but a colonel in the Artillery on whom Cupid's darts can have the effect of cannonballs. This is where these charming ruins come to grief. Or rather, since they themselves are past such things, where they cause their disciples to come to grief. Balzac never at any point criticizes this spirit of the Ancien Régime. On the contrary, he writes of it with evident sympathy. What he does condemn is its survival. What he criticizes, what he shows as leading inevitably to disaster, is the application of this Louis Quinze mental furniture to the problems of Louis XVIII people. The immorality of men like Pamiers and Valois, though delightful in them, when applied to young men like Victurnien or Maulincour simply turns them into spineless, cowardly, bewildered creatures, one of whom ends up dead and the second of whom only just avoids trial for fraud and a prison sentence. Because times have changed. The disciples must face temptations different from those of their advisers, and when they encounter these temptations they realize too late that those advisers have put nothing in their hands to fight them with but old and rusty weapons, principles that are no longer of the slightest use. They have been taught how to fence: suddenly they find themselves in drawing-rooms where everyone is playing whist. Balzac is in favor of fencing. But he has nothing but harsh words for those who attempt to apply its rules to whist. It is another form of his hatred for the absolute, of his belief in the necessity to adapt to one's surroundings. And in order to prevent this hatred of the absolute from itself becoming an absolute, he introduces an exception: the same eighteenth century principles when applied to Emilie de Fontaine lead, not to failure, but to victory, at least on a social level.

The lawyer Chesnel (Choisnel in *la Vieille Fille*) is another survivor from the past. But a middle-class survivor, a "representative" in Balzac's words, "of that great and noble class of family retainers" that existed before the Revolution (*Cabinet des Antiques*, p.462), all of them animated by that sentiment of loyalty to the great aristocratic families that "did equal honor to the Nobility that could inspire such affection and to the Bourgeoisie that could conceive it" (*id.* p.462). A former steward on the Esgrignon estate, Chesnel has become a lawyer only in deference to the pressures of the age. In the depths of his heart he has remained a steward. In the depths of his heart, but not in his head. Though his loyalty to the Marquis is such that he is prepared to ruin himself, he is not without clearsightedness. He has gauged the changes that have taken place in society. There are times when he tries to act accordingly. But the Marquis only has to say to him: "What are these new doctrines if they've spoiled you, my lad" and he desists. Loyalty is a stronger argument for him than reason. And by the way, that "my lad" to a sixty-nine-year-old lawyer is worth noting.

THE ÉMIGRES

The Marquis d'Esgrignon, the Baron du Guénic and the Comte de Mortsauf

Born in 1749, Charles-Marie-Victor-Ange, Marquis Carol d'Esgrignon, Victurnien's father, is a member of one of the most noble families in Normandy, "provincial nobility, not heard of at Court for two hundred years, but untainted by any baser stock, and owing allegiance to no higher power but the King" (*Cabinet des Antiques*, p.335). During the Revolution, he becomes one of the heads of the underground royalist movement in the Orne (*Chouans*, p.816). Upon his return to Alençon, he marries a Mlle de Nouastre, who has been living abroad during the Revolution, "the prettiest human creature in the world" (*Cabinet des Antiques*, p.337). She dies shortly afterwards. This grief, the failure of the underground movement, his loyalty to the crown, all these things combine to make the Marquis a man who has ceased to live in the real world. He is frozen in his "Frankish stubbornness" (*id.* p.338). And he remains exactly the same until his death in 1830.

The Baron du Guénic, Calyste's father, is cast in the same mold. After a stint with the chouans, he goes into exile in Ireland, marries an Irish girl there and does not come back until 1814. Ireland in one case, Alençon in the other: the gesture is the same. One leaves the country, the other shuts himself up on his estate; both have retired from French life. Both have taken their leave of absence. And that absence lasts for twenty years. Once you are twenty years behind you can never catch up again. Or at least, you could only do so with the help of an intellectual agility that neither d'Esgrignon nor du Guénic possesses. All exiles (whether abroad or at home) have a tendency to consider that the history of their country stopped the moment they left it. And when an exile returns, whether after ten months or ten years, he always has the feeling that it is still the day after he left. And even more so when History seems to be proving this to be so, when the cause for which he was exiled has triumphed at last. When the Bourbons return, both du Guénic and d'Esgrignon sing the song of Simeon. Who is there to tell them, in their provincial towns, in the narrow circle in which they move, that the King who has come back is not exactly the one for whom they fought? At the height of the Restoration, the Marquis still wears his blue coat with fleurs de lys on the skirt and his eighteenth-century breeches. When his son gets out of hand, he threatens him with *lettres de cachet* (*Cabinet des Antiques*, p.364). Who is to tell him that things have changed, that the King doesn't issue the dreaded *lettres de cachet* any more? A short visit to Paris would have sufficed to open his eyes to these things. But he never goes to Paris. Other returned exiles, the Chaulieus, the Navarreins, since they live in the capital, are able to gauge the changes that have occurred and adapt themselves accordingly. Some of them even accept office under the Empire. Others at least apply to be struck off the list of émigrés, thus recognizing the fact of the new régime, if not its legality. Du Guénic and d'Esgrignon have never recognized anything at all in any way. When, in 1814, du Guénic receives notification that he has been made a colonel, he says: "The King has remembered!" (*Béatrix*, p.335). In reality, the King has signed a piece of paper put in front of him by the Duc de Feltre, one of Napoleon's generals, a man whose father was heaven knows who. How is du Guénic to know that? The Chaulieus know it. So does the Comte de Fontaine, even though he was once a chouan. And he draws certain conclusions from what he knows. He marries his children to Mongenods and to Grossetêtes. He has understood what's happened. Du Guénic and d'Esgrignon don't even know the facts, so they don't even have anything to understand. What? Weren't they in the right, fighting in the underground against the Republic? Yes, a thousand times yes. They would have been certain about that even if it had all ended in disaster. But it hasn't. They are victorious, because the King is on the throne again, because he recognizes their services, because the ex-chouans and the émigrés are all being honored, lauded, decorated. So there you are. Twenty years have gone by, you say? What do twenty years matter beside a truth? A principle is a principle, and those twenty years have nothing to do with it. They are the champions of an absolute truth, of a truth that must be true in every age. Despite their nobility, despite their greatness of soul, despite the respect with which he writes of them, Balzac condemns them for this. Their sentence is the failure of their sons. These two fathers, so full of honor and energy and pride, only succeed in producing two cowardly, spineless sons, one of whom, Victurnien, also comes very near to dishonoring his name. And the same failure is also in store for Savinien de Portenduère, the son of another exile, a stubborn old woman who shuts herself up on her estates and refuses to admit that anything has changed in the world. Balzac condemns any survival of outworn principles. And being a true "realist" he also condemns those absences, those exiles, those prolongued leaves of absence that were so many challenges thrown down by the absolute to the relative. He makes all this clear during the discussion that takes place in *Une Ténébreuse Affaire* (pp. 556 to 559) between the wise Marquis de Chargeboeuf and the four young men who have just returned from exile. "Compromise," the old Marquis tells them. That is Balzac's advice. "The truest consecrations of the Law, and those most worthy of respect, those that Louis XVIII was attempting to express by dating his Charter from the twenty-first year of his reign, cannot exist unless ratified by a universal consent: the d'Esgrignon family lacked the main persuasive force in the political arena today, money, that great source of prominence for the modern nobility; they also lacked *historical continuity*, that special kind of fame that is acquired at Court as well as on fields of battle, in the drawing-room conferences of diplomats as well as in parliamentary debates, with the aid of a book as well as from an expedition, and which is like the Holy Oil anointing the head of each new generation" (*Cabinet des Antiques*, pp. 351 and 352). The education of a noble under the Ancien Régime, Balzac also says, was not complete until it had been supplemented by "the instruction provided by Society, the customs of the Court, and the exercise of the great offices of the Crown" (*Lys dans la Vallée*, p.809). This second education is lacking in Mortsauf, just as it is in Victurnien, in Calyste and in Savinien. They are stumbling in the dark. Because, like their fathers, they are ignorant of the new laws, the real laws of existence. Balzac could not show us the disadvantages inherent in this ignorance of their own times in the fathers, since they all live retired, inactive lives in the provinces and do not really come into contact with those times. Instead, we see these disadvantages demonstrated in the careers of their sons, who, armed only with this outworn kind of education they have had, venture forth into Paris and into the year 1830. They are doomed because they are doubly lost: in time as well as in space.

This was the beginning of the long misunderstanding—of which one can still find traces even today—between the French nobility and the rest of the country. It was a misunderstanding caused, not by the stubbornness of that nobility, but by the shortness of the time at their disposal in which to recover from the effects of their foreign or internal exiles, to bring themselves back into step with the march of history. The survivors from the Empire (whose roots were in any case much less deep) had the reign of Louis-Philippe and then the Second Empire in which to get back onto their feet. In consequence, the spirit of the Empire vanished altogether. The Restoration, on the other hand, was too short, so that the spirit of the Ancien Régime persisted. The two old noblemen that Montherlant depicts for us in his *Célibataires* are exactly the same: survivors, men left behind by time. Léon de Coantré is Victurnien d'Esgrignon grown slightly older. Whenever I return to France, Costals says (and Costals certainly shares some of the features of Montherlant's own character), I feel lost, as though everything is rubbing me the wrong way. In times of war, France is at one with its nobility again, thanks to the profession of arms, for which that nobility is better trained than any other class; but it is not at one with it in every sphere. The nobility can share its country's military courage, but not its country's passions. Proust's Robert de Saint-Loup conducts himself like a hero, but nothing can prevent him saying: the Emperor Wilhelm, and not Wilhelm, as the true patriots do. What is nonconformism? It is the presence, in the midst of all the run-of-the-mill stupidities, of an idea either younger or older than the passions of the age. Thanks to this disharmony, there continues to flourish amid the French nobility today a nonconformism that was already present in the words of du Guénic and the Marquis d'Esgrignon. After 1830, the old Marquis cries out in grief: "The Gauls have won!" (*Cabinet des Antiques*, p.463). After the failure of the Duchesse de Berry's expedition to la Vendée, du Guénic says simply: "All the barons did not do their duty" (*Béatrix*, p.337). We find this gamey flavor, this exotic note, this aristocratic nonconformism, echoed later on in the novels of La Varende, a Normandy nobleman himself, and doubtless related to the d'Esgrignons. We also find them again in the words of the Baron de Charlus when he blames the Hohenzollerns much more for taking Hanover than for annexing Alsace. And in Alphonse de Chateaubriant when he saw Hitler's victories not as the defeat of France but as the return of the druids.

The Comte de Mortsauf, Félix de Vandenesse writes, "finally completed in my mind the portrait of that great figure, one of the most imposing types of our era, the émigré" (*Lys dans la Vallée*, p.1024). In reality, Mortsauf is before everything else an invalid. It's true that it was the miseries of exile that ravaged his health, but the cause, in this case, is of little importance when compared with the result. The result is this nervous, irascible man, this neurasthenic whose illness, one finally comes to realize, is something quite other than neurasthenia, alas! Like du Guénic and d'Es-grignon, Mortsauf is living cut off from his own times. The policies of Louis XVIII leave him aghast. But this is merely an accessory detail in his case. The important thing about Mortsauf, I repeat, is the state of his health.

Born in 1759, Mortsauf was twenty at the beginning of all those notori-ous events that did so much to disturb the lives of so many people. Which means that he too was deprived of that second education which can hardly be begun before that age. Instead of the brilliant offices that he had been destined by his high birth to fill, he experiences the wretched life of the émigré. He almost dies of hunger. And moreover, convinced that the Revolution cannot last, instead of adapting himself to his exile (another absolutist, you see), he waits, he lets things drift. "His exile had been spent in the most deplorable kind of idleness" (*id.* p.810). And of all the kinds of idleness there are, the poor man's idleness is the worst. Mortsauf gives himself up to "low debaucheries that not only endangered his life at the time but also ruined its future" (*id.* p.810).

After returning to France, he marries, in 1804, Blanche-Henriette de Lenoncourt-Givry. The two children born from this marriage are both frail and sickly. It is notorious that nothing makes a man more bitter than to know he is responsible for his own misfortune. Mortsauf becomes "as harsh as a power that knows itself to be in the wrong" (*id.* p.804). It begins to dawn on him that his life has been ruined. It is only a step from being a failure to becoming a torturer. Mortsauf becomes his wife's tor-turer. Yet he is neither a commonplace man nor a petty one. On occasion, he can be chivalrous. There are patches of good in him. But his inner despair turns him into a gloomy being who takes pleasure in laying waste whatever lies around him. And in addition, he is possessed by the mysteri-ous stranger created inside him by his malady. He has strange spells during which the well-brought-up nobleman disappears altogether. Unbalanced, disoriented, he is a character entirely composed of contradictions, some-times yielding to ignoble fits of anger, forgetting himself so far as to reveal secrets that have no business outside a bedchamber, but also capable of understanding and respecting his wife's friendship for Félix, never once allowing himself to taint it with the slightest suspicion. A constant plague to others, he is no less so to himself. He ferrets through medical diction-aries, discovers symptoms in himself, lives in a state of alarm, gnaws at himself with his own anxiety. In short, a gentlemanly murderer. And they are the worst murderers of all.

THE REVOLUTION

Du Bousquier

After such a pretty bunch of survivors from the Ancien Régime, one is rather surprised to find that the *Comédie humaine* has almost no other survivors from the Revolution to offer us except the solitary du Bousquier. And even then he is more a survivor from the Directory than the Revolution itself. It is true, of course, that the men who emerged from the Revolution mostly turned into Empire men later on, and also that the Revolution, as we all know, had a habit of devouring its own children. But all the same, I am astonished not to find, as in *les Misérables*, some old regicide, growing old in a little corner somewhere, nostalgically humming a *Carmagnole*. There is Malin de Gondreville, of course; but he's the very opposite of a survivor in the sense I use the word here, since he adapts himself immediately to every régime.

"*Quèsaco*, my pretty one?" (*Vieille Fille*, p.230). Enter du Bousquier, ex-friend of Barras, ex-army contractor, ex-speculator extraordinary, one of those get-rich-quickers who spring up in the wake of any war or revolution: a carpetbagger.

Born of an old Alençon family, du Bousquier managed to make quite a tidy pile for himself under the Terror and the Directory. He didn't count his pennies in those days, that's for sure. But later on, Balzac tells us, he "squeezed the orange of pleasure to excess" (*id.* p.230). He has an illegitimate daughter, Flavie Minoret, who later marries Colleville and whom we have the pleasure of meeting in *les Employés* and *les Petits Bourgeois*. After Marengo, du Bousquier plays a losing game, and finds himself, from one day to the next, reduced to an income of two thousand two hundred francs a year. Another man might have been able to fight his way back. Du Bousquier retires to Alençon and stagnates. Twenty years later he is still there, still living off his two thousand and two hundred francs per annum. Even now, he still has the look of a bull, "a torso like the Farnese Hercules," huge broad shoulders, tufts of hair on every finger joint, a flattened nose, bristles sticking out of his nostrils, thick eyebrows, abrupt, energetic, sparing with his words, frightening in his appearance, "as impotent as an insurrection in reality" (*id.* pp. 226 and 228). Make a note of that metaphor. Du Bousquier wears a false hairpiece. His voice sounds like "the noise that a saw makes biting through soft, damp wood" (*id.* p.226). Invaluable clues. This great bull is, alas, merely an ox. Which is the whole tragedy of *la Vielle Fille*. Because it's that bull-like air of du Bousquier's that Mlle Cormon marries him for. Because he has the reputation of being a libertine. Because he's always stunning her with his connoisseur's compliments. "I've never seen a more beautiful figure of a woman in my life," he tells her . . . "Women with plenty of flesh do have this to be said for them, they're magnificent to look at; they only have to show themselves and it's a triumph!" (*id*. p.304). The poor girl's disappointment may be imagined. As for du Bousquier, he doesn't give a damn. He was looking for a rich wife and he's got one. The rest is a matter of complete indifference to him. And this triumph even restores the way with people that he'd lost. He takes over the leadership of liberal society in Alençon. He's full of plans and little plots. We see him at work in *le Cabinet des Antiques*, in which book, for complicated and mysterious reasons, he is known as du Croisier. After 1830, he is made district head of the Internal Revenue service. He marries his niece to Victurnien d'Esgrignon. Du Bousquier is a very strong man, people say. "Unhappily for his wife, this word is a horrible misconception" (*Vieille Fille*, p. 325).

THE EMPIRE

The National Guard, the soldiers, Cottin, officers in retirement, Philippe Bridau, Max Gilet, Giroudeau, Chabert, Castanier, Gouraud, Montcornet, Genestas, Gondrin, Goguelat, Hulot de Forzheim

And here, marching in serried ranks, come the survivors from the Empire, the survivors of Wagram, of Austerlitz, of the Napoleonic Code, of the Council of State. Needless to say, we shall pass over those who were able to adapt themselves to the return of the Bourbons; the Sérizys, the Malins, the Cariglianos. De Trailles was a page to the Emperor himself. It has left no mark upon him. Generally speaking, in fact, it is only the soldiers who were scarred by the Empire, because for Balzac, Empire and soldier are pretty well synonymous. Even a civil servant like Hulot has something about his character, something in the way his mind functions, that suggests the ex-soldier.*

---

* There are a few civilian survivors from the Empire, however: the Baron du Chatelet in *les Illusions*, cousin Pons, and also M. Gravier in *la Muse du Département,* who failed to grasp "the enormous difference between the morals of the Restoration and those of the Empire." But Gravier is a character of no importance, and in both Pons and Chatelet the fact that they are survivors from the Empire is of merely secondary importance.

Now Balzac doesn't like soldiers. I have already touched on the lengths to which he was prepared to go in order to avoid his stint in the National Guard, the selective service of those days. And he has exacted vengeance for those persecutions. Almost all the fools in his work hold some rank or other in that institution. The whole of the first page or two of *la Cousine Bette* is taken up with a very caustic description of the Captain-scent-maker Célestin Crevel. "Among the ranks of those Parisians who are accused of being so witty, there are some who believe themselves to look infinitely better in a uniform than in their ordinary clothes, and who suppose women to have such depraved tastes that they imagine the ladies will be favorably impressed by the sight of a bearskin and military accoutrements" (*Cousine Bette*, p.135). In *l'Envers de l'Histoire contemporaine* (p. 363) Balzac refers to someone who is an idiot. The man must be at least a lieutenant in his local company, he adds. Pierre Grassou, "that infamous mediocrity," is "head of a battalion" (*Pierre Grassou*, pp. 129-131), and the good-natured idiot Phellion, in *les Petits Bourgeois*, also holds a rank of some sort.

Balzac is scarcely more affectionate towards the regular army. Though we should note at this point that he intended to devote a considerable portion of his total works to military life. In a project published in 1845, he promised twenty-two works to be grouped under the heading: *Scènes de la vie militaire*. Of these twenty-two he actually wrote only two: *Les Chouans* and *Une Passion dans le Désert*. But the first is a story of civil war, and though the hero of the second is a soldier the action of the story has nothing to do with the army. All we have in the way of genuine army scenes are Balzac's frequent visits to the various battlefields. At various times he takes us as camp-followers in this way to Germany (*l'Auberge Rouge*), Egypt (*Une Passion dans le Désert*), into the departments rebelling against the Revolution (*les Chousans*), to Jéna (*Ténébreuse Affaire*), to Eylau (*Colonel Chabert*), to Wagram (*Paysans*), to Spain (*Marana, Muse du Département, El Verdugo, autre Etude de Femme*), to the Tyrol (*Oeuvres ébauchées*, p.1100), and several times to the well-known crossing of the Bérésina (*Adieu, Médecin de Campagne, Autre Etude de Femme*).

Although Balzac certainly displays both an awareness and an appreciation of the heroism that is displayed in such circumstances, on the other hand, he is extremely quick to insist on the looting and the excesses of Napoleon's troops. In *El Verdugo* we are shown a massacre of hostages. In *le Médecin de Campagne*, the upright Genestas makes no attempt whatever to restrain his soldiers from making off with the inhabitants' possessions. And when an Allied soldier disturbs him he kills him without pausing to draw breath. Montcornet is a good fellow, but he squeezes Pomerania for more than a million—which he keeps for himself. In *les Marana*, we see Captain Diard stealing pictures. In *Echantillons de Causeries Françaises*, an unfinished work, General Rusca is to be observed having civilians shot whether they give the right answers or not. In *Adieu*, there are several soldiers on a raft. An officer attempts to push one of the soldiers into the water in order to make room for himself. The soldier loses his temper and sends the officer to the bottom. Elsewhere, this same soldier comes upon the corpse of one of his cousins. The sight fails to extract even a single sigh from him (*Adieu*, pp. 778 and 774). Balzac often refers to the Légion Italienne. "For a surprise raid, there were no better troops in the whole army," he writes, but "they were such rogues they'd have robbed the good Lord above . . . real cannibals, a pack of cunning hounds" (*Oeuvres ébauchées*, p.1086). Among other beautiful natures, this Légion Italienne included in its ranks the notorious Captain Bianchi, who one day ate the heart of a sentry, and also the colonel in *Autre Etude de Femme* who made use of his rank to snatch away a captain's wife. In short, war, in the *Comédie humaine*, appears above all else as a frightful midwife to dishonesty, brutality and egoism: "There is good reason to shudder when one ponders all the misfortunes that are caused, all the crimes that are committed by the army, after battles, when the savagery of so many savage natures is free to display itself with impunity" (*Oeuvres ébauchées*, p.1099).

So much for war. As for the military profession, for Balzac it is the lowest of the low. "Lucien," he writes, "felt himself drained of all pride and all strength. For the sake of a little money, he would even have enlisted as a soldier" (*Illusions Perdues*, p.875). Just as he might say of a woman that she has resigned herself to going on the streets. "When I picked him up he was a beggar on the highroad, ready to turn soldier," Vautrin says in the play that bears his name. When sunk deep into the direst poverty, Mongenod begs for a loan. If you refuse, he says, I'll sign up as a soldier. "You a soldier!" his friend replies. "You, Mongenod!" (*Envers de l'Histoire contemporaine*, p.277). When in despair at having no more money to give to his daughters, even Goriot considers enlisting. His daughters protest in horror "No, no" (*Père Goriot*, p.1045). "There are no bad men in our valley," Benassis says. "And if any do turn up, I send them into the army, where they make excellent soldiers" (*Médecin de Campagne*, p.420). And it was only when he'd failed at everything else, you will remember, that young Husson finally joined up.

The officers are not handled any more kindly. Here are the reflections inspired by the career of the ex-Captain Castanier: "Military life requires few ideas . . . (Soldiers) passively obey the being who is in command of them and kill the men in front of them much as the woodcutter chops down the trees in a forest . . . They fight and drink, they fight and eat, they fight and sleep." Back in civilian life again, they "prove uneducated, without faculties, without vision . . . as devoid of intelligence as the humblest clerk might be" (*Melmoth réconcilié*, pp. 301 and 302). Still, Castanier did rise from the ranks, so too much can't be expected of him. But here is the brilliant Colonel Marquis d'Aiglemont: "He is one of those men whom heaven has created to eat and digest four meals a day, sleep, make love to the first woman who comes along, and fight . . . One day, you will lament bitterly over his nullity, his lack of order, his egoism, his uncouthness, his ineptitude in matters of love." (*Femme de Trente Ans*, pp. 684 and 685). The military man has physical courage, of course (though Montefiore in *les Marana* is a coward), but this physical courage may often not be accompanied by moral courage, which is the one essential. "In the rabble of men enlisted by Napoleon, there were a great many who . . . possessed the purely physical courage of the battlefield without the moral courage that has the power to make a man as great in the field of crime as he could have been in that of virtue" (*Melmoth réconcilié*, p.275).

Against Philippe Bridau, Max Gilet and Castanier, who are all three scoundrels, it is of course possible to set Montriveau, Genestas and the Marshal Hulot, who are all honest. But one should also note that out of these three honest army men there are two, Genestas and Marshal Hulot, who are depicted as being of very limited intelligence. As for Montriveau, he is in the artillery, and that branch of the army, according to Balzac, is more civilian in nature than the others (*Rabouilleuse*, p.947). Though that may well have been nothing more than a simple rhetorical precaution on the author's part, intended to spare the feelings of his friends Periolas and Carraud, both artillery men. Above all, though, it should be noted that whereas Bridau and Gilet are ex-soldiers, Montriveau and Genestas are still in service. Furthermore, though Balzac describes these failings so prevalent among army men, he at no point gives any indication that he disapproves of them. He seems to have looked upon them as necessary evils inherent in the nature of war and the military profession in general. In the same way, it will be remembered, we never found him criticizing either the spirit of the Ancien Régime or the émigré attitude in themselves. Again, what he condemns is the survival of these attitudes and the application of the principles behind them to eras in which they have become out of date. Bridau, Gilet and their ilk are condemned, not for behaving like soldiers when they were in fact soldiers, but for having continued to behave like soldiers after their return to civilian life. In the case of the Ancien Régime, the hiatus in time obliged Balzac to divide his proof of its ill effects into two stages, to follow it through two generations. The principles that led Valois to success in 1785 lead Victurnien to disaster in 1820. Here, on the other hand, since the Restoration followed directly after the Empire, the proof can be embodied in a single character. The same qualities and the same defects that made Bridau an excellent soldier in 1815 make him a contemptible civilian in 1820. And the same thing with Hulot. Oh nonsense, someone may say, Bridau and Hulot would have turned out badly in any case. I don't think so. Had Napoleon not been defeated at Waterloo, Bridau would have become a general. He would never have needed to become dishonest. And as for Hulot, under the Empire he was "one of the most upright and most active workers in his corps" (*Cousine Bette*, p.155). If he becomes dishonest and criminal, it is entirely due to his lust; but that lust would never have taken a hold on him were it not for the fall of Napoleon. "Forced into idleness from 1818 to 1823, the Baron Hulot drafted himself into active service with the ladies" (*id.* p.156). Moreover, Balzac makes it clear that it is precisely the lessons learned while serving under the Emperor that later lead Hulot into the misappropriation of funds that seals his fate. He chooses this way because he is still under the influence of habits acquired as an administrator of occupied countries where anything went, where there was hardly any control over the administrator's actions, and where the Emperor demanded that the methods used be efficacious rather than that they be honest. What, after all, does it amount to, this business of the fodder supplies that forces Hulot to resign? It is in fact just that: malversation by the administrator of an occupied country, the sort of skullduggery it is only too easy to get away with in such circumstances. And let us also note that the two men from whose good offices Hulot benefits in this undertaking are also former followers of Napoleon: his uncle Fischer and Marshal Cottin. And again, both of these men, though fundamentally honest, have been tainted by their Imperial pasts. I have to have a hundred thousand francs, Hulot tells Fischer. What does the honest old fellow reply? "I can't see any harm in taking it off the Bedouins. That's how things were done under the Empire" (*id.* p.255). "That's how things were done under the Empire." That's all there is to the whole business, you see. That's how they did things under the Empire . . . only unfortunately they are under Louis-Philippe.

Fischer is simply a good old man who has never learned how to split hairs. But the same attitude is to be found, scarcely changed at all, at the very top of the social scale. Of all the army men in the *Comédie humaine*, we now come to the highest in rank, Cottin, Prince of Wissembourg, Duke of Orfano, Minister for War, Marshal of France, and a marshal of the first Imperial promotion too, the companion in arms of Ney, of Murat, of Lannes, a man who might have been a king, like Bernadotte, one of those giants built on the same scale as history itself, the Condé of the Republic. Balzac never mentions him without respect. Read the pages of *la Cousine Bette* in which he appears. Every time we meet him we seem to hear the trumpets of victory sounding in the distance. Cottin has "the eyes of an eagle, whose pride, lucidity and perspicacity made it clear that, despite his years, this great soul had remained still firm and vigorous" (*id.* p.386). He has "a brow of such breadth that the imagination could picture it a field of battle"; and "eyes of a Napoleonic blue, usually sad, full of bitter thoughts and regrets" (*id.* p.415). Yet even in this aging lion we find the brutality of a Bridau and the lack of scruples of a Baron Hulot. His anger is the anger of a bargee. "Your brother is a j . . . f . . . ," he yells at the elder Hulot (*id.* p.417). Yet when the aforesaid *jeanfoutre* asks to have his mistress's husband appointed to a post he has no right to, the renowned old Marshal simply laughs. "What's this! You're still at it? Ah! you do honor to the Imperial Guard!" and he approves the promotion "with a smile" (*id.* p.386 and p.388). After all, it's only a matter of doing down civilians. "I don't give a damn" (*id.* p.387). "Such," Balzac sums up, "is the effect of the comradeship that binds together the glorious remnants of the Napoleonic host; they still think of themselves as being under canvas in the field, obliged to protect one another against the whole world" (*id.* p.388). "One of the particular features of the Bonapartist character is a faith in the power of the saber, a secure belief in the superiority of the army man over the civilian" (*id.* p.374). However different they may be in other ways, the revered Cottin and the lamentable Hulot do at least have this in common, that they both look back nostalgically to the days when civilians had to keep their mouths shut. "Oh, Napoleon, where are you?" Hulot cries. It is the same cry as the one we hear from Philippe Bridau: "When one thinks that Napoleon is on St. Helena!" (*Rabouilleuse*, p.908). It is the cry of all these demobilized officers, all these army men on half-pay in whose honor Georges d'Esparbès wove such glorious garlands, but who must also have been, on occasion, rather hard to put up with. "If you have served in the army," George Sand wrote in *Indiana*, "then you will know exactly what the soldiers mean by the term *culotte de peau* (an officer risen from the ranks) and you will admit that there is a vast number of them to be found among the débris of the old Imperial cohorts. These men, drawn together and directed by a powerful hand, accomplished magical feats and towered like giants in the smoke of battles; but having returned to civilian life again, these heroes became no more than soldiers, bold and coarse comrades who reasoned like so many machines; one was fortunate when they did not behave in society as though in a conquered country." This character is met with frequently in the literature of the time. The *Moniteur de l'Armée* complained of the fact in 1844: "The Empire officer . . . is one of the obligatory types, hackneyed though it may be, in every new play or novel to which the author wishes to give, as they say in their modern jargon, an exciting topical interest." Balzac was not one to let any matter of topical interest escape him, and he has devoted several stories to these half-pay soldiers, the most important of which is *la Rabouilleuse*. We meet several of them in that novel, bitter, disappointed, belligerent, always grousing, hanging around in cafés, deliberately provoking the royalists. We find Potel and Renard, Mignonnet and Kouski, and above all, Philippe Bridau, Max Gilet and Giroudeau.

This Philippe Bridau is the brother of Joseph, the painter. Born in 1796, by 1815, when he is still less than twenty years old, Philippe is already a lieutenant-colonel. Such a brilliant career justifies us in thinking that he possesses all the qualities that go to make a first-class officer. Waterloo forces him back into civilian life. He is uprooted, forced to change his environment. And that, according to Balzac, is a test from which only really strong men emerge victorious. Bridau goes under. He goes away to America, then returns "brutal, a drinker, a smoker, self-centered, impolite" (*Rabouilleuse*, p.880). What is more, he thinks of himself as persecuted, which always makes "unintelligent people into intolerant persecutors themselves" (*id.* p.880). He drinks and he gambles. In order to drink and gamble he steals. He steals from his brother, from his mother, and from his old aunt Descoings, who dies as a result. He becomes treasurer to a newspaper. His principle task is to provoke any reader ill-advised enough to complain about an article into fighting a duel (*Illusions perdues*, p.766). He leads a life of debauchery. We see him at Coralie's (*id.* p.801), at Esther's (*Splendeurs*, p.863), and at the theater with women of easy virtue (*id*. p.840). He is the preferred lover of Mariette, who leads him a dance. "Philippe doesn't know how to manage Mariette," Lucien comments (*Illusions perdues*, p.803). Needless to say, he ends up embezzling money from the newspaper. He is also a political conspirator. He is implicated in a Bonapartist plot; though his exact role in it is never made clear. At one point, Balzac tells us that he betrayed his fellow-conspirators; at another, he insinuates that he was used as a screen by important personages (*Rabouilleuse*, pp. 1045 and 1052).

Whatever the truth of the matter, Bridau gets off with nothing more serious than a term of probation, which he goes to spend in Issoudun. His visit to prison has changed him. In *la Comédie humaine*, the characters who have been in prisons are always slightly superior to the rest. Bridau has acquired a more serious attitude towards evil there, a hidden cunning, rather coarse but effective nonetheless. He has also learned that flying in the face of society is dangerous. The wicked young scapegrace who used to steal from his mother's drawers has become "one of those deep-dyed villains who mask their plots and misdeeds behind a screen of legality and beneath the blameless roof of their family home" (*Rabouilleuse*, p.897). Henceforth, those who talk with him are able to sense that his actions are the product of careful calculation and an implacable will. When he arrives at his cousin Rouget's house, Flore Brazier experiences "a sort of shiver in her heart" and Max Gilet feels "within himself that shuddering of the intelligence and the sensibility which is nature's warning to us of some latent enmity or imminent peril" (*id*. p.1047).

It will be remembered that Philippe is the cousin and heir of a mental defective, Rouget, who lives under the thumb of a servant-cum-mistress who is herself under the domination of Max Gilet. Philippe has flushed this covey in less time than it takes to tell it. He kills Gilet, marries the uncle to the servant girl, arranges the uncle's death, marries his widow, eliminates her in her turn, and thus ends up with complete control over the mental defective's fortune (one million, six hundred thousand francs). The details of these machinations are all to be found in *la Rabouilleuse*. They are all managed by Bridau with the brutality and the elementary cunning that, according to Balzac, are typical of the military mind. He never finesses; he never bluffs. Rouget runs away: Bridau brings him back by force. Gilet is in the way: he kills him. Rouget has served his purpose: he kills him. His wife becomes an encumbrance: he kills her. Cunning? Yes, if you like, but it is a coarse, barrack-room kind of cunning. Bridau handles people with cowhide gloves, not kid ones. Not for an instant, for example, does he think of concealing his intention to kill Gilet. The only way in which he tricks the others concerned in this business is by always acting more quickly and more savagely than they expect. They think he won't dare—but he dares. That he won't do it yet—he does it then and there.

Once he has acquired the necessary wealth, Bridau goes over to the Bourbons. He renews his military activities and is made Comte de Brambourg. His mother is dying. He sends her an atrociously cruel letter that hastens her death. In 1830, he puts his money on the Bourbons, ends up stagnating as a result, and finally gets himself killed in Algeria in 1839. His beautiful town house on the Rue Taitbout is inherited by Joseph: the first sign of revenge on the part of a Providence that has scarcely shown its face at all in the story up till then.

Born in 1788, and therefore slightly older than Bridau, Max Gilet is a bastard whose mother was a cobbler's wife and whose father was an army officer. Enlisted in the army himself, then taken prisoner during the Peninsula War, he spends several years in the celebrated Spanish prison hulks. In 1815 he is a commandant. Or rather an ex-commandant, for Gilet is now, for his sins, back in civilian life. He is the victim of the same uprooting, the same change of environment as Bridau. He was destined to do great things, Balzac tells us, "had he remained in the environment that was favorable to him" (*Rabouilleuse*, p.1085). "The Emperor would have possessed in this lad one of those men so necessary to vast undertakings" (*id.* p.1067). But Gilet has neither enough moral courage nor enough intelligence to enable him to transform these military virtues into civil ones. He goes under, he becomes a gigolo, and what a gigolo! The gigolo of Rouget's servant-mistress. Pocketing his pride, this former commandant moves into the Rouget house and allows himself to be coddled there with the whole of Issoudun looking on.

Base though he is, Gilet nevertheless seems to me less contemptible than Bridau. Balzac himself says as much: "His opponent who was worth less than him" (*id.* p.1085). At one point, he says that Bridau might have made a good general. In Gilet's case, that "might" disappears. "He would certainly have made a magnificent general in command of a division" (*id.* p.957). In Bridau's case, Balzac talks only about the "usual cavalry officer's gallantry"; in Gilet's he evokes "the courage, the cool-headedness, and the political astuteness of a Cesare Borgia" (*id.* pp. 874 and 1085). If there does exist a hierarchy of the ignoble, perhaps it may also be thought less base to sponge off a servant-girl than to steal from one's mother. Lastly, Gilet is a bastard, and bastards, in the *Comédie humaine*, are rarely mediocrities. One senses again in him that inward effervescence, that constantly bubbling source of activity that the Empire seems to have created in so many of those who came to manhood under it. Idleness weighs heavy on him. Nero, bored with life in Rome, founded an association of practical jokers called the Knights of Augustus. Gilet, the Nero of Issoudun, founds the Knights of Idleness for exactly the same reasons, and spends his time devising tricks to play on the inhabitants. A very silly way in which to expend one's energy; but at least it is better, in a way, than mere stagnation. Bridau is merely a mercenary. Gilet is a condottiere, a leader of a gang. Balzac talks of his coolheadedness. And justly so. When Gilet is wounded by Fario, he still remains sufficiently master of himself to think of throwing suspicion onto Joseph Bridau. He's no fool. But then, faced with Philippe Bridau, he is seized with vertigo. His cool head deserts him and he dies in a duel.

Giroudeau's character is not drawn on quite such bold lines. "Beginning as a simple cavalry soldier in the army of the Sambre-et-Meuse, five years a master at arms in the First Hussars, Army of Italy" (*Illusions perdues*, p.670), a captain in the Dragoons of the Guard, retired with the rank of major, given the job of treasurer to a newspaper, thanks to his nephew Finot, Giroudeau does not seem to be intrinsically a rotter. But he too has been tainted by the gang morality that makes any enterprise undertaken by one's comrades automatically legitimate. Out of friendship for Bridau he helps him kill off his uncle (*Rabouilleuse*, p.1096). Out of gratitude to Finot, he sometimes involves himself in very shady deals (*Illusions perdues*, p.798). But at least he does these things more in order to help his comrades than for personal profit. Moreover, whereas Bridau and Gilet both regret the end of the Empire only for strictly personal reasons, Giroudeau's regrets seem to be the product of a mystical belief. An idiotic mystical belief, of course. "God of Gods," he says, "you're nothing but a beggarly knave, you let the Emperor down" (*id*. p.670). He is the old grouser dragging his cane behind him, angry, bitter, spiteful sometimes, but straightforwardly so, dishonest on occasion, but more out of simpleness of mind than fundamental lack of probity. After 1830, he returns to the army, becomes a general, and takes advantage of this fact to send his former friend Bridau, with whom he has fallen out, to his death.

Colonel Chabert is a different matter. According to Balzac, he is sublime. Though I must confess I can't see why. Seriously! A foundling, Hyacinthe, known as Chabert, enlists in the army and makes a brilliant career for himself. Meanwhile, though I'm not sure at quite what point, he marries Rosine Chapotel, a lady who rooms in a brothel. The devil he does! Is he a Tolstoy hero then, this Chabert? But Rose Chapotel is none of your sad little St. Petersburg whores. She is vulgar and she is mean. Which doubtless means, since Chabert decided to marry her, that he himself is vulgar and would not feel at home with any other kind of wife. Unless he's a weakling who just gives way to the first strong will he comes across. Possibly it was the wife who decided on the marriage. And if, among all those clients of hers, she picked on Chabert, then it must mean that she sensed a weakness in him that would make him consent without too much trouble. Whatever the truth of the matter, up till this point there has certainly been nothing sublime. Then, having been wounded at Eylau, Chabert is buried. He digs himself out, wanders around for a while, and eventually returns to Paris. I suppose you can call that sublime, if you like. The events are sublime. But Chabert is only sublime by association, at second hand, as it were. Just as, today, we think a man sublime who has been shot or imprisoned for his opinions. And it is true that his death, or his ordeal, give him the right to our respect. But everyone will agree that among so many martyrs there may very well have been a few who were mediocrities. And furthermore, in the case of the man shot or imprisoned for his opinions there has always, at some point, been a moment of choice. The analogy here is rather with the man who is shot or imprisoned by mistake, without having done anything to invite such a fate. Because that is Chabert's case. He is buried alive; but he did not choose to be buried alive. So any sublimity he has comes from outside, from a misfortune he did not invite, not from within himself. Back in France, he finds that his wife has remarried. He tries to get her back. The wife smothers him with caresses: he gives up the attempt. I warned you that she had sensed a weakness in him that would make him agree to anything. Chabert's claims dwindle. "Can't I live here, in your little lodge, as though I were one of your relations?" (*Colonel Chabert*, p.1139) It's very touching, but it's also not very different from Max Gilet moving in with the Rougets. "All I need is a little tobacco and *le Constitutionnel*" (*id.* p.1139). Sublime! Balzac cries. Why? In *Pierrette* (p.730), he condemns Sylvie Rogron because "this horrible woman took exhaustion, submission and the silence of poverty for virtues!" In what way is Chabert's case different? Why have submission and renunciation become sublime in him? One could just as well take them as signs of diminishing vitality. "I'm as worn out as an old cannon on the junkheap," Chabert says. "When I think that Napoleon is on St. Helena, nothing in this world seems to matter any more" (*Colonel*

Chabert, pp. 1139 and 1144). If nothing matters to him, where is the hero-ism? What would Chabert do with his money? All he needs is a quiet corner in which to smoke his pipe. Or with his title? Though Chabert does not actually say so, there is some justification for thinking that his count's coronet has always seemed to him rather like a kind of fancy dress that fell from the sky one day, and that heaven is quite likely to take back again. "I can no longer be a soldier, that's my whole misfortune" (*id.* p.1144). His trade has been taken away from him so his whole life col-lapses. Like Bridau, like Gilet, Chabert is a soldier incapable of being any-thing but a soldier. They're brave fellows, these army men, but they haven't the energy to change their rifles over to the other shoulder. Once the Empire has crumbled under them, they have nothing left but the blinkered dreams of the retired captain. A little tobacco and the newspa-per, Chabert says. A lot of tobacco and Mariette, says Bridau. Tobacco and Flore, says Gilet. So where's the difference? Chabert is more moder-ate in his desires; but I'm inclined to think that that's simply because he's much older. He must be at least fifty. In 1815, Bridau was not yet twenty and Gilet certainly under thirty. That's the only essential difference. Gilet and Bridau still have a store of vital energy left that gets out of hand and makes them go to the bad. Chabert has nothing left. He is a piece of flotsam. Having been fobbed off by his wife, he disappears. We might perhaps expect to meet him again as an honest old cashier in some quiet corner, or as a conscientious night watchman, or as a diligent doorkeeper. But no. Chabert lets himself go. In 1840, he is still dragging out his exist-ence in a home for hoboes in Bicêtre.

The ex-Captain Castanier of *Melmoth réconcilié* and the ex-Colonel Gouraud of *Pierrette* are simply two counterparts of Giroudeau; his sa-tanic counterpart and his provincial counterpart. Castanier I have already mentioned.

Colonel Baron Gouraud lives in Provins. He has thin legs, a strong torso, a thick mustache, sidewhiskers like fins, earrings and a nose that has been shortened by a saber wound (*Pierrette*, p.690). Like his colleagues, he is notable for "a total contempt for the social conventions" and by a careless brutality beneath which, one eye always half-open, there dozes the coarse cunning that, according to Balzac, exists in every soldier. He is considering marriage with Sylvie Rogron, an excessively ugly, but rather rich old maid. The 1830 revolution saves him from this frightful peril. He marries Mlle Matifat, the daughter of the pharmacist. He becomes a peer of France. He becomes a sleeping partner in a theater (*Cousin Pons*, p.689). I shall avoid the obvious pun, but I'm afraid that access to the less exalted actresses is indeed his only reason for this enterprise.

Do you recall what Philippe Bridau was like in the beginning? When he still hadn't been in prison and was just a dishonest drunkard? There's another young fellow cast in just the same mold to be found in *Echantillons de Causeries françaises,* one of the works that Balzac didn't have time to finish. This fellow is a lieutenant-colonel, another one on half-pay, like Bridau employed on a newspaper, dirty, always smoking, always drunk, hair never combed. Bianchon is attending the fellow's mistress, who is very ill. One day the doctor comes in and finds her in a smoke-filled room where the soldier "finding Clarisse admirable in her death-throes had doubtless wanted to wish her goodbye . . . The disorder of the bed," Bianchon comments, "made it clear to me . . ." (*Oeuvres ébauchées,* p.1099). An incident worthy of Philippe Bridau.

Having managed to take advantage of the Empire in order to amass himself a tidy fortune, the General Comte de Montcornet is never reduced to the expedients that bring such dishonor on the Gilets and the Bridaus. But he nevertheless displays the same military and Imperial character that is unable to cope with even the slightest difficulties of civilian life. The same low cunning, the same brutality. "That particular cunning to be found in veteran campaigners," Balzac writes when describing him (*Paysans,* p.99). "Accustomed to cutting his way through every difficulty with a saber, full of contempt for civilians," he is always ready to go off into "one of those fits of anger so characteristic of these nation-tamers" (*id.* p.100). Alas! These methods are useful when dealing with the alcaldes, the podestas and the burgomasters of occupied countries, but Montcornet is completely nonplussed when faced with French peasants. They get the better of him entirely, and he is forced to sell his beautiful château. This is the theme of *les Paysans.*

Like Castanier and Bridau, Montcornet is one of those military men with a great deal of physical courage but very little moral courage. A hero of the Empire, magnificent as long as he's wielding a saber, showered with honors by the Little Corporal, he rushes over to join the Bourbons when they return, goes back to Napoleon during the Hundred Days, then back to the Bourbons after Waterloo. Though even this notable dexterity in turning his cape does not save him from temporary disgrace during the early Restoration. He then buys himself back into royal favor by marrying Virginie de Troisville, who is poor but a member of an émigré family.

His attitude to his wife is as pusillanimous as his attitude towards authority, and this hero puts up with the liaison between Virginie and Blondet without a single protest. When Virginie is alone in a room with her lover one day and tells Montcornet not to come in, the old soldier "executed a right-about turn in the best military fashion" (*id*. p.26). "People think of him as a Titan, but there's a dwarf inside" (*id*. p.25). He has the head of a lion however, the shoulders of a locksmith, and is five foot nine inches tall. Born in 1774, he is the son of a cabinet-maker in the Faubourg Saint-Antoine. In *la Paix du Ménage*, in 1809, we see him at a ball, a colonel in the Imperial Guard, brilliant, knowing, witty, flirting with Mme de Vaudremont, who (alas) dies shortly afterwards. It was at about this time too no doubt that he was keeping a young lady named Fortin, by whom he has a daughter, Valérie, the future Mme Marneffe. Being a goodhearted fellow at bottom, he looks out for the young couple, slips them a few banknotes now and then, and has the husband appointed to a post in the Ministry for War. Having been made a Marshal under Louis-Philippe, he dies in 1837. After his death, a statue is put up in his honor (*Cousine Bette*, p.223). An equestrian one, I imagine.

It will have been noticed that the nostalgia running through all these truncated careers is only secondarily political. Bridau goes over to the Bourbons: it does not improve his character. What destroys, what sours all these half-pay soldiers is not so much their political rage, though that does come into it too, but the fact that they have been transplanted from the field of battle into civilian flowerbeds. A man like Genestas, for example, in *le Médecin de Campagne*, has ten times as much Napoleonic fervor as Bridau and Gilet put together. Yet he displays none of their failings. Thrown back into civilian life, this "simple and faithful soldier" (*le Médecin de Campagne*, p.319) might perhaps have suffered the same disappointments and slithered down the same slopes as his former colleagues. But he has remained a soldier; he has stayed in the environment to which he is suited. And in consequence, he has also remained honest and upright. Balzac does not imply that this transplantation is inevitably fatal, mark you. The inference is simply that it takes character and intelligence to overcome it. Neither Bridau nor Gilet is particularly well endowed in these respects. But on the other hand, also in *le Médecin de Campagne*, we have Gondrin, the only survivor of those celebrated pontoneers at the crossing of the Beresina, a soldier from 1792 to 1814, returning to his native Dauphiné without a pension, without even a medal, and reduced to the trade of roadmender. And we have Goguelat too, the postman, an other old soldier, rather more jovial, rather more quick witted. Both of these men have preserved a feeling of adoration for Napoleon beside which the nostalgic reveries of a Giroudeau are as nothing. In 1829, Gondrin still believes that the Man is not dead, and "convinced that his captivity is due to the English, I believe that, given the slightest excuse, he would slaughter even the kindliest of Aldermen traveling here for pleasure" (*id.* p.388). As for Goguelat, he gathers the peasants together in the evening in order to tell them that admirable Life of Napoleon of which the text is to be found in *le Médecin de Campagne.* "To begin by giving you something of how extraordinary it all is, his mother, who was the most beautiful woman of her time and a shrewd one, had the idea that she would promise him to God in order to have him escape all the dangers of his childhood and his life, because she had dreamed that the world was on fire the day she was brought to bed of him" (*id.* p.453). Now in neither of these two old soldiers, of whom one at least has very good reason to be bitter, do we find any trace of the ignoble failings to be observed in a Bridau. Not once do we hear them invoke the fall of Napoleon as justification for even so much as the theft of a chicken. Why is this? Because they are good, honest folk? Yes, of course. But above all, because these two old soldiers, without wasting their energy on regrets or grumbles, have courageously gone back to civilian life and taken on a trade, because they have proved capable of carrying on that trade, because they have understood that times are no longer the same, because they have been able to come to terms with a new order and adapt to it.

So that these three, Genestas who remains in the army, and Gondrin and Goguelat who transplant themselves firmly back into civilian life, escape the degradation that befalls the other demobilized soldiers. And here again we are forced to recognize the invariable verdict that Balzac brings in against those who think they can abolish time, deny the progress of history, and ignore their circumstances; against those who refuse to come to terms or don't know how to; against all champions of the absolute, in short. For Bridau and for Giroudeau, the Empire is an absolute. Its law alone is the good law. The Restoration, for them, is bad. Hence, allowing their predilections to affect their judgment, they assume it to be a passing thing to which it would be pointless to adapt. Bridau and Giroudeau are exiles at home in exactly the same way as the old Marquis d'Esgrignon is. The Marquis d'Esgrignon is of course too honorable a man to descend as low as a Bridau does. But having said that, we should immediately add, first, that his age and the remains of his fortune spare him the same temptations, and secondly, that he does suffer the same bankruptcy, the same downfall as a Gilet in fact, but in the person of his son, Victurnien. Obviously we have to take into account the differences in character that are operating here; but there is a common denominator that runs through all of them, through Victurnien as well as the Gilets, the Hulots, the Chaberts. And that common denominator is unawareness, ignorance of the law. Victurnien commits a fraud almost without realizing it. Chabert can't believe his ears when Derville explains to him that he will have to go to court to recover his fortune. "The social and legal worlds were weighing down on his chest like a nightmare" (*Colonel Chabert*, p.111). He is so disheartened that he gives up the idea. The others, as may be imagined, give up less easily than Chabert; but since their understanding of the law is no better than his, they all end up behaving more or less illegally. The great hero Cottin finds it the most natural thing in the world to ratify unfair promotions. Hulot robs the government. Max Gilet destroys a stock of wheat that doesn't belong to him. Bridau steals from his mother. Castanier steals from his employer. Giroudeau helps his friends in their criminal activities. Irresponsibility, malversation, malicious practical jokes, theft pure and simple, aiding and abetting, we have samples of practically every possible form of lawbreaking. Nor need we exclude murder, sometimes in a more or less camouflaged form, sometimes not. Bridau kills Gilet. But at least he kills him in a duel, so there is a gesture in the direction of legality there. But Diard, the ex-quartermaster, does his killing quite openly, in the street (*les Marana*). Such are the results, according to Balzac, of the uprooting, the transplanting of mediocre beings. Such is the fate, if it does not have the energy or the intelligence to avoid it, of any "creature forced to live elsewhere than in its own proper sphere" (*Médecin de Campagne*, p.408).

The energy or the intelligence, I said. But the ex-soldier can also be saved by uprightness and simplicity of character. For now we come to the third Marshal of the *Comédie humaine*, the Comte Hulot. He presents almost none of the characteristics of the retired soldier. And the reason is not hard to find. Hulot is honesty personified. He is as simple and forthright as a child. He is modest. He has had honors showered on him without ever intriguing for them. Consequently there is nothing bitter, nothing vengeful in his tone, as there is in that of the others. He does not consider himself to be suffering under an injustice. Moreover, he is a republican. If there is any deformation of character there, then it is entirely military and has nothing to do with the Empire. Also, he does not leave the army. And finally, I should add that Balzac does not introduce us to him until after the Restoration. When we first meet him, in 1838, it is twenty years after the fall of the Empire. So it is possible that Hulot did mutter a little to begin with; but in any case he has had time to quiet down.

I hope it is clear by now that there are two Hulots brothers: the elder, Comte Hulot de Forzheim, Marshal of France, and the younger, Baron Hulot d'Ervy, civil servant and skirt-chaser. The Hulot with the saber, born in 1766, is to be found in 1799, in *les Chouans*, at the head of a half-brigade on active service in the rebellious departments. He takes part in the Peninsula War (*Muse du Département*, p.107). In 1809, he is a general and a count. After 1830, having been made a marshal by Louis-Philippe, he goes into retirement, lives a quiet bachelor life, without liaisons, asking nothing of anybody, rather deaf, and confining his social activities to an occasional evening spent with his sister-in-law, whom he worships. He is short, thickset and very chivalrous in manner (*Cousine Bette*, p.177). It was he who brought up his younger brother, and he took great pains to inculcate in him a "love of Country, of Family, and of the Poor" (*id.* p.425). He might have saved his breath. His pupil steals from his country, ruins his family, and takes only as much interest in the poor as will enable him to seduce their daughters. Old Hulot has also taken under his wing the young Montauran, whose brother he once had shot. A true sign of nobility that, for it is rarely that a man does not hate his victims. Resolutely republican, even under Napoleon, Hulot is of a "divine probity" (*id.* p.427). But his intelligence is only average. "Without education, a son of the people, his military career was achieved by courage alone, and his common sense had always supplied his lack of wit," (*id.* p.177). In this respect he is much inferior to Cottin. Hulot is much more the orders-are-orders type of officer. In *les Chouans*, when he is sent a female spy who could be of more use to him than a hundred extra men, Hulot looks his gift horse nervously in the mouth and then starts leafing through his copy of Regulations. He is full of honor, but it is the limited honor of a soldier who can see no further than the end of his saber. His brother has stolen from his country: the only advice he can find to give him is to shoot himself. There's presence of mind for you! When the brother proves recalcitrant to this idea, he dies himself. He too meets with failure. The education he gave his younger brother has done nothing to save that brother from disaster, and he himself, despite his position, is unable to save his sister-in-law. All of which does not prevent the old marshal from being a fine and noble figure. He forces us to respect him. He is Plutarch's soldier. He is the soldier of *Grandeurs et Servitudes*, at once diminished and made greater by the discipline of his profession. He has less stature than Cottin, but he is more pure. Despite all the honors he has received, he has remained poor. Cottin, on the other hand, is a very wealthy man (*id.* p.416). Balzac does not tell us whether these riches are the result of thrifty saving or whether, like Montcornet's, they were extorted from the occupied countries.

It is evident enough that all these characters are the prisoners of time. Their lives have come to a halt at a certain point, a point that is always, it will have been noticed, that of their triumphs. Just as Mme de la Chanterie is imprisoned with her tragedy, in perpetual tête à tête with that tragedy, so Bridau remains forever in tête à tête with that moment in his life when, at Waterloo, he first became aware of the marvelous possibility within him. Mme de Blamont-Chauvry was once the mistress of Louis XV; the Chevalier de Valois was once the lover of the Princess Goritza. Neither of them has ever got over those events. Literally. Since no further triumphs, no other moments of self-affirmation have occurred in their lives, they have stopped there, rather like people who have been born in a castle and spend the rest of their lives feeling lost in an apartment. D'Esgrignon and du Guénic have both been chouans. Out in the forests and the fields where they risked their lives, and where those lives took on their full meaning, they were living at the full stretch of their faculties. Nothing will ever again bring them the same feeling of exaltation. Under the Directory, du Bousquier was one of the kings of Paris. He stopped there. Under the Empire, Bridau and Giroudeau rode in triumph. They stopped there. As a woman, when giving us a photograph of herself, will choose the one in which she looks her best, so each of these characters clings to the noblest image of himself. Only a nobler one can erase that image. Only a greater triumph can liberate them from those past triumphs in which they continue to live. But there are no more triumphs. Neither for Mme de Blamont-Chauvry, d'Esgrignon and du Guénic, because they are too old; nor for Bridau or Giroudeau, because they are not capable of them. The petrifaction of age for the first group, the petrifaction of the intelligence for the second. It took an intervention from outside, an exterior event, the sudden social rearrangements brought about by the Empire to make Montcornet a count, or Bridau a major, or Giroudeau a commandant. It took exceptional circumstances to make the Marquis d'Esgrignon into a chouan. It even took fairly exceptional circumstances to make Mme de Blamont-Chauvry Louis XV's mistress and Valois the lover of the Princess Goritza. No longer surrounded by those circumstances, they are forced to fall back on their own resources, which do not, in many of these cases, amount to very much. Hence their loyalty to the conception of life, to the social organization, prevalent at the moment of their triumphs. If, by some chance, a fresh triumph does occur, then they are able to regain their foothold in the world. Look at du Bousquier, for example. Until 1815 he remains merely a survivor from the Directory. Then he succeeds in marrying a rich woman. The Directory is eclipsed. Du Bousquier becomes a man like other men once more. He re-affirms himself. His new triumph gives him a new lease on life. Moreover, du Bousquier changes his name. He becomes du Croisier. For other reasons no doubt; but the coincidence is a curious one.

CHAPTER 18

Religion

ALMOST as soon as we have opened the *Comédie humaine*, we come across this sentence in the *Avant-Propos:* "I write in the light of two eternal verities, Religion and the Monarchy." How now, what's this? we cry. Two such different values on exactly the same footing? Though it is true that Balzac speaks of religion in more emphatic terms elsewhere. "The sublime Catholic religion" (*Vieille Fille*, p.260), "the sublime prayer of Catholics" (*César Birotteau*, p.534), "the sublime and divine idea of the Catholic communion" (*Médecin de Campagne*, p.438), or, speaking of a plaster figure of the Virgin Mary: this "sublime token" (*id.* p.324). But all that sublimity doesn't reassure me. Is sublime the word that a genuine Catholic would use?

We will discount the wicked Abbé Gudin in *les Chouans*, the pious and odious Mlle Gamard in *le Curé de Tours*, and also that good but very stupid Abbé Birotteau. Where would we be, after all, if the novelist was only allowed to show us religious women and Abbés worthy of haloes? But in *la Duchesse de Langeais* there is even worse in store. This Mme de Langeais, it will be remembered, in order to avoid yielding to the attentions of Montriveau, conjures up "the terrors of religion . . . Death seemed to her preferable to a criminal happiness" (*Duchesse de Langeais*, p.185). Very laudable sentiments indeed, you will say. Yes, but Balzac condemns her outright: she was a depraved woman, he tells us. A horrible coquette, an imbecile, a titled courtesan (*id.* pp. 184, 192, 199). She goes to her confessor for help. "That Abbé of yours turns my stomach," Montriveau tells her. "Either you stop going to confession or I shan't set foot here again" (*id.* pp. 184 and 188).

Even then, it may be objected that the example is a bad one, that Mme de Langeais' piety is in fact a somewhat doubtful quantity, and that Montriveau, who is a good liberal, could scarcely be expected to take any other attitude. Very well, let it pass then. Let us move on instead to *Une Double Famille*. The intensity of Mme de Granville's piety forces her to decorate her house in only the very darkest colors. Her husband grows tired of the gloom and goes off to furnish an apartment in much lighter shades for a little working girl. In this struggle between the Henri III dower chest and the Louis XV commode, who is in the wrong? For Balzac, the wife. Everything in the text tends to condemn Mme de Granville and excuse her husband. "Granville abandoned his own house where everything was becoming intolerable to him . . . He at least saved his sons from that hell" (*Double Famille*, p.976). That hell? A woman who never thinks of anything but making herself worthy of paradise? I am aware, of course, that Mme de Granville is stupid and ungracious. And that these are not qualities necessarily enjoined by the Catholic religion. But though some of her demands may be ridiculous, there are others that are legitimate. Yet Balzac makes no distinctions between them. On Fridays, she fasts: she is wrong. She has hung a crucifix over her bed: that's odious. She brings her daughters up to be believers: that's stupid (*Fille d'Eve*, pp. 63 to 65). But to be honest, which of them is the more intolerant? The excessively cantankerous wife, or the husband who objects to the crucifix? And here again, though even more seriously, the influence of the confessor is called into question: Mme de Granville doesn't become really impossible until after she finds the Abbé Fontanon again.

Those are only two examples. We can immediately put our finger on others that contradict them. Beside the possibly hypocritical society beauty and the indubitably clumsy wife, here are the Baronne Hulot, Mme Birotteau, Mme Graslin, Mme de Mortsauf, Mme de la Chanterie. All women whose religious beliefs produce excellent results. Balzac speaks of them all with infinite respect. Faced with Mme Hulot, even a bounder like Crevel is "dazzled, dumbfounded" (*Cousine Bette*, p.405). And after having, apparently, condemned the interference of confessors in marital affairs, Balzac shows us Mme Claës receiving a great deal of spiritual comfort from hers (*Recherche de l'Absolu*). While in *la Muse du Département*, he laments the fact that Mme de la Baudraye does not have the good Abbé Duret there to help her.

It should be noted, however, that none of these women is in exactly the same situation as Mme de Granville. Mme Graslin and Mme de la Chanterie are both widows, while the lecherous habits of the Baron Hulot and the delicate health of M. de la Baudraye have reduced their wives also to a kind of celibacy. As for Mmes de Mortsauf, Claës and Birotteau, though they are all deeply religious, it is with the approval of their husbands. The true nature of Mme de Granville's "crime" is now, I think, apparent: her religious beliefs are infringing the laws of marriage. Mme de Granville has ignored one of the most important circumstances in her particular situation: her husband. Her religion is therefore in opposition to her environment; so Balzac condemns her. Whereas Mme Hulot's religion not only does not bring her into conflict with her husband but actually turns her into a sort of super-wife, a total wife, who finds in the purity of her Catholic faith yet one more reason far accepting the laws of the conjugal state, even including the Baron's infidelities: "I am your wife and not your judge . . . I shall always be useful to you in some way, even if it is only by sparing you the expense of hiring a servant" (*Cousine Bette*, p.430).

There is no need for me to point out how far this Catholicism is from being truly Catholic. To regard religious faith as merely a contributory factor to a happy marriage is scarcely any better than regarding it as merely a contributory factor to political stability. Though it is true that *Une Double Famille* appeared in 1830 and *la Duchesse de Langeais* in 1834. They are therefore both early works. And it is well known that Balzac's attitude to Catholicism developed during the course of his career from a vague hostility at the beginning to a fairly emphatic adherence, though perhaps not a very deep one, at the end (on this subject, see *Balzac et la Religion* by the Abbé Philippe Bertault). This development is perceptible in his work. Though on the question of the priest's influence on home life he does not ever seem to have changed his mind. In one of his very last works (*Petits Bourgeois*, p.211), we still find Félix Phellion saying: "Nothing is more deadly . . . believe me, than the interference of priests in marital affairs." On this point, the authoritarian always maintained an ascendancy over the Christian.

Apart from this one particular point, however, it will be noted that almost all the "sympathetic" characters in the *Comédie humaine* are practicing Christians.

César Birotteau's death is an apotheosis in which he is borne aloft in the combined embrace of Commercial Probity and Religious Fervor. And there is another apotheosis at the end of *le Curé de Village*, in which Mme Graslin, torn from her adultery by force, toils slowly up the hard path that leads her from repentance to a hair-shirt, and finally attains saintliness. Mme de la Chanterie and Mme de Mortsauf we already know well enough. The Abbé Bertault, in his book mentioned above, is rather hard on Mme de Mortsauf. A true Christian, he says, would have sent Félix away right at the start. The Abbé Bertault is certainly more qualified to pass judgment in this matter than I am; but I'm afraid I persist in finding a great deal of merit in Mme de Mortsauf all the same. Then there is the honest Savarus: he goes every morning to hear Mass. Mlle d'Esgrignon too. Eugénie Grandet is a pious girl, just like her mamma. And then there is Ursule Mirouët, glowing like a gentle alabaster lamp, lit from within by prayers and her unfailing attendance at Communion. And Benassis. And the good Alain. Then another great soul, another being lit from within by his own goodness: the water-carrier Bourgeat in *la Messe de l'Athée*. He too is a practicing Catholic, and has a particular devotion to the Virgin Mary. On the other hand, we have Desplein, the atheist. He is a man of eminence; but in Balzac's eulogy of him there is one reservation: "Perhaps (his) talent was all of a piece with his beliefs, and consequently deadly" (*Messe de l'Athée*, p.1149). And it is possible that their indifference in religious matters is one of the reasons for the secret disgrace that, according to Balzac, hangs over all that tribe of middle-class liberals, the Camusots, the Cardots, the Matifats and their ilk. "What is the origin of this hidden sickness?—Lack of religious beliefs" (*Cousine Bette*, p.501).

It has often been pointed out that though the Catholic "foundations" of Balzac's characters are solid enough, all his attempts at expressing religious enthusiasm or sublimity tend to smack of a rather suspect illuminism. This is possibly true. But those are regions into which I think it would be unwise for me to venture. It has also been said that he had very little sense of sin. Here I must express surprise. What does the entire story of *le Curé de Village* rest on, if not a sense of sin? Is there no sense of sin in the long expiation undergone by Benassis, or in the terrible punishments, quite evidently proceeding from the hand of God, with which Balzac overwhelms several of his characters, from the Polish plait of Bourlac's daughter to the explosion that disfigures Rosalie de Watteville? Needless to say, there is no sense of sin to be found in a Mme de Maufrigneuse or in a Henri de Marsay. How can Balzac be expected to describe what isn't there? Should he have broken off for a moment in order to exclaim: "Oh heavens, what a pity that Mme de Maufrigneuse has no sense of sin!"? Up to a certain point, the true novelist must identify with his characters. When he is writing about worldly people, Balzac becomes a worldly person. And a man-about-town when describing men-about-town. Marsay never gives God a thought. Therefore Balzac can't give God a thought either, when writing about Marsay. Nor is their any reason why he should smuggle in between the lines a presence who does not exist in the reality he is describing, or underline for his readers an absence to which Marsay himself certainly never paid the slightest attention. Doubtless this absence, this void, this gap would have been emphasized by a Bernanos or a Mauriac. But Balzac isn't Bernanos. There is nothing of the Catholic novelist about him at all. God exists. God rewards and punishes. Balzac indicates these facts. But what really interests him is something quite different. Not man's relations with God but their relations with other men. Man as a social animal. Man's life here on earth.

We should also note, in passing, the amazing number of conversions to be found in the *Comédie humaine.* Doctor Minoret, his nephew, Mme Graslin, Esther, Benassis, Valérie Marneffe, Mlle de Watteville, Savarus, Mlle des Touches, Dinah Piedefer, Melmoth, Castanier, the Brothers of Consolation—all of these are converts (taking the word in its widest sense, that is, and including conversion from indifferent or tepid religious attitudes to a more fervent form of belief). The causes of these conversions are various: emotional disasters, remorse, imminent death, fear of the devil, even simple ambition (Dinah Piedefer).

The churchmen

There are numerous members of the Church to be found in the *Comédie humaine.* At a quick glance, I would say there are certainly a good forty. Is this abundance of cassocks an argument in favor of Balzac's Catholicism? I think not. Of Stendhal's three leading male characters created during the same period (Julien Sorel, Fabrice del Dongo and Lucien Leuwen), one is a seminarist and another a priest. Yet no one is likely to call Stendhal a Catholic novelist.

Julien and Fabrice, however, occur in stories that are set between 1815 and 1830. Both have dreamed of galloping across Europe in the wake of Napoleon and arrived too late to do so. They turn to the Church, not because they feel a religious vocation, but because it is the Church that has, in a sense, replaced Napoleon. They are living in an age when the Church is triumphant, when it is the great power. And it is also a power that has retained something secret, something intimate and cloaked about it. In other words, we are back once more with two of Balzac's favorite themes. For a man like him, a man who doesn't like simple-minded cavalry officers, who prefers the devious approach, the tortuous mind, how tempting it must have been, the opportunity to evoke, behind the visible power, that other, invisible power that extends from the secret councils of the Vatican to the secret counsels of the confessional!

It may be imagined with what delight Balzac set about augmenting the power of the Church and also its secrecy. In *le Curé de Tours,* for example, it seems to me that Birotteau, since he is in the right and has powerful patrons, should have won the day. In order to ensure his defeat, Balzac makes Troubert into the man of the Congregations, the "anonymous proconsul of the Touraine. Archbishop, General, Prefect, the great and the humble alike were all under his arcane dominion" (*Curé de Tours*, p.834). Similarly, in order to justify the marriage of a Mlle Piedefer to a Baudayer (*Muse du Département*), the social position achieved by Rubempré (*Splendeurs et Misères*), and Baudoyer's successful career (*les Employés*), Balzac again turns to the Church for aid, in one case invoking the power of a kindly Archbishop, in the other two that of the Grande Aumônerie. In fact, of course, the second two examples are fraudulent. The Grande Aumônerie has no interest whatever in either Rubempré or Baudoyer. But Balzac deplores this fact. "Unfortunately," he writes, "its influence was wielded neither by a Cardinal de Richelieu nor a Cardinal Mazarin" (*Employés*, p.1037). Richelieu and Mazarin. They, quite obviously, are the kind of churchmen that Balzac likes, the statesman-prelate, the priest whose breviary is the works of Machiavelli, who conceals beneath the folds of his scarlet robe not only the Church's omnipotence and unction, but also its discretion and its mystery. It is certainly not by chance, for instance, that he chooses the cassock as a disguise for Vautrin, that perfect incarnation of the will to power. Nor is it by chance that of all the politicians who emerged from the Revolution he admires only Talleyrand and Fouché, the two unfrocked priests. "As unfathomable as a monk, as silent as a Benedictine, as wily as a priest," he says of another unfrocked ecclesiastic, his Grégoire Rigou in *les Paysans*.

I have already mentioned Troubert, the odious vicar-general in *le Curé de Tours*. His activities in that book amount to no more than the sordid eviction of a tenant from an apartment. Yet we must not judge him too hastily. "There is no doubt," Balzac himself writes, "that Troubert would have been a Hildebrandt or an Alexander VI had he lived in another age . . . The apparent egoism of men whose hearts are entirely devoted to a science, to a nation, or to the law should perhaps be regarded as the most noble of the passions . . . In order to give birth to new peoples or to produce new ideas, are they not obliged to unite within their powerful minds the breasts of the woman and the energies of God? The life stories of the Innocent III's, and the Peter the Greats and all such leaders of ages or nations, though on a higher plane, are the examples that convey, should comparisons be necessary, the vast scope of thought that Troubert represented in the seclusion of the cloisters of Saint-Gatien" (*Curé de Tours*, p.846). Now I'd like you, if you would, to reread that amazing sentence.

Do you perceive a single term in it that has any connection at all with religion? It is entirely concerned with the will to power. God is mentioned, but only just, and only as being a source of energy and as a sort of stepping-stone. A stepping-stone of which Troubert makes use with signal success. He becomes a bishop (*Député d'Arcis*, p.70), just as another churchman, Marsay's tutor Abbé de Maronis, becomes a bishop. If we are to judge the tree by its fruits, what ought we to think of a tutor whose pupil develops into such an ungodly monster? It is true of course that this Abbé used very individual educational methods, that he took his pupil "extremely rarely into churches" but "occasionally backstage in theaters and rather more often to visit courtesans" (*Fille aux Yeux d'Or*, p.271). This is what Balzac terms "providing a virile replacement for his mother." And then, quite seriously, he adds: "Is the Church not the mother of all orphans?" "This corrupt but politic priest," he also says, "an unbeliever but extremely learned, treacherous but likeable . . . was of such genuine use to his pupil, so ready to condone his vices . . ." (*id.* p.271). And Balzac says this approvingly! He practically shouts his enthusiasm—though not, I imagine, without a touch of wilful provocation. "A true priest, an admirable example of the type of man whose genius will save the Catholic, Apostolic and Roman Church." (Here again, mark you, we are dealing with one of Balzac's early works.)

There are, of course, other, and more edifying, examples of the priestly profession in the *Comédie humaine*. Even in them, however, we still find the same will to power, or rather the awareness, the consciousness of being a power, or of representing a power. And nowhere, I think, does this power show itself so forcefully as in *le Curé de Village*. From her cradle to her grave, Mme Graslin is led every step of the way by priests, by the Church. Her adultery estranges her from it for a moment. But then her lover's crime leads her back onto the right path. And the Church alone sees clearly in this whole affair. Where the police and the legal profession break their backs at the task in vain, the Church triumphs. It is the Church that guesses the name of the accomplice, that secures restitution of the stolen money. After Troubert and Maronis, what a relief to meet the Abbé Bonnet! He is a saint, this man, a true saint. And no fool either, not even God's. He has both feet firmly on the ground. At one point, he even transforms himself into an authority on economics and explains to Mme Graslin exactly the best way to run her estate. "There is an immense fortune . . . waiting there" (*Curé de Village*, p.654). Elsewhere, he ventures into the realm of politics, He praises Charles X's last measures, laments his departure, condemns the liberty of the press, deplores the system of deliberative assemblies, regrets the disappearance of the law of primogeniture, and finally expresses a desire for the advent of "a providential leader" (*id.* pp. 711 to 717).* And beside the Abbé Bonnet, the Abbé Dutheil, another saint. Though "without pride or ambition," he does have ambition for the Church. He would like "by means of certain concessions . . . to associate the Church with the interests of the people in order to help it win back . . . its former influence over the masses, which it could then link once again to the monarchy" (*id.* p.569). And as for the third priest involved in this affair, the Abbé de Rastignac, he is simply a becassocked counterpart of his brother Eugène, a pretty specimen of the staff-headquarters priest, solely concerned with his own advancement, as lost in a country parish as a pen-pushing army officer on garrison duty.

Another parish priest: the Abbé Brossette in *les Paysans*. An excellent churchman. Although of middle class birth and delicate health, he has accepted being buried away in a country village where the peasants make life very difficult for him. "One does not desert the cause of God any more than one does that of an Emperor" (*Paysans*, p.88). Even with him, however, one senses the perpetual concern with power. He deplores the blindness of the rich; but the reason he deplores it is above all because it is harmful to the social order. What he condemns is not the egoism of the rich but their inconsistency. "Egoism" is the word he himself uses, for example, when speaking of a certain landowner, rather a charitable one I should have thought, who is thoughtless enough, as the Abbé Brossette sees it, to allow his peasants to abuse their gleaning and woodgathering rights. "You are only the depositaries of the power conferred by wealth, and if you do not fulfil the obligations of your charge then you will not hand it on to your children as it came down to you. You are robbing your own descendants" (*id.* p.184). Where is the young man whom Jesus told to sell all his goods and give the proceeds to the poor? "A truly Catholic impulse of charity," Balzac cries. Where is the charity? "These people are simply trying to get a living at your expense," Brossette tells the landowners. "These people" being the peasants. "If your good works are not tempered with due consideration, you will run the risk of paying wages to your enemies" (*id.* pp. 73-76). Where is the divine folly of the Gospels in

---

* Which does not prevent him from saying elsewhere: "There are some men who find it possible to regard the priesthood as a means of regenerating our country; but, in the light of my feeble understanding, the patriot priest is a contradiction in terms" (*id.* p. 625).

all this? The Abbé Brossette's words are the words of a man, not those of a priest. "Your enemies." Is this Christ's teaching? It is not a star the Abbé Brossette sees rising in the East, it is the class struggle.

We meet Brossette again in the latter part of *Béatrix*, where he gives the Duchesse de Grandlieu the benefit of some advice in which concern for the attitudes of Society is far more prominent than the rigors of Christian morality. At this time, Balzac writes, he was "one of the most distinguished members of the Parisian clergy . . . Two dark eyes, burning with faith, but softened by an expression more mysterious than mystical, lit up his apostle's face" (*Béatrix*, p.570). I hope you don't mind my calling your attention to that "more mysterious than mystical."

In the case of the Abbé Gudin, in *les Chouans*, politics has devoured everything else. He is the soldier-priest, the partisan-priest—in short, no longer a priest at all. And the Abbé de Sponde in *la Vieille Fille*, excellent man though he is, has been contaminated too. He leads an ascetic life, all prayer, alms and mortifications (*Vieille Fille*, p.258); but that does not prevent him from playing his part in the cruel ostracism inflicted on the poor Abbé François, who is a saint, but who has sworn allegiance to the wrong leader. Their piety should unite them. They are divided by politics.

With the Abbé Fontanon, in *Une Double Famille*, we are back with the will to power in its crude state. He is a black crow, croaking out his anathemas, leading his flock in much the same way as Vautrin leads his gang of accomplices, and already foreshadowing the sooty ecclesiastics of Barbey d'Aurevilly.

There are also several abbés who are purely and simply good priests: the Abbé Loraux in *Honorine*, the Abbé Duplanty in *le Cousin Pons*, the Abbé de Vèze in *l'Envers de l'Histoire contemporaine*. But one has the feeling that this very modesty of theirs has done them a disservice in the eyes of their creator, for Balzac tells us very little about them and makes very sparing attempts to give them a third dimension. For that, we have to turn to the picturesque type of priest, the priest who's a good enough fellow but plagued with one or two little eccentricities. Example: Birotteau in *le Curé de Tours*, who is an old bachelor more than he is a priest. (A fact that Balzac himself underlined, I might add, by classifying *le Curé de Tours* under the general heading *les Célibataires*.) For how is he shown to us, old Birotteau? In his slippers, not in his chasuble. Not that I wish to imply that he is in any way a bad priest. We discover later on that he has even had his moment of heroism; that he has lived the hunted life of the non-juring priest. But the residential tragedy that earns him the right to a novella of his own is the tragedy of an old bachelor, not that of a priest. With Birotteau and his friend Chapeloud, we have stumbled into that amiable fraternity of ecclesiastics who are partial to their game of *wisk* in the evenings. The Abbé Cruchot in *Eugénie Grandet* is another member of that fraternity, as is the Abbé de Quélus in *le Lys dans la Vallée*. Ah, the virtue of a well-chosen name! The Abbé de Quélus is never described, but thanks to his name we can see him all the same, affable, white haired, speaking very little, but always to the point. And I would even say the same of Mgr. de Persépolis, of whom we catch a glimpse at the end of *le Bal de Sceaux*.

There are also two or three bishops. The only one who is at all memorable is the Bishop of Limoges in *le Curé de Village*. There's a charming scene there, delicately presented behind a gauze of ecclesiastical finesse, I don't know if you remember it, in which, one beautiful clear evening, the Bishop and his intimates see from a distance the lights that reveal to them the secret of the Tascheron affair (*Curé de Village*, p.594).

Balzac's churchmen, as you will have realized, are more the active than the contemplative kind. Consequently you will not find any monks in the *Comédie Humaine*, with the one exception of Albert Savarus, who is driven into a convent by his despair. There are rather more nuns, however. *La Duchesse de Langeais* involves a visit to a Spanish convent, and the *Mémoires de deux Jeunes Mariées* includes a few reminiscences of a convent school for young ladies. Moreover, Félicité des Touches also goes into a convent, as does her cousin, the eldest Grandlieu girl, and her aunt Faucombe. In *Un Episode sous la Terreur*, we see two bewildered, terrified nuns who have been abruptly ejected into the world by the Revolution. They are Sister Agathe de Langeais and Sister Marthe de Beauséant.

CHAPTER 19

Balzac's View
of Politics

*Technique of the coup d'état—willful extremism—the
theme of the leader—Benassis—The parliamentary
system—the liberals.*

THERE EXISTS in the *Comédie humaine*, very clearly drawn, a blueprint
for a coup d'état: Marsay's letter to Manerville in *le Contrat de Mariage*.

Henri de Marsay wants to seize power. What means does he contemplate using to achieve this end? Riots? No. Elections? No. Assassination?
Stirring the masses to an uprising against a tyrant? Nothing could be further from his thoughts. And in any case, he himself writes: "Personal
preferences in the matter of who is actually king are nothing more these
days than sentimental stupidity" (*Contrat de Mariage*, p.200). Is he relying on propaganda, on a political doctrine? Marsay has no doctrine. There
is nothing he believes in. "The softhead party" is his own term for the
liberal party of which he is a member. The whole business, as far as he is
concerned, consists quite simply in bringing together a number of men
with clear heads and strong wills. It is not a technique of revolution but of
conspiracy, of the coup d'état.

If this is how power is won, how is it to be kept? Again, by conspiracy,
by the use of ruses and maneuvers borrowed from the arsenal of the political plot. And Balzac triumphantly quotes this phrase of Casimir Périer's:
"All power is a permanent conspiracy."

It should be noted that Balzac has no a priori repugnance to violence in
itself. He is not, he tells us, one of those "hypocritical writers ready to
shed tears over two hundred rogues killed for the right reason" (*Sur
Catherine de Médicis*, p.17). To the sacred right of rebellion he adds the
sacred right of repression. This is a subject he deals with in his preface to
Sur Catherine de Médicis. Nevertheless, if violence is not necessary he
would always prefer some more cunning method, and if his Catherine is a

"great and magnificent figure" it is because she constantly employed such methods. Similarly, of all the politicians of his own age, the two he mentions most frequently are Talleyrand and Fouché. Always, be it added, with the utmost admiration. They are, in his eyes, "the only two great politicians that the Revolution produced" (*Splendeurs,* p.754). Marsay adds: Talleyrand is "one of the most extraordinary men of our time" (*Ténébreuse Affaire,* p.632). And here again, these two favorites of Balzac's are both outstanding for their cunning; they are both men who follow the dictates of intelligence alone, of intelligence never fettered by an excess of loyalty or an excess of scruples. And what is more, one is a diplomat and the other a policeman, with everything that those professions imply, for Balzac, in the way of cunning, trickery, secrecy, cloaked figures and secret files. It is still the theme of invisible power. Malin de Gondreville is made after their image. Less brilliant than Talleyrand, shrewder than Fouché, entirely without superfluous grudges or useless scruples, he rises to the top under every regime. And the fact that politicians of this kind scarcely ever have any place in the affections of the people, the fact that neither Talleyrand nor Fouché was ever a popular figure is for Balzac only one more reason for regarding them with esteem. Popularity is merely another form of the appeal to the masses that Balzac so frequently condemns. (And throughout this chapter we must never lose sight of how much in Balzac's work, and in his political ideas particularly, must be recognized as being largely a matter of deliberate provocation, of defiance, or even of simply laughing up his sleeve. Every strong temperament has a tendency to oppose the thought of its age. The age one lives in is exasperating, by definition. Even the sanest and soundest ideas, when they become the property of everyone, and therefore of the imbeciles as well, become infected with an aura of stupidity. At the time when Balzac was writing, stupidity happened to be wearing its middle class, liberal, democratic face. So Balzac felt a revulsion against these things. It was only natural. Just as he felt a revulsion from the "jesuitical" ideas of Mme de Langeais, ideas that were expressed in a novel written still in the shadow of the reign of Charles X. When he writes a eulogy of Fouché or of absolutism, when he talks about those "two hundred rogues killed for the right reason," I picture him snickering behind his coffee pot, jubilant at the thought of people's faces as they read it. And then there is that mysterious law, so inexplicable and yet so constant, that turns almost all writers into extremists as soon as they venture in politics. They seem to like to go too far. They are attracted by the bold and clearcut. Does all this really matter? Since when did the political opinions of novelists become so serious a consideration? Perhaps you are right. If I have digressed here on the subject of Balzac's it is solely because they give us a valuable insight into the way his mind works.)

For us, the word politics—regardless of our preferences in that sphere—immediately conjures up the idea of a party, elections, polling booths or riots, processions, murmuring crowds, the sound of multitudinous feet. For Balzac, it conjures up simply the image of one man or a few men, the group, the clique. The March on Rome, the Ten Days in October, or just a local election campaign, whatever the precise context involved, politics for us is fundamentally and invariably a matter of numbers. For Balzac, it is the leader. Marsay wants to overthrow the existing régime. To whom does he turn for his aid? To the embittered, to the martyrs, to the dreamers in their attics or to the angry students? Oh no! Look at his list. There is Ronquerolles, who is already a cabinet minister; Sérizy, who is already a Councilor of State; Montriveau, who is already a lieutenant-general; Martial de la Roche-Hugon, who is already a peer of France; Granville, who is one of the most highly placed magistrates in the country; and the Grandlieus, who are already "admirably in favor at Court." And this is in 1828. Two years before their revolution all these conspirators are already people in very high positions. A conspiracy yes, but a conspiracy of leaders. Something like the Communist cell. It is a question of infiltrating the corridors of power, then taking advantage of the first opportunity to sweep aside all their opponents. "We are Ronquerolles, Montriveau, etc. We wish to overthrow the two Vandenesses, the Dukes of Lenoncourt, Navarreins, etc." (*Contrat de Mariage*, p.200). Leaders versus leaders. The control of the State being fought for by two cliques already in the arena. Where does the consent of the people enter into a contest of that sort? Where is the need even to exploit it, or rig it? Marsay and his friends do of course take advantage of the riots of 1830. But only because those riots happen to be the opportunity they are waiting for. It could equally well have been an assassination they took advantage of; or a change of royal mistress; or a foreign invasion. It is a revolution at the top. An insurrection; but in the sphere of power. The barricades go up; but only in the corridors of the ministries. It is a revolution the masses only know about from the posters that go up afterwards. It is the Mayor of the Palace seizing the throne. Or the Prince-President seizing power in 1851. It is also, if you like, though minus the war, Marshal Pétain in 1940, the other Fascist leaders against Mussolini in 1943, the generals against Hitler in 1944.

Balzac explains this technique of the coup d'état: he does not say that he approves of it. But, on the other hand, he is unstinting in his admiration of Doctor Benassis, who shares all Marsay's views in this sphere. "In my opinion," he says, "a man who has conceived a political system ought, if he feels he has the strength to apply it, to remain silent, to seize power, and to put it into effect" (*Médecin de Campagne*, p.439). To remain silent: always the same secrecy. Seize power: the conspiracy. Put it into effect: the authoritarian. And according to this same Benassis, power is the more perfect "the more restricted the privilege it has been established to defend," the word privilege signifying here "the social circle within which the developments of power are enclosed." Leaders against leaders. Not the people against the tyrant, not the liberals against the legitimists, but Marsay against Vandenesse. Extend this privilege, Benassis goes on, and "you will have enlarged the wound of social inequalities." Extend it to everyone and you will have "suffrage extended without any limitation to the masses. Voting implies choice and preliminary disputation. There is no such thing as disputed power."

Note that Benassis is presented to us as the benefactor and the Providence of his district. It would be unjust to regard him as a man who does not love the people. But there are two ways of loving the people: like a much-cherished mistress whose every wish must be respected, or like a child whose caprices one disregards. Why would a father who is confident in his system of education, or an authoritarian ruler who is confident in his program, waste his time seeking approval for his actions? And the approval of whom? Of the children? Of the masses? For Benassis, children and masses, it's all the same thing. "The proletariat," he says, "seem to me to be the minors of any nation, and should always remain the wards of the state." Balzac elaborates on this: the masses are "unintelligent, only clever at understanding disorder" (*Employés*, p.980). The workers, "those grown up children," he says elsewhere (*Interdiction*, p.24). He praises Napoleon for having, in 1814, "chosen to risk his own downfall rather than arm the masses" (*Paysans*, p.21). He blames the chouans for not having foreseen the "danger of stirring up the scarcely civilized masses" (*Chouans*, p.779). Obviously, then, he is politically impartial in this matter. Whether it is used in support of the right or in support of the left, power in the hands of the masses appears to him as invariably harmful.

Let us therefore beware, he continues, of "that stupid collective love that ought to be called *humanitareism*" (*Employés*, p.928). Equality is a joke. "Equality may perhaps be a *right*, but no power on earth can ever turn it into a *fact*" (*Duchesse de Langeais*, p.145). "And does not education, if equally and unrestrictedly dispensed to the masses, lead these days to the son of a minister's concierge giving his opinions on the career of the man of merit, or on the life of the great landowner in whose house his father was once a doorkeeper?" (les Employés, p.875). And what are the invisible mental connections that so often result in a contempt for women being accompanied by a certain contempt for the people? I have no idea; but those connections do exist. Or they exist in Balzac and in Marsay at any rate. Europe capable of thought? "It is a thing impossible for the masses, for nations, and for women" (Physiologie du Mariage, p.742). "For the woman who loves him, a man should be a being full of strength and grandeur, always imposing. The family cannot exist without despotism. Nations, remember that!" (id. p.686). "Peoples, like women . . ." (Duchesse de Langeais, p.146). Marsay—who is of course a leader of the liberals—reasons in just the same way. "What is woman?" he asks. "A little thing, a collection of fatuities" (Fille aux Yeux d'Or, p.286). And corresponding to this contempt for women there is "his hatred of the masses" (Fille d'Eve, p.129).

Given these conditions, given that the majority is composed solely of "the fools, the envious, etc.," what possible value could there be in the representation of that majority in parliament? None, needless to say. It is "the falsest, the most fickle, the most oppressive" power there is (Vieille Fille, p.319). "The power of all takes no one at all into account, the power of one man is obliged to take all its subjects into account" (Sur Catherine, p.17). "A nation that has two houses of representatives and a woman who listens with two ears are both heading for disaster" (Illustre Gaudissart, p.13). "To place one's trust in an assembly of any sort, even one composed of honest men, is madness," cries the Abbé Bonnet "in an excess of divine patriotism" (Curé de Village, pp. 710-721). And Balzac himself, in his Avant-Propos (p.9): "Without being an enemy of the election, which is an excellent principle for the drawing up of laws, I reject the notion of election as the only governing principle of society, and above all when the electoral system is as badly organized as it is today . . . The election, applied in every field, gives us government by the masses, the only form of government that has no responsibilities and of which the tyranny is unrestricted."

How could it be otherwise, when parliament represents only a majority "of fools" and a public opinion that is "often stupid" (Curé de Village, p.594)? "The more faithfully the assembly represents the opinions of the crowd, the less it will be in agreement with Government, the less far-sighted its views will be, the less clearcut and the more vacillating its legislation will be . . . How can this notion, that five hundred men collected

together from all corners of the Empire will produce good laws, be anything but a bad joke?" (*Médecin de Campagne*, p.433). Moreover, does
parliament even represent the people in the first place? In *le Député d'Arcis*, it was Balzac's intention to give us a detailed picture of an election in
the reign of Louis-Philippe. The work was unfortunately never finished.
But it is evident, even from the beginning we have, that the will of the
people in this affair is going to be directed into some rather unlikely channels (Stendhal shows us the same process in *Lucien Leuwen*). Balzac's
criticism in this matter thus takes two quite different forms. Firstly, the
electoral system is bad because it represents the majority; secondly, it is
bad because it does not represent it. Such contradictions are frequent in
polemics. But this one serves to prove that Balzac's hostility to elections
was total.

Nor has Balzac much good to say for what he considers to be the results
of the electoral system, or those of the liberalism that spawned it. "The
product of free choice, of religious liberty and of political liberty . . . is
the France of today . . . a country exclusively concerned with material
interests, without patriotism, without a conscience, in which the governing power is powerless, in which Election . . . bestows office only on
mediocrities, in which brute force has become the necessary antidote to
popular violence, and in which the principle of debate, extended even to
the smallest matters, is stifling all powers of action in the body politic; in
which money is the governing factor in all questions, and in which indi-
vidualism, that horrible product of the progressive division of inheritances
that is destroying the family unit, will eventually devour everything, even
the nation itself, which will finally be so sapped by egoism that it will lie
entirely at the mercy of a foreign invasion. People will say to themselves:
why not the Czar?" (*Sur Catherine*, p.18). "*Man the social animal . . .
ought not to profess the dogma of liberty of conscience, or possess political liberty. But, since no society can exist without guarantees to the subjects against the sovereign, the subjects are therefore allowed *liberties* curtailed by certain restrictions" (*id.* p.181).

Erroneous in principle, baneful in its results, the parliamentary system
appears to Balzac above all absurd in its methods. Time and time again, he
condemns the notion of debate, not only in public life but in private life as
well. "There is no kind of choice between alternatives that cannot be
made in a moment. Whatever one does, the moment of decision must
come. The longer the conflict one permits between the reasons for and the
reasons against, the less sound the verdict will be" (*Employés*, p.873). Still
the mystique of power. Speed is an essential element of the authoritarian

technique. Better a bad decision than no decision at all. It is also a military
principle. "All political activity is incompatible with permanent debate"
(*Sur Catherine*, p.20). In *la Rabouilleuse*, (p.872), Balzac gives a verbatim
account of an idiotic conversation. "This discussion," he then says,
"which is the image of all human discussions . . ." Debate and discussion
are founded on a belief in the existence of perfect solutions. It is a belief
that Balzac rejects. "The human race is not situated, socially speaking,
between the good and the bad but between the bad and the worse" (*Physiologie du Mariage*, p.890). This being so, the best solution is always, quite
simply, the quickest. From which it necessarily follows that one leader is
better than three hundred. "The magnificent rule of one man," sighs
d'Arthez (*Secrets de la Princesse de Cadignan*, p.31). "A despot would do
it tomorrow," Balzac himself wrote in an article advocating a reorganization of the literary profession.* Look at England, Gérard says in *le Curé
de Village* (p.718), "everything concerning the action of the government,
everything to do with the choice of men or means is so swift." But also
"the elections are not in the hands of the stupid middle classes," and debate is used only as "a political comedy intended to satisfy the people and
mask the government's actions." That is the only use that Balzac will allow to deliberative assemblies: to be a sideshow, a diversion. "It is a measure of the highest diplomacy to silence a nation by throwing it a bone to
chew" (*Physiologie du Mariage*, p.742).

Since the masses are mere children, their representation in parliament
therefore valueless, and all forms of debate in any case pernicious, simply
because discussion is pernicious by definition, what are we left with? The
leader. His the decisions. And his, too, the responsibility. Or rather: the
leaders. For here too, Balzac remains faithful to the mystique of the group.
The dictator is alone. Balzac, as we have seen, fears and condemns solitude. He admires Napoleon (though not without reservations), and he
allows his Abbé Bonnet to cry out for "a providential leader." But nevertheless—though I don't think he ever said it in so many words—one feels
very definitely that his personal taste is for less personal forms of power;
that his own preference would go, not to Napoleon, but to Louis XVIII
and his cabinet, to Talleyrand and his collaborators, to Fouché and his
police, to Marsay and his gang. The solitary head of state appeals to him
less than the group, the clique, "the social circle within which the developments of power are enclosed" (*Médecin de Campagne*, p.440). A restricted circle, it goes without saying, and progressively more efficient as

* Pierre Descaves: *Le Président Balzac*.

it is more restricted. In *les Employés*, we find Balzac putting forward a plan for the reform of the administration. This plan is based above all on a reduction in the number of ministers and a similar reduction in the number of civil servants under them. It is within this restricted circle that policies are to be hammered out, within this restricted circle that what is good for the people will be decided, even if the people themselves disagree. I belong to that small number of men, the Duc de Chaulieu says, who wish to oppose the power of the people—in its own interest, needless to say (*Mémoires de deux Jeunes Mariées*, p.173). Similarly, Benassis says: "The legislator, gentlemen, should be superior to the age he lives in" (*Médecin de Campagne*). It is interesting to compare these remarks with those of Gandhi: "It is not enough to protest against the general opinion. It is necessary, in important questions, for the leaders to act contrary to the opinion of the masses, if that opinion does not appear to them to be reasonable" (*Young India*). Not that I am going to waste my time here drawing a parallel between Balzac and Gandhi. Though both had notions of what is "reasonable," those notions probably had very little in common. Both, however, do seem to work from the same principle: that the leader, whether by divine right, through prayer, or because of his superior intelligence, knows better than the people what its true interests are, and that it may be the leader's duty to go against the wishes of the people.

Given these attitudes, it may be imagined what a small place the liberals hold in Balzac's affections. He inveighs against the "stupid discussions of the left" (*Employés*, p.888), he refers to that "ignoble and middle-class liberalism" (*Massimila Doni*, p.345), to the "duplicity of the liberals," to "that party of hypocrites" (*Rabouilleuse*, pp. 882 and 881). Issoudun is a loathsome town in his eyes. As is only understandable, considering it harbors all "those middle class, loose-tongued, ignorant liberals" (*id.* p.940). And we find that the antipathetic characters in the *Comédie humaine* are very often liberal in their views: du Croisier in *le Cabinet des Antiques*, the scurvy Vinet, the cretinous Rogron, the dishonest du Tillet, the loathsome Cérizet, the petty bourgeoisie of *les Paysans*. And the grotesque Crevel is another. He has "sucked at the breast of the Revolution" (*Cousine Bette*, p.508). This is only a tendency of course. Balzac would be but a dismal kind of novelist had he divided all his characters up neatly into nasty liberals and good legitimists. So there are also a few liberals with excellent, or at least sympathetic characters: Bianchon, Rabourdin, Pillerault, Athanase Granson. But even so, reservations often loom up before long. The liberal Rabourdin, for example, has opinions about how to run the Civil Service that are as non-liberal as opinions can possibly be. And

Athanase Granson's liberalism is depicted as really little more than adolescent mental acne. "He was unaware that at thirty-six . . . opinions are bound to change" (*Vieille Fille*, p.276). As for Pillerault, Balzac insinuates that his intelligence is by no means on the same level as his character: "He believed that his political freedom and standing were compromised by the Jesuits . . . He believed in all the republican virtues, he thought of Manuel as free from all excess, of General Foy as a great man, of La Fayette as a political prophet . . . In short, he was a victim of noble fantasies" (*César Birotteau*, p.404).

On the other hand, Balzac seems to have entertained a weakness for republicans: the charming Michel Chrestien in *les Illusions perdues*, old Niseron in *les Paysans*, or the elder Hulot. "Such men are the honor of the parties they have embraced. There was no one who did not come to pay homage to that noble virtue, to that immaculate probity, to that glory so entirely pure. It is not every man that the people will follow to his grave" (*Cousine Bette*, p.427). The last sentence is somewhat surprising, coming from Balzac's pen. But *Cousine Bette* is one of his last works. The partisan in him had calmed down. In the same novel (p.310), twenty years after his paean of praise to "the benefits of despotism" (*Ferragus*, p.114), he tells us: "despotism is the insanity of power."

I should also add that, just as Balzac sometimes presents us with a nice liberal, so he occasionally shows us a rotten or fatuous legitimist. The liberal journalists in *les Illusions perdues* are none of them worth the two bits for which they sell themselves, but their ultra colleagues are all tarred with exactly the same brush. In that particular case it is the entire profession that is being attacked. Elsewhere, we find the Duchesse de Langeais expressing views that are more or less those of Balzac. In her mouth, however, they become ridiculous. She produces nothing but a string of "stupidities, platitudes and pure nonsense" (*Duchesse de Langeais*, p.172). This is the victory of the novelist over the polemicist. (In the same way, Gaudissart is made to express farcical and ridiculous versions of ideas concerning the organization of energy that are substantially Balzac's own.)

CHAPTER 20

Law and the Police

Le Cabinet des Antiques—*absence of a legal mystique*
—appeal to divine justice—criticism of the law—the
magistrates: Granville, Blondet, Camusot, Popinot,
Bourlac—absence of a police mystique—Corentin,
Peyrade, Contenson.

IT IS always amusing to bring great men to life again. To attempt to work out what their reactions would have been to certain questions, or what side they would have taken in certain arguments that they did not live to see. Amusing. But risky too. There is no evidence that would permit us to say, for example, on which side Balzac would have been in the Dreyfus affair, had he lived fifty years later. That said, however, I don't think I'm really making an excessive claim when I say that the *Cabinet des Antiques* already provides us with a short of prefiguration of the Dreyfus affair.

I know, of course, that here there is no possible doubt about the defendant's guilt. Victurnien d'Esgrignon has indubitably committed a fraud. But for Balzac that is not the important point. The question for Balzac is whether or not it is worth meting out to the culprit a punishment that will dishonor the nobility and consequently undermine the established order of things. And that was what lay behind the Dreyfus affair too. If the whole of France was divided by that affair, it was because, above the captain himself, above the baying packs of anti-Semites and anti-militarists who became involved in the matter, there was taking place a confrontation between the two great principles that stir the minds of men: order and justice. There was a mystical belief in order that refused to allow the possibility of dishonoring the General Staff and threatening the established order, or France itself, for the sake of a single man—even an innocent one. And there was a mystical belief in justice that rejected the notion of an order based on injustice, or that was prepared to sacrifice that order to the supremacy of justice.

These two mystiques are to be found also in the debate between du

Croisier on the one hand and his wife and the lawyer Chesnel on the other. What does du Croisier say? "It is a question of letting these aristocratic gentlemen of yours know that there is a justice, that there are laws . . . Is it not a sacred mission to enlighten the people? That people will open its eyes . . . when it sees the aristocrats walking up into the dock just like Tom, Dick or Harry. And people will say to themselves that humble and honorable folk are better than great folk that dishonor themselves . . . Here I stand . . . the supporter of the laws" (*Cabinet des Antiques*, p.422). These are words that one would have supposed to be beyond reproach. But Balzac condemns them. Simple though they are, they appall not only Chesnel but even Mme du Croisier herself. They gave her, Balzac says, "a *horrible* insight into her husband's character" (*id.* p.422). All her own opinions have been "cruelly trampled" (*id.* p.424). And Balzac applauds her for betraying her husband in this affair and for acting, not according to her marriage bond, not in accordance with the mystique of justice, but in accordance with "her duties towards the Throne and the Altar" (*id.* p.427). Victurnien's fraud will go unpunished? What does that matter, provided the nobility, the foundation of a social order only so recently re-established, emerges safe and unharmed from this sudden danger? Was I wrong to evoke the Dreyfus affair? Though there is a slight difference: Balzac sacrifices no more than the punishment of a legal offender to his mystique of order. The anti-Dreyfus faction were prepared to sacrifice the life of an innocent man to theirs. That is a much more serious matter. But the principle remains the same.

It is above all in his conception of justice, it seems to me, that Balzac shows how far he was from having the democratic turn of mind. (Once more, there is nothing to indicate that Balzac would not have been entirely different had he been born a little later. In a chapter such as this, it is imperative that we never lose from sight one of his own key-phrases: "Everything is modified by events.") For the democrat, justice is a value in itself, sacred, absolute. For the authoritarian, on the contrary, it is no more than a weapon put into the hand of the Prince as a means of defending the order of his state. The power of justice cannot, in that case, extend beyond the limit set by that order. At the end of *Tartuffe*, the King's decision, which we hear announced with such relief, is, as far as one can tell, totally illegal. It is an action on the part of the Prince, nothing more. For the Catholic too, human justice must remain a very relative value. The punishments imposed by earthly courts can never be anything more than imperfect prefigurations of the true punishments to come: hell, the sentence of the supreme judge; remorse, the sentence of our own conscience; the reprobation of our peers, the sentence of a society in which moral values are both strong and undisputed. The democrat, on the other hand, is by definition mistrustful of the Prince. He therefore requires a justice that can outface that Prince. And since he approves of religious liberty, he is also forced to recognize that there is a certain number of citizens for whom a fear of hell is no longer a deterrent. Then, as the severity of people's consciences also diminishes, as the power of remorse wanes, as the effect of public reprobation loses its power, the democrat finds himself with no means left to check criminal activities in the state except that state's own courts. Hence the mystique of justice that is an essential characteristic of democracy, a mystique that has sunk so deeply by now into our minds that we have almost reached the point where we do not consider it possible for any action to be culpable that has not been specifically labeled as such by the law, and for which an officially formulated punishment is known to exist. If you go round saying that you have seen so-and-so making free with a shepherdess in a field, people will smile. But if you say that he has been convicted of indecency, those same people will shut their door in his face, or at least send their daughter up to her room when he calls. Instead of the reprobation of a moral society rejecting the offender, we have the fear of a conformist society rejecting the man condemned by the law. Similarly, remorse and the fear of hell have been replaced by an obsession with the police. Take the criminals we see in our films or our detective novels. Is it their consciences that are bothering them? Not at all, it's just a fear of the fuzz. Their guilty starts are not caused by *the still small voice of conscience*, but by the doorbell ringing. And though Nemesis still prowls after them, her name today is Maigret. And since all societies need to believe that no crime goes unpunished, since it is essential for democracy that the criminal should not escape the only kind of punishment it can still conceive of, the policeman inevitably assumes gigantic proportions. He is the God of Vengeance. He is infallible, because he must be so. He triumphs because it is necessary that he triumph. (Until such times as he is replaced in his turn—a development already looming on the horizon—by the blithe attitude of a neo-primitive society for which the criminal alone is in the right, a society that requires the criminal to win. See any number of recent detective novels.)

All these notions are notable in the *Comédie humaine* for their absence. Nowhere do we find the slightest hint of a mystique of justice. I mean, needless to say, of law-court justice, not of justice as a virtue. The law court kind of justice Balzac limits immediately by telling us that it must always, in any case, yield precedence to natural feelings. He praises Royer-

Collard for having "courageously" proclaimed this doctrine and for having stated, in particular, that the laws of hospitality automatically void the
binding power of a legal oath. (*Splendeurs*, p.991). Rubempré, when
questioned by representatives of the law, tells the truth, the whole truth
and nothing but the truth. Balzac condemns him. "Lucien had just ignored
. . . the law of solidarity . . . He had lost everything by his lack of
understanding . . ." (*id.* p.991). Tascheron, on the other hand, in *le Curé
de Village*, refuses to give the name of his accomplice. Balzac praises him.
And the Abbé Bonnet, in this same affair, refuses outright to aid the cause
of justice: he is presented to us as one of the noblest figures in the whole
Comédie Humaine. And his bishop has this comment to add: "We have no
fealty to human justice" (*Curé de Village*, pp. 599-633).

Having first set limits to the courtroom kind of justice in this way,
Balzac then takes pleasure in showing us into the bargain what very tenuous connections it in fact has with true justice. "Human justice," he
writes, "is a feeble reflection of divine justice, merely a pale imitation of it
applied to the needs of society" (*Curé de Village*, p.650). But there is
worse to come. Human justice does not always limit itself to being only a
pale imitation of divine justice or justice as a virtue: it is often the negation of it. Victurnien d'Esgrignon commits a fraud: the case is dismissed.
Sylvie Rogron murders Pierrette: that case is dismissed too. But in those
cases, at least the machinery of justice is actually set in motion. Even that
does not happen when du Tillet steals from Birotteau's till, or when Mme
Cibot robs cousin Pons. Vautrin, it is true, is finally arrested. But for the
one crime he did not in fact commit (Esther's death). Whereas he has
only to kill a policeman and the next day he is appointed Chief of Police.
In *l'Auberge Rouge*, there is another murder: the man convicted for it is
innocent. David Séchard and Mme de la Chanterie are both excellent human beings: they both go to prison. In *Une Ténébreuse Affaire*, the
Simeuses, the Hauteserres and Michu are all innocent: they are all convicted.

Even when there is no outright error, there is always a grave disproportion—so grave that it amounts to almost the same thing as injustice.
"Why," Vautrin asks, "why should it be two months in prison for the
dandy who, in the space of a night, despoils a child of half its fortune, and
the prison hulks for a poor devil who steals a thousand-face note?" (*Père
Goriot*, p.941).

And apart from the crimes that go unpunished, how many others that
evade the letter of the law! Philippe Bridau murders Max Gilet, his uncle
Rouget, then his own wife, in relentless succession; yet there is nothing

there on which the police could even begin to base a case. It is true that we do see Bridau in the dock. But he has been brought there, not by his crimes, but by that which is best in him: his loyalty to Napoleon. Nucingen ruins I don't know how many families. But none of that has anything to do with the law. And yet, Mme du Tillet says, "there are murders committed on the highroad that seem to me to be acts of charity when compared with certain financial combines" (*Fille d'Eve*, p.74). Franchessini kills young Taillefer in a duel: there is nothing the law can do to prevent him. "It is slow murder!" Vandenesse cries, referring to Mme de Mortsauf (*Lys dans la Vallée*, p.875). Where is the warrant for the murderer's arrest? Old Pons's heritage is descended upon by a pack of looters. There is a magistrate involved. He is the one who carries off the booty. De Trailles is openly called a murderer (*Gobseck*, p.647). Yet he is never involved in even the slightest difficulty with the law. "Oh, the weakness and the impotence of human justice," cries Vandenesse . . . "Why should it allot death and shame to the murderer who kills with a single blow? . . . Why does it allow a happy life and the esteem of his fellows to the murderer who pours his venom drop by drop into the soul and slowly saps the body with a determination to destroy it? How many murderers go unpunished! . . . What acquittal for the homicide brought about by moral persecution." (*Lys dans la Vallée*, p.995). Well, here is the opinion of two practicing members of the legal profession! "Justice is powerless," cries the barrister Derville (*Colonel Chabert*, p.1147). And Popinot, the model judge, speaking of unjustifiable applications for legal interdictions, adds: "We are accustomed to seeing these little plots . . . According to present day morality one is not dishonored by attempts of this kind; whereas we send a poor devil who has broken the pane of glass between him and a dish of gold straight off to the galleys" (*Interdiction*, p.57).

Indeed, one is fortunate when this law-court justice, the negation of true justice, does not actually become the instrument of crime, when it does not actually rush to the criminal's aid and furnish him with weapons. The eviction of the Abbé Birotteau in *le Curé de Tours*; the fleecing of Chabert; the theft of which David Séchard is a victim in *les Illusions perdues*; all these are examples of the pleasure Balzac takes in showing us a criminal justice, a justice that backs the aggressors and not the victims. Gobseck could have betrayed his trust. D'Espard and Octave de Camps could both have kept the fortunes stolen by their ancestors. The law would have been on their side. And when Ursule Mirouët is deprived of her inheritance, once more the law is on the side of those who rob her.

And even when it does happen to direct its powers against the real culprit, what good is it, this justice? Is it even efficient? Balzac says that it is not. Human law, he writes, "possesses neither the means of preventing crimes, nor the means of preventing their recurrence in the culprits it has already punished" (*Curé de Village*, p.651). Even when given a fresh scent to follow, is it efficient in its pursuit? Rarely. "Out of every hundred criminal cases, there are not ten the law really gets to the bottom of" (*Ténébreuse Affaire*, p.591). Has it any meaning? "The penal laws are made by people who have never known what misfortune is" (*Lys dans la Vallée*, p.823). "Ah! young man, only those who are wretched themselves can be judge of wretchedness in others." Here again, it is a member of the legal profession speaking, the former judge, Bourlac. And he confesses: "Formerly, I was too strict" (*Envers de l'Histoire contemporaine*, p.374). And in any case, Gobseck tells us, the law courts are an invention of the rich (*Gobseck*, p.633). The facts justify that opinion. Back from the tomb, Chabert asks nothing more than to recover possession of his own property. Is that too much to ask? Yes, it is too much. Penniless though he is, he is asked for "twelve or fifteen thousand francs" for expenses before the lawyer will even undertake the case (*Colonel Chabert*, p.1117). Is it surprising then, in view of all this, that we find no trace in the *Comédie humaine* of that feature so characteristic of contemporary conformist societies, the horror of the man who has been sentenced in a court of law? Tascheron is genuinely a murderer and indisputably a thief. Balzac writes of him with a sympathy not entirely devoid of admiration.

Ought we then to regard Balzac as one of those grimly snickering novelists who take pleasure in holding up to us the picture of an unjust, absurd world in which evil is always triumphant and virtue an invariable victim? Proust shows us Charlie Morel, once a kept man of the worst sort, transformed into an eminent and respected man. And he takes pleasure in showing us this picture. It is a development, one feels, that at the same time delights him and helps to complete his vision of the world. Balzac, on the other hand, never snickers. The world he shows us is cruel, but it is not absurd. He points out the injustices of that world unflinchingly, but far from delighting in them, he deplores them, he expresses indignation at them, and quite often he even indicates ways in which they could be avoided. If he depicts these things, it is because that is how things are. The novelist is not God the Father. He cannot, without indulging in sentimental inanity, take it upon himself to redress the errors of fate. He is not a prisoner of that strictly partial justice to be found in children's books, in which the naughty little boy must necessarily break his leg and the vain little girl must necessarily marry a "sporting type who beats her" (Vicomtesse de Pitray). It is simply, as I have already pointed out, that Balzac does not have any mystic belief in the power of human law. Being an authoritarian, he regards the law as no more than a weapon in the hands of order. Being a Catholic, he sees it as no more than a pale approximation of the true justice. But this true justice is present. Let us take another look at some of the criminals in the *Comédie humaine*. They escape the law courts. They do not escape punishment. Victurnien d'Esgrignon doesn't serve his six months in jail. But God makes up for this by sentencing him to six years in Alençon. Rosalie de Watteville is disfigured by an explosion. Minoret is racked by remorse. Bourlac is removed from office and his daughter is attacked by a frightful disease. Benassis once deserted a girl he had seduced: he pays for this with a whole lifetime of grief. Mme Marneffe dies in the most appalling agony. Rubempré commits suicide. Bridau is killed in Algeria. Justice does exist. Only it does not reside in the law courts; it resides in the will of God and in our own consciences. "Let us admit amongst ourselves, where social knavery is concerned, that the notion of legality would be a very fine but very hollow thing if God did not exist" (*Pierrette*, p.782).

Corresponding to this absence of faith in the justice of the law we also find, naturally enough, a total absence of faith in the judge and the police. Neither Granville nor Corentin is presented to us with that halo conventionally worn by the detective from Scotland Yard in our paperback detective novels. And yet, in *Splendeurs et Misères*, at the time of his interview with Vautrin, Granville, the attorney general, was introduced to us as the very embodiment of justice. I have already quoted the phrase: "These two men, CRIME and JUSTICE, stood face to face." But despite being the embodiment of justice, despite his right to the dignity of upper case, Granville is quite prepared to lower himself, in the very same work, to the extent of putting pressure on an examining magistrate, and finds it perfectly natural that an influential countess should use his office, the attorney general's office, to burn the incriminating documents in a criminal case. Furthermore, by a singular twist of fate, it is the embodiment of crime, the ex-convict Vautrin, who becomes the instrument of immanent justice. For it is Vautrin—and not a law court—who eventually repairs the judicial error committed in *l'Auberge Rouge* by instigating the death of young Taillefer, the unpunished murderer's son. It is Vautrin who avenges Mme de la Chanterie by throwing her informer of a son-in-law off a roof. Vautrin who avenges Nucingen's victims by stealing a nice fat sum off him. And we find Vautrin's hand too, or that of his henchmen, in the punishment of Valérie Marneffe. Vautrin the instrument of justice—that stroke should clear up any lingering doubts we may have had about the distinction that Balzac makes between human justice and divine justice.

There are also several other magistrates in the *Comédie humaine*. Camusot does not bear lingering over. He is simply compliance incarnate. The elder Blondet seems to have rather more integrity at first sight. But in *le Cabinet des Antiques* he deliberately confuses the d'Esgrignon case because his son's marriage depends on it. Popinot, on the other hand, is beyond reproach, and Bourlac too is conscientious. But when Popinot tries to conduct the d'Espard case according to the rules laid down by law, his superiors hurriedly take it out of his hands. As for Bourlac, it is his very conscientiousness in judicial matters that renders him responsible for Mme de la Chanterie's misfortune. A zealous judge, a too zealous judge; his old age is racked with remorse, and he ends up throwing himself at the feet of his former defendant (*Envers de l'Histoire contemporaine*). So much for Balzac's faith in judges.

Nor is there any trace in the *Comédie humaine* of that obsession with the police or that panic on the part of the criminal that, in our contemporary novelists, have replaced remorse. We are able to follow the course of Vautrin's career over a period of several years. Is his existence poisoned by fear? Does he start whenever he hears a bell? Never. And look at that famous trio of policemen, Corentin, Peyrade and Contenson. Are they infallible? No, they spend their entire time making mistakes. Are they successful? Occasionally. But they are also quite often defeated. They set out to hunt Vautrin down: two of them are killed and the third survives to see Vautrin made Chief of Police. Bibi-Lupin hangs on like grim death: Vautrin takes his job from under him. "However shrewd they may be," Balzac writes, "the police have innumerable disadvantages . . . One conspirator an outwit the whole police force singlehandedly, despite its immense powers of action" (*Ténébreuse Affaire*, p.518). "As though human passions and personal interest could not outmatch all the police in the world for cunning," he says in *le Curé de Village* (p.634). A way does exist, then, for the individual or the group to stand up against the police. There is hope. The struggle is not entirely one-sided. It is interesting to compare this attitude with that of a writer like Emile Zola, who is nevertheless thought of as a revolutionary writer. In *le Ventre de Paris*, he shows us a group of conspirators setting themselves up in opposition to a régime that Zola, like them, abhors. But how pitiful their attempt is. They have barely made their first move before the police are fully informed. The police play with these conspirators like a cat with a mouse; they let them continue their activities while looking on with quizzical indulgence; then, finally, they arrest every single one of them, having had the advantage, throughout the whole affair, of the total infallibility of their own spies and the unanimous support of the whole neighborhood (even though it is a working-class one) in which the plot was being hatched.

But let us look at the three celebrated policemen of the *Comédie humaine* a little more closely. Corentin, Peyrade and Contenson. What appallingly low creatures they are. All three of them! A hundred times more loathsome than their victims. How could any reader not hope for the defeat of a police force represented by such utterly crapulous fellows as these? Though it is only fair to point out that none of the trio belongs to that tranquil public force whose heavy and regular footsteps reassure the belated passer-by at night. They are policemen, yes, but much closer to the hired political agent than to the precinct commissioner. Their job is arresting conspirators, not thieves. Which means, in other words, that nine times out of ten they are attacking people a hundred times better than they are. In *les Chouans*, Corentin arranges the murder of Montauran, whose only crime is fighting on behalf of his king. In *Une Ténébreuse Affaire*, he secures the conviction of Michu and the Simeuses, all of whom are innocent. And he knows they are: he committed the crime himself.

Those activities might be covered by the term "political necessity." But in *Splendeurs et Misères*, the trio finally sets out to capture a genuine criminal: Vautrin. They are the police hunting down crime. Or are they? In reality, if you take another look, you realize that it is a story of gang warfare, with the same low tricks being pulled by both sides. And we should also note that Balzac sees nothing to stop them changing from one gang to the other. The ex-convict Bibi-Lupin becomes Chief of Police. Then Vautrin does exactly the same thing in his turn. But though he changes sides, note that he doesn't change either his methods or his accomplices. His aunt Jacqueline was his assistant when he was a criminal, and she continues to be his assistant when he becomes a policeman (*Cousine Bette*, pp. 460 and 476).

Born in about 1771, Corentin's origins are obscure. It is whispered in some quarters that he is the illegitimate son of Fouché (*Ténébreuse Affaire*, p.499 and *Splendeurs*, p.749). Balzac himself hastens to add that this conjecture is an extremely unlikely one; but simply by giving it voice he has managed to provide the character with a distinctive aura. We have already encountered another use of this same device in *les Employés,* when Balzac denies that the Grande Aumônerie had anything to do with securing Baudoyer's appointment, even though he has already used it as an explanation of that appointment. But in any case, son of Fouché or not, Corentin certainly enjoys the entire confidence of that formidable minister. He is "the secret Tristan of that miniature Louis XI" (*Ténébreuse Affaire,* p.499). At the age of twenty-two he finds himself already charged with a delicate mission (*Chouans*). At this period in his life he presents the appearance of a young dandy, dressed after the fashion of the *incroyables:* coat with short tails and long front flaps, red waistcoat, boots à la Souvaroff, hair in ringlets (*Chouans,* p.823). He has a pallid complexion, green eyes, and is distinguished, as Malin puts it, by a face that "looks like a carafe of lemonade" (*Ténébreuse Affaire,* p.469). This remark is made in 1803, at a time when he has been entrusted with a second mission, the details of which are to be found in *Une Ténébreuse Affaire.*

With age, the green eyes turn blue. In 1830, Vautrin recognizes him as "one of those fair-haired, blue-eyed natures, terrible and cold" (*Splendeurs,* p.857). As for the face, it has turned from pallid to chalky: "His plaster mask" (*id.* p.783). Having continued to exercise his functions throughout the Empire period, Corentin nevertheless manages to survive the changeover in 1815. Louis XVIII takes him onto his personal staff. Perhaps Corentin had been playing a double game the whole time. There is a phrase in *les Chouans* (p.1012) that indicates his readiness to do so. But Corentin is mendacity incarnate. Even his pretended treachery is probably another treachery. I think, more simply, that he is just a born police-spy, prepared to serve any power with exactly the same zeal and exactly the same indifference. "He's not one of those imbeciles who hang on to their opinions," as Vautrin puts it (*Père Goriot,* p.940). Worse still, I don't believe he is even capable of having any. Which means, of course, that he is also not capable of betraying them. Even treachery presupposes some minimal degree of human warmth. Corentin has none. His presence alone is sufficient to chill any atmosphere.

Moreover, the cold Corentin judges other men according to his own image. "Men," he says, "are worth no more than I esteem them at, almost nothing" (*Chouans,* p.1012). Cunning himself, he believes only in cunning, and that is his limitation. Why do intelligent people make so many mistakes? Precisely because they always think before they act and therefore assume that other people do the same. In consequence, they are always left bewildered and aghast by the erratic leaps of passion or the inspirations of stupidity. Marie de Verneuil says as much: "You have a cold heart, Corentin. You are able to work out intricate equations and predict the outcome of human affairs, but not that of a passion" (*id.* p.1014). Corentin has no passion anywhere in him. It is true that he asks for Marie de Verneuil's hand in marriage, but that, I suspect, is simply because he needs an assistant. Nor has he any vices. From 1797 to 1830, he does not once, as far as we know, sleep with a woman or get drunk. He is a police spy, and that's all. No anger, no grief. Nothing. He has a sort of friendship for Peyrade. That's the only human thing it's possible to discern in this carafe of lemonade. His colleague's death seems to touch him. He even takes in young Lydie and goes to live with her, under an assumed name. That definitely is something to be said in his favor, and heaven knows one is only too glad to find something at last. Though it seems unlikely that Corentin has given up his former devious activities, since we see him again later on in conference with La Roche-Hugon (*Petits Bourgeois*, p.227).

Corentin seems to be a policeman by vocation. Peyrade probably became one more from necessity. Talent, not a penny to his name, and vices. A combination that obviously doomed him to equivocal employment of some sort. Born in about 1755 of a good family belonging to the lesser nobility of Provence, Peyrade becomes a member of the police in 1775 (*Splendeurs*, p.754) or 1778 (*id.* p.856). Though involved, amongst others, in the affair of the Queen's Necklace, he is still only a subordinate in 1804, and it is in the capacity of an assistant that he accompanies Corentin, his junior in years, on the latter's well-known mission in *Une Ténébreuse Affaire*. It is still necessary to apply oneself seriously even in the lowest of trades. But Peyrade can't apply himself seriously. "Ah!" he laments, "why have I got into the habit of eating at Véry's, of drinking the finest wines . . . of singing drunken songs . . . of gambling as soon as I have money?" (*Splendeurs*, p.758). We see him, on one occasion, disguising himself as a rich libertine with the greatest delight, and performing his role with infinite pleasure (*Splendeurs*). Moreover, his vices are writ in large on his face. Peyrade has a large red nose, an erupting face, no teeth, and small, piglike eyes "full of a mocking and almost merry cruelty" (*Ténébreuse Affaire*, p.459). He is none too clean, and he neglects his appearance. Though much inferior to Corentin, he nevertheless manages to attain the post of Commissioner General of Police in Antwerp. He makes the most of this, lives it up, and keeps la Beaumesnil, who leaves him after bearing him a baby girl: Lydie. Dismissed from office in 1809, he goes away to live quietly out of the public eye under the assumed name of Canquoëlles. Corentin continues to employ him in various murky dealings. He also does a little private police work: shadowing, information obtained, swiftness, discretion. During one of his missions he makes trouble for Vautrin. Furious at this interference, Vautrin kidnaps his daughter then poisons him. These events take place in 1830. Despite his vices—or because of them—Peyrade, I must confess, appears to me less odious than Corentin. Or at any rate, he seems more human. He loves his daughter. That's not nothing.

A vocation for Corentin, a financial necessity for Peyrade, police work for Contenson is the last step in a progressive social degradation. He is the underling, the spy plain and simple, without talent, without intelligence, without a trace of dignity. Yet he started much higher than the others. His real name is Bernard-Polydor Bryond, Baron des Tours-Minières. It's true that Balzac also slips in the insinuation that no one really knows where he came by such a name. But he is a chouan, he is fighting for the right cause. That suffices to earn him the hand of Henriette de la Chanterie, a girl from a family of irreproachable nobility. When being a chouan ceases to be profitable, Bryond betrays his wife to the Revolution and calmly climbs over the fence to enjoy the greener grass represented by a job in Fouché's police. He has his needs to meet, you see, poor fellow. He has vices. And he will shrink from nothing in order to satisfy them. His vices, Balzac writes, "his depraved habits . . . had caused him to fall lower than his two friends" (*Splendeurs*, p.757). He has no useless pride. No task is too low for him if it allows him to pick up a few pennies. We see him accepting twenty-franc tips. Of the three, it is Contenson, the aristocrat, who uses the vulgarest language. "Aren't you going to grease my palm, Monsieur le Baron?" he asks of Nucingen (*id*. p.749). He is the lackey of the police force. When Peyrade disguises himself as a rich Englishman, the idea of disguising Contenson as his servant presents itself to him quite naturally. Contenson is also occasionally referred to by the nickname of "the philosopher," because he is given to making sententious pronouncements. "I have great talents," he says, "but such things serve no purpose, I might as well be a cretin" (*id*. p.746). Born in 1763, he dies in 1830, thrown off a roof by Vautrin.

CHAPTER 21

The Use of History

THE STORY of *les Proscrits* is set in the fourteenth century. *Sur Catherine de Médicis* begins in 1560. They are both historical novels on the most conventional lines, obeying all the rules of the genre. The story of *les Chouans* takes place in 1799, that of *Une Ténébreuse Affaire* begins in 1803. The tone of these two books is already freer. By the time we reach *Une Double Famille* and *le Lys dans la Vallée*—the first of which begins in 1806, the second in 1809—there is no "historical" flavor at all. Both books are simply novels, period. This development in time has nothing to do with the development of the author. It is a function of the chronology of the plots, not of the order of their composition. Balzac wrote *Une Ténébreuse Affaire* long after *Une Double Famille*.

Right to the end of his career, however, whether by means of references to events or by giving descriptions of furniture, Balzac continued taking great pains to see that his stories should reflect the color of the times in which they took place. Each story has its particular background shade. And those varying shades represent the presence of history. Alain defines *le Lys dans la Vallée* as: "The story of the Hundred Days seen from a château on the Loire." But more than that, by showing us men like de Valois or Bridau still acting in 1820 on principles that ceased to be valid in 1789 or 1815, Balzac even uses history as an element in the creation of his characters themselves. Valois and Bridau too, are historical figures in their way.

There are others who are historical simply in the sense that they did really exist: Napoleon, Talleyrand. Since Balzac's time, we have grown accustomed to this device. Proust used it, and Jules Romains, and Aragon, and many others besides. Balzac, for his part, used it very boldly (he even goes so far as to make one of his leading female characters Danton's widow) and also, I imagine, with something like a chuckle on occasion (as when he mentions his own tailor, Buisson, in *le Cabinet des Antiques*, his friend Laurent-Jan in *la Cousine Bette*, or the coachmaker Bernus in *Béatrix*). But there is one very interesting fact that we have to thank

[463]

Marcel Bouteron for pointing out: often, in later editions of his works, Balzac replaced these historical characters with characters taken from his own works. Canalis is substituted for Lamartine, Nucingen for the Maréchal Oudinot. This gives us a great deal of insight, it seems to me, into the function that Balzac intended his historical characters to fulfill: they are there simply as references, and as a stop-gap. When Balzac tells us that Franchessini is a friend of Maxime de Trailles, he is giving us, with scarcely any expense of words at all, a clear indication of the man's character. We know Maxime de Trailles. We can tell right away what class of character Franchessini must fall into. And the device is exactly the same when, elsewhere, Balzac tells us that Jacqueline Collin has been the mistress of Marat. Marat . . . Immediately we have a general picture in our heads of what's involved. We know this Marat, we've already met him. Whether the information comes from la Cousine Bette, from the David painting, or from some hidden recess of our memory doesn't make any difference. The image still appears before us. And that is all Balzac asks. It is the device of recurring characters again. It is one more example of Balzac's economy of means. Franchessini is a shady character. Instead of wasting ten lines describing that shadiness, Balzac conveys it in the concise form: a friend of Maxime de Trailles. Similarly, in order to throw a dramatic aura over Jacqueline's life, he needs no more than the phrase: she was once Marat's mistress. Already the character takes on a certain relief. One pictures her drying Marat as he gets out of his bath, opening the door to Charlotte Corday. And the same is true when Balzac makes Marie de Verneuil Danton's widow. Just that one phrase, and the character already has a kind of density. The density of Danton's historical existence. It is, of course, entirely an optical illusion. And it is also a fine example of the use that a novelist can make of the irrational. When Balzac shows us Laurence de Saint-Cygne whipping Corentin, when Proust shows us Oriane de Guermantes with Gilberte Swann, when Jules Romains shows us Gurau going to bed with Germaine Baader, we are able to believe in all these scenes. They could have happened. Laurence and Corentin, Gurau and Baader all inhabit the same world, a world that we have been able to forget is imaginary and which, for the moment, is real. On the other hand, when Laurence throws herself at the feet of Napoleon, when the Duchesse de Guermantes smiles at Detaille, when Gurau goes to visit Jaurès, then we know that those meetings did not take place. Where could Oriane have met Detaille? In what drawing-room hovering on the borders of the real and the imagined worlds? On what cloud? No, it is impossible. Marie de Verneuil can have done anything in the world she wants. Anything—except be married to Danton. Unless, that is, Gurau and Marie and Oriane are all disguises for real-life people, which Balzac, Proust and Romains all firmly deny. Well then? If we are to be strictly logical, ought not such inventions suffice to destroy the reality of a novel? It is as though I were to tell you that I'd just had lunch with Savonarola. Yet as it happens, preposterous though it may seem, the reality of a novel can actually be strengthened by such devices. Marie de Verneuil and Danton? All right. Fine. We'll accept that. Such are the powers of illusion wielded by the great creators of fiction.

There are several real personages, however, that Balzac never attempted to replace with fictional equivalents. And this despite the fact that the *Comédie humaine* constitutes a complete and completely populated social structure in itself. From the Premier, Marsay, down to old Pons's concierge, every social niche has been filled. And every single unit in that structure has been invented. Except the sovereigns. There we are reduced to the real Napoleon, the real Louis XVIII.

This is because they exist in a region where invention fails, or rather, in a region where the pressure of history on the novel becomes so strong that the two quickly become confused. This pressure even makes things difficult in the case of Henri de Marsay. He is an invented, an imaginary character. And almost as soon as Marsay succeeds in becoming Premier, Balzac kills him off. Why? Marsay could still have been of use. And certainly this death was not a matter of artistic necessity: it serves no purpose whatever. But Balzac must have come to realize, I imagine, that as soon as he had seized power, as soon as he had become that unique social personage the Premier of France in the year 1833, Marsay began to acquire a dangerous tendency to burst the bounds of his own fictional character and merge with that other, but historical personage, the real Premier of France in 1833. Or, if you prefer it the other way around, the real Premier was beginning to intrude into Balzac's world of fiction.

The same is true in the cases of Napoleon and Louis XVIII. The one with his brisk and forceful step, the other in his wheelchair, they both make their personal appearances in the *Comédie humaine*.

By the drive that he imparted to his age, by the tremendous political and social upheaval he provoked, by the changes he made in the laws, and by the deformation of which he was the cause in many minds, Napoleon is present throughout almost the entire work. *La Vieille Fille* takes place in Alençon under the Restoration. Athanase Granson, whom we meet in this work, is still only a very young man. On the surface, there can be no pos-

sible connection with the Little Corporal. And yet, Balzac tells us, "Athanase was the product of an Imperial education. The notion of fatality, the
Emperor's own religion, had spread from the throne . . . even as far as
those college benches" (*Vieille Fille*, p.308).

The memory of Napoleon prowls above all through the pages of *le
Colonel Chabert* and *le Médecin de Campagne*. "We no longer have our
father," Genestas says (*Médecin de Campagne*, p.391). "Ever since *the
other* got the push, I don't care about anything much any more," Gondrin
says (*id.* p.392). "Those fellows say that he's dead," Goguelat adds, eight
years after the Emperor's death. "Oh yes, dead! I can just see it! It's obvious they don't know the first thing about him" (*id.* p.469). "When I
think that Napoleon is on St. Helena, nothing seems to matter any more,"
Chabert sighs (*Colonel Chabert*, p.1144). "Did you see him then?" la
Fosseuse asks Genestas (*Médecin de Campagne*, p.417). It is the simple
souls and the people who seem to have kept the cult for him alive. It is
noticeable, for instance, in *le Médecin de Campagne*, with what rapt attention his peasant audience listens to Goguelat's account of Napoleon's life
story. Characters such as Montcornet and Bridau, on the other hand, only
regret his disappearance because of the advantages they had enjoyed under
his rule. And Mme de l'Estorade cries out in joy: "There won't be two
Bonapartes in this century: I shall be able to keep my children" (*Mémoires de deux Jeunes Mariées*, p.153).

In *la Vendetta*, we see Bonaparte the First Consul, in his red jacket, as
in the Ingres painting. In *Une Ténébreuse Affaire* (p.542), he presides
over a council; then, on the eve of Jena, he gives audience to Laurence de
Cinq-Cygne. It is a charming scene, so simple, so natural that it could
almost have been written by Stendhal. Napoleon talks rather brusquely,
at moments quite kindly, then suddenly more seriously "with his own
particular eloquence that could make brave men out cowards" (*Ténébreuse Affaire*, p.625). Towards the end, however, the interview declines
slightly in tone. "That's the second lieutenant showing through," Laurence
says. "Our sovereign has a prodigious self-regard," says Talleyrand . . .
"He is a great soldier who has the power to change the laws of both space
and time; but he has no means of changing men, though he would like to
remold them all to his convenience" (*id.* p.619). We see the Emperor
again in 1813 too, at a review, "a short rather fat man . . . surrounded by
so much love, enthusiasm, devotion, good wishes," his face imbued with
"so great a confidence in his power" that the women are jealous of him.
"Seeing her lover so intent on catching a glance from Napoleon, Julie
experienced an instant's jealousy" (*Femme de Trente Ans*, pp. 679 to 682).

There are further appearances—though only background ones—of the Ogre of Corsica in *l'Envers de l'Histoire contemporaine* (p.327), and in *le Cabinet des Antiques* (p.431). "Who will ever succeed in explaining, in depicting, or in understanding Napoleon?" Canalis exclaims . . . "The noblest power ever known, the most concentrated power, the most corrosive, the most acid power that ever was; a singular genius who marched a civilization in arms far and wide over the earth without ever finding it a resting place . . . Hypocritical and generous, a lover of both glitter and simplicity, without taste yet a patron of the arts; but despite these antitheses, whether by instinct or by constitution, great in everything" (*Autre Etude de Femme*, p.234). "The true king!" Says Marsay (*id.* p.235). "A good man," says Genestas (*Médecin de Campagne*, p.413). "An Italian, very fond of dressing up" (*Cousine Bette*, p.161).

The case of Louis XVIII seems to me even more interesting. For Balzac did after all live under the reigns of Charles X and Louis-Philippe as well. Yet Louis XVIII is the only one of these three kings to appear in the *Comédie humaine*. With Louis-Philippe, there is justification for supposing that the reason was pure antipathy. But what about Charles X? Balzac must surely have found the policies of Charles X very much to his taste. Yet Charles X is given the benefit of only very infrequent allusions. Perhaps this is just a matter of plot requirements? Obviously a character like Pons is less likely to meet his sovereign than, say, the Duc de Navarreins. But it is also during the reign of Louis-Philippe that Marsay, that Rastignac, that Popinot all become members of the government. It would have been quite natural for Balzac to depict them in their relationship with the sovereign. But he doesn't. Was it that he knew more about Louis XVIII? Did he want to make use of the confidences of the Duchesse d'Abrantès? The objection to this argument is that Mme d'Abrantès, if we are to believe the author of *Balzac mis à nu*, "served up to M. de Balzac an apocryphal Louis XVIII, a figure having nothing in common with the Louis XVIII described by the Comte Beugnot, by M. de Chateaubriand and by M. Fournay . . . By one of those prodigies of self-deception of which he constantly gave such incredible examples, M. de Balzac imagined that he had known the King personally, that he had worked with him."

What a ninny that fellow was! He has an example like that of the novelist's gift thrust under his nose, and all he can do is talk asininely about "prodigies of self-deception!" Of course, he's absolutely right. Only it is precisely to the extent that this Louis XVIII is apocryphal that he interests us. Precisely to the extent that he has been transmuted from a historical personage into a Balzac character. If, given three kings, Balzac chose to use only one of them in his work, then the evidence suggests that it was because he saw in that particular one certain of the features by which a novelist recognizes his particular kind of character. Because—whether rightly or wrongly—Balzac discerned something in Louis XVIII that he needed, that he could find a place for in his work. It does not take long to find out why. In a letter to Zulma Carraud, Balzac makes a comparison between Louis XVIII and Napoleon. "Both held all the parties in France together, the one by force, the other by cunning." By cunning . . . So there we are. Louis XVIII, in the *Comédie humaine*, is not just a king imposed on this fictional world by History, he is a king after Balzac's own heart, a king probably very close to the one that he himself would have invented. "A great king," Vautrin calls him, and one who owes his crown to "deep and secret schemes" (*Illusions perdues*, p.1027). Schemes that the novelist does not divulge, and about which the King himself, according to Balzac, was equally secretive. The theme of silence, of secrecy. "Louis XVIII," he writes, "died in possession of secrets that will always remain secrets even to the best informed historians" (*Splendeurs*, p.756). He repairs the misfortunes caused in *Une Ténébreuse Affaire*, but he "remained silent on the causes of the disaster" (*Ténébreuse Affaire*, p.627). He sees to it that Mme de la Chanterie is vindicated, but he keeps her accuser "in his counter-police throughout the whole of his reign" (*Envers de l'Histoire contemporaine*, p.329). All examples of behavior that would suit Marsay's character equally well.

Louis XVIII is also particularly present in *le Lys dans la Vallée*. His teachings and his example play a definite part in the drying up process that takes place, before our very eyes, in the soul of his secretary, Félix de Vandenesse. When the latter asks for leave of absence in order to rush to Mme de Mortsauf's bedside, the King throws him "a look full of those royal ironies, overwhelming in their subtlety, the purport of which seemed to be: 'If you want to be someone in the world of politics, come back! Don't idle away your time chattering to the dead.'" (*Lys dans la Vallée*, p.994). Skeptical, unfeeling in the way that was customary under Louis XV, his indulgence is reserved wholly for people who are witty, or, better still, for people who give him the opportunity to be witty himself. "'Away with you then, my lord,'" he says to Félix, "sparing him a reprimand in recognition of his wit" (*id.* p.993). And his help in finding suitable matches for the Comte de Fontaine's children, that too is a royal thank you for the witty shafts with which the astute father takes care to regale him. But you have to be on your guard: one bon mot will delight him, the next will cause a royal frown. "Though I perceive the rhyme, the reason escapes me," he remarks curtly in *le Bal de Sceaux* (p.77).

Napoleon: energy and power. Louis XVIII: cunning, secrecy, intelligence. In other words, Balzac's two favorite themes. And when great power is also great in cunning, then he is in his seventh heaven. This is doubtless the reason why, out of all the female sovereigns available, it was Catherine de Médicis he chose to make the heroine of one of his novels. And also I imagine, the reason for his singling out of Talleyrand and Fouché, who are the only two historical characters, aside from the sovereigns, who play roles of any importance in the *Comédie humaine*. For here again we have two characters after Balzac's own heart. Two schemers. Two representatives of power in its most secret and devious forms: diplomacy and the police. And both unfrocked priests, what's more, with everything that implies in the way of hidden motives, unction of manner, and contempt for both man and principles. No doctrines, no scruples. Talleyrand becomes rich in office, but, as Blondet puts it: "Is a prime minister who takes a hundred million francs for himself and in return makes France great and happy not preferable to a minister who has to be buried at the expense of a state he has brought to ruin?" (*Maison Nucingen*, p.640). But aren't they treacherous? No, Balzac says, because "everything is modified by events" (*César Birotteau*, p.492). In differing degrees, and on different levels, Talleyrand and Fouché were both men who always chose cunning instead of violence, the path of intelligence rather than that of honor. In 1814, they were both in favor, not of loyalty, but of peace. And not for humanitarian reasons, but because war to them was something irrational, inimical to order, wasteful. We meet Talleyrand, among others, in one of the scenes in *Une Ténébreuse Affaire*. Of all the politicians present, he is the only one concerned with peace. It is in much the same spirit that his disciple Marsay later writes: "We will stop at nothing to secure the happiness of our country" (*Contrat de Mariage*, p.200). For the happiness . . . That is worth noting. Not the greatness, as a man of genuine magnanimity or a fool would have said. Marsay is neither magnanimous nor a fool. The happiness! And in consequence, peace. Peace no matter how, no matter at what price. "There is nothing we will not stop at." On the horizon, already distantly silhouetted, we glimpse the Thiers-Rastignac of 1870, the Pierre Laval of 1940.

Most of Talleyrand's appearances are made in *Une Ténébreuse Affaire*. He appears in two meetings. He also grants audience to Chargeboeuf and Bordin at one point. He gives them a quantity of useful advice which he then spoils somewhat by adding: "Don't go and get yourselves mixed up with that clownish gamekeeper of yours." A little later we see him at daggers drawn with Corentin (*Ténébreuse Affaire*, p.619). In *le Contrat de Mariage* he is the soul and the spiritual father of the clique that Marsay assembles. I look upon him "as a politician of genius," this latter says, "a complete prince in the same way that a great artist can be" (*Contrat de Mariage*, p.200). "Whom I admire as one of the most extraordinary men of our times" (*Ténébreuse Affaire*, p.632). "That inimitable man," Balzac also remarks in *Un Prince de la Bohème* (p.828).

As for Fouché, apart from two scenes in *Une Ténébreuse Affaire* (pp. 542 and 632), he does not appear much in person. But his wan shadow hovers over all the misadventures of that celebrated police trio, Corentin-Peyrade-Contenson. Read *l'Envers de l'Histoire contemporaine*, *les Chouans*, *Une Ténébreuse Affaire*, and even the end of *Splendeurs*, which takes place ten years after his death. Whenever any of the trio appears, Fouché is there like a watermark in the page, his pallid face, the bags under the eyes, that white rabbit's gaze. Balzac even allows it to be insinuated that he is possibly Corentin's father (*Splendeurs*, p.749). Another startling touch, and one to be compared with that of making Marie de Verneuil into Danton's widow. And they are touches, I must confess, that never cease to amaze me. That mixture of the real with the more than real; that marriage—quite literally in Marie's case—of the real with the invented . . . What a pity that our novelists no longer possess this kind of daring. Can you see Thérèse Desqueyroux married to Julien Benda?

There are two further historical characters who play a certain role: Mme de Staël, in *Louis Lambert*, and the executioner Sanson, in *Un Episode sous la Terreur*. The son of this Sanson appears very briefly in *Splendeurs*. The remaining real-life characters only appear very breifly, and in passing. We see Benjamin Constant and Général Foy (*Illusions perdues*, p.704); the actor Bouffé (*id.* p.729); Berthier; Napoleon's man-servant Constant and his mameluke Rustan (*Ténébreuse Affaire*, pp. 623-624); Sieyès, Carnot and the prefect Dubois (*id.* pp. 634 and 542); Rapp (*Vendetta*, p.861) and Lacépède (*César Birotteau*, p.546). Then there are others who are mentioned but do not actually appear.

CHAPTER 22

Money

Obsession with money—its limits—the misers—Gob-seck—the world of Money—Business: Célestin Crevel —banking and usury—the speculators—the notaries— the lawyers.

KATHERINE MANSFIELD once wrote, in a letter, that she always felt an especially horrid kind of exasperation when reading Balzac, because the whole of existence, according to him, is based on money.

It isn't true, of course. There is a whole list of Balzac's works I could name in which money plays no part; a whole list of characters who scarcely give it a thought. But society today has acquired a singular reticence in this respect. I have intimate friends whom I would not dream of asking how much they earn. And this reticence is reflected in our novels. In *A la Recherche du Temps perdu*, Odette and Mme Cottard are discussing their dresses: "How much do you think it was?" Mme Cottard asks . . . "No, change the first figure." "What!" Odette exclaims, "it was practically a gift then. I was told three times that much." It is quite evident that the figure in question was actually spoken aloud in this conversation. Yet Proust had not dared to reproduce it. And the same attitude is prevalent in our films. They show us a great many people drinking in bars or getting out of taxis. The people pay, but they never inquire a price, and they never wait for change. The act of paying is always reduced to the absolutely bare essentials. Money is eliminated.

Balzac has no such reticence. For him, a man's income and expenses are as much a part of him as his character, his family, his vices and his virtues. Money is first and foremost one of those "circumstances" that, for Balzac, make the man. "When you live in Paris, what you're always up against in the end is that figure at the foot of the bill" (*Employés*, p.868).

Though it must immediately be added that Balzac is always quite ready to talk about it, and that he even takes a certain satisfaction in doing so. One feels that he is adding up all those bills with a certain pleasure, that his pen is quite quivering with delight. A man who has difficulty in making both ends meet is always more ready to talk about money than other people. And I don't need to remind you here of all the difficulties and anxieties that Balzac suffered in that respect. He is, I think I am right in saying, the only writer whose account books have earned the honor of two whole books all to themselves (*Balzac homme d'affaires* by René Bouvier, and *les Comptes dramatiques de Balzac* by René Bouvier and Edouard Maynial).

We should add, too, that this intrusion of money into Balzac's work often occurs in the most startlingly brutal manner. In *le Cousin Pons* (p.598), when introducing her guests, Mme Camusot says: "May I present M. le Comte and Mme la Comtesse Popinot, whose son turned out not to be rich enough for Cécile." "My daughter has a dowry of sixty thousand francs," says another mother in the middle of an evening reception. The deputy public prosecutor Vinet, with no intention but flattery, expresses himself in these terms: "I knew already that Mademoiselle possessed as much wit as she does money" (*Député d'Arcis*, p.702). There are a thousand examples one could quote of such calm immodesty. In general, though, they are found only in the "bourgeois" novels of the *Comédie humaine*. It is not that the Grandlieus and the Chaulieus are disinterested; but in their case, in addition to the importance of money, there exist other assets as well, and particularly that supreme asset: the name, the title. Before agreeing to let Rubempré marry his daughter, Grandlieu certainly cross-questions him about his finances. But even so, it's still necessary for the suitor to be a Rubempré and a marquis. A Nucingen, for all his money, would have been sent packing back behind his teller's window immediately. And respect for the prestige attaching to a title is not limited to those who actually have them: Nucingen considers himself extremely honored to be invited to Mme d'Espard's, even though her income barely exists in comparison with his. César Birotteau is very proud to have the Comte de Fontaine in his house. Twenty years later, the reign of the aristocracy having come to an end, that same Birotteau's son-in-law, Popinot, doesn't care a rap one way or the other whether he has counts or marquises visiting him. His snobbery is directed elsewhere. In *Splendeurs*, we see Mme Camusot running to do the bidding of Mme de Maufrigneuse. Twenty years later, we meet Mme Camusot again, in *le Cousin Pons*. She is no longer interested in duchesses. These middle-class people have now become aristocratic themselves. Instead of remaining content to entertain countesses, Popinot has made himself into a count, and Mme Camusot has become Mme Camusot de Marville.

In this new aristocracy it is money that counts. Though again, it is not simply because Balzac's middle-class people are more grasping than his dukes. But once the prestige of the great name has lost its power, once the hierarchy founded on quarterings has vanished, what is there left by which to judge a man? Personal merit, you may say. Very well, but in the eyes of this middle-class aristocracy there can be no better gauge of a man's personal merit than the use to which he puts it, and the yardstick by which they measure that is how much money he earns. A poor duke is always a duke (if you happen to believe in that sort of thing). Whereas there can be no such thing as a poor bourgeois: the phrase is a contradiction in terms. So that in this middle-class aristocracy of Balzac's, the person who is poor is always treated rather like someone hovering in a limbo world between being and non-being. The only thing that can save him is being related to the right people. *Poor Relations* is one of the subheadings of the *Comédie humaine*. There are two books that come under this heading, and both of them take place in this middle-class world. For two reasons: because, according to Balzac, as I have already said, the middle-class world is the only one in which family connections have any great importance, and also because it is the only class of society in which it is a serious matter to be poor. Even though they are made welcome in their relatives' houses, Bette and Pons are nonetheless treated as not quite socially acceptable. In the case of Pons, this can be explained by the Camusots' thoroughly unpleasant characters. But Bette's relatives, the Hulots, are very good, kindly folk, yet even their manner towards their cousin has a certain nuance of disrespect in it. And the cruelty of this attitude is even further increased by the fact that it is certainly unconscious (Hortense Hulot makes a great deal of fun of the idea that Bette could possibly be in love with anyone). Whereas under the Restoration, in *la Vieille Fille*, we have seen a man like the Chevalier de Valois treated with infinite respect, even though he is as poor as Job, and solely on account of his name. A new reign has begun, that of "the holy, the venerated, the solid, the kindly, the gracious, the beautiful, the noble, the young, the all-powerful five-franc piece"(*Cousine Bette*, p.400).

That said, this tyranny of money once recognized, this obsession duly noted, I confess that I can't really see much more to be said on the subject. Is that just inadequacy on my part? I could say that it's because I'm not really very interested. But I think the real reason is that, contrary to what many people think, money is in fact the inspiration for rather few of Balzac characters or plots. We find money everywhere, that I admit. But how many characters are there in whose lives it is the essential drama or the primordial passion? I can see Birotteau, Nucingen, Gobseck, Grandet, Cérizet . . . And who else? Nobody else. What? Yes, seriously, I assure you. We thought we were plunging into a dense forest, and here we are on the other side of a little spinney. And Crevel? you may say. We don't meet him until he's retired. Du Tillet? He's mentioned a great deal, but he is never a principal character.

And furthermore, everything considered, I think that money must always remain a rather unfruitful field for the novelist. It's such a meager subject, so clearcut, so easily exhausted. And capable of so few variations. Once you have depicted a miser, what is there to add? What would be the point of starting in on another? In his book on Balzac, André Bellessort writes very aptly: "The passions that have merely inanimate things as their object and their goal, such as the love of gold, the frenzy of the gambler or the folly of the inventor, never attain to the variety of tone or the depth of pathos to be found in those that aim at dominion over men's minds or the conquest of another soul."

There is no denying that money is ubiquitous in the *Comédie humaine;* but it is often only present in order to perform a subsidiary function, the character or the plot being colored primarily by some quite different passion. Rastignac complains of not having any money; but as soon as he acquires any he rushes out to spend it on gloves and cabs. His driving passion is ambition, not greed. "Money is life. Gold is everything," Goriot cries (*Père Goriot,* p.1037). And it is a cry that has not gone unquoted. But do we see Goriot becoming a man of money, a man whose whole life is governed by money? On the contrary, he is the most generous, the most disinterested of fathers. Money has its role to play; but the play is about something quite different. "The moment money finds its way into a student's pocket, that student has an inner vision of himself standing high on an imaginary column" (*id.* p.927). A column, that's nicely put. Writing the life of St. Siemon Stylites, how much space would I devote to his column? It's important that the money should be there, but that's all. It is a means and nothing more. Only in the case of misers does it become an end. And when you come down to it, just how many misers are there in the *Comédie humaine?* Nucingen? Nucingen is a classic example of conspicuous consumption. Hochon in *la Rabouilleuse?* He is miserly, but not a miser. His stinginess is an eccentricity rather than a vice. Rigou, in *les Paysans?* He wears a cheap topcoat, but the shirt underneath is of the finest quality. He is more the cautious peasant, a stubborn believer in the country precept: better a neighbor's pity than his envy. Magus? He spends untold fortunes on his collection. Which leaves us with Grandet, the only genuine miser in the canon, or at any rate the only important one, since Pingret in *le Curé de Village*, Orgemont in *les Chouans* and Molineux in *César Birotteau* are only very minor characters. But what am I expected to say about Grandet? He's a miser. Everyone agrees? But now what? Money, whatever people may say about it, is a dead thing. And misers are dead people. Yes, I know I still haven't mentioned Gobseck. But is Gobseck really a miser?

"Born in about 1740 on the outskirts of Antwerp, the son of a Jewish mother and a Dutch father" (*Gobseck*, p.626), Jean-Esther Van Gobseck, having knocked about the world for a while, has settled in Paris and set up as a moneylender. He lives on nothing at all in a wretched little room. From the sound of that, he must be a miser. But, Derville says, "away from his business, he is the most scrupulous and upright man you will find in Paris" (*id*. p.654). And as proof of this, we actually see him restoring young Restaud's fortune to him when he is not obliged to do so by any power other than that of his own conscience. So the sway of money is not absolute. "I am rich enough," Gobseck says, "to buy the consciences of those who control the country's ministers, from their office boys up to their mistresses: is that not power? I can command possession of the most beautiful women and their most tender caresses: is that not pleasure? And are not power and pleasure the sum total of your social order? There are ten or so of us like that in Paris, so many anonymous and silent kings, the arbiters of your destinies" (id. p.636). Where is the avarice there? It is the will to power. "Anonymous and silent kings." Gobseck is mysterious, he is at the head of a conspiracy of usurers, he has the gift of second sight. All the attributes of power are there for us to see. It is only at the end of the story that he becomes a genuine miser. Then, it is true, money takes possession of him, devours him, becomes an absolute for him. And, almost immediately, annihilates him.

THE MONEY WORLD

The passion that we term love is sometimes taken up by certain members of society as a trade, a trade by which they often earn their living without ever experiencing the passion themselves. And so it is with money. It is a passion for the miser, a mirage for the poor, but it can also appear, more simply, in the guise of a king, a minister that one serves with more or less zeal, with more or less conviction. Here are that passion's courtesans: the businessmen, the bankers, the moneylenders. Here are that minister's administrators: the notaries, the lawyers.

THE BUSINESS WORLD

Let us limit ourselves to one of the most remarkable representatives of this species: Célestin Crevel.

Having started his career as a clerk employed by the perfumer Birotteau, Crevel later buys up his employer's business and, within the space of a few years, makes a fortune out of it. Yet he is much inferior to Birotteau as a man, and he himself is aware of this. So aware that he always retains his former employer, despite Birotteau's bankruptcy, and possibly not entirely consciously, as a model. "Have you noticed how in childhood, or at the time of our first entry into society, we create a model for ourselves with our own hands, often without our own knowledge . . . Crevel became deputy mayor because his employer had been deputy mayor, he had now become a major because of the envy he once felt for César Birotteau's epaulettes" (*Cousine Bette*, p.234). Like Birotteau too, Crevel is stupid, conceited, and is always taking the floor in order to make asinine remarks. From the one to the other, however, there is that sharp step down so often found in Balzac between two characters of the same kind of whom one lived before 1830 and the other after that date. Despite his stupidity, Birotteau had stature. His death is depicted as the apotheosis of a just man. There is no apotheosis for Crevel. He is a man with "petty motives" (*id.* p.143). Birotteau is pious and virtuous. Crevel poses as a freethinker. "I was suckled at the breast of the Revolution," he says (*id.* p.508). He is a libertine. He tries to be "Regency, gray musketeer, Abbé Dubois, and Maréchal de Richelieu, damn it!" (*id.* p.508). He is above all profoundly vulgar. He is Flaubert's bourgeois, the man whose every thought is base. "What a woman!" he says, "she stirs me up inside like a colic" (*id.* p.306). "Little mother," he says to the Baronne Hulot, "twenty-five years of virtue, that's always going to repel people like a disease that's been left to spread" (*id.* p.403). His wife, moreover, was "rather ugly, very vulgar, and stupid" (*id.* p.269). And his daughter, who has married Baron Hulot's son, is "vulgar and utterly insignificant," as well as being the possessor of a "cold and commonplace face" (*id.* pp. 176 and 445). We are a long way from the sympathetic Birotteau family.

Crevel, however, succeeds. Crevel triumphs. Another good example of Balzac's moral impartiality. We are shown Crevel between Birotteau, his employer, and Hulot, his crony. The former is virtuous but stupid, the other is intelligent but loose-living. The one's stupidity and the other's lust lead them both to the same end: ruin. While Crevel, who unites the defects of both these men, who is stupid like Birotteau and loose-living like Hulot, without possessing any of their good qualities, Crevel succeeds. He makes a fortune in the same business that brought Birotteau to bankruptcy, and he manages not to ruin himself in the same life of debauch that swallows up Hulot's entire fortune. He achieves all those commercial triumphs that Birotteau had once dreamed of, he marries the Mme Marneffe that Hulot is so infatuated with. How can all this be? Can it be explained by strength of character on Crevel's part? No, because he doesn't have that either. Having been deceived by Mme Marneffe, having acquired certain knowledge of that fact, having decided to leave her, he goes back to her. It is at this point that there occurs that extraordinary scene in which Hulot and Crevel, both made fools of by the same woman, go off to spend the night together, exchanging reminiscences of their mistress's charms and swearing to one another that they will neither of them ever see her again. Next day, they meet face to face again outside her door. "They looked at one another and dissolved into gloomy laughter" (*id*. p.314). That sentence is, for me, one of the peaks of the *Comédie humaine*.

The two men have thus both been brought to the same point. But Hulot continues on his downward path after that, whereas the other, the stupider of the two, succeeds in effecting a sort of recovery. And the reason for this, I think, is precisely that he is stupid. Hulot is powerless against his lust because it is absolute. There is nothing else inside him but lust, so he is annihilated by it. Whereas the same passion in Crevel is kept within bounds by his vulgarity, by his baseness, by his pettiness of soul. Far from reinforcing one another, stupidity and passion in Crevel's case act as counterweights; they cancel one another out. Crevel is incapable of any but base thoughts. That is at least a safeguard against ever falling from too great a height. We are back once more to Balzac's condemnation of the absolute, of the all-devouring passion. In Hulot, the passion in question has nothing to limit it. In Crevel, it is limited by the man's pettiness. "Crevel is a *rat!*" Josépha says, "a nice old rat who always says yes and always does just as he pleases" (*id*. p.433). He has the petty sort of will-power displayed by those who go whoring just as much as the next man, but who empty their wallets before they leave home. A libertine, but with "ideas as set as the staves on a sheet of music paper" (*id*. p.143). He sets up a young lady in an establishment, but he takes care to pick one so young that she still hasn't started to get ideas about money. Later on, having been seduced by

Valérie Marneffe, he marries her rather than allow her to ruin him. In short, he is the man who comes to terms with his passions. And in consequence, he triumphs. Though only temporarily, for he dies prematurely, having caught the frightful disease given to his wife. I should also add that at some time or another, I'm not sure when, he has had a liaison with Héloïse Brisetout (*Cousin Pons*, p.740).

BANKING AND USURY

The worlds of banking and moneylending are abundantly represented. Balzac does not look upon them as different in kind, merely as different levels of the same activity. "At the top, the house of Nucingen, the Kellers, the du Tillets, the Mongenods; a little lower down, the Palmas, the Gigonnets, the Gobsecks; lower still, the Samanons, the Chaboisseaus, the Barbets; then, last of all, below the pawnshop, there is that king of usury who sets his snares on street corners so that he can be sure of wringing the neck of every poor devil in existence, so that not one shall escape—Cérizet" (*Petits Bourgeois*, p.168).

Although very frequently mentioned, the Baron Frédéric de Nucingen does not, to my way of thinking, call for much in the way of commentary. He is a banker the way other creatures are elephants, by nature, without any other motives for action than those that might animate a strongbox disguised as a man. In *Splendeurs et Misères*, he loses his head over Esther, but that is certainly the only example of such a thing in his life. Moreover, once away from his bank he is just a rather ordinary man who allows himself to be cheated by old ladies selling second-hand clothes. Born in Strasbourg in 1767, "the son of some Jew who had been converted for reasons of ambition" (*Maison Nucingen*, p.601), created Baron I'm not quite sure when, he eventually marries Delphine Goriot, who is unfaithful to him and to whom he is unfaithful. Apart from the Esther business, however, his adulterous activities must be matters entirely without importance to him. He quite simply goes to whores for his diversions. He visits Suzanne du Val-Noble (*Illusions perdues*, p.785), Florine (*Fille d'Eve*, p.105), Josépha (*Béatrix*), and even Carabine (*Comédiens sans le savoir*). I say "even" Carabine because he must be almost eighty at the time. There's food for thought there.

Du Tillet's antecedents are not known. He was found by a priest on St. Ferdinand's day, 1793, abandoned on a doorstep in a village called du Tillet, which is situated in the department of the Eure. Hence the gentleman's first and family names. Though raised by the priest in question,

Ferdinand has retained none of the good principles his benefactor took pains to inculcate in him. Having come to Paris and been taken on as a clerk by Birotteau, he attempts to rob his employer's wife. Escaping with no more than a reprimand, he then steals from the till. Birotteau forgives him. But du Tillet never forgives Birotteau for his forgiveness. That's the way men with base natures are made. But then, having become Mme Roguin's lover, du Tillet decides that it is time he gave up petty crime. I mean, of course, time he gave up the pettiness, not the crime. So he starts a bank. With Mme Roguin's money, needless to say. "Young men sometimes find themselves forced into the most frightful positions," he says (*César Birotteau*, p.502). As you see, we are a long way from the rough, honest language of a Vautrin. Du Tillet has the art of humbug. Moreover, he succeeds. But he always remains base, spiteful, a bearer of grudges for no reason. He likes to do harm. He blithely pushes his former employer on towards his ruin. He helps Nathan get his fingers burnt in the friendliest possible way (*Un Fille d'Eve*). The upsets of 1830 make him a deputy. He takes up his position on the center left, the political sector that was the object of all Balzac's antipathies. He has meanwhile married Marie-Eugénie de Grandlieu, a sweet, resigned little woman whom he neglects in favor of Mme Roguin, until the day when he leaves Mme Roguin in her turn for Carabine. And I was forgetting to mention that he also indulges in some vaguely unpleasant, rather cruel, and, furthermore, rather ill-defined behavior towards Malvina d'Aldrigger, in *la Maison Nucingen*. This Malvina's father, the Baron d'Aldrigger, is also a banker, but an honest one. Moreover, he dies a ruined man. Ought we to conclude from this that, for Balzac, all successful bankers must necessarily be rogues? Not at all. Mongenod is both honest and successful. His story is to be found in *l'Envers de l'Histoire contemporaine*. The house of Mongenod is a sedate kind of bank, a bank for steady people: Mme de la Chanterie (*Envers de l'Histoire contemporaine*), Mme de la Baudraye (*Muse du Département*), Mme d'Espard (*Interdiction*, p.34), Hochon (*Rabouilleuse*, p.1060). As for François Keller, he is the banker who goes in for politics. He is a liberal deputy.

Now we go down one flight. Here we have the discount bankers, the speculators, the moneylenders, a whole little world of its own dominated by that famous foursome Gobseck-Werbrust-Palma-Gigonnet. This Gigonnet—his real name is Bidault—owes his surname to the "nervous and convulsive movement with which he was wont to lift his leg" (*Employés*, p.903). We see him at work in *les Employés*, in *la Maison Nucingen*, in *César Birotteau*, and in *Ursule Mirouët*. I have already dealt with Gobseck.

Palma and Werbrust are often mentioned but we have few details about them. All of these people are little old men, modest in appearance, with dead eyes. In the evenings, they all meet at the Café Thémis. Chaboisseau also goes there from time to time. He has a speciality: discounting in the book trade. He also has an eccentricity: his apartment on the Quai Saint-Michel is decorated in Greek style. "It is worth remarking that the most whimsical and fantastic men in the world are to be found amongst those who are concerned in the money trade. These eccentrics are, as it were, the libertines of the mind. Able to possess everything, and consequently surfeited, they are prepared to go to monstrous lengths to overcome their indifference" (*Illusions perdues*, p.835). Barbet is another who operates in the book trade. As for Samanon, he is simply a pawnbroker (*id*. p.837). Though he does sell obscene engravings too, on occasion. Vauvinet is a moneylender of the new school, young, elegant, sprightly, who gives a false impression of wearing his heart on his sleeve.

But of them all, the worst, the vilest, the slimiest, is Cérizet, the poor man's moneylender. He hangs out in a squalid hole on the Rue des Poules, where he does business from three o'clock in the morning onwards in summer, from five o'clock onwards in winter (*Petits Bourgeois*, p.169). It is there that he sits, jovial as an undertaker's mute, listening to his clients' moans. When Maxime de Trailles goes to see Gobseck, he can at least still afford to hide his penury beneath a cloak of light-hearted indifference. The poor people who go to see Cérizet can't afford a cloak of any sort. They are on their knees. The moneylender is their king. He rules over them, cuts them short, scolds them. "It can't go on like this, you know, papa Lantimèche," he cries (*id*. p.174). Do you remember Peachum, the king of the beggars in the *Threepenny Opera*? Cérizet is another Peachum. He began life as an apprentice in the Séchard printing works in Angoulême. At that time, he was a sly, malicious, vicious little urchin who used to seduce the little laundry-girls, then later betrayed his employer (*Illusions perdues*, part 3). These brilliant qualities, later on in life, make him just the man to be manager of a liberal newspaper (*id*. p.1056). Having been somewhat ill-treated by the powers that be, he acquires a certain reputation. That brave Cérizet, people call him. In 1830, he is made a prefect. When this appointment is rescinded, he goes into business, whereupon he finds himself clapped into jail for two years. When the sentence expires, he turns moneylender.

There is not much to be said about the two or three remaining speculators. Couture is a financier-journalist and journalist-financier who is ruined in about 1840, then more or less rehabilitated by Mme Schontz. She even dallies for a moment with the idea of making him her husband. Mme Schontz has a thirst for respectability, you will remember. During his moments of glory, Couture also kept Jenny Cadine (*Béatrix* and *César Birotteau*). Then there's Charles Claparon. He's the eternal man of straw. A former traveling salesman, stupid, coarse, bald, and a drunkard. During successive periods of his life, he is to be seen trailing along in the shadows of Roguin (*César Birotteau*), du Tillet and Nucingen (*Maison Nucingen*), Cérizet (*Homme d'Affaires*), and the Devil, to whom he eventually sells his soul (*Melmoth réconcilié*). As for Georges d'Estourny, he is just a crook. He cheats at cards, keeps Esther for a short while, seduces and abandons Bettina Mignon, and ends up in the police courts.

THE NOTARIES

The notaries, I need hardly say, are legion. For Balzac, society is fundamentally organized around the family unit. Hence the importance that he attaches to the notary, who becomes a sort of legal extension of the family, a high priest of contracts, a sacristan of wealth, a verger in charge of wills, an adviser for mothers and a surrogate tutor for their sons. There is no family that does not have its notary. We have Chesnel and Lepressoir in Alençon, Mathias, Solonet and Lécuyer in Bordeaux, Cruchot in Saumur, Lupin in Soulanges, Pierquin in Douai, Héron in Issoudun, Grévin and Herbellot in Arcis. In general, all these notaries are notaries and nothing else. They are there, but their presence, like that of the family furniture, seems to require no comment. The only exceptions I would make to this remark are Chesnel and Grévin, both of whom I have discussed elsewhere.

Though mention must also be made of the charming professional scene that occurs between the two notaries Mathias and Solonet in *le Contrat de Mariage*. Mathias is the old, classic notary figure, prudent and wily. Solonet represents the new school. He's livelier, he drives a cabriolet, he speculates. The first is Manerville's notary, the second is Mme Evangelista's. "We took no inventory after the death of our husband," says Solonet, speaking with the identity of his client. "We were Spanish, a creole, and we did not know the French laws . . . It is public knowledge that we were adored by the deceased." "Ta ta ta," the older man replies. "Tell us frankly . . . what you have left . . . If we are too much in love, we'll see" (*Contrat de Mariage*, p.1180). Then, the battle over, having roundly insulted one another in the proper manner, the two notaries walk off arm in arm.

The Parisian notaries in the *Comédie humaine* are more distinctive.

There is Roguin, for example, who absconds in about 1820, thus precipi-
tating the ruin of Birotteau, of Grandet's brother, and of Mme Descoings
and Mme Bridau. In *la Vendetta*, in 1815, he had made really a rather good
impression. But having been repulsed by his wife on account of a slight
physical affliction, hungry for affection, poor man, he falls back on la
belle Hollandaise, a notorious cocotte, a woman less demanding in the
matter of a lover's physical endowments, but a great devourer of patrimonies.

Cardot is another notary afflicted by passion. He keeps Malaga (*Muse
du Département*, p.156). Though there is some excuse, for Mme Cardot's
function in some departments of the marital relationship could only be,
as her irrepressible rival puts it, that of "a scubbing-brush for one's sins."
This notary Cardot should not be confused with his father, who keeps
Coralie and is a silk merchant. When the notary Cardot's daughter is
discovered to be pregnant by the head clerk, by then unhappily deceased,
the notary first offers her to Lousteau, then, observing the laws of senior-
ity, to his second clerk, Berthier, who later succeeds him in his professional
capacity. It is an extremely flourishing practice, but one with a somewhat
heterogeneous clientele: the Camusots de Marville, Schwab, in *le Cousin
Pons*, the Thuilliers (*Petits Bourgeois*), Mme Marneffe, Nucingen (*Splendeurs*, p.814), Victurnien d'Esgrignon (*Cabinet des Antiques*, p.371), M.
Vervelle and his future son-in-law Grassou.

Of all these notaries, the one most deserving of recommendation is undoubtedly Léopold Hannequin. There is a man in whom one could really
place one's confidence. He is "heavy and pedantic," Héloïse Brisetout
says . . . "I call him Old Rat Poison, because he's been infecting all my
girl friends with thrifty principles . . . He's a notary all the time, waking
or sleeping." Among his clients are the Grandlieus, Florine, the du Bruels,
and the Maréchal Hulot. A great friend of Albert Savarus, he accompanies
the latter on the trip to Switzerland of which Savarus gives a transposed
account in the short story that he has published in a Besançon review. As
for Alexandre Crottat, he's the fat, kindly, clumsy type. In *la Femme de
Trente ans* (p.781), we see him flounder his way from gaffe to gaffe.
Clients: the Comte de Sérizy (*Un Début dans la Vie*), the Comtesse Ferraud (*Colonel Chabert*, p.1110), Charles de Vandenesse. His poor parents
were murdered in about 1830 by a robber (*Splendeurs*, p.1042). There
was at one point some question of his marrying Césarine Birotteau, but the
wife he does in fact take is a Mlle Lourdois, the daughter of a contractor.

THE LAWYERS

There are two sorts of lawyers, Blondet says in *la Maison Nucingen* (p.618). The honest lawyer "who advises his clients with strict regard to the truth," and who "sees that they compromise on any doubtful points." And "the predatory lawyer, who doesn't mind what happens as long as he's sure of his fees." Derville, on the Rue Vivienne, is one of the first kind. Desroches, on the Rue de Béthizy, is one of the second. Derville, the Duc de Chaulieu says is "an upright man, a man who carries weight, a man of honor. He is shrewd, he is cunning, but only in the sense that a good lawyer needs to be" (*Splendeurs*, p.870). By which the duke means that he is honest. Despite the gratitude he feels towards Gobseck for having lent him the money to set up in practice, he nevertheless refuses to abet the old moneylender in one of his dishonest affairs. He is a hard worker and has a thorough mastery of his profession. He is, Balzac says, "one of the ablest brains in the whole Palais de Justice" (*Employés*, p.910). He demonstrates the uprightness of his mind, as well as the generosity of his heart, in his dealings with Chabert. He is also a brilliant conversationalist: it is to him that we owe the biography of Gobseck. He is as open as a child, and never attempts to gloss over the fact that he has married a young working-class girl. And in Balzac's day that was something that hadn't become fashionable yet. By this working-class girl, née Fanny Malvaut, he has a daughter, Mathilde, who in 1842 marries Augustin Bongrand, the crown prosecutor in Château-Chinon (*Oeuvres ébauchées*, p.1074). Derville is lawyer to the Grandlieus, to the Comte de Restaud, to César Birotteau, to de Sérizy, and to Félix de Vandenesse. Lastly, it was in Derville's chambers that Desroches acquired his training.

This Desroches is the son of a civil servant whom we glimpse for a moment in *la Rabouilleuse*. In 1822, though I don't know where he got the money, he sets up his own practice. He has his former employer's finesse, but not his probity. A "wily clown" he is called on one occasion (*Splendeurs*, p.810). "A little man on the make, a fellow poorly regarded by the courts and his colleagues" (*Interdiction*, p.32). He is perfectly prepared to take on clients with questionable cases: des Lupeaulx, whose cases are always shady; Mme d'Espard, who is bringing the most despicable suit against her husband; Charles de Vandenesse, who is suing his own brother without justification; Philippe Bridau. For the rest, his clientele is composed above all of artists and strumpets. On occasion, he goes to visit them.

He is friendly with both Bixiou and Blondet (*Illusions perdues*, p.874). In *Un Homme d'Affaires*, we see him attending a supper at Malaga's during which he proves himself to be another brilliant conversationalist. But he is antipathetic. Having fallen in love with Malvina d'Aldrigger, he drops her like a hot brick as soon as he discovers that she has lost all her money (*Maison Nucingen*). At that time, Couture says, "he gave me the impression of a tiger escaped from the Jardin des Plantes. Thin, sandy haired, eyes the color of Spanish tobacco, a sour complexion, a cold and phlegmatic air . . . well educated, devious, two-faced, honey-tongued, never losing his temper, concealing all the hate he felt in true lawyer's fashion" (*id*. p.618). He is "the ablest lawyer in Paris" Goupil says (*Ursule Mirouët*, p.342). But just what exactly does a scurvy creature like Goupil mean by "the ablest"? However, Desroches is a hard worker, that we can't deny him. "We work day and night here," he tells young Husson when he takes him on as a clerk (*Un Début dans la Vie*, p.708).

Godeschal has been employed as a clerk by both of these lawyers in succession. He's a fine fellow this Godeschal, serious, thrifty, hard-working, and also, despite all that, jolly good company at times. In *le Colonel Chabert* he shows that he has quite a witty way with him when he tries. In *Un Début dans la Vie* (p.714), he treats all his colleagues to a lunch, as a consequence of which, so the minutes of the meeting inform us, "Godeschal was proclaimed the very flower of the Bazoche and above all a jolly good fellow." At the time of this lunch, he is sharing an apartment with his sister, Mariette, who is a ballet dancer. Something of each seems to rub off on the other. The legal file borrows a little of the tutu's gaiety, and the tutu a little of the file's legal gravity. In 1840, Godeschal becomes a lawyer in his turn.

But that is enough about these lawyers, none of whom ever plays a leading role anyway. There are several others I haven't mentioned, but none of them are really worth commenting on, except Petit-Claud, and I've dealt with him elsewhere. Nor shall I linger any longer over the stockbrokers: Jules Desmarets, the husband of the exquisite Mme Jules, in *Ferragus*; Foullepointe in *les Petites Misères de la Vie conjugale*; Jacques Falleix, who was for a short while the lover of Suzanne du Val-Noble, then disappeared after his financial collapse in 1828 (*Splendeurs*, p.813 and *Maison Nucingen*). Then we have two District Heads of Internal Revenue: Grossetête in Bourges (*Curé de Village*) and Marion in Troyes (*Député d'Arcis*). An Excise Tax collector: Gravier in Sancerre (*Muse du Département*). A Civil Service collecting clerk: the imbecile Saillard of *les Em-*

ployés; a bank teller: the diabolic Castanier of *Melmoth réconcilié;* a cashier in a store: the insignificant Gabusson of *les Illusions perdues;* a messenger boy in a bank: Lemprun in *les Petits Bourgeois;* a doorman: Plissoud in *les Paysans.*

III

INDEX OF CHARACTERS OCCURRING IN *LA COMÉDIE HUMAINE*

Rather than limit myself to an index of the Balzac characters mentioned in the body of this work, I decided that it would be of more use to the reader if I provided a complete list of all the characters that occur in the *Comédie Humaine*. The numbers following each entry indicate the pages of the present work on which the character in question is mentioned. Numbers in italics refer to pages on which an individual study of the character is to be found.

Unless otherwise indicated, all characters may be taken to be French. Similarly, unless otherwise indicated, all characters may be taken to reside in Paris.

Where dates are concerned, the reader will do well to remember that although Balzac specifies many of them precisely, others are merely indicated in sentences of this sort: "At this time, he was a vigorous old man of eighty-two." Which is to say that they are not always accurate in the very strictest sense.

ABRAMKO, Polish, doorkeeper to Magus (*Cousin Pons*).

ACHILLE, a character in *la Physiologie du Mariage*.

ADÈLE, a servant to the Rogrons, in Provins (*Pierrette*).

ADÈLE, Suzanne du Val Noble's maid (*Splendeurs et Miséres des Courtisanes*).

ADOLPHE, a clerk employed by Fritot (*Gaudissart II*).

ADOLPHUS, German, a banker in Mannheim (*Maison Nucingen*).

Has one daughter who marries Aldrigger (See Aldrigger).

AGATHE (Sister), née Langeais, a nun (*Episode sous la Terreur*): 441.

AGATHE, mistress of Benassis, by whom she

has a child who dies in infancy (*Médecin de Campagne*).

AIGLEMONT (Marquis Victor d'), a soldier, born 1783, dies 1833 (*Femme de trente ans*, etc.): 82, 94, 103, 133, 144, 145, 259, 342, 343, 416.

Marries Julie de Chastillonnest, born 1797, dies 1844 (*id.*): 57, 130, *144*, *145*, 156, 157, 171, 258, 338, 342, 466.

Issue:

1) Hélène, born 1817, dies 1833 approx. (*id.*): 144, 145, 152, *156*, *157*, 160, 342. Carried off by the pirate Victor, by whom she has four children all of whom die young;

2) Charles, killed by Hélène: 144, 145;

AIGLEMONT (*cont.*)
3) Gustave, dies young leaving a widow and children;
4) Moïna, who marries Saint-Héreen (See Saint-Héreen);
5) Abel, killed at siege of Constantine.

It is reasonable to suppose that all these children, with the exception of Hélène, were the issue of their mother's liaison with Charles de Vandenesse. Where this family is concerned, all dates are approximate.

AJUDA, a noble Portuguese family represented by:
1) a Mlle Ajuda who marries the Duc de Grandlieu (See Grandlieu);
2) the Marquis Miguel d'Ajuda-Pinto (*Père Goriot*, etc.): 5, 7, 8, 15, 70, 82, 85, 127, 128, 129, 170, 259, 262, 394;
Marries Berthe de Rochefide, who dies in 1834 approx.: 70, 128, 131.
Ajuda then marries Joséphine de Grandlieu: 70, 156.

ALAIN (Frédéric), a clerk, accountant, member of the Brothers of the Consolation (*Envers de l'Histoire contemporaine*): 324, 325, 435.

ALBERTINE, a maid in Mme de Bargeton's household (*Illusions Perdues*).

ALBON (Marquis d'), a magistrate and deputy (*Adieu*).

ALBRIZZI (Comtesse), a Venetian (*Massimila Doni*).

ALDRIGGER (Baron Jean-Baptiste d'), a banker, born in 1764, dies in 1823 (*Maison Nucingen*): 68, 479.
Marries Théodora-Marguerite-Wilhelmine Adolphus: 68, 387.
Issue:
1) Malvina, born 1801: 68, 156, 479, 484;
2) Isaure, born 1807, who marries Beaudenord (See Beaudenord).

ALEXANDRE, a character in *la Physiologie du Mariage*.

ALEXANDRINE, a character in *les Petites Misères de la Vie conjugale*.

ALINE, Mme Graslin's maid (*Curé de Village*).

ALPHONSE, a friend of Charles Grandet (*Eugénie Grandet*).

AL-SARTCHILD (house of), a bank (*Cousin Pons*).

ALTHOR (Jacob), a banker from Hamburg settled in le Havre (*Modeste Mignon*).

Has a son, Francisque, who marries a Mlle Vilquin.

AMANDA, a dressmaker (*Homme d'Affaires*).

AMAURY (Mme), a landowner at Ingouville (*Modeste Mignon*).

AMBERMESNIL (Comtesse de l'), a boarder in Mme Vauquer's pension. Probably no more a countess than I am a bishop (*Père Goriot*).

ANASTASIE, a chambermaid (*Physiologie du Mariage*).

ANCHISE (le père), a young servant in employ of La Palférine (*Prince de la Bohème*).

ANGARD, a doctor (*Cousine Bette*).

ANGÉLIQUE (Sister), a nun in Blois (*Mémories de deux Jeunes Mariées*).

ANGLAISE (une), an English courtesan (*Splendeurs et Misères des Courtisanes*): 227, 388, 392.

ANICETTE, a pretty maid in employ of Mme de Cadignan (*Député d'Arcis*).

ANNETTE, an old servant to Lady Brandon (*Grenadière*).

ANNETTE, family name not known, mistress of Charles Grandet (*Eugénie Grandet*): 147.

ANNETTE, a servant to the Rigou family (*Paysans*).

ANTOINE, an usher at the Ministry of Finance and uncle to the ushers Laurent and Gabriel (*Employés*).

ANTOINE, an old servant in employ of Mme de Rochefide (*Béatrix*).

ANTONIA (see Chocardelle).

AQUILINA, a kept woman (*Melmoth réconcilié, Peau de Chagrin*): 228, 328.

ARCHBISHOP OF BOURGES, intervenes in *la Muse du Département*: 109.

ARCOS (Comte d'), a Spanish nobleman (*Marana*).

ARGAIOLO (Duc d'), an Italian nobleman, dies in 1835 (*Albert Savarus*).
Married a Soderini: 78, 155, 173, 312.
When widowed, she marries the Duc de Rhétoré.

ARMAND, a character in *les Petites Misères de la Vie conjugale*.

ARRACHELAINE (see Ruffard).

ARTAGNON (Baron d'), a soldier in the 17th century (*Enfant Maudit*).

ARTHEZ (Daniel d'), a writer and politician, born in 1794 (*Illusions Perdues, Secrets de la Princesse de Cadignan*, etc.): 23, 25, 29, 35, 63, 86, 88, 89, 97, 147, 185, 186, 208, 210, 211, 212, 214,

215, *216*, 217, 218, 219, 220, 240, 241, 251, 276, 295, 311, 314, 326, 354, 356, 369, 448.

ASIE (see Collin) (Jacqueline).

ATHALIE, a cook in the employ of Mme Schontz (*Muse du Département*).

AUBRION (Marquis d'), a gentleman who appears briefly with his wife in *Eugénie Grandet*. They have a daughter, Mathilde, who marries Charles Grandet, thus making him Comte d'Aubrion (see Grandet).

AUFFRAY, a grocer in Provins, born about 1723, dies in 1813 (*Pierrette*).
Married, but wife's name unknown. They have a daughter who marries the innkeeper Rogron and is mother of Sylvie and Jérôme (see Rogron).
After death of first wife, marries again (wife's name not known) in 1792. A daughter born in 1793, who marries Lorrain. They have one daughter, Pierrette (see Lorrain).
The second Mme Auffray, when widowed, marries Docteur Néraud.
Another Auffray, great-great-nephew of the grocer and husband of a Guénée is a lawyer in Provins (*Pierrette*).

AUGER, a journalist (*Illusions Perdues*).

AUGUSTE, a valet in employ of Montriveau (*Duchesse de Langeais*).

AUGUSTE, a murderer (*Splendeurs et Misères des Courtisanes*).

AUGUSTE, a character in *Physiologie du Mariage*.

AUGUSTE (Madame), a dressmaker (*Splendeurs*).

AUGUSTIN, a valet in Sérizy household (*Début dans la Vie*).

AUGUSTINE, a maid in the Manerville household (*Contrat de Mariage*).

AURÉLIE, a courtesan mentioned in *Béatrix*

AUVERGNAT (see Sélérier).

BABYLAS, a groom to Amédée de Soulas (*Albert Savarus*).

BANCKER (Mme), a Norwegian peasant (*Séraphita*).

BAPTISTE, a servant in the Lenoncourt-Chaulieu household (*Splendeurs*).

BARBANTI, a Corsican family mentioned in *la Vendetta*.

BARBET, a bookseller (*Illusions Perdues*).
Probably the same character as the Barbet who appears in *Petits Bourgeois* and *l'Envers de l'Histoire contemporaine*: 478, 480.

Another Barbet, his nephew, is a publisher (*Petits Bourgeois*).

BARCHOU DE PEN-HOEN, a writer and politician (1801-1855) (*Louis Lambert*). Did exist.

BARGETON (Mirault de), an aristocratic family of the Angoulême district represented by the Marquis de Bargeton, born 1761 approx., dies 1821 (*Illusions Perdues*): 16, 113, 114.
Marries Marie-Louise-Anaïs de Nègrepelisse, born 1783 approx. (*id.*): 16, 22, 23, 24, 74, 95, 103, 104, *112-115*, 273, 295, 296, 311, 326, 351, 375, 378.
When widowed, she remarries with Sixte du Chatelet.

BARILLAUD, a relative of Alain's (*Envers de l'Histoire contemporaine*).

BARIMORE (Lady), husband unknown, daughter of Lord Dudley (*Autre Etude de Femme*): 388, 391.

BARNIOL, director of a teaching establishment (*Petits Bourgeois*).
Marries a Mlle Phellion.
A sister of this Barniol is married to Pron.

BARRY (John), English, a stableman (*Modeste Mignon*): 388, 392.

BARTAS (Adrien du) and his wife Joséphine, live in Angoulême, are great friends of the Brébians, the two husbands being generally supposed to be the lovers of each other's wives (*Illusions Perdues*).

BASTIENNE, a milliner (*Illusions Perdues*).

BATAILLE, a tradesman (*Petits Bourgeois*).

BAUDOYER, a tanner (*Employés*).
Marries a Mitral.
They have one son: Isidore, born 1787, a civil servant, then a tax-collector and mayor (*id.* and *Cousin Pons*): 72, 232, 307, 326, 331, 437, 460.
Marries Elisabeth Saillard, born 1794: 146, 147.
They have a daughter, Elise.

BAUDRAND, a theater cashier (*Cousin Pons*).

BAUDRY (Planat de), a tax official (*Bal de Sceaux*).
Marries a daughter of the Comte de Fontaine.

BAUVAN, an aristocratic family represented by:
1) The Comte de Bauvan (*Chouans*) and his wife, later his widow (*Cabinet des Antiques*). She is possibly to be identified with "the mare of Charette" who appears in *les Chouans* as Mme du Gua-Saint-Cyr;

BAUVAN (*cont.*)

2) the Comte and Comtesse de Bauvan who die in about 1815 (*Honorine*);

3) Octave, their son, "famous pro-Government orator" (*id.*): 15, 103, 136, 137, 172, 326.

Marries Honorine X., born 1794, dies in 1831 approx.: 13, 135, *136*, *137*, 172, 214, 326.

They have one son.

BEAUDENORD (Godefroid de), born 1800 (*Maison Nucingen*, etc.): 20, 21, 67, *68*, 259, 392.

Marries Isaure d'Aldrigger, born 1807: 68.

They have four children.

BEAUMESNIL, an actress (*Splendeurs et Misères des Courtisanes*): 150, 461.

From a liaison with Peyrade she has one daughter, Lydie (See La Peyrade).

BEAUMINET (Suzanne), a character in *les Petites Misères de la Vie conjugale*).

BEAUPIED (see Falcon).

BEAUPRÈ (Fanny), an actress (*Illusions Perdues*).

BEAUSÉANT, an aristocratic family represented by a Marquis de Beauséant who dies at the beginning of the Restoration (*Père Goriot*).

Had married a Champignelles. Issue:

1) a Comte de Beauséant;

2) a Vicomte (later Marquis) (*Père Goriot* etc.): 7, 82.

Marries Claire de Bourgogne, born approx. 1791 (*id.* and *Femme abandonnée*): 4, 5, 15, 21, 30, 32, 46, 70, 83, 84, 94, 97, 102, *127-129*, 170, 171, 258, 260, 261, 273, 282, 311, 312.

Another female Beauséant, born 1733, is a nun (*Episode sous la Terreur*).

BEAUSSIER, a couple living in Issoudun. They have a son (*Rabouilleuse*).

BEAUVISAGE, a doctor in Blois (*Mémoires de deux Jeunes Mariées*).

BEAUVISAGE, a farmer at Gondreville (*Ténébreuse Affaire*).

Has one son, Philéas, born 1792, a milliner (*Député d'Arcis*): 50.

Philéas marries Séverine Grévin.

They have a daughter, Cécile-Renée, who is in reality the daughter of Melchior-René de Chargeboeuf: 50.

Cécile probably marries Maxime de Trailles.

BEAUVOIR (Chevalier de), a character mentioned in *La Muse du Département*.

BEAUVOULOIR, a 16th century family comprising a bonesetter named Antoine, his wife, née Gertrude Marana, and their daughter Gabrielle (*Enfant Maudit*).

BECKER, a Norwegian pastor (*Séraphita*).

Has one daughter, Minna, the first lady skier in French literature.

BECKER (Edmé), a medical student (*Interdiction*).

BEDEAU, a clerk employed by Bordin (*Un Début dans la Vie*).

BEGA, an army doctor, principal character of an anecdote told in *La Muse du Département*.

BELLEFEUILLE (Caroline de), name assumed in her career as a cocotte by Caroline Crochard (See Crochard).

BELLE HOLLANDAISE (see Gobseck).

BELLEJAMBE, a servant to Oscar Husson (*Début dans la Vie*).

BELOR (Mlle de), a young lady living in Bordeaux (*Contrat de Mariage*).

BELVIDERO, an aristocratic Italian family of 15th century comprising: Bartolomeo, his wife Juana, their son Don Juan, their daughter-in-law Elvire, and their grandson Philippe (*Elixir de longue vie*).

BEMBONI (Mgr.), an Italian prelate (*Mémoires de deux Jeunes Mariées*).

BENARD (Pièri), a correspondent of Birotteau's in Germany (*César Birotteau*).

BENASSIS, a doctor, born 1783, dies 1829 (*Médecin de Campagne*): 155, 307, 312, 324, 373, 377, 415, 435, 436, 445, 449, 457.

Has an illegitimate son by a certain Agathe. The child does not survive.

BENJAMIN, a servant employed by Philippe Bridau (*Rabouilleuse*).

BENOIT, a manservant (*Petites Misères*).

BÉRÉNICE, Coralie's maid (*Illusions Perdues*): 24, 242, 295.

BERGERIN, a doctor in Saumur (*Eugénie Grandet*).

BERGMANN (M. and Mme), a Swiss couple. Characters in Savarus's short story (*Albert Savarus*).

BERNUS, a coachmaker in Guérande (*Béatrix*). Did exist (Billy, *Vie de Balzac*, II, 6): 463.

BERQUET, a workman in Besançon (*Albert Savarus*).

BRISETOUT (Héloïse), a dancer (*Cousin Pons*, etc.): 207, 221, *232, 233,* 241, 478, 482.

BRISSET, a doctor (*Peau de Chagrin*).

BROCHON, a domestic employed by Moreau (*Début dans la Vie*).

BROSSARD (Mme du), an inhabitant of Angoulême. Has a daughter, Camille (*Illusions Perdues*).

BROSSETTE (Abbé), a parish priest, first in Blangy then in Paris (*Paysans, Béatrix*): 261, *439,* 440.

BROUET (Joseph), a Chouan, killed in 1799 (*Les Chouans*).

BROUIN (Jacquette), wife of Pierre Cambremer (*Drame au bord de la Mer*).

BROUSSON, a doctor (*Auberge Rouge*).

BRUCE (Gabriel), a royalist condemned to death for desertion in 1809 (*Envers de l'Histoire contemporaine*).

BRUEL (du), a civil servant glimpsed in *la Rabouilleuse,* dies in 1821. His widow is mentioned in *Un Prince de la Bohème.*

They have a son, Jean-François, born 1797, civil servant, playwright, Count and Peer of France (*Employés, Illusions Perdues,* etc.): 55, 187, 191, 194, *197, 198,* 208, 214, 240, 242, 251, 276, 304, 312, 482.

Marries in 1829 Claudine Chaffaroux, known as Tullia, a dancer (*Illusions Perdues, Un Prince de la Bohème,* etc.): 55, 77, 78, 81, 187, 193, *197, 198,* 225, 229, 236, 241, 242, 243, 276, 312.

BRUNET, an usher in Soulanges (*Paysans*).

BRUNNER (Gédéon), German, a hotelkeeper in Frankfurt, dies in 1844 (*Cousin Pons*).

Marries first a Virlaz, then a shrew.

By the first, has a son, Fritz, who becomes a banker in Paris (*Cousin Pons*): 387.

BRUNO, a manservant to Corentin (*Splendeurs et Misères des Courtisanes*).

BRUTUS, an innkeeper in Alençon (*Chouans*).

BRYOND DES TOURS MINIÈRES (Baron Bernard-Polydor), better known under name of Contenson, born 1763, or 1772, dies 1830, a Chouan, then a policeman (*Envers de l'Histoire contemporaine, Splendeurs,* etc.): 143, 144, 307, 327, 458, *459, 462,* 470.

BUISSON, a tailor (*Cabinet des Antiques*).
Did exist: 463.

BULOT, a "great imbecile" (*Illustre Gaudissart*).

BUNEAUD, an owner of a family boarding house (*Père Goriot*).

BUTIFER, a huntsman in the Dauphiné (*Médecin de Campagne*).

BUTSCHA (Jean), son of a Swedish sailor and a Mlle Jacmin, born 1804, a lawyer's clerk in le Havre (*Modeste Mignon*): *183, 184,* 307.

CABIROLLE, a coachman in Nemours. Has a son, also a coachman.

Marries second wife, Antoinette Patris, also known as la Bougival (*Ursule Mirouët*).

CABIROLLE (Mme), a concierge and mother of Florentine (see Florentine): 241.

CABOT, a hairdresser (*Comédiens sans le savoir*).

CABOT (Marie-Anne), alias La Jeunnesse, a Chouan. He is executed in 1809 (*Envers de l'Histoire contemporaine*).

CACHAN, a lawyer in Angoulême, then mayor of Marsac (*Illusions Perdues, Splendeurs*).

CADENET, a wine merchant (*Petits Bourgeois*).

CADIGNAN, an aristocratic family represented by an old Prince de Cadignan who dies in 1830 (*Modeste Mignon,* etc.): 8, 77.

Married (wife's name unknown).
Issue:

1) A daughter who marries the Duc de Navarreins;

2) A son, the Duc de Maufrigneuse until 1830, then Prince de Cadignan, born about 1776 (*Illusions Perdues, Secrets de la Princesse de Cadignan*): 8, 77, 81, 82, 85, 89, 196, 212, 259.

Marries in 1814 Diane d'Uxelles, born 1796, Duchesse de Maufrigneuse, then Princesse de Cadignan (*Cabinet des Antiques, Secrets de la Princesse de Cadignan, Splendeurs et Misères des Courtisanes,* etc.): 7, 13, 15, 20, 25, 27, 33, 40, 43, 46, 62, 63, 64, 65, 70, 77, 80, 81, 82, *84 to 90,* 94, 95, 96, 98, 107, 113, 147, 211, 216, 217, 242, 259, 273, 276, 283, 302, 317, 325, 334, 355, 402, 435, 472.

She has one son, Georges de Maufrigneuse, born about 1815: 85, 304.

He marries Berthe de Cinq-Cygne.

Another female Cadignan marries,

first Firmiani, then Octave de Camps (see Firmiani).

CADINE (Jenny), an actress, born in 1814 (*Cousine Bette, Comédiens sans le savoir*): 221, *229, 230,* 235, 239, 242, 281, 481.

CADOT (Mlle), a housekeeper employed by the judge Blondet (*Cabinet des Antiques*).

CALVI (Théodore), alias la belle Madeleine, a murderer, then a policeman, born 1803 (*Splendeurs et Misères des Courtisanes*): 291, 294, *301.*

CAMBACÉRÈS (Jean-Jacques), a real life political figure (1753-1824) (*Ténébreuse Affaire*).

CAMBON, a wood merchant in the Dauphiné (*Médecin de Campagne*).

CAMBREMER (Pierre), a fisherman at le Croisic (*Drame au bord de la Mer*).
Marries Jacquette Brouin.
They have a son, Jacques.
Cambremer also has a brother, Joseph, who is the father of a Pierrette or Pérotte (*id.*) (not the heroine of *Pierrette*).

CAMÉRISTUS, a doctor (*Peau de Chagrin*).

CAMPS (Octave de), born about 1802 (*Madame Firmiani*, etc.): 62, 130, 266, 332, 455.
Marries a Cadignan, widow of Firmiani, born before 1797: 7, 15, 62, *129, 130,* 266.

CAMUSOT, a silk dealer, later Baron, born 1765 (*Illusions Perdues, César Birotteau*, etc.): 13, 16, 23, 187, 195, 242, 333.
Marries first a Pons, then a Cardot. The second marriage produces three or four offspring never mentioned again.
From the first marriage there is one son, Camusot de Marville, born 1794, magistrate (*Cabinet des Antiques, Splendeurs, Cousin Pons*, etc.): 97, 98, 99, 100, 266, 267, 268, 312, 313, 331, 333, 458, 482.
Marries in 1819 Marie-Cécile-Amélie Thirion, born 1798 (*id.*): 13, *97 to 100,* 148, 266, 267, 268, 312, 313, 472.
Issue:
1) Charles, dies young;
2) Cécile, born 1821 (*Cousin Pons*): *148, 149,* 387, 472.
Marries Vicomte Popinot.

CANALIS (Constant-Cyr-Melchior, Baron de), poet, born 1800 (*Modeste Mignon, Mémoires de deux Jeunes Mariées*, etc.): 6, 116, 152, 172, 184, 186, 191, 221, *223 to 226,* 239, 240, 266, 304, 307, 366, 464, 467.
Marries a Moreau.

CANE (Marco-Facino), Prince of Varese, dies in 1820 (*Facino Cane*): 227, 258, 300, 379.

CANQUOËLLE, assumed name of Peyrade (see La Peyrade).

CANTAL (Armand du), a character in *Petites Misères de la Vie conjugale.*

CANTE-CROIX (colonel de), a suitor to Mme de Bargeton, killed at Wagram (*Illusions Perdues*).

CANTINET, a beadle, married to a chair-attendant, father of a bit-player (male) at the Cirque Olympique (*Cousin Pons*).

CAPRAJA, a music lover living in Venice (*Massimila Doni*): 288.

CAPITAINE PARISIEN (le) (see Victor).

CARABÈS (Mme), a character in *Petites Misères de la Vie conjugale.*

CARABINE, a courtesan, born 1820, real name Séraphine Sinet (*Cousine Bette*, etc.): 185, 229, 237, 240, 478, 479.

CARBONNEAU, a doctor in Tours (*Lys dans la Vallée*).

CARCADO (Mme de), a charity worker (*Muse du Département*).

CARDANET (Mme de), an old lady living in Angoulême. Her granddaughter Zéphirine marries Senonches (*Illusions Perdues*).

CARDINAL, a porter in a Paris market, deceased (*Petits Bourgeois*).
Wife's maiden name Poupillier.
They have a daughter, Olympe, born 1824, actress (*id.*): *230, 231,* 241.

CARDOT (Jean-Jérôme-Séverin), a silk merchant, born 1755 (*Illusions Perdues, Début dans la Vie*, etc.): 13, 16, 187, 195, 334.
Wife's maiden name Husson, dies 1816. Issue:
1) A daughter who marries Camusot (see Camusot);
2) Marianne, who marries Protez;
3) A lawyer son, born 1794 (*Muse du Département*, etc.): 149, 234, 332, 333, *482.*
Marries a Chiffreville: 149, 307, 482. Issue:
a) a son in love with literature;
b) Félicie or Félicité marries Ber-

CARDOT (*cont.*)
thier (see Berthier); c) a daughter.
4) Joseph, partner of the pharmacist Matifat (*Début dans la Vie*).

CARIGLIANO (Maréchal duc de), a character little known to any but his wife, née Malin de Gondreville. She was born about 1778 (*Maison du Chat-qui-pelote*, etc.): *133*, 138, 221, 271, 277, 413.

CARMAGNOLA, a gondolier in Venice (*Massimila Doni*).

CARNOT (Lazare), a real life French politician (1753-1823), (*Ténébreuse Affaire*): 470.

CAROLINE (Mlle), governess to the Vandenesse children (*Lys dans la Vallée*).

CAROLINE, a servant employed by Mme de Listomère (*Etude de Femme*).

CAROLINE, a servant employed by the Thuilliers (*Petits Bourgeois*).

CARON, a lawyer in Tours (*Curé de Tours*).

CARPENTIER, a retired army officer living in Issoudun (*Rabouilleuse*): 388.
Maiden name of wife Borniche-Hereau.

CARPI, a jailer in Venice (*Facino Cane*).

CARTHAGENOVA, a bass at the Fenice Theater in Venice (*Massimila Doni*).

CARTIER (M. and Mme), gardeners (*Envers de l'Histoire contemporaine*).

CASA-REAL, a Spanish title borne by Mme Claës's brother (*Recherche de l'Absolu*).
Mme Evangelista is also a Casa-Real by birth (*Contrat de Mariage*).

CASTAGNOULD, second of the "Mignon" (*Modeste Mignon*).

CASTANIER (Rodolphe), an ex-officer, teller employed by Nucingen (*Melmoth réconcilié*): 228, 328, 341, 342, 353, 416, 424, 428, 436, 485.
Married, but wife's maiden name not known.

CASTERAN "pronounced Catéran," an aristocratic Normandy family represented by:
1) A female Casteran-la-Tour who has married a Milaud de la Baudraye (*Muse du Département*);
2) Blanche de Casteran who had an illegitimate daughter by the Duc de Verneuil (Marie de Verneuil) and who becomes a nun (*Chouans*);
3) The Marquis and Marquise de Casteran who live in Alençon (*Cab-*

inet des Antiques, Vieille Fille) and have three children:
a) The Comte de Casteran. Probably the same Casteran who is a prefect in Burgundy and who married a Troisville (*Paysans*).
b) a daughter.
c) Béatrix-Maximilienne-Rose, who marries Arthur de Rochefide (see Rochefide).

CATANEO (Le Duc), a Sicilian music lover (*Massimila Doni*): 262, 287, *288*, 381, 393.
Married to Massimila Doni.

CATHERINE, a housemaid employed by Laurence de Cinq-Cygne (*Ténébreuse Affaire*).

CATHERINE, a servant to the Sillards (*Employés*).

CAVALIER (see Fendant et Cavalier).

CAVATOLINO (Bianca), a courtesan in Ferrara during 16th century (*Elixir de longue vie*).

CAYRON, an umbrella dealer (*César Birotteau*).

CÉLESTIN, Birotteau's cashier (*César Birotteau*).

CÉLESTIN, Rubempré's manservant (*Splendeurs*).

CÉLESTINE, a housemaid (*Physiologie du Mariage*).

CÉLINE, a housemaid (*Physiologie du Mariage*).

CÉNACLE (le) (see 207, *209* to 220, 221, 298).

CÉRIZET, a foreman, then a sub-prefect, then a moneylender, born 1802 (*Illusions Perdues, Petits Bourgeois, Homme d'Affaires*, etc.): 169, 180, 231, 241, 326, 327, 357, 359, 362, 391, 449, 474, 478, *480*.

CÉSARINE, a laundress in Alençon. Possibly marries the Chevalier de Valois (*Vieille Fille*).

CÉSARINE, a dancer (*Rabouilleuse*).

CHABERT (known as Hyacinthe), a colonel and Comte (*Colonel Chabert*): 134, *422* to *424*, 428, 455, 456, 466, 483.
Marries Rose Chapotel who later, believing herself a widow, marries Ferraud (see Ferraud).

CHABOISSEAU, a former bookseller and discounter (*Illusions Perdues, Homme d'Affaires*, etc.): 478, 480.

CHAFFAROUX, a family represented by a rich contractor (*Prince de la Bohême* and *Petits Bourgeois*) and also by Claudine Chaffaroux, known as Tullia, who marries du Bruel (see Bruel).

CHAMAROLLES (Mlles), heads of a boarding school in Bourges (*Muse du Département*).

CHAMPAGNAC, a boilermaker in Limoges (*Curé de Village*).
Has a daughter who marries Saviat.

CHAMPIGNELLES, an aristocratic Normandy family represented by:
1) A Marquis de Champignelles who lives in Bayeux (*Femme abandonnée and Envers de l'Histoire contemporaine*);
2) A Champignelles (f.) who marries a Beauséant (see Beauséant);
3) Another Champignelles (f.) who marries La Chanterie (see La Chanterie).

CHAMPION (Maurice), Mme Graslin's confidential agent (*Curé de Village*).

CHAMPLAIN, a winegrower at Vouvray (*Illustre Gaudissart*).

CHANDOUR (Stanislas and Amélie de), townsfolk in Angoulême (*Illusions Perdues*).

CHANOR (see Florent et Chanor).

CHANTONNIT, mayor of les Riceys, near Besançon (*Albert Savarus*).

CHAPELOUD (Abbé), a canon in Tours (*Curé de Tours*): 441.

CHAPERON (Abbé), a parish priest in Nemours (*Ursule Mirouët*): 346, 347, 357.

CHAPOTEL (Rose), a prostitute in a brothel who marries first Chabert and then the Comte Ferraud (see Ferraud).

CHAPOULOT, a former passementerie maker and co-tenant of Pons together with his wife and his daughter Victorine (*Cousin Pons*).

CHAPUZOT (M. and Mme), Malaga's porter and concierge (*Fausse Maîtresse*).

CHAPUZOT, a divisional chief at Police headquarters (*Cousine Bette*).

CHARBONNON DE MAULINCOUR (see Maulincour).

CHARDIN, an interesting Parisian family represented by:
1) An old mattress maker (*Cousine Bette*);
2) His son, a storekeeper in Algeria (*id.*);
3) A great-nephew of 1), known as Idamore, works as a theater claqueur (*id.*): 238, 240;
4) A sister of 3), Elodie: 53, 238, 281.

CHARDIN DES LUPEAULX (see Lupeaulx).

CHARDON, an army doctor, then a pharmacist in Angoulême, dies 1816 (*Illusions Perdues*): 13, 21.
Wife, née Rubempré, dies 1827: 21. Issue:
1) Lucien, known as de Rubempré (see Rubempré);
2) Eve, who marries Séchard (see Séchard).

CHAREL (M. and Mme), a farmer and his wife who live near Alençon.
Their daughter Olympe marries Michaud (*Paysans*).

CHARGEBOEUF (Duineff de), a noble family, "one of the most illustrious of the old county of Champagne," represented by:
1) The Marquis de Chargeboeuf, born about 1737 (*Ténébreuse Affaire*): 409, 469;
2) A Mlle de Chargeboeuf sometimes visited by Talleyrand (*Mémoires de deux Jeunes Mariées*);
3) Melchior-René de Chargeboeuf, sub-prefect in Arcis, then in Sancerre, probably the father of Cécile Beauvisage (*Député d'Arcis, Muse du Département*);
4) A Chargeboeuf who is secretary to the Attorney General, Granville (*Splendeurs*). Possibly the same Chargeboeuf mentioned in *Pierrette;*
5) A Chargeboeuf (f.), possibly the sister of 4), seduced, then married by Vinet (*Pierrette*): 178;
6) A widow living in Provins with her daughter Bathilde. The latter marries Rogron (*Pierrette*): 48, *159*.
The Cinq-Cygnes are a junior branch of the Chargeboeuf family.

CHARGEGRAIN (Louis), an innkeeper in Normandy (*Envers de l'Histoire contemporaine*).

CHARLES, a young man killed in a duel by Raphaël de Valentin (*Peau de Chagrin*).

CHARLES, a domestic servant employed by the Montcornets (*Paysans*).

CHARLES, a painter (*Père Goriot*).

CHARLES, a captain (*Physiologie du Mariage*).

CHARLOTTE, mistress of Henri de Marsay. Names of first husband and of the duke she marries when widowed both unknown (*Autre Etude de Femme*): 39, 40, 57, 147.

1799. This cousin leaves a wife and a son (*Chouans*).

CIBOT, a tailor and concierge, dies 1845 (*Cousin Pons*).

Has a wife, born 1788, a former oyster seller (*id.*): viii, 13, 180, 252, 262, *307*, 345, 346, 454.

After Cibot's death, she marries Rémonencq.

CIGOGNARA (Cardinal), a prelate in Rome (*Sarrasine*).

CINQ-CYGNE (Duineff de), a noble family of the Champagne represented by:
1) A widow Cinq-Cygne who, under Louis XIV, remarries with a Simeuse (*Ténébreuse Affaire*);
2) Berthe de Cinq-Cygne, who marries Jean de Simeuse. They have two sons, Marie-Paul and Paul-Marie (see Simeuse);
3) a Comte de Cinq-Cygne, brother of Berthe, dies before 1789, leaving a widow who dies in 1793 and two children: a) Jules, killed in the Armée des Princes; b) Laurence, born 1781 (*Ténébreuse Affaire*, etc.): viii, 89, 143, *157*, *158*, 159, 259, 464.

She marries Adrien de Hauteserre, who takes her name. Issue:
1) Berthe, who marries Georges de Maufrigneuse: 304.
2) Paul (*Député d'Arcis*).

CIPREY, a deputy guardian of Pierrette Lorrain (*Pierrette*).

CLAËS-MOLINA DE NOURHO, a noble family originating in Ghent, now settled in Douai, represented by Balthazar Claës, born 1761, dies 1832 (*Recherche de l'Absolu*): 53, 304, 306, 336, 353, 358, 368, 377.

Marries Joséphine de Tenninck, born 1770, dies 1816: 53, 146, 277, 318, 353. 433. Issue:
1) Marguerite who marries Emmanuel de Solis (see Solis).
2) Félicie who marries Pierquin.
3) Gabriel who marries a Mlle Conynckx.
4) Balthazar.

CLAGNY (de), a magistrate in Sancerre, then in Paris (*Muse du Département*).

CLAPARON, a civil servant who dies in 1820 (*Rabouilleuse*).

Has son, Charles, born 1790, a business man (*Melmoth réconcilié* and *Petits Bourgeois*): *481*.

CLAPART, an office worker, dies in 1835 (*Début dans la Vie*): 182.

Married to the widowed Mme Husson, born 1780: 181, 182, 334.

CLARIMBAULT (Maréchal de), a common ancestor of the Beauséants and the Rastignacs. Married a Rastignac (*Père Goriot*).

CLAUDE, an idiot living in the Dauphiné (*Médecin de Campagne*).

CLEF-DES-COEURS (la) a republican soldier (*Chouans*).

CLÉRETTI, an architect (*Cousine Bette*).

CLERGEOT, a civil servant (*Employés*).

CLERGET (Basine), a laundrywoman in Angoulême (*Illusions Perdues*).

CLOTILDE, a dancer (*Sarrasine*).

CLOUSIER, a justice of the peace in Montégnac. Another Clousier, his nephew, is a court clerk, then a notary, also in Montégnac (*Curé de Village*).

COCHEGRUE, a farmer in the Limousin, murdered by the Farrabesche gang (*Curé de Village*).

COCHEGRUE (Jean), a Chouan killed in 1799 (*Chouans*).

COCHET (Mlle), maid to Mlle Laguerre, born 1763 (*Paysans*).

Marries Soudry, the police sergeant in Soulanges (see Soudry).

COCHET (Françoise), maid to Modeste Mignon in le Havre (*Modeste Mignon*).

COCHIN (Emile-Louis-Lucien-Emmanuel), a clerk, then a business man and a Baron (*Employés*, *César Birotteau*, *Petits Bourgeois*).

Has a wife and a son, Adolphe. Another Cochin, brother of Emile-Louis, is also a clerk (*Employés*).

COEUR-LA-VIROLE, a prisoner being held in the Conciergerie (*Splendeurs et Misères des Courtisanes*).

COFFINET, a grocer in Arcis (*Député d'Arcis*).

COFFINET (M. and Mme), porter and concierge to the Thuilliers (*Petits Bourgeois*).

COGNET (le père), and COGNETTE (la mère), innkeepers in Issoudun (*Rabouilleuse*).

COINTET (Boniface), a printer in Angoulême, later a minister (*Illusions Perdues* and *Maison Nucingen*):

Marries a daughter of Anselme Popinot.

Has a brother, Jean (*Illusions Perdues*).

COLAS (la mère), a peasant woman living in le Dauphiné (*Médecin de Campagne*).

Has a son, Jacques (1813-1829).

COLLEVILLE, a civil servant (*Employés, Petits Bourgeois,* etc.): 242, 251, 276, 286, 287, 306.

Marries Flavie Minoret, born 1798, daughter of a dancer and (probably) du Bousquier (*id.*): 276, 286, 287, 306, 352, 412.

Issue:

1) A daughter.

2) Charles, son of Charles Gondreville.

3) François, son of François Keller.

4) Céleste, daughter of Thuillier: 160, 286.

5) Théodore or Anatole, probably the son of an ecclesiastic: 286.

COLLIAU, a tradesman (*Illusions Perdues*).

COLLIN (Jacques) (see Vautrin).

COLLIN (Jacqueline), aunt of Vautrin, born in Java in 1774 (*Splendeurs, Cousine Bette,* etc.): 27, 240, 242, 290, 298, 299, 325, 459, 464.

COLLINET, a musician (*César Birotteau*).

COLLINET, a grocer in Arcis (*Député d'Arcis*).

COLLINET, a businessman in Nantes (*Pierrette*).

COLONNA, an old Genoese (*Vendetta*).

COLONNA (Prince and Princesse), characters in the story written by Savarus. Their daughter, Francesca, married the Prince Gandolphini (*Albert Savarus*).

COLOQUINTE, an invalid (f.) (*Illusions Perdues*): 241.

COLORAT (Jérôme), an overseer of Mme Graslin's estate at Montégnac (*Curé de Village*).

COMBABUS, nickname of Montès. See *Cousine Bette*, p. 478, for explanation.

CONSTANCE, a maid employed by Mme de Restaud (*Père Goriot*).

CONSTANT (Benjamin), a real life writer and politician (1767-1830) (*Illusions Perdues*): 470.

CONSTANT, a manservant to Napoleon (*Ténébreuse Affaire*): 470.

CONSTANTIN, a groom to the Laginskis (*Fausse Maîtresse*).

CONTENSON (see Bryon).

CONTI (Gennaro), a composer of Italian birth (*Béatrix,* etc.): 107, 131, 226, 236, 241, 259, 260, 261.

CONYNGHAM, leader of Louis XI's Scotch Guards (*Maître Cornelius*).

CONYNCKX, great-uncle and deputy guardian of the Claës children (*Recherche de l'Absolu*). Has a daughter who marries Gabriel Claës.

COQUART, Camusot's clerk in court (*Splendeurs*).

COQUELIN (M. and Mme), a hardware merchant and his wife (*César Birotteau*).

COQUET, a civil servant (*Cousine Bette*).

CORALIE, family name unknown, an actress, born 1803, dies 1822 (*Illusions Perdues*): 13, 23, 24, 25, 26, 28, 40, 53, 187, 193, 194, 195, 202, 206, 207, 212, 214, 216, 229, 242, 243, 258, 262, 295, 396, 397, 419.

CORBIGNY (de), prefect in the Loir-et-Cher (*Louis Lambert*).

CORBINEAU (Abbé), confessor of the Duc d'Hérouville in the 16th century (*Enfant Maudit*).

CORBINET, a notary in Soulanges (*Paysans*). Has a son, a judge in the court of la Ville-aux-Fayes (*id.*).

A brother of the notary is head of the post office in la Ville-aux-Fayes (*id.*).

CORDE-A-PUITS, a young artist (*Rabouilleuse*).

CORENTIN, a police officer, born about 1777 (*Chouans, Ténébreuse Affaire, Splendeurs,* etc.): 150, 327, 457, 458, 459, 460, 461, 462, 464, 470.

CORET (Augustin), a clerk employed by Bordin (*Début dans la Vie*).

CORMON, an eminent citizen of Alençon, date of death unknown (*Vieille Fille*).

Leaves a daughter, Rose-Marie-Victoire, born 1773 (*id.* and *Cabinet des Antiques*): 16, 100, 163 to 165, 168, 252, 253, 259, 271, 272, 275, 332, 355, 358, 359, 366, 377, 404, 413.

Rose Cormon marries du Bousquier in 1816.

CORNEVIN, foster father of Mme Michaud (*Paysans*).

CORNOILLER, a gamekeeper in Saumur. Marries la grande Nanon (*Eugénie Grandet*).

CORRET, partner in the des Grassins bank in Saumur (*Eugénie Grandet*).

CORROY, marries Reybert (see Reybert).

COTTEREAU, a Chouan leader. Did exist (*Chouans*).

COTTIN (Maréchal, Prince de Wissembourg, Duc d'Orfano), Minister of War under Louis-Philippe, born 1771 (*Cousine Bette*): 281, 417, *418*, 428, 429, 430.

COTTIN (Francine), a friend and maid of Marie de Verneuil (*Chouans*). Has an uncle, Thomas (*id.*).

COTTIN and his wife Brigitte, servants in the home of Mme de Dey in Carentan (*Réquisitionnaire*).

COUDRAI (du), a mortgage registrar in Alençon. Appears with his wife in *la Vieille Fille* and *le Cabinet des Antiques.*

COUPIAU, known as Mène-à-Bien, a stagecoach driver in Fougères (*Chouans*).

COUPIAU (Sulpice), a Chouan killed in 1799 (*Chouans*).

COURAND (Jenny), a flowerseller, friend of Gaudissart (*Illustre Gaudissart*): 228.

COURCEUIL (Félix), a surgeon in the armies of the Vendée, implicated in the affair of the chauffeurs de Mortagne (*Envers de l'Histoire contemporaine*).

COURNAND (or Cournant), a notary in Provins (*Pierrette*).

COURTECUISSE (known as Courtebotte), an overseer at les Aigues. Appears with his wife in *les Paysans*. Their daughter is a domestic servant in Auxerre (*id.*).

COURTEL, an usher in Arcis (*Député d'Arcis*).

COURTEVILLE (Mme de), the widow of a judge. She is mentioned, together with her daughter Amélie, in *Honorine.*

There is also some mention of a Courteville family living in Douai (*Recherche de l'Absolu*).

COURTOIS (M. and Mme), a miller and his wife in Marsac (*Illusions Perdues, Splendeurs*).

COUSSARD or GOUSSARD (Laurent), a carpenter in Arcis (*Député d'Arcis*).

COUTELIER, one of Maxime de Trailles' creditors (*Homme d'Affaires*).

COUTURE (Mme de), a widow and adoptive mother of Victorine Taillefer (*Père Goriot*).

COUTURE, a speculator, born in 1797 (*Béatrix, Maison Nucingen*, etc.): 34, 68, 229, 230, 480, 481, 484.

COUTURE, a lawyer (*Cousin Pons*).

COUTURIER (Abbé), a parish priest in Alençon (*Vieille Fille* and *Cabinet des Antiques*).

CRÉMIÈRE-CRÉMIÈRE, a tax-collector in Nemours (*Ursule Mirouët*).

Married to a Massin-Massin, niece of Doctor Minoret.

They have at least one daughter. (See Minoret).

CRÉMIÈRE-DIONIS, a notary mayor of Nemours after 1830 (*Ursule Mirouët*). Has a wife and a daughter. (See Minoret).

CRÉMIÈRE-LEVRAULT-DIONIS, a forage dealer in Nemours, guillotined (*Ursule Mirouët*). Had married a Massin-Levrault.

One daughter, who marries Levrault-Minoret, a farmer at Montereau. (See Minoret).

CREVEL (Célestin), a perfumer, then deputy mayor, born 1786, dies 1843 (*César Birotteau, Cousine Bette*, etc.): 14, 16, 78, 166, 205, 214, 231, 232, 242, 281, 282, 283, 284, 285, 308, 350, 351, 355, 357, 414, 433, 449, 474, *476* to *478*.

Marries a farmer's daughter who dies in 1833.

They have one daughter, Célestine, who marries Victorin Hulot (see Hulot).

When widowed, Crevel marries Valérie Fortin, widow of Marneffe. (See Marneffe).

They have one son that dies in infancy.

Crevel also had a maternal aunt (*Cousine Bette*): 231.

CROCHARD, a dancer, then a colonel, dies in 1814 (*Double Famille*). Wife's name unknown. She dies in 1822: 228, 241, 340.

They have a daughter, Caroline, known as de Bellefeuille: 61, 214, *228*, 241.

From a liaison with the Attorney General, Granville, Caroline has two children, Charles and Eugénie.

CROISIER (du) (see Bousquier).

CROIZEAU, a former coachmaker (*Homme d'Affaires*).

CROTTAT (M. and Mme), a farmer and his wife murdered by La Pouraille (*Splendeurs*).

They had a son, Alexandre, a notary (*César Birotteau, Femme de Trente Ans*): 183, *482*.

He marries a Lourdois.

CRUCHOT, a family living in Saumur represented by:
1) The Abbé Cruchot (*Eugénie Grandet*): 441.
2) His brother, a notary (*id.*): 481.
3) Their nephew, Cruchot de Bonfons, a magistrate, born 1783, dies 1829 (*id.*): 151.
In 1828, marries Eugénie Grandet, born 1796 (see Grandet).

CURÉ DE SAINT-LANGE, an ecclesiastic in Nemours. Took holy orders after having lost his wife and three sons, the latter all killed at Waterloo. (*Femme de Trente Ans* and *Ursule Mirouët*).

CUREL, a goldsmith. Appears with his wife and daughter in *César Birotteau.*

CURIEUX, a peasant family in the Limousin. One of the four daughters, Catherine, marries Jacques Farrabesche after having had an illegitimate child by him called Benjamin (*Curé de Village*).

CURSY, a pseudonym used by du Bruel (see Bruel).

CYDALISE, a courtesan, born 1827 (*Cousine Bette*): 237, 238, 285.

CYRUS (de), a character in *Petites Misères de la Vie conjugale.*

DALLOT, a mason (*Adieu*).

DANNEPONT, known as La Pouraille, a murderer. Was "married" to La Gonore (*Splendeurs*): 285.

DANTON (Georges-Jacques), a politician (1759-1794) (*Chouans*): 157, 464, 465, 470.
Marries Marie de Verneuil (see Verneuil).

DAUPHIN, a pastrycook in Arcis (*Député d'Arcis*).

DAURIAT, a bookseller (*Illusions Perdues*, etc.): 187, 240.

DAVID (M. and Mme), a farmer and his wife near Brive (*Curé de Village*).

DAVID, a Norwegian manservant (*Séraphita*).

DELBECQ, a businessman, then a magistrate (*Colonel Chabert*).

DELSOUCQ, a convict (*Splendeurs*).

DENISART, assumed name of Cérizet (*Homme d'Affaires*).

DERVILLE, a lawyer, born 1794 (*Gobseck, Colonel Chabert*, etc.): 9, 134, 139, 328, 349, 428, 455, 475, *483.*
Marries Fanny Malvaut: 483.

They have a daughter, Mathilde, who marries Augustin Bongrand (*Oeuvres ébauchées*).

DESCHARS (M. and Mme and Jules), characters in *Petites Misères de la Vie conjugale*).

DESCOINGS, a wool broker in Issoudun. Dies, together with his wife, before 1799 (*Rabouilleuse*). Issue:
1) A daughter who marries Rouget (see Rouget).
2) A son who is a grocer, guillotined in 1793. "A measure that did at least have the good effect of frightening all the other grocers and keeping them out of politics until 1830." Marries a widow Bixiou, born 1744, dies 31 December 1821 (*Rabouilleuse*): 206, 344, 356, 357, 358, 419, 482.
By Bixiou, Mme Descoings had had a son, a colonel, whose son is the caricaturist (see Bixiou).

DESFONDRILLES, a magistrate in Provins (*Pierrette*).

DESLANDES, a doctor in Azay-le-Rideau (*Lys dans la Vallée*).

DESMARETS (Jules), a stockbroker (*Ferragus*, etc.): 69, 139, 453.
Marries Clémence, illegitimate daughter of the convict Bourignard and of a married woman who dies in 1819 (*Ferragus*): 13, 69, 135, *139,* 258, 321.
Another Desmarets, the brother of Jules, is a notary (*id.*).

DESPLEIN, "the greatest surgeon of both ancient and modern times" (*Messe de l'Athée*, etc.): 13, 214, 219, 220, 311, 344, 355, 435.
Married, but wife's maiden name not known. They have a daughter, who is engaged to marry the Prince de Loudon (*Modeste Mignon*).

DESROCHES, a civil servant, dies 1823 (*Rabouilleuse*).
His wife is also mentioned in *La Maison Nucingen.*
They have a son, a lawyer, born 1796 (*Un Début dans la Vie, Maison Nucingen*, etc.): 182, 183, *483,* 484.

DESROYS, a civil servant (*Employés*).

DESROZIERS, a printer in Moulins (*Muse du Département*).

DESTAINS, a journalist (*Illusions Perdues*).

DÉVORANTS (les), a secret society (see preface to *l'Histoire des Treize*).

DEY (Comtesse de), a widow who has

taken refuge in Carentan, born 1755, dies 1793 (*Réquisitionnaire*): 377.

Has a son, Auguste, who goes into exile and is shot in 1793 (*id.*).

DIARD (Pierre-François), a soldier, then a businessman, killed by his wife in about 1826 (*Marana*): 260, 276, 415, 428.

Marries Juana Mancini in 1811 (*id.*): 260, 276, 332, 380. Issue:

1) Juan, in reality the son of Montefiore (*id.*).

2) Francisque.

DIAZ (Jan), pseudonym of Mme de la Baudraye (*Muse du Département*).

DIODATI, a character in the short story by Savarus (*Albert Savarus*).

DIONIS (see Crémière-Dionis).

DIX-MILLE (the Ten Thou'): 301, 320.

DIXON, a ship's captain (*Séraphita*).

DOGUEREAU, a bookseller-publisher (*Illusions Perdues*): 240.

DOISY, a porter in the Pension Lepitre (*Lys dans la Vallée*).

DOMINIS (Abbé de), tutor of Jacques de Mortsauf at Clochegourde (*Lys dans la Vallée*).

DOMMANGET, a doctor (*Béatrix*).

DONI (Massimila), a lady of Florence, born 1800 (*Massimila Doni*): 266, 277.

Marries first the Duc Cataneo, then Emilio Memmi, Prince de Varèse (*id.*).

DORSONVAL (Mme), an inhabitant of Saumur (*Eugénie Grandet*).

DOUBLET, a clerk employed by Desroches (*Début dans la Vie*).

DOUBLON (Victor-Ange-Herménégilde), an usher in Angoulême (*Illusions Perdues*).

DROLLING, a painter mentioned in *Pierre Grassou*.

DUBERGHE, a wine merchant in Bordeaux (*Maison Nucingen*).

DUBOURDIEU, a painter (*Comédiens sans le savoir*): 222, 241.

DUBUT, a Normandy wholesale dealer who names his three sons after the three properties he owns:

1) Dubut de Boisfranc, President of the Board of Excise (*Envers de l'Histoire contemporaine*).

2) Dubut de Boisfrelon, councillor to Parlement, then a lodger with Mme de la Chanterie (*id.*). Was married once.

3) Dubut de Boislaurier, a Chouan,

promoted lieutenant-general under the Restoration (*id.*).

4) Dubut, cousin to the three brothers, first president of a Royal Court. He later takes over the name Boisfranc (*id.*).

DUDLEY (Lord), an English politician (*Lys dans la Vallé, Fille aux Yeux d'Or*, etc.): 39, 42, 44, 82, 194, 242, 332, 388, 389, 390, *391*.

Marries Arabelle X., also English (*Lys dans la Vallée, Fille d'Eve*, etc.): 42, 58, 60, 61, 83, 119, 120, 144, 382, 388, *389* to *390*.

They have two children.

Dudley also has two illegitimate children: Henri de Marsay (see Marsay) and Euphemia Porraberil, who marries San Real (see San Real). He also has another daughter, whether legitimate or not we do not know, who marries Lord Barimore.

DUFAU, a justice of the peace in the Dauphiné (*Médecin de Campagne*).

DUFAURE, a student at the Collège de Vendôme (*Louis Lambert*).

DUMAY, a lawyer in Vannes (*Modeste Mignon*).

Has a wife and also a son, Anne-François-Bernard, a retired army officer living in le Havre (*id.*): 223.

This son marries a Miss Grummer, an American: 395.

DUMETS, a clerk employed by Desroches (*Début dans la Vie*).

DUNCKER, a Norwegian fisherman (*Séraphita*).

DU PETIT-MÉRÉ (Frédéric), a journalist (1785-1827) (*Illusions Perdues*). Did exist.

DUPLANTY (Abbé), a curate (*Cousin Pons*): 440.

DUPLAY (Mme), Robespierre's landlady (*Rabouilleuse*). Did exist.

DUPOTEL, a banker in le Croisic (*Drame au bord de la mer*).

DUPUIS (Adèle), an actress (*Illusions Perdues*).

DURAND, a shadowy figure mentioned in *le Bal de Sceaux*.

DURAND, owner of the Château de Frapesle. Having married a Chessel, he has himself called de Chessel and drops Durand altogether (*Lys dans la Vallée*).

DURET, a parish priest in Sancerre (*Muse du Département*).

DURIAU, a doctor (*Muse du Département*).

EVELINA, a girl engaged to be married to Benassis (*Médecin de Campagne*): 155.

EVÊQUE D'ANGOULÊME (the Bishop of Angoulême) and his deputy both appear in *les Illusions Perdues*.

EVÊQUE DE LIMOGES (the Bishop of Limoges), plays a certain rôle in *Le Curé de Village*: 441.

FAILLE and BOUCHOT, perfumers (*César Birotteau*).

FALCON, known as Beaupied, a soldier (*Chouans* and *Muse de Département*), then a domestic servant employed by Marshal Hulot (*Cousine Bette*).

FALLEIX (Jacques), a stockbroker (*Ferragus* and *Splendeurs*): 199, 484.

His brother, Martin, born 1796, is a brass-founder (*Employés*).

FANANDELS (les grands), a secret society (*Splendeurs et Misères des Courtisanes*): 301, 320.

FANCHETTE, a servant employed by Doctor Rouget in Issoudun (*Rabouilleuse*).

FANJAT, a doctor, uncle to Mme de Vandières (*Adieu*).

FANNY, a young girl (*Auberge Rouge*).

FARIO, a Spanish businessman settled in Issoudun (*Rabouilleuse*): 394, 422.

FAROUN, an Arab (*Physiologie du Mariage*).

FARRABESCHE, a family of the Limousin that includes:

1) a captain killed in 1796 (*Curé de Village*);

2) a sergeant killed at Austerlitz (*id.*);

3) Jacques, a deserter in good health (*id.*)

In about 1831 he marries Catherine Curieux.

They have one son, Benjamin.

FATME, Faroun's wife (*Physiologie du Mariage*).

FAUCOMBE (de), a noble family that comprises:

1) an old gentleman (1734-1814) (*Béatrix*), who had a wife;

2) a niece of 1) who marries a des Touches. Their daughter is Félicité des Touches (see Touches).

3) a sister of 2), a nun (*Béatrix*).

FAUSTINE, a young woman living in Argentan mentioned in *la Vieille Fille*.

FÉLICIE, a housemaid employed by Mme Diard (*Marana*).

FÉLICITÉ, a servant employed by Mme Vauthier (*Envers de l'Histoire contemporaine*).

FÉLIX, an office boy employed by Grandville (*Splendeurs et Misères des Courtisanes*).

FENDANT and CAVALIER, publishers (*Illusions Perdues*).

FERDINAND, a character in *Petites Misères de la Vie conjugale*.

FERDINAND, a Chouan leader mentioned in *Béatrix*, in *les Chouans*, and in *le Cabinet des Antiques*.

FEREDIA (Comte Bagos de), a Spanish prisoner in France who dies of being walled up (*Autre Etude de Femme*): 382.

FÉRET, a clerk, possibly imaginary (*Début dans la vie*).

FERGUS, a Norwegian shepherd (*Séraphita*).

FERRAGUS (see Bourignard).

FERRARO (Comte), a soldier (*Melmoth réconcilié*).

FERRAUD (Comte), an émigré, then a Councillor of State (*Colonel Chabert, etc.*): 134, 322.

Marries Rose Chapotel, supposed widow of Chabert (*id.*): 81, *133, 134,* 135, 423, 482.

They have two children. One of them is called Jules.

FESSARD, a grocer in Saumur (*Eugénie Grandet*).

FICHET (Mme), an inhabitant of Issoudun. Has a daughter (*Rabouilleuse*).

FIL-DE-SOIE (see Sélérier).

FINOT, a hatter (*César Birotteau*).

Has a son, Andoche, a publicist (*id., Illusions Perdues, Maison Nucingen, etc.*): 29, 32, 41, 67, 103, 116, 187, *194, 195,* 200, 202, 203, 208, 241, 250, 422.

FIRMIANI, a tax official who disappeared in about 1822 (*Madame Firmiani*): 82, 129.

Married to a Cadignan: 8, 15, 62, *129, 130,* 266.

When officially a widow she marries Octave de Camps.

FISCHER, an Alsatian family comprising three brothers:

1) Pierre, killed in 1815. He has a daughter, Lisbeth, known as la cousine Bette, born 1796, dies 1843 (*Cousine Bette*): *165, 166,* 167, 168, 305, 308, 311, 317, 383, 473;

2) André, dies in 1820. Has a

FISCHER (*cont.*)
 daughter, Adeline, who marries Baron Hulot (see Hulot);
  3) Johann, commits suicide in 1841 (*Cousine Bette*): 301, 417, 418.
FISCHTAMINEL (Comte and Comtesse de), characters in *Petites Misères de la Vie conjugale:* 147.
FITZ-WILLIAM (Lord) and his daughter Margaret. Relations of Mme du Guénic (*Béatrix*).
FLAMET DE LA BILLARDIÈRE (see La Billardière).
FLEURANT (la mère), a tavern keeper in le Croisic (*Drame au bord de la mer*).
FLEURIOT, a soldier who dies in about 1816 (*Adieu*).
FLEURY, a soldier, then a civil servant, then publisher of a newspaper (*Employés*).
FLORE, a character in *Physiologie du Mariage*.
FLORENT and CHANOR, goldsmiths (*Cousine Bette*, etc.).
FLORENTINE (real name Agathe-Florentine Cabirolle), a dancer, born 1804 (*Illusions Perdues, Début dans la Vie,* etc.): 13, 187, 193, 195, *196*, 229, 241.
FLORIMOND (Madame), a haberdasher (*Cousin Pons*).
FLORINE (real name Sophie Grignoult), an actress, born 1805 (*Illusions Perdues, Fille d'Eve,* etc.): 13, 56, 72, 186, 187, *193, 194*, 196, 197, 202, 229, 237, 241, 242, 244, 391, 478, 482.
 Marries Raoul Nathan in about 1845.
FLORVILLE (Mlle), an actress (*Illusions Perdues*).
FOEDORA (Comtesse), "a woman without a heart," married to a mysterious and possibly nonexistent husband (*Peau du Chagrin*): 34, 38, 82, 84, *93*, 94, 299.
FOIX-GRAILLY, a great family alluded to in passing (*Cabinet des Antiques, Prince de la Bohème*).
FONTAINE (de), a noble family of Poitou represented by a Comte de Fontaine who is a Chouan, then a deputy, and dies in 1824 or 1828 (*Chouans, Bal de Sceaux,* etc.): 33, 158, 334, 339, 408, 468, 472.
 Married a Kergarouët. Issue:
  1) a son, a magistrate, who marries the daughter of a salt millionaire (*Bal de Sceaux,* etc.).

  2) a son, a soldier, who marries a Mongenod (*id.*).
  3) a son, a civil servant, who marries Anna Grossetête (*id.* and *Muse du Département*).
  4) a daughter who marries Director of Inland Revenue Planat de Baudry (*Bal de Sceaux*).
  5) a daughter who marries the Baron de Villaine, a magistrate (*id.*).
  6) Emilie (*Bal de Sceaux, Ursule Mirouët,* etc.): 16, 33, 57, 65, 68, *158, 159*, 257, 331, 405, 406.
 Marries first Admiral de Kergarouët, her uncle, then Charles de Vandenesse.
FONTAINE (Madame), a fortune teller (*Cousin Pons, Comédiens sans le savoir*): 345.
FONTANGES, a character in *Physiologie du Mariage*.
FONTANIEU (Mme), "the merriest gossip" in Vouvray (*Illustre Gaudissart*).
FONTANON (Abbé), a priest in Bayeux, then in Paris (*Double Famille,* etc.): 433, 440.
FORTIN (Mlle), a woman kept by Montcornet (*Cousine Bette*): 283, 426.
 She has a daughter, Valérie, by him who marries first Stanislas Marneffe, then Célestin Crevel (see Marneffe).
FORZHEIM (see Hulot).
FOSSEUSE (la), daughter of a gravedigger and a housemaid. Lives in the Dauphiné (*Médecin de Campagne*): 161.
FOUCHÉ (Joseph), a politician (1753-1820). Did exist. (*Chouans, Ténébreuse Affaire*): 157, 437, 443, 448, 459, 469, 470.
FOUILLEPOINTE, a character in *Petites Misères de la Vie conjugale*.
FOUQUEREAU, the concierge of M. and Mme Desmarets (*Ferragus*).
FOURCHON, a handyman living in Blangy, born 1753 (*Paysans*): 101.
 Has two daughters (mother unknown): 1) Philippine, who marries Tonsard (see Tonsard); 2) a daughter who has an illegitimate son, little Mouche (*Paysans*).
FRAISIER, a lawyer, then a judge in a criminal court (*Cousin Pons*): 13, 99, *179*, 180.
FRANCHESSINI (Comte), a colonel (*Père Goriot,* etc.): 48, *55*, 144, 298, 393, 455, 464.
FRANÇOIS (Abbé), a parish priest in Alençon (*Vieille Fille*): 440.

GASTON (*cont.*)

Married the widow of an English merchant. There were two children by this marriage.

2) Marie-Gaston, man of letters, born about 1810 (*id.*): 127, 144, 191, 264, 266.

Marries Louise de Chaulieu in 1833, after the death of Macumer, her first husband (see Chaulieu).

GATIENNE, a servant employed by Mme Bontems in Bayeux (*Double Famille*).

GAUBERT (Général), a soldier (*Début dans la Vie*): 103.

Married Léontine de Ronquerolles who, after his death, remarries with Sérizy (see Sérizy).

GAUBERTIN, a judge in Soulanges, later Public Prosecutor (*Paysans*).

Has a son, François, born 1770, steward at les Aigues, then mayor of la Ville-aux-Fayes (*id.*).

Marries Isaure Mouchon. Issue:

1) Claude, lawyer at la Ville-aux-Fayes (*id.*).

2) Jenny, who marries Leclercq, a deputy (*id.*).

3) Elise, betrothed to the sub-prefect des Lupeaulx (*id.*).

Gaubertin also has an illegitimate son, Bournier, by Mme Socquard (*id.*).

GAUBERTIN-VALLAT (Mlle), an old maid in la Ville-aux-Fayes (*Paysans*).

She has a sister married to Sibilet, a court clerk.

GAUCHER, a servingboy to the Michus in Gondreville (*Ténébreuse Affaire*).

GAUDIN, Baron de Wistchnau, a soldier, listed as missing in 1812, then reappears during the Restoration (*Peau de Chagrin*).

While waiting for him, his wife runs a hotel (*id.*).

They have a daughter, Pauline, born 1812, godchild of Pauline Borghese, engaged to marry Raphaël de Valentin (*id.*): 38, 160.

GAUDISSART (Félix), a traveling salesman, then a theater manager, born 1792 (*César Birotteau, Illustre Gaudissart, Cousin Pons*, etc.): 195, 228, 232, 241, 349, 363, 375, 377, 450.

GAUDRON (Abbé), a priest (*Début dans la Vie* and *Employés*).

GAUDRY (Simon), a native of le Croisic known only for having given la

grande Frelu a child (*Un Drame au bord de la mer*).

GAULT, governor of a prison (*Splendeurs et Misères des Courtisanes*).

GAY, a cobbler (*Illusions Perdues*).

GAZONAL (Sylvestre-Palafox-Castel), a manufacturer of lace, cousin of Léon de Lora (*Comédiens sans le savoir*): 200, 221, 230, 237, 242, 327, 375.

GENDRIN, a magistrate in la Ville-aux Fayes (*Paysans*).

Married to one of the daughters of Mouchon, a former member of the National Convention.

They have a son, who is a registrar of mortgages (*id.*).

There is another Gendrin, related to the two above, who is also a magistrate (*id.*).

GENDRIN, a draughtsman (*César Birotteau*).

GENDRIN-WATTEBLED, a former overseer at Soulanges, born 1733, dies at an unspecified time leaving behind a daughter who marries Doctor Gourdon (*Paysans*).

GENESTAS (Pierre-Joseph), a soldier, born 1779 (*Médecin de Campagne*): 327, 388, 397, 401, 414, 416, 426, 466, 467.

Marries Judith, a Polish girl, born 1795, dies 1814 (*id.*).

Genestas has recognized his wife's son by Renard. The son's name is Adrien, born 1813.

GENEVIÈVE, a servant in the Phellion household (*Petits Bourgeois*).

GENEVIÈVE, a madwoman (*Adieu*).

GENOVESE, an Italian tenor (*Massimila Doni* and *Albert Savarus*).

GENTIL, a domestic servant employed by Mme de Bargeton (*Illusions Perdues*).

GENTIL, a domestic servant in Grandlieu household (*Splendeurs*).

GENTILLET (Mme), grandmother of Mme Félix Grandet (*Eugénie Grandet*).

GENTILLET, a man who rents out carriages in Besançon (*Albert Savarus*).

GEORGES, a manservant to Nucingen (*Splendeurs et Misères des Courtisanes*).

GEORGES, a coachman employed by the Gaudin de Wistchnau family (*Peau de Chagrin*).

GEORGES, a manservant of the Comtesse Foedora (*Peau de Chagrin*).

GÉRARD (Baron), a painter (1770-1837) (*Rabouilleuse* and *Béatrix*). Did exist.

GÉRARD, a soldier killed in 1799 (*Chouans*).

GÉRARD (Mme), a landlady (*Splendeurs et Misères des Courtisanes*). Has two daughters.

GÉRARD (Grégoire), an engineer, later Mayor of Montégnac. (*Curé de Village*): 448.
    Marries Denise Tascheron in 1844 (*id.*).

GIACOMO, a Corsican (*Vendetta*).

GIARDINI, an Italian, keeps a restaurant in Paris (*Gambara*).

GIBOULARD, a carpenter in Auxerre (*Paysans*).
    He has a pretty daughter, Gatienne.

GIGELMI, an Italian, a musician in Paris (*Gambara*).

GIGONNET, nickname of Bidault (see Bidault).

GIGUET, a family living in Champagne and comprising:
    1) a police officer (*Ténébreuse Affaire* and *Député d'Arcis*);
    2) his sister, who marries Marion;
    3) his brother, a colonel.
    The colonel marries a woman from Hamburg who dies in 1814.
    Issue:
    a) Simon, a lawyer (*Député d'Arcis*): 388;
    b) a son who dies in 1818;
    c) a son who dies in 1825.

GILET, a clogmaker in Issoudun whose wife, from a liaison with an army officer, has a son, Max Gilet, a soldier, born 1788, dies 1822 (*Rabouilleuse*): 279, 280, 324, 363, 416, 417, 419, 420, *421*, 422, 423, 424, 425, 426, 428, 454.

GILLE, a printer (*Illusions Perdues*).

GILLETTE, mistress of Nicolas Poussin in the 17th century (*Chef-d'oeuvre inconnu*).

GINA, a character in the story written by Savarus (*Albert Savarus*).

GINETTA, Calvi's mistress (*Splendeurs*): 301.

GIRARD ("old mother"), former lessee of an eating-joint (*Envers de l'Histoire contemporaine*).

GIRARD, a forger (*Splendeurs*).

GIRARD, a moneylender (*Gobseck*).

GIRARDET, a lawyer in Besançon (*Albert Savarus*).

GIRAUD (Léon), a politician (*Illusions Perdues, Comédiens sans le savoir*): 210, *211*, 218, 226.

GIREL, a businessman in Troyes (*Ténébreuse Affaire*).
    Has a daughter who marries Michu.

GIRIEX, a cousin of Farrabesche (*Curé de Village*).

GIROUD, a priest in Besançon (*Albert Savarus*).

GIROUDEAU, a former army officer, a cashier, then a general (*Illusions Perdues, Rabouilleuse*, etc.): 26, 195, 208, 241, 280, *422*, 424, 427, 428, 430.

GOBAIN (Mme), Mme de Bauvan's housekeeper (*Honorine*).

GOBENHEIM, a banker, brother-in-law of the Kellers (*César Birotteau*, etc.).
    Has a nephew, a banker in le Havre (*Modeste Mignon*).

GOBET (Mme), a shoemaker's wife in le Havre (*Modeste Mignon*).

GOBSECK (Jean-Esther van), a Jew from Antwerp, a moneylender, born in 1740, dies in 1830 (*Gobseck, Employés*, etc.): 72, 253, 298, 323, 328, 353, 354, 356, 357, 358, 394, 396, 397, 455, 456, 474, *475*, 478, 479, 483.
    Has a great-niece, Sara, known as la Belle Hollandaise, murdered in 1818 (*César Birotteau*, etc.): 28, 49, 227, 482.
    Sara has a daughter (father not known) named Esther, known as la Torpille, a prostitute, born 1805, kills herself in 1830 (*Splendeurs et Misères des Courtisanes*, etc.): 13, 24, *25-26*, 27, 28, 33, 40, 72, 215, 221, 227, 237, 240, 241, 243, 258, 260, 284, 291, 326, 364, 365, 387, 396, 419, 436, 478, 481.

GODAIN (la), a female peasant in Blangy (*Paysans*).
    Has a son, a short man (*id.*). He marries Catherine Tonsard.

GODART (Manon), a housemaid employed by Mme de la Chanterie (*Envers de l'Histoire contemporaine*).

GODART (Joseph), a civil servant and musican (*Employés*).
    Has a sister who sells flowers (*id.*).

GODART, a domestic servant in household of Mme d'Espard (*Splendeurs*).

GODDET, an army surgeon living in retirement at Issoudun (*Rabouilleuse*).
    Has a son who is engaged to Mlle Fichet and sleeping with her mother.

GODEFROID, a young man whose family name is not known (*Envers de l'Histoire contemporaine*): 324, 325, 374.

GODEFROID, a theology student in the fourteenth century (*Proscrits*).

GODENARS (Abbé de), a priest in Besançon (*Albert Savarus*).

GODESCHAL (François-Claude-Marie), a clerk, then a lawyer, born 1804 (*Colonel Chabert, Début dans la vie*, etc.): 196, *484*.

Has a sister, Marie, known as Mariette, a dancer, born 1803 (*Début dans la Vie, Rabouilleuse, Illusions Perdues*, etc.): 77, 81, 180, 187, 193, *196*, 241, 420, 424, 484.

GODET, a convict (*Splendeurs et Misères des Courtisanes*).

Has a sister who is a laundress.

GODIN, a shadowy figure (*Prince de la Bohème*).

GODIVET, the registrar in Arcis (*Député d'Arcis*, p. 658). Does Arcis have two registrars? On p. 701 the same office is assigned to Miley.

GOGUELAT, a former private soldier, a postman in the Dauphiné (*Médecin de Campagne*): 388, *426*, 427, 466.

GOGUELU, a peasant mentioned, together with his daughter, in *les Chouans*.

GOHIER, a goldsmith (*César Birotteau*).

GOMEZ, captain of the "Saint Ferdinand" (*Femme de Trente Ans*).

GONDRAND (Abbé), a priest (*Duchesse de Langeais*).

GONDREVILLE (see Malin).

GONDRIN (Abbé), a curate (*Petits Bourgeois*).

GONDRIN, an old soldier, a roadmender in the Dauphiné (*Médecin de Campagne*): 388, *426*, 427, 466.

GONDUREAU, assumed name of Bibi-Lupin (*Père Goriot*).

GONORE (la), "widow" of Moïse, mistress of La Pouraille and manageress of a brothel (*Splendeurs*): 301.

GORDES (de), a family in Normandy mentioned in *la Vieille Fille*.

GORENFLOT, a mason in Vendôme (*Autre Etude de Femme*).

GORIOT (Jean-Joachim), a former manufacturer of vermicelli, Italian pastas and starch, born about 1750, dies in 1820 (*Père Goriot*): 4, 9, 32, 33, 58, 60, 102, 214, 252, 304, *335* to *338*, 339, 352, 353, 354, 356, 358, 360, 474.

Married the daughter of a farmer in la Brie (*id.*): 336.

Issue:

1) Anastasie, born about 1791, who marries the Comte de Restaud (see Restaud).

2) Delphine, born 1792, who marries the Baron de Nucingen (see Nucingen).

GORITZA (Princesse), a Hungarian lady frequently mentioned in *la Vieille Fille*: 147, 403, 430.

GORJU, mayor of Sancerre. Has a wife and a daughter. The latter is named Euphémie (*Muse du Département*).

GOTHAUD, a servant to Laurence de Cinq-Cygne (*Ténébreuse Affaire*), then a steward (*Député d'Arcis*).

Has a sister who marries Poupart (*Député d'Arcis*).

GOUGET (Abbé), parish priest of Cinq-Cygne, then Bishop of Troyes (*Ténébreuse Affaire* and *Député d'Arcis*).

Has a sister who lives with him.

GOULARD, mayor of Cinq-Cygne (*Ténébreuse Affaire*).

Has a son, Antonin, sub-prefect in Arcis (*Député d'Arcis*).

GOUNOD, a gardener at les Aigues (*Paysans*).

GOUPIL (Jean-Sébastien-Marie), a clerk, then a notary in Nemours, born 1802 (*Ursule Mirouët*): 176, 177, 178, 179, 181, 484.

Marries a Massin-Levrault: 177.

They have horrible children.

GOURAUD (Baron), an army officer under the Empire, retired in Provins, born 1781 (*Pierrette*): 424.

Marries a daughter of Matifat (*id.*).

GOURDON, a doctor in Soulanges (*Paysans*).

Marries a Gendrin-Wattebled (*id.*).

A brother of this doctor is a clerk of the court and is married to a niece of Abbé Taupin (*id.*).

GOUSSARD (see Coussard).

GRADOS, an individual alluded to in *le Colonel Chabert*.

GRAFF (Johann), a German living in Paris, owner of the Hotel du Rhin (*Cousin Pons*): 384, 387.

Has a daughter, Emilie, who marries Wilhelm Schwab (*id.*).

Wolfgang, Johann's brother, is a tailor (*id.*): 387.

GRANCEY (Abbé de), a high-ranking ecclesiastic in Besançon (*Albert Savarus*).

GRANCOUR (Abbé de), a high-ranking ec-

GRANSON (*cont.*)

She has one son, Athanase, born 1793, kills himself 1816 (*id.*): 164, 165, 198, 199, 258, 269, *271*, 272, 273, 340, 354, 449, 465, 466.

GRANVILLE (see Grandville).

GRASLIN (Pierre), a banker in Limoges, born 1775, dies 1831 (*Curé de Village*): 115, 302.

Marries in 1823 Véronique Sauviat, born 1802, dies 1844 (*id.*): *115*, 152, 176, 214, 258, 260, 273, 303, *355*, 378, 433, 434, 436, 438.

GRASSET, a bailiff (*Cousine Bette*).

GRASSINS (des), a banker in Saumur, a deputy (*Eugénie Grandet*): 194.

Has a plump wife, a son named Adolphe, and a daughter.

GRASSOU (Pierre), a painter (*Pierre Grassou*, etc.): 202, 213, *220*, 221, 241, 302, 360, 414, 482.

Marries Virginie Vervelle in about 1832 (*id.*).

They have two children.

GRAVELOT (brothers), wood merchants (*Paysans*).

GRAVIER, a civil servant in Grenoble (*Médecin de Campagne*).

Married to a woman with "a narrow brain."

They have a daughter.

GRAVIER, a tax-collector in Sancerre (*Muse du Département*): 484.

GRENIER (Charles), a Chouan executed in 1809 (*Envers de l'Histoire contemporaine*).

GRENOUVILLE, a merchant (*Cousine Bette*): 238.

GRENVILLE (Arthur Ormond, Lord), an Englishman deceased in 1823 (*Femme de Trente Ans*): 146, *171*, 172, 382, 388, 392.

GRÉVIN, a notary in Arcis, born 1763 (*Ténébreuse Affaire* and *Député d'Arcis*): 313, 315, 326, 481.

Married to a Varlet.

They have one daughter, Séverine, born 1795.

She marries Philéas Beauvisage.

GRÉVIN, an old sailor living in retirement at Alençon (*Vieille Fille*).

GRIBEAUCOURT (Mlle de), an inhabitant of Saumur (*Eugénie Grandet*).

GRIFFITH (Miss), English, governess of Louise de Chaulieu (*Mémoires de deux Jeunes Mariées*): 388, 393.

GRIGNOULT (see Florine).

GRIMBERT, a messenger (*Père Goriot*).

GRIMM (Frédéric-Melchior), German, a man of letters, born 1723, died 1807 (*Ursule Mirouët*). Did exist.

GRIMONT (Abbé), a priest of Guérande. (*Béatrix*).

GRIMPEL, a doctor (*Père Goriot*).

GRINDOT, an architect (*César Birotteau, Béatrix*, etc.): 13.

GRITTE (Marguerite so-called), a servant to the Hochon family in Issoudun (*Rabouilleuse*).

GROISON, a rural policeman in Blangy who appears with his wife in *les Paysans*.

GROLLMAN (Dinah), a German (*Ursule Mirouët*) who marries Joseph Mirouët (see Mirouët).

GROS (Antoine), a painter, born 1771, died 1835 (*Rabouilleuse*). Did exist.

GROSLIER, a police inspector in Arcis (*Député d'Arcis*).

GROSMORT (Mme), an inhabitant of Alençon mentioned, with her son, in *la Vieille Fille*.

GROSSETÊTE, a family originating from the Limousin and comprising:

1) a Grossetête (m.) of the banking house of Grossetête et Perret in Limoges who appears with his wife in *le Curé de Village;*

2) another Grossetête (m.), District Director of Internal Revenue in Bourges, who dies in 1828 and whose daughter, Anna, marries one of the Comte de Fontaine's sons (*Bal de Sceaux* and *Muse du Département*).

GROZIER (Abbé), a learned priest (*Illusions Perdues, Interdiction*).

GRUGET (widow Etienne), a passementerie maker and nurse (*Ferragus, Employés, Rabouilleuse*).

Has a daughter, Ida, a corset- and dressmaker who kills herself in 1819 (*Ferragus*).

GRUMMER (Miss), an American (*Ursule Mirouët*).

Marries Dumay.

GUA-SAINT-CYR (du), a young man and his mother killed by the Chouans in 1799 (*Chouans*).

This name was usurped at about the same time by the Marquis de Montauran and by a woman companion of his, possibly the Comtesse du Gua (*id.*).

GUDIN (Abbé), a parish priest in Brittany, killed in 1799 (*Chouans*): 432, 440.

Has a nephew, a republican soldier (*id.*).

GUÉNÉE, a haberdasher (*Pierrette*).

Married to a Tiphaine (*id.*).

Issue:

1) a daughter who marries Lesourd, Crown prosecutor in Provins (*id.*).

2) a daughter who marries Martener, a doctor in Provins (*id.*).

3) a daughter who marries Auffray, a notary in Provins (*id.*).

When widowed, Mme Guénée marries Galardon, tax-collector.

GUÉNIC or GUAISNIC (du), a noble Brittany family represented by:

1) Zéphirine, born 1756, unmarried (*Béatrix*): *163*, 168.

2) Gaudebert-Calyste-Charles, Baron du Guénic, brother of Zéphirine, born 1763, dies 1836 (*id.*): 13, 16, 107, 163, 376, *407-410*, 411, 430.

Marries in 1813 Fanny O'Brien, Irish, born 1792 (*id.*): 163, 261, 331, 393, 407.

They have one son, Calyste, born 1814 (*id.*): 108, 131, 135, 136, 160, 163, 205, 259, 260, 261, 262, 278, 282, 286, 326, 374, 376, 409.

He marries Sabine de Grandlieu, born 1816 (*id.*): 108, 131, 132, *135*, *136*, 153, 155, 259, 261, 262, 395.

They have one son and the promise of a second.

GUÉPIN, a haberdasher in Paris who later retires to Provins (*Pierrette*).

Has a daughter who marries Garceland, the mayor (*id.*).

He also has a grandson.

GUÉPIN, a deserter and convict (*Curé de Village*).

GUERBET, the postmaster in Couches (*Paysans*).

Married to a Mouchon.

His brother is a tax-collector in Soulanges and has a son who is a judge at la Ville-aux-Fayes (*id.*).

GUERBET, a prosecutor at the Châtelet (*Début dans la Vie*).

GUILLAUME, a domestic servant in the Aiglemont household (*Femme de Trente Ans*).

GUILLAUME, a cloth merchant (*Maison du Chat-qui-pelote*): 251, 369.

Married to a Cheverel (*id.*): 265, 277, 340.

Issue:

1) Virginie, born 1783 (*id.*), who marries Joseph Lebas, a merchant.

2) Augustine, born 1793, dies 1820 (*id.*). Marries Théodore de Sommervieux, a painter.

GUINARD (Abbé), a parish priest in Sancerre (*Muse du Département*).

GYAS (Marquis and Marquise de), a couple living in Bordeaux who have a daughter to marry (*Contrat de Mariage*).

HABERT (Abbé), a priest in Provins (*Pierrette*).

Has a sister, Céleste.

HADOT (Mme), an inhabitant of la Charité-su-Loire (*Muse du Département*).

HALGA (Chevalier du), a former sailor, mayor of Guérande (*Bourse* and *Béatrix*).

HALMER, a banker in Calcutta (*Mémoires de deux Jeunes Mariées*).

HALPERSOHN (Moïse), Polish, a doctor, born 1782 (*Envers de l'Histoire contemporaine*): *384*, 397.

HANNEQUIN (Léopold), a notary, born about 1799 (*Albert Savarus, Cousin Pons*, etc.): 183, *482*.

HAPPE and DUNCKER, bankers in Amsterdam (*Recherche de l'Absolu*).

HARDOUIN (le Père), a monk in the seventeenth century (*Chef-d'oeuvre inconnu*).

HAUDRY, a doctor (*Rabouilleuse, Ferragus, Cousin Pons, César Birotteau*, etc.)

HAUGOULT (Abbé), a teacher at the Collège de Vendôme (*Louis Lambert*).

HAUTESERRE (de), a noble family of the Champagne, represented by:

1) an Abbé de Hauteserre, killed in 1792 (*Ténébreuse Affaire*).

2) An old gentleman, born 1751, and his wife, born 1763 (*id.*).

Their issue:

1) Robert, an émigré, then a colonel, killed in 1812 (*id.*): 352.

2) Adrien, an émigré, then a general, dies in 1829 (*id.*): 157, 352.

Marries Laurence de Cinq-Cygne and takes her name.

HAUTOY (M., Mme and Mlle), people who live in Saumur (*Eugénie Grandet*).

HAUTOY (Francis du), a former consul, lives in Angoulême (*Illusions Perdues*): 151.

From a liaison with the future Mme de Senonches, has had an ille-

HAUTOY (*cont.*)
gitimate daughter, Françoise de la Haye (*id.*).

HECTOR, a character in *Petites Misères de la Vie conjugale.*

HENAREZ, patronymic of the Dukes of Soria used by one of them during his exile in Paris (see Macumer).

HERBELOT, a notary in Arcis (*Député d'Arcis*): 481.
Has a sister, Malvina (*id.*).

HERBOMEZ (d'), known as Général-Hardouin, a Chouan, executed in 1809 (*Envers de l'Histoire contemporaine*).
His brother is made a count and appointed a Director of Taxation under the Restoration (*id.*).

HÉREAU (Mlle), an inhabitant of Issoudun (*Rabouilleuse*).

HÉRÉDIA (Maria), Spanish, betrothed to the Duke of Soria but marries his brother instead. The latter, still not content, takes his brother's title as well (*Mémoires de deux Jeunes Mariées*).

HÉRISSON, a clerk employed by Desroches (*Début dans la Vie*).

HERMANN, a German merchant (*Auberge Rouge*).

HÉRON, a notary in Issoudun (*Rabouilleuse*): 481.

HÉROUVILLE (d'), one of the greatest names in France. In the 16th and 17th centuries, this family is represented by:
1) a bibliophile cardinal (*Enfant Maudit*);
2) the Comte, then Duc d'Hérouville, great-nephew of 1), born 1537 (*id.*).
Marries Jeanne de Saint-Savin, born 1573, dies 1593 (*id.*).
Issue:
1) Etienne, dies in 1617 (*id.*).
2) Maximilien, killed in 1617 (*id.*). When widowed, the Duke marries a Grandlieu (*id.*).
From a liaison with a courtesan, known as La Belle Romaine, the Duke has previously had a daughter who marries Beauvouloir (*id.*).
In the 19th century, the family is represented by:
1) an old Marshal who dies in 1819 (*Modeste Mignon*);
2) an old maid sister of the Marshal who dies in 1819 (*id.*): 78;

3) a son of the Marshal born in 1796, a small, ailing man (*Modeste Mignon*, etc.): 8, 78, 153, 231, 266, 272, 273;
4) a sister of 3), Héléne (*Modeste Mignon*): 78.

HERRERA (Abbé Carlos), a Spanish ecclesiastic and diplomat murdered by Vautrin, who then takes the Abbé's identity (*Illusions Perdues, Splendeurs et Misères des Courtisanes*): 25, 291.

HERVÉ, a teacher in la Ville-aux-Fayes (*Paysans*).
Married to a Sibilet.

HEURTAULT (Caroline), a character in *Petites Misères de la Vie conjugale.*
Marries Chodoreille.

HICLAR, a musician (*Comédiens sans le savoir*).

HILEY, a Chouan, executed in 1809 (*Envers de l'Histoire contemporaine*).

HIPPOLYTE, an officer killed in 1812 (*Adieu*).

HIRAM (see Mirah).

HOCHON, a retired Inland Revenue official living in Issoudun, born 1748 (*Rabouilleuse*): 474, 479.
Married to Maximilienne Lousteau, born 1750: 213, 357.
Issue:
1) a son killed in 1814 (*id.*).
Married, though wife's maiden name unknown. The wife also dies in 1814, leaving a son François.
2) a son who dies young;
3) a daughter who marries Borniche. Both die young, leaving two orphans, Baruch and Adolphine (*id.*).
All three children are taken in by M. and Mme Hochon.

HONORINE (see Bauvan).

HOOGWORST (Cornélius), silversmith to Louis XI (*Maître Cornelius*).
Has a sister, Jeanne.

HOPWOOD (Lady), English (*Duchesse de Langeais*).

HOREAU (Jacques), a Chouan executed in 1809 (*Envers de l'Histoire contemporaine*).

HORTENSE, a kept woman (*Homme d'Affaires*): 50, 391.

HOSTAL (Maurice de l'), secretary to Bauvan and nephew of the Abbé Loraux, born 1802 (*Honorine*): 172.
Marries Onorina Pedrotti, an Italian (*id.*).
They have two children.

JEAN, a domestic servant in the Merret household (*Autre Etude de Femme*).

JEAN, a domestic servant in the Listomère household (*Lys dans la Vallée*).

JEAN, a workman in Saumur (*Eugénie Grandet*).

JEAN, a peasant in the Dauphiné (*Médecin de Campagne*).

JEAN, an attendant at Père Lachaise (*Ferragus*).

JEAN, Beauvouloir's valet (*Enfant Maudit*).

JEANNETTE, cook in the Ragon household (*César Birotteau*).

JEANNETTE, Soudry's servant-mistress in Soulanges (*Paysans*).

JEANRENAUD, a Protestant family ruined by one of the Marquis d'Espard's ancestors. This family is represented by a Lady Jeanrenaud of "repulsive ugliness" and by her son, the Baron Jeanrenaud, a soldier, born 1792 (*Interdiction*).

JENNY, a maid employed by Aquilina (*Melmoth réconcilié*): 242.

JÉRÉMIE, a domestic servant employed by Marie de Verneuil (*Chouans*).

JÉRÔME, a bookseller (*Illusions Perdues*).

JÉRÔME, a domestic servant employed by Albert Savarus in Besançon. Marries Mariette (*Albert Savarus*).

JOLIVARD, an office worker (*Cousin Pons*).

JONATHAS, Raphaël de Valentin's steward (*Peau de Chagrin*).

JORDY (de), an ex-captain in the Royal Swedish, living in retirement in Nemours, where he dies in 1825 (*Ursule Mirouët*): 327, 328.

JOSEPH (M.) (see Lecamus).

JOSEPH, a footman employed by the Wistchnaus (*Peau de Chagrin*).

JOSEPH, a domestic servant employed by Rastignac (*Etude de Femme* and *Peau de Chagrin*).

JOSEPH, a manservant in the Fontaine household (*Bal de Sceaux*).

JOSEPH, a manservant in the Montcornet household (*Paysans*).

JOSEPH, a domestic servant in the du Tillet household (*César Birotteau*).

JOSEPH, a stove-setter (*Cousine Bette*). Has a son.

JOSÉPHA (see Mirah).

JOSÉPHIN, a servant to Victurnien d'Esgrignon (*Cabinet des Antiques*).

JOSÉPHINE, a housemaid in Desmarets household (*Ferragus*).

JOSÉPHINE, a domestic servant in the Thuillier household (*Petits Bourgeois*).

JOSETTE, a housemaid in the Maufrigneuse household (*Splendeurs et Misères des Courtisanes*).

JOSETTE, housekeeper to the notary Mathias in Bordeaux (*Contrat de Mariage*).

JOSETTE, cook to the Claës family in Douai (*Recherche de l'Absolu*).

JOSETTE, a housemaid employed by Mlle Cormon. Sometimes referred to as Perotte also, probably inadvertently. Josette or Perotte, she marries Jacquelin (*Vieille Fille*).

JUDICI or JUDIX, Italian, a stove-setter in Paris, dies 1819 (*Cousine Bette*).

Has a son who dies young, leaving a widow and a daughter, Atala, who at the age of 14 becomes the aged Baron Hulot's "little wife" (*id.*): 281.

JUDITH, a Polish Jewess, who dies in 1814 (*Médecin de Campagne*).

Marries Genestas.

Had previously had a son, Adrien, by Renard, a sergeant major.

JUGAULT (Claire), a character in *Petites Misères de la Vie conjugale*.

Marries La Roulaudière.

JULIA, maid to Clara Tinti (*Massimila Doni*).

JULIEN, a warder in the Conciergerie (*Splendeurs et Misères des Courtisanes*).

JULIEN, a domestic servant employed by Mme de Langeais (*Duchesse de Langeais*).

JULIEN, a domestic servant employed by Antoine in Arcis (*Député d'Arcis*).

JULIETTE, a cook in the Michaud household at les Aigues (*Député d'Arcis*).

JULIETTE, a milliner in Paris (*Illusions Perdues*).

JULLIARD, a haberdasher in Paris, later living in retirement in Provins (*Pierrette*). Marries a Peroux.

They have a son, married and the father of several children (*id.*).

JUSSIEU (Julien), a conscript (*Réquisitionnaire*).

JUSTE, a student then a doctor "in Asia" (*Z. Marcas*).

JUSTIN, manservant to the Vidame de Pamiers. Murdered in 1819 (*Ferragus*).

JUSTINE, a maid employed by the Comtesse Foedora (*Peau de Chagrin*).

JUSTINE, a housemaid in *Petites Misères de la Vie conjugale.*
Marries Chavagnac, a water carrier.

KATT, Flemish, nurse to Lydie Peyrade (*Splendeurs*): 150, 394.

KELLER (brothers), bankers. Three brothers, we are told in *le Cabinet des Antiques* (p. 350). In fact, two brothers and a brother-in-law, Gobenheim-Keller.
1) François, a liberal deputy, then Comte and peer of France (*César Birotteau,* etc.):16, 286, 313, 314, 315, 478, 479.
Marries Cécile Malin de Gondreville (*id.*): 133.
They have a son, Charles, born 1809, a soldier, killed 1839 (*Député d'Arcis,* etc.): 222, 352.
2) Adolphe, a banker, period (*César Birotteau*): 313, 315.
3) Probably a sister who marries Gobenheim.

KERGAROUËT, a noble family of Brittany represented by:
1) a Kergarouët (f.) who marries a Portenduère, the father of Savinien (*Ursule Mirouët*);
2) her sister, who marries the Comte de Fontaine (*Bal de Sceaux*);
3) the vice-admiral Comte de Kergarouët, uncle of 1) and 2), born 1755, dies about 1835 (*id., Bourse,* etc.): 158, *405.*
Marries wife of unknown origins while an émigré abroad (*Bourse*).
When she dies, he marries his great-niece, Emilie de Fontaine, who upon his death remarries with Charles de Vandenesse (see Fontaine).
4) the Vicomte de Kergarouët, nephew of the vice-admiral (*Béatrix*). Marries a Pen-Hoël (*id.*).
They have four daughters, among them Charlotte, born 1820 (*id.*): *160.*

KOLB, David Séchard's factotum in Angoulême (*Illusions Perdues*): 385.
Marries Marion.

KOUSKI, a Polish manservant employed by Max Gilet (*Rabouilleuse*).

KROPOLI, (Zéna), a Montenegrin. (*Paysans*).
Was to have married Auguste Niseron.

Both of them die young, leaving a daughter, Geneviève (*id.*).

LA BASTIE (see Mignon and La Brière).

LA BAUDRAYE (Milaud de), a noble family represented by several ancestors and by a farmer-general who marries a Casteran-la-Tour (*Muse du Département*).
They have a son, Jean-Athanase-Polydore, born 1780. His health is poor and he becomes a Comte and a peer of France (*id.*): 71, 89, 109 to 112, 115, 259, 433, 437.
Marries Dinah Piedefer, born 1807 (*id., Prince de la Bohème,* etc.): 81, 104, *108* to *113,* 114, 115, 123, 153, 187, 189, 190, 214, 215, 259, 266, 273, 351, 376, 378, 379, 433, 436, 437, 479.
She has a son, Polydore, another son, and a daughter, all of them fathered by Etienne Lousteau.

LA BERTELLIÈRE (de), a soldier who dies in 1806 (*Eugénie Grandet*).
Has a daughter who marries a La Gaudinière.
This daughter's daughter marries Félix Grandet (*id.*).

LA BILLARDIÈRE (Athanase-Jean-François-Michel, Baron Flamet de), a Chouan, then head of a department in the Ministry of Finance, dies in 1828 (*Chouans, Employés,* etc.): 13, 214.
Has a son, Benjamin, born 1802, a civil servant (*Employés*).

LA BLOTTIÈRE (Mlle Merlin de), an old maid living in Tours (*Curé de Tours*).

LABRANCHOIR (Comte de), landowner in the Dauphiné (*Médecin de Campagne*).

LA BRIÈRE (Ernest de), born 1800, secretary to the Minister of Finance first, then to Canalis (*Employés, Modeste Mignon*): 6, 152, *172,* 251, 266.
Marries Modeste Mignon de la Bastie in 1830 and thereafter calls himself Vicomte de la Bastie-la Brière: 78, *152,* 153, 154, 160, 172, 184, 225, 226, 266, 272, 273, 326, 356.

LABROSSE, clerk of the court in le Havre (*Modeste Mignon*).
Has two daughters of whom one dies young and the other marries Latournelle, a notary (*id.*).

LACÉPÈDE (Etienne de), a scientist, born 1756, died 1825 (*César Birotteau*).
Did exist: 470.

LA CHANTERIE (Le Chantre de), a noble Normandy family represented by:

1) an old Baron (*Envers de l'Histoire contemporaine*);

2) his son, Henri, born 1753, Clerk of Appeals, then President of a revolutionary court, then a bigamist. Dies in 1828 (*id*.): 143, 259.

Marries Barbe-Philiberthe de Champignelles, born 1772 (*id*.): *143, 144,* 239, 259, 324, 355, 358, 359, 363, 364, 430, 433, 434, 454, 457, 468, 479.

They have a daughter, Henriette, who marries Bryond des Tours-Minière (see Bryond).

LACHAPELLE, a clerk of the court (*Père Goriot*).

LA-CLEF-DES-COEURS, a soldier (*Chouans*).

LACROIX, a restaurant keeper in Issoudun (*Rabouilleuse*).

LADVOCAT, a bookstore owner (*Illusions Perdues*). Did exist.

LA FERTE (Nicolas), a Chouan (*Chouans*).

LA FIN DE DIEU, a Swiss landowner (*Albert Savarus*).

LA GAUDINIÈRE (de), a timber merchant in Saumur (*Eugénie Grandet*).

Marries a La Bertellière.

Their daughter marries Félix Grandet.

LAGINSKI (Comte Adam), a Pole living in exile in France, born about 1806 (*Fausse Maîtresse*, etc.): 142, 214, 234, *383.*

Marries in 1835 Clémentine du Rouvre, born 1816 (*id*.): *55, 142, 143,* 232, 383, 384.

Allusion is also made to the Comte Adam's mother, the Comtesse Laginska who dies in 1832 (*id*.).

LAGOUNIA (Perez de) and his wife, Spaniards from Tarragona, adoptive parents of Juana Mancini (*Marana*): 380, 394.

LAGRAVE (Mlles), headmistresses of a school (*Employés* and *Petits Bourgeois*).

LAGUERRE (Sophie), an actress, a kept woman, and owner of les Aigues before Montcornet. Born 1740, dies 1815 (*Paysans*).

LA HAYE (Françoise de), a young girl living in Angoulême, born 1805, illegitimate daughter of Francis du Hautoy and the future Mme de Senonches (*Illusions Perdues*): *151,* 177, 178.

Marries Petit-Claud.

LALLIER, a goldsmith in the 16th century (*Sur Catherine de Médicis*).

Has a daughter, Babette, who marries Christophe Lecamus (*id*.).

LAMARD, "a little shrimp" (*Illustre Gaudissart*).

LAMBERT, a tanner in Montoire (*Louis Lambert*).

Married to a Lefebvre.

They have a son, Louis, a student at the Collège de Vendôme, then a thinker, born 1797, dies 1824 (*id*.): 210, 269, 270, 311, 345, 353, 354, 356.

Was engaged to marry Pauline Salomon de Villenoix.

A maternal great-grandmother is also mentioned (*id*.).

LAMBERT (Mme), an inhabitant of Troyes and aunt of Mme Mollot (*Député d'Arcis*).

LAMBREQUIN (Marie), a Chouan killed in 1799 (*Chouans*).

LANGEAIS (de), a noble family represented by:

1) a Langeais who is a nun. In religious order, Sister Agathe (*Episode sous la Terreur*): 441;

2) an old duke, who dies in 1812 (*id*. and *Duchesse de Langeais*);

3) a Marquis, later Duc, son of 2), dies before 1823 (Duchesse de Langeais): 78, 79, 82, 90, 259.

Marries Antoinette de Navarreins, born 1794, dies about 1823 (*id*.): 4, 9, 15, 20, 42, 46, 47, 48, 69, 82, 83, 84, *90* to *93,* 94, 97, 103, 106, 147, 226, 258, 259, 273, 287, 288, 322, 323, 331, 340, 362, 363, 401, 402, 403, 405, 406, 432, 443, 450.

It is to be supposed that the duke mentioned above 3) had a brother and that it is he who is alluded to in passing in *le Contrat de Mariage.* There is also a Marquis de Langeais mentioned, together with his daughter, in *la Rabouilleuse.*

LANGLUME, a miller in Blangy (*Paysans*).

LANSAC, junior branch of the Navarreins family, represented by a Duchesse de Lansac (*Paix du Ménage*).

LANTIMÈCHE, nickname of a locksmith (*Petits Bourgeois*).

LANTY (Comte de), a little man (*Sarrasine*): 133.

Married to a niece of the castrato Zambinella.

They have two children, Marianina and Filippo.

LEBRUN (*cont.*)
in the Ministry of War (*Cousine Bette*).
LEBRUN, a doctor (*Splendeurs*). Probably the same Doctor Lebrun as the one in *Cousin Pons*.
LEBRUN (M. and Mme), characters in *Physiologie du Mariage*.
LECAMUS, a furrier in the 16th century (*Sur Catherine de Médicis*).
Has a wife (*id.*).
They have one son, Christophe, who marries Babette Lallier (*id.*).
LECAMUS (Baron de Tresnes), possibly a descendant of the preceding family, President of a Royal Court, later, under the name of M. Joseph, a member of Mme de la Chanterie's philanthropic organization (*Envers de l'Histoire contemporaine*): 324.
LECHESNEAU, a former Attorney General living in retirement in Troyes (*Ténébreuse Affaire*).
LECLERQ (Théodore), a journalist (*Illusions Perdues*).
LECLERCQ, a wine dealer and deputy (*Paysans*).
Marries Jenny Gauvertin.
He has a brother who is a property manager in Burgundy (*id.*).
LECOCQ, a businessman (*Maison du Chat-qui-pelote*).
LECOEUR, an usher in Nemours (*Ursule Mirouët*).
LÉCUYER, former clerk of Solonet's in Bordeaux (*Contrat de Mariage*): 481.
LEFEBVRE (Abbé), a juring priest, parish priest of Mer, born about 1740 (*Louis Lambert*).
One of his sisters is married to Lambert the tanner (*id.*).
LEFEBVRE (Robert), a painter (*Ténébreuse Affaire* and *Cousine Bette*). Did exist.
LÉGANÈS, a noble Spanish family comprising the Marquis de Léganès, his wife, and their five children: Clara, Juanito, Filippo, Manuel and Mariquita. All, except Juanito, are executed in 1808 (*El Verdugo*): 394.
LÉGER, a farmer at Beaumont-sur-Oise (*Début dans la Vie*): 213.
Marries a Reybert.
Their daughter marries Joseph Bridau (*id.*).
LEGRAS, a teller employed by du Tillet (*César Birotteau*).
LEMIRE, a drawing master (*Rabouilleuse*).

LEMPEREUR, a clerk employed by Claparon (*César Birotteau*).
LEMPRUN, an employee of the Banque de France, born 1745, dies 1815 (*Petits Bourgeois*): 485.
Marries a Galard.
Their daughter, Céleste, marries Thuillier.
LEMULQUINIER, a domestic servant in the Claës household in Douai (*Recherche de l'Absolu*).
LENONCOURT, a noble family represented, in the 16th century, by a cardinal (*Sur Cathérine de Médicis*) and, in the 19th century, by the Duc Henri, First Gentleman of the King's Bedchamber, who dies in 1836 (*Lys dans la Vallée*, etc.): 15, 116, 117, 119, 339, 444.
Married, I think, to a Blamont-Chauvry (*id.*): 116, 117, 339.
Their daughter, Blanche-Henriette, marries Mortsauf (see Mortsauf).
Another Lenoncourt is referred to in *les Chouans*: 157.
LENONCOURT-CHAULIEU (Duc de), name and title assumed by the Comte de Chaulieu after his marriage with Madeleine de Mortsauf, born 1805, the grand-daughter of the last Duc de Lenoncourt (*Lys dans la Vallée, Splendeurs*): 8, 60, 117, *160, 161.*
LENORMAND, a clerk of the court (*Honorine*).
LÉON, a non-commissioned officer executed in 1822 (*Melmoth réconcilié*): 228, 300.
LÉOPOLD, a character in the story written by Savarus. Modeled on the notary Hannequin (*Albert Savarus*).
LEPAS (les), innkeepers in Vendôme (*Autre Etude de Femme*).
LEPITRE, a headmaster of a school (*Lys dans la Vallée*).
LEPRESSOIR, a notary in Alençon (*Vieille Fille, Cabinet des Antiques*): 481.
LEPRINCE, an appraiser who dies in 1822 (*Employés*): 116.
Has a daughter, Célestine, who marries Rabourdin (see Rabourdin).
LEROI (Pierre), known as Marche-à-Terre, a Chouan (*Chouans*, etc.).
His mother is also mentioned in *les Chouans*.
LESCAULT (Catherine), a courtesan in the 17th century (*Chef-d'oeuvre inconnu*).
LESEIGNEUR DE ROUVILLE (Baron), a ship's

captain who dies in about 1796 (*Bourse*).
Married. Wife's origins unknown. They have a daughter, Adélaïde: 160, 221, 277.
She marries the painter Schinner.
LESOURD, Crown prosecutor in Provins (*Pierrette*).
Marries a Guénée.
LÉVEILLÉ, a notary and a Chouan, executed in 1809 (*Envers de l'Histoire contemporaine*).
LEVRAULT-CRÉMIÈRE, an innkeeper in Nemours (*Ursule Mirouët*).
Has a daughter who marries Minoret-Levrault.
Another Levrault-Crémière, a miller, was mayor of Provins until 1830 (*id.*).
He also has a daughter. (See Minoret).
LEVRAULT-LEVRAULT, an iron merchant, dies in about 1813 (*Ursule Mirouët*).
Has a son who is a butches (*id.*). (See Minoret).
LEVRAULT-MINORET, a farmer at Montereau, dies in 1814 (*Ursule Mirouët*).
Marries a Crémière-Levrault-Dionis.
Their daughter marries Massin-Levrault, a clerk in Montargis (*id.*). (See Minoret).
LEVRAULT or LEVROUX, a lawyer in Mantes (*Cousin Pons*).
LIAUTARD (Abbé), director of an educational establishment (*Envers de l'Histoire contemporaine*).
LIÉNARD, a sculptor (*Cousin Pons*).
LINA (Duc de), an Italian, lover of la Marana (*Marana*).
LISIEUX (François), a defaulter who dies in 1809 (*Envers de l'Histoire contemporaine*).
LISTOMÈRE (de), a noble family of Touraine represented by a variety of characters whose kinship to one another Balzac does not make clear:
1) an old Marquise de Listomère, née Grandlieu (*Lys dans la Vallée*): 142.
She has a son who is a "grave man" (*Etude de Femme*, etc.): 142.
He marries a Vandenesse, his cousin, the sister of Charles and Félix (*Lys dans la Vallée, Etude de Femme*, etc.): 33, *142*, 214;
2) a Listomère (f.) who marries a Vandenesse (m.).

Their children are Félix, Charles and the Vandenesse bride mentioned above (*Lys dans la Vallée*);
3) an old Comtesse de Listomère-Landon who lives in Tours and dies there in 1814 (*Femme de Trente Ans*). There is also an "old Comtesse de Listomère" whom we meet in *le Député d'Arcis* in 1839. Did Balzac forget that she was dead? Or is this a different person?: 141;
4) an old Baronne de Listomère who also lives in Tours, and who dies there in 1826 (*Curé de Tours*): 142, 253;
5) a Baron de Listomère, the nephew of the Baronne above (*id.*);
6) a Demoiselle de Listomère (*Mémoires de deux Jeune Mariées*).
LIVINGSTON, a manufacturer (*César Birotteau*).
LOLOTTE, a kept woman (*Rabouilleuse*): 280.
LONGUEVILLE, an illustrious family that died out in 1793 (*Bal de Sceaux*).
LONGUEVILLE (Vicomte Guiraudin de), a deputy (*Bal de Sceaux*). Issue:
1) Auguste.
2) Maximilien.
3) Clara.
LONGUY (de), a Chouan (*Chouans* and *Envers de l'Histoire contemporaine*).
LORA (Didas y or de), a Spanish family settled in Roussillon and represented by:
1) Juan (*Comédiens sans le savoir*);
2) Léon, Juan's brother, born 1806, a painter (*id., Début dans la Vie, Honorine*, etc.): 108, 200, *221*, 222, 232, 237, 241, 327;
3) a demoiselle de Lora, aunt of the preceding two (*Comédiens sans le savoir*).
LORAIN (Mme.), a concierge (*Employés*).
Her daughter, Zélie, married Minard.
LORAUX (Abbé), an ecclesiastic, born 1752, the uncle of Maurice de l'Hostal (*Honorine, César Birotteau*, etc.): 338, 440.
LORRAIN, a tradesman in Pen-Hoël, then living in retirement in Nantes. Dies in 1826 (*Pierrette*).
His wife dies in 1829.
Their one son, a soldier, dies in 1814.
He has married an Auffray, who dies in 1819.

LORRAIN (*cont.*)
They have one daughter, Pierrette, who dies in 1828 (*id.*): 13, 161, 168, 214, 343, 454.
LOUCHARD, a bailiff (*Splendeurs et Misères des Courtisanes*, etc.).
LOUDUN (Prince de), a title belonging to the Verneuil family and borne successively by:
1) a general of the Vendée guillotined during the Terror (*Modeste Mignon*, etc.) and
2) Gaspard de Verneuil, who is engaged to Desplein's daughter (*Modeste Mignon*).
LOUIS XVIII, a king of France (1754-1824) (*Bal de Sceaux, Lys dans la Vallée*, etc.): 60, 72, 85, 158, 218, 408, 409, 411, 448, 460, 465, *467, 468,* 469.
LOUISA (see Wimphen).
LOUISE, maid employed by the Steinbocks (*Cousine Bette*).
LOUISE, a peasant woman in the Dauphiné (*Médecin de Campagne*).
LOUISE, a character in *Physiologie du Mariage*.
LOURDOIS, a contractor (*Maison du Chat-qui-pelote, César Birotteau*).
Has a daughter who marries the notary Crottat: 482.
LOUSTEAU, a subdelegate in Issoudun who dies in 1800 (*Rabouilleuse*): 187, 279.
Married. Wife's origins unknown.
They have one son, Etienne, born 1799, a journalist (*Illusions Perdues, Muse du Département*, etc.): 23, 26, 38, 105, 110, 111, 112, 123, 147, 149, 186, *187* to *190*, 191, 193, 194, 200, 201, 204, 206, 207, 208, 209, 210, 211, 215, 220, 232, 235, 239, 241, 242, 243, 250, 266, 279, 283, 295, 307, 327, 375, 376, 377, 482.
Etienne is the father of all Mme de la Baudraye's children.
Maximilienne, sister of the subdelegate, marries Hochon.
LOUSTEAU-PRANGIN, a magistrate in Issoudun (*Rabouilleuse*).
Has a son.
LUCAS, a domestic servant in the l'Estorade household (*Mémoires de deux Jeunes Mariées*).
LUDOVICO, a character in *Physiologie du Mariage*.
LUPEAULX (Clément Chardin Comte des), Clerk of appeals, then chief undersecretary to the Minister of Finance, born 1785 (*Employés, Illusions Per-*

dues, etc.): 25, 32, 41, 71, 72, 73, 94, 95, 116, 195, 327, 483.
Has a nephew who is sub-prefect in la Ville-aux-Fayes (*Paysans*): 73.
LUPIN, a steward in Soulanges (*Paysans*).
Has a son, a notary, who marries a certain Bebelle, the daughter of a salt dealer.
They have one son, Amaury (*id.* and *Début dans la Vie*): 183.
LUSTRAC (M. and Mme de), characters in *Petites Misères de la Vie conjugale*.

MACHEFER (Mlle), a character in *Petites Misères de la Vie conjugale*.
MACHILLOT (Mme), owner of a family boarding-house (*Envers de l'Histoire contemporaine*).
MACUMER (Baron de), a Sardinian title used by the Duke Felipe de Soria, a Spaniard, during his exile in France. Dies 1829 (*Mémoires de deux Jeunes Mariées*): 126, 127, 263, 264, 269, 270, 316, 394, 395.
Marries in 1825 Louise de Chaulieu (see Chaulieu).
MADELEINE (la belle) (see Calvi).
MADOU (Angélique), a hazelnut seller (*César Birotteau*).
MAGALHENS, a noble family of Douai (*Recherche de l'Absolu*).
MAGNAN (Prosper), an army surgeon shot in 1799 (*Auberge Rouge*).
Had a mother, mentioned in the same work.
There is another Prosper Magnan who occurs in *Physiologie du Mariage*.
MAGUS (Elie), a picture dealer, born 1770 (*Pierre Grassou, Cousin Pons*, etc.): 303, 394, 396, *397, 398,* 475.
Has a daughter, Noémi (*Cousin Pons*).
MAHAUT (Comtesse), mother of Godefroid in 14th century (*Proscrits*).
MAHOUDEAU (Mme), a moneylender, friend to Mme Cardinal (*Illusions Perdues* and *Petits Bourgeois*).
MAHUCHET (Mme), a cobbler's wife (*Comédiens sans le savoir* and *Petites Misères de la Vie conjugale*).
MALAGA, real name Marguerite Turquet, a bareback rider, born 1816 (*Fausse Maîtresse, Homme d'Affaires*, etc.): 47, 81, 143, *233, 234,* 238, 240, 241, 242, 283, 384, 482, 484.
MALASSIS (Jeanne), a servant in the Pin-

MARIE, a little girl (*Petites Misères de la Vie conjugale*).

MARIE-JEANNE, a servant employed by Mme Madou (*César Birotteau*).

MARIETTE (see Godeschal).

MARIETTE, a servant employed by la Fosseuse in the Dauphiné (*Médecin de Campagne*).

MARIETTE, a servant in the Watteville household in Besançon (*Albert Savarus*).

Marries Jérôme.

MARIETTE, a cook in the Hulot household (*Cousine Bette*).

MARIETTE, a cook employed by Mlle Cormon in Alençon (*Vieille Fille*).

MARIGNY (Duc and Duchesse de), a 17th century couple mentioned in *Modeste Mignon*.

One of their descendants, a Duchesse, and her son, a Duc de Marigny, are mentioned in *la Duchesse de Langeais*.

MARIN, a workman (*Envers de l'Histoire contemporaine*).

MARIN, a manservant to the young Duc de Maufrigneuse (*Député d'Arcis*).

MARION, a servant employed by old Séchard (*Illusions Perdues*).

Marries Kolb.

MARION, a lawyer in Arcis, then President of a court (*Ténébreuse Affaire* and *Député d'Arcis*).

Has a wife (*Ténébreuse Affaire*).

Also a brother, District Internal Revenue Director for the Aube, who dies in about 1815 (*id.* and *Député d'Arcis*): 484.

Marries a Giguet (*id.*).

MARIOTTE, a servant in the du Guénic household (*Béatrix*).

MARIOTTE, a property dealer in Auxerre (*Paysans*).

His mother is mentioned in the same work.

MARIUS, a hairdresser (*Comédiens sans le savoir*).

MARNEFFE (Jean-Paul-Stanislas), an employee of the Ministry of War, born 1796, dies 1842 (*Cousine Bette*): 180, 242, 276, *283, 284,* 285, 286, 287, 332, 382, 426.

Marries Valérie Fortin, illegitimate daughter of Mlle Fortin and Montcornet, born 1815, dies 1843 (*id.*): 71, 136, 166, 167, 205, 214, 232, 237, 238, 239, 242, 276, 281, *282-285,* 286,

311, 317, 381, 383, 426, 436, 457, 458, 477, 478, 482.

Issue:
1) Stanislas
2) a stillborn child.

When widowed, Mme Marneffe remarries with Crevel.

MAROLLES (Abbé de), an ecclesiastic (*Episode sous la Terreur*).

MARONIS (de), an Abbé, tutor to Henri de Marsay, later a bishop (*Fille aux Yeux d'Or*): 39, *438*.

MARRON (Abbé), a parish priest in Marsac (*Illusions Perdues, Splendeurs*).

Has a nephew who is a doctor.

The nephew has a daughter, Léonie, who marries Postel.

MARSAY (de), an old gentleman who dies at an unspecified date (*Fille aux Yeux d'Or*): 39, 391.

Married a Mlle X., already pregnant by Lord Dudley, who later, after Marsay's death, remarries with the Marquis de Vordac (see Vordac).

She has a son, Henri (in fact the son of Lord Dudley), born 1792 or 1801 (*Fille aux Yeux d'Or, Contrat de Mariage, Autre Etude de Femme, Illusions Perdues,* etc.): 3, 4, 13, 15, 18, 19, 21, 35, 37, *38-45,* 46, 48, 49, 50, 51, 54, 56, 57, 58, 60, 61, 65, 66, 67, 69, 72, 76, 80-87, 89, 95, 102, 119, 174, 218, 222, 273, 282, 289, 293, 298, 302, 304, 310, 311, 321, 322, 324, 329, 330, 340, 341, 342, 388, 390, 391, 392, 395, 435, 438, 442, 443, 444, 445, 446, 448, 465, 467, 469.

Marries, in about 1827, Dinah Stevens, born 1791 (*Contrat de Mariage*): 42, 388, *392*.

The elder Marsay had a sister, an old maid (*Fille aux Yeux d'Or*): 39.

MARTAINVILLE (Alphonse-Louis), a journalist (1777-1830), creator of the character Nigaudinos ("Nigaudinos!" old Goriot exclaims at one point.) and originator of that very just remark: "The man who pays his debts grows rich? Bah, that's just a rumor put around by creditors." (*Illusions Perdues*). Did exist.

MARTELLENE, a linguist (*Peau de Chagrin*).

MARTENER, a doctor in Provins (*Pierrette*).

Has a son, also a doctor, who marries a Guénée.

Their son is an examining magistrate in Arcis (*Député d'Arcis*).

MARTHA, a servant in the Claës household in Douai (*Recherche de l'Absolu*).

MARTHE (Sister), née Beauséant, a nun (*Episode sous la Terreur*).

MARTHE (Sister), a Carmelite nun in Blois (*Mémoires de deux Jeunes Mariées*).

MARTHE (Sister), a grey sister in Limoges (*Curé de Village*).

MARTIN (Mme), a woman who takes care of children in the Dauphiné (*Médecin de Campagne*).

MARTINEAU, a keeper employed by the Mortsaufs at Clochegourde. (*Lys dans la Vallée*).

Has a son. Also a brother, who is a tenant farmer.

MARVILLE (see Camusot).

MARY, an English nurse employed by the l'Estorades (*Mémoires de deux Jeunes Mariées*).

MASSIN-LEVRAULT (Jean), a common ancestor of the Minoret, Massin, etc. tribe (see Minoret).

MASSIN-LEVRAULT, a locksmith in Montargis (*Ursule Mirouët*).

Wife's origins unknown.

Issue:

1) a daughter who is a postmistress;

2) a son who is a clerk of the court in Nemours.

He marries a Levrault-Minoret.

Issue:

a) Paméla, who marries Goupil: 177.

b) Aline.

MASSOL (Léon), a lawyer then a councilor of state (*Splendeurs et Misères des Courtisanes, Fille d'Eve*, etc.): 230, 239.

MASSON, a counsel in a commercial court (*Illusions Perdues*).

MASSON (Publicola), a chiropodist (*Comédiens sans le savoir*).

MATHIAS, a notary in Bordeaux (*Contrat de Mariage*): 481.

Has a wife, who dies in 1826, a son, who is a magistrate, and a married daughter (*id.*).

MATHILDE, a character in *Petites Misères de la Vie conjugale*.

MATHILDE, a friend of Jenny Courand's (*Illustre Gaudissart*).

MATHURINE, a cook employed by the Marneffes (*Cousine Bette*).

MATIFAT, a pharmacist (*Illusions Perdues, César Birotteau*, etc.): 13, 187, 194, 242, 435.

Has a wife: 363.

And a daughter who marries the General Baron Gouraud: 424.

(See Minoret).

MAUCOMBE, a noble Provençal family represented by a Comte de Maucombe (*Illusions Perdues, Mémoires de deux Jeunes Mariées*): 122.

Wife's origins unknown.

Issue:

1) a son;

2) Jean;

3) Renée, who marries Louis de l'Estorade (see l'Estorade).

MAUFRIGNEUSE, (Duc de), a title belonging to the Cadignan family. (See Cadignan).

MAUGREDIE, a doctor (*Peau de Chagrin*).

MAULINCOUR (Charbonnon de), a noble family represented by:

1) an old dowager (*Ferragus, Contrat de Mariage*): 69, 70.

2) Auguste, her grandson, a soldier, born 1796 (*id.*): 42, 46, *69*, *70*, 103, 405.

These two characters both die at about the same time. In 1819, according to *Ferragus*, after 1822, according to *Contrat de Mariage*.

MAUNY (Baron de), an old man living in Versailles who is murdered by Victor le Parisien (*Femme de Trente Ans*).

MAUPIN (Camille), the pen name of Félicité des Touches (see Touches).

MAURICE, a manservant employed by the Restauds (*Père Goriot* and *Gobseck*).

MÉDAL (Robert), an actor mentioned in *le Cousin Pons* who was to have been the leading character in *Le Théâtre comme il est*, an unfinished work: 241.

MELIN, a keeper of an inn near Mortagne (*Envers de l'Histoire contemporaine*).

MELMOTH (John), an Englishman who dies in 1822 (*Melmoth réconcilié*): 388, *392*, 436.

MEMMI (Emilio), Prince of Varese, a Venetian (*Massimila Doni*): 266.

Marries Massimila Doni after death of her first husband the Duc Cataneo: 266.

MERGI (de), a magistrate (*Envers de l'Histoire contemporaine*).

Has a son who dies in about 1823. The son marries Wanda Bourlac: 13, 146, 214, 226, 332, 344, 435.

Issue:

Index

MERGI (*cont.*)
1) Auguste, born 1822;
2) a stillborn child.

MERLE, a captain, killed in 1799 (*Chouans*).

MERLIN (Hector), a journalist (*Illusions Perdues*): 187, 199, *200*, 207, 208, 218, 241.

MERLIN, Attorney General (*Ténébreuse Affaire*).

MERLIN DE LA BLOTTIÈRE (see la Blottière).

MERRET (Comte de), a "handsome man" but a scurvy person, inhabitant of Vendôme, dies about 1816 (*Autre Etude de Femme*).
His wife, of unknown origins, dies in about 1816 too (*id.*): 258.

MERKSTUS, a banker in Douai (*Recherche de l'Absolu*).

MÉTIVIER, a paper merchant (*Illusions Perdues*, etc.)
Issue:
1) a daughter who marries her cousin, also named Métivier, who takes over his father-in-law's business (*Petits Bourgeois* and *Envers de l'Histoire contemporaine*).
2) another daughter.

MEYNARDIE (Mme), a corset seller (*Ferragus*) and manageress of a brothel (*Splendeurs et Misères des Courtisanes*): 240, 242.

MEYRAUX, a scientist and member of the Cénacle (*Illusions Perdues, Louis Lambert*): 210.

MICHAUD (Justin), a soldier, then an overseer at les Aigues, murdered in 1823 (*Paysans*).
Marries Olympe Charel, who dies in 1823.

MICHEL, a café waiter in Soulanges (*Paysans*).

MICHONNEAU (Christine-Michelle), a boarder in Mme Vauquer's pension (*Père Goriot, Splendeurs*, etc.): *168, 169*.
Marries the elder Poiret.

MICHU, steward to the Simeuse family, guillotined in 1806 (*Ténébreuse Affaire*): 300, 454, 459.
Married Marthe X., who dies in 1806.
They leave a son, François, born 1793, who becomes Crown prosecutor in Arcis (*Député d'Arcis*).
He marries a Girel.

MIGEON, a concierge (*Muse du Département*).

Has a wife and a daughter, Paméla.

MIGNON DE LA BASTIE, a noble family of the Vaucluse region all the members of which are murdered in about 1794, except one son, Charles, born 1776, an army officer, then a shipowner (*Modeste Mignon*): 273.
Marries, in 1804, Bettina Wallenrod, a German: 13.
Issue:
1) a child that dies in infancy;
2) another child that dies in infancy;
3) Bettina-Caroline, born 1805, dies in about 1827: 152, 481;
4) Marie-Modeste, born 1808 (*id.*): 78, *152, 153*, 154, 160, 172, 184, 225, 226, 266, 272, 273, 326, 356.
Marries, in 1830, Ernest de la Brière.

MIGNONNE, a panther in Egypt (*Passion dans le désert*): x, 259, 288.

MILAUD, a middle-class branch of the Milaud de la Baudrayes, represented by a magistrate, his wife, and their son (*Illusions Perdues* and *Muse du Département*).

MILEY, a registrar in Arcis (*Député d'Arcis*).

MILLET, a grocer (*Envers de l'Histoire contemporaine*).

MILLOT (Mlle), mistress of Braulard (*Illusions Perdues*).

MINARD (Auguste-Jean-François), an office worker, then a businessman (*Employés, Petits Bourgeois*): 251, 306.
Marries Zélie Lorain.
Issue:
1) Julien, a lawyer (*Petits Bourgeois*).
2) Prudence (*id.* and *Cousin Pons*).

MINARD (Louis), a defaulter who is executed in 1809 (*Envers de l'Histoire contemporaine*).

MINISTRE, the Minister of Finance and his wife play a certain part in *les Employés*.

MINISTRE ALLEMAND (a German minister), appears in *Illusions Perdues*.

MINORET, a food supplier (*Paysans*).

MINORET (Mlle), a dancer (*Employés*): 286.
Has a daughter, probably by du Bousquier, who is called Flavie and marries Colleville.

MINORET. For clarity's sake, I shall give here not only the Minorets themselves, but also the various related branches that are themselves listed separately elsewhere. The common ancestor is a certain Jean Massin-Levrault who has two daughters. The first of these marries a Minoret.

Issue:

1) a son whose son, François Minoret-Levrault, born 1769, is a postmaster of Nemours (*Ursule Mirouët*): 457.

He marries Zélie Levrault-Crémière, who dies in 1841.

Issue:

1) Désiré, born in 1805, who dies in 1836. 177, 194, 346;

2) a sailor son who dies without issue (*id.*);

3) a son who is a captain, also dies without issue (*id.*);

4) Denis, born 1746, dies 1835, a doctor, later living in retirement in Nemours (*id.*): 153, 326, 346, 347, 377, 436.

Marries an Ursule Mirouët, who dies in 1793.

He adopts his niece, Ursule Mirouët, who marries Portenduère (see Mirouët).

5) a daughter who marries Massin-Massin, the steward of Saint-Lange (*id.*).

They have a daughter who marries Crémière-Crémière, a tax-collector in Nemours.

They have a daughter, Angélique.

The second of Jean Massin-Levrault's daughters marries a Crémière-Levrault-Dionis, a supply contractor (*id.*).

They have a daughter who marries a Levrault-Minoret, a farmer.

They have a daughter who marries a Massin-Levrault who is a clerk of the court in Nemours.

They have two daughters: Aline, and Paméla who marries Goupil. They have issue.

Others members of the family are:

1) a Massin-Levrault who is a sister of the clerk of the court and herself a postmistress (*Ursule Mirouët*).

2) a Levrault-Levrault who is an iron merchant (*id.*).

3) a son of the former, a butcher (*id.*).

4) a Levrault-Crémière who is

mayor of Nemours till 1830 and has a daughter (*id.*).

5) a Crémière-Dionis who is a notary, mayor after 1830, and has a wife and a daughter (*id.*).

6) a Levrault (Levroux in the Conard edition), a lawyer in Mantes apparently totally unrelated to all the foregoing (*Cousin Pons*).

MIRAH (Josépha), real name Hiram, an opera singer (*Cousine Bette*, etc.): 34, 53, 65, 78, 212, 229, *231*, 232, 235, 237, 241, 281, 396, 477, 478.

MIROUËT (Valentin), a harpsichordist who dies in 1815 (*Ursule Mirouët*).

Issue:

1) a legitimate daughter, Ursule, who dies in 1793.

She marries Denis Minoret and has children, all of whom die in infancy.

2) an illegitimate son, Joseph, who dies in 1814.

He marries Dinah Grollman, a German, who dies in 1814.

They have a daughter, Ursule, born 1814, adopted by her uncle Minoret (*id.*): 65, 66, 136, *153*, 154, 160, 177, 226, 266, 267, 331, 346, 347, 355, 385, 387, 395, 435, 455.

She marries, in 1837, Savinien de Portenduère.

MISTIGRIS, nickname of Léon de Lora.

MITANT ("old mother"), a peasant woman living in Couches (*Paysans*).

MITOUFLET, an innkeeper in Vouvray (*Illustre Gaudissart*).

MITOUFLET, an usher at the Ministry of War (*Cousine Bette*).

MITRAL, an usher and moneylender (*César Birotteau* and *Employés*).

His sister is married to the tanner Baudoyer.

MIZERAL, a restaurateur (*Z. Marcas*).

MODINIER, a steward of the Wattevilles, near Besançon (*Albert Savarus*).

MOINOT, a postman. "My name is spelt exactly like a sparrow (moineau in French): M-o-i-n-o-t, n-o-t, Moinot." "So it is," Laurent said. "I live on the Rue des Trois-Frères, No. 11, on the fifth floor; I have a wife and four children" (*Fille aux Yeux d'Or*).

MOÏSE, a highwayman, date of death unspecified. Leaves a "widow," la Gonore (*Splendeurs et Misères des Courtisanes*): 301.

Marries, in about 1804, Blanche-Henriette de Lenoncourt, born 1786, dies 1823 (*id.*): 58-61, *116-122,* 160, 161, 176, 258, 259, 260, 273, 275, 316, 339, 347, 362, 363, 389, 411, 433, 434, 435, *455,* 468.

Issue:

1) Jacques, who dies in 1836: 117, 316;

2) Madeleine, who marries the Comte de Chaulieu, thus becoming the Duchesse de Lenoncourt-Chaulieu (see Lenoncourt-Chaulieu).

MOUCHE (le petit), illegitimate son of one of Fourchon's daughters (*Paysans*).

MOUCHON, a family in Burgundy represented by three brothers:

1) Mouchon the elder, a former member of the National Convention. Has two daughters. One marries Gaubertin, the other Gendrin;

2) Mouchon the younger, postmaster (*id.*).

Has a daughter who marries Guerbet;

3) Mouchon the Abbé (*id.*).

MOUGIN, known as Marius, a hairdresser (*Comédiens sans le savoir*).

MOUILLERON, Crown prosecutor in Issoudun (*Rabouilleuse*).

MOUSQUETON, a kept woman (or another nickname for Carabine) (*Comédiens sans le savoir*).

MURET, a businessman (*Père Goriot*).

NANON (la grande), the Grandets' servant (*Eugénie Grandet*).

Marries Antoine Cornoiller.

NAPOLEON I, emperor of France (1769-1821) (*Vendetta, Ténébreuse Affaire,* etc.): 9, 18, 19, 23, 53, 171, 206, 216, 218, 320, 322, 329, 356, 388, 416, 417, 418, 423, 425, 427, 429, 445, 448, 462, 464, *465-466,* 467, 468, 469.

Has a brother, Lucien Bonaparte (1775-1840) (*Vendetta, Ténébreuse Affaire*).

NAPOLITAS, a policeman (*Splendeurs et Misères des Courtisanes*).

NARZICOFF, a Russian princess (*Gaudissart II*).

NATHAN (Raoul), a writer and journalist (*Fille d'Eve, Illusions Perdues,* etc.): 5, 11, 15, 55, 62, 85, 101, 138, 186, 187, 189, *191-193,* 194, 197, 202, 208, 209, 210, 212, 218, 220, 226, 232, 239, 240, 241, 242, 243, 249, 326, 343, 396, 479.

Marries Sophie Grignoult, known as Florine (see Florine).

NAVARREINS or NAVARREINS-LANSAC (de), a noble family represented by the Duc de Navarreins, born about 1767 (*Duchesse de Langeais, Peau de Chagrin,* etc.): 8, 15, 90, 333, 334, 408, 444, 467.

Marries a Cadignan, a sister of the Duc de Maufrigneuse (*Cousine Bette*).

They have a daughter, Antoinette, who marries the Marquis, later Duc de Langeais (see Langeais).

The Duc de Navarreins has a sister who marries the Prince de Blamont-Chauvry.

NÈGREPELISSE (de), a noble family of the South of France whose name and estates passed to the d'Espards by marriage. This is why the eldest son of the Comte d'Espard has the title Comte de Nègrepelisse.

There is still a junior branch in existence represented by an old count who lives near Barbezieux (*Illusions Perdues*).

He has a daughter, Anaïs, who marries Bargeton first, then Chatelet (see Bargeton).

NÉGRO (Marquis de), a Genoese nobleman (*Honorine*).

NÉPOMUCÈNE, a domestic servant employed by Mme Vauthier (*Envers de l'Histoire contemporaine*).

NÉRAUD, a doctor in Provins (*Pierrette*).

Marries the widow Auffray.

NICOLA (M.), see Montauran (Nicholas de).

NICOLLE, a groom employed by Benassis in the Dauphiné (*Médécin de Campagne*).

NINETTE, a young ballet dancer (*Comédiens sans le savoir*).

NIOLLANT (Abbé), tutor of Anaïs de Nègrepelisse (*Illusions Perdues*).

NISERON (Abbé), parish priest of Blangy before the Abbé Brossette (*Paysans*).

Has a nephew, Jean-François, a beadle, a gravedigger and a republican (*id.*).

The nephew has a wife, who dies in 1794. Issue:

1) Geneviève, who dies in 1794;

2) Auguste, a soldier, killed in 1814.

By a Montenegrin, Zéna Kropoli, who dies in 1810, Auguste has a

NISERON (*cont.*)
daughter, Geneviève, born 1810, who is taken in by her grandfather (*id.*).

NOCÉ (Comte de), a character in *la Physiologie du Mariage*.

NOËL, a clerk of the court (*Interdiction*).

NOIRMOUTIER (Marquise de), sister of the Comtesse de Grandlieu in the 17th century (*Enfant Maudit*).

NOSWELL (Mrs.), an Englishwoman (*Gaudissart II*): 385, 393.

NOUASTRE (de), an émigré back in Alençon, dies in 1802 (*Cabinet des Antiques*).
Has a daughter "the prettiest human creature in the world," who marries the Marquis d'Esgrignon.

NOURRISSON (Mme), a secondhand dress dealer, moneylender, procuress, owner of a brothel on the Rue Sainte-Barbe, and a nest of love-boxes in the Pâté des Italiens (*Cousine Bette, Comédiens sans le savoir*, etc.): 237, *240*, 242, 298.

NOUVION (Comte de), a friend of the Marquis d'Espard (*Interdiction*).

NUCINGEN (Baron Frédéric de), a banker, born about 1767 (*Maison Nucingen, Splendeurs et Misères des Courtisanes*, etc.): 7, 13, 15, 26, 27, 33, 34, 35, 68, *75*, 85, 86, 95, 102, 107, 139, 178, 214, 215, 227, 239, 240, 275, 276, 299, 302, 303, 335, 337, 349, 350, 385, 386, 387, 396, 397, 455, 457, 462, 464, 472, 474, *478*, *481*, 482.
Marries Delphine Goriot, born 1792 (*id.*): 10, 13, 15, 32, 33, 34, 35, 36, 38, 40, 81, 84, 86, *101* to *103*, 139, 150, 275, 276, 299, 311, 313, 321, 335, 337, 340, 341, 342, 353, 354, 355, 356, 478.
They have a daughter, Augusta, who marries Eugène de Rastignac.

NUEIL, a noble Normandy family represented by a Comte de Nueil who dies in 1825 (*Femme abandonnée*).
Wife's maiden name unknown. Issue:
1) a son, who dies in 1825;
2) Gaston, born 1799, dies 1831 (*id.*): 127, 128, *170*, *171*, 260, 273, 282.
Gaston marries Stéphanie de la Rodière: 128, 171.

O'BRIEN (Fanny), an Irish girl, born 1792, who marries the Baron du Guénic (see du Guénic).

OCTAVE (see Bauvan).

O'FLAHERTY (Martin), an Irish major (*Peau de Chagrin*).
Has a sister, Barbe-Marie, who marries the Marquis de Valentin, Raphaël's father.

OIGNARD, a clerk employed by Bordin (*Début dans la Vie*).

OLIVET, a lawyer in Angoulême (*Illusions Perdues*).

OLIVIER, a policeman in Arcis (*Ténébreuse Affaire*).

OLIVIER (M. and Mme), Mme Marneffe's concierges (*Cousine Bette*).
They have three children, the eldest a notary's clerk.

OOSTERLINCK, a banker in Bruges in the 15th century (*Maître Cornelius*).

OGREMONT (d'), a banker in Fougères (*Chouans*): 475.
Has a brother, a juring priest, who dies in 1795 (*id.*).

ORIGET, a doctor in Tours (*Lys dans la Vallée*).

ORMOND (Arthur), later Lord Grenville (see Grenville).

ORSONVAL (Mme d'), an inhabitant of Saumur (*Eugénie Grandet*).

OSSIAN, a footman employed by the hairdresser Marius (*Comédiens sans le savoir*).

OSSUNA (Duc d'), a Spaniard, natural father of the Abbé Herréra, murdered by Vautrin (*Splendeurs et Misères des Courtisanes*).

OSTROEM (Comtesse van), a character in *Physiologie du Mariage*.

OTTOBONI, an Italian composer (*Gambara*).

OZALGA, a Spanish friend of Macumer's (*Mémoires de deux Jeunes Mariées*).

PACCARD, Vautrin's factotum (*Splendeurs et Misères des Courtisanes*): 298.
Probably marries Prudence Servien.
Has a sister, Jéromette or Romette (*id.*).

PADDY (see Toby).

PALMA, a moneylender (*Gobseck*, etc.): 478, 479, 480.

PAMIERS (Vidame de), former Commander of the Order of Malta (*Cabinet des Antiques, Ferragus*, etc.): 7, 401, *402*, 405, 406.

PANNIER, a businessman in Alençon who dies in prison (*Envers de l'Histoire contemporaine*).

PARADIS, Maxime de Trailles' tiger (*Député d'Arcis*).

PARQUOI (François), a Chouan killed in 1799 (*Chouans*).

PASCAL (Abbé), a prison chaplain in Limoges (*Curé de Village*).

PASTELOT (Abbé), a priest in Paris (*Cousin Pons*).

PASTOUREAU (Jean-François), a peasant in the Dauphiné (*Médecin de Campagne*).

PATRAT, a notary in Fougères (*Chouans*).

PATRIS (see Bougival).

PAUL, a domestic servant in Petit-Claud household in Angoulême (*Illusions Perdues*).

PAULINE (see Salomon).

PAULINE, a maid in employ of the Aiglemonts (*Femme de Trente Ans*).

PAULMIER, a civil servant employed in the Ministry of Finance (*Employés*).

PAZ (Comte Thaddée), a Pole living in exile in France (*Fausse Maîtresse*, etc.): 142, 143, 233, 234, 383.

PÉCHINA, from "piccina," little, nickname of Geneviève Niseron (see Niseron).

PEDROTTI (Comte), a Genoese banker (*Honorine*).

Has a daughter, Onorina, who marries Maurice de l'Hostal.

PELLETIER (Mme), a peasant woman in the Dauphiné (*Médecin de Campagne*).

She has two sons.

PÉNÉLOPE, Mlle Cormon's mare, born 1792, dies 1816 (*Vieille Fille*).

PEN-HOËL (de), a noble Brittany family, represented by:

1) Jacqueline de Pen-Hoël, born 1780 (*Béatrix*): 162, 163, 168;

2) Her sister, who marries the Vicomte de Kergarouët (*id.*).

She has four daughters, the eldest being named Charlotte (see Kergarouët).

PEREZ (see Lagounia).

PERNETTI (Comtesse), a character in *Physiologie du Mariage*.

PÉROTTE, a servant employed by Mlle Cormon. The same person, I think, as Josette (*Vieille Fille*).

PÉROUX (Abbé), a parish priest in Provins (*Pierrette*).

Has a sister who marries Julliard.

PERRACHE (M. and Mme), concierges (*Petits Bourgeois*).

PERRET, a banker in Limoges, the partner of Grossetête (*Curé de Village*).

Has a wife.

PERROTET, a farmer on Grandet's land (*Eugénie Grandet*).

PERSEPOLIS (Mgr. de), a bishop in partibus and a piquet player (*Bal de Sceaux*): 441.

PETIT-CHATEAU, the legitimist élite (see *Splendeurs et Misères* p. 730).

PETIT-CLAUD (Pierre), a clerk, then a lawyer in Angoulême, born 1807 (*Illusions Perdues*): 151, 177, 178, 179, 180, 181, 484.

Marries Françoise de la Haye, natural daughter of Francis du Hautoy and the Comtesse de Senonches: *151, 177*.

PEYRADE (see La Peyrade).

PHELLION, a civil servant in the Ministry of Finance and a teacher (*Employés, Petits Bourgeois*): 251, 360, 414.

Married to a piano teacher whose maiden name is not known. Issue:

1) Félix, born 1817: 434;

2) Marie-Théodore (m.);

3) a daughter who marries Barniol.

PHILIPPART, a porcelain manufacturer in Limoges (*Curé de Village*).

PHILIPPE, a manservant employed by Mme de Vaurémont (*Mémoires de deux Jeunes Mariées*).

PICHARD, a servant employed by the Abbé Niseron (*Paysans*).

She has a niece, Arsène, who marries Grégoire Rigou.

PICQUOUSEAU (Comtesse), a shadowy figure (*Père Goriot*).

PIE VII, Pope Pius VII (1740-1823) (*Double Famille*).

PIÉDEFER, a Protestant family in Bourges represented by:

1) Moïse, who dies in 1819 (*Muse du Département*).

Married, but wife's maiden name unknown.

They have one daughter, Dinah, born 1807, who marries Milaud de la Baudraye (see La Baudraye).

2) Silas, brother of Moïse, who dies in New York in 1837 (*id.*).

PIERQUIN, a notary in Douai, born 1786 (*Recherche de l'Absolu*): 481.

Marries Félicie Claës.

The notary has a brother who is a doctor (*id.*).

A distant cousin of the foregoing,

PIERQUIN (*cont.*)
one of the Antwerp Pierquins, had married Balthazar Claës' grandfather.

PIERRETTE (see Lorrain).

PIERROTIN, a coachmaker (*Début dans la Vie*): 183.
Has a daughter, Georgette, who marries Oscar Husson.

PIÉTRO, a domestic servant in the Piombo household (*Vendetta*).

PIGEAU (Mme), a widow murdered by Calvi in about 1829 (*Splendeurs et Misères des Courtisanes*).

PIGERON, a resident of Auxerre who dies in about 1823, possibly poisoned by his wife (*Paysans*).

PIGOULT, a magistrate in Arcis (*Ténébreuse Affaire, Député d'Arcis*).
Has a son, a hosier (*Député d'Arcis*).
And a grandson, a notary (*id.*).

PILLE-MICHE, nickname of the Chouan Jean Cibot who is executed in 1809 (*Chouans* and *Envers de l'Histoire contemporaine*).

PILLERAULT (Claude-Joseph), a hardware merchant born in about 1756 (*César Birotteau*, etc.): 449.
After losing his wife, his son and then an adopted child, he takes care of his niece, Constance-Barbe-Joséphine, who marries César Birotteau (see Birotteau).

PIMENTEL (Marquis and Marquise de), residents of Angoulême (*Illusions Perdues*).

PINGRET, a resident of Limoges murdered in 1829 by Tascheron (*Curé de Village*): 475.

PIOMBO (Baron Bartolomeo di), a Corsican born about 1740 (*Vendetta*): 331.
Marries Elisa X.
Issue:
1) Gregorio, killed in a vendetta;
2) Ginevra, born 1791, dies 1820. She marries Luigi Porta, born 1793, dies 1820.
They have a son, Bartolomeo, who dies very young.

PIQUETARD, a kitchen maid employed by the Hulot d'Ervy family (*Cousine Bette*).
Marries, in 1846, the Baron Hulot.

PIQUOIZEAU, Nucingen's concierge (*Melmoth réconcilié*).

PLAISIR, a hairdresser (*Double Famille*).

PLANAT DE BAUDRY, an Inland Revenue official (*Bal de Sceaux*).

Marries one of the Comte de Fontaine's daughters.

PLANCHETTE, a teacher of mechanics (*Peau de Chagrin*).

PLANTIN, a publicist (*Fille d'Eve*).

PLISSOUD, an usher and court-crier in Soulanges (*Paysans*): 485.
Marries Euphémie Vattebled.

POÈTE INCONNU (unknown poet): 239.

POIDEVIN, a clerk employed by Bordin (*Début dans la Vie*).

POINCET, a scribe and interpreter (*Fille aux Yeux d'Or*).

POIREL (Abbé), a priest in Tours (*Curé de Tours*).

POIRET (Mme), a woman given to "disastrous misbehavior" (*Employés*).
Issue:
1) Poiret the elder, a civil servant at the Ministry of Finance, then retired (*id., Père Goriot*, etc.): 169.
Marries, late in life, Christine-Michelle Michonneau: 168, *169*.
2) Poiret the younger, civil servant at the Ministry of Finance and an accountant (*Employés*, etc.): 206.

POLISSARD, a contractor who exploits the woods on the Ronquerolles estate (*Paysans*).

POMBRETON (Marquis de), a character who is often referred to (*Vieille Fille* and *Illusions Perdues*), but who does not, in all probability, really exist.

PONS (M. and Mme), owners of an embroidery business (*Cousin Pons,* etc.)
They have a son, Sylvain, known as le Cousin Pons, a musician, born about 1784, dies 1845 (*Cousin Pons*): ix, 100, 149, 227, 241, 252, 302, 317, 331, 333, 343, 344, 360, 366, 368, 382, 385, 386, 399, 413, 454, *455*, 467, 473.
Another Pons, the brother of the embroidery maker, becomes the latter's partner (*id.*).
He has a daughter who marries Camusot.

POPINOT, a municipal magistrate in Sancerre (*César Birotteau*).
Issue:
1) a daughter who marries the perfumer Ragon;
2) Anselme, a dealer in woolens. Dies young, as does his wife (*id.*).
They have a son, Anselme, born 1797, who becomes one of Birotteau's clerks, then a pharmacist, then Minister of Trade, a count and a peer of

France, "one of the most influential statesmen of the dynasty" (*César Birotteau, Cousin Pons*, etc.): 16, 160, 265, 266, 267, 268, 271, 304, 312, 334, 467, 472.

Marries, in 1823, Césarine Birotteau born 1801 (*id.*): 10, 11, 160, 265, 266, 267, 268, 304, 312, 472.

Issue:

a) the Vicomte Popinot (*Cousin Pons*) who marries Cécile Camusot de Marville;

b) a lawyer son (*Cousine Bette*);

c) a daughter who marries Boniface Cointet (*Illusions Perdues*);

3) Jean-Jules, a magistrate, dies in 1833 or 1840 (*Interdiction*, etc.): 9, 95, 216, 324, 357, 359, 361, 455, 458.

Marries a Bianchon, Horace's aunt, who dies in 1823.

Mention should also be made of the Popinot-Chandier family, also of Sancerre and related to the Popinots. This family includes a Mme Popinot-Chandier who has a son and a daughter; also a Mlle Popinot-Chandier who marries Boirouge (*Muse du Département*).

POPOLE, the godson of Mme Madou (*César Birotteau*).

PORCHON (see Vidal and Porchon).

PORRABERIL (Margarita-Euphémia), illegitimate daughter of Lord Dudley and an unknown woman (*Fille aux Yeux d'Or*).

Marries the Marquis de San-Real (see San-Real).

PORRIQUET, teacher of Raphaël de Valentin (*Peau de Chagrin*).

PORTA, a Corsican family consisting of seven members. Six are exterminated by Bartolomeo di Piombo. The seventh, Luigi, a soldier, born 1793, dies in 1820 (*Vendetta*).

He marries Ginevra di Piombo, the daughter of the savage mentioned above. She dies in 1820.

They have one child, Bartolomeo, who dies in infancy.

PORTAL (du), false name used by Corentin (*Petits Bourgeois*).

PORTENDUÈRE (de), a noble Provençal family represented by:

1) a lieutenant-general in the naval forces, deceased (*Gobseck, Ursule Mirouët, Bourse*);

2) Luc-Savinien, deputy, grandson

of the foregoing and father of three children (*Ursule Mirouët*): 65;

3) a Vicomte de Portenduère, nephew of the lieutenant-general, who dies at an unspecified time (*id.*).

Marries a Kergarouët-Ploëgat who, when widowed, settles in Nemours (*id.*): 65, 66, 153, 409.

They have a son, Savinien, born 1807 (*Ursule Mirouët*, etc.): viii, 20, 65, 66, 67, 69, 72, 103, 153, 154, 158, 177, 266, 267, 272, 300, 346, 351, 355, 409.

He marries Ursule Mirouët, born 1814: 65, 66, 136, *153, 154*, 160, 177, 226, 266, 267, 331, 346, 347, 355, 385, 387, 395, 435, 455.

POSTEL, a pharmacist in Angoulême (*Illusions perdues*): 21.

Marries Léonie Marron.

They have one son.

POTEL, retired army officer living in Issoudun (*Rabouilleuse*).

POUGAUD (la petite), a little girl in le Croisic (*Drame au bord de la mer*).

POULAIN (Mme), a widow and breeches maker (*Cousin Pons*): 180.

Has a son, a doctor, born in 1815 (*id.*): 179, *180*.

POUPART, an innkeeper in Arcis (*Député d'Arcis*).

Marries a Gothard.

POUPILLIER, a Parisian family consisting of three sisters and four brothers "all destined to live the most absurd lives." One of them, born in 1775, is successively a drum-major, a hall-porter, one of the "good poor," and a bogus centenarian (*Petits Bourgeois*). One of his nieces marries Cardinal (see Cardinal).

POURIN, a soldier (*Cousine Bette*).

PRÉLARD, a harware dealer and mayor's assistant (*Splendeurs et Misères des Courtisanes*).

Marries "La Rousse," the former doxy of Auguste, a convict who is guillotined.

They have two children.

PRÉVOST (Mme), a florist (*Splendeurs et Misères des Courtisanes*).

PRIEUR (Mme), a laundress in Angoulême (*Illusions Perdues*).

PRON, a teacher (*Petits Bourgeois*).

Marries a Barniol.

PROTEZ, a druggist, partner of Chiffreville (*Recherche de l'Absolu*, etc.)

Marries Marianne Cardot.

PROUST, a clerk employed by Bordin
(*Début dans la Vie*).

PROVENÇAL (le), a soldier (*Passion dans le
Désert*): x, 259, 288.

QUELUS (Abbé de), an ecclesiastic in Touraine (*Lys dans la Vallée*): 441.

QUEVERDO, a Spaniard, very strict, Macumer's steward (*Mémoires de deux
Jeunes Mariées*).

QUILLET (François), an office boy (*Fille
d'Eve*).

RABOUILLEUSE, nickname of Flore Brazier
who marries, first Jean-Jacques Rouget, then Philippe Bridau (see Bridau).

RABOURDIN (Xavier), born in 1784, a head
clerk at the Ministry of Finance (*Employés*, etc.): 116, 251, 266, 267, 303,
307, 327, 449.

Marries Célestine Leprince, born
1796 (*id.*): 15, 104, *115*, 116, 130, 214,
266, 302, 312, 363, 368, 372.

Issue:

1) Charles, born 1815 (*Employés*
and *Z. Marcas*);

2) a daughter.

RAGON, a perfumer, born 1748 (*César
Birotteau, Episode sous la Terreur*):
326, 328.

Marries a Popinot, sister of the
magistrate and aunt of Anselme.

RAGOULLEAU, a shadowy figure (*Père Goriot*).

RAGUET, an odd-job boy employed by the
Birotteaus (*César Birotteau*).

RAMACHARD (Mme), a character in *Petites
Misères de la Vie conjugale*).

RAPARLIER, a notary in Douai (*Recherche
de l'Absolu*).

Has a nephew who is an usher.

RAPP (General), a soldier (1772-1821)
(*Vendetta* and *Ténébreuse Affaire*).
Did exist: 470.

RAQUETS (des), Pierquin's uncle (*Recherche de l'Absolu*).

RASTIGNAC, a noble family of the Angoulême region represented by a
Baron de Rastignac who lives just
outside Angoulême (*Illusions Perdues*): 30.

Married to a wife of unknown
origin: 30.

Issue:

1) Eugène, born 1798, a law student, then a cabinet minister and a
count (*Père Goriot, Illusions Perdues, Etude de Femme, Peau de
Chagrin, Maison Nucingen*, etc.): x,
7, 10, 13, 15, 18, 19, 20, 21, *29-37*, 38,
40, 41, 49, 50, 52, 53, 56, 57, 59, 72, 74,
76, 81-87, 93, 94, 101-104, 128, 150,
151, 153, 174, 176, 181, 205, 215, 229,
263, 270, 273, 290, 292, 293, 294, 296,
298, 302, 303, 304, 311, 312, 313, 321,
335, 337, 340, 341, 349, 350, 351, 354,
355, 356, 364, 372, 373, 467, 469, 474.

Marries, in 1838, Augusta de Nucingen (*Député d'Arcis*, etc.): 10, 35,
335.

2) Laure-Rose, born 1801 (*Père
Goriot, Illusions Perdues*): 35, 148.

3) Agathe, born 1802 (*Père Goriot*).

Both girls marry. One of them
(either Laure or Agathe) with Martial de la Roche-Hugon, the other
with a person unknown.

4) Gabriel, born 1804, an abbé,
then a bishop (*Curé de Village*,
etc.): 35, 439.

5) Henri.

Mention must also be made of a
great-aunt of Eugène (possibly to be
identified with Mme de Marcillac)
and of a vice-admiral, Eugène's great-
uncle, who marries a Marcillac and
whose daughter marries the Maréchal
de Clarimbault (*Père Goriot*).

RATEL, a policeman who commits suicide
in 1809 (*Envers de l'Histoire contemporaine*).

RAVENOUILLET, a concierge and a moneylender. (*Comédiens sans le savoir*).

Has a wife and also a daughter,
Lucienne.

RÉGNAULD DE SAINT-JEAN D'ANGELY, a clerk
employed by Bordin (*Début dans la
Vie*).

REGNAULT, a notary in Vendôme (*Autre
Etude de Femme*).

RÉGNIER (Claude-Antoine, Duc de Massa),
Chief Justice (1746-1814). Did exist.
(*Ténébreuse Affaire, Double Fa-
mille*).

RÉGULUS, a hairdresser's assistant (*Comédiens sans le savoir*).

REMONENCQ, a second-hand dealer who
dies in 1846 (*Cousin Pons*): 262, 307,
308.

Marries the widow Cibot.

He has a sister (*id.*).

RENARD, a wholesale grocer (*Médecin de
Campagne*).

Has a son, a non-commissioned officer, killed in 1813, who has a son by the Polish woman Judith. This illegitimate son, Adrien, is later recognized by Genestas (*id.*).

RENARD, a retired army officer living in Issoudun (*Rabouilleuse*).

RENÉ, a domestic servant employed by du Bousquier in Alençon (*Vieille Fille*).

RESTAUD (de), a noble family (there was a Restaud who commanded the *Warwick* before 1789) represented by the Comte de Restaud, born 1774, dies 1824 (*Père Goriot, Gobseck*): 139, 140, 259, 335, 337, 483.

Marries Anastasie Goriot, born about 1792 (*id.*): 4, 20, 32, 49, 53, *139, 140,* 259, 335, 336, 337.

Issue:

1) Ernest, born 1818 (*Gobseck*): *155,* 335, 349.

Marries Camille de Grandlieu.

2) Georges, probably the son of Maxime de Trailles.

3) Pauline, probably the daughter of Maxime de Trailles.

REYBERT (de), an army officer, then the Comte de Sérizy's manager (*Début dans la Vie*).

Marries a Corroy.

They have one daughter. She marries Léger.

RHÉTORÉ (Duc de), title borne by the eldest sons of the Chaulieus and, from about 1820 onwards, by Alphonse de Chaulieu (*Mémoires de deux Jeunes Mariées, Illusions Perdues*, etc.): 7, 41, 77, *78,* 85, 197, 225, 236, 242, 243.

Marries, in 1836, Francesca Soderini, widow of the Duc d'Argaiolo (see Argaiolo).

RICHARD (widow), a resident of Nemours (*Ursule Mirouët*).

RIDAL (Fulgence), a farce writer, a member of the Cénacle (*Illusions Perdues,* etc.): 207, 208, 210, *211,* 218, 240.

RIFFÉ, a civil servant working at the Ministry of Finance (*Employés*).

RIFOEL (see Vissard).

RIGANSON, known as le Biffon, and his wife, known as la Biffe, both highway robbers (*Splendeurs et Misères des Courtisanes*): 293, *301.*

RIGOU (Grégoire), a former Benedictine, the mayor of Blangy (*Paysans*): 363, 437, 474.

Marries Arsène Pichard, the ser-

vant, mistress, and heiress of the Abbé Niseron.

They have a daughter, Arsène, who marries Soudry.

RIVABARELLA (la), a courtesan in Ferrara in the 16th century (*Elixir de longue vie*).

RIVAUDOULT D'ARSCHOOT, a family mentioned in *la Duchesse de Langeais.*

RIVET, a dealer in passementerie and embroidery (*Cousine Bette*).

ROBESPIERRE (Maximilen), a politician (1758-1794) (*Rabouilleuse, Ursule Mirouët, Sur Catherine de Médicis*): 157, 178.

ROCHEFIDE (de), "upstart nobility," if we are to believe Mme de Beauséant.

The family is represented by:

1) a young lady who marries Ajuda-Pinto and dies somewhat swiftly (see Ajuda);

2) Arthur, the foregoing's brother (*Béatrix*, etc.): 131, 132, 235, *236,* 237, 242, 286.

Marries, in 1828, Béatrix-Maximilienne-Rose de Casteran, born 1808 (*id.*): 81, 107, 108, *130-132,* 135, 136, 147, 160, 191, 226, 235, 236, 259, 260, 261, 262, 278, 282, 285, 286, 374.

They have one son.

ROCHEGUDE (Marquis de), an old gentleman mentioned in *Illusions Perdues.* "Rochefide alias Rochegude" Balzac writes in *Splendeurs* (p. 729). From which it is permissible to conclude that this Rochegude is the father of the two Rochefides above.

RODOLPHE, the hero of Savarus's short story (*Albert Savarus*).

ROGER, personnel director at the Ministry of War (*Cousine Bette*).

ROGRON, an innkeeper in Provins who dies in about 1820 (*Pierrette*).

Marries an Auffray, born 1743, who dies before her husband.

Issue:

1) Sylvie, born 1781, haberdasher in Paris, then retired in Provins: 14, *167, 168,* 306, 308, 371, 375, 377, 423, 424, 454.

2) Jérôme-Denis, born 1783, haberdasher, then retired on his savings in Provins: 159, 167, 306, 371, 375, 377, 449.

Marries Bathilde de Chargeboeuf, born 1803: 48, *159.*

ROGUIN, a notary, born in about 1768

SARATAS, a policeman in Arcis (*Ténébreuse Affaire*).

SABATIER, a detective (*Ténébreuse Affaire*).

SABATIER (widow), a nurse (*Cousin Pons*)
Marries one of her patients.
Has one child by him.

SAGREDO, a Venetian senator, born 1730, dies 1760 (*Facino Cane*)
Marries Bianca Vendramini, born 1742.

SAILLARD, a cash clerk at the Ministry of Finance (*Employés*): 251, 484.
Marries a Bidault.
They have one daughter, Elisabeth, who marries Baudoyer (see Baudoyer).

SAINT-DENIS (M. de), a false name used by Corentin (*Splendeurs et Misères des Courtisanes*).

SAINT-ESTÈVE, a false name used by both Corentin and Jacqueline Collin (*Splendeurs et Misères, Cousine Bette*).

SAINT-FONDRILLE (M. and Mme de), characters in *les Petits Bourgeois*.

SAINT-GERMAIN, a false name used by Peyrade (*Splendeurs et Misères*).

SAINT-HÉRÉEN (Comte de), a character notable for his absences.
Marries Moïna d'Aiglemont (*id.* and *Fille d'Eve*): 146, 147.

SAINT-MARTIN (M. de), a philosopher (1743-1803). Did exist. His memory and influence are evoked in *Lys dans la Vallée*: 117, 119, 347.

SAINT-SAVIN (de), president of a Court of Justice in the 16th century (*Enfant Maudit*).
Has a wife.
They have one daughter, Jeanne, who marries the Duc d'Hérouville.
The President also has a sister, a nun.

SAINTE-SÉVÈRE (Mme. de), a resident of Bayeux (*Femme abandonnée*).

SAINTOT (M. and Mme de), residents of Angoulême (*Illusions Perdues*).

SAINT-VIER (Mme de), a resident of Besançon (*Albert Savarus*).

SALMON, a former valuer (*Curé de Tours*).

SALOMON, a Jewish family represented by:
1) Joseph (*Louis Lambert*);
2) a brother who marries a wife whose origins we don't know. They have one son, Joseph, Baron Salomon de Villenoix. The Baron has an illegitimate daughter, Pauline, though by whom we do not know. Pauline, born 1800, is engaged to marry Louis Lambert (*Louis Lambert, Curé de Tours*, etc.): 397.

SAMANON, a pawnbroker (*Illusions Perdues*, etc.): 13, 239, 478, 480.

SAN-ESTERAN (Marquise de), a false name used by Jacqueline Collin (*Splendeurs*).

SAN-LUCAR (Abbé de), an ecclesiastic in the 15th century (*Elixir de longue vie*).

SAN-REAL (Marquis de), a Spaniard born in 1735 (*Fille aux Yeux d'Or*).
Marries Euphémia Porraberil, illegitimate daughter of Lord Dudley: 40, 259, 289, 293, 382, 391, 394.

SANSON (Charles-Henri), an executioner (1740-1793). Did exist (*Episode sous la Terreur*): 470.
Had a son, Henri (1767-1840), also an executioner (*Splendeurs et Misères des Courtisanes*): 470.

SARCUS, a magistrate in a criminal court in Soulanges (*Paysans*).
Marries a Vermut.
They have a daughter, Adeline, who marries Adolphe Sibilet.
Another Sarcus, known as Sarcus-le-Riche, a cousin of the above, is a deputy (*id.*).
He marries a Vallat.
They have a son, an engineer.
Lastly, another cousin, Sarcus-Taupin, a miller (*id.*).
He has a daughter.

SARRASINE (Ernest-Jean), a sculptor, born 1736, murdered in 1758 (*Sarrasine*): 222, 241, 259, 288, 289, 305, 306, 343.

SAUTELOUP, a clerk of the court at the Conciergerie (*Splendeurs et Misères des Courtisanes*).

SAUVAGE (Mme), a servant employed by Fraisier (*Cousin Pons*): 179.

SAUVAGER, a deputy Crown prosecutor in Alençon (*Cabinet des Antiques*).

SAUVAGNEST, a lawyer (*Début dans la Vie*).

SAUVAIGNOU, a carpenter (*Petits Bourgeois*).

SAUVIAT (Jérôme-Baptiste), an iron merchant in Limoges, born 1747, dies 1827 (*Curé de Village*): 115, 304.
Marries a Champagnac, born 1763.
They have a daughter, Véronique, who marries Graslin (see Graslin).

SAVARUS (Savaron de), a noble family of Flanders, represented by:

Index

1) Adolphe, born 1791, a clerk in the Land Registry, then a steward. Marries Adeline Sarcus.

They have two children.

2) a son who is a police inspector;

3) a daughter who marries the teacher Hervé;

4) a son who is a clerk;

5) a son who is a civil servant employed in land administration;

6) a daughter engaged to Corbinet.

Sibilet-père also has a sister who marries Vigor.

SIBUELLE, an army contractor (*Ténébreuse Affaire*).

Has a daughter who marries Malin de Gondreville.

SIEYÈS (Emmanuel-Joseph), a politician (1748-1836) (*Ténébreuse Affaire*): 470.

SIGNOL (Henriette), a woman who irons clothes in Angoulême (*Illusions Perdues*).

SIMEUSE (de), "Ximeuse is a fief situated in Lorraine. The name is pronounced Simeuse." Under Louis XIV, there was a Marquis de Simeuse who married a widowed Cinq-Cygne (*Ténébreuse Affaire*).

They had a son, a vice-admiral (*Ténébreuse Affaire*, etc.)

He has a son, Jean, who marries Berthe de Cinq-Cygne, both of whom are executed in 1792.

They have twin sons, Marie-Paul and Paul-Marie, born 1773, both killed in 1808 (*id.*): 300, *352*, 454.

SIMON, a clerk in the Palais de Justice (*Début dans la Vie*).

SIMONNIN, an errand-boy employed by Derville (*Colonel Chabert*).

SINARD, a doctor (*Splendeurs et Misères des Courtisanes*).

SINET (Séraphine), (see Carabine).

SINOT, a lawyer in Arcis (*Député d'Arcis*).

SOBOLEVSKA (Wanda), a Polish woman who marries general Tarlowski (*Envers de l'Histoire contemporaine*).

SOCQUARD (Alcide), a café owner in Soulanges (*Paysans*).

Has a wife, Junie.

They have a daughter, Aglaé.

From a liaison with Gaubertin, Junie also has a son named Bournier (*id.*).

SODERINI (Prince), an Italian (*Albert Savarus*).

Has a daughter, Francesca, who marries the Duc d'Argaiolo, then the Duc de Rhétoré (see Argaiolo).

SOLIS (Abbé de), a Spanish ecclesiastic who has taken refuge in Douai (*Recherche de l'Absolu*).

Has a nephew, Emmanuel, a professor, then Comte de Nourho (*id.*): 154, 268, 344, 345.

Marries Marguerite Claës, born 1796: *154*, *268*, *344*, *345*.

They have one son, Joseph.

SOLONET, a notary in Bordeaux (*Contrat de Mariage*): 481.

Marries a mulatto girl.

"A notary marrying a mulatto girl? What an age!"

SOLVET, lover of Caroline Crochard (*Double Famille*): 228.

SOMMERVIEUX (Théodore, Baron de), a painter, born 1792 (*Maison du Chat-qui-pelote*, etc.): 133, 138, *221*, 241, 259, 264, 265, 266, 271, 276, 354.

Marries Augustine Guillaume, born 1793, dies in 1820 (*id.*): 133, *138*, 148, 221, 259, 265, 266, 271, 276, 354.

They have one son.

SONET, a marble dealer (*Splendeurs et Misères des Courtisanes*, *Cousin Pons*).

Has a wife.

SOPHIE, cook employed by Anselme Popinot (*Cousin Pons*).

SORBIER, a notary, Cardot's predecessor, dies about 1822 (*Cabinet des Antiques*).

Has a wife.

SORIA (de), a noble Spanish family represented by a Duc de Soria and his wife Doña Clara (*Mémoires de deux Jeunes Mariées*).

Issue:

1) Felipe, Baron de Macumer, who marries Louise de Chaulieu (see Macumer);

2) Fernand, Duc de Soria, who marries Maria Hérédia.

SORMANO, an Italian, servant to the Argaiolos in Switzerland (*Albert Savarus*).

SOUCHET (François), a sculptor (*Bourse*).

SOUCHET, a stockbroker (*Eugénie Grandet*).

SOUDRY, a policeman, then mayor of Soulanges (*Paysans*).

Marries Françoise Cochet, a former housemaid, born 1763.

SOUDRY (*cont.*)
They have a son, who is legitimized, then becomes Crown prosecutor.
He marries Arsène Rigou.

SOULANGES (de), a noble Burgundian family represented by the Comte Léon de Soulanges, born 1777, a soldier and a peer of France (*Paix du Ménage, Paysans,* etc.): 16, 207.
Marries, in 1807, Hortense X., a relation of the Duchesse de Lansac.
Issue:
1) a son who becomes a soldier (*Ursule Mirouët*);
2) Amélie, whose hand is refused to both Montcornet and Philippe Bridau in succession (unless there are in fact two daughters involved).
We must also mention two ancestors, a Maréchal and a Marquis de Soulanges-Hautemer (*Paysans*).

SOULAS (Amédée, Comte de), a resident of Besançon, born 1809 (*Albert Savarus*): 76, 303.
Marries, in 1837, Clotilde du Rupt, widow of Watteville.
They have two children.

SPARCHMANN, a German doctor in Heilsberg (*Colonel Chabert*).

SPENCER (Lord), an Englishman (*Recherche de l'Absolu*).

SPIEGHALTER, a German mechanic (*Peau de Chagrin*).

SPONDE (de), an old gentleman who lives in Alençon and has two children:
1) the Abbe de Sponde, born 1746, dies 1819 (*Vieille Fille*): 332, 440;
2) a daughter who marries Cormon.
They have a daughter, Rose-Marie (see Cormon).

STAËL (Mme de), a woman of letters (1766-1816) (*Louis Lambert*): 470.

STANHOPE (Lady), an Englishwoman (*Lys dans la Vallée*).

STAUB, a tailor who is mentioned several times. Did exist.

STEIBELT, a musician in Nantes (*Béatrix*).

STEINBOCK (Wenceslas, Comte), Polish and a sculptor, born 1809 (*Cousine Bette,* etc.): 71, 135, 136, 166, 167, 203, 204, 222, 240, 259, 276, 282, 284, 300, 305, 317, 351, *382, 383.*
Marries, in 1838, Hortense Hulot, born 1816 (*id.*): 135, *136,* 148, 153, 166, 222, 259, 383, 473.
They have one son, Wenceslas.

STEINGEL, a general (*Paysans*).

Has an illegitimate son who becomes a gamekeeper at les Aigues.

STÉPHANIE, a character in *Petites Misères de la Vie Conjugale.*

STEVENS, an English brewer (*Contrat de Mariage*).
Has a daughter, Dinah, who marries Henri de Marsay (see Marsay).

STIDMANN, a sculptor (*Cousine Bette,* etc.): 136, *222,* 232, 240.

STOPFER (M. and Mme), characters in Savarus's short story (*Albert Savarus*).

SUCY (General Baron Philippe de), a soldier, born 1789, dies 1830 (*Adieu*).

SUZANNE (see Val-Noble).

SUZETTE, a maid in the employ of Mme de Langeais (*Duchesse de Langeais*).

SUZON, a manservant employed by Maxime de Trailles (*Homme d'Affaires*).

SYLVIE, a cook employed by Mme Vauquer (*Père Goriot*): 169.

TABAREAU, an usher (*Cousin Pons*).
Has a daughter.

TABOUREAU, a seedmerchant in the Dauphiné (*Médecin de Campagne*).

TAILLEFER (Frédéric), a food supplier, then a banker, born about 1779, dies in 1831 (*Auberge Rouge,* etc.): 149.
Marries twice. Issue from the first marriage:
1) Frédéric, who is killed in a duel by Franchessini in 1820 (*Père Goriot*): 55, 455, 457;
2) Victorine (*id.* and *Auberge Rouge*): 32, *149,* 150, 151, 153.

TALLEYRAND-PÉRIGORD (Charles-Maurice de), Prince of Benevento, a statesman (1754-1838) (*Ténébreuse Affaire,* etc.): 43, 95, 392, 437, 443, 448, 463, 466, *469, 470.*

TARLOWSKI, a Polish general (*Envers de l'Histoire contemporaine*).
Marries Vanda Sobolevska.
They have a daughter who marries Bourlac.

TARNOWICKI, a Polish general who has fled to Paris (*Envers de l'Histoire contemporaine*).

TASCHERON, a Montégnac family that emigrates to America (*Curé de Village*):
The family comprises:
1) a grandfather and his wife;
2) a father and his wife;
3) two daughters, their husbands, and five children;
4) Jean-François, a workman, born

TOUCHES (des), a noble family of Brittany represented by a soldier who dies in 1792 (*Béatrix*).

He marries a Faucombe, who dies in 1793. Issue:

1) a Chevalier des Touches, killed in 1793;

2) Félicité, born 1791, a woman of letters, then a nun (*Béatrix, Honorine, Illusions Perdues*, etc.): 7, 15, 46, 81, 82, *104* to *108*, 110, 113, 115, 130, 131, 152, 163, 186, 192, 204, 205, 222, 226, 241, 259, 260, 261, 274, 436, 441.

TOUPINET, a poor man helped by Popinot (*Interdiction*).

Has a wife.

TOURILLON, a glovemaker in Orléans in the 16th century (*Sur Catherine de Médicis*).

TOURNAN, a hatter (*Employés*).

TOURS-MINIÈRES (Baron Bryond des) (see Bryond).

TOUSARD (Reine), a maid employed by the Marneffes (*Cousine Bette*).

TRAILLES (Comte Maxime de), born about 1792 (*Gobseck, Député d'Arcis, Béatrix*, etc.): 20, 21, 35, *48* to *52*, 53, 54, 55, 81, 85, 86, 105, 139, 140, 178, 221, 227, 238, 262, 299, 321, 328, 335, 413, 455, 464, 480.

Marries a wife we have every reason for supposing to be Cécile Beauvisage, born 1820.

TRANS (Mlle de), a young girl living in Bordeaux (*Contrat de Mariage*).

TRANSON (M. and Mme), dealers in pottery (*Employés*).

TREIZE (le) (the Thirteen), a secret society: 20, 42, 46, 47, 50, 103, 288, 298, *321, 322*, 323, 340, 341.

TROGNON, a notary (*Cousin Pons*).

TROISVILLE (de), a noble Normandy family ("pronounce it Tréville") which includes:

1) a commodore under Louis XV (*Vieille Fille*);

2) a son of the above, Vicomte de Troisville, an émigré who joined the Russian army (*id*.): 100.

He marries a Sherbelloff: 100.

They have four or five children. One of them, Virginie, marries Montcornet (see Montcornet);

4) a Marquis de Troisville, a peer of France, who has two children (*id*.);

5) a Chouan leader (*Chouans*), possibly the same person as 4);

6) a female Troisville, possibly the daughter of either the Vicomte or the Marquis, who marries a Casteran (*Paysans*);

7) two deputies with children.

TROUBERT (Hyacinthe), an ecclesiastic in Tours, later Bishop of Troyes (*Curé de Tours*, etc.): 363, 437, 438.

TROUSSENARD, a doctor in le Havre (*Modeste Mignon*).

TRUDON, a grocer (*César Birotteau*).

TULLIA (see Bruel).

TULLOYE, owner of a meadow near Angoulême (*Illusions Perdues*).

TURQUET (Marguerite) (see Malaga).

URBAIN, a domestic servant in the Soudry household in Soulanges (*Paysans*).

URRACA, a Spanish woman, Macumer's nurse (*Mémoires de deux Jeunes Mariées*).

URRACA Y LORA (Mlle), Léon de Lora's aunt (*Comédiens sans le savoir*).

URSULE, a servant employed by the Abbé Bonnet in Montégnac (*Curé de Village*).

URSULE, a cook employed by the Ragons, a "lascivious woman" and Birotteau's first mistress (*César Birotteau*).

UXELLES (d'), a family represented by:

1) the dowager duchess d'Uxelles, born 1769 (*Secrets de la Princesse de Cadignan*, etc.): 15, 77, 89.

She has a daughter, Diane, who marries the Duc de Maufrigneuse. He later succeeds to the title of Prince de Cadignan (see Cadignan).

2) a Marquise d'Uxelles (*César Birotteau*).

VAILLANT (Mme), a charwoman who works for the Pilleraults (*César Birotteau*) and also for the narrator of *Facino Cane*.

VALDÈS (Paquita), a young girl born in the Antilles in 1793 of a Georgian mother and an unknown father. She is killed by the Marquise de San-Real in 1815 (*Fille aux Yeux d'Or*): 40, 42, 81, 259, 262, 289, 293, 382, 394.

VALENTIN (de), a noble family of the Auvergne represented by a Marquis de Valentin who dies in 1826 (*Peau de Chagrin*).

He marries Barbe O'Flaherty, an Irish girl, who dies in 1814.

VICTOIRE, a servant (f.) in the Claparon household (*César Birotteau*).

VICTOIRE, a maid employed by the Restauds (*Père Goriot*).

VICTOR, a pirate who dies in about 1843 (*Femme de Trente Ans*): 157, 342, 368.

Carries off Hélène d'Aiglemont.

They have four children.

VICTORINE, a dressmaker (*Mémoires de deux Jeunes Mariées*).

VIDAL and PORCHON, booksellers (*Illusions Perdues*).

VIEUX-CHAPEAU, a soldier (*Chouans*).

VIGNEAU, a tiler in the Dauphiné (*Médecin de Campagne*).

Has a wife, a mother, and a stepmother.

VIGNON (Claude), a critic and professor, born 1799 (*Béatrix, Honorine, Cousine Bette*, etc.): ix, 15, 108, *203* to *205*, 207, 208, 209, 210, 222, 240, 260, 261, 308.

VIGOR, a police lieutenant in la Ville-aux-Fayes (*Paysans*).

Marries a Sibilet.

They have a son, a judge.

A brother of this Vigor is the director of the post horse relay station (*id.*).

VILLAINE (Baron de), a magistrate (*Bal de Sceaux*).

Marries a Fontaine.

VILLEMOT, a clerk employed by Tabareau (*Cousin Pons*).

VILLENOIX (see Salomon).

VILLEPAINE (Adolphe de), a character in *Physiologie du Mariage*.

VILQUIN, a businessman in le Havre (*Modeste Mignon*).

Has a wife.

They have a son and two daughters. One of the latter marries Francisque Althor.

VIMEUX, a clerk of the court (*Employés*).

Has a son, Adolphe, who is employed at the Ministry of Finance. (*id.*).

VINET, a lawyer in Provins, then Attorney General and a deputy (*Pierrette*, etc.): 14, *178*, 179, 449.

Marries a Chargeboeuf: 178. Issue:
1) Olivier, a magistrate (*Député d'Arcis*, etc.): 178, 307, 472;
2) a daughter.

VIOLETTE, a farmer in Champagne (*Ténébreuse Affaire*).

He has a grandson, Jean, a hosier (*Député d'Arcis*).

VIOLLET, a policeman in Soulanges (*Paysans*).

VIRGINIE, a maid in the employ of the du Tillets (*Fille d'Eve*).

VIRGINIE, former mistress of le Provençal (*Passion dans le Désert*).

VIRGINIE, a cook employed by the Birotteaus (*César Birotteau*).

VIRGINIE, a milliner (*Illusions Perdues*).

VIRLAZ, a furrier in Leipzig (*Cousin Pons*).

VISSARD (Charles-Amédée-Louis-Joseph Rifoël, Chevalier du) a Chouan, executed in about 1810 (*Chouans, Envers de l'Histoire contemporaine*).

Has a brother who becomes a peer of France and Marquis (*Envers de l'Histoire contemporaine*).

VISSEMBOURG (see Wissembourg).

VITAGLIANI, Italian, a tenor in Rome (*Sarrasine*).

VITAL, a hatter (*Comédiens sans le savoir*). Has a wife.

VITEL, a judge in a criminal court (*Cousin Pons*).

Has a daughter.

VITELOT, partner of the marble dealer Sonet (*Cousin Pons*).

Has a wife.

VITREMONT, a character in *Petites Misères de la Vie conjugale*.

VIVET (Madeleine), a maid employed by the Camusots de Marville (*Cousin Pons*): 363.

VOLFGANG, a cashier in Nucingen's bank (*Splendeurs et Misères des Courtisanes*).

VORDAC (Marquis de), a vague character (*Fille aux Yeux d'Or*).

Marries the widow of old Marsay, Henri's mother (*id.* and *Contrat de Mariage*): 39, 42.

VOUILLON (Lucienne), a character in *Petites Misères de la Vie conjugale*.

VULPATO (la), a Venetian (*Massimila Doni*).

WADMANN, an Englishman who lives near Marville (*Cousin Pons*).

WAHLENFER, a German businessman who is murdered in 1799 (*Auberge Rouge*).

WALLENROD-TUSTALL-BARTENSTILD (Baron de), a German banker who dies in 1814 (*Modeste Mignon*).

Has a daughter, Bettina, who marries Mignon (see Mignon).

Index

This book was set on the linotype in Janson, a type dating from about 1700. Its origins are rather obscure, but it probably came from a Dutch design, though it was almost certainly not cut by Anton Janson, whose name it bears. The display type used is Perpetua, designed by Eric Gill, and is his most popular roman design.

Composed, printed and bound by H. Wolff Book Manufacturing Company, Inc., New York.

Designed by Jacqueline Schuman.

This is a thorough study of Balzac and *La Comédie Humaine*, written by one of France's leading contemporary novelists and playwrights. It is neither a biography nor a work of criticism as we know it; it is rather a guided visit, a voyage to the world of Balzac, an exploration of the works of a writer the author calls the most secret of novelists. It is, beyond that, an attempt to explain the creation of a great novel.

Combining scholarship with the creative insights that only one novelist could bring to the work of another, Marceau has succeeded in writing what must be considered a definitive book on France's great literary master.

FÉLICIEN MARCEAU was born in Cortenberg, Belgium, in 1913. After efforts in the worlds of publishing, radio, and art, he turned his attention to literature and the theatre. Well known in Europe as a novelist, he is best known in America as a playwright, author of *The Egg* and *La Bonne Soupe*. At the present time, he lives in Paris.